Dictionary of Literary Biography

1 *The American Renaissance in New England,* edited by Joel Myerson (1978)

2 *American Novelists Since World War II,* edited by Jeffrey Helterman and Richard Layman (1978)

3 *Antebellum Writers in New York and the South,* edited by Joel Myerson (1979)

4 *American Writers in Paris, 1920-1939,* edited by Karen Lane Rood (1980)

5 *American Poets Since World War II,* 2 parts, edited by Donald J. Greiner (1980)

6 *American Novelists Since World War II, Second Series,* edited by James E. Kibler Jr. (1980)

7 *Twentieth-Century American Dramatists,* 2 parts, edited by John MacNicholas (1981)

8 *Twentieth-Century American Science-Fiction Writers,* 2 parts, edited by David Cowart and Thomas L. Wymer (1981)

9 *American Novelists, 1910-1945,* 3 parts, edited by James J. Martine (1981)

10 *Modern British Dramatists, 1900-1945,* 2 parts, edited by Stanley Weintraub (1982)

11 *American Humorists, 1800-1950,* 2 parts, edited by Stanley Trachtenberg (1982)

12 *American Realists and Naturalists,* edited by Donald Pizer and Earl N. Harbert (1982)

13 *British Dramatists Since World War II,* 2 parts, edited by Stanley Weintraub (1982)

14 *British Novelists Since 1960,* 2 parts, edited by Jay L. Halio (1983)

15 *British Novelists, 1930-1959,* 2 parts, edited by Bernard Oldsey (1983)

16 *The Beats: Literary Bohemians in Postwar America,* 2 parts, edited by Ann Charters (1983)

17 *Twentieth-Century American Historians,* edited by Clyde N. Wilson (1983)

18 *Victorian Novelists After 1885,* edited by Ira B. Nadel and William E. Fredeman (1983)

19 *British Poets, 1880-1914,* edited by Donald E. Stanford (1983)

20 *British Poets, 1914-1945,* edited by Donald E. Stanford (1983)

21 *Victorian Novelists Before 1885,* edited by Ira B. Nadel and William E. Fredeman (1983)

22 *American Writers for Children, 1900-1960,* edited by John Cech (1983)

23 *American Newspaper Journalists, 1873-1900,* edited by Perry J. Ashley (1983)

24 *American Colonial Writers, 1606-1734,* edited by Emory Elliott (1984)

25 *American Newspaper Journalists, 1901-1925,* edited by Perry J. Ashley (1984)

26 *American Screenwriters,* edited by Robert E. Morsberger, Stephen O. Lesser, and Randall Clark (1984)

27 *Poets of Great Britain and Ireland, 1945-1960,* edited by Vincent B. Sherry Jr. (1984)

28 *Twentieth-Century American-Jewish Fiction Writers,* edited by Daniel Walden (1984)

29 *American Newspaper Journalists, 1926-1950,* edited by Perry J. Ashley (1984)

30 *American Historians, 1607-1865,* edited by Clyde N. Wilson (1984)

31 *American Colonial Writers, 1735-1781,* edited by Emory Elliott (1984)

32 *Victorian Poets Before 1850,* edited by William E. Fredeman and Ira B. Nadel (1984)

33 *Afro-American Fiction Writers After 1955,* edited by Thadious M. Davis and Trudier Harris (1984)

34 *British Novelists, 1890-1929: Traditionalists,* edited by Thomas F. Staley (1985)

35 *Victorian Poets After 1850,* edited by William E. Fredeman and Ira B. Nadel (1985)

36 *British Novelists, 1890-1929: Modernists,* edited by Thomas F. Staley (1985)

37 *American Writers of the Early Republic,* edited by Emory Elliott (1985)

38 *Afro-American Writers After 1955: Dramatists and Prose Writers,* edited by Thadious M. Davis and Trudier Harris (1985)

39 *British Novelists, 1660-1800,* 2 parts, edited by Martin C. Battestin (1985)

40 *Poets of Great Britain and Ireland Since 1960,* 2 parts, edited by Vincent B. Sherry Jr. (1985)

41 *Afro-American Poets Since 1955,* edited by Trudier Harris and Thadious M. Davis (1985)

42 *American Writers for Children Before 1900,* edited by Glenn E. Estes (1985)

43 *American Newspaper Journalists, 1690-1872,* edited by Perry J. Ashley (1986)

44 *American Screenwriters, Second Series,* edited by Randall Clark, Robert E. Morsberger, and Stephen O. Lesser (1986)

45 *American Poets, 1880-1945, First Series,* edited by Peter Quartermain (1986)

46 *American Literary Publishing Houses, 1900-1980: Trade and Paperback,* edited by Peter Dzwonkoski (1986)

47 *American Historians, 1866-1912,* edited by Clyde N. Wilson (1986)

48 *American Poets, 1880-1945, Second Series,* edited by Peter Quartermain (1986)

49 *American Literary Publishing Houses, 1638-1899,* 2 parts, edited by Peter Dzwonkoski (1986)

50 *Afro-American Writers Before the Harlem Renaissance,* edited by Trudier Harris (1986)

51 *Afro-American Writers from the Harlem Renaissance to 1940,* edited by Trudier Harris (1987)

52 *American Writers for Children Since 1960: Fiction,* edited by Glenn E. Estes (1986)

53 *Canadian Writers Since 1960, First Series,* edited by W. H. New (1986)

54 *American Poets, 1880-1945, Third Series,* 2 parts, edited by Peter Quartermain (1987)

55 *Victorian Prose Writers Before 1867,* edited by William B. Thesing (1987)

56 *German Fiction Writers, 1914-1945,* edited by James Hardin (1987)

57 *Victorian Prose Writers After 1867,* edited by William B. Thesing (1987)

58 *Jacobean and Caroline Dramatists,* edited by Fredson Bowers (1987)

59 *American Literary Critics and Scholars, 1800-1850,* edited by John W. Rathbun and Monica M. Grecu (1987)

60 *Canadian Writers Since 1960, Second Series,* edited by W. H. New (1987)

61 *American Writers for Children Since 1960: Poets, Illustrators, and Nonfiction Authors,* edited by Glenn E. Estes (1987)

62 *Elizabethan Dramatists,* edited by Fredson Bowers (1987)

63 *Modern American Critics, 1920-1955,* edited by Gregory S. Jay (1988)

64 *American Literary Critics and Scholars, 1850-1880,* edited by John W. Rathbun and Monica M. Grecu (1988)

65 *French Novelists, 1900-1930,* edited by Catharine Savage Brosman (1988)

66 *German Fiction Writers, 1885-1913,* 2 parts, edited by James Hardin (1988)

67 *Modern American Critics Since 1955,* edited by Gregory S. Jay (1988)

68 *Canadian Writers, 1920-1959, First Series,* edited by W. H. New (1988)

69 *Contemporary German Fiction Writers, First Series,* edited by Wolfgang D. Elfe and James Hardin (1988)

70 *British Mystery Writers, 1860-1919,* edited by Bernard Benstock and Thomas F. Staley (1988)

71 *American Literary Critics and Scholars, 1880-1900,* edited by John W. Rathbun and Monica M. Grecu (1988)

72 *French Novelists, 1930-1960,* edited by Catharine Savage Brosman (1988)

73 *American Magazine Journalists, 1741-1850,* edited by Sam G. Riley (1988)

74 *American Short-Story Writers Before 1880,* edited by Bobby Ellen Kimbel, with the assistance of William E. Grant (1988)

75 *Contemporary German Fiction Writers, Second Series,* edited by Wolfgang D. Elfe and James Hardin (1988)

76 *Afro-American Writers, 1940-1955,* edited by Trudier Harris (1988)

77 *British Mystery Writers, 1920-1939,* edited by Bernard Benstock and Thomas F. Staley (1988)

78 *American Short-Story Writers, 1880-1910,* edited by Bobby Ellen Kimbel, with the assistance of William E. Grant (1988)

79 *American Magazine Journalists, 1850-1900,* edited by Sam G. Riley (1988)

80 *Restoration and Eighteenth-Century Dramatists, First Series,* edited by Paula R. Backscheider (1989)

81 *Austrian Fiction Writers, 1875-1913,* edited by James Hardin and Donald G. Daviau (1989)

82 *Chicano Writers, First Series,* edited by Francisco A. Lomelí and Carl R. Shirley (1989)

83 *French Novelists Since 1960,* edited by Catharine Savage Brosman (1989)

84 *Restoration and Eighteenth-Century Dramatists, Second Series,* edited by Paula R. Backscheider (1989)

85 *Austrian Fiction Writers After 1914,* edited by James Hardin and Donald G. Daviau (1989)

86 *American Short-Story Writers, 1910-1945, First Series,* edited by Bobby Ellen Kimbel (1989)

87 *British Mystery and Thriller Writers Since 1940, First Series,* edited by Bernard Benstock and Thomas F. Staley (1989)

88 *Canadian Writers, 1920-1959, Second Series,* edited by W. H. New (1989)

89 *Restoration and Eighteenth-Century Dramatists, Third Series,* edited by Paula R. Backscheider (1989)

90 *German Writers in the Age of Goethe, 1789-1832,* edited by James Hardin and Christoph E. Schweitzer (1989)

91 *American Magazine Journalists, 1900-1960, First Series,* edited by Sam G. Riley (1990)

92 *Canadian Writers, 1890-1920,* edited by W. H. New (1990)

93 *British Romantic Poets, 1789-1832, First Series,* edited by John R. Greenfield (1990)

94 *German Writers in the Age of Goethe: Sturm und Drang to Classicism,* edited by James Hardin and Christoph E. Schweitzer (1990)

95 *Eighteenth-Century British Poets, First Series,* edited by John Sitter (1990)

96 *British Romantic Poets, 1789-1832, Second Series,* edited by John R. Greenfield (1990)

97 *German Writers from the Enlightenment to Sturm und Drang, 1720-1764,* edited by James Hardin and Christoph E. Schweitzer (1990)

98 *Modern British Essayists, First Series,* edited by Robert Beum (1990)

99 *Canadian Writers Before 1890,* edited by W. H. New (1990)

100 *Modern British Essayists, Second Series,* edited by Robert Beum (1990)

101 *British Prose Writers, 1660-1800, First Series,* edited by Donald T. Siebert (1991)

102 *American Short-Story Writers, 1910-1945, Second Series,* edited by Bobby Ellen Kimbel (1991)

103 *American Literary Biographers, First Series,* edited by Steven Serafin (1991)

104 *British Prose Writers, 1660-1800, Second Series,* edited by Donald T. Siebert (1991)

105 *American Poets Since World War II, Second Series,* edited by R. S. Gwynn (1991)

106 *British Literary Publishing Houses, 1820-1880,* edited by Patricia J. Anderson and Jonathan Rose (1991)

107 *British Romantic Prose Writers, 1789-1832, First Series,* edited by John R. Greenfield (1991)

108 *Twentieth-Century Spanish Poets, First Series,* edited by Michael L. Perna (1991)

109 *Eighteenth-Century British Poets, Second Series,* edited by John Sitter (1991)

110 *British Romantic Prose Writers, 1789-1832, Second Series,* edited by John R. Greenfield (1991)

111 *American Literary Biographers, Second Series,* edited by Steven Serafin (1991)

112 *British Literary Publishing Houses, 1881-1965,* edited by Jonathan Rose and Patricia J. Anderson (1991)

113 *Modern Latin-American Fiction Writers, First Series,* edited by William Luis (1992)

114 *Twentieth-Century Italian Poets, First Series,* edited by Giovanna Wedel De Stasio, Glauco Cambon, and Antonio Illiano (1992)

115 *Medieval Philosophers,* edited by Jeremiah Hackett (1992)

116 *British Romantic Novelists, 1789-1832,* edited by Bradford K. Mudge (1992)

117 *Twentieth-Century Caribbean and Black African Writers, First Series,* edited by Bernth Lindfors and Reinhard Sander (1992)

118 *Twentieth-Century German Dramatists, 1889-1918,* edited by Wolfgang D. Elfe and James Hardin (1992)

119 *Nineteenth-Century French Fiction Writers: Romanticism and Realism, 1800-1860,* edited by Catharine Savage Brosman (1992)

120 *American Poets Since World War II, Third Series,* edited by R. S. Gwynn (1992)

121 *Seventeenth-Century British Nondramatic Poets, First Series,* edited by M. Thomas Hester (1992)

122 *Chicano Writers, Second Series,* edited by Francisco A. Lomelí and Carl R. Shirley (1992)

123 *Nineteenth-Century French Fiction Writers: Naturalism and Beyond, 1860-1900,* edited by Catharine Savage Brosman (1992)

124 *Twentieth-Century German Dramatists, 1919-1992,* edited by Wolfgang D. Elfe and James Hardin (1992)

125 *Twentieth-Century Caribbean and Black African Writers, Second Series,* edited by Bernth Lindfors and Reinhard Sander (1993)

126 *Seventeenth-Century British Nondramatic Poets, Second Series,* edited by M. Thomas Hester (1993)

127 *American Newspaper Publishers, 1950-1990,* edited by Perry J. Ashley (1993)

128 *Twentieth-Century Italian Poets, Second Series,* edited by Giovanna Wedel De Stasio, Glauco Cambon, and Antonio Illiano (1993)

129 *Nineteenth-Century German Writers, 1841-1900,* edited by James Hardin and Siegfried Mews (1993)

130 *American Short-Story Writers Since World War II,* edited by Patrick Meanor (1993)

131 *Seventeenth-Century British Nondramatic Poets, Third Series,* edited by M. Thomas Hester (1993)

132 *Sixteenth-Century British Nondramatic Writers, First Series,* edited by David A. Richardson (1993)

133 *Nineteenth-Century German Writers to 1840,* edited by James Hardin and Siegfried Mews (1993)

134 *Twentieth-Century Spanish Poets, Second Series,* edited by Jerry Phillips Winfield (1994)

135 *British Short-Fiction Writers, 1880-1914: The Realist Tradition,* edited by William B. Thesing (1994)

136 *Sixteenth-Century British Nondramatic Writers, Second Series,* edited by David A. Richardson (1994)

137 *American Magazine Journalists, 1900-1960, Second Series,* edited by Sam G. Riley (1994)

138 *German Writers and Works of the High Middle Ages: 1170-1280,* edited by James Hardin and Will Hasty (1994)

139 *British Short-Fiction Writers, 1945-1980,* edited by Dean Baldwin (1994)

140 *American Book-Collectors and Bibliographers, First Series,* edited by Joseph Rosenblum (1994)

141 *British Children's Writers, 1880-1914,* edited by Laura M. Zaidman (1994)

142 *Eighteenth-Century British Literary Biographers,* edited by Steven Serafin (1994)

143 *American Novelists Since World War II, Third Series,* edited by James R. Giles and Wanda H. Giles (1994)

144 *Nineteenth-Century British Literary Biographers,* edited by Steven Serafin (1994)

145 *Modern Latin-American Fiction Writers, Second Series,* edited by William Luis and Ann González (1994)

146 *Old and Middle English Literature,* edited by Jeffrey Helterman and Jerome Mitchell (1994)

147 *South Slavic Writers Before World War II,* edited by Vasa D. Mihailovich (1994)

148 *German Writers and Works of the Early Middle Ages: 800-1170,* edited by Will Hasty and James Hardin (1994)

149 *Late Nineteenth- and Early Twentieth-Century British Literary Biographers,* edited by Steven Serafin (1995)

150 *Early Modern Russian Writers, Late Seventeenth and Eighteenth Centuries,* edited by Marcus C. Levitt (1995)

151 *British Prose Writers of the Early Seventeenth Century,* edited by Clayton D. Lein (1995)

152 *American Novelists Since World War II, Fourth Series,* edited by James R. Giles and Wanda H. Giles (1995)

153 *Late-Victorian and Edwardian British Novelists, First Series,* edited by George M. Johnson (1995)

154 *The British Literary Book Trade, 1700-1820,* edited by James K. Bracken and Joel Silver (1995)

155 *Twentieth-Century British Literary Biographers,* edited by Steven Serafin (1995)

156 *British Short-Fiction Writers, 1880-1914: The Romantic Tradition,* edited by William F. Naufftus (1995)

157 *Twentieth-Century Caribbean and Black African Writers, Third Series,* edited by Bernth Lindfors and Reinhard Sander (1995)

158 *British Reform Writers, 1789-1832,* edited by Gary Kelly and Edd Applegate (1995)

159 *British Short-Fiction Writers, 1800-1880,* edited by John R. Greenfield (1996)

160 *British Children's Writers, 1914-1960,* edited by Donald R. Hettinga and Gary D. Schmidt (1996)

161 *British Children's Writers Since 1960, First Series,* edited by Caroline Hunt (1996)

162 *British Short-Fiction Writers, 1915-1945,* edited by John H. Rogers (1996)

163 *British Children's Writers, 1800-1880,* edited by Meena Khorana (1996)

164 *German Baroque Writers, 1580-1660,* edited by James Hardin (1996)

165 *American Poets Since World War II, Fourth Series,* edited by Joseph Conte (1996)

166 *British Travel Writers, 1837-1875,* edited by Barbara Brothers and Julia Gergits (1996)

167 *Sixteenth-Century British Nondramatic Writers, Third Series,* edited by David A. Richardson (1996)

168 *German Baroque Writers, 1661-1730,* edited by James Hardin (1996)

169 *American Poets Since World War II, Fifth Series,* edited by Joseph Conte (1996)

170 *The British Literary Book Trade, 1475-1700,* edited by James K. Bracken and Joel Silver (1996)

171 *Twentieth-Century American Sportswriters,* edited by Richard Orodenker (1996)

172 *Sixteenth-Century British Nondramatic Writers, Fourth Series,* edited by David A. Richardson (1996)

173 *American Novelists Since World War II, Fifth Series,* edited by James R. Giles and Wanda H. Giles (1996)

174 *British Travel Writers, 1876-1909,* edited by Barbara Brothers and Julia Gergits (1997)

175 *Native American Writers of the United States,* edited by Kenneth M. Roemer (1997)

176 *Ancient Greek Authors,* edited by Ward W. Briggs (1997)

177 *Italian Novelists Since World War II, 1945-1965,* edited by Augustus Pallotta (1997)

178 *British Fantasy and Science-Fiction Writers Before World War I,* edited by Darren Harris-Fain (1997)

179 *German Writers of the Renaissance and Reformation, 1280-1580,* edited by James Hardin and Max Reinhart (1997)

180 *Japanese Fiction Writers, 1868-1945,* edited by Van C. Gessel (1997)

181 *South Slavic Writers Since World War II,* edited by Vasa D. Mihailovich (1997)

182 *Japanese Fiction Writers Since World War II,* edited by Van C. Gessel (1997)

183 *American Travel Writers, 1776-1864,* edited by James J. Schramer and Donald Ross (1997)

184 *Nineteenth-Century British Book-Collectors and Bibliographers,* edited by William Baker and Kenneth Womack (1997)

185 *American Literary Journalists, 1945-1995, First Series,* edited by Arthur J. Kaul (1998)

186 *Nineteenth-Century American Western Writers,* edited by Robert L. Gale (1998)

187 *American Book Collectors and Bibliographers, Second Series,* edited by Joseph Rosenblum (1998)

188 *American Book and Magazine Illustrators to 1920,* edited by Steven E. Smith, Catherine A. Hastedt, and Donald H. Dyal (1998)

189 *American Travel Writers, 1850-1915,* edited by Donald Ross and James J. Schramer (1998)

190 *British Reform Writers, 1832-1914,* edited by Gary Kelly and Edd Applegate (1998)

191 *British Novelists Between the Wars,* edited by George M. Johnson (1998)

192 *French Dramatists, 1789-1914,* edited by Barbara T. Cooper (1998)

193 *American Poets Since World War II, Sixth Series,* edited by Joseph Conte (1998)

194 *British Novelists Since 1960, Second Series,* edited by Merritt Moseley (1998)

195 *British Travel Writers, 1910-1939,* edited by Barbara Brothers and Julia Gergits (1998)

196 *Italian Novelists Since World War II, 1965-1995,* edited by Augustus Pallotta (1999)

197 *Late-Victorian and Edwardian British Novelists, Second Series,* edited by George M. Johnson (1999)

198 *Russian Literature in the Age of Pushkin and Gogol: Prose,* edited by Christine A. Rydel (1999)

199 *Victorian Women Poets,* edited by William B. Thesing (1999)

200 *American Women Prose Writers to 1820,* edited by Carla J. Mulford, with Angela Vietto and Amy E. Winans (1999)

201 *Twentieth-Century British Book Collectors and Bibliographers,* edited by William Baker and Kenneth Womack (1999)

202 *Nineteenth-Century American Fiction Writers,* edited by Kent P. Ljungquist (1999)

203 *Medieval Japanese Writers,* edited by Steven D. Carter (1999)

204 *British Travel Writers, 1940-1997,* edited by Barbara Brothers and Julia M. Gergits (1999)

205 *Russian Literature in the Age of Pushkin and Gogol: Poetry and Drama,* edited by Christine A. Rydel (1999)

206 *Twentieth-Century American Western Writers, First Series,* edited by Richard H. Cracroft (1999)

207 *British Novelists Since 1960, Third Series,* edited by Merritt Moseley (1999)

208 *Literature of the French and Occitan Middle Ages: Eleventh to Fifteenth Centuries,* edited by Deborah Sinnreich-Levi and Ian S. Laurie (1999)

209 *Chicano Writers, Third Series,* edited by Francisco A. Lomelí and Carl R. Shirley (1999)

210 *Ernest Hemingway: A Documentary Volume,* edited by Robert W. Trogdon (1999)

211 *Ancient Roman Writers,* edited by Ward W. Briggs (1999)

212 *Twentieth-Century American Western Writers, Second Series,* edited by Richard H. Cracroft (1999)

213 *Pre-Nineteenth-Century British Book Collectors and Bibliographers,* edited by William Baker and Kenneth Womack (1999)

214 *Twentieth-Century Danish Writers,* edited by Marianne Stecher-Hansen (1999)

215 *Twentieth-Century Eastern European Writers, First Series,* edited by Steven Serafin (1999)

216 *British Poets of the Great War: Brooke, Rosenberg, Thomas. A Documentary Volume,* edited by Patrick Quinn (2000)

217 *Nineteenth-Century French Poets,* edited by Robert Beum (2000)

218 *American Short-Story Writers Since World War II, Second Series,* edited by Patrick Meanor and Gwen Crane (2000)

219 *F. Scott Fitzgerald's* The Great Gatsby: *A Documentary Volume,* edited by Matthew J. Bruccoli (2000)

220 *Twentieth-Century Eastern European Writers, Second Series,* edited by Steven Serafin (2000)

221 *American Women Prose Writers, 1870-1920,* edited by Sharon M. Harris, with the assistance of Heidi L. M. Jacobs and Jennifer Putzi (2000)

222 *H. L. Mencken: A Documentary Volume,* edited by Richard J. Schrader (2000)

223 *The American Renaissance in New England, Second Series,* edited by Wesley T. Mott (2000)

224 *Walt Whitman: A Documentary Volume,* edited by Joel Myerson (2000)

225 *South African Writers,* edited by Paul A. Scanlon (2000)

226 *American Hard-Boiled Crime Writers,* edited by George Parker Anderson and Julie B. Anderson (2000)

227 *American Novelists Since World War II, Sixth Series,* edited by James R. Giles and Wanda H. Giles (2000)

228 *Twentieth-Century American Dramatists, Second Series,* edited by Christopher J. Wheatley (2000)

229 *Thomas Wolfe: A Documentary Volume,* edited by Ted Mitchell (2001)

230 *Australian Literature, 1788-1914,* edited by Selina Samuels (2001)

231 *British Novelists Since 1960, Fourth Series,* edited by Merritt Moseley (2001)

232 *Twentieth-Century Eastern European Writers, Third Series,* edited by Steven Serafin (2001)

233 *British and Irish Dramatists Since World War II, Second Series,* edited by John Bull (2001)

234 *American Short-Story Writers Since World War II, Third Series,* edited by Patrick Meanor and Richard E. Lee (2001)

235 *The American Renaissance in New England, Third Series,* edited by Wesley T. Mott (2001)

236 *British Rhetoricians and Logicians, 1500-1660,* edited by Edward A. Malone (2001)

237 *The Beats: A Documentary Volume,* edited by Matt Theado (2001)

238 *Russian Novelists in the Age of Tolstoy and Dostoevsky,* edited by J. Alexander Ogden and Judith E. Kalb (2001)

239 *American Women Prose Writers: 1820-1870,* edited by Amy E. Hudock and Katharine Rodier (2001)

240 *Late Nineteenth- and Early Twentieth-Century British Women Poets,* edited by William B. Thesing (2001)

241 *American Sportswriters and Writers on Sport,* edited by Richard Orodenker (2001)

242 *Twentieth-Century European Cultural Theorists, First Series,* edited by Paul Hansom (2001)

243 *The American Renaissance in New England, Fourth Series,* edited by Wesley T. Mott (2001)

244 *American Short-Story Writers Since World War II, Fourth Series,* edited by Patrick Meanor and Joseph McNicholas (2001)

245 *British and Irish Dramatists Since World War II, Third Series,* edited by John Bull (2001)

Dictionary of Literary Biography Documentary Series

1 *Sherwood Anderson, Willa Cather, John Dos Passos, Theodore Dreiser, F. Scott Fitzgerald, Ernest Hemingway, Sinclair Lewis,* edited by Margaret A. Van Antwerp (1982)

2 *James Gould Cozzens, James T. Farrell, William Faulkner, John O'Hara, John Steinbeck, Thomas Wolfe, Richard Wright,* edited by Margaret A. Van Antwerp (1982)

3 *Saul Bellow, Jack Kerouac, Norman Mailer, Vladimir Nabokov, John Updike, Kurt Vonnegut,* edited by Mary Bruccoli (1983)

4 *Tennessee Williams,* edited by Margaret A. Van Antwerp and Sally Johns (1984)

5 *American Transcendentalists,* edited by Joel Myerson (1988)

6 *Hardboiled Mystery Writers: Raymond Chandler, Dashiell Hammett, Ross Macdonald,* edited by Matthew J. Bruccoli and Richard Layman (1989)

7 *Modern American Poets: James Dickey, Robert Frost, Marianne Moore,* edited by Karen L. Rood (1989)

8 *The Black Aesthetic Movement,* edited by Jeffrey Louis Decker (1991)

9 *American Writers of the Vietnam War: W. D. Ehrhart, Larry Heinemann, Tim O'Brien, Walter McDonald, John M. Del Vecchio,* edited by Ronald Baughman (1991)

10 *The Bloomsbury Group,* edited by Edward L. Bishop (1992)

11 *American Proletarian Culture: The Twenties and The Thirties,* edited by Jon Christian Suggs (1993)

12 *Southern Women Writers: Flannery O'Connor, Katherine Anne Porter, Eudora Welty,* edited by Mary Ann Wimsatt and Karen L. Rood (1994)

13 *The House of Scribner, 1846-1904,* edited by John Delaney (1996)

14 *Four Women Writers for Children, 1868-1918,* edited by Caroline C. Hunt (1996)

15 *American Expatriate Writers: Paris in the Twenties,* edited by Matthew J. Bruccoli and Robert W. Trogdon (1997)

16 *The House of Scribner, 1905-1930,* edited by John Delaney (1997)

17 *The House of Scribner, 1931-1984,* edited by John Delaney (1998)

18 *British Poets of The Great War: Sassoon, Graves, Owen,* edited by Patrick Quinn (1999)

19 *James Dickey,* edited by Judith S. Baughman (1999)

See also DLB 210, 216, 219, 222, 224, 229, 237

Dictionary of Literary Biography Yearbooks

1980 edited by Karen L. Rood, Jean W. Ross, and Richard Ziegfeld (1981)

1981 edited by Karen L. Rood, Jean W. Ross, and Richard Ziegfeld (1982)

1982 edited by Richard Ziegfeld; associate editors: Jean W. Ross and Lynne C. Zeigler (1983)

1983 edited by Mary Bruccoli and Jean W. Ross; associate editor Richard Ziegfeld (1984)

1984 edited by Jean W. Ross (1985)

1985 edited by Jean W. Ross (1986)

1986 edited by J. M. Brook (1987)

1988 edited by J. M. Brook (1989)

1989 edited by J. M. Brook (1990)

1990 edited by James W. Hipp (1991)

1991 edited by James W. Hipp (1992)

1992 edited by James W. Hipp (1993)

1993 edited by James W. Hipp, contributing editor George Garrett (1994)

1994 edited by James W. Hipp, contributing editor George Garrett (1995)

1995 edited by James W. Hipp, contributing editor George Garrett (1996)

1996 edited by Samuel W. Bruce and L. Kay Webster, contributing editor George Garrett (1997)

1997 edited by Matthew J. Bruccoli and George Garrett, with the assistance of L. Kay Webster (1998)

1998 edited by Matthew J. Bruccoli, contributing editor George Garrett, with the assistance of D. W. Thomas (1999)

1999 edited by Matthew J. Bruccoli, contributing editor George Garrett, with the assistance of D. W. Thomas (2000)

2000 edited by Matthew J. Bruccoli, contributing editor George Garrett, with the assistance of George Parker Anderson (2001)

Concise Series

Concise Dictionary of American Literary Biography, 7 volumes (1988-1999): *The New Consciousness, 1941-1968; Colonization to the American Renaissance, 1640-1865; Realism, Naturalism, and Local Color, 1865-1917; The Twenties, 1917-1929; The Age of Maturity, 1929-1941; Broadening Views, 1968-1988; Supplement: Modern Writers, 1900-1998.*

Concise Dictionary of British Literary Biography, 8 volumes (1991-1992): *Writers of the Middle Ages and Renaissance Before 1660; Writers of the Restoration and Eighteenth Century, 1660-1789; Writers of the Romantic Period, 1789-1832; Victorian Writers, 1832-1890; Late-Victorian and Edwardian Writers, 1890-1914; Modern Writers, 1914-1945; Writers After World War II, 1945-1960; Contemporary Writers, 1960 to Present.*

Concise Dictionary of World Literary Biography, 10 volumes projected (1999-): *Ancient Greek and Roman Writers; German Writers; African, Caribbean, and Latin American Writers; South Slavic and Eastern European Writers.*

Dictionary of Literary Biography® • Volume Two Hundred Forty-Five

British and Irish Dramatists Since World War II

Third Series

Dictionary of Literary Biography® • Volume Two Hundred Forty-Five

British and Irish Dramatists Since World War II

Third Series

Edited by
John Bull
University of Reading

A Bruccoli Clark Layman Book
The Gale Group
Detroit • San Francisco • London • Boston • Woodbridge, Conn.

Matthew J. Bruccoli and Richard Layman, Editorial Directors
Karen L. Rood, Senior Editor

Printed in the United States of America

The paper used in this publication meets the minimum requirements of American National Standard for Information Sciences–Permanence Paper for Printed Library Materials, ANSI Z39.48-1984.∞™

Library of Congress Cataloging-in-Publication Data

British and Irish dramatists since World War II. Third series / edited by John Bull.
p. cm.–(Dictionary of literary biography: v. 245)
"A Bruccoli Clark Layman book."
Includes bibliographical references and index.
ISBN 0-7876-4662-8 (alk. paper)
1. English drama–20th century–Bio-bibliography–Dictionaries. 2. English drama–Irish authors–Bio-bibliography–Dictionaries. 3. Dramatists, English–20th century–Biography–Dictionaries. 4. Dramatists, Irish–20th century–Biography–Dictionaries. I. Bull, John (John Stanley). II. Series.

PR736.B68 A3966 2001b
822'.91409'03–dc21 2001040163
[B]

10 9 8 7 6 5 4 3 2 1

For my parents with immense
love and gratitude

Contents

Plan of the Series

. . . Almost the most prodigious asset of a country, and perhaps its most precious possession, is its native literary product—when that product is fine and noble and enduring.

Mark Twain*

The advisory board, the editors, and the publisher of the *Dictionary of Literary Biography* are joined in endorsing Mark Twain's declaration. The literature of a nation provides an inexhaustible resource of permanent worth. Our purpose is to make literature and its creators better understood and more accessible to students and the reading public, while satisfying the needs of teachers and researchers.

To meet these requirements, *literary biography* has been construed in terms of the author's achievement. The most important thing about a writer is his writing. Accordingly, the entries in *DLB* are career biographies, tracing the development of the author's canon and the evolution of his reputation.

The purpose of *DLB* is not only to provide reliable information in a usable format but also to place the figures in the larger perspective of literary history and to offer appraisals of their accomplishments by qualified scholars.

The publication plan for *DLB* resulted from two years of preparation. The project was proposed to Bruccoli Clark by Frederick G. Ruffner, president of the Gale Research Company, in November 1975. After specimen entries were prepared and typeset, an advisory board was formed to refine the entry format and develop the series rationale. In meetings held during 1976, the publisher, series editors, and advisory board approved the scheme for a comprehensive biographical dictionary of persons who contributed to literature. Editorial work on the first volume began in January 1977, and it was published in 1978. In order to make *DLB* more than a dictionary and to compile volumes that individually have claim to status as literary history, it was decided to organize volumes by topic, period, or genre. Each of these freestanding volumes provides a biographical-bibliographical guide and overview for a particular area of literature. We are convinced that this organization—as opposed to a single alphabet method—constitutes a valuable innovation in the presentation of reference material. The volume plan necessarily requires many decisions for the placement and treatment of authors. Certain figures will be included in separate volumes, but with different entries emphasizing the aspect of his career appropriate to each volume. Ernest Hemingway, for example, is represented in *American Writers in Paris, 1920–1939* by an entry focusing on his expatriate apprenticeship; he is also in *American Novelists, 1910–1945* with an entry surveying his entire career, as well as in *American Short-Story Writers, 1910–1945, Second Series* with an entry concentrating on his short fiction. Each volume includes a cumulative index of the subject authors and articles.

Since 1981 the series has been further augmented by the *DLB Yearbooks,* which update published entries, add new entries to keep the *DLB* current with contemporary activity, and provide articles on literary history. There have also been nineteen *DLB Documentary Series* volumes which provide illustrations, facsimiles, and biographical and critical source materials for figures, works, or groups judged to have particular interest for students. In 1999 the *Documentary Series* was incorporated into the *DLB* volume numbering system beginning with *DLB 210: Ernest Hemingway.*

We define literature as the *intellectual commerce of a nation:* not merely as belles lettres but as that ample and complex process by which ideas are generated, shaped, and transmitted. *DLB* entries are not limited to "creative writers" but extend to other figures who in their time and in their way influenced the mind of a people. Thus the series encompasses historians, journalists, publishers, book collectors, and screenwriters. By this means readers of *DLB* may be aided to perceive literature not as cult scripture in the keeping of intellectual high priests but firmly positioned at the center of a nation's life.

DLB includes the major writers appropriate to each volume and those standing in the ranks behind them. Scholarly and critical counsel has been sought in

**From an unpublished section of Mark Twain's autobiography, copyright by the Mark Twain Company*

deciding which minor figures to include and how full their entries should be. Wherever possible, useful references are made to figures who do not warrant separate entries.

Each *DLB* volume has an expert volume editor responsible for planning the volume, selecting the figures for inclusion, and assigning the entries. Volume editors are also responsible for preparing, where appropriate, appendices surveying the major periodicals and literary and intellectual movements for their volumes, as well as lists of further readings. Work on the series as a whole is coordinated at the Bruccoli Clark Layman editorial center in Columbia, South Carolina, where the editorial staff is responsible for accuracy and utility of the published volumes.

One feature that distinguishes *DLB* is the illustration policy–its concern with the iconography of literature. Just as an author is influenced by his surroundings, so is the reader's understanding of the author enhanced by a knowledge of his environment. Therefore *DLB* volumes include not only drawings, paintings, and photographs of authors, often depicting them at various stages in their careers, but also illustrations of their families and places where they lived. Title pages are regularly reproduced in facsimile along with dust jackets for modern authors. The dust jackets are a special feature of *DLB* because they often document better than anything else the way in which an author's work was perceived in its own time. Specimens of the writers' manuscripts and letters are included when feasible.

Samuel Johnson rightly decreed that "The chief glory of every people arises from its authors." The purpose of the *Dictionary of Literary Biography* is to compile literary history in the surest way available to us–by accurate and comprehensive treatment of the lives and work of those who contributed to it.

The *DLB* Advisory Board

Introduction

The period covered by the *British and Irish Dramatists Since World War II* volumes of the *Dictionary of Literary Biography*–a series that thus far comprises *DLB 233* (2001) and the present volume–embraces the work of writers working in theatrical traditions ranging from the classic well-made play to the most radical avant-garde pieces. This variety is indicative of the fact that this period is one of the most important in British drama, comparable to the late-Elizabethan/Jacobean and post-Restoration eras in terms of the quantity and quality of new work and surpassing both of them in the sheer variety of theatrical fare on offer.

More than a decade passed from the end of World War II before any real challenge to the continuity of the prewar theater emerged. This challenge is usually dated as having begun on 8 May 1956, the opening night of John Osborne's *Look Back in Anger;* this first "new wave" was challenged by a new generation of writers after 1968, which, in its turn, was challenged by successive generations of writers from the 1980s onward. At any particular moment, however, alongside the work of new and ideologically adventurous writers, versions of essentially the same kind of plays that could be found at the end of the war continued to be produced, their social mores only slightly modified by the changing society that they still sought to mirror.

These volumes will, thus, give the reader a sense not only of the strength of British and Irish theater in the postwar period but also of its rich variety, a variety that owes much to the circumstance that theater in Ireland, Scotland, and Wales has evolved partly in parallel and partly in opposition to that in England, a country perceived by many of the writers as a locus of colonial oppression and would-be hegemony. Similarly, in Liverpool, in Stoke, and in Hull–to take but three English examples–playwrights have seen as an important part of their function the creation of a theater that reflects the particular concerns of their locale and opposes the centralizing cultural control of London and the Home Counties. The struggle for survival of many non-London theaters and the determination of some of them to reflect regional differences are discussed in some of the entries in these volumes, as is the continuing development of television–and, to a lesser extent, radio–drama as media capable of finding audiences who are aware in their day-to-day lives of such regional disparities.

Regionality has combined with differences in class, ethnicity, gender, and sexual preference to produce the wide variety of drama in the British Isles. A play about the lives of three working-class women in Protestant Belfast, such as Marie Jones's *The Hamster Wheel* (1990), offers quite different perspectives from those in a play about a middle-class vicar's wife undergoing a nervous breakdown in suburbia, such as Alan Ayckbourn's *Woman in Mind* (1985); or those in a play also set in the London suburbs but dealing with the struggle for control of their own lives by lesbian mothers, such as Sarah Daniels's *Neaptide* (1982); or those in a play set in London about the tensions between a West Indian woman and her English-born daughters, such as Winsome Pinnock's *Leave Taking* (1987)–and yet, all four are centrally concerned with female experience.

So, above all, these volumes will celebrate this sense of disparity and diversity, whether it be thought to be a product of essentially ideological forces or a result of the uniqueness of the individual writers–and these playwrights disagree on this issue, as they do on so much else. The series will obviously not encompass every playwright active in the period, but every effort has been made to make the volumes as representative as possible, with an emphasis not only on the established and "canonical" writers but also on newer and potentially exciting talents. The inevitable omissions will, one hopes, engender debate rather than recrimination.

In his foreword to Peter Noble's *British Theatre* (1946) Laurence Olivier characterized postwar theater as so full of "notable talents . . . vitality and enthusiasm" that it was comparable to what he saw as the previous golden age, "the glorious Restoration period." This remark reads now as a somewhat strange one, given the fairly general acceptance of the official line enshrined in the critical writings of Kenneth Tynan, who wrote in 1954 in an essay collected in his *Curtains* (1961), "The bare fact is that, apart from the revivals and imports, there is nothing in the London theater that one dares discuss with an intelligent man for more than ten minutes" and no sign "of a native playwright who might set the boards smouldering." He was not alone in this feeling: in an account of the first five years of theatrical activity after the war J. C. Trewin concluded, "As I write now, in the spring of 1950, the need for new playwrights with something to say and the means to say it, is still the first anxiety of the theatre."

How are these diametrically opposed opinions to be reconciled? First, by realizing that in one sense Olivier was correct. At the outbreak of war in 1939 the government's first instinct had been to close the London theaters. With the help of the Council for the Encouragement of Music and Arts (CEMA), formed in 1940 and the forerunner of the Arts Council, many of these London productions toured the provinces. Almost immediately, however, the London theaters began to reopen. January 1940 brought the return of Noel Coward's *Design for Living* to the Savoy Theatre after a provincial tour, and by the summer of 1941, after the air Battle of Britain had been won, London theater began to revive in earnest, with Coward's *Blithe Spirit,* directed by the author and opening that year, enjoying the longest wartime run. Audiences diminished in 1944 with the arrival of the V-bombs; but on the day the war ended, thirty-six theaters were open in London's West End.

The end of the war brought a continuation of a tradition of theatrical activity that was virtually unbroken. When Olivier speaks of a new golden age, he is referring to the revival of classical plays–in particular, the plays of William Shakespeare, which Olivier himself interpreted brilliantly in this period–and he is conceiving of the theater almost exclusively in terms of the panoply of actors who trod the boards. In 1975 Tynan recalled of the 1940s and early 1950s: "theatres . . . belonged to the actors." They also belonged, however, to the impresarios, the most important of whom, Binkie Beaumont of the H. M. Tennant Company, had twelve plays running in eight theaters as the war ended. Within a year the number had doubled. The control of the theater by Beaumont–who was interested in it as, above all, a vehicle for star actors–and his rivals was the major factor in the resistance to innovation. At the beginning of 1946 just two new plays were running in London, and neither was in the West End; one was at the experimental Swiss Cottage Embassy and the other, by Ted Willis, at the Unity Theatre in King's Cross.

New native writers did begin to emerge, although not in great numbers at first. One was William Douglas Home, whose career started in 1947 with *The Chiltern Hundreds,* a country-house comedy with an aristocratic Labour candidate being opposed in an election by his horrified Conservative-supporting butler, a somewhat obvious plot device in a West End theater not looking forward to the kind of change promised by the postwar Labour administration of Clement Atlee. Home's play serves well as an indication of the way in which postwar theater in England was intent on preserving the links with prewar society, with only the most token gestures toward the present. Hugh Hunt puts the point well in his, Kenneth Richards's, and John Russell Taylor's *The Revels History of Drama in English: 1880 to the Present Day* (1978): "Between 1946 and 1956 British theatre was largely living on its past both in subject matter and in staging." In 1946 Barry Jackson was installed for two important years as director of the Shakespeare Memorial Theatre, where he helped bring the actor Paul Scofield and the director Peter Brook to public recognition. Before finding a London base at the Theatre Royal, Stratford East, in 1952 and playing an important part in the theatrical "new wave" in the late 1950s, Joan Littlewood had worked with the Theatre Workshop on tour beginning in 1945; the Theatre Workshop, in turn, was a continuation of the work done by the Theatre Union in Manchester from 1936 to 1942. The activity of Unity Theatre in presenting politicized drama in London and Glasgow in the 1940s and 1950s was also extremely important. Avant-garde work was being done at venues such as the Mercury Theatre in Notting Hill, which put on verse dramas by the likes of Ronald Duncan and T. S. Eliot, so that Philip Barnes is right to stress the importance of "the less sensational, and certainly less known or popular, experimental theatre which emerged in the years immediately following the war."

More generally, however, the stress was on the perpetuation of a theatrical world that began to look increasingly out of kilter with the political and cultural changes of the postwar period. The basic fare was provided by writers who had already been established before the outbreak of hostilities, by revivals, by American musicals–fourteen American plays and musicals were running in London in 1955–and by European imports. Indeed, one of the more-heartening features of the late 1940s and early 1950s was the tours of companies to Europe under British Council sponsorship, part of the movement toward a reconstitution of a sense of a united Europe; and in 1951 the impresario Peter Daubeny started to bring European companies to London, including the famous visit of the Berliner Ensemble in 1956 and culminating in the first of several highly successful World Theatre Seasons at the Aldwych Theatre in 1964.

As far as the new writing of the period was concerned, Tynan wickedly–if a little unfairly, in light of the occasional playwright such as Terence Rattigan, who attempted to use the tradition of the well-made play more subversively–summarized the typical plot in 1954 in an essay collected in *Curtains:*

> If you seek a tombstone, look about you; survey the peculiar nullity of our drama's prevalent genre, the Loamshire play. Its setting is a country house in what used to be called Loamshire but is now, as a heroic tribute to realism, sometimes called Berkshire. Except when somebody must sneeze, or be murdered, the sun invariably shines. The inhabitants belong to a social class derived partly from romantic novels and partly from the leisured life he will lead after the play is a success–this being the only effort of imagination he is called upon to make. Joys and sorrows are giggles and whimpers; the crash of denunciation dwindles into "Oh, stuff, Mummy!" and "Oh, really, Daddy!" And so grim is the continuity of the thing that the foregoing paragraph might have been written at any time during the last thirty years.

Apart from revivals, musicals, and foreign imports, theater in the immediate postwar years came to rely on a diet of thrillers, farces, and drawing-room dramas and comedies that did nothing to threaten a status quo clearly out of tune with the changing cultural climate. "The drawing-room comedy was above all a theatrical pattern based on a social pattern; essential to its effect was the imaginative presence of a rigid convention of behaviour against which everything (in certain classes at least) would always be measured and judged," wrote John Russell Taylor in 1967.

This background helps to explain the inordinate importance placed on 8 May 1956, the date of the first performance of Osborne's first staged play, *Look Back in Anger*–the event that marks "'then' off decisively from 'now,' as Taylor wrote in *Anger and After* (1962)–at the Royal Court Theatre in London, the most important venue then and now for the presentation of new plays in England. Perhaps an easier way to stress the perceived significance of Osborne's play and the others that were seen as part of the movement is to repeat the words of a critic of the old order, Ivor Brown, from his review of that year's theater: "I am not for a moment saying that bombed-site scenery is inexcusable . . . All I suggest is . . . a reluctance to accept railing against life in a rag-and-bone setting as essentially and mentally more truthful than the tolerance, even–dare we say it–the cheerfulness of 'civilised' people not deeming personal cleanliness to be reactionary and undemocratic." In his foreword to the first published history of the Royal Court, Martin Esslin reinforced the way in which the success of Osborne's play acted as a catalyst for new writing: by revealing "the fact, hitherto unsuspected by the commercial entrepreneurs of the theatre, that plays dealing with lower class characters speaking a non-standard English and flouting the conventions of the 'who's for tennis' school of playwriting could actually become profitable theatrical ventures."

Esslin's emphasis on the profit motive is important. Since 1945 the Arts Council had subsidized the work of the Old Vic and other "noncommercial" theaters, which were, in addition, exempted from paying the entertainment tax. Commercial theater impresarios were quick to seize on the loophole: "by spreading their activities to embrace non-profit-distributing companies, commercial managements were able, under the 1916 Finance Act, to [also] claim exemption," according to Hunt, Richards, and Taylor. The result, however, had been a proliferation of revivals of classics rather than–except rarely–the promotion of new work; as a result, the Arts Council withdrew its support from such ventures in 1951. But commercial managements began to realize the potential of transferring successful new works from the subsidized sector to the mainstream, which was a major factor in the careers of many writers, and the commercial and noncommercial theater were bound in an increasingly symbiotic relationship over the years. "It was in the interest of the West End Managers to take some plays for which they did not have to pay rehearsal costs, which had an established reputation and for which there was already a known audience. Such transfers were often "more in the interest of the West End establishments than of the 'revolutionary' theatres," according to John Pick's *The West-End: Mismanagement and Snobbery* (1983). The possibility had been heralded by the unexpected success of Samuel Beckett's *Waiting for Godot* in 1955, which had opened at the subsidized Arts Theatre before becoming the first subsidized transfer to the West End. Donald Albery of Donmar Productions said in *The Times* (London) for 26 March 1961: "I always maintain that *Waiting for Godot* was unquestionably the start of the new wave, better than anything since. It was the first stirring of anything new and its nine-month run at the Criterion was unheard of in those days for that sort of thing, not a thriller, or a drawing-room comedy or the revival of a classic."

Look Back in Anger also transferred, going to the Lyric Theatre in Hammersmith, thus generating revenue for the Royal Court experiment and continuing the pull for wider audiences that *Waiting for Godot* had initiated. The English version of Brendan Behan's *The Quare Fellow* also premiered in 1956, and the English version of his *The Hostage* and Shelagh Delaney's *A Taste of Honey* followed in 1958; all of them were directed and reworked by Littlewood at Stratford East. Debuts by such exciting writers as John Arden, Arnold Wesker, Harold Pinter, and Ann Jellicoe followed in quick succession, guaranteeing a consensus that a new dawn had risen. Perhaps the most significant aspect of the work of the new English Stage Company at the Royal Court, from the point of view of these volumes, is the emphasis it came to place on the promotion of new writing. The careers of many playwrights of later generations, including Edward Bond, Caryl Churchill, Maureen Duffy, and Timberlake Wertenbaker, owed much to the encouragement of George Devine and subsequent directors of the theater.

The impact of Beckett's work and of that of Eugène Ionesco (whose *The Lesson,* his first play to be staged in the British professional theater, ran at the Arts Theatre in the same year as *Waiting for Godot*) was to be seen at first mostly in avant-garde circles as a conscious opposition to the newly dominant mode of naturalism–as evidenced by N. F. Simpson's *A Resounding Tinkle* (1957), for instance, and Pinter's *The Birthday Party* (1958). But throughout the 1960s absurdism was increasingly appropriated by a mainstream that saw in it an opportunity to satirize middle-class mores in an adapted version of the classic comedy format. *The Times* (London) of 22 July 1960 made the point strongly when it compared the fate of the first staged plays of Simpson and Pinter with the much different reception accorded two of their later plays: "Two years ago *The Birthday Party* was thought so obscure that the critics despaired of it; today *The Caretaker* is a solid commercial hit. . . . Not so long ago *A Resounding Tinkle* was one of the Royal Court's less patronised ventures; this year *One Way Pendulum* became a notable West End success." That same year David Turner had a hit with a play whose very title, *Semi-Detached,* proclaims the connection between absurdism and the mainstream, and playwrights such as Giles Cooper with *Everything in the Garden* (1962) continued to develop the tradition. The plays of Joe Orton, the early work of Peter Shaffer and of Tom Stoppard, and, most obviously, the by-that-time impressive oeuvre of Ayckbourn, whose first big success was *Absurd Person Singular* in 1972, are all a part of that particular piece of the theatrical narrative.

In his 1946 foreword Olivier lays stress on the imminent creation of a National Theatre. It was another five years before the foundation stone was laid alongside the Royal Festival Hall, constructed as part of the 1951 Festival of Britain celebrations on the South Bank of the Thames in London. Twelve years later Olivier established the National Theatre Company at the Old Vic, and it was another thirteen years before the actual building was opened in 1976; its first commissioned work was *Weapons of Happiness* by Howard Brenton, who was four years old when Olivier's optimistic words of 1946 were written.

In Ireland, however, the Irish National Theatre Company had been formed in 1903, followed the next year by the opening of the Abbey Theatre in Dublin. The Irish National Theatre Company's first production was a double bill of plays by William Butler Yeats and Lady Isabella Augusta Persse Gregory, and the Abbey followed a rigorous policy of staging both Irish and foreign drama. John Millington Synge's *The Well of the Saints* was the second play performed there, and Henrik Ibsen was actively promoted. Indeed, the first production at Dublin's Gate Theatre, which opened in 1928, was Ibsen's *Peer Gynt,* and beginning in 1923 with *Shadow of a Gunman* Sean O'Casey was an imposing presence in the Abbey Theatre. The Dublin theater scene has long since established its independence from its English counterpart; Brian Friel's reputation was established at the 1964 Dublin Festival, for instance, with a first staging of *Philadelphia Here I Come!* at the Gaiety Theatre.

In Northern Ireland the efforts of the Ulster Group Theatre were responsible for nearly fifty new productions from 1940 to 1955 and also for staging the first production of Friel's *This Doubtful Paradise.* The Lyric Players' Theatre was founded in Ulster in 1951 to present poetic dramas; the theater's first productions were Yeats's *At the Hawk's Well* and *The Dreaming of the Bones.* But even before the opening of the Abbey Theatre the Irish theater establishment was split on the need to create a specifically Irish dramatic tradition, as opposed to looking elsewhere–particularly to England–for models and themes, as well as for playwrights. Indeed, not until 1901 was the first play in Irish staged at a recognized venue, the Irish Literary Theatre.

In an abrasive essay, "Groundwork for an Irish Theatre," the young Thomas Kilroy looked across the water from Ireland in 1959 at what had been happening at the Royal Court and the Theatre Royal, Stratford East theaters and lamented the lack of vigor in his own country's theater: "During the last twenty years few Irish dramatists have been in any way exciting technically. More often, however, our dramatists today are guilty of a worse defect than mere lack of technical proficiency. They are inclined to shirk the painful, sometimes tragic problems of a modern Ireland which is undergoing considerable social and ideological stress." With a few notable exceptions, it was not until the 1980s that the issues raised by Kilroy–technique and theme–became central to Irish drama, but when they did, they brought an exciting new generation of writing talent to the fore.

Similar debates were occurring in Scotland and in Wales. The historian of Edinburgh's Traverse Theatre, Joyce McMillan, concluded in 1988 that "it often seems that it's only in the past quarter of a century that there's been much Scottish Theatre to celebrate at all." One might set against that assessment James Bridie's launching in 1943 of the company that moved into Glasgow's Citizens Theatre two years later. Bridie's ambition was to create the Scottish national theater, taking his inspiration and the name of his theater from a 1909 declaration of intent by the Glasgow Repertory: "It is a citizens' theatre in the fullest sense of the term. Established to make Glasgow independent of London for its dramatic supplies, it provides plays which the Glasgow playgoers would otherwise not have an opportunity of seeing." Like its Irish counterparts, it survived on a mixture of new native work and revivals until the 1970s and was embroiled in essentially the same debate about the need to advance Scottish drama against the incursions of an English-oriented program.

The Welsh Theatre Company was formed in 1962, and not until the late 1970s can a discernibly Welsh theatrical movement be traced. The important changes in Welsh theater date from about the same time as the next great explosion in English playwriting talent, and comparable changes can be found in Scotland and Ireland. The second "new wave," which dates from around 1968, had resonances that were felt across the British Isles. That was the year in which theater censorship was abolished, the last attempts to retain it having foundered against the change in public sensibilities and, in the theater, by the challenge posed by such writers as Joe Orton and Edward Bond. The context of the 1956 "revolution" had been disillusionment with the Conservative administration of Harold Macmillan; in 1968 the impetus was the failure of the Labour administration of Harold Wilson to effect real socialist change. A framework of alternative oppositional theater rapidly grew, with writers and companies "frequently and violently in disagreement about the forms and aims of the new drama, but in agreement on one thing, the desire to create a drama that would stand in the vanguard of political and social change," as I put it in *New British Political Dramatists* (1984). Writers such as Brenton, John McGrath, Trevor Griffiths, David Hare, and David Edgar emerged from this cauldron, as did companies such as CAST in 1967; Moving Being, McGrath's 7:84, and John Fox's Welfare State in 1968; and the Pip Simmons Company in 1969.

The early work of these writers and companies was neither aimed at the mainstream theaters of London's West End nor welcomed by them. The Working Men's Clubs, community centers, hastily created small theaters above pubs, student unions, and Arts Labs that arose in response to the demand for the new drama formed a circuit that came to be known as "alternative theater." Possibly the first, and certainly the most famous, of these venues was the original Arts Lab founded in London's Drury Lane in 1968 by Jim Haynes. Its life was brief, but its example was quickly followed. "One of the interesting things about the Arts Lab is the number of other Arts Lab-like places that grew up in Britain within six months of our opening. People were arriving from virtually every town in Britain–Manchester, Birmingham, Brighton, Coventry, from all over the country–to consult us about setting up an Arts Lab in their own towns," Haynes recalls in *Thanks for Coming!* (1984). Many of the writers (McGrath most famously) and many of the companies (Fox's Welfare State International most spectacularly) remained–and still remain–resolute in their determination to stay independent of the conventional theater circuit.

One of the most fascinating developments to come out of the 1970s–although it was anticipated by Arden and Margaretta D'Arcy with *The Business of Good Government* (1960) and *Ars Longa, Vita Brevis* (1963)–has been the growth of community-based theater. This movement is usually dated from the first self-described "community play," Ann Jellicoe's *The Reckoning* (1979), about the Monmouth Rebellion, written to be performed by the pupils at a comprehensive school in Lyme Regis, Dorset.

Throughout the 1970s the money available through the Arts Council and the regional arts bodies to fringe companies and writers associated with them increased steadily, if not spectacularly. In contrast, the sums available to the subsidized theaters rose dramatically. In 1977–1978 the National Theatre and the Royal Shakespeare Theatre received £4.2 million, all of the rest £6 million. And of the latter figure, nearly £5 million went to theater buildings, leaving less than £1 million for thirty-three designated touring companies and just over a quarter of a million pounds for fifty-eight new projects. Increasingly, the subsidized theaters throughout Britain were able to offer the new writers commissions, transfers, and reruns. Richard Eyre's directorship of the Nottingham Playhouse in the 1970s, for instance, resulted in important new works such as Brenton's *The Churchill Play* (1974), Brenton and Hare's *Brassneck* (1973), Griffiths's *Comedians* (1975), and Brenton, Griffiths, Hare, and Ken Campbell's *Deeds* (1978). In Wales, Moving Being has been based in Cardiff since 1972, although not until 1981 can a significant movement, in terms of new companies dedicated to producing new work, be traced with the formation of Brith Gof and Made in Wales. In Scotland the Traverse Theatre, which had opened in 1963, was producing a healthy output of new work by the mid 1970s, and a similar pattern can be found throughout Britain and Ireland. Edward Bond's *Lear* (1971), *The Sea* (1973), *Bingo* (1973), *The Fool* (1975), *The Bundle* (1978), *The Woman* (1978), and *The Worlds* (1979) were staged in venues that not only included important regional theaters such as The Northcott in Exeter and the Newcastle Playhouse but also the Royal Court and the National Theatre, where Bond directed *The Woman.* By 1976 Brenton and Hare were in the National Theatre as writer and director, respectively. In 1979 Brenton calculated that about seven hundred new plays had been performed in Britain since 1965 (roughly equivalent to the total produced in the great Elizabethan/Jacobean period of 1582 to 1618), adding, provocatively, "and what is the drift, the chorus of this explosion of new work in the theatre? It is socialist." That same year Edgar, who had had some forty plays produced since his writing career started in 1970, had three plays running simultaneously in London.

The year 1979 was also when Prime Minister Margaret Thatcher came to power with the first of her Conservative governments, and the climate in the theater rapidly changed. The new administration immediately instituted decreases in Arts Council funding, and many of the alternative companies faced large funding cuts or even total elimination of their subsidies. For many of the writers whose earliest work dates from the late 1960s, the 1980s proved an increasingly difficult period with the subsidized theaters unwilling, or economically unable, to take a chance on large-scale epic dramas on political themes. For other writers whose origins were also in the 1960s, however, the 1980s proved to be a golden decade. Michael Frayn produced a steady stream of intelligently commercial hits. Alan Bennett, whose first professional work was with Peter Cooke, Dudley Moore, and Jonathan Miller in *Beyond the Fringe* (1961–1966), had his first stage play, *Forty Years On,* produced in 1970 and continued to gain in popularity and critical status with his subsequent work–particularly on television, a spawning ground for many of the playwrights who will be treated in these volumes, including Dennis Potter, Simon Gray, and Frayn, as well as offering a home for writers, such as John Mortimer, who had lost favor in the theater. Tom Stoppard wrote a series of highly acclaimed plays. Ayckbourn became, second only to Shakespeare, the most successful British playwright of all time as his works moved from the Stephen Joseph Theatre in Scarborough to the subsidized and commercial theaters of London, to the regional theaters, and, finally, to the flourishing amateur theatrical circuit. Other playwrights found a local audience that became a national one: Willy Russell in Liverpool, for instance, and, in Hull, John Godber, the most successful contemporary playwright after Ayckbourn.

Another seismic change occurred in the 1980s. The Royal Court Theatre had played a great part in launching the careers of Jellicoe, Churchill, and Duffy, and it continued to do so with women writers such as Wertenbaker and Pinnock; but for the majority of the theatergoing public in the 1960s the idea of a female playwright was probably enshrined in the work of Agatha Christie, whose *The Mousetrap* continues to play in London in an ever-increasingly longest theatrical run. But when Daniels's blisteringly exciting treatment of pornography, *Masterpieces,* opened at the Royal Exchange Theatre in Manchester in 1983 (later transferring to the Royal Court), it constituted a proclamation that new writing in the 1980s would be centered on a reexamination of gender roles. It heralded the emergence of a new generation of female writers who were responsible for some of the most exciting theater of the last two decades of the twentieth century. In Scotland, Liz Lochhead really began her theatrical career with *Blood and Ice* (1982), although she had earlier collaborated with Marcella Evaristi on a revue, *Sugar and Spice* (1978). Rona Monro's *Piper's Cave* (1985) announced another exciting new Scottish talent. In Northern Ireland, Marie Jones cofounded the Charabanc Theatre Company in 1983, the same year Christina Reid had her first play staged; Anne Devlin's first play, *Ourselves Alone,* premiered two years later. In England, Charlotte Keatley's highly successful *My Mother Said I Never Should* (1987) was preceded by five years of theatrical experience as a writer, and she was surrounded by many other new young female playwrights, including Sharman Macdonald, whose *When I Was a Girl, I Used to Scream and Shout* shot her into public prominence in 1984. Two of the most exciting pieces of theatrical opposition to the fiscal policies of the Thatcher years, *Top Girls* (1982) and *Serious Money* (1987), came from Churchill, whose first staged work dates from 1972–an earlier generation.

Serious Money transferred from the subsidized to the commercial theater, but in the 1980s and 1990s the subsidized theaters were forced to think harder about the scale and the extent of new work that could be reduced and the suitability of such productions as a source of much-needed revenue. These considerations tended to favor the use of established writers from a nonradical tradition, and two stalwarts of the commercial mainstream, Bennett and Frayn, had their first National Theatre productions in the 1990s with *The Madness of George III* (1991) and *Copenhagen* (1998), respectively. On the other hand, Terry Johnson, whose playwriting career began in 1979 but really took off with *Insignificance* in 1982, was welcomed into the National Theatre in 1998 as the director of Edward Ravencroft's *The London Cuckolds* and of his own *Cleo, Camping,* and *Emmanuelle and Dick.* Other National Theatre discoveries include Patrick Marber, with his exciting *Dealer's Choice* (1995) and *Closer* (1997).

Throughout the 1980s and into the 1990s the theater became more than ever a site of cultural confrontation between managements who felt economically forced to opt for a safe product and a new generation of writers who, cut off from the earlier traditions of middle-class theater, drew their models from the cinema, television, and other aspects of popular culture. If it was a political confrontation, it was one envisaged in quite different terms from those of the post-1956 and post-1968 generations. In 1986 Jim Cartwright brought the despair of the unemployed and dispossessed in a small Lancashire town to the rapt attention of well-to-do audiences at the Royal Court with his *Road;* Alan Bleasdale had done the same for the poor of Liverpool four years earlier with his television series *Boys from the Blackstuff* (1982), and it is easy to see that the fragmented structure of Cartwright's play owed more to his knowledge of television soap operas than to the venerable tradition of the well-made play.

The last ten or so years of the twentieth century brought the emergence of yet another new and exciting generation of writers who see the theater as the best place to work, and the amount of writing that has found a venue in this period is without precedent. These writers have not been supported by the nonsubsidized theater but have relied largely on a network of regional theater studios, fringe venues, and stages outside the conventional theatrical circuit, as well as on the strenuous activities of a substantial number of regionally based touring companies, most of which do not receive any form of financial backing. The problem for the new playwright is obvious: for all the excitement of getting a first play on, wherever and how briefly it may appear, the need to find a wider audience and longer runs for subsequent work is paramount in terms both of establishing a reputation that might invite future commissions and of sheer economic survival. As Kate Harwood says in *First Run* (1989), a collection of plays first produced in 1988:

> In most [regional theatres] new plays are shunted into studios for shorter and shorter runs where they cause less financial damage if they fail. Few theatres expect a premiere to be the season's big "earner." Gradually new writing is acquiring a medicinal flavour–theatres do it because they "ought" to, or because it is "good" for their audiences. There are also, of course, the small-scale touring companies that specialize in new work. But two of these, Joint Stock and Foco Novo, had their grants removed in 1988. The rest are forced to dash round the country on a series of one-night stands, with the consequence, at the box office, that there is no time for favourable word of mouth to build audiences. . . . This means small casts in simple sets, performing plays written for small spaces and expecting short runs.

Harwood's collection reinforces the point about the proliferation of new work. It also shows that the nature of that work has changed in accordance with the demands and limitations of the contemporary theater. It is pointless for theater directors and others to bemoan the absence of large-cast epic plays on public issues, such as were to be found in the 1970s, when the larger theaters lack the willingness or the economic capability to take on such work. As Harwood says:

> What keeps British theatre vibrant is the delight with which so many of the writers have risen to the challenge of limitation. There has long been an aesthetic of poverty in contemporary British theatre. . . . However, it is notable that newer writers are re-engaging with the benefits that this can bring. One can observe several encouraging factors. Writers seem to be wringing as many characters as possible out of six or so actors and making genuine creative use out of the need for doubling. There is both an interest in using the set as a dramatic image and a weariness with writing plays that demand the endless carting on and off of furniture. Even the one-set drama is being re-explored in inventive and theatrical ways. Most of all there is a sense of new delight in the dramatic power of language, as young writers investigate poetic or heightened forms of language.

In the contemporary postmodernist theater adaptations of Brechtian theory sit excitingly alongside the rediscovery of expressionism and surrealism–one thinks, for example, of the wonderful moment in Johnson's *Hysteria* (1993) when Sigmund Freud's study is startlingly reconfigured into a three-dimensional representation of a Salvador Dali painting. The result is a drama that is continually redefining the boundaries. It is worth stressing the way in which–as always–an integral part of the presentation of the new involves a dialogue, or a confrontation, with the old. One of the playwrights featured in *First Run* is Paul Godfrey, with *Inventing a New Colour;* six years later he recalled that his first experience of the theater came when he was living in Exeter at the time Jane Howells was running the Northcott Theatre there:

> One of the Plays that she'd commissioned and directed and premiered was Edward Bond's *Bingo,* and I saw it there at the age of thirteen. There were just six of us in the audience, and I seem to remember the local paper wrote an editorial saying: We want no more of this kind of thing in Exeter. Now that play's a modern classic, isn't it? And I remember by equal chance Joint Stock tried out their productions of *The Ragged-Trousered Philanthropists* and *Cloud Nine* in Exeter and the

vigour and the vitality of this work made an impression on me at that age.

All three of the plays that Godfrey recalls are concerned with redefining a past against a present social reality–a dominant theme in much of the "committed" writing of the last thirty years of the twentieth century.

In 1993 Methuen published *Frontline Intelligence I: New Plays for the Nineties.* In her introduction to the volume Pamela Edwardes discusses the way in which the plays selected offer "frontline intelligence of what has excited theater audiences in London, Liverpool, Dublin and Glasgow over the last year," stressing that the venues for new writing have become less centralized in London and, by implication, the significance of a continuing development of a network of smaller venues that are not designed to feed the demands of a mainstream tradition. She comments on her criteria for choosing plays to include: "Every decision I have taken in selecting plays for the volume has been a decision about the quality of a piece of writing. I find it intriguing to discover how, speaking in many dialects and styles, these plays all comment on the rapid social change of the last thirteen years [that is, since the formation of Thatcher's first Conservative regime] and ask 'Is this the world we wanted to create?' Not one of the plays seeks to lay out a Marshall Plan for economic and social recovery but all point to defeats and victories of the spirit which suggest where some kind of positive movement could have been made or might yet be made." Postmodernism's dialogue with the past is, then, not always to be thought of in ironic or self-referential terms; in investigating and interrelating earlier theatrical models and genres, the debates that shaped them are themselves reanimated and cross-pollinated with the currently contemporary.

In a second volume, *Frontline Intelligence II: New Plays for the Nineties* (1994), Edwardes included a play that was yet to be staged, one that emerged as a signpost for the way in which much new drama of the 1990s has developed. The play was Sarah Kane's *Blasted,* which opened at the Royal Court in 1995. Its depiction of war as the natural state and violent excess as the only message worth proclaiming caused a controversy the likes of which the Court had not known since the objections to the stoning of the baby in Bond's *Saved* (1965). Set in a Leeds hotel room, *Blasted* is one of several recent plays that may be thought to reflect the terrible escalation of fighting and genocide in Europe since the destruction of the Berlin Wall and the disintegration of the Russian empire. These events have been reflected in much recent writing. In 1985 Edgar staged his *Pentecost,* set in an unnamed Eastern European country; Brenton and Tariq Ali collaborated on *Moscow Gold* (1990), tracing Mikhail Gorbachev's rise to power; and in the same year Churchill produced her play about Romania, *Mad Forest.* In 1992 Griffiths's *The Gulf between Us,* a protest against what he saw as the obscenity of the Persian Gulf War, was produced at the West Yorkshire Playhouse.

Struggles are taking place that are rather less distant, however. In 1972 Brenton, Edgar, Hare, Tony Bicat, Howard Brian Clark, Francis Fuchs, and Snoo Wilson collaborated on a play about the Irish "Troubles," *England's Ireland,* for the Portable Theatre Company. No theater would touch it, and its failure to reach audiences proved the final straw that broke the back of Portable. In 1980 Brenton's *The Romans in Britain* brought the problematic history of Irish colonization onto the stage of the National Theatre in London, against the backdrop of its director being threatened with private prosecution for the simulated depiction of male rape on the stage. Although Arden and D'Arcy had written a stream of plays on this and related matters in Ireland, Brenton's play was a lone voice in the London theater at the time. But outside of England–and particularly outside of London, where the musical reigned supreme in the 1980s and the 1990s–new writing flourished. In Ireland the Troubles were a subject of debate by young playwrights of vastly different persuasions. In Scotland and in Wales, the continuing debate about nationalism, devolution, and the decolonization of culture produced a batch of fine new work. Where there were real public issues to discuss and to agonize over, the theater was able to demonstrate once more its power as a medium of argument, of persuasion, and of dissent.

Newspapers, when they consider the theater at all, agree that the institution is in a parlous state, that audiences are getting ever older, and that young people are no longer attracted to buy tickets for an "entertainment" that not only does not reflect their own lives but is also priced beyond their means. The same argument has been heard at least since the 1950s, but it is not any less true for being perennial. A tourist in London's West End will be hard put to find much that is new or contemporary among the wares on offer. But even there, exceptions can be found. The real strength of contemporary theater lies elsewhere. Despite all the economic struggles facing the theater, and notwithstanding an avant-garde position that resists the significance of "texted" plays in favor of performance art, the groundswell of new playwrights continues to grow. Although many of them, Sebastian Barry perhaps most notably, have continued to find a place in the large subsidized theaters, many have not done so yet, and some never will. The impetus behind the work of many of these fresh talents is the realization that there are still theaters willing to take a chance, and performance venues away from the mainstream still available, that there is a space for the making of plays that is not held hostage to the economic demands of alternative outlets such as television and movies.

Each of the *British and Irish Dramatists Since World War II* volumes will offer a mixture of the old and the new, incorporating both playwrights who were active before the war and continued to be active after it and writers whose careers started after 1945–in many cases, considerably after. So, in addition to offering a series of extensive accounts of the work of individual playwrights, each volume offers key signposts through the period. This treatment will reveal the way in which each new generation of writers works with the "ghosts" of the past on its shoulders; sometimes it quietly annexes its immediate past, and sometimes it sets out to oppose that past. Either way, lines of historical connection can be drawn.

Just how far these lines may reach can be easily demonstrated. Four of the playwrights discussed in this volume, though still quite active after 1945, were born in the nineteenth century. Although all were born within two years of each other, however, they can be seen to represent quite separable strands of theatrical development.

In 1952 Agatha Christie's *The Mousetrap* opened in London. In 2001, nearly fifty years later, this classic "whodunit" was still there, having been seen by more than ten million people during the longest run in West End history. Though better known as a writer of crime fiction, Christie enjoyed a considerable stage career in addition to the many motion-picture and television adaptations of her novels and short stories. Her work is at the center of a popular twentieth-century theater tradition, and she, more than anyone else, was responsible for the development of the crime and thriller genres as staples of both professional and amateur stage productions.

Coward, a stalwart of popular theater of a quite different kind, was born in 1889–just one year before Christie. His first theatrical successes came in the 1920s, and he was soon established–as a writer and performer, as well as in regard to his personal life–as the epitome of the excesses of the privileged rich during the interwar years. His success continued after World War II, and although his reputation was somewhat dimmed in the immediate aftermath of the post-1956 "new wave," he found new fame after the National Theatre revival of his *Hay Fever* in 1964: on the opening night the actress Maggie Smith claimed, "There seemed to be no generation gap with Noel, he just seemed to leap right into the sixties."

Coward had, of course, not been untouched by the war–his most famous contribution to the war effort is his screenplay for the 1941 movie *In Which We Serve*–but the effect of the conflict on the writing of other playwrights of the older generation was more obvious. George Tabori did not begin writing for the stage until 1952; he was born in Budapest in 1914, the year in which World War I began, and though he became a British citizen in 1941, he still regarded himself as a European rather than a British writer, and much of his work reflects the horrors of warfare through which he lived.

Eliot was born a year earlier than Coward, in 1888. Better known as a poet than as a playwright, he wrote for the theater between 1939 (*The Family Reunion*) and 1958 (*The Elder Statesman*), although his *Murder in the Cathedral* (1935), written to be performed not on a commercial stage but at Canterbury Cathedral, where the actual events occurred, should also be regarded as a part of his dramatic oeuvre. Like the Romantic poets of the early nineteenth century, including George Gordon, Lord Byron; Percy Bysshe Shelley; William Wordsworth; and John Keats, who tried to reintroduce poetry to drama, Eliot can be seen as contributing to a latter-day urge to bring verse back into the drama–an urge that looks back both to Classical Greek drama and to the Renaissance theater of Shakespeare and his contemporaries in a movement away from the everyday and the mundane that sought to embrace a spiritual sense of human potential. Opinion is still divided on the merit of Eliot's stage work; certainly, it shares the increasingly High Tory/High Anglican Church mores of his poetry, which has fallen out of favor. But his drama is indicative of a continuing desire on the part of theater periodically to reinvent itself.

Eliot's deployment of verse in the theater was echoed by several other writers in the 1950s, notably Christopher Fry, but it stands in stark contrast to the work of the poet Tony Harrison, whose first English play was staged at the Old Vic by the National Company in 1973. He has largely stayed with that company since then, revisiting classical and biblical myths in ways that seek to move away from the elitist treatment of playwrights such as Eliot in favor of a more accessible language.

The fourth Victorian considered in this volume, however, points most neatly to the connections and disconnections of theatrical tradition. Much has been made of the impact of a new generation of playwrights, whose work was chiefly produced at the Royal Court Theatre and the Theatre Royal, Stratford East in London dating from the latter half of the 1950s–a generation that changed the course of theater history. In this regard the key year is 1956, now best remembered theatrically as the year of *Look Back in Anger;* but Osborne's was by no means the most successful play of the year. That honor goes to *The Chalk Garden,* by Enid Bagnold, who was born in 1889. Her style in the play "harks back," according to Lib Taylor in her entry on Bagnold in this volume, "to the prewar West End and the well-made plays of the 1920s and 1930s," and it was precisely the sort of piece to which the "new wave" was opposed. But although Bagnold's theater, set in a declining upper-class world, rapidly went out of favor–as did those of Rattigan and Coward–the format continued to be reworked in the mainstream; and it is worth noting that both Rattigan's and Coward's plays have not only recently started to reemerge in performance but have also undergone something of a critical reevaluation.

It is clear, then, that, to a considerable extent, the "new wave" was largely a construction by cultural analysts anxious to mark the fact of change. Some highly unlikely practitioners were called upon to do service, if only because they started to write plays at this moment, perhaps in part as a result of a perceived audience for new writing. John Mortimer–who is now best known for his television creation Rumpole of the Bailey, a comic character in the tradition of Charles Dickens–is an example. His first stage play, *The Dock Brief* (1958), a surreal drawing on his own experiences as a barrister, started life as a radio drama before being televised and, eventually, becoming a movie vehicle for Peter Sellers. At the suggestion of the theater producer Michael Codron, Mortimer wrote another short piece, *What Shall We Tell Caroline?* The double bill opened at the Lyric Hammersmith before transferring to the Garrick to make way for Pinter's first London production, *The Birthday Party.* The slight elements of absurdism in both plays allowed the reviewer in *The Times* (22 May 1958) to make an approving comparison between *What Shall We Tell Caroline?* and Ionesco's *The Bald-Headed Prima-Donna;* and by 24 September the newspaper was able to define a new theatrical school and, indeed, to draw up lines of distinction–talking, on the one hand, of a party in opposition to the prevalent mode of naturalism and citing Osborne, Shaffer, and Robert Bolt as its examples, and, on the other hand, of a "comedy of menace" deriving from Ionesco and including Mortimer and Dennis. With the advantage of hindsight, the writer might have taken the opening stage directions for Mortimer's play as a more reliable clue to what might follow and, furthermore, to the direction from which the playwright was really coming: "The Loudon's living room at Highland Close School, Coldsands," a room complete with the requisite three doors that constituted a minimal requirement for conventional farce, and the "tall French windows" that were de rigeur for the well-made drawing-room comedy.

Following Raymond Williams, Simon Baker, in an article in *Staging Wales: Welsh Theatre 1979–1997,* edited by Anna-Marie Taylor, has identified two distinct movements in British theater from this period–the first loosely socialist and concerned with class, the second more experimental and drawing from a Continental avant-garde–and has identified these two strands in Wales with the work of Gwyn Thomas and Dannie Abse, respectively. And, indeed, the mid 1950s did bring the beginning of that Continental invasion of absurdist drama, epitomized most importantly by the 1955 production of Beckett's *Waiting for Godot,* a production that was seen and enjoyed by a young actor of the time, Harold Pinter. His early plays owe a considerable debt to the emerging absurdist tradition and also to the emphasis on the new naturalism, and they explored social territory previously virtually uncharted in the British theater. Pinter's was not an overnight success, however, and his first London production, *The Birthday Party,* met largely with baffled incomprehension and limped out of the Lyric Theatre, Hammersmith, in May 1958 after less than a week. By 1960 *The Caretaker* had established him as a major writer, and his stature has continued to grow with a succession of important scripts for both the stage and the screen.

Ayckbourn's roots as a playwright are also to be found in the English response to Continental absurdism–his first play was staged in 1959–although the domestic location of most of his work places it as a kind of disrupted version of the "well-made play." His first real success came in 1972 with the suitably named *Absurd Person Singular,* a play that, like virtually all his subsequent work, opened in Scarborough, Yorkshire–where many of David Campton's early plays were first produced–before successfully transferring to London. Soon, Ayckbourn's plays were offered a home at the National Theatre–as, later, he himself was as a director.

Whatever the truth of claims for a coherently organized movement in the latter half of the 1950s may be, however, there is no doubt that a sense of its existence, together with an increasing emphasis by the Arts Council on the promotion of new work, did encourage new writing, and not just in London or even in England. The early years of the Royal Court experiment are represented in this volume by the entry on Arden, whose excitingly disturbing and ambiguous antiwar play, *Serjeant Musgrave's Dance,* was first staged there in 1959, followed by *The Happy Haven* in 1960. One of the important developments at the Court was the development of the Writers' Group, and many playwrights were able to start on a career through its support. A note of caution is in order, however. A great deal of mythology has been created in connection with the early years of the English Stage Company at the Royal Court. The first two plays of the first (1956) season were *The Mulberry Bush* and *The Crucible,* the first by the quintessentially English novelist Angus Wilson and the second by the well-established and world-renowned American dramatist Arthur Miller. Osborne's play then followed, but it was succeeded by two plays by Ronald Duncan, a writer whose roots lay in the Verse Drama movement represented by Eliot. But, just as Eliot looked to the poets for a rejuvenation of the theater, the founder of the English Stage Company, George Devine, originally looked to the novelists. That subsequent history proved him mistaken is beside the point. Some of the best-received plays of the latter half of the 1960s at the Royal Court were by David Storey, who regarded himself as a novelist first and a playwright only second and the screen version of whose first novel, *This Sporting Life* (1960), was one of the high points of the short-lived British Cinema Revival. The moment of 1956, however, was, more than is usually recognized, part of a continuum rather than an overnight revolution.

In this continuum television had a major role to play in the development of drama, as the series titles of the weekly televised productions suggest: *The Wednesday Play, Armchair Theatre,* and so on. But, inevitably, television developed its own dramatic styles and conventions, to the extent that by the present day the influence may frequently be seen to be working in the opposite direction: *Road* (1986), the exciting first produced play by Jim Cartwright, for instance, is clearly the product of a writer for whom television, rather than the theater, provided models of narrative structure. For many writers of an earlier period, Pinter included, radio had provided a first access to an audience, as had television for many others, such as Frayn and Peter Nichols. Frayn owed much of his initial success to the availability of television as a dramatic medium, as did two other playwrights featured in this volume: Tony Marchant, who is most widely thought of as a television writer, and Alan Bleasdale, one of the most important British dramatists to work in that medium. Frayn's career dates from the 1970s, and since then he has produced a mixture of farces and serious mainstream pieces that led finally to his own *Copenhagen* appearing at the National Theatre in 1998, after he had been a frequent visitor with his translations of the works of the Russian playwright Anton Chekhov.

The next great "moment," which can be dated from around 1968, was more profound in its reshaping of the theatrical agenda and more far-reaching geographically in its scope. That such is the case clearly owes much to the pioneering efforts of earlier "new" writers, as well as to a redefinition of what was permissible onstage as a result of the abolition of theater censorship in that year. Griffiths's *The Party* was first staged by the National Theatre Company at the Old Vic in 1973. Its recall of the events of 1968 placed him as one of several writers, including Hare and Brenton, whose careers can be dated from this period and who were united in an opposition to both mainstream politics and mainstream theater. Probably the most important single figure in the development of the gay theater movement in Britain, Noël Greig, started in 1970 with the Brighton Combination–a company with which Brenton was also briefly associated at this time–before moving to General Will, the Bradford agitprop group that staged Edgar's early work. He then went on to form a long-lasting relationship with Gay Sweatshop and in 1977, in collaboration with Drew Griffiths, he provided that company with its first full-length production, *As Time Goes By.*

The second "new wave" is also attributable to a change in the political climate that coincided with increased public subsidies that encouraged the creation of what came to be known as the alternative theater movement, with writers working for venues outside of the conventional theatrical circuit. Some of the most innovative and long-lasting examples of this change in the theatrical climate are provided by the works of John Fox, cofounder and director of the now internationally renowned Welfare State company, which is dedicated to the production of site-specific work in which ritual, music, dance, and many other carnivalesque elements rarely found in conventional theater are brought together in a series of "events" that critique the values of contemporary society, reevaluate the past, and celebrate alternatives.

The earlier discussion of Christie's *The Mousetrap* serves to illustrate another important change. In 1952, and for a considerable period afterward, most theatergoers would have been hard-pressed to come up with the name of another contemporary female British or Irish playwright. The situation was altered somewhat in the late 1950s and early 1960s with the emergence of writers such as Ann Jellicoe and Shelagh Delaney, and the beginning of the development of Caryll Churchill into one of the greatest contemporary British playwrights followed shortly thereafter. The 1980s, however, was the decade in which female rather than male dramatists led the way. Daniels's blast against the effects of pornography, *Masterpieces* (1983), was but one of a host of new plays by female playwrights that took positions from militant feminism to a more centrist position. Their work is represented in this volume by writers from most areas of the British Isles: Daniels, Shirley Gee, and Keatley from England; Devlin and Marina Carr from Ireland; and Sharman Macdonald from Scotland. An important development has been the increasingly significant impact that women writers have had in the last twenty years in the two islands. Gee's promising career, dating from 1983, has, sadly, been cut short by ill health. She was but one of many highly talented women playwrights who seized the 1980s as their decade.

This sense of a new drama developing in several distinctly different centers and with varying and often conflicting agendas can easily be verified in the entries in this volume. A change in the relationship of the writer to his or her regional base has become ever more important. The extraordinary high quality and variety of work coming from Cardiff-based companies by writers such as Dic Edwards has led to a perceived renaissance in Welsh drama. And in Ireland, on both sides of the border, the works of writers of the calibre of Frank McGuiness, Tom Mac Intyre, and Stewart Parker marks the last twenty years of the twentieth century as a major period of Irish drama. Seamus Finnegan has yet to find an audience in Ireland, but Sebastian Barry has emerged as a major playwright whose work is equally valued on both sides of the Irish Sea.

One of the first productions mounted by John McGrath's Scottish company 7:84 was a reworking of Arden's classic of that period, *Serjeant Musgrave's Dance* as *Musgrave Dances On,* a production that marked a more directly political position on Arden's part. Shortly after this production the playwright announced that he had lost patience with English theatrical managements, and he left for Ireland. There he wrote a series of plays in collaboration with his wife, D'Arcy, that sought to address the history of Irish struggle directly.

Certainly, it had been difficult to get British theaters to take on anything that questioned the official British government line on Ireland. Portable Theatre had been killed off when its collaborative project *England's Ireland* was rejected by more than fifty theaters, but the question of Ireland would not go away; and, gradually and inexorably, the theater was forced to offer an arena for the debate. As well as Ireland slipping onto the theater agenda, the theater in Ireland itself, both north and south of the border, began to develop new playwrights who were interested in looking at Ireland from various points of views. In this volume this renaissance of Irish playwriting is represented by Carr, whose first play, *Ullaloo,* was given a rehearsed reading at the Peacock Theatre as part of the Dublin Theatre Festival in 1989, and by Devlin, McGuinness, Mac Intyre, Parker, Finnegan, and Barry. Their work, and that of many others, marks the last twenty years of the twentieth century as a major period of Irish drama.

Despite the not infrequent cry of doom about the state of the contemporary theater, the truth is that while there is, as always, a great deal being staged that is best not remembered, the profession of playwriting has never been in a more healthy situation–although anyone wishing to test this claim should not assume that London's West End or, indeed, even that London is the only place to look. Nor, for that matter, should one's examination be confined to the theater, including that outside England. Much of the best new work is to be found in what would once have been called "alternative" venues, but much of it is not to be found in theatrical spaces at all. Many writers continue to work exclusively on plays for the stage, but others, including Marchant, whose career dates from 1980, and Hanif Kureishi, who began writing in 1976, are equally at home, if not more so, working for television and movies. If recent developments have demonstrated anything, it is that the lines of demarcation between the three media are more fluid than they have ever been. Much new and exciting work is to be anticipated from their continuing borrowings and collisions.

A Note on the Structure of the Volumes

A decision was made early in the planning of the *British and Irish Dramatists Since World War II* series not to follow a straight alphabetical ordering from volume to volume. Thus, each volume has its own alphabetical order. The intention was to make each volume a mixture in which the old and the new sit alongside each other. This arrangement has the further advantage of allowing some "breathing space" for playwrights who, as the first volumes are published, may not yet have produced a body of work sufficient to justify inclusion but in the interim may well do so. The entries have been commissioned from a wide variety of theater scholars, all of them experts in their field. Many of the pieces have been written in collaboration with their subjects, and we are extremely grateful to all the playwrights who have responded to detailed questions about the exact dates of production and the like, to their agents, and, in some cases, members of their families who have done likewise. Although the present volume is designated *Third Series* in acknowledgment of *DLB 13: British Dramatists Since World War II* (1982), it is really the second volume in a new series that began with *DLB 233.*

–John Bull

Acknowledgments

This book was produced by Bruccoli Clark Layman, Inc. Karen L. Rood is senior editor. Philip B. Dematteis was the in-house editor; he was assisted by Tracy Simmons Bitonti, Charles Brower, Penelope M. Hope, Nikki La Rocque, Karen L. Rood, Angela Shaw-Thornburg, and Teresa D. Tynes.

Production manager is Philip B. Dematteis.

Administrative support was provided by Ann M. Cheschi, Amber L. Coker, and Angi Pleasant.

Accountant is Ann-Marie Holland.

Copyediting supervisor is Sally R. Evans. The copyediting staff includes Phyllis A. Avant, Brenda Carol Blanton, Worthy B. Evans, Melissa D. Hinton, William Tobias Mathes, Rebecca Mayo, Nancy E. Smith, and Elizabeth Jo Ann Sumner.

Editorial associates are Michael Allen, Michael S. Martin, and Jennifer Reid.

Database manager is José A. Juarez.

Layout and graphics supervisor is Janet E. Hill. The graphics staff includes Karla Corley Brown and Zoe R. Cook.

Office manager is Kathy Lawler Merlette.

Photography supervisor is Paul Talbot. Photography editor is Scott Nemzek.

Digital photographic copy work was performed by Joseph M. Bruccoli.

The SGML staff includes Frank Graham, Linda Dalton Mullinax, Jason Paddock, and Alex Snead.

Systems manager is Marie L. Parker.

Typesetting supervisor is Kathleen M. Flanagan. The typesetting staff includes Jaime All, Patricia Marie Flanagan, Mark J. McEwan, and Pamela D. Norton. Freelance typesetter is Wanda Adams.

Walter W. Ross did library research. He was assisted by Jaime All and the following librarians at the Thomas Cooper Library of the University of South Carolina: circulation department head Tucker Taylor; reference department head Virginia W. Weathers; Brette Barclay, Marilee Birchfield, Paul Cammarata, Gary Geer, Michael Macan, Tom Marcil, Rose Marshall, and Sharon Verba; interlibrary loan department head John Brunswick; and interlibrary loan staff Robert Arndt, Hayden Battle, Barry Bull, Jo Cottingham, Marna Hostetler, Marieum McClary, Erika Peake, and Nelson Rivera.

Dictionary of Literary Biography® • Volume Two Hundred Forty-Five

British and Irish Dramatists Since World War II

Third Series

Dictionary of Literary Biography

Dannie Abse

(22 September 1923 –   )

Linden Peach
Loughborough University

See also the Abse entry in *DLB 27: Poets of Great Britain and Ireland, 1945–1960.*

PLAY PRODUCTIONS: *Fire in Heaven,* London, Group 28, 21 November 1949; rehearsed reading, London, Institute of Contemporary Arts, 1952; revised in prose as *Is the House Shut?* London, Questors Theatre, 21 June 1964; revised as *In the Cage,* London, Questors Theatre, 1967;

Hands around the Wall, London, Embassy Theatre, 1950;

House of Cowards, London, Questors Theatre, 9 June 1960;

The Eccentric, London, Mountview Theatre, 1961;

Gone (one-act version), London, Questors Theatre, 19 June 1962; revised in a three-act version as *Gone in January,* Edinburgh, Edinburgh Festival, Ensemble Theatre Company, 23 August 1977; London, Young Vic, January 1978;

The Joker, London, Questors Theatre, 14 June 1962;

Is the House Shut? London, Questors Theatre, 1964;

The Dogs of Pavlov, London, Questors Theatre, 17 June 1969; New York, Cubiculo Theatre, 18 April 1974;

Pythagoras, Birmingham, Birmingham Repertory, 22 September 1976.

BOOKS: *After Every Green Thing* (London & New York: Hutchinson, 1948);

Walking under Water (London: Hutchinson, 1952);

Ash on a Young Man's Sleeve (London: Hutchinson, 1954; New York: Criterion, 1954);

Some Corner of an English Field: A Novel (London: Hutchinson, 1956; New York: Criterion, 1956);

Fire in Heaven (London: Hutchinson, 1956);

Dannie Abse (photograph © John Harris)

Tenants of the House (London: Hutchinson, 1957; New York: Criterion, 1959);

The Eccentric (London: M. Evans, 1961);

Dannie Abse (London: Vista, 1963);
Three Questor Plays (Lowestoft: Scorpion Press, 1967)–comprises *House of Cowards, Gone,* and *In the Cage; House of Cowards* republished in *Twelve Great Plays,* edited by Leonard F. Dean (New York: Harcourt, Brace & World, 1970), pp. 739–786;
Medicine on Trial (London: Aldus, 1967 [i.e., 1968]; New York: Crown, 1969);
A Small Desperation: Poems (London: Hutchinson, 1968);
Demo: A Poem (Frensham, Surrey: Sceptre Press, 1969);
O. Jones, O. Jones (London: Hutchinson, 1970);
Selected Poems (London: Hutchinson, 1970; New York: Oxford University Press, 1970);
Funland: A Poem in Nine Parts (Portland, Ore.: Portland University Library, 1971);
The Dogs of Pavlov (London: Vallentine, Mitchell, 1973);
Funland and Other Poems (London: Hutchinson, 1973; New York: Oxford University Press, 1973);
A Poet in the Family (London: Hutchinson, 1974);
Dannie Abse, D. J. Enright, Michael Longley, edited by Anthony Thwaite, Penguin Modern Poets, no. 26 (Harmondsworth, U.K. & Baltimore: Penguin, 1975);
Collected Poems, 1948–1976 (London: Hutchinson, 1977; Pittsburgh: University of Pittsburgh Press, 1977);
More Words, by Abse and others (London: British Broadcasting Corporation, 1977);
Pythagoras (London: Hutchinson, 1979);
Way Out in the Centre (London: Hutchinson, 1981); republished as *One-Legged on Ice* (Athens: University of Georgia Press, 1983);
Miscellany One (Bridgend, Wales: Poetry Wales Press, 1981)–includes *The Courting of Elsie Glass;*
A Strong Dose of Myself (London: Hutchinson, 1982);
"Under the Influence of . . . ": The Annual Gwyn Jones Lecture, Friday, 4th May, 1984 in the Humanities Building, University College, Cardiff (Cardiff: University College, Cardiff Press, 1984);
Ask the Bloody Horse (London: Hutchinson, 1986);
Journals from the Ant-Heap (London: Hutchinson, 1986);
White Coat, Purple Coat: Collected Poems, 1948–1988 (London: Hutchinson, 1989; New York: Persea, 1991);
Remembrance of Crimes Past: Poems, 1986–1989 (London: Hutchinson, 1990); republished as *Remembrance of Crimes Past: Poems* (New York: Persea, 1993);
The View from Row G: Three Plays, edited by James A. Davies (Bridgend, Wales: Seren, 1990)–comprises revised version of *House of Cowards; The Dogs of Pavlov;* and *Pythagoras (Smith);*
There Was a Young Man from Cardiff (London: Hutchinson, 1991);
On the Evening Road (London: Hutchinson, 1994);
Selected Poems (Harmondsworth, U.K.: Penguin, 1994);
Intermittent Journals (Bridgend, Wales: Seren, 1994);
Welsh Retrospective (Bridgend, Wales: Seren, 1997);
Arcadia, One Mile (London: Hutchinson, 1998);
Be Seated, Thou: Poems 1989–1998 (Riverdale-on-Hudson, N.Y.: Sheep Meadow Press, 1999);
Encounters (London: Hearing Eye, 2001).

PRODUCED SCRIPTS: *Conform or Die,* radio, BBC, 5 December 1956;
No Telegrams, No Thunder, radio, BBC, 10 January 1962;
You Can't Say Hello To Anybody, radio, BBC, 7 February 1964;
A Small Explosion, radio, BBC, 5 March 1964;
Dylan Thomas Lived Here, television, BBC One, 1975;
Like Poetry, television, BBC Two, 16 November 1977;
Pythagoras, BBC Radio 3, 1978;
Return to Cardiff, television, BBC Wales, 10 March 1985;
Bookmarks, television, BBC Two, 1986;
A Welsh Life, television, HTV, 1990;
Case History, BBC Wales, 1999.

OTHER: *New Poems, 1956,* edited by Abse, Stephen Spender, and Elizabeth Joan Jennings (London: Joseph, 1956);
Mavericks: An Anthology, edited by Abse and Howard Sergeant (London: Editions Poetry and Poverty, 1957);
Modern European Verse, edited by Abse (London: Vista, 1964);
Corgi Modern Poets in Focus, volumes 1, 3, and 5, edited by Abse (London: Corgi, 1971–1973);
Thirteen Poets, edited by Abse (London: Poetry Book Society, 1972);
Poetry Dimension 2: The Best of the Poetry Year, edited by Abse (London: Robson, 1974; New York: St. Martin's Press, 1974);
Poetry Dimension: The Best of the Poetry Year, volume 3, edited by Abse (London: Robson, 1975);
Poetry Dimension Annual: The Best of the Poetry Year, volume 4, edited by Abse (London: Robson, 1976);
My Medical School, edited by Abse (London: Robson, 1978);
Poetry Dimension Annual: The Best of the Poetry Year, volume 5, edited by Abse (London: Robson, 1978);
Poetry Dimension Annual: The Best of the Poetry Year, volume 6, edited by Abse (London: Robson, 1979);
Poetry Dimension Annual: Best of the Poetry Year, volume 7, edited by Abse (London: Robson, 1980);
Poems for Shakespeare 9, edited by Abse (London: Globe Playhouse, 1981);
Wales in Verse, edited by Abse (London: Secker & Warburg, 1983);
Doctors & Patients, edited by Abse (Oxford & New York: Oxford University Press, 1984);

THE DOGS OF PAVLOV 85

Pink light ~~is~~ has faded and is replaced by white spotlight.

JONES 59, 60, 61. (*Pause*) 1,2,3,4,5,6,7,8.

SALLY 180.

JONES 72, 77, 79. (*Pause*) 1,2,3,4,5,6,7,8,9,10. PULL THE PURPLE.

Harley-Hoare pulls the purple lever and purple spot comes on Sally.

SALLY Oh hell, that's too much. TOO MUCH. Oh dear, oh dear, oh dear. Oh . . . ah . . .

HARLEY-H That was OK, wasn't it? I did do that right.

JONES Yes, quite right.

HARLEY-H ~~Ah yes,~~ I'm getting the hang of it, ~~This is a shocking business, isn't it, ha ha ha? This is very interesting~~ but . . er. I'm worried about her.

JONES 80, 84, 86. (*Pause*) 1,2.

SALLY 250.

JONES 97, 98, 104. (*Pause*) 1,2,3,4,5,6,7,8,9,10. PULL. THE

Harley-Hoare pulls the blue lever and blue light bathes Sally's distorted face.

SALLY Aw, aw, aw, aw, STOP. Please, please. Stop, stop. Oh dear, oh dear. No. Aaah.

Blue light begins to fade and Sally, in chair, closes her eyes and breathes heavily.

HARLEY-H That was quite a shock. Are you all right?

JONES It was 160 volts.

HARLEY-H 160. Shall I go on?

JONES Yes, yes. The experiment must continue.

SALLY I think I can go on.

HARLEY-H Fine, good. If you think you can go on.

SALLY It was very powerful though. I don't think I'd like much more.

HARLEY-H You must add up properly. Please try. Please.

SALLY I'll do my best. Can I have a drink?

JONES Are you ready, Mr Harley-Hoare?

HARLEY-H Yes, yes.

SALLY I'd like a drink first.

Harley Hoare is now sweating and becomes more agitated as the scene continues

You're the expert, doctor. I mean are you sure? I don't want to . . . .

Page from the script for one of Abse's plays, with his handwritten revisions (Collection of Dannie Abse)

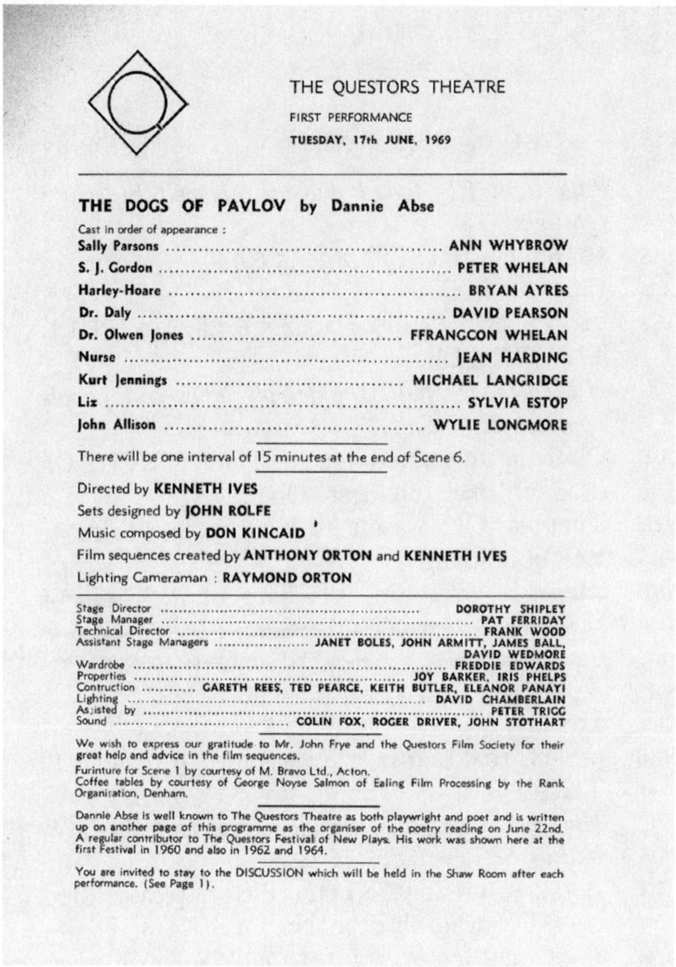

THE QUESTORS THEATRE
FIRST PERFORMANCE
TUESDAY, 17th JUNE, 1969

THE DOGS OF PAVLOV by Dannie Abse

Cast in order of appearance :

Sally Parsons	ANN WHYBROW
S. J. Gordon	PETER WHELAN
Harley-Hoare	BRYAN AYRES
Dr. Daly	DAVID PEARSON
Dr. Olwen Jones	FFRANGCON WHELAN
Nurse	JEAN HARDING
Kurt Jennings	MICHAEL LANGRIDGE
Liz	SYLVIA ESTOP
John Allison	WYLIE LONGMORE

There will be one interval of 15 minutes at the end of Scene 6.

Directed by KENNETH IVES
Sets designed by JOHN ROLFE
Music composed by DON KINCAID
Film sequences created by ANTHONY ORTON and KENNETH IVES
Lighting Cameraman : RAYMOND ORTON

Stage Director	DOROTHY SHIPLEY
Stage Manager	PAT FERRIDAY
Technical Director	FRANK WOOD
Assistant Stage Managers	JANET BOLES, JOHN ARMITT, JAMES BALL, DAVID WEDMORE
Wardrobe	FREDDIE EDWARDS
Properties	JOY BARKER, IRIS PHELPS
Contruction	GARETH REES, TED PEARCE, KEITH BUTLER, ELEANOR PANAYI
Lighting	DAVID CHAMBERLAIN
Assisted by	PETER TRIGG
Sound	COLIN FOX, ROGER DRIVER, JOHN STOTHART

We wish to express our gratitude to Mr. John Frye and the Questors Film Society for their great help and advice in the film sequences.

Furinture for Scene 1 by courtesy of M. Bravo Ltd., Acton.
Coffee tables by courtesy of George Noyse Salmon of Ealing Film Processing by the Rank Organisation, Denham.

Dannie Abse is well known to The Questors Theatre as both playwright and poet and is written up on another page of this programme as the organiser of the poetry reading on June 22nd. A regular contributor to The Questors Festival of New Plays. His work was shown here at the first Festival in 1960 and also in 1962 and 1964.

You are invited to stay to the DISCUSSION which will be held in the Shaw Room after each performance. (See Page 1).

Page from the program for Abse's play about a sadistic psychological experiment (Collection of Dannie Abse)

Voices in the Gallery: Poems & Pictures, edited by Abse and Joan Abse (London: Tate Gallery, 1986);

The Music Lover's Literary Companion, edited by Abse and Joan Abse (London: Robson, 1988; New York: Parkwest, 1989);

The Hutchinson Book of Post-war British Poetry, edited by Abse (London: Hutchinson, 1989);

The Gregory Anthology, 1991–1993, edited by Abse and Anne Stevenson (London: Sinclair-Stevenson, 1994);

"The Ass and the Green Thing," in *How Poets Work,* edited by Tony Curtis (Bridgend, Wales: Seren, 1996);

Twentieth Century Anglo-Welsh Poetry, edited by Abse (Bridgend, Wales: Seren, 1997).

Although he was long well known as a poet, the writer/physician Dannie Abse only belatedly came to be seen as a major theatrical voice. Despite generally favorable reviews, his plays were regarded as aloof from the main trends in English theater in the 1960s and 1970s; as ignoring the influences of Eugene O'Neill, Samuel Beckett, and Eugène Ionesco; and as having most affinity with radio plays, a genre in which Abse also worked. His career as a dramatist reflects his concern with complex philosophical issues, and his Jewish background has exerted an increasingly powerful influence on his work.

The youngest of four children, Abse was born on 22 September 1923 in Cardiff, the capital of Wales. His family provided a stimulating creative and artistic environment: his father, Rudolf, was part-owner and manager of a chain of movie theaters and played the violin; his mother, Kate, née Shepherd, was fond of the arts and spoke Welsh and Hebrew in addition to English. One of his brothers became a physician, and another, Leo, became a lawyer and a Labor Party member of Parliament.

Although he was Jewish, Abse attended St. Illtyd's College, a Roman Catholic secondary school in

Cardiff, from 1935 to 1941. He studied medicine at the University of South Wales and Monmouthshire (now Cardiff University) in 1941–1942; King's College in London from 1942 to 1944; and Westminster Hospital in London from 1944 to 1947 and in 1949–1950. From 1949 to 1954 he served as editor of *Poetry and Poverty* magazine. In 1951 he married Joan Mercer, with whom he has three children: Keren, Susanna, and David. In the year of his marriage he enlisted in the Royal Air Force, in which he became a squadron leader, and was assigned to the Central Medical Establishment chest clinic in London. He continued to work there as a part-time physician after his discharge from the air force in 1955, retiring in 1989. He served as a visiting professor at Princeton University in 1973–1974 and as president of the Poetry Society from 1978 to 1992. He was elected a fellow of the Royal Society of Literature in 1983 and received an honorary D.Litt. from the University of Wales in 1989. Although he has lived most of his adult life in London, Abse has maintained close links with South Wales and has a second home there.

Abse submitted his first play, the verse drama *Fire in Heaven,* to the Questors Theatre in London in 1947; it was not accepted there (an earlier version, a poetry-drama, was produced in London in 1948) but was produced by Group 28 in London the following year and presented in a rehearsed reading in 1952 and produced in 1964 in a revised prose version titled *Is the House Shut?* It was revised again as *In the Cage* in 1967. The play is reputedly based on a Honoré de Balzac's story "El Verdigo" (The Executioner): as a reprisal for a raid on a munitions dump in which two soldiers are killed, a partisan leader's family is ordered to select one member, who will then be freed, to kill the others; otherwise, other families will be slaughtered. The leader's pacifist brother, Christian, is chosen to kill the leader, their sister, and their parents. The play's focus on the central moral dilemma is underscored by the lack of any identifiable historical or political context: neither the time nor the locale of the action is identified.

Comparison of the initial verse drama and the later prose versions shows Abse bringing wider perspectives to bear on the situation. While *Fire in Heaven* focuses on Christian's moral dilemma from his perspective and overidealizes him, the subsequent versions explore themes such as the nature of humanity, the complex reasons why individuals become involved in violence, and whether war causes, or merely reveals, moral schizophrenia. The final version, *In the Cage,* begins with two army officers discussing, in the wake of the raid, how this is what "humanity" leads to, while a sentry is disgusted at the wanton violence.

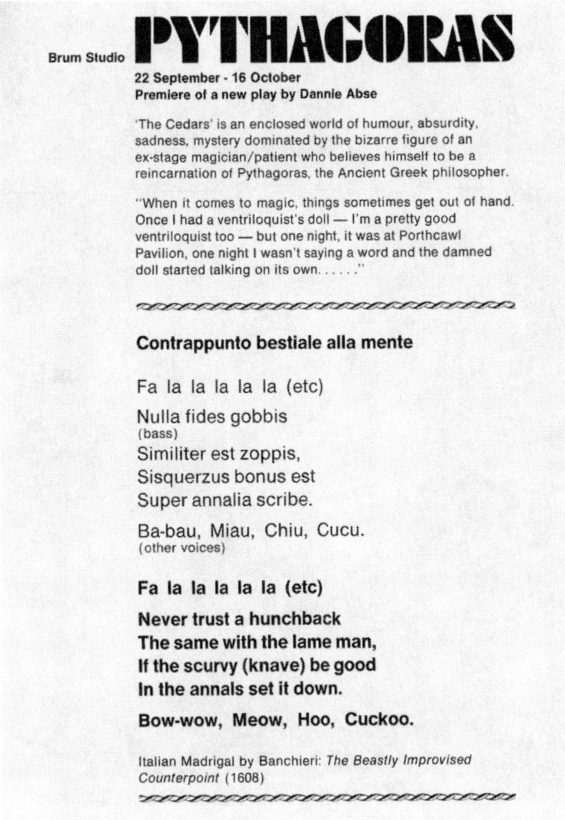
Brum Studio **PYTHAGORAS**

22 September - 16 October
Premiere of a new play by Dannie Abse

'The Cedars' is an enclosed world of humour, absurdity, sadness, mystery dominated by the bizarre figure of an ex-stage magician/patient who believes himself to be a reincarnation of Pythagoras, the Ancient Greek philosopher.

"When it comes to magic, things sometimes get out of hand. Once I had a ventriloquist's doll — I'm a pretty good ventriloquist too — but one night, it was at Porthcawl Pavilion, one night I wasn't saying a word and the damned doll started talking on its own. . . . ."

Contrappunto bestiale alla mente

Fa la la la la la (etc)

Nulla fides gobbis
(bass)
Similiter est zoppis,
Sisquerzus bonus est
Super annalia scribe.

Ba-bau, Miau, Chiu, Cucu.
(other voices)

Fa la la la la la (etc)

Never trust a hunchback
The same with the lame man,
If the scurvy (knave) be good
In the annals set it down.

Bow-wow, Meow, Hoo, Cuckoo.

Italian Madrigal by Banchieri: *The Beastly Improvised Counterpoint* (1608)

Page from the program for the 1976 premiere of Abse's play about the struggle between a patient in a mental hospital and the superintendent of the institution (Collection of Dannie Abse)

In the bodies of his dead friends he sees the reality of war–a point reinforced shortly afterward by another soldier who argues that the "heroic" military code is predicated on death. A glimmer of hope emerges when the Captain, in putting the scheme to the family, begins to break down: he hesitates, repeats himself, changes his line of attack, resorts to rhetorical questions, succumbs to emotional outbursts, and answers questions he has not been asked. But in the closing moments of the play the Captain's face is, according to the stage directions, "utterly expressionless" as he tears up the report that he had intended to send to the field marshal about what has happened.

The one-act play *Gone* (1962), revised as the three-act *Gone in January* (1977), begins after Peter's wife, Connie, has left him for a younger man. Peter's anxiety about aging and his obsession with not allowing his body to go to seed are symbolized by the cry of the rag-and-bone man (a collector of castoff items for resale), which comes nearer and nearer in the street outside. The play is structured as a conversation between Peter and his younger coworker, Aubrey, who arrives as Peter is contemplating suicide. In

Abse in 1983

emphasizing that it is their employer, Mr. Tanner, who has asked him to check on Peter, Aubrey demonstrates his loyalty to the business; the fact that Peter's job is at risk is of more concern to Aubrey than is Peter's state of mind. The play ends with Peter, his head in a noose, sobbing and repeating the rag-and-bone man's cry. *In the Cage* and *Gone* are linked in their concern with organizations–the army in the former play, the business in the latter one–that require absolute allegiance.

House of Cowards (1960) is based on Abse's poem "The Meeting," first published in *Tenants of the House* (1957). Commissioned by the Questors Theatre thirteen years after it rejected *Fire in Heaven, House of Cowards* concerns the expected visit of an enigmatic character, the Speaker, to a washed-up industrial town whose inhabitants see him as their savior. The play focuses on one family, the Hickses, who are susceptible to delusions; they convince themselves that the suitcase the Journalist has left in their house belongs to the Speaker, even though it is empty. Although it won the Charles Henry Foyle New Play Award, the production exposed faults that Abse himself recognized, and thirty years later he published a revised version in which the characters are more complex and believable and the dialogue is more taut and dynamic. Even the revision, however, includes familiar, almost clichéd, elements: from absurdist drama, the situation of the wait for a mysterious visitor who is expected to deliver an important message but who, like Samuel Beckett's Godot, fails to appear; and from radio drama, the family with a crotchety father, a long-suffering mother, a rebellious son, and two eccentric lodgers. Abse's professional medical interest in mental disorders is evident in the character of Nott, whose conversation and circumstances suggest that he is a recently released psychiatric patient; he may, however, be the Speaker. Confusion of the real and the imaginary is not just a matter of individual psychology but also a social problem produced by the mass media, as is shown by the way the Hicks household is seduced by the Journalist. The play can also be read as a religious allegory: Jews await the arrival of the Messiah, who, like the Speaker, seems to be long overdue; and the Journalist's empty suitcase can be seen as analogous to the empty tomb of Jesus.

In *The Dogs of Pavlov* (1969) Kurt and Sally are lovers who volunteer to take part in a psychological experiment. They are separated, and Sally is strapped to an electrically wired chair and asked to perform a series of arithmetical calculations. If she gets an answer wrong, a volunteer in another room, who can hear but not see her, is instructed to give her a shock; the shocks become increasingly powerful with each wrong answer. The experiment is supposedly designed to test the effect of negative reinforcement on learning; in fact, the ostensible subject, Sally, is a confederate of the experimenter and is not being shocked at all but is screaming in simulated pain. The real purpose of the experiment is to see the degree to which the actual subject–the person administering the "shock"–will ignore his own moral code and carry out the instructions of the experimenter. One of these subjects, Gordon, is so anxious to win the approval of the experimenters that he apologizes for not inflicting as much pain as he could have. In the second half of the play Kurt is placed at the controls of the machine that purportedly generates the shock; neither he nor Sally is aware of the other's identity. The ironic twist is that in the end Kurt inflicts an emotional torture on Sally that, unlike the electric shocks he supposedly administered, is real. The play developed out of Abse's thinking in the 1960s–reflected in poems such as "Postmark," "Not Beautiful," and "No More Mozart"–about how ordinary Germans during the Holocaust could obey orders to commit atrocities; the experimenter in the play, Dr. Michael Daly, worked as a medical student in the Nazi death camps. The play was also inspired by W. H. Auden's essay "The Joker in the Pack" (1961), concerning the practical joker's contempt for others and need for power, and most directly by Stanley Milgram's nearly identical experiments at Yale University in the 1960s. Comparisons are drawn within the play between the Holocaust and contemporary situations such as the My Lai massacre in Vietnam and the actions of the British army in Northern Ireland. The play also reflects Abse's concern, as a doctor, with the blurring of boundaries between medical practice and scientific experiment, between healing and the infliction of pain, and between patient and clinical exhibit.

Pythagoras (1976) received the Welsh Arts Council Literature Award on its publication in 1979; it was revised in 1990 as *Pythagoras (Smith)*. The play is set in The Cedars, a psychiatric hospital, and centers on the struggle between the superintendent, Aquillus, and a patient, Tony Smith, a former stage magician who thinks that he is the reincarnation of the ancient philosopher, mathematician, and mystic Pythagoras and that he possesses magical powers–for instance, he can make the telephone ring by pointing at it. The same kind of contempt that Daly has for his experimental subjects in *The Dogs of Pavlov* reveals itself here in Aquillus's use of patients in demonstration lectures. In cruelly scratching the arm of a patient known as X to prove to him that he is not dead, and in humiliating another in front of a student audience, Aquillus behaves in ways that contradict the ideals of medicine. X's belief in his own death is a result of the reductive way in which patients are seen: "They call me X because I'm an ex-person, an ex-human being. So I'm dead." In the scene in which the other patient, Marian, is forced to perform a striptease, Aquillus's students and the audience of the play are made complicit in her reduction to a sex object. When Pythagoras is mistaken for Aquillus because he is wearing a white coat, he portrays the superintendent as a psychopath. In a final confrontation with Aquillus, Pythagoras collapses, emerging as a normal person–but, significantly, he is described in the stage directions as "reduced." The doctors convince him that he is ready to return to society; he is to take a job as a temporary clerk, thereby exchanging the reductive discourse of psychiatry for that of bureaucracy. But the conclusion of the play leaves things open: the audience is left, like Pythagoras himself, uncertain as to the significance of the ringing telephone.

Pythagoras includes carnivalesque elements that hint at a kind of illegitimate power that refuses to go away. These elements serve as reminders that the English theater was initially regarded as a site of subversion and associated with magic and with the supernatural. *Pythagoras* celebrates the magical and the irrational, dimensions of life that are excluded by the rationalism on which the doctors in the play insist.

As critics have pointed out, Abse's most lively, original, and verbally inventive characters are those who pose questions or are tormented by their consciences: Christian in *In the Cage;* Nott in *House of Cowards;* Goldstein, the tobacconist in *The Eccentric* (1961), who, while resisting a takeover bid by a chain store, refuses to sell his customers what they want; and Pythagoras. A price is, however, invariably to be paid for not conforming: for example, Christian becomes insane, and Nott may well be no more than a released psychiatric patient. The least original and verbally exciting characters are those who conform to some external system of thought and manipulate others accordingly: the General in *In the Cage,* the Journalist in *House of Cowards,* Daly and Gordon in *The Dogs of Pavlov,* and Aquillus in *Pythagoras.*

References:

John Cassidy, "The Plays of Dannie Abse: Responsibilities," in *The Poetry of Dannie Abse: Critical Essays and Reminiscences,* edited by Joseph Cohen (London: Robson, 1983), pp. 85–96;

Tony Curtis, *Dannie Abse* (Cardiff: University of Wales Press, 1985);

James A. Davis, introductory essay to *The View from Row G: Three Plays,* edited by Davis (Bridgend, Wales: Seren, 1990);

John Elsom, "Dannie Abse," in *Contemporary Dramatists,* edited by James Vinson (London: St. James Press / New York: St. Martin's Press, 1973), pp. 13–16.

John Arden

(26 October 1930 -)

Frances Gray
University of Sheffield

See also the Arden entry in *DLB 13: British Dramatists Since World War II.*

John Arden (photograph by Roger Mayne)

PLAY PRODUCTIONS: *All Fall Down,* Edinburgh, Edinburgh College of Art Theatre Group, student production, 1955;

The Waters of Babylon, London, Royal Court Theatre, 20 October 1957; Washington, D.C., Washington Theatre Club, April 1967;

When Is a Door Not a Door? London, Embassy Theatre, Swiss Cottage, 2 June 1958;

Live Like Pigs, London, Royal Court Theatre, 30 September 1958; New York, Actor's Playhouse, 7 June 1965;

Serjeant Musgrave's Dance: An Unhistorical Parable, London, Royal Court Theatre, 22 October 1959; New York, Theatre de Lys, 8 March 1966;

The Happy Haven, by Arden and Margaretta D'Arcy, Bristol, University Drama Studio, April 1960; London, Royal Court Theatre, 14 September 1960; New York, 1967;

A Christmas Play, by Arden and D'Arcy, Brent Knoll, Somerset, Church of St. Michael, 25 December 1960; retitled *The Business of Good Government: A Christmas Play,* New York, 1970;

The Workhouse Donkey: A Vulgar Melo-drama, Chichester, Chichester Festival Theatre, 8 July 1963;

Ironhand, adapted from Johann Wolfgang von Goethe's *Götz von Berlichingen,* Bristol, Bristol Old Vic, 12 November 1963;

Ars Longa, Vita Brevis, by D'Arcy and Arden, Kirkbymoorside, Yorkshire, 1964; London, London Academy of Music and Dramatic Art, 28 January 1964;

Armstrong's Last Goodnight: An Exercise in Diplomacy, Glasgow, Glasgow Citizens' Theatre, 5 May 1964; Boston, Theatre Company of Boston, 10 December 1966;

Left-Handed Liberty: A Play about Magna Carta, London, Mermaid Theatre, 14 June 1965;

Fidelio, libretto by Arden, music by Ludwig van Beethoven, London, Sadler's Wells, 16 September 1965;

Friday's Hiding (mime), by D'Arcy and Arden, Edinburgh, Royal Lyceum Theatre, 29 March 1966;

The Royal Pardon; or, The Soldier Who Became an Actor, by Arden and D'Arcy, Beaford, Devon, Beaford Arts Centre, 1 September 1966;

Harold Muggins Is a Martyr, by D'Arcy, Arden, and the Cartoon Archetypical Slogan Theatre, London, Unity Theatre Club, 14 June 1968;

The True History of Squire Jonathan and His Unfortunate Treasure, London, Ambiance Lunch Hour Theatre, 17 June 1968; New York, AMDA Theater, 21 December 1974;

The Hero Rises Up: A Romantic Melodrama, by Arden and D'Arcy, London, Round House Theatre, 6 November 1968;

The Soldier's Tale, libretto adapted from that of Charles Ramuz, music by Igor Stravinsky, Bath, Bath Festival, 1968;

Granny Welfare and the Wolf, by Arden, D'Arcy, and the Muswell Hill Street Theatre, London, Ducketts Common, Turnpike Lane, March 1971;

My Old Man's a Tory, by D'Arcy, Arden, and the Muswell Hill Street Theatre, London, Wood Green, March 1971;

Two Hundred Years of Labour History, by D'Arcy, Arden, Roger Smith, and the Socialist Labour League, London, Alexandra Palace, April 1971;

Rudi Dutschke Must Stay, by D'Arcy, Arden, and Writers against Repression, London, British Museum, spring 1971;

The Ballygombeen Bequest, by Arden and D'Arcy, 7.84 Theatre Company, Edinburgh, Edinburgh Festival, 21 August 1972; London, Bush Theatre, 11 September 1972;

The Island of the Mighty: A Play on a Traditional Theme in Three Parts, by Arden and D'Arcy, London, Aldwych Theatre, 5 December 1972;

Serjeant Musgrave Dances On, by Arden and John McGrath, Sheffield, Crucible Theater, 1972;

The Devil and the Parish Pump, by D'Arcy, Arden, and the Corrandulla Arts Entertainment Club, Galway, Gort, Roe, Corrandulla Arts Centre, April 1974;

The Non-Stop Connolly Show: A Dramatic Cycle of Continuous Struggle in Six Parts, by D'Arcy and Arden, Dublin, Liberty Hall, 29–30 March 1975; London: Ambiance Lunch Hour Theatre, 17 May 1976;

The Crown Strike Play, by D'Arcy, Arden, and the Galway Theatre Workshop, Galway, Eyre Square, December 1975;

Sean O'Scrudu, by D'Arcy, Arden, and the Galway Theatre Workshop, Galway, Coachman Hotel, February 1976;

The Hunting of the Mongrel Fox, by D'Arcy, Arden, and the Galway Theatre Workshop, Galway, Regional Technical College, October 1976;

No Room at the Inn, by D'Arcy, Arden, and the Galway Theatre Workshop, Galway, Coachman Hotel, December 1976;

Silence, by D'Arcy, Arden, and the Galway Theatre Workshop, Galway, Eyre Square, April 1977;

Mary's Name, by D'Arcy, Arden, and the Galway Theatre Workshop, Galway, University College, May 1977;

Blow-In Chorus for Liam Cosgrave, by D'Arcy, Arden, and the Galway Theatre Workshop, Galway, Eyre Square, June 1977;

The Little Grey Home in the West: An Anglo-Irish Melodrama, by D'Arcy and Arden, London, Sugawn Theatre, 1 May 1978;

Vandaleur's Folly: An Anglo-Irish Melodrama, by D'Arcy and Arden, Lancaster, Lancaster University Nuffield Studio, 10 October 1978;

The Menace of Ireland . . . ? by Arden and D'Arcy, Bradford, Bradford Art College, 1979.

BOOKS: *Serjeant Musgrave's Dance: An Un-historical Parable* (London: Methuen, 1960; New York: Grove, 1962);

The Business of Good Government: A Christmas Play, by Arden and Margaretta D'Arcy (London: Methuen, 1963; New York: Grove, 1967);

Three Plays: The Waters of Babylon, Live Like Pigs, The Happy Haven, by Arden and D'Arcy, introduction by John Russell Taylor (Harmondsworth: Penguin, 1964; Baltimore: Penguin, 1965);

The Workhouse Donkey: A Vulgar Melo-Drama (London: Methuen, 1964; New York: Grove, 1967);

Armstrong's Last Goodnight: An Exercise in Diplomacy (London: Methuen, 1965; New York: Grove, 1967);

Ars Longa, Vita Brevis, by D'Arcy and Arden (London: Cassell, 1965);

Left-Handed Liberty: A Play about Magna Carta (London: Methuen, 1965; New York: Grove, 1966);

Ironhand, adapted from Johann Wolfgang von Goethe's play *Götz von Berlichingen* (London: Methuen, 1965);

Soldier, Soldier and Other Plays, by Arden and D'Arcy (London: Methuen, 1967)–comprises *Soldier, Soldier: A Comic Song for Television; Wet Fish: A Professional Reminiscence for Television; When Is a Door Not a Door?* and *Friday's Hiding;*

The Royal Pardon; or, The Soldier Who Became an Actor, by Arden and D'Arcy (London: Methuen, 1967);

The Hero Rises Up: A Romantic Melodrama, by Arden and D'Arcy (London: Methuen, 1969);

Two Autobiographical Plays (London: Methuen, 1971)–comprises *The True History of Squire Jonathan and His Unfortunate Treasure* and *The Bagman; or, The Impromptu of Muswell Hill;*

The Island of the Mighty: A Play on a Traditional British Theme in Three Parts, by Arden and D'Arcy (London: Eyre Methuen, 1974);

To Present the Pretence: Essays on the Theatre and Its Public, by Arden and D'Arcy (London: Eyre Methuen, 1977; New York: Holmes & Meier, 1979);

The Non-Stop Connolly Show: A Dramatic Cycle of Continuous Struggle in Six Parts, by D'Arcy and Arden, 5 volumes (London: Pluto, 1977–1978)–comprises volume 1, *Part 1 and 2: Boyhood, 1868–1889: Apprenticeship, 1889–1896* (1977); volume 2, *Part 3:*

Professionals, 1896–1903 (1978); volume 3, *Part 4: The New World, 1903–1910* (1978); volume 4, *Part 5: The Great Lockout, 1910–1914* (1978); volume 5, *Part 6: World War and the Rising, 1914–1916* (1978);

Pearl: A Play about a Play within the Play. Written for Radio (London: Eyre Methuen, 1979);

Vandaleur's Folly: An Anglo-Irish Melodrama. The Hazard of Experiment in an Irish Co-operative, Ralahine, 1831, by D'Arcy and Arden (London: Eyre Methuen, 1981);

The Little Gray Home in the West: An Anglo-Irish Melodrama, by Arden and D'Arcy (London: Pluto, 1982);

Silence among the Weapons: Some Events at the Time of the Failure of a Republic (London: Methuen, 1982; revised and corrected, 1983); republished as *Vox Pop: Last Days of the Roman Republic* (San Diego: Harcourt Brace Jovanovich, 1982);

Books of Bale: A Fiction of History (London: Methuen, 1988);

Awkward Corners: Essays, Papers, Fragments; Selected, with Commentaries, by the Authors, by Arden and D'Arcy (London & New York: Methuen, 1988);

Whose Is the Kingdom? by Arden and D'Arcy (London & New York: Methuen, 1988);

Cogs Tyrannic: Four Stories (London: Methuen, 1991);

Jack Juggler and the Emperor's Whore: Seven Tall Tales Linked Together for an Indecorous Toy Theatre (London: Methuen, 1995).

Collections: *Plays One* (London: Eyre Methuen, 1977; New York: Grove, 1978)–comprises *Sergeant Musgrave's Dance, The Workhouse Donkey,* and *Armstrong's Last Goodnight;*

Plays, volume 1, by Arden and D'Arcy (London: Methuen, 1991)–comprises *The Business of Good Government; Ars Longa, Vita Brevis; Friday's Hiding; The Royal Pardon; The Little Gray Home in the West; Vandaleur's Folly;* and *Immediate Rough Theatre;*

Plays: One, by Arden and D'Arcy (London: Methuen, 1994)–comprises *The Waters of Babylon, When Is a Door Not a Door? Live Like Pigs, Serjeant Musgrave's Dance,* and *The Happy Haven;*

Plays: Two (London: Methuen, 1994)–comprises *The Workhouse Donkey, Armstrong's Last Goodnight, Left-handed Liberty, The True History of Squire Jonathan and His Unfortunate Treasure,* and *The Bagman.*

PRODUCED SCRIPTS: *The Life of Man,* radio, BBC Home Service, 16 April 1956;

Soldier, Soldier: A Comic Song for Television, BBC TV, 16 February 1960;

Wet Fish: A Professional Reminiscence for Television, BBC TV, 3 September 1961;

Death of a Cowboy, BBC Radio, 1961;

The Bagman; or, The Impromptu of Muswell Hill, BBC Radio 3, 7 March 1970;

Keep Those People Moving, by Arden and Margaretta D'Arcy, BBC Radio, 1972;

Portrait of a Rebel, by Arden and D'Arcy, television, Dublin, Radio-Telefis Eireann, 1973;

To Put it Frankly . . . , BBC Radio 4, 19 May 1979;

Pearl: A Play about a Play within a Play, BBC Radio 4, 3 July 1979;

The Adventures of the Ingenious Gentleman, Don Quixote de la Mancha, adapted from Miguel de Cervantes's *Don Quixote,* 2 parts, BBC Radio 4, 29 September 1980 and 6 October 1980;

Garland for a Hoar Head, BBC Radio 3, 25 March 1982;

The Old Man Sleeps Alone, BBC Radio 4, 22 October 1982;

The Manchester Enthusiasts, by Arden and D'Arcy, 3 parts, BBC Radio, 18–25 June 1984;

Whose Is the Kingdom? by Arden and D'Arcy, 9 parts, BBC Radio 3, February 1988;

A Suburban Suicide, by Arden and D'Arcy, BBC Radio, 1994.

OTHER: Michael Horowitz, ed., *Children of Albion*–includes poems by Arden (Harmondsworth: Penguin, 1969);

The Old Man Sleeps Alone, in *Giles Cooper Award Plays 1982* (London: Methuen, 1982), pp. 26–56.

SELECTED PERIODICAL PUBLICATION–UNCOLLECTED: *The Ballygombeen Bequest, Scripts,* 9 (September 1972).

To encounter the work of John Arden is to join a debate about theater: what it is for and whom it is for. These questions are the subject of most of his articles, more than one of his novels, and several of his plays. The debate has been joined by critics who have responded with some passion to both the form and the content of his work: some in favor, some against, and a substantial number with a sort of perpetually delayed gratification that derides his newer work in relation to his early "masterpieces"–which were, at the time, equally vilified. It has also been joined, on a less theoretical basis, by Arden's chosen audiences and performers, between whom the dividing line is not always fixed. They have been drawn not only from the subsidized theater, in which the fairly well-heeled perform for the extremely well-heeled, but also from labor unionists, children, church congregations, and students. All of these have joined with Arden and his wife and frequent collaborator, Margaretta D'Arcy, to erode the boundaries and question the relationships between performance and politics and between art and action.

One of the so-called New Wave of British playwrights who came to prominence in the wake of John Osborne's *Look Back in Anger* (1956), Arden was born in Barnsley, Yorkshire, on 26 October 1930 to Charles Alwyn Arden, a glassworks manager, and Annie Elizabeth Layland Arden. His parents sent him to Sedbergh, a country public (American private) school, to escape bombing during World War II. He earned his B.A. at King's College of the University of Cambridge in 1953 and received a diploma in architecture from the Edinburgh College of Art in 1955. His understanding of theater was shaped more by reading and by student experimentation than by formal instruction. Of his first performed play, *All Fall Down,* a student production in Edinburgh in 1955, he says in *To Present the Pretence: Essays on the Theatre and Its Public* (1977): "If someone were to turn up the MS of this play and present it somewhere today I would no doubt be embarrassed by its technical ineptitude but I would not disown its fundamental conception." *All Fall Down* was inspired by the Victorian Toy Theater, with its crude twopence colors, glitter, and strained heroic poses. The same motif appears in Arden's novel *Jack Juggler and the Emperor's Whore: Seven Tall Tales Linked Together for an Indecorous Toy Theatre* (1995); the central characters, all working in the theater, deceive and betray one another in their work, their politics, and their personal lives, but the toy theater is a more or less truthful means of communication among them despite–or because of–the fact that it deals in fantastic stories performed with elaborate artifice.

Artifice is central to Arden's idea of theater. A theater that acknowledges that it is a theater and not real life can become a mirror for society, as it was for Arden's acknowledged role models, Ben Jonson, Sean O'Casey, and John Millington Synge. In this theater, Arden says in "Telling a True Tale," a 1960 essay for *Encore* that was collected in *Drama Criticism: Developments since Ibsen* (1979) and edited by Arnold P. Hinchcliffe, a playwright can translate "the concrete life of today into terms of poetry that shall at the one time both illustrate that life and set it within the historic and legendary tradition of our culture." Rather than accept that the everyday speech that produced a William Shakespeare or a John Bunyan had vanished in "A sludgy uninterested nation married to its telly and its fish and chips," Arden, in this same essay, considered that a playwright can recapture this linguistic excitement through the stylization of language and action that the emblematic theater can offer. Now that almost everyone has a television, he suggests, stage naturalism will be seen as the false creation it is; if people were not to desert the theater, they needed to be offered something else. Then they might begin to come to performances not in spite of the artifice but because of it.

Ian Bannen in the title role in the original 1959 production at the Royal Court Theatre of Arden's Serjeant Musgrave's Dance *(photograph by Bernand)*

This notion implies considerable faith in the possibility of communication: faith that it is possible to express complex social and political meaning in speech and spectacle and that this expression can be understood and enjoyed by its audience. This view was not a fashionable one in the late 1950s and early 1960s, when many plays were primarily concerned with the difficulty of communicating, with the inadequacy of language. Harold Pinter's early plays are full of ambiguities and ellipses; Osborne's Jimmy Porter in *Look Back in Anger* raves in front of uncomprehending friends; Arnold Wesker devotes an entire play (*Roots,* 1959) to the process by which a young woman becomes articulate for the first time in her life in a family that does not understand what she is saying. Arden assumed from the outset that a complex assault on the intellect is possible only through a full-blooded attack on the senses, and that theater language should be both verbally and visually rich.

After graduating from the Edinburgh College of Art, Arden took a position as an architect's assistant in London. He married the Irish playwright D'Arcy, with whom he has five children, on 1 May 1957. That same year he left architecture and began his theatrical career as the result of an invitation from George Devine at the Royal Court Theatre; Devine had been impressed by Arden's first radio play, *The Life of Man* (1957), a richly textured piece with overtones of Samuel Taylor Coleridge's *The Rime of the Ancient Mariner* (1798) that won the BBC Northern Region Prize. Devine had leased the Royal Court for the English Stage Company with the avowed intent of establishing a "writers' theater." Arden's first play for the Royal Court, a work based on the King Arthur legends, was rejected, but Arden became a member of the Court Writers' Group, which included Ann Jellicoe, Edward Bond, and David Cregan. The group undertook a series of practical explorations into theater organized by William Gaskill and Keith Johnstone that did a great deal to open up the more consciously theatrical writing styles Arden already favored; he benefited especially from the workshops on masks. These explorations were an outgrowth of the Royal Court's commitment to the plays of German dramatist Bertolt Brecht; Arden, although he later claimed that Brecht was less important to his work than the medieval and Jacobean Irish traditions, has cited *Mutter Courage und ihre Kinder* (Mother Courage and Her Children, 1941) as the play he would most like to have written and has found himself more than once labeled "the English Brecht." The new theatrical techniques, however, were not always fully understood or well received by audiences and critics. The Royal Court's production of Brecht's *The Good Woman of Setzuan* (November 1956) was a failure; so, at least in financial terms, were Arden's early plays, which cost the theater around £15,000.

The enormous success of *Look Back in Anger* helps to account for Arden's chilly reception. Osborne's play is set in a sordid London flat as is Arden's first play accepted by the Royal Court, *The Waters of Babylon,* produced in the Theatre Upstairs as a Sunday-night play-without-decor in October 1957. But in the Osborne play a small group of people speak in a style that resembles everyday conversation and work through changes in their personal relationships in a structure that is not very different from that of the plays of Terence Rattigan or William Douglas-Home. In *The Waters of Babylon,* on the other hand, a whole underclass is brought together: an East European refugee pimp, a corrupt Yorkshire politician, a West Indian tart, and a black local councillor are caught up in a rigged-lottery scheme. They speak in a poetic language that sometimes blossoms into verse or even song; it is a language that is aware of its own theatricality and that speaks directly to the audience, as well as to the onstage characters. In so doing, it engages the audience members in a complex inner debate. The spectators are invited to judge the characters and their context and constantly to rethink and revise those judgments. The corrupt mayor, Charlie Butterthwaite, for instance, is a product of the materialism that sprang out of the postwar boom, but his wheeling and dealing produces benefits for the hospitals and orphanages over which he exercises his power. He is on the side of the unions, not the mill owners; but he refers to them as "The Adverse Power," like the hero of a medieval morality play. He presents himself in a blank-verse soliloquy like a villain from Jacobean tragedy, but he does so with such energy and inventiveness that the audience finds him likable. Similarly, the most plangent and memorable song in the play is that sung by the Polish refugee brothel owner, Sigismanfred Krankiewicz–known as Krank–about the Bergen-Belsen concentration camp:

> As I went down by Belsen town
> I saw my mother there
> She said go by, go by, my son, go by
> But leave with me here
> Your lovely yellow hair.

Like the folk songs after which it is patterned, Krank's song contains the pain and violence of its subject through lyricism, but the names of the camps are too real to make the containment comforting. The hair, the blood, and the strong teeth celebrated in the song add up to a stylized picture of a beautiful person, as in many a traditional ballad, but they are also a reminder of the way the camps reduced human beings to cash commodities such as hair, teeth, and blood. The song requires a complex evaluation of Krank, who first claims to be a victim of Buchenwald, then admits to being a guard, and finally challenges the audience's right to judge anyone for keeping himself alive by so doing. It explains Krank's greed and lack of affect as products of his wartime suffering but does not invite the audience to excuse him on that account.

The *Daily Mail* (London, 21 October 1957) hailed *The Waters of Babylon* as promising, despite its "haze of words." The *Liverpool Post* (4 October 1958) greeted Arden's play of the following year, *Live Like Pigs,* about a gypsylike family, the Sawneys, who are forced out of the abandoned trolley car in which they have been living and into a public-housing project, as showing "considerable talent," while headlining the review: "My most sordid evening in the theatre." The assumption seemed to be that Arden could produce the kind of play that the theater of the 1950s expected but that he was perversely refusing to do so.

Arden's next play, *Serjeant Musgrave's Dance: An Unhistorical Parable,* made no concessions to popular taste. Devine, however, aware that Arden had made a

Arden and his wife and frequent collaborator, Margaretta D'Arcy, in the 1960s (photograph by Roger Mayne)

considerable leap forward on his own terms, staged the play at a loss in 1959 and published a pamphlet in which Osborne, Wesker, and N. F. Simpson declared their belief in Arden's work.

Serjeant Musgrave's Dance has long been acknowledged as one of the most significant plays since World War II; it is Arden's most frequently revived work and is widely studied in schools and universities. Thus, today the incomprehension with which the play's premiere was greeted is difficult to imagine. The clarity of its structure, the simplicity of its visual design, and the balladlike images and story have a rightness about them that seems unchallengeable. One may dislike the play, but it is nearly impossible to deny its coherence or its power, though some of its earliest critics did so.

Sergeant Musgrave's Dance is the first play by an English-speaking author in which the work of Brecht is truly absorbed and refracted rather than merely copied in terms of surface detail. Peter Thomson suggests that it springs from Arden's intense admiration of *Mutter Courage und ihre Kinder:* "The symbiotic relationship . . . is unique. . . . Without copying its methods, and perhaps beyond his consciousness, Arden apprehended *Mother Courage* and transfigured it." Both plays choose the relatively distant past to explore the theme of war: Brecht's play is set during the Thirty Years' War (1618–1648), Arden's during the British colonial wars of the 1880s. Both feature family or quasi-family groups: Courage and her children, Musgrave and his men, respectively. Both have at their center characters who think that they have room to maneuver in the complexities of the power structure–Courage by putting survival above everything, Musgrave by outright confrontation–but who find that they have unwittingly colluded with that power structure to destroy their "families." Echoes of Brecht's play appear in Arden's: for example, Eilif's war dance in *Mutter Courage und ihre Kinder* and Musgrave's death dance. Both plays use props and costumes whose beauty derives from their practical functions rather than from sheer decorativeness. Finally, like Brecht, Arden turned to ballads for his images and structure; in so doing, he rooted the play unmistakably in his own British culture.

In ballads, as Arden points out in "Telling a True Tale," colors are central, and *Serjeant Musgrave's Dance* is painted in red, white, and black. At the beginning of the play these colors are in simple opposition. Musgrave and his three fellow soldiers are rumored to have come to the snowbound town to break the coal miners' strike; in fact, they are deserters from the colonial wars. Musgrave holds a "recruiting" meeting at which he displays the skeleton of a local boy, Billy, and announces his "logic": Billy was killed by a sniper in the wars, and five natives were executed in reprisal; he intends to take the lives of the town's figures of power who set the murderous cycle in motion. His surviving comardes–whether pacific or violent–both refuse his logic. The barmaid, Annie, then produces the tunic of Sparky, a trooper who had defied Musgrave and was accidentally killed in a scuffle with another soldier. Shocked by the murder, the miners start to leave too. Suddenly, the dragoons summoned by the mayor to break the strike arrive and restore "order." The townspeople dance, and Musgrave and his last loyal comrade, Attercliffe, are taken to be hanged; but the rejoicings are policed by the dragoons, and the future is uncertain.

The moral and political complexity of the play can be seen in the connotational shifts undergone by Arden's apparently simple color pattern. Red, the color of a soldier's jacket, is, as the satirical figure of the bargeman reminds Musgrave, also the color of the stripes on his back, the scarred remnants of any soldier who has been flogged in the past. "Bloodred roses . . . whack, whack, whack." It is also the color of Sparky's blood; Annie licks it, almost ritualistically, and it gives her speech authority when she identifies Sparky with the miners: "A Bayonet is a raven's beak. This tunic's a collier's jacket." The mayor in his red coat of office and the dragoons in their own red jackets surround the town, cutting it off more dangerously than the snow has; the red of the oppressor and the red of the oppressed have become one. Black, the color of the death-symbolizing ace of spades that keeps appearing in Sparky's card tricks, is also the color of the lettering on Black Jack Musgrave's plan and of the miners' coats. And white is the color of the snow that locks up the town, of Billy's skeleton, and of the "word" of Musgrave ("Our shining white word, let it dance!" he repeats). The shifting meanings of color force the audience to question other images: the soldier, the archetype of many stories and ballads, is not a fighting machine or a dashing young hero but the bearer of a terrible knowledge. Annie is not a stereotypical whore with a heart of gold but a visionary who articulates bitter political truths. The play does not take simple attitudes to war and pacifism, but it does make clear that the oppressed cannot afford to collude with the techniques of their oppressors. Arden leaves his audience not with answers but with a question: as Attercliffe and Musgrave wait to be hanged, Attercliffe sings a song about a green apple, then says: "They're going to hang us up a length higher nor most apple-trees grow, Serjeant. D'you reckon we can start an orchard?"

When *Serjeant Musgrave's Dance* was first produced, critics fretted about the psychology of the characters and tried to explain Musgrave's madness or find depth of characterization in the soldiers rather than a typology that illuminates the world of which they are a part. The complaint that "you never know where he stands" became a refrain that haunted Arden productions, to the point that it was invoked as a sort of shorthand review. "This is an Arden play!" wrote Edwin Morgan in *Encore* (7 August 1964) of *Armstrong's Last Goodnight: An Exercise in Diplomacy* (1964), about the sixteenth-century Scottish outlaw James Armstrong of Glinockie, in 1964. "Sympathy never develops very far." The accusation seems odd in the face of characters such as Charlie Butterthwaite from *The Waters of Babylon,* reincarnated in corrupt splendor in *The Workhouse Donkey* (1963), in which he struggles against a rigidly legalistic chief of police, Colonel Feng, or of Armstrong himself, the sexy, treacherous, and naive border raider destroyed by Renaissance politics, roles in which the actor is given all he needs to charm the audience. The point of the criticism was that Arden was not interested in creating figures with whom the audience might straightforwardly identify. Rather, he chose to lay bare power structures; his use of colorful and passionate characters was theatrically enlivening and reminded the politically committed that energy had value and should be channeled but never repressed.

After *Armstrong's Last Goodnight,* perhaps partly in response to the repeated complaints, Arden turned from the subsidized theaters, with their clear demarcation between performer and audience, and extended and developed another kind of work that he had begun to explore with D'Arcy in 1959, when he was awarded a fellowship in creative writing at the University of Bristol. During their two years in the West Country they wrote for students and for their parish church, St. Michael's at Brent Knoll, for which they developed *A Christmas Play* (1960). In this work they set out to re-create something of the relationship between performer and watcher that had existed in the preprofessional theater of the medieval mystery plays. The action was set in the church itself; the angel announced the birth of Christ from the pulpit; all of the performers, regardless of role, sat in the choir stalls when not involved in the action and joined in the songs. The focus of the play was not on acting-as-imitation, a skill reserved for an elite, but on the direct communication of a story of importance to both audience and players.

Arden and D'Arcy's community activities became more ambitious after they moved to Kirkbymoorside, Yorkshire, in 1963. A project to make a movie about the town evolved into a month-long festival centered in their home and included movies, music, and plays; one of the plays, developed in cooperation with a Girl Guide group in 1964, was *Ars Longa, Vita Brevis.* This short piece, partly improvised around objects found lying around the house, is an example of Arden's belief that theater belongs to everyone: rather than patronizing the children, it makes use of their natural energy to explore the nature of authority and subversion; at its heart is a figure not too different from Serjeant Musgrave, an art teacher who dreams of "the glowing brutalities" of war but is controlled by the children he

Henry Woolfe as Admiral Horatio Nelson and Bettina Jonic as Lady Emma Hamilton in the original 1968 production at the Round House Theatre in London of Arden and D'Arcy's The Hero Rises Up *(photograph by Donald Cooper)*

disciplines and by his exuberantly erotic young wife. (The director Peter Brook found the play challenging for the actors who were working on his experimental Theatre of Cruelty season at the London Academy of Music and Dramatic Art that same year.)

In 1966 Arden further explored the relationships between power and theater as co-author of and actor in *The Royal Pardon; or, The Soldier Who Became an Actor,* a play written for the Beaford Festival in Beaford, Devon. Like Salman Rushdie later in *Haroun and the Sea of Stories* (1990) he found a children's story a useful form in which to couch a passionate defense of artifice. The play is about an actress, Esmeralda, and Luke, a soldier-turned-carpenter, who find themselves entertaining royalty; they struggle with pretentious professionals on the one hand and literal-mindedness on the other. Arden played their chief adversary, the Constable, an enemy of pretense who is turned to stone. The "happy ending" comes not when they are offered a huge government subsidy, but when they reject it:

We two will attempt together a far more dangerous thing:
We will travel, hand in hand,
Across water and dry land–
We will entertain the people.

Arden had by this time consolidated his belief in theater as a democratic, communal art, and a play, as he wrote in *Plays One* (1977), as "something of interest" for "a whole crowd of people whom I would have liked to believe my friends." Soon another dimension was added to this conception: although his work had always been more political than that of most of his contemporaries, politics became a driving force in them. The watershed years were 1968 and 1969.

The year 1968 brought the Soviet invasion of Czechoslovakia, the Tet Offensive in Vietnam, student revolutions in Paris, and Bloody Sunday in Derry. It marked the end of censorship in the British theater and the beginning of a new wave of playwrights who, unlike the socialists who had spearheaded the Royal Court renaissance of 1956, dealt overtly with politics in their work. They evolved a fruitful symbiosis with theater companies such as CAST, 7.84, and Red Ladder, which, like Arden and D'Arcy, played not only in established venues but also in pubs, clubs, and local halls.

Arden's theater was more at home with this new generation than with his own, and his antinaturalistic approach had an impact on companies such as 7.84. His 1970 radio play, *The Bagman,* explores some of the implications of political theater in a fable about a well-meaning liberal playwright, "John Arden," who refuses to make a real commitment to politics in his work. Arden and D'Arcy's play about Admiral Horatio Nelson, *The Hero Rises Up: A Romantic Melodrama* (1968), brought struggles with the management of the Institute of Contemporary Arts. In a preface to the published version (1969) they trace parallels between their administrative battles and the action of the play, in which they deconstruct the national hero and the society that had no better use for his anarchic energies than to set him to killing on its behalf.

Arden's most radical rethinking came the following year, when he and D'Arcy visited India. Weeklong performances in Bengal that depicted gods and heroes in giant, spangled glory not only reflected their own preoccupation with theater as a community activity but also gave them a new vision of the scale on which it might be practiced. More important, for the first time they encountered genuine poverty, which caused them to realize that in this society the poorest British worker could be seen as an emblem of the capitalistic West. Losing their way on a tour of a "model" factory, they witnessed a side of Indian industry they were not meant to see: workers on the edge of starvation, struggling in near-swamp territory with huge loads. As a result, Arden found himself jailed briefly on charges of possessing "subversive literature." They also made contact with revolutionary groups who were, for the first time, beginning to work with those at the bottom of the caste system. The trip clarified Arden's understanding of socialism and of the power of literature; in the preface to the published edition of *The Bagman* in *Two Autobiographical Plays* (1971) he wrote:

> I recognise as the enemy the fed man, the clothed man, the sheltered man, whose food, clothes and house are obtained at the expense of the hunger, the nakedness and the exposure of so many millions of others: and who will allow anything to be *said* . . . so long as the food, clothes and house remain undiminished in his possession.

Inspired by his experience in India, Arden returned to the subject of his first rejected play for the Royal Court Theatre, and he and D'Arcy composed an allegorical Arthurian trilogy, *The Island of the Mighty: A Play on a Traditional Theme in Three Parts* (1972), about a decaying outpost of the Roman Empire defended by a war leader who is too rigid to change. The kingdom is grounded in Roman values, capitalistic, and savagely patriarchal. It is menaced by the threat of an Anglo-Saxon invasion; one possible means of salvation lies in forming an alliance with the Picts, who are devious, matriarchal, and capable of change. The action is seen not only through the perspective of the ruling class but also through that of the ordinary people, the underclass of slaves, bondwomen, and poor peasants who are too busy trying to survive to be able to afford the luxury of political opinions. In the end, concludes Merlin, who survives the deaths of King Arthur and Medraut (Mordred), they are the ones whose voices should be heard: "They have so much to say."

The Royal Shakespeare Company had reservations about the length of the piece, which was ultimately truncated into a one-night play, but agreed to allow D'Arcy to observe the final rehearsals. When she did so, she saw that the production had changed its focus: Arthur had become a tragic hero rather than an oppressor; the sets and costumes were spectacular but did not reflect the precisely imagined power relationships that the authors intended; and many of the ordinary characters had been cut out, with those who remained depicted as mindless and violent. After fruitless confrontations Arden and D'Arcy picketed the theater and mounted a protest at the first preview. Shouted down when he attempted to speak, Arden promised that "We will never write for you again," and shortly thereafter he and D'Arcy moved to Ireland. On the opening night of *The Island of the Mighty* Arden and D'Arcy attended instead 7.84's production of their play *The Ballygombeen Bequest* (1972).

The Ballygombeen Bequest had its roots in a highly local issue: in 1971 a tourist boom had begun in Galway, where Arden and D'Arcy were spending much of their time; the land became attractive to the big hotel chains, and the tenant farmers, whose rights were grounded in tradition rather than legalities, were subjected to considerable harassment to leave. Lacking other help, many of them turned to the Irish Republican Army (IRA). Bulldozers were blown up, and shots were fired at the police. Arden and D'Arcy constructed a tale about a British landowner, Hollidey-Cheype, who inherits an Irish property after World War II–a gold mine in the days of mainland shortages. As the 1950s boom unites the capitalists of England, Ireland, and Northern Ireland, Seamus, the tenant of the property, is evicted. In the late 1960s his son, Padraic, who has studied Marxism, turns to the IRA for help; but the IRA is not interested in the petty squabbles of the poor. The way is then clear for Hagan, his corrupt builder, to double-cross Hollidey-Cheype: he uses his IRA contacts to blow up the property; it is then "marked" by the IRA, and he is able to buy it at a knockdown price. Padraic is set up by both Hollidey-Cheype and Hagan: driving to the border to sell Hagan's horses, he is arrested by troops acting for British Intelligence and the Dublin Special Branch, tortured, and killed. His body is dumped after being doctored to look like a victim of IRA internecine strife.

The play provided a lively evening's entertainment as the arguments were buttressed by audacious swings in

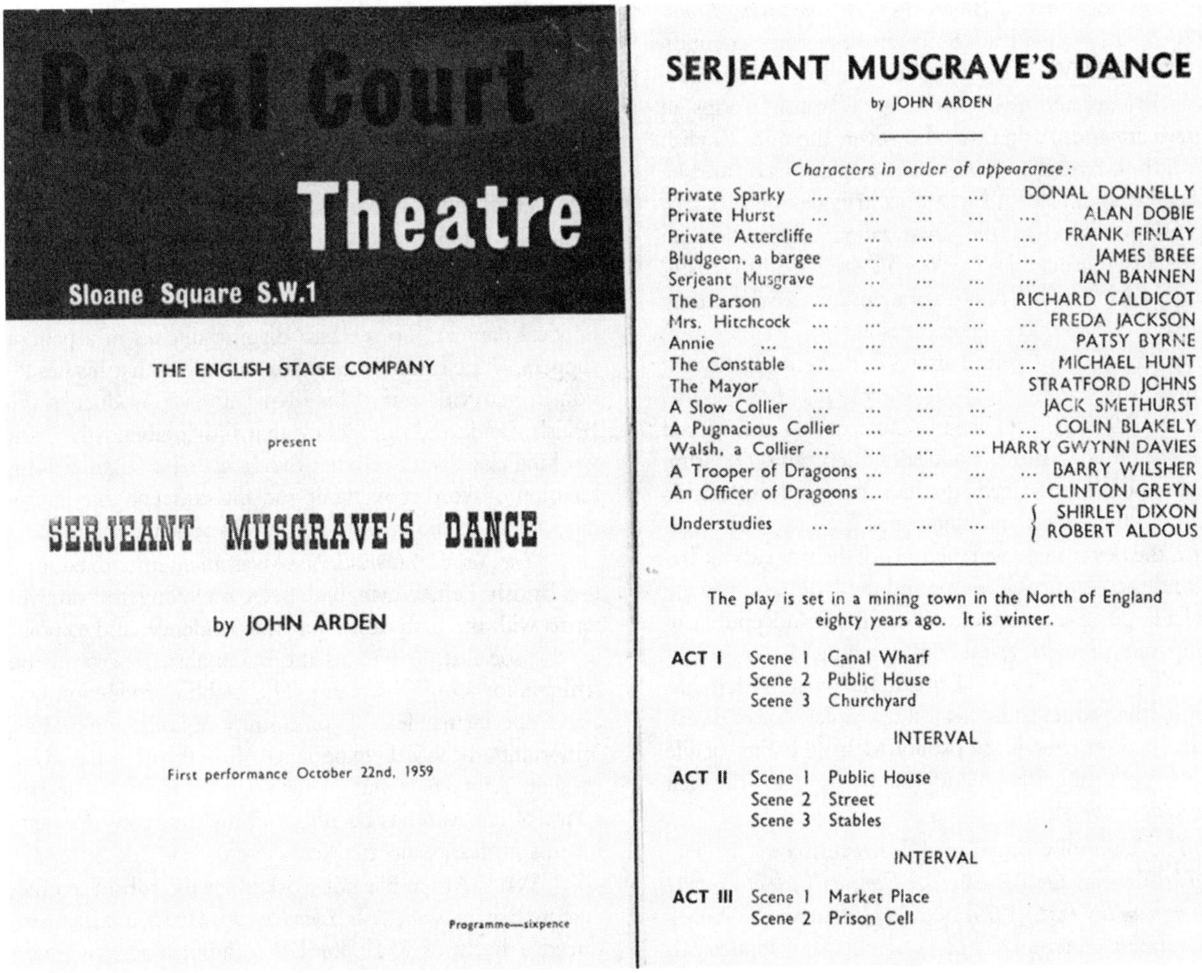

Royal Court Theatre

Sloane Square S.W.1

THE ENGLISH STAGE COMPANY

present

SERJEANT MUSGRAVE'S DANCE

by JOHN ARDEN

First performance October 22nd, 1959

Programme—sixpence

SERJEANT MUSGRAVE'S DANCE

by JOHN ARDEN

Characters in order of appearance:

Private Sparky	DONAL DONNELLY
Private Hurst	ALAN DOBIE
Private Attercliffe	FRANK FINLAY
Bludgeon, a bargee	JAMES BREE
Serjeant Musgrave	IAN BANNEN
The Parson	RICHARD CALDICOT
Mrs. Hitchcock	FREDA JACKSON
Annie	PATSY BYRNE
The Constable	MICHAEL HUNT
The Mayor	STRATFORD JOHNS
A Slow Collier	JACK SMETHURST
A Pugnacious Collier	COLIN BLAKELY
Walsh, a Collier	HARRY GWYNN DAVIES
A Trooper of Dragoons	BARRY WILSHER
An Officer of Dragoons	CLINTON GREYN
Understudies	SHIRLEY DIXON ROBERT ALDOUS

The play is set in a mining town in the North of England eighty years ago. It is winter.

ACT I Scene 1 Canal Wharf
Scene 2 Public House
Scene 3 Churchyard

INTERVAL

ACT II Scene 1 Public House
Scene 2 Street
Scene 3 Stables

INTERVAL

ACT III Scene 1 Market Place
Scene 2 Prison Cell

Cover and cast list from the program for the first production of Arden's play about a British soldier who terrorizes a mining community in the 1880s

mood: Hollidey-Cheype is a comic villain, but the British soldiers are real men trapped by unemployment into work they never wanted; the torture scene is brutal, but Padraic's ghost returns to pelt Hagan and Hollidey-Cheype with custard pies; the closing song is a cheerful jig, but its last lines remind the audience that "there are more of us than them." The atmosphere of the production became a trademark of 7.84, one of the most successful political companies of the 1970s.

In Edinburgh, however, the production ran into trouble. The problem lay less in the play than in an accompanying leaflet, which gave details about an actual case in Galway. It was not written by Arden or D'Arcy, but they were sued anyway by a British gentleman who owned property in the West of Ireland and thought that he recognized himself in Hollidey-Cheype. Under British law, once a character has been "recognized," everthing he or she does on stage becomes an accusation that the same thing happened in real life. The basis for the suit was the text of the play, to which attention had been drawn by the leaflet. The suit was brought in London, because the threatrical company was based there. The plaintiff's main complaint was that Hollidey-Cheype is shown getting Seamus drunk in order to exploit him. Arden and D'Arcy replied that the play was an allegory and tried to outline the history of the British in Ireland. The judge expressed his regret that the jury "should have to read this turgid piece of prose," a phrase that might have been taken from the uncomprehending reviews of *Serjeant Musgrave's Dance* twelve years earlier. The suit was settled out of court after five ruinously expensive years.

Arden and D'Arcy were not the only English playwrights to encounter problems in attempting to write about the political situation in Northern Ireland in the 1970s. In 1972 Howard Brenton, David Hare, David Edgar, Tony Bicat, Francis Fuchs, Brian Clark, and Snoo Wilson wrote *England's Ireland;* more than fifty theaters refused to stage it. Caryl Churchill's *The Legion Hall Bombing* was only broadcast by the British Broadcasting Corporation (BBC) in 1978 after cuts that led her to remove her name from the credits. Brenton's *The Romans in Britain* (1980) was prosecuted for obscenity, diverting attention from the explicit parallels drawn between the Roman invasion of Britain and the stationing of British troops in Northern Ireland. Arden was, however, the only English playwright to return so consistently to the subject, and he has written at some length about his struggle to do so. In a pamphlet published by the organization Information on Ireland, later reprinted in *The New Statesman* (13 July 1979), he and D'Arcy point out several instances when they believed they had encountered censorship: 7.84 met difficulties with the Arts Council after *The Ballygombeen Bequest;* Irish performers in their play *Vandaleur's Folly: An Anglo-Irish Melodrama* (1978) felt the need to cut speeches considered pro-IRA and to remove political posters and literature from the theater; managements had conveyed to Arden's agent that they were not interested in his work with D'Arcy, the better-informed member of the team about Ireland; and the National Theatre and the BBC rejected the idea of a large project about the life of the Irish Republican leader James Connolly, the BBC stating that it might "inflame" passions. They also outline what Arden has called in the same pamphlet "the whole obsessed distressed uncomprehending hostility to Irish habits of life and their political embodiment" that has crippled the Left as much as the Right.

The Connolly project did, however, come to fruition. *The Non-Stop Connolly Show: A Dramatic Cycle of Continuous Struggle in Six Parts* (1975) became Arden and D'Arcy's most ambitious attempt to open up political dialogue with an audience on the scale of the Indian epics or the mystery plays of the Middle Ages. Like the mystery plays, it is a cycle rather than a single play and is constructed to resonate with a particular time and place. Although readings were held in Ireland and at the Almost Free Theatre in London, the staging closest to the authors' design took place at Liberty Hall in Dublin, once the center of Connolly's Citizen Army, on the fifty-ninth anniversary of the Easter Rising in 1916. Like the mystery plays, too, it sought to involve the whole community. The cast included professional actors; students; labor union members; and members of Na Fianna Éireann, the youth scouting movement founded in 1909 by Countess Constance Markievicz that had played an important role in the Easter Rising. The cycle is enormously wide-ranging, setting Connolly in a world context with episodes involving the Dublin General Strike of 1913, labor disputes in the United States at the turn of the twentieth century, and the silencing of socialist dissenters during World War I. The theatrical techniques include slapstick, cartoonish melodrama, and masks: Connolly's antagonist, a composite capitalist named Grabitall from cartoons of the 1930s, is a protean figure who, for example, can organize the Boer War as a toilet-paper-roll battle fought by whites over the heads of black Africans or summon up masked war demons whose dances are genuinely frightening. Alongside the depiction of world events ran a purely Irish strain, including dream sequences in which Connolly's dilemmas find a parallel in Irish mythology, staged with all the musical and dance resources available, and the lampooning of William Butler Yeats and Maud Gonne as figures of patronizing whimsy. Connolly is portrayed in a naturalistic style, but the milestones of his life–the low points of poverty and the more joyful moments, such as his courtship–are placed in a political context. To see him digging ditches in a pair of slippers, all he can afford, or reasoning out that his hesitation in marrying out of his own faith is a product of the British divide-and-rule policy that has inhibited the Irish working class, is to see what Brecht called a *Gestus*–a combination of word movement and mis-en-scène that illuminates social relations–within a purely personal moment.

The Non-Stop Connolly Show was an attempt to educate the British Left, which had been unwilling to come to terms with the Irish desire for independence, and to point up the socialist, as well as the nationalist, aspects of the struggle for a united Ireland. The Dublin production was also a spectacular feat of community organization and an important theatrical experience for those who were present. As such, it has never received its due: the language of criticism has been that of the uninvolved spectator of a professionally marketed event.

While Arden has not worked for the subsidized theater in Britain since *The Island of the Mighty,* he has produced a body of work for BBC radio, alone and with D'Arcy, that has continued to explore the themes of artifice, representation, and politics and to revise his listeners' perspectives on history. The most interesting of these have also opened up questions of gender in new ways.

Pearl: A Play about a Play within the Play (1979) explores the issues raised by *The Island of the Mighty* dispute, along with questions Arden has asked throughout his career: What is theater for? Whom is it for? And, in this case, to whom does a play belong? The central character is an actress and a secret agent, and when she meets the disaffected playwright Tom Backhouse, the two parts of her being fuse. She inhabits a moment of history when the "obsessed distressed uncomprehending hostility" of England to the Irish is at a point of crisis, the beginning of the 1640s. Politically, she is struggling to bring about an alliance of English Puritans, Scots Presbyterians, and Irish Catholics–in short, a people's revolution that will defeat the oppressive Royalist regime by establishing the understanding that wars about religion are only a mask for wars about land, and that the oppressed belong together. As Pearl and Backhouse begin to write a play based on the biblical story of Esther, with which they hope to win over the Puritans not only to the cause but to the theater, her desires as an artist work their own revolution. Pearl is a

Scene from the 1972 Belfast production of D'Arcy and Arden's The Ballygombeen Bequest, *about a greedy British landowner in Ireland (photograph by Brian McAvera)*

logical development of Esmeralda in *The Royal Pardon,* one who thinks out her situation in more adult and politicized terms. Scratching out a living as an entertainer all over Europe, she hungers for the magic, the passion, and the craftsmanship of the all-male English theater. In claiming an equal place with Backhouse and his leading actor, she asserts the right of women to speak for and about themselves without the distortions inherent in male intervention; she also claims the existential adventure and the sensual pleasure of the act of performance:

> I stand here bold upright stripped to my brown skin
> I turn over and over one question: just who I am. . . .
> Who would have dreamed my brimstone blood would rage
> At dance of so-called devils on a stage?
> Yet never before did I so yearn and groan
> In hope one day to set to them their tune. . . .

The counterpoint to Pearl's growing power is the Royalist plot by which the Esther play is robbed of its significance. The spy Captain Catso acts as producer and reduces it to a piece of flashy garbage that can only offend the Puritans. At the climax of the play he seizes Pearl as she is changing into the costume in which she will deliver the polemical epilogue and drags her naked onto the stage; turning dialectic into obscene spectacle, he not only brings about the downfall of the hoped-for alliance of dissidents but also wrecks the prospects of the theater as an instrument of learning and pleasure for the oppressed. *Pearl* is an alternative history in which gender, class, and national boundaries are eroded.

The ideas of alternative history and of the blurring of boundaries are taken further in Arden and D'Arcy's most ambitious project for the BBC to date, the nine-play cycle *Whose Is the Kingdom?* (1988). The work was initiated by Richard Imison, deputy head of drama at the BBC, in 1981, the fortieth anniversary of *The Man Born to be King,* a cycle of radio plays on the life of Christ by Dorothy L. Sayers. The Sayers cycle had not only stretched the resources of radio but had also broken new ground in terms of subject matter and had sparked a lively controversy: some people found the very act of representing Jesus on radio blasphemous (it was forbidden on stage for years to come); others found that it led them to reimagine their faith. Imison hoped for a similar impact on a generation that was both more accustomed to such representations and less unified in belief. After six years of research Arden and D'Arcy wrote a series of linked plays that chart the growth of Christianity from persecuted sect to official religion of a state–the Roman Empire under Constantine in the third century–that was already crumbling.

Like *The Island of the Mighty, The Non-Stop Connolly Show,* and *Pearl,* the plays grow out of the assumption that "history" is constructed by those in power, and that the responsible narrator should uncover the aspects that have been repressed or censored because they conflict with that construct. The main narrative strands track Constantine, holding his world together with an ideology he himself barely understands, and the Christian leaders who collaborate with him to present their faith as not inconsistent with Roman rule; among them is Paul of Tarsus, presented as a mocking spirit inside Constantine's mind. As a counterpoint to them runs the story of Fausta, Constantine's queen, whose disappearance has never been adequately explained. Fausta discovers a text that relates to the faith of women, both Christian and non-Christian, and through her encounters with real and imagined characters the audience is gradually made aware of a multifaceted and complex religion in which the hierarchies of gender and class are dissolved and love and plurality are celebrated; it is a faith dangerous enough to be rigidly forced into alien patriarchal and hierarchical lines.

Whose Is the Kingdom? is narrated by a woman, Kybele, a philosopher in exile who has come to Ireland, where the Druids have persecuted Christian women as Constantine persecuted Fausta. Lacking faith herself, she is all too aware of the dangers of faith that collude with power and of the magic and healing that are inherent not in any one religion but in the freedom to practice the faith of one's choice. While awaiting judgment as to whether or not she may remain in Hibernia, she reviews the history of a Rome "fallen in on its empty-hearted self" and looks ahead to the "frustrated energy" of the Irish kingdoms whose struggles with the Christian faith are yet to come.

Since 1982 Arden has written three novels–*Silence among the Weapons: Some Events at the Time of the Failure of a Republic* (1982), republished in the United States as *Vox Pop: Last Days of the Roman Republic* (1982); *Books of Bale: A Fiction of History* (1988); and *Jack Juggler and the Emperor's Whore*–and a collection of four short stories, *Cogs Tyrannic* (1991). As of 2001 he has not written again for the major subsidized theaters in England.

Interview:

Georg Gaston, "An Interview with John Arden," *Contemporary Literature,* 32 (Summer 1991): 147–170.

References:

Michael Anderson, *Anger and Detachment: A Study of Arden, Osborne and Pinter* (London: Pitman, 1976), pp. 50–87;

John Russell Brown, *Theatre Language: A Study of Arden, Osborne, Pinter, and Wesker* (London: Allen Lane, 1972), pp. 190–234;

Michael Cohen, "A Defence of D'Arcy and Arden's *Non-Stop Connolly Show,*" *Theatre Research International,* 15 (Spring 1990): 78–88;

Cohen, "The Politics of the Earlier Arden," *Modern Drama,* 28 (June 1985): 198–210;

Diana Culbertson, "Sacred Victims: Catharsis in the Modern Theatre," *Cross Currents,* 41 (Summer 1991): 179–194;

P. C. David, "Poetry in the Drama of John Arden," *Panjab University Research Bulletin (Arts),* 17 (April 1986): 41–50;

Ishwar Dutt, "The Rebel and the Tyrant: An Analysis of Violence in *Serjeant Musgrave's Dance,*" *Panjab University Research Bulletin (Arts),* 14 (October 1983): 143–155;

Frances Gray, *John Arden* (Basingstoke: Macmillan, 1982; New York: Grove, 1982);

Ronald Hayman, *John Arden* (London: Heinemann, 1968);

Albert Hunt, *Arden: A Study of His Plays* (London: Eyre Methuen, 1974);

Andrew K. Kennedy, *Six Dramatists in Search of a Language: Studies in Dramatic Language* (Cambridge: Cambridge University Press, 1975), pp. 213–229;

Glenda Leeming, *John Arden,* edited by Ian Scott-Kilvert, Writers and Their Work, no. 238 (Harlow: Published by Longman for the British Council, 1974);

Javed Malick, *Toward a Theatre of the Oppressed: The Dramaturgy of John Arden* (Ann Arbor: University of Michigan Press, 1995);

Redmond O'Hanlon, "The Theatrical Values of John Arden," *Theatre Research International,* 5 (Autumn 1980): 218–236;

Malcolm Page, *John Arden* (Boston: Twayne, 1984);

Page, ed., *Arden on File* (London & New York: Methuen, 1985);

Henry I. Schvey, *From Paradox to Propaganda: The Plays of John Arden* (Munich: Hueber, 1981);

Helena Forsas Scott, "Life and Love and Serjeant Musgrave: An Approach to Arden's Play," *Modern Drama,* 26 (March 1983): 1–11;

John Russell Taylor, *Anger and After* (London: Methuen, 1969), pp. 83–105;

Peter Thomson, *Mother Courage: Plays in Production* (Cambridge: Cambridge University Press, 1997), pp. 159–162;

Simon Trussler, *John Arden* (New York: Columbia University Press, 1973);

Jonathan Wike, *John Arden and Margaretta D'Arcy: A Casebook* (New York: Garland, 1995);

Elizabeth Hale Winkler, "Modern Melodrama: The Living Heritage in the Theatre of John Arden and Margaretta D'Arcy," in *Melodrama,* edited by James Redmond (Cambridge: Cambridge University Press, 1992), pp. 255–267;

Katherine Worth, ed., *Revolutions in Modern English Drama* (London: Bell, 1972), pp. 126–135.

Alan Ayckbourn

(12 April 1939 -)

Trevor R. Griffiths
University of North London

See also the Ayckbourn entry in *DLB 13: British Dramatists Since World War II.*

PLAY PRODUCTIONS: *The Square Cat,* as Roland Allen, Scarborough, Library Theatre, 30 July 1959;

Love after All, as Allen, Scarborough, Library Theatre, 21 December 1959;

Dad's Tale, as Allen, Scarborough, Library Theatre, 19 December 1960;

Standing Room Only, as Allen, Scarborough, Library Theatre, 13 July 1961;

Xmas v. Mastermind, Stoke-on-Trent, Victoria Theatre, 26 December 1962;

Mr. Whatnot, Stoke-on-Trent, Victoria Theatre, 12 November 1963; revised version, London, Arts Theatre, 6 August 1964;

Meet My Father, Scarborough, Library Theatre, 8 July 1965; retitled *Relatively Speaking,* London, Duke of York's Theatre, 29 March 1967; Washington, D.C., Arena Stage, June 1974;

The Sparrow, Scarborough, Library Theatre, 13 July 1967;

Countdown, in *We Who Are About To . . . ,* by Ayckbourn, David Campton, Harold Pinter, John Bowen, Alun Owen, and others, London, Hampstead Theatre Club, 6 February 1969; *We Who Are About To . . .* revised as *Mixed Doubles,* London, Comedy Theatre, 9 April 1969;

How the Other Half Loves, Scarborough, Library Theatre, 31 July 1969; London, Lyric Theatre, 5 August 1970; New York, Royale Theatre, 29 March 1971;

The Story So Far, Scarborough, Library Theatre, 20 August 1970; revised as *Me Times Me Times Me,* Leicester, Haymarket, 25 August 1971; revised as *Family Circles,* Richmond, Surrey, Orange Tree Theatre, 24 November 1978;

Time and Time Again, Scarborough, Library Theatre, 8 July 1971; London, Comedy Theatre, 16 August 1972;

Alan Ayckbourn (photograph © The Cambridge Evening Sun*)*

Ernie's Incredible Illucinations, London, Arts Theatre, 17 September, 1971;

Absurd Person Singular, Scarborough, Library Theatre, 26 June 1972; London, Criterion Theatre, 4 July 1973; New York, Music Box Theatre, 8 October 1974;

Mother Figure, in *Mixed Blessings,* by Ayckbourn and others, Horsham, Sussex, Capitol Theatre, 1973;

The Norman Conquests: Table Manners, Living Together, Round and Round the Garden, Scarborough, Library Theatre, 18 and 25 June and 2 July 1973; London, Greenwich Theatre, 9 and 21 May and 6

June 1974; New York, Morosco Theatre, 1 December 1975;

Absent Friends, Scarborough, Library Theatre, 17 June 1974; London, Garrick Theatre, 23 July 1975; Washington, D.C., Kennedy Center, 11 July 1977;

Confusions: Mother Figure, Drinking Companion, Between Mouthfuls, Gosforth's Fete, A Talk in the Park, Scarborough, Library Theatre, 30 September 1974; London, Apollo Theatre, 19 May 1976; Chicago, Body Politic Theatre, Spring 1982;

Jeeves, adapted from the stories by P. G. Wodehouse, music by Andrew Lloyd Webber, London, Her Majesty's Theatre, 22 April 1975; revised as *By Jeeves,* Scarborough, Stephen Joseph Theatre, 1 May 1996; London, Duke of York's Theatre, 2 July 1996;

Bedroom Farce, Scarborough, Library Theatre, 16 June 1975; London, National Theatre, 16 March 1977; New York, Brooks Atkinson Theatre, 29 March 1979;

Just between Ourselves, Scarborough, Library Theatre, 28 January 1976; London, Queen's Theatre, 20 April 1977; Princeton, N.J., McCarter Theater Company, 30 September 1981;

Ten Times Table, Scarborough, Stephen Joseph Theatre, 18 January 1977; London, Globe Theatre, 5 April 1978;

Joking Apart, Scarborough, Stephen Joseph Theatre, 11 January 1978; London, Globe Theatre, 7 March 1979;

Men on Women on Men, music by Paul Todd, Scarborough, Stephen Joseph Theatre, 17 June 1978;

Sisterly Feelings, Scarborough, Stephen Joseph Theatre, 10 and 11 January 1979; London, National Theatre, 3 and 4 June 1980;

Taking Steps, Scarborough, Stephen Joseph Theatre, 28 September 1979; London, Lyric Theatre, 2 September 1980; New York, York Theatre Company, 28 October 1986;

Suburban Strains, music by Todd, Scarborough, Stephen Joseph Theatre, 18 January 1980; London, Round House Theatre, 5 February 1981;

First Course, music by Todd, Scarborough, Stephen Joseph Theatre, 8 July 1980;

Second Helping, music by Todd, Scarborough, Stephen Joseph Theatre, 5 August 1980;

Season's Greetings, Scarborough, Stephen Joseph Theatre, 25 September 1980; London, Round House Theatre, 14 October 1980; revised version, London, Greenwich Theatre, 28 January 1982; Berkeley, Cal., Berkeley Repertory Theatre, 7 December 1983; transferred to New York, Joyce Theatre, 6 July 1985;

Me, Myself, and I, music by Todd, Scarborough, Stephen Joseph Theatre, 2 June and 8 and 9 July 1981;

Way Upstream, Scarborough, Stephen Joseph Theatre, 2 October 1981; Houston, Texas, Alley Theatre, 24 February 1982; London, National Theatre, 4 October 1982;

Making Tracks, music by Todd, Scarborough, Stephen Joseph Theatre, 16 December 1981; London, Greenwich Theatre, 14 March 1983;

Intimate Exchanges, Scarborough, Stephen Joseph Theatre, 3 June 1982; London, Greenwich Theatre, 11 June 1984;

A Trip to Scarborough, adapted from Richard Brinsley Sheridan's play, which was based on John Vanbrugh's *The Relapse; or, Virtue in Danger,* Scarborough, Stephen Joseph Theatre, 8 December 1982;

Incidental Music, music by Todd, Scarborough, Stephen Joseph Theatre, 12 January 1983;

It Could Be Any One of Us, Scarborough, Stephen Joseph Theatre, 5 October 1983;

The Seven Deadly Virtues, music by Todd, Scarborough, Stephen Joseph Theatre, 12 January 1984;

A Chorus of Disapproval, Scarborough, Stephen Joseph Theatre, 2 May 1984; London, National Theatre, 1 August 1985; Seattle, Contemporary Theatre, 14 July 1988;

The Westwoods, music by Todd, Scarborough, Stephen Joseph Theatre, 29 and 31 May 1984; London, Etcetera Theatre, 19 May 1987;

Boy Meets Girl, music by Todd, Scarborough, Stephen Joseph Theatre, 23 May 1985;

Girl Meets Boy, music by Todd, Scarborough, Stephen Joseph Theatre, 25 May 1985;

Woman in Mind, Scarborough, Stephen Joseph Theatre, 30 May 1985; London, Vaudeville Theatre, 3 September 1986; New York, Manhattan Theatre Club, 17 February 1988;

Tons of Money, adapted from Will Evans and Valentine's play, Scarborough, Stephen Joseph Theatre, 11 December 1985; London, National Theatre, 6 November 1986;

Mere Soup Songs, music by Todd, Scarborough, Stephen Joseph Theatre, 22 May 1986; London, Lyttleton Theatre Buffet of the National Theatre, 13 December 1986;

A Small Family Business, London, Olivier Theatre of the National Theatre, 5 June 1987;

Henceforward . . . , Scarborough, Stephen Joseph Theatre, 30 July 1987; Houston, Texas, Alley Theatre, 4 October 1987; London, Vaudeville Theatre, 21 November 1988;

Man of the Moment, Scarborough, Stephen Joseph Theatre, 10 August 1988; London, Globe Theatre, 14 February 1990;

Mr. A's Amazing Maze Plays, Scarborough, Stephen Joseph Theatre, 30 November 1988; London, National Theatre, 4 March 1992;

The Revengers' Comedies, Scarborough, Stephen Joseph Theatre, 13 June 1989; London, Strand Theatre, 16 and 17 October 1991;

The Inside Outside Slide Show, Scarborough, Stephen Joseph Theatre, 22 July 1989;

Wolf at the Door, adapted from David Walker's translation of Henry Beque's play *Les Corbeaux,* Scarborough, Stephen Joseph Theatre, 3 October 1989;

Invisible Friends, Scarborough, Stephen Joseph Theatre, 23 November 1989; London, National Theatre, 13 March 1991;

Body Language, Scarborough, Stephen Joseph Theatre, 21 May 1990;

This Is Where We Came In, Scarborough, Stephen Joseph Theatre, 4 August 1990;

Callisto 5, Scarborough, Stephen Joseph Theatre, 12 December 1990; revised as *Callisto #7,* Scarborough, Stephen Joseph Theatre, 4 December 1999;

Wildest Dreams, Scarborough, Stephen Joseph Theatre, 6 May 1991; London, The Pit, Barbican Theatre, 14 December 1993;

My Very Own Story, Scarborough, Stephen Joseph Theatre, 10 August 1991;

Time of My Life, Scarborough, Stephen Joseph Theatre, 21 April 1992; London, Vaudeville Theatre, 3 August 1993;

Dreams from a Summer House, music by John Pattison, Scarborough, Stephen Joseph Theatre, 26 August 1992;

Communicating Doors, Scarborough, Stephen Joseph Theatre, 2 February 1994; London, Gielgud Theatre, 7 August 1995;

Haunting Julia, Scarborough, Stephen Joseph Theatre, 20 April 1994;

The Musical Jigsaw Play, music by Pattison, Scarborough, Stephen Joseph Theatre, 1 December 1994;

A Word from Our Sponsor, music by Pattison, Scarborough, Stephen Joseph Theatre, 20 April 1995;

The Champion of Paribanou, Scarborough, Stephen Joseph Theatre, 4 December 1996;

Things We Do for Love, Scarborough, Stephen Joseph Theatre, 29 April 1997; London, Gielgud Theatre, 3 March 1998;

Cheap and Cheerful, Scarborough, Stephen Joseph Theatre, 18 December 1997;

Comic Potential, Scarborough, Stephen Joseph Theatre, 4 June 1998; London, Lyric Theatre, 13 October 1999;

Gizmo, Scarborough, Stephen Joseph Theatre, 1998;

The Boy Who Fell Into A Book, Scarborough, Stephen Joseph Theatre, 4 December 1998;

The Forest, adapted from Alexander Ostrovsky's play, London, Royal National Theatre, 28 January 1999;

House & Garden, Scarborough, Stephen Joseph Theatre, 12 June 1999; London, Royal National Theatre, 9 August 2000; Chicago, Goodman Theatre, 5 February 2001;

Virtual Reality, Scarborough, Stephen Joseph Theatre, 8 February 2000;

Whenever, music by Denis King, Scarborough, Stephen Joseph Theatre, 5 December 2000;

Damsels in Distress: GamePlan, Scarborough, Stephen Joseph Theatre, 29 May 2001;

Damsels in Distress: FlatSpin, Scarborough, Stephen Joseph Theatre, 3 July 2001;

Role Play, Scarborough, Stephen Joseph Theatre, 4 September 2001.

BOOKS: *Relatively Speaking* (London: Evans Plays, 1968; New York: S. French, 1968);

Ernie's Incredible Illucinations (London & New York: S. French, 1969);

How the Other Half Loves: A Play in Two Acts (New York: S. French, 1971); republished as *How the Other Half Loves: A Comedy* (London: Evans Plays, 1972);

Time and Time Again: A Comedy in Two Acts (London & New York: S. French, 1973);

Absurd Person Singular (London & New York: S. French, 1974);

The Norman Conquests (London & New York: S. French, 1975); republished as *The Norman Conquests: A Trilogy of Plays* (London: Chatto & Windus, 1975; New York: Grove, 1979)–*comprises Table Manners, Living Together,* and *Round and Round the Garden;*

Absent Friends: A Play (London & New York: S. French, 1975);

Bedroom Farce: A Comedy (London & New York: S. French, 1977);

Confusions: Five Interlinked One-Act Plays (London & New York: S. French, 1977)–comprises *Mother Figure, Drinking Companion, Between Mouthfuls, Gosforth's Fête,* and *A Talk in the Park*; republished as *Confusion: Five Interlinked One-Act Plays* (London & New York: Methuen, 1983);

Just between Ourselves: A Play (London & New York: S. French, 1978);

Ten Times Table: A Play (London & New York: S. French, 1978);

Joking Apart (London & New York: S. French, 1979);

Sisterly Feelings: A Related Comedy (London & New York: S. French, 1981);

Taking Steps: A Farce (London & New York: S. French, 1981);

Suburban Strains: A Musical Play, book and lyrics by Ayckbourn, music by Paul Todd (London & New York: S. French, 1982);

Season's Greetings: A Play (London & New York: S. French, 1982);

Way Upstream: A Play (London & New York: S. French, 1983);

Intimate Exchanges: A Play, 2 volumes (London & New York: S. French, 1985);

A Chorus of Disapproval: A Play; with Additional Material from the Original Libretto and Music of the Beggar's Opera by John Gay (London & New York: S. French, 1985); republished as *A Chorus of Disapproval* (London & Boston: Faber & Faber, 1986);

Woman in Mind: December Bee (London & Boston: Faber & Faber, 1986);

A Small Family Business (London & Boston: Faber & Faber, 1987; London & New York: S. French, 1988);

Henceforward–: A Play (London & New York: S. French, 1988; London & Boston: Faber & Faber, 1988);

Me, Myself, and I, book and lyrics by Ayckbourn, music by Todd (New York: S. French, 1989);

Mr. A's Amazing Maze Plays (London & Boston: Faber & Faber, 1989; London & New York: S. French, 1993);

Man of the Moment (London & Boston: Faber & Faber, 1990);

Invisible Friends (London & Boston: Faber & Faber, 1991);

A Cut in the Rates: A Play (London & New York: S. French, 1991);

The Revengers' Comedies (London & Boston: Faber & Faber, 1991; revised edition, London & New York: S. French, 1993);

Mr. Whatnot: A Comedy (London & New York: S. French, 1992);

Wildest Dreams (London: Faber & Faber, 1993);

Time of My Life (London & Boston: Faber & Faber, 1993);

This Is Where We Came In: A Play (London & New York: S. French, 1995);

Callisto 5: A Play (London & New York: S. French, 1995);

My Very Own Story: A Play for Children (London & New York: S. French, 1995);

Communicating Doors (London & Boston: Faber & Faber, 1995);

Family Circles: A Comedy (London & New York: S. French, 1997);

It Could Be Any One of Us: A Comedy (London & New York: S. French, 1998);

A Word from Our Sponsor: A Musical Play, book and lyrics by Ayckbourn, music by John Pattison (London & New York: S. French, 1998);

Things We Do For Love (London: Faber & Faber, 1998);

Comic Potential (London & New York: Faber & Faber, 1999);

The Forest, adapted from Alexander Ostrovsky's play (London: Faber & Faber, 1999);

House & Garden (London: Faber & Faber, 2000);

Body Language (London & New York: S. French, 2001).

Collections: *Three Plays* (London: Chatto & Windus, 1977; New York: Grove, 1979)–comprises *Absurd Person Singular, Absent Friends,* and *Bedroom Farce;*

Joking Apart, Just between Ourselves, Ten Times Table (London: Chatto & Windus, 1979);

Sisterly Feelings and Taking Steps (London: Chatto & Windus, 1981);

Ayckbourn: Plays One (London & Boston: Faber & Faber, 1995)–comprises *A Chorus of Disapproval, A Small Family Business, Henceforward . . . ,* and *Man of the Moment;*

Ayckbourn: Plays Two (London & Boston: Faber & Faber, 1998)–comprises *Ernie's Incredible Illucinations, Invisible Friends, This Is Where We Came In, My Very Own Story,* and *The Champion of Paribanou.*

PRODUCED SCRIPTS: *Relatively Speaking,* television, BBC, 2 March 1969;

"Service Not Included," *Masquerade,* television, BBC, 20 May 1974;

Time and Time Again, television, Anglian, 18 May 1976;

The Norman Conquests, television, Thames, 5, 12, and 19 October 1977;

Just Between Ourselves, television, Yorkshire, 23 July 1978;

Bedroom Farce, television, Granada , 28 September 1980;

A Cut in the Rates, television, BBC, 27 January 1984;

Absurd Person Singular, television, BBC, 1 January 1985;

Absent Friends, television, BBC, 29 September 1985;

Season's Greetings, television, BBC, 24 December 1986;

Ernie's Incredible Illucinations, television, BBC, 11 November 1987;

Way Upstream, television, BBC, 31 December 1987;

A Chorus of Disapproval, motion picture, screenplay by Ayckbourn and Michael Winner, Palisades Entertainment Group, 1988;

Smoking/No Smoking, motion picture, screenplay by Ayckbourn and Jean-Pierre Bacri, adapted from Ayckbourn's play *Intimate Exchanges,* Vega Film Productions, 1993.

OTHER: *Countdown,* in *Mixed Doubles: An Entertainment on Marriage,* by Ayckbourn, David Campton,

Scene from the 1972 Scarborough production of Ayckbourn's Absurd Person Singular, *with Matyelok Gibbs, Peirs Rogers, Christopher Godwin, and Philippa Urquhart (photograph © Ken Boden)*

Harold Pinter, John Bowen, Alun Owen, and others (London: Methuen, 1970), pp. 59–64;

Will Evans and Valentine, *Tons of Money,* adapted by Ayckbourn (London & New York: S. French, 1988?);

Henry Beque, *Wolf at the Door,* translated by David Walker, adapted by Ayckbourn (London: S. French, 1993).

Alan Ayckbourn is the most performed of contemporary British dramatists; his plays are a staple of repertory theaters, frequently translated, and usually highly successful. Their very success–and the fact that, although he is endlessly technically innovative, he works with the core ingredients of farce and light comedy–have contributed to a certain amount of critical suspicion of his work. Like Trevor R. Griffiths, however, he has preferred to operate along broadly traditional lines, while at the same time stretching the notion of what makes a play suitable for the theater. The subject matter of the plays is largely domestic and even parochial, as Ayckbourn returns again and again to the nuances of the class system and the often phatic rituals by which people define their social existence, shoring themselves up against their own ineffectiveness and their sense of a void beneath the social surface.

Alan Ayckbourn was born in the Hampstead area of London on 12 April 1939. His father, Horace, was an orchestral violinist; his mother, Irene Maud Worley Ayckbourn, was a romance novelist. They were divorced when Ayckbourn was five; three years later his mother married a bank manager, Cecil Pye. Ayckbourn's childhood was spent moving around Sussex as his stepfather was transferred to branches in Lewes, Uckfield, and Staines. From 1952 to 1956 he attended Haileybury School and Imperial Service College in Hertfordshire, where he became heavily involved in drama. One of the teachers, Edgar Matthews, toured school productions in which Ayckbourn acted to the Netherlands, Canada, and the United States.

On Matthews's recommendation Donald Wolfit, one of the last actor-managers, took Ayckbourn on as an assistant stage manager for the 1956 Edinburgh Festival. After working as an assistant stage manager and bit player for Wolfit in Worthing, Leatherhead, Scarborough, and Oxford, Ayckbourn joined Stephen Joseph's company in Scarborough in 1957; working there meant playing in the round, an aspect of theatrical production that has had a profound influence on his approach to dramaturgy. In 1957 and 1958 he worked with Frank Hauser's company in Oxford, returning to Scarborough for the summer season and touring with the Joseph company in the winter.

On 9 May 1959 Ayckbourn married Christine Helen Roland, an actress in the Joseph company; they have two sons, Steven Paul and Philip Nicholas. Ayckbourn has said that the sometimes tempestuous relationship of his mother and stepfather and his own early marriage contributed to his astringent depiction of marriage as an institution.

Dissatisfied with the roles in which he was being cast and recognizing that good stage managers were hard to find, Ayckbourn developed his technical skills. He also responded to Joseph's challenge to write a play with a good part in it for himself. Most of his early plays are unpublished and unavailable for performance, but the scripts reveal some of the themes that have fascinated him throughout his career. For example, *Standing Room Only* (1961) takes a comic view of phlegmatic British responses to a dystopian London traffic jam.

In 1962 Ayckbourn was a cofounder and associate director of the New Victoria Theatre in Stoke-on-Trent, Staffordshire, which was led by another of Joseph's protégés, Peter Cheeseman. Ayckbourn's *Mr. Whatnot,* which was not published until 1992, premiered there in 1963. The play, which draws heavily on the techniques of silent-film comedy, is a farce that concentrates on the antagonism between the nonspeaking title character and a group of stereotypical aristocrats who attempt to thwart his love for the ingenue.

By 1964, when Ayckbourn stopped acting, his roles had included Aston in Harold Pinter's *The Caretaker* (1960), Vladimir in Samuel Beckett's *Waiting for Godot* (1952), and Sir Thomas More in Robert Bolt's *A Man for All Seasons* (1960). He returned to Scarborough that year, and from 1964 to 1970 he combined his stage work with producing radio dramas for the BBC in Leeds, where, he says, he was responsible for "more plays in a year than I'd done in ten years in the theatre." His career as a dramatist began to take off with the success of *Relatively Speaking* in London in 1967.

Originally titled *Meet My Father* when it was performed in Scarborough in 1965, *Relatively Speaking* uses two naturalistic sets and one time frame to tell an apparently simple story. It covers some of what has become Ayckbourn's most familiar territory, the war between the sexes. Somewhat daring for its period in opening with the young unmarried lovers, Greg and Ginny, having shared a bed for the night, *Relatively Speaking* is a tightly knit farce in which the suspicious Greg pursues Ginny to the country, where she has gone to break off her affair with Philip, her older married lover. Ginny has told Greg that she is going to visit her parents; Greg, arriving before her, mistakes Philip and his wife, Sheila, for the parents. English reticence decrees that no one can disabuse him, and misunderstandings proliferate and spiral out of control. Greg asks Philip for permission to marry his nonexistent daughter, but Philip believes that Greg wants to marry Sheila because the two are having an affair. Sheila eventually works out what is going on and, without revealing the true situation to Greg, thwarts her husband's attempt to have one more fling with Ginny. One of the mainsprings of the action of the play is Greg's discovery of a pair of slippers under his girlfriend's bed. Ginny explains them away as her father's; but at the end of the play the audience, but not the characters, discovers that they belong to a third man, unseen and previously unsuspected. Sheila uses them to further persuade her husband that she may be having an affair. The revelation of the source of the slippers is an effective coup de théâtre, throwing into doubt the apparent closure of the play. Here Ayckbourn does not move beyond a technically adroit and apparently morally neutral presentation of events; subsequently, he developed innovative approaches to staging and dramaturgy to push his audiences in particular directions in their evaluation of what they are watching.

Modern farce has traditionally depended on the manipulation of settings and situations to create a world in which multiple opportunities for error and confusion arise from, for example, a proliferation of doors. In *How the Other Half Loves* (1969) Ayckbourn, working in the round, collapses two rooms into one to show two dinner parties taking place simultaneously in theatrical space and time but at different "real" locations and times; one couple attends both functions, during the course of which it is revealed that the hostess of the Thursday-night party is having an affair with one of her husband's employees, who is the host of the Friday-night gathering. Mealtimes and the social rituals associated with them play an important part in Ayckbourn's dramaturgy. Generally, he avoids the trap of making his social observations so precisely detailed that they become dated; thus, it is rare to find something like the ingredients of the intercut shopping lists for the two dinner parties in *How the Other Half Loves,* which reflect not only class differences but also a specific historical moment. A contemporary production would need to update the ingredients or run the risk of introducing a new layer of perhaps unwanted connotations.

Ayckbourn's mentor, Joseph, had died in 1967. In 1970 Ayckbourn became artistic director of the Stephen Joseph Theatre, saving the company from extinction. He has remained in that capacity ever since.

Ayckbourn' s career is a lifelong dialogue with the Aristotelian unities in which he tests their value in various ways and extends them to show both their elasticity and their inflexibility in dealing with the flux of life. The few critical disappointments in Ayckbourn's career have tended to be those in which technical and thematic explorations have been mismatched: for example, *The Story So Far* (1970), revised as *Me Times Me Times Me* (1971) and as *Family Circles* (1978), has never established itself, because its multiple partner-swapping–three sisters are each paired with three different men–is so technically dazzling that audiences are unable to follow it.

Absurd Person Singular (1972) is typically inventive. The play deals with three successive Christmas Eve parties in three different homes, where middle-, lower-, and upper-class couples take turns entertaining each other. Offstage characters, including a dog, populate the other rooms; but the action stays in the kitchen, where, in the second act, one woman's successive attempts to commit suicide are consistently misinterpreted as good housewifely behavior. The basic format of three Christmases derives from Charles Dickens's *A Christmas Carol* (1843), but the redemptive moral of Dickens's tale is absent. The London production of the play won the *Evening Standard* Best New Comedy Award in 1973.

Ayckbourn's work reflects changes in social structures over the decades, but he is always particularly acute on the gap between aspiration and achievement in the lives of women and on the ways in which women are forced to bear patriarchal burdens. His view of marriage is usually bleak, and he returns again and again to the question of repression and its effects on women who are forced to become guardians of the patriarchal traditions and attempt to impose a fantasy of domestic and social order through "a cosy family meal." One such woman is Sarah in *The Norman Conquests* (1973). *The Norman Conquests* attracted much praise for the way in which Ayckbourn developed a weekend's events in one house over three locations and three separate plays–a dining-room play, *Table Manners;* a living-room play, *Living Together;* and a garden play, *Round and Round the Garden*–each scene in one play intercutting with scenes in the others so that an exit in one is an entrance in another. The work poses a major challenge to traditional theatergoing habits, however, since the only way to get the full picture is to see all three plays on three nights. The title character, Norman, is an assistant librarian who believes that his mission in life is to make women happy, and he does so with all of the women in the play: Sarah; her sister-in-law, Annie; and Annie's sister, Ruth, who is married to Norman. The play won the *Evening Standard* and *Plays and Players* awards as Best Play of the Year, and Ayckbourn won the Variety Club of Great Britain Award for it.

Ayckbourn is deeply concerned with the status and roles of women in society and with the ways that social forces, usually mediated through men, limit their potential in ways that are destructive for both the women and men involved. In *Absent Friends* (1974), for example, the dramaturgy perfectly matches the woman's experience: the key speech is one in which Diana, a downtrodden wife, speaks about her childhood desire to run away to join the Mounties and then has a nervous breakdown. Since it is incongruous with its context–the polite facades of a tea party given by Diana to console her old friend Colin after the drowning death of his fiancée, Carol, whom none of the guests had ever met–the speech evokes laughter; but it also reveals the accommodation and repression that are demanded of women who try to find their own voice.

Many of Ayckbourn's plays are set in what might seem to be a peripheral place or told from the viewpoint of what might seem to be a peripheral character. Ayckbourn's experience as an actor may be a significant factor here, since he often provides a view of an action that one might associate not with a leading player but with one in a more minor role. For example, in "Service Not Included," his 1974 television play for the *Masquerade* series, the story is told from the viewpoint of a waiter who circulates among the other characters and their developing stories of familial treacheries.

Ayckbourn's musicals generally deal with the same themes as his straight plays, using musical devices to comment on personal relationships–usually marriages–with a significant use of competing voices. The major exceptions to this rule are *Jeeves* (1975) and *By Jeeves* (1996), the two versions of a musical based on P. G. Wodehouse's characters Jeeves and Bertie Wooster. Although it was a collaboration between two of the most successful figures in contemporary British theater, Ayckbourn and the composer Andrew Lloyd Webber, *Jeeves* flopped: bloated in length and presented in a West End theater far too big for it, it failed to capture Wodehouse's style. Although *By Jeeves,* which opened the new Scarborough theater in 1996, worked better than the first version, the use of metatheatrical trickery seemed more defensive than exploratory. Perhaps the most significant element in this regard is that Ayckbourn constructed the play so that the audience seemed to be watching a charity fund-raiser in a village hall; while this ploy justified the lack of the elaborate stage machinery that has come to be associated with musicals, it also initiates the way in which the implicit contract with the audience has been addressed more directly in Ayckbourn's later works. The relative failure of Ayckbourn's work with Lloyd Webber–although *Time* magazine voted the American production of *By Jeeves,* which Ayckbourn directed, one of the ten best productions of 1996–contrasts with the success of his sustained involvement with two lesser-known composers, Paul Todd and John Pattison.

While many of Ayckbourn's contemporaries have dealt with politics in their plays, his concern has always been with the mundane evasions and betrayals of everyday family life. Ayckbourn's male characters often indulge in displacement activities, using hobbies–from do-it-yourself projects to amateur dramatics–to avoid engagement with reality or to compensate for their lack of control elsewhere in their lives. Do-it-yourself comes in for scorn as a means of displacing emotional energies into physical activity in *Just between Ourselves* (1976): Vera goes quietly mad as her husband, Dennis, indulges in one failed project after another, resulting in a garage door that will not open, a kettle that explodes, and a car that does not run. The play won the *Evening Standard* award for best play of 1977.

When Ayckbourn does engage with politics, his work tends to occupy a middle ground and to derive fairly directly from his own experience with theatrical politics; *Ten Times Table* (1977), for example, is a committee-room play that the author has described as "a predominantly sedentary farce with faintly allegorical overtones." The play was written when Ayckbourn was heavily involved in negotiating his theater's move from the library to the old grammar school in Scarborough. Unsympathetic caricatures of right- and left-wing figures attempt to dominate the staging of a pageant to commemorate an obscure eighteenth-century event that the assiduous historical researches of an old lady, whose poor hearing has contaminated most of the minutes of the meeting, suggest did not actually happen, anyway.

In the first scene of *Sisterly Feelings* (1979) two sisters compete for the favors of the same man by tossing a coin to see which will walk home with him from their mother's funeral since there is not enough room in the car. The second scene thus differs, depending on the result of the toss; and at the end of that scene the actress playing the victorious sister is allowed a spur-of-the-moment choice of whether to continue the affair or give up the lover to the other sister, so that the third scene also differs at different performances. The final scene in the play is the same, however, whatever has happened in the interim. Ayckbourn used the device to investigate the relationship between free will and fate; but the actors in the National Theatre production made their task easier by creating a two-headed coin to rig the decision, defeating Ayckbourn's desire for randomness.

Most of Ayckbourn's work has been conceived and initially produced in the round, and many of his technical innovations can be seen as an attempt to achieve proscenium-arch effects in this theatrical form. In his best plays, however, a necessary connection exists between technical and formal innovation on the one hand, and subject matter on the other hand. For example, in *Taking Steps* (1979) three floors of a building are superimposed upon each other rather than being presented vertically. This collapsing of levels is required to make the action visible in the round and is not necessary in a conventional staging. The collapsing of levels, however, also symbolizes the overlapping demands and needs of the characters and was retained in the London production, which was performed on a conventional proscenium stage. The farce is about a hard-drinking manufacturer named Roland who is thinking of buying a Victorian house that was formerly a brothel. He spends the night there along with his wife, Lizzie, a former dancer who is planning to leave him; her brother, Mark; Mark's suicidal fiancée, Kitty; Roland's solicitor, Tristram; and the seller of the house. Much of the comedy arises from the characters running "up and down stairs" to the various rooms that are, in fact, on the same level.

Many of Ayckbourn's plays mirror Scarborough's small-town social and sexual politics; but he also draws on the social nuances typically associated with the Home Counties, in which he spent his early years. Characters' lives are bounded by the low-key events that define social normality: birthdays, mealtimes, parties, family rituals, and rites of passage. Christmas is a key event, since it allows Ayckbourn to bring together families and acquaintances in an atmosphere of strained bonhomie as they attempt to perform the behaviors appropriate to their sentimental image of a "proper" Christmas. In *Season's Greetings* (1980) the holiday brings together the usual crew of ill-assorted relatives and dreamers who swirl around the house, coalescing and reforming into dissatisfied groups. Chekhovian parallels include the failing doctor, the would-be artist–albeit in this case the two are the same person, and the art is puppetry–and the inappropriate affair; Ayckbourn even goes so far as a Chekhovian gunshot.

Me, Myself, and I (1981), with music by Todd, splits Ayckbourn's female protagonist along Freudian lines, with id, ego, and superego sometimes competing musically, sometimes cooperating, to present a portrait of repressed fantasies and unfulfilled aspirations. The husbands in Ayckbourn's nonmusical plays are almost uniformly incapable of recognizing their wives' distress, but here the husband realizes that something is wrong and decides to make an effort to change for the better.

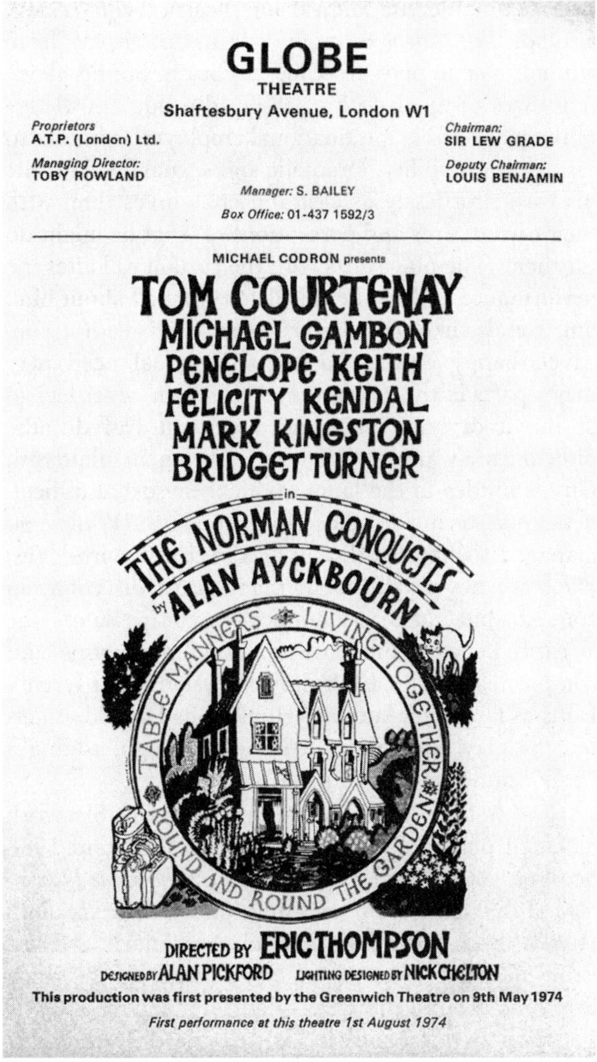

Title page and cast list from the program for Ayckbourn's acclaimed trilogy

By the time of *Way Upstream* (1981) the Conservative leader Margaret Thatcher was prime minister, some prominent members of the Labour Party had created the Social Democratic Party because they believed that the Labour Party was moving too far to the left, and Ayckbourn had become concerned about political polarization. The play is a political allegory set on a cabin cruiser on a river called the Orb; the aim of the trip is to reach Armageddon Bridge, the limit of navigation. As the captain becomes increasingly concerned about problems at work, and his secretary appears intermittently on the river bank with news of escalating confrontation at his factory, the boat becomes a version of the ship of state. Piracy, walking the plank, and mutiny occur, and offstage militancy matches onstage fascism. It is left to Alistair, the reasonable man, finally to stand up and be counted. The journey ends in the calm waters beyond Armageddon Bridge. There Alistair's wife, Emma, who cannot swim, sheds the life jacket that has been her comfort throughout the journey, and the two of them take off their clothes and plunge into the Edenic baptismal waters. The formal problems of allegory in *Way Upstream* were matched in the National Theatre production by difficulties with the huge water tank and control of the cabin cruiser. The combination of technical challenge and political engagement with the concerns of a specific period has meant that the play has remained largely unproduced, although a 1987 television production directed by the dramatist Terry Johnson avoided many of the technical difficulties.

Way Upstream is an example of how Ayckbourn's control over the whole production process at Scarborough allows him to set huge dramatic and theatrical challenges for his actors and technical crew and also to demand from audiences a radically different approach to theatergoing. *Intimate Exchanges* (1982) is one of the most extreme examples. The setting and characters derive from Ayckbourn's early experiences as a weekly boarder at a decaying prep school on the verge of closing down. Written for two long-standing members of his company, Robin Herford and Lavinia Bertram, each of whom played five parts, *Intimate Exchanges* consists of sixteen different plays with a shared first scene from which choices multiply depending on whether or not a woman decides to have a cigarette. In one case the gardener calls her, in the other a male friend does. A further choice is made at the end of the second scene, and so on, until there are sixteen possible final scenes. The plays are grouped into eight pairs, each of which has a different title and two possible endings; to see the full range, one would have to attend all sixteen. Clearly, the work is a massive technical tour de force. Since only two actors are involved, sometimes one addresses the other, who is hidden offstage, under a table, or in a shed doing a quick change into another character. On one occasion an actress fights herself behind a curtain, popping out from time to time as one character or the other. The titles of the thirty-two scenes include "A Garden Fête," "A Pageant," "A Cricket Match," and "A Game of Golf." The final scenes of all the versions take place outside a church and include "A Funeral" (two different ones), "A Service of Thanksgiving," "A Christening," "A Wedding" (two different ones), "A Midnight Mass," and "Easter Greetings." Each marks an appropriate conclusion to a radically different set of events as the actors play multiple permutations on the characters' lives, with friendships and sexual relationships developing and dissolving across a wide spectrum. In his Author's Note Ayckbourn points out that the plays can be performed with larger casts and can be presented separately, but that such productions would be "infinitely less satisfying" and "far less theatrically exciting"; he also asks that in such cases the audience be told what his original preferences were.

Ayckbourn's success in developing traditional models of comedy for his own purposes has not been matched in his attempts in the thriller genre. Two Scarborough productions of *It Could Be Any One of Us* (1983), a sort of theatrical version of the board game Clue, did not establish its theatrical viability. This failure contrasts starkly with the success of his use of the stock plot of the understudy who becomes a star in *A Chorus of Disapproval* (1984). Ayckbourn adds an extra dimension by making the play within the play John Gay's *The Beggar's Opera* (1728), an attack on corruption that itself uses various theatrical and musical devices to undercut political and theatrical convention. Guy, the hero, rises through the ranks of the cast from a minor role to play the lead, Macheath; but his elevation owes as much to his perceived inside knowledge of the plans of his multinational employer as it does to his histrionic ability. Dramatic and sexual favors come his way effortlessly as cast and crew invest him with their own desires and perceptions of what he might do for them. The play starts with the curtain call after the performance and the hero isolated from all about him, but it ends, like *The Beggar's Opera* itself, with a contrived happy ending. Greed and sexual need play major parts in the action, but Ayckbourn never lets go of the underlying pain. At one point Dafydd, the director, unaware that his wife is having an affair with Guy, confides in the latter about their sexual difficulties. Guy, trying to cheer him up, says "Well. You managed to have twins." The director's reply–"Yes. Well, we never talk about that. Never"–is comic in context but also economically encapsulates the anguish beneath the outward accommodations and compromises. The 1988 movie version, with Jeremy Irons as Guy and Anthony Hopkins as Dafydd, opens out the play and locates it in Scarborough, adding a further dimension to its metatheatricality.

Although Ayckbourn's early, unavailable work included plays for children, between 1961 and 1988 he wrote only two such pieces: *Ernie's Incredible Illucinations* (1969) and the television play *A Cut in the Rates* (1984). Both deal with typical Ayckbourn themes: Ernie has the power to fantasize scenarios in which everyone around him gets caught up, and in *A Cut in the Rates* a local official is terrorized by ghostly goings-on involving a reenactment of a failed theatrical illusion that had apparently resulted in violent death. After the woman is scared away, it turns out that the whole apparently supernatural business was staged to avoid the payment of property taxes.

Woman in Mind (1985) marks a further development in Ayckbourn's astringent approach to contemporary suburban living and his technical interest in making visible and audible that which is normally unseen and unspoken. He creates one of his typical families: Susan, a frustrated suburban housewife; her desiccated husband, a vicar who is writing a pamphlet on the history of the parish; a grimly repressed and domestically incompetent sister-in-law; and an embarrassed son. When Susan first appears, however, she is suffering from a concussion after stepping on a rake, so that instead of her real family the audience meets a fantasy family that represents everything her real life is not. Although the play elicits early laughter, it gradually becomes clear that her stifling domestic circumstances are literally driving Susan mad. The fantasy family becomes increasingly satanic, invading the real world and refusing to stay under control, until, at the end of the play, Susan is about to be declared insane. Ayckbourn initially encourages the audience to share Susan's point of view, since the imaginary characters are visible to them but not to the "real" characters. As the action proceeds and the fantasy family becomes more and more disruptive, however, the audience can scarcely maintain that identification. The audience's discomfort grows because it can scarcely identify with the other "real" characters any more than it can with the increasingly dangerous fantasy ones. In a curiously Brechtian way, the effect is to destroy any opportunity to lose oneself in the action while posing awkward questions about one's own social role.

Ayckbourn spent the years 1986 to 1988 at the National Theatre in London, directing his own adaptation of the 1927 Will Evans and Valentine farce *Tons of Money* (1985), John Ford's Caroline tragedy *'Tis Pity She's a Whore,* and an award-winning production of Arthur Miller's *A View from the Bridge.* His writing career since then has generally taken the pattern of a Scarborough premiere one year followed by a London opening, usually directed by Ayckbourn himself, the subsequent year.

The most chilling expression of Ayckbourn's opposition to Prime Minister Thatcher's conservative policies is *A Small Family Business* (1987), in which Ayckbourn clearly sees the family as a metaphor for a corrupted wider society. The play was written for the open stage of the National Theater's Olivier Theatre. It needs a set that shows two stories of a single house, with four rooms, stairs, and hallways; the house is the home of various branches of the eponymous family and provides an apt physical location for a dissection of the interconnections between family values and business practices. The family itself is the cornerstone of corruption as Jack, initially an upholder of honesty and the importance of the family, ends up as a Mafia boss importing heroin, while, unnoticed in another room, his daughter gets high on the drug. Business corruption is a theme that permeates Ayckbourn's work, from the minor-key treatment of the would-be adulterous older lover in *Relatively Speaking* who proposes to take his mistress away on his expense account, through the "you scratch my back" antics of *Absurd Person Singular,* to the endemic corruption of *A Chorus of Disapproval* and *A Small Family Business.*

Ayckbourn has consistently played with traditional ideas about certainty and closure in ways similar to the practices of such contemporaries as Michael Frayn and Tom Stoppard. He is fascinated by the means individuals use to attempt to impose order on the flux of life, to compensate for their dissatisfactions, and to work toward some kind of imagined wholeness, often at the expense of others. While the title and the ingenious handling of the various witty deaths in *The Revengers' Comedies* (1989) draw on the ways in which the revenge theme is developed in such Jacobean plays as Thomas Middleton's *The Revenger's Tragedy* (1606), the idea of strangers swapping revenges derives from Patricia Highsmith's novel *Strangers on a Train* (1950) or Alfred Hitchcock's 1951 movie version of it. The thriller elements of *The Revengers' Comedies,* however, take second place to the comedy of watching the shape-changing female revenger as she finally overreaches herself. While the plays were respectfully received, critics were unconvinced that the development of the revenges required two evenings in the theater.

Since 1988 Ayckbourn has once again added plays for children to his output. Many of the children's plays pursue the same themes as his adult plays but in less pessimistic ways, since he argues that children's plays cannot end unhappily. In the adult play *Henceforward . . .* (1987), for example, an absent father ultimately rejects his child; but in the children's plays *Mr. A's Amazing Maze Plays* (1988) and *Callisto 5* (1990) the return of a missing father resolves the situation positively. Both *Henceforward . . .* and *Callisto 5* feature a malfunctioning domestic robot; but whereas *Callisto 5* is set on a space station in the distant future, *Henceforward . . .* is set in London in the near future. Jerome, the father in *Henceforward . . . ,* is a composer who places secret microphones in every room of his home with the goal of converting human activity into art. The endeavor is sterile: Jerome attempts to synthesize sounds that will express love; in his search for artistic purity he spurns his wife and child in favor of computer-generated art. In *Callisto 5* the computer generates an imaginary monster to entertain the child while the parents attempt to return to it. The *Callisto 5* computer is more humane than the human Jerome. In *Mr. A's Amazing Maze Plays,* as in *Sisterly Feelings* and *Intimate Exchanges,* the development of the action is partly dependent on random elements: two narrators encourage the children in the audience to vote on what the heroine and her faithful dog should do. Some critics thought that the choices offered were loaded in particular directions; but regardless of how the votes come out, the journey always concludes with the same final scene, in which the girl and the dog find the object of their quest. And whereas *Woman in Mind* ends with the imaginary family taking over the protagonist's existence, in *Invisible Friends*

(1989), a treatment of the same theme for children, the situation is resolved happily.

Ayckbourn's reworking of some of his adult themes in children's plays may have played a role in his development toward a more optimistic adult dramaturgy. Adultery and marital failure remain staples of his plays, often standing in for wider social breakdown; but he has begun to explore the possibility of redemptive actions. Just as David Hare's dissatisfaction with describing and analyzing social and political decline led him to move away from "question" plays to "answer" plays, so Ayckbourn's long-standing view of the patriarchal family as the source of social discontent has begun to lead him to explore alternative models of the family that could serve as the basis for a new form of social organization. In *Wildest Dreams* (1991) four of the characters are involved in a long-running fantasy board game similar to Dungeons and Dragons. Two of the players are Stanley and Hazel, a typical Ayckbourn childless, middle-aged, middle-class couple with an interfering live-in relative, Hazel's brother Austen, who does not play the game. The other players are less-familiar figures: Rick is a lesbian with some dark secrets revealed in the course of the play (prior to *Wildest Dreams* Ayckbourn scarcely mentions male homosexuality, except in one of the strands of *Intimate Exchanges* and, marginally and obliquely, in *The Norman Conquests;* similarly, lesbianism had not previously figured significantly in his work); Warren is a computer freak who believes that he is an alien from outer space. The arrival of Marcie, a battered wife who works with Rick and seeks refuge from her abusive husband in Rick's home, is the catalyst for the revelation and deepening of the various characters' neuroses and frustrations. The game, like the garage and do-it-yourselfism in *Just between Ourselves,* is a refuge where broken or ineffective individuals can conceal their inadequacies; but, unlike previous refuges, which usually allowed men to hide from their own inability to relate to their wives, it is a haven for both men and women who cannot cope with the world. Although there is some humor in the contrast between the heroic fantasy personas the characters assume and their everyday personalities, in *Wildest Dreams* the underlying horrors are spelled out with much greater clarity than before: child abuse, incest, impotence, and childlessness, in addition to wife battering, are all part of the mix. Despite the horrors the characters face in the real world, which are much more difficult to deal with than those in the game, there are some positive outcomes: Marcie and Rick form a relationship, and Rick dispatches the threat from Marcie's husband with a virtuoso martial-arts display. Such an unequivocally positive outcome is highly unusual for Ayckbourn, and it is telling that it takes place outside the norms of the conventional family. Equally telling, and far more disturbing, is Ayckbourn's treatment of Hazel, the barren wife. Unable to have a child, she gradually reverts to a childlike state, lying under the game table dressed in outsized baby clothes; but, unlike the uncomprehending husbands in Ayckbourn's earlier plays, Stanley shows awareness and understanding of the situation. The paradox is that he refuses to get her treated for her growing mental disturbance, because she is happier than she has ever been.

Ayckbourn has always been interested in the dramatic possibilities of playing with time. The technique allows him some of the technical freedom of nonnaturalistic modes while preserving a basic commitment to everyday realism. Time shifts also permit the kinds of moral evaluation that result from the contrast between past actions and present consequences that Henrik Ibsen, for example, generally achieves by using the arrival of a stranger or the return of a prodigal. In *Time of My Life* (1992) three related couples live time in different ways: one is in "real time"; one goes backward, showing the audience what has happened over the past two months; and the third goes forward more rapidly than in normal time, revealing what will happen over the next two years, so that events that are in the future for one couple are in the past for another. Ayckbourn also plays with space here, since all three couples use tables in the same restaurant. This technique is fairly straightforward and operates as the equivalent of a cinematic flashback or like J. B. Priestley's time plays, *Time and the Conways* (1937) and *I Have Been Here Before* (1937).

Ayckbourn's musical *Dreams from a Summer House* (1992), with score by Pattison, pursues the same kinds of issues as *Woman in Mind* but reverses the usual pattern in which a polite facade crumbles under the onslaught of reality; instead, it shows a disagreeable reality of misogyny and dysfunctional families succumbing to the influence of the Romance tradition. The antiwoman diatribe of the former husband, who is illustrating a book of fairy tales in a summer house, causes Beauty to materialize, while his former wife's attack on men does the same for the Beast. Neither of the fairy-tale characters can understand spoken English, so the others have to resort to song. Technically, this device allows for parody of many of the more-bizarre conventions of the musical, while underpinning a contrast between reality and fantasy. Here, however, the fantasy characters perform the traditional role of reordering reality more favorably, and the play ends more or less happily.

Josephine Tewson, Martin Jarvis, and Julia McKenzie in the 1986 Vaudeville Theatre production of Woman in Mind

In *Communicating Doors* (1994) three women move among the years 1974, 1994, and 2014 through a time lock, cooperating to prevent one another from being killed. *Communicating Doors* is successful as a thriller, since the audience is genuinely interested in whether the multiple murders will take place or whether the time travelers will be able to prevent them. In the original production the hotel room in which all of the action takes place did not change over the forty-year period, which detracted from the overall effect.

Michael Billington has called Ayckbourn "a left-wing writer using a right-wing form"; but although Ayckbourn is an acute commentator on social and sexual politics, his work has usually avoided overtly political themes. An exception is *A Word from Our Sponsor* (1995), which was a response to the same kinds of issues that led to *Ten Times Table* in the 1970s: once again Ayckbourn's involvement in the politics of trying to get a new theater led to a play attacking the absurdities of arts funding. In the musical, set in a dystopian near future in a railway station where the privatized trains no longer stop, a clergyman's attempt to stage a Nativity play is hijacked by a devil who appears in both male and female form with an offer to sponsor the needy production in exchange for a few script changes: Mary is to become Herod's wife and give birth to a girl named Jasmine. In 1997 Ayckbourn used the proscenium-arch theater at Scarborough to stage his *Things We Do for Love,* a complex reworking of themes from Noel Coward's *Private Lives* (1930) with a set that shows just the top of one room, the whole of the room on the floor above, and just the bottom of the one above that. Also in 1997 Ayckbourn was divorced from his wife, from whom he had been separated for many years, and married his longtime companion, actress Heather Stoney. That same year his contribution to the theater was recognized with a knighthood.

Ayckbourn's plays generally cover similar social, moral, and geographical terrains: the plays are set in domestic interiors, sometimes in gardens, but rarely in shops, factories, or offices. The characters who inhabit these settings tend to come from a fairly narrow stratum of society: they are mainly white middle- and lower-middle-class married couples engaged in the precarious business of negotiating social status in terms of relative degrees of aspiration or achievement. There are occasional exceptions, such as the macho, medallioned Vince and the decadent aristocrat Fleur in *Way Upstream,* but otherwise the plays largely deal with small family businesses, ineffectual lower-middle management, struggling teachers, and the like. There are few manual workers and, despite the emphasis on family, no onstage children.

Part of Ayckbourn's strength as a dramatist is his sustained testing of the limits of what is theatrically possible. He does not share Bertolt Brecht's Marxist political ideology, but his theater uses a similar distancing approach to make audiences question their beliefs. Many theatrical practitioners have challenged the traditional boundaries of performance, but Ayckbourn does so in one of the most subversive ways of all: by adapting and extending old forms until their elasticity finally gives out and by stressing the amount of fun to be had by doing so. Theatrical audiences traditionally expect to see a self-contained event during one attendance at a venue; two-part plays and trilogies are generally regarded as special-event anomalies. Ayckbourn has consistently challenged such assumptions about the nature of the theatrical event: his playing with conventions, his use of multiple settings, his creation of multiple choices within one text, and the necessity to attend on more than occasion to see the full picture demand a spectatorship that is more alert than that usually expected of farce, comedy of manners, musical, or comedy thriller. Ayckbourn's dramaturgy and theatrical practice involve shape-changing at every level: he has changed actor-audience relationships; he has widened the scope of comic genres; he has played variations on the theme of identity and how it is constituted. He has pursued a career-long interest in deconstructing traditional forms so that the ways in which they efface contradictions in favor of spurious closures and completions can be made the object of a detached and amused scrutiny.

Interview:

Ian Watson, *Conversations with Ayckbourn* (London: Macdonald, 1981; revised edition, London & Boston: Faber & Faber, 1988).

References:

Michael Billington, *Alan Ayckbourn* (Basingstoke: Macmillan, 1990);

John Bull, *Stage Right: Crisis and Recovery in Contemporary British Mainstream Theatre* (Basingstoke: Macmillan, 1994);

R. A. Cave, *New British Drama in Performance on the London Stage, 1970–1985* (Gerrard's Cross: Colin Smythe, 1987);

John Elsom, *Post-War British Theatre* (London: Routledge & Kegan Paul, 1976);

Ronald Hayman, *British Theatre since 1955* (Oxford: Oxford University Press, 1979);

A. E. Kalson, *Laughter in the Dark: The Plays of Alan Ayckbourn* (Cranbury, N.J.: Associated University Presses, 1993);

Oleg Kerensky, *The New British Drama* (London: Hamilton, 1977);

Malcolm Page, comp., *File on Ayckbourn* (London: Methuen, 1989);

Joseph Stephen, *Theatre in the Round* (London: Barrie & Rockliff, 1967);

J. R. Taylor, *The Second Wave* (London: Methuen, 1971);

S. H. White, *Alan Ayckbourn* (Boston: G. K. Hall, 1984);

Duncan Wu, *Six Contemporary Dramatists,* revised edition, (Basingstoke: Macmillan, 1996).

Enid Bagnold

(27 October 1889 - 31 March 1981)

Lib Taylor
University of Reading

See also the Bagnold entries in *DLB 13: British Dramatists Since World War II; DLB 160: British Children's Writers, 1914–1960;* and *DLB 191: British Novelists Between the Wars.*

PLAY PRODUCTIONS: *Lottie Dundass,* Santa Barbara, California, 21 August 1941; Brighton, Theatre Royal, 1942; London, Vaudeville Theatre, July 1943;

National Velvet, adapted by Bagnold from her novel, London, Embassy Theatre, 23 April 1946;

Poor Judas, Bradford, Bradford Civic Theatre, November 1946; London, Arts Theatre, 18 July 1951;

Gertie, New York, Plymouth Theatre, 30 January 1952; produced again as *Little Idiot,* London, Q Theatre, 10 November 1952;

The Chalk Garden, New York, Ethel Barrymore Theatre, 26 October 1955; London, Haymarket Theatre, 11 April 1956;

The Last Joke, London, Phoenix Theatre, 28 September 1960;

The Chinese Prime Minister, New York, Royale Theatre, 2 January 1964; London, Globe Theatre, 20 May 1965;

Call Me Jacky, Oxford, Oxford Playhouse, 27 February 1968; revised as *A Matter of Gravity,* New York, Broadhurst Theatre, 3 February 1976.

BOOKS: *A Diary without Dates* (London: Heinemann, 1918; Boston: Luce, 1918);

The Sailing Ships, and Other Poems (London: Heinemann, 1918);

The Happy Foreigner (London: Heinemann, 1920; New York: Century, 1920); republished in *The Girl's Journey, Containing The Happy Foreigner and The Squire* (London: Heinemann, 1954; Garden City, N.Y.: Doubleday, 1954);

Serena Blandish; or, The Difficulty of Getting Married, as A Lady of Quality (London: Heinemann, 1924; New York: Doran, 1925);

Enid Bagnold (photograph by Tara Heinemann)

Alice and Thomas and Jane (London: Heinemann, 1930; New York & London: Knopf, 1931);

"National Velvet" (London: Heinemann, 1935; New York: Morrow, 1935);

The Squire (London: Heinemann, 1938); republished as *The Door of Life* (New York: Morrow, 1938); republished in *The Girl's Journey, Containing The Happy Foreigner and The Squire* (London: Heinemann, 1954; Garden City, N.Y.: Doubleday, 1954);

Lottie Dundass: A Play in Three Acts (London: Heinemann, 1941);

Two Plays (London: Heinemann, 1951); republished as *Theatre* (Garden City, N.Y.: Doubleday, 1951)–comprises *Lottie Dundass* and *Poor Judas;*

The Loved and Envied (London: Heinemann, 1951; Garden City, N.Y.: Doubleday, 1951);

The Chalk Garden (London: Heinemann, 1956; New York: Random House, 1956);

National Velvet: A Play in Three Acts (New York: Dramatists Play Service, 1961);

The Chinese Prime Minister (New York: Random House, 1964);

Enid Bagnold's Autobiography (London: Heinemann, 1969; Boston: Little, Brown, 1970);

Four Plays (London: Heinemann, 1970; Boston: Little, Brown, 1971)–comprises *The Chalk Garden, The Last Joke, The Chinese Prime Minister,* and *Call Me Jacky;*

Poems (Andoversford: Whittington Press / London: Heinemann, 1978);

A Matter of Gravity, revised version of *Call Me Jacky* (London: Heinemann, 1978; New York: S. French, 1978);

Early Poems (Andoversford: Whittington Press / London: Heinemann, 1987).

Editions: *The Loved and Envied* (Westport, Conn.: Greenwood Press, 1970; London: Chatto & Windus, 1970);

A Diary without Dates (London: Virago / Heinemann, 1978).

OTHER: Marthe Bibesco, *Alexander of Asia,* translated by Bagnold (London: Heinemann, 1935);

National Velvet [play], in *Embassy Successes II. 1945–46* (London: Sampson Low, Marston, 1946);

Call Me Jacky, in *Plays of the Year,* no. 34 (London: Elek, 1968);

"In Germany Today: Hitler's New Form of Democracy," in *Enid Bagnold: The Authorized Biography,* by Anne Sebba (London: Weidenfeld & Nicolson, 1986), pp. 267–269–first published in *Sunday Times* (London), 6 November 1938.

SELECTED PERIODICAL PUBLICATION–UNCOLLECTED: "The Flop," *Atlantic Monthly,* 4 (October 1952): 53–57.

Enid Bagnold's *The Chalk Garden* was the most commercially successful play in Great Britain in 1956, the year of John Osborne's *Look Back in Anger,* but in many ways Bagnold's form of theater belongs to a generation eclipsed by the changes wrought by Osborne and his generation. Her sharp, witty, epigrammatic style harks back to the prewar West End and the well-made plays of the 1920s and 1930s. In its representation of class and gender if not in its form of audience address, however, Bagnold's work is remarkably modern. Her plays feature women who are independent and, as Lenemaja Friedman asserts, "sexually emancipated"; certainly her female characters do not conform to conventions of family life. While her male characters are often disabled by strokes or in some other way rendered inactive and dependent, her women, particularly mothers and elderly women, are strong and active. Her plays have autobiographical elements. Written during the last four decades of her life and usually set in her own upper-class milieu, they draw on her experience of aging and express her acute awareness of the inevitable decay of her class.

Enid Algerine Bagnold was born on 27 October 1889 in Rochester, Kent, the elder of the two children of Arthur and Ethel Alger Bagnold. Her father was a colonel in the Royal Engineers, and her mother was the daughter of William Alger, the mayor of Plymouth. The Bagnolds' younger child, Ralph, was born in 1896.

The family lived in Jamaica from 1899 until 1902, when they returned to England and Enid was enrolled in the unconventional Prior's Field school in Surrey. Her parents sent her to finishing schools in Switzerland and France in 1906–1907, and in the summer of 1910 she was sent to learn German by living with a family in Marburg. The following year she became a student at Walter Sickert's school of drawing and began to move in the artistic circles of pre–World War I London.

In late 1912 Bagnold began working for Frank Harris at his magazine *Hearth and Home,* later joining the staff of *Modern Society* after he bought that periodical in 1913. Harris was more than thirty years her senior, and Bagnold's fascination with him led to her first love affair. During World War I, while she worked as a Voluntary Aid Detachment auxiliary nurse in the Royal Herbert Hospital, she wrote her first books, *A Diary without Dates* (1918), based on her wartime nursing experiences, and *The Sailing Ships, and Other Poems* (1918), which collects poems published in newspapers and magazines during those years. After the war she worked as an ambulance driver in France, helping to transport wounded soldiers. She returned to England in April 1919. On 8 July 1920 she married Sir Roderick Jones, owner and director of Reuters News Agency. They had four children between 1921 and 1930. In 1920 Bagnold also published her first novel, *The Happy Foreigner,* based on her experiences in France just after the war. It was followed in 1924 by one of her most popular books, *Serena Blandish; or, The Difficulty of Getting Married* (published anonymously, under the pseudonym A Lady of Quality).

Serena Blandish paved the way for Bagnold's first encounter with theater, when S. N. Behrman adapted the novel for the stage. Produced by Jed Harris and starring Ruth Gordon, the play opened in New York in January 1929 and ran for ninety performances. Bagnold never saw the play, but Harold Freedman, who later became her agent, wrote to her on 25 January, "I hope that now this is on you will write a play of your own and send it to me as soon as you have finished it."

During the 1930s Bagnold visited Germany and was impressed with what she saw, writing journalistic pieces extolling the virtues of Nazism, for which she was heavily criticized. In 1935 she wrote the novel for which she is best known, *National Velvet,* and in 1938 she published *The Squire,* based on her experiences of motherhood.

Bagnold's first original play for the theater, *Lottie Dundass,* was first produced in the United States. Directed by David O. Selznick, it opened in Santa Barbara, California, on 21 August 1941 and included Dame May Whitty in the cast. The first British production was at the Theatre Royal Brighton in 1942 with Ann Todd in the title role. The following year, it moved to the Vaudeville Theatre in London, where Dame Sibyl Thorndike took over the role of Mrs. Dundass. The play is a fanciful thriller that draws on Bagnold's experience as a disappointed understudy in the theater. While in terms of setting it is markedly different from her later plays, *Lottie Dundass* sets in place motifs that recur in much of Bagnold's drama. Women are the driving forces of the plot, and, in Mrs. Dundass, Bagnold created an older woman of strength and courage. Set in Brighton, the play depicts Lottie Dundass, a psychotic girl who dreams of following her grandfather into the theater but is prevented from doing so by a heart condition. One day, the star at the Theatre Royal in Brighton is ill, and her understudy is delayed, giving Lottie the chance to step into the leading role. When the understudy unexpectedly arrives in time to play the part, it is assumed Lottie will stand down. Determined to continue in the role, however, she strangles the understudy and goes on stage, where she achieves great success. When her mother discovers what Lottie has done and confronts her, the unrepentant Lottie suddenly collapses from heart failure. Aware of what Lottie will have to go through in court, her mother allows her to die rather than face the consequences.

Bagnold shortly before her marriage to Sir Roderick Jones in 1920

The play is melodramatic in its language and presentation of character. Lottie is a two-dimensional figure whose selfish callousness is unsubtle. While it demonstrates extensive evidence of her instability, the play lacks the psychological insight that would help the audience to understand Lottie. Like much high naturalist drama, Bagnold's first dramatic effort turns on questions of hereditary and biological determinism. Lottie is fatally linked to her father, who five years earlier was found guilty of strangling a young actress. Lottie follows in the footsteps of her father, whom she despises, rather than those of her grandfather, whom she venerates. The significance of the play is in the portrayal of Lottie's mother, Mrs. Dundass, the mainstay of the family, bringing up her children alone. She is the first in the line of independent mother figures in Bagnold's plays, and any hope for the future resides in this character. Though it now seems structurally flawed and melodramatic, *Lottie Dundass* was quite well reviewed. It did not, however, have a long run.

Bagnold's second play followed five years later. Like *Lottie Dundass, Poor Judas,* which opened in Bradford in November 1946, is about the selfishness of the artist and his betrayal of others. The play focuses on writer Edward Mission Walker, who is the translator on a lengthy scholarly project led by the elderly Jules Pasdeloupe Calas. The play opens in France at the beginning of World War II, and then Walker and his daughter return to England with the troops retreating from Dunkirk in June 1940, bringing part of the manuscript notes with them. In England, Walker apparently continues to work on the manuscript, but he is resentful, feeling that he is unable to express himself as a poet in such a project. In act 3 Calas arrives four years later, demanding the finished work, but he discovers that Walker has not touched the notes since he left France. Everyone assumes that Walker has been working on his own creative project instead, but he confesses to Smithie, a young Canadian soldier, that he has not done so. He has betrayed everyone: his daughter, Calas, and, most of all, himself.

As in *Lottie Dundass,* the characters in *Poor Judas* are somewhat two-dimensional. The audience is given little information about the their pasts or the motivations for their actions. Plot development consists of sudden reversals and unexpected events, while the language is self-consciously literary. This play is the only one of Bagnold's dramatic works that has a man at its center, and the unsympathetic Walker is weak and unproductive. Calas, the other central male figure, has a stroke at the end of the play, introducing the motif of the emasculating stroke that became another recurring image in Bagnold's plays. The lack of a strong central woman character leaves *Poor Judas* with only weak and weakened men to carry it. Nevertheless, in 1951, when *Poor Judas* was performed at the Arts Theatre in London as part of the Festival of Britain, Bagnold received the Arts Theatre Prize for the play.

Eleven years after the enormous success of *National Velvet* in Britain and America, Bagnold adapted her novel into a play, which was presented at the Embassy Theatre in London on 23 April 1946. Not as well-known as the motion-picture version that launched the career of the young Elizabeth Taylor in 1944, Bagnold's stage version, like her novel, is the story of Velvet Brown's bid to win the Grand National horse race. Disguised as a boy, Velvet wins the race, but then she falls from her horse, and her secret is discovered. She is disqualified but eventually exonerated from charges of fraud. Without the staging of the race itself or the appearance of the horse, Piebald, the play lacks dramatic effect. Both *Lottie Dundass* and *National Velvet* were produced as radio plays in 1950.

Bagnold's last novel, *The Loved and Envied,* was published in 1951. From then on she concentrated on writing for the theater, and her next play, *Gertie,* opened at the Plymouth Theatre, New York in 1952. It had only five performances in America, but it was produced as *Little Idiot* at the Q Theatre in London later that year.

In 1955 Bagnold's highly regarded play *The Chalk Garden* opened at the Ethel Barrymore Theatre in New York, with Gladys Cooper as Mrs. St. Maugham and Siobhan McKenna as Miss Madrigal. George Cukor, and later Albert Marre, directed the play, and set designs were by Cecil Beaton. In 1956 *The Chalk Garden* opened at the Haymarket Theatre in London, with Dame Edith Evans as Mrs. St. Maugham and Dame Peggy Ashcroft as Miss Madrigal. Directed by Sir John Gielgud, it ran for 658 performances. In 1964 the play was adapted for the screen with Dame Edith Evans, Deborah Kerr, and Hayley Mills in the leading roles. The success of *The Chalk Garden* was partly the result of Bagnold's collaboration with the American producer Irene Selznick, who worked indefatigably on the script, disciplining Bagnold into producing more-direct forms of dialogue.

The title of *The Chalk Garden* refers to the infertile garden at the house owned by the imperious Mrs. St. Maugham, but it is also a metaphor for the climate in which Laurel, Mrs. St. Maugham's wild and unstable granddaughter, is reared. Having run away from her biological mother, Olivia, Laurel is brought up by surrogate mother figures, including her grandmother, who fail to restrain her. This unorthodox "family" is controlled by an unseen figure, Pinkbell, the family butler, who resides in the attic. Despite the fact that Pinkbell has been disabled by a stroke, he governs house and garden with a rigid set of laws that nurture neither Laurel nor the garden. At the beginning of the play Mrs. St. Maugham hires the enigmatic Miss Madrigal to help her with Laurel. As Madrigal's unconventional methods challenge Pinkbell's authority, both Laurel and the garden begin to flourish. In act 2 the arrival of a judge causes Madrigal to become uneasy, and the audience realizes that she has been implicated in a past crime. In act 3 Madrigal is revealed as a convicted murderer who has recently been released from prison. As she prepares to leave, Pinkbell dies, and Olivia arrives to take her daughter away. Supported by Madrigal, Laurel realizes that her mother cares for her more than she has thought, and they leave together. The play ends with Madrigal staying on with Mrs. St. Maugham to tend the chalk garden in her own unconventional but effective way.

The Chalk Garden masquerades as a realistic piece of theater, but symbolic action, setting, and relationships are of great significance in the play. Suspense rests on the question of Madrigal's past, but a modern audience is most interested in staging of the dynamics of authority and the unconventional representation of motherhood. Pinkbell and the judge are archetypes of patriarchal authority, with the judge admitting, "My demeanour on the Bench *is* Pinkbell's." The decay of Pinkbell's physical body, however, signals the aridity of his rule, which is challenged by an alternative female authority located in the maternal figure of Madrigal. She represents a new order, one that sustains the garden and Laurel with tender care.

In *The Chalk Garden* the function of the mother is separated into several roles, splitting the economic caregiver and the emotional caregiver from the biological mother. The play challenges the definition of woman as "natural" mother. Related to this re-evaluation of the mother's role is Bagnold's interest in the Oedipal complex. Laurel claims that she ran away because she was the victim of a sexual attack on the night of her mother's second marriage. This story is a fabrication, which symbolically represents Laurel's Oedipal anxieties about separation from her mother and the intervention of her stepfather. In accepting her mother and her stepfather at the end of the play Laurel conforms to conventions of family life, but *The Chalk Garden* nonetheless challenges patriarchal authority. Both Laurel's resistance to fatherly control and Madrigal's challenge to Pinkbell's authority propose a family organized around matriarchal formulations.

Bagnold followed *The Chalk Garden* with another play that splits the role of the mother. *The Last Joke,* which opened at the Phoenix Theatre in London in 1960, featured Gielgud and Ralph Richardson and was directed by Glen Byam Shaw. The play, which ran for only sixty-one performances, depicts the search for an Edouard Vuillard portrait of a woman, which was stolen from her sons, Romanians Hugo and Prince Ferdinand Cavanati. Rose–the daughter of Edward Portal, a self-made, shady millionaire–is in love with Hugo, but his energies are devoted to preventing Ferdinand, who has had a stroke, from committing suicide. Ferdinand is obsessed with finding the picture of his mother and suspects that it is in Edward Portal's house. Rose makes a bargain with Ferdinand: she will help him gain entry to her father's house if he promises that Hugo will attend her coming-out ball. Disguised as a Turkish art dealer, Ferdinand meets Portal and realizes that he is the son of the appraiser who was in the

Dame Edith Evans as Mrs. St. Maugham and Dame Peggy Ashcroft as Miss Madrigal in the 1956 London production at the Haymarket Theatre of Bagnold's The Chalk Garden *(Angus McBean/ Raymond Mander and Joe Mitchenson Theatre Collection)*

Cavanati household on the day the picture disappeared. After Ferdinand manages to take the painting from its hiding place in Portal's room, there is a confrontation between the two men. In the course of this scene the audience discovers that on the day Portal stole the painting he killed his father in a shooting accident. He has kept the picture as an ideal image of motherhood and family life. It is also revealed that Mrs. Webster, Portal's austere housekeeper, is Rose's biological mother. Because she does not meet his ideals of motherhood, Portal has not allowed her to bring up Rose. Finally reunited with his mother's image, Ferdinand commits suicide by drinking hemlock. Hugo, freed from the responsibility of his brother, undertakes to marry Rose.

Like *The Chalk Garden, The Last Joke* centers on Oedipal relationships. All the major male characters desire the mother: Portal kills his father and sleeps with the portrait of the idealized mother above his bed; Ferdinand and Hugo seek reunification with their mother. This reunion can be achieved only through Rose: she ensures that the portrait is returned to Ferdinand before his death, and, in agreeing to marry Hugo at the end of the play, she also

Anna Massey, Paul Curran, John Gielgud, and Ralph Richardson in the 1960 production at the Phoenix Theatre in London of Bagnold's The Last Joke

secures Hugo's reunion with the mother, symbolized in her wearing of his mother's ring. Two significant themes in Bagnold's work resurface in the play. First, although the majority of characters are male, they are weak and disabled: Ferdinand has had a stroke and desires death; Portal is dependent on an idealized image of an unattainable mother; Hugo is inactive and absorbed by his brother's problems. Rose propels the narrative, and her actions enable the sterile situation to be resolved. Second, the maternal role is again separated, this time into a functional biological mother and an idealized representation of motherhood. The maternal role is restored to the biological mother in *The Chalk Garden,* but in *The Last Joke* the parts cannot be reconciled.

Like its predecessor, *The Last Joke* employs witty language, but without the restraining influence of Selznick, the artificial, epigrammatic dialogue becomes cloying. The play was not well received. Bernard Levin summed up the critical response in the *Daily Express* (29 September 1960): "How shall we excuse Miss Enid Bagnold whose paper-thin, star-stuffed little play is smothered under bales of sham writing, mock-metaphor, nothing-over-sixpence aphorisms and poetry of a quality to set the teeth aching?"

In 1962 Bagnold's husband died. Their marriage had been unconventional, but Bagnold and Jones had been tolerant and unfailingly supportive of each other. Bagnold's next play, *The Chinese Prime Minister,* may be seen as a response to this loss, an expression of many of her feelings about the aging process and her desire to shed unnecessary responsibilities. *The Chinese Prime Minister* opened in New York at the Royale Theatre on 2 January 1964, with Margaret Leighton as She. Reviews were lukewarm, but it ran for 108 performances. The play opened in London at the Globe Theatre in 1965, with Dame Edith Evans playing the central character, whose name had been changed to Mrs. Forrest.

The Chinese Prime Minister has another strong, elderly woman at its center. An actress, She, decides just before her seventieth birthday to give up the stage in order to find time for herself. Without her husband, from whom she is effectively separated, she feels she has devoted too much time to the needs of others, particularly her sons and her public. On her birthday her estranged husband, Sir Gregory, arrives to reclaim her. She agrees to leave with him. In act 3 she returns to her house, dissatisfied with her husband and resolving to live on her own.

The meaning of the title is revealed when She refers to the Chinese prime minister in Eastern tradition as someone who has acquired wisdom and the daring to live as a free spirit. The play is elliptical in its mode of expression and includes familiar Bagnold motifs. Once again, male characters are weak: the two sons display an Oedipal dependence on their mother and are incapable of sustaining relationships with women; the husband is unreliable. Characteristically, a butler figure is at the center of the play. Like Pinkbell, Bent suffers from strokes. The weakened Bent and She are left together, interdependent, at the rather ambiguous ending of the play. While the tenuous family structure has disintegrated, leaving time for She to devote to herself, she is isolated in an old house with nothing but a retainer for company.

Although the New York production of *The Chinese Prime Minister* had some success, the London production did not. Bagnold's disappointment, however, did not prevent her from working on her last play. *Call Me Jacky* was first produced at the Oxford Playhouse in 1968, with Dame Sibyl Thorndike as Mrs. Basil, Paul Eddington as Herbert, and Edward Fox as Niggie. Mrs. Basil, the old woman at the center of *Call Me Jacky* is far less imperious than Mrs. St. Maugham or She, and this play, written when Bagnold was nearly eighty, presents a far less assured image of old age than either *The Chalk Garden* or *The Chinese Prime Minister.*

The play begins with Mrs. Basil refusing to give up her dilapidated house. She is opposed by her grandson, Niggie, and a group of his left-leaning friends, who consider ownership of property to be immoral. Bizarre events ensue: one of Niggie's homosexual friends attempts suicide; Mrs. Basil's cook is taken back to the asylum from which she has just been released; and Niggie falls in love with the lesbian lover of another of his friends, a mixed-race woman called Elizabeth. The final act takes place eight years later, when Elizabeth and Niggie return from Jamaica with their two children, one black and one white. Elizabeth has always desired Mrs. Basil's house, and finally Mrs. Basil agrees to give it to her, even though it is unlikely that Niggie will stay there with the family.

The house is a potent metaphor. As in most Bagnold's plays, it represents the structure of society, which is crumbling. In giving up the house at the end Mrs. Basil is supplanted by a younger woman, but in

Margaret Leighton, Alan Webb, and John Williams in the 1964 production at the Royale Theatre in New York of The Chinese Prime Minister, *which expresses Bagnold's feelings about the aging process*

Elizabeth she has found someone who is like herself, independent and alone. Mrs. Basil secures a matriarchal succession that does not conform rigidly to patriarchal circumscription. If the dilapidated house and the society it represents are to survive, then they must be rebuilt to accommodate a new and different form of family unit.

Call Me Jacky was a failure. With critics calling it Tory and racist, it ran for two weeks in Oxford, and there was no hope of moving the production to London. The play was significantly revised as *A Matter of Gravity* for a 1976 Broadway production with Katharine Hepburn in the central role and Christopher Reeve as her grandson. This version had more success than the first. It ran for ten weeks on Broadway and later toured nine American cities with Hepburn in the cast.

Call Me Jacky marked the end of Bagnold's playwriting. In 1969 she produced *Enid Bagnold's Autobiography,* and in 1976 she was made a Commander of the Order of the British Empire (CBE). During the last decade of her life, Bagnold became more dependent on morphine, which she had started to take for continuing arthritic pain after hip-replacement surgery in 1970, and she suffered a series of small strokes. She died of bronchopneumonia on 31 March 1981.

Bagnold's plays create a bridge between the drawing-room theater of the prewar period and the drama of the New Wave. Her plays are outmoded in form and in their poetic language; her characters are from a bygone age. Yet, her focus on the wealthy upper classes cannot be dismissed as antiquated. In most Bagnold plays class and gender are under threat. The remnants of the old ruling system are crumbling, and alternative futures are envisioned. With assertive women pitted against weakened men, masculinity is in crisis in her plays, which propose what might be regarded as feminine models of organization. While Bagnold's plays do not fit easily into the theater of the 1960s and 1970s, her work is a precursor of the concerns of those decades.

Letters:

Letters to Frank Harris & Other Friends, edited by R. P. Lister (Andoversford: Whittington / London: Heinemann, 1980).

Interviews:

"Enid Bagnold Talks to Keith Harper," *Guardian,* 20 August 1965;

"Just the Type for H. G. Wells," *Observer,* 26 October 1969.

Biography:

Anne Sebba, *Enid Bagnold: The Authorized Biography* (London: Weidenfeld & Nicolson, 1986).

References:

Lenemaja Friedman, *Enid Bagnold* (Boston: Twayne, 1986);

Irene Mayer Selznick, "The Chalk Garden," in her *A Private View* (New York: Knopf, 1983), pp. 341–356;

Lib Taylor, "Early Stage: Women Dramatists 1958–68," in *British and Irish Women Dramatists Since 1958: A Critical Handbook,* edited by Trevor R. Griffiths and Margaret Llewellyn-Jones (Buckingham: Open University Press, 1993), pp. 9–25;

Kenneth Tynan, "'The Chalk Garden,' by Enid Bagnold at the Haymarket," in his *Curtains* (New York: Atheneum, 1961), pp. 127–128;

Gerald Weales, "The Madrigal in the Garden," *Tulane Drama Review,* 3 (December 1958).

Papers:

Enid Bagnold's papers are in the Beinecke Rare Books and Manuscripts Library, Yale University.

Sebastian Barry

(5 July 1955 -)

Margaret Llewellyn-Jones
University of North London

PLAY PRODUCTIONS: *The Pentagonal Dream,* music by Roger Doyle, Dublin, Damer Theatre, 1986;

Boss Grady's Boys, Dublin, Abbey Theatre, Peacock Stage, 22 August 1988; Chester, New Hampshire, Miniature Theatre, 1992; Edinburgh, Traverse Theatre, March 1998;

Prayers of Sherkin, Dublin, Abbey Theatre, Peacock Stage, 20 November 1990; London, Old Vic Theatre, 18 May 1997; Boston, Poets' Theatre, 1993; New York, 78th Street Lab Theatre, 24 March 2001;

White Woman Street, London, Bush Theatre, 23 April 1992; transferred to Dublin, Abbey Theatre, Peacock Stage;

The Steward of Christendom, London, Royal Court Upstairs, 30 March 1995; transferred to Royal Court Downstairs, 2 September 1995; Dublin, The Gate, 25 April 1995; Brooklyn, N.Y., Brooklyn Academy of Music, January 1997;

The Only True History of Lizzie Finn, Dublin, Abbey Theatre, October 1995; [staged reading] Chicago, Organi Touchstone, 2 September 1997;

Our Lady of Sligo, London, National Theatre, Cottesloe Studio, 9 April 1998; Dublin, Gate Theatre, September 1998; New York, Irish Repertory Theatre, 2000.

Sebastian Barry; from the dust jacket for The Whereabouts of Eneas McNulty *(1998)*

BOOKS: *Macker's Garden* (Dublin: Irish Writers' Cooperative, 1982);

The Water-Colourist (Mountrath, Ireland: Dolmen, 1982);

Time out of Mind, and Strappado Square (Dublin: Wolfhound, 1983);

The Rhetorical Town: Poems (Mountrath, Ireland: Dolmen, 1985);

Elsewhere: The Adventures of Belemus (Mountrath, Ireland: Dolmen, 1985);

The Engine of Owl-Light (Manchester: Carcanet, 1987);

Fanny Hawke Goes to the Mainland Forever (Dublin: Raven Arts Press, 1988);

Boss Grady's Boys (Dublin: Raven Arts Press, 1989);

Prayers of Sherkin and Boss Grady's Boys (London: Methuen, 1991);

The Steward of Christendom (London: Methuen/Royal Court Theatre, 1995; New York: Dramatists Play Service, 1998);

The Only True History of Lizzie Finn, The Steward of Christendom, and White Woman Street: Three Plays (London: Methuen, 1995);

Our Lady of Sligo (London: Methuen, 1998; New York: Dramatists Play Service, 1999);

The Whereabouts of Eneas McNulty (London: Picador, 1998; New York: Penguin, 1999).

Collection: *Plays: 1* (London: Methuen, 1997)–comprises *Boss Grady's Boys, Prayers of Sherkin, White*

Woman Street, The Only True History of Lizzie Finn, and *The Steward of Christendom.*

OTHER: *The Inherited Boundaries: Younger Poets of the Republic of Ireland,* edited, with an introduction, by Barry (Mountrath, Ireland: Dolmen, 1985).

Sebastian Barry started his career as a playwright in his thirty-first year and did not achieve wide acclaim until his fortieth year, when *The Steward of Christendom* (1995), had a sellout run in the Royal Court Theatre Upstairs, and then transferred, after a tour, to the Royal Court Theatre Downstairs. As reviewers praised the poetic language and vision of this play that poignantly links personal memory and history, Barry was firmly established as an important member of the new generation of Irish writers.

While some reviewers have dwelled on the so-called typical Irish characteristics of Barry's plays, Barry dislikes the label "Irish writer," commenting in an unpublished November 1996 interview that it is an "awful phrase–which I resist." As Fintan O'Toole has pointed out in his introduction to *The Only True History of Lizzie Finn, The Steward of Christendom, and White Woman Street: Three Plays* (1995), although Barry's plays seem "utterly Irish," they "also acknowledge the terrifying truth that Ireland is not a fixed place." The postmodern notion that grand narratives such as language and history are unstable and personal identities fluid is particularly significant in postcolonial drama. Long-term effects of previous British rule in Ireland are made evident in Irish plays, including Barry's, through characteristic dramatic strategies. These strategies include disruption of space and time; reworking of indigenous myths, cultural practices, and historical accounts; and, especially, emphasis on the performing body, since this can embody both resistance to, and the effect of, colonizing power.

Barry–a Catholic married to a Presbyterian–employs an extremely personal voice, particularly in his evasion of conventional conflict-driven narrative and the main stage of history and contemporary politics: "I'm not looking for utopias: I'm looking for sites of peace," he told Sarah Hemmings (*Independent,* 2 October 1995). As O'Toole commented, "These plays happen in the space between the ordered serenity of language on one hand and the instability of the world in which they are spoken on the other." Although Barry's plays may seem to some observers to allude to Irish canonical drama, their fluid form and introspective elements disrupt the conventional realistic structures that are typical in earlier Irish plays, including the early work of the Celtic revivalists at the Abbey Theatre. Focusing on misfits, characters with ambiguous identities, Barry's plays are concerned with the spiritual journeying of individual human beings rather than overtly ideological issues. He said in November 1996: "I don't believe in history as an antidote to misunderstanding."

Barry was born on 5 July 1955 in Dublin. His father, Francis Barry, was a poet who became an architect, and his mother, Joan O'Hara, was a well-known Abbey Theatre actress. His creative and somewhat bohemian family also included a sculptor uncle, a singer aunt, and a paternal grandfather who was a painter. Growing up in Monkstown, South Dublin, Barry studied English and Latin at Trinity College, Dublin, earning a B.A. in 1977. After graduation he lived mostly in France, Switzerland, England, Greece, and Italy before going to the University of Iowa, where he was an honorary fellow in writing in 1984. He returned to Dublin in 1985, and later moved to the coastal area of County Wicklow, near Greystones. Married to actress Alison Deegan on 4 May 1992, Barry has three children, including a set of twins.

In 1989 Barry was elected to Aosdána, an affiliation of Irish artists in literature, music, and the visual arts, and the following year he became Ansbacher Writer-in-Residence at the Abbey Theatre, where he was a member of the board of directors in 1990–1991. Another member of the board was novelist Jennifer Johnston, who has been supportive of his work. In 1995–1996 Barry was Writer-In-Association at Trinity College, Dublin.

As Barry wrote in a personal interview (1991), when he returned to Dublin, he felt that "none of the available identities of Irishness seemed to fit," so he decided, "Since I was now to be an Irishman, it seemed I would have to make myself up as I went along." This observation suggests two key elements of his plays: the exploration of his wider family and ancestors as a means of clarifying his identity and the elliptical relationship of personal memory to history that permeates his work and makes it different from that of Irish dramatists such as John Millington Synge, whose poetic style is often compared to Barry's.

Having begun his career by writing poetry and novels, Barry had become by 1986 "slightly impatient with the medium and the way fiction makes its journey." Commenting on his choice of a new literary form in November 1996, he emphasized that the discipline of seeing and hearing is preliterate; thus, in writing for the theater, the playwright is joining his "expertise as a mature individual to unconscious experience as a child. . . . as a human being." The "forms of plays predate writing," he claimed, and in this sense they are archaic, with an interior form that is natural to the writer. This form has the quality of a waking dream, like the thoughts of a child on the edge of sleep, and characters' illuminating reveries are typical throughout his plays. Although critics tend to emphasize the verbal elements of Barry's plays, striking visual moments–often created through lighting effects indicated in the text–are equally significant in establishing their powerful characteristic atmosphere. Barry has disputed the description of his plays as "poetic," emphasizing that they show how humans speak about ordinary but powerful experiences: "Poetic things do not reside in language, but within us." He has acknowledged that there may be some "accidental links" between his intense boyhood experiences of seeing his mother perform the Irish dramatic canon and his feeling for theater. For example, as a child, he believed that when his mother played the title role in William Butler Yeats's play *Cathleen Ni Houlihan* (1902), the character was somehow in "a greater, non-explicable, non-rational way . . . more than my mother," though he was aware that the role was not real. His sense of the theatrical is also evident in his attention to writing roles, seeing the parts as embodied in their "suits of clothes."

Barry's first foray into the theater was his collaboration with composer Roger Doyle on *The Pentagonal Dream,* an experimental piece performed by Olwen Fovere at the Damer Theatre in Dublin in 1986. Two years later he completed his first full-fledged play, *Boss Grady's Boys* (1988), which–like his next two dramatic efforts, *Prayers of Sherkin* (1990) and *White Woman Street* (1992)–was directed at the Abbey Theatre by Caroline Fitzgerald. In the introduction to *Prayers of Sherkin and Boss Grady's Boys* Barry acknowledges that he wrote *Boss Grady's Boys* "to repay a human debt to a pair of real brothers in a real corner of Cork, where I had lived for a while in 1982." The phenomenon of elderly brothers living together is by no means unusual in rural Ireland, and Barry's sympathetic treatment of the quasi-marital bonds between them provides an interesting comparison with Martin McDonagh's brutally comic look at the same subject in *Lonesome West* (1997).

In *Boss Grady's Boys* the brothers' forty-acre hill farm on the border of Cork and Kerry is represented by minimal props and broad lighting effects that employ selective pools of light to suggest sky and mountains outside or interior spaces such as the bedroom or fireside. Sixty-year-old Mick is protective of, yet frustrated by, his elder brother, Josey. Either slightly simpleminded or suffering from Alzheimer's disease, Josey repeats his worries about the horse out in the rain; a beloved (but dead) dog; and when his long-dead father will return from the fair. Mick sees Josey as a deep, dry well: "I throw stones into the poor man that echo with a deep, lost sort of echo. I love him, I love his idiocy."

The form and style of the play are not confined to classic realism. Impressionistic and atmospheric rather than driven by a linear plot, the play flows through episodes touching on details of the brothers' daily lives (such as shoeing the horse or going to bed), individual moments of reverie, separate dream sequences, and memories of the past (such as Josey's thoughts of fishing with his father and Mick's recollections of his dumb mother's gardening and the moment of their father's death). Because the audience sees the substance of some of these dreams and memories performed by actors, there is a blurring of the line between imagined and "real" events. For example, the brothers' repressed sexuality is shown in two encounters with girls, and it is not clear whether these scenes are fantasies or actual happenings in the past. There are other surreal touches, such as the masks that lie in the bed instead of the brothers during their dreams and the dancers who appear to accompany Josey's fiddle playing and are suddenly and briefly revealed as cancan dancers. Running through the brothers' conversation are allusions to Marx Brothers and Charlie Chaplin movies, contributing some of the comedy in the play but also creating a sense of Mick and Josey's remoteness from modern, urban existence. Mick's memories of meeting Irish revolutionary leader Michael Collins creates the impression that the brothers' forgotten lives, like those of others in their rural community, are marginal to history. A sense of the Irish landscape and the harsh poverty of rural life permeates the play in a way that evokes aspects of Synge's works. The brothers' comic awareness of their situation is tempered by an underlying tenderness, such as Mick's prayer for his dead father: "Accept this most beautiful, most wayward father amongst other fathers." Such moments reveal Barry's humanity, which is deeply emotional but never indulgent in its offsetting of pathos with the absurd.

Boss Grady's Boys won the first BBC/Stewart Parker Award in 1988 but did not have its premiere in the United Kingdom until March 1998, when a touring production from the Glasgow Arches Theatre performed the play at Traverse Theatre in Edinburgh. "Apocalypse Plough," Lyn Gardner's review for *The Guardian* (12 March 1998), stresses the "blessedness of acceptance" that she detected in the moments of happiness in the play, as well as the poetic and "luminous intensity" with which the play explores the fading lives of brothers "lost far beyond history."

Prayers of Sherkin is one of the plays in which Barry explores and develops the fragmented history of his ancestors. His preface to the 1997 collection of his plays reveals that the heroine is drawn from his great-grandmother Fanny Hawke, who left the Protestant religious community on Sherkin Island: "The thought struck me

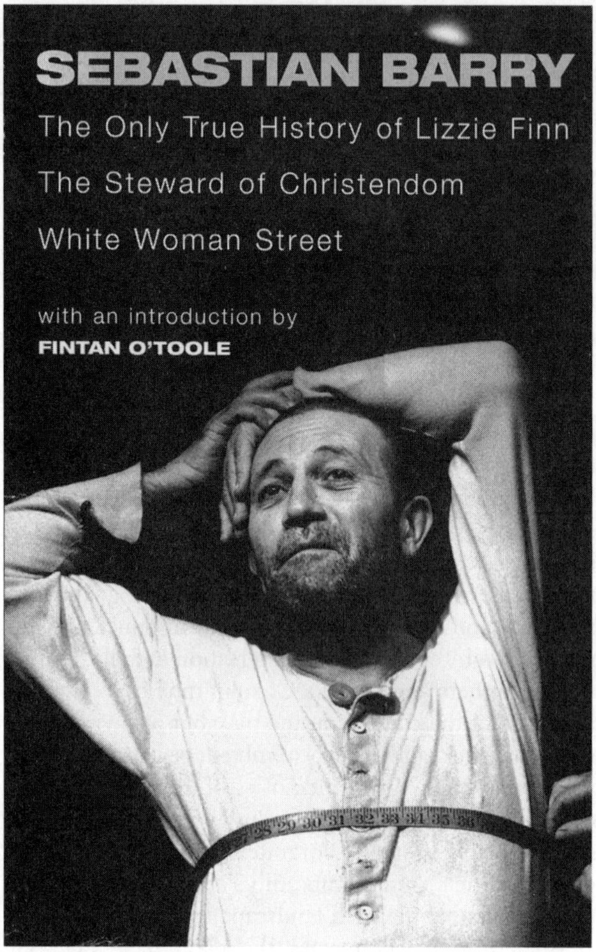

Cover for the 1995 Methuen collection of Barry's plays

that if she hadn't crossed that narrow stretch of water, I wouldn't exist myself. . . . therefore the play is a sort of coming over the water to her, to come, to come." Having previously written about her in his poems, Barry created the character from a few scraps of family history, "the very shadow of her true life, a piece of olde thread"; yet, his characterization rang true with those who remembered her. As he told Mic Moroney, Barry first heard her mentioned at a family funeral, when his sister "was told not to talk about this woman who had been married–out of her culture–to my great grandfather. . . . My father didn't know much about her, because his father had never spoken of her, his own mother" (*Independent on Sunday,* 21 May 1997). The play is set in 1890, by which time the Sherkin community, founded by Matt Purdy of Manchester with a group of three families one hundred years previously, has dwindled to five members of the Hawke family, candle makers who sell their wares on the mainland. Only Fanny and her brother Jesse are of marriageable age. The play focuses on Fanny's decision to marry lithographer Patrick Kirwin of Cork, a Catholic of half-Jewish ancestry, who falls in love with her when she visits the mainland. Marrying out of the community means that she must leave it and the island forever. Whereas other writers might have made the religious conflict central, Barry emphasizes that reconciliation and forgiveness are essential.

Small moments in the interchanges between characters–little details such as the old aunt's weakness for ribbons or Jesse's fascination with telescopes–indicate the plain nature of life on Sherkin. The location of the island off the coast of Ireland, which is itself off the coast of Europe, is analogous to the characters' situation on the edge of history. Linear time is broken by the appearance of the ghost of Matt Purdy, who gives Fanny his blessing: "They are the voices of thy children. They wait for you up the years and you must go. . . . I steer you back into the mess of life because I was blinder than I knew." There is no overt conflict. The restrained tenderness of the community makes it clear that Fanny is loved and will be missed; there is also gentle humor in Jesse's reaction to his sister's suitor. The strongest elements of the play are the images of nature, especially the sea and the light, which permeate the written text. In the Old Vic production perhaps the most evocative moment was the final fading of the light as Fanny is rowed ashore while her lover waits on the far bank.

O'Toole commented on the "luminously beautiful" quality of the original Dublin production of this evocative work. Seeing *Prayers of Sherkin* after the phenomenal 1995 success of *The Steward of Christendom,* British critics were more divided when the play was performed by the Peter Hall Company at the Old Vic in London during 1997. Nick Curtis, the reviewer for the *Evening Standard* (20 May 1997), said this haunting play exhibited "parochial quaintness and narrative slenderness" while Maggie Gee, writing for *TLS: The Times Literary Supplement* (6 June 1997) thought it lacked the "conflict that added depth and vigour" to *The Steward of Christendom.* Such readings of *Prayers of Sherkin* undervalue the economy of the tale and its manner of telling, which–through a sparse Shaker-style setting, fluid lighting, and poetic language–conveys moments of quiet transcendence. Other critics recognized these qualities. As Robert Butler said in his review for the *Sunday Independent* (25 May 1997), "The richness is elsewhere: explicitly in the lyrical dialogue, and implicitly in the quality of the relationships which has a rare gentleness."

Barry's London debut play, *White Woman Street,* which was later transferred to the Abbey Theatre, is set in Ohio during Easter 1916. Again, the characters seem to be on the far edge of history. The distant, momentous events of the Easter Rising in Ireland impinge only briefly on life in the United States, when, near the end of the play Clarke, an American storekeeper, mentions the events in Ireland and alludes to the American Civil War: "Place there burning like Richmond, I hear. Some big mail depot or someplace. Fire and ruin in Dublin. Fellas put in jail and likely to be shot. Fighting the English." Trooper O'Hara, an Irish outlaw, who seems not to be listening, replies: "That right?" Like most of Barry's characters, O'Hara and his band of outlaws are in different ways marginal characters with a sense of cultural displacement.

O'Hara says "Indian towns . . . put me in mind of Sligo hills and certain men in certain Sligo hills. The English had done for us I was thinking, and now we're doing for the Indians." This acknowledgment of colonial dispossession, however, is not the major plot element in this somewhat mythic Western tale, which centers on O'Hara's need, after twenty years, to revisit the small town that was once known for having the only white prostitute for five hundred miles. He and his gang also intend to rob a gold train, which should be loaded with the local soldiers' Easter pay. At key points during the play, reveries illuminate the history and thoughts of different characters, so that the audience appreciates how each one has been exiled from his place of origin. Some London critics complained about what they saw as a relative lack of narrative drive and the "political correctness" of the outlaw gang, which includes a Russian with a Chinese mother, a black man, an American Indian, an Englishman from Grimsby, and Mo, a former member of the Amish sect. The sense of drifting within the form of the play seems analogous to the outlaws' lifestyle, which has within it some comedy about their quasi-domestic routine and a sense of the fading romance of the West. Not all reviewers responded favorably to the poetic passages, set, and imaginary horses; but others praised Shaun Davey's music, Kendra Ullyart's hyperrealistic set, "the marvellously atmospheric direction," and Barry's skill at "making tragic and comic feelings grate against each other." It is eventually revealed that, against audience expectations, O'Hara did not kill the white prostitute. In fact, he found that he had taken the virginity of a young Indian girl, who had immediately slit her own throat. He has long borne a sense of guilt about the incident, but Mo persuades him finally to lay it to rest. After their raid on the golden train fails, Trooper O'Hara dies as–encouraged by Mo–he imagines he sees Ireland again. Throughout the play, shifts in time and location, as well as moments of reverie are signified by modulations of lighting. In spite of the critics' reservations, praise for the haunting and memorable quality of the play came from Paul Taylor (*Independent,* 30 April 1992) and John Peter (*Sunday Times,* 3 May 1992), with Peter suggesting that Barry's writing was "tense with feeling and intelligence" and exclaiming that he "couldn't wait for his next play."

The Only True History of Lizzie Finn was Barry's next play. Although written before *The Steward of Christendom,* it was premiered on the Abbey Theatre main stage in October 1995, and received poor reviews, while *The Steward of Christendom* was playing to a rave reception in London. Barry's wife and mother both appeared in the original Abbey production of *The Only True History of Lizzie Finn,* which is loosely based on the life of an actress who was Barry's ancestor. What O'Toole has called "the ambiguity of belonging" is evident in this play. An actress in England when the play opens, Lizzie Finn was brought up in Corcaguiney as the daughter of a poor, hardworking mother and a traveling-singer father. Because of her profession, she now belongs fully nowhere. Set in the 1890s, the play opens while she is on tour with her friend and dancing partner, Jelly Jane, in Weston-super-Mare. After Lizzie's marriage to Robert Gibson, the surviving son of a fading Protestant Irish landlord dynasty, the play moves to the big family house in Inch, Kerry. Robert is also something of a misfit and has unusual views for a member of his class: "It is only history chooses a person's circumstances. . . . We are all very much equal under the clothes history lends us." His decision to marry Lizzie at first upsets his mother, who later grows to love her daughter-in-law. Yet, ultimately the couple is ostracized in Inch because of their "unsuitable" marriage and Robert's views. Robert has shocked Lord Castlemaine and local society by revealing the truth about the deaths of his three brothers during the Boer War: "It's true Frank and Harry died as nobly as people can die, when your general is a fool and the cause is unjust. . . . Charlie died of drink in Cape Town. That's how he took the news." Robert, who also fought in the war, became disillusioned and crossed over to fight for the Boers. Once this news gets about in Inch, his mother, who has been prevented from attending the chapel by the priest, drowns herself. The hypocrisy at her funeral, where those indirectly responsible speak of "a freak wave," is the final straw for Lizzie and Robert, who leave for Cork, where they can be "foreigners" away from the conventional, restrictive expectations of the landlord class and its association with colonization. Their return from exile–a common theme in Irish writing–has left them feeling estranged from home.

The play flows quickly through the early scenes about Lizzie's theatrical career to the Irish scenes, again through lighting changes and sound effects that suggest location and atmosphere, in particular the wind and the seashore. The relationship between the lovers and Lizzie's friendship with Jelly Jane are convincingly, yet economically, shown. Clothing is a key indicator of position and character. For example, Lizzie's warm-hearted and energetic bohemianism is indicated by the gold stars under the crotch of her stage cancan knickers, which later the maid Teresa, whom Lizzie has befriended, puts on to complement the splendid gown Lizzie has made for her. Robert also shocks Bartholomew, the gardener, by wearing rough working clothes and repairing fences. Lucinda, Robert's mother, gets increasingly disheveled as her world and her previous attitudes gradually fall apart. Small details–such as Jane's parting gift to Lizzie, a little stone angel from Yorkshire that she later places on Lucinda's tombstone, or the use of dance as an indicator of Lizzie's energy–underpin characterization. The doubling of roles, as with Jelly Jane and Lady Castlemaine, across class, indicated in the printed text suggests the common characteristics of humanity beneath the superficial social distinctions implied by clothing. Lizzie's assertion about her father–"Singing or dancing to him were the highest things a person could put himself to"–is finally supported by her later statement that "There'll be nobody in the wide world to remember us, child, and all that will remain of us is an echo, a strain of dancing music, and the memory of a man that loved his brothers and his people, who was given a heart as restless as a frightened dog by wars and accidents. So what odds where we are?"

The Steward of Christendom, an Out of Joint production in conjunction with the Royal Court Theatre, opened in London at the Royal Court Theatre Upstairs in March 1995 and was directed by Max Stafford-Clark. Its success marked a watershed in Barry's career. The play earned unanimous praise for Barry and for Donal McCann, who played the main role–that of Barry's great-grandfather Thomas Dunne, the last head of the Dublin Metropolitan Police, as high a position as any Catholic could reach in his era, just before the transfer of power in 1922. The play explores the slippages among memory, history, and identity, indicative of Barry's concern that the personal should not be erased by official history. As he commented in November 1996, "I believe more in how the mind remembers things than I do in that masculine surety written history."

In the Royal Court Theatre Downstairs, where the play moved in September 1995, the grimy walls of the Baltinglass Asylum, County Wicklow, where Dunne is confined in 1932, become partly translucent as the borders between past and present dissolve. Traces of golden light suggest aspects of landscape, echoing his happier and rural past. This disruption of linear time permits the appearance of his daughters, his son, and other characters–interspersed with interchanges with the warders Smith and Mrs. O'Dea. Sometimes the language seems to echo the poetic rhythms of Synge or James Joyce. The body of Dunne, especially as played by McCann, captures the pathos and past powers of the protagonist. In dingy long johns suggestive of the bodily residues accumulated from rare washing, big-framed Dunne's repetitive gestures, as he alternates between an almost fetal crouch and a quasi-military erect posture, suggest his confusion and his repressed guilt.

Gradually the audience learns that Dunne's beloved wife died in childbirth, leaving him to bring up three little girls and a son with whom he was not close and who died young during World War I. Dunne's position as superintendent damaged the lives of his beloved daughters. Their social opportunities were limited because of his job. As Dolly suggests, "People are cold towards me Papa . . . . Because–because of you Papa, I suppose." One escaped through marriage, another through exile, and Annie, crippled by polio, stayed single, looking after her father. Dunne is proud that his loyalty to the British Crown, and to Queen Victoria in particular, ran counter to the spirit of nationalism during the period: "Her mark was everywhere, Ireland, Africa, Canada, every blessed place. And men like me were there. . . . to keep order in her kingdoms. . . . Ireland was hers for eternity, order was everywhere, if we could but honour her example." Despite his pride in doing his duty to control violence, he feels the charisma of Michael Collins. At the moment when Dunne had to hand over the castle to Collins, "for an instant . . . I felt a shadow of that loyalty pass across my heart." His dislocated memories and repressed admiration often return to the assassination of Collins: "'I think the last order I gave to the men was to be sure to salute Mr. Collins's coffin as it went by." This inner contradiction is echoed in his feelings of failure as a father and his regret that his grandchildren are not allowed to see him. His memory re-creates key scenes, such as the moment when his daughters helped him don his uniform to relinquish the castle, or the moment when his favorite daughter, Dolly–born when her mother died "just as the need for candlelight fails"–showed him her travel ticket to Ohio.

From the early moment in the play when he is stripped for washing, Dunne's regrets about "things of my own doing and damned history" are embodied in his wordless roaring and beating of bed or table, as he imagines fellow countrymen coming to punish him for his role in imposing the rules of the colonizers. These fears and his request that Annie strike him with his ceremonial sword were the immediate causes of his con-

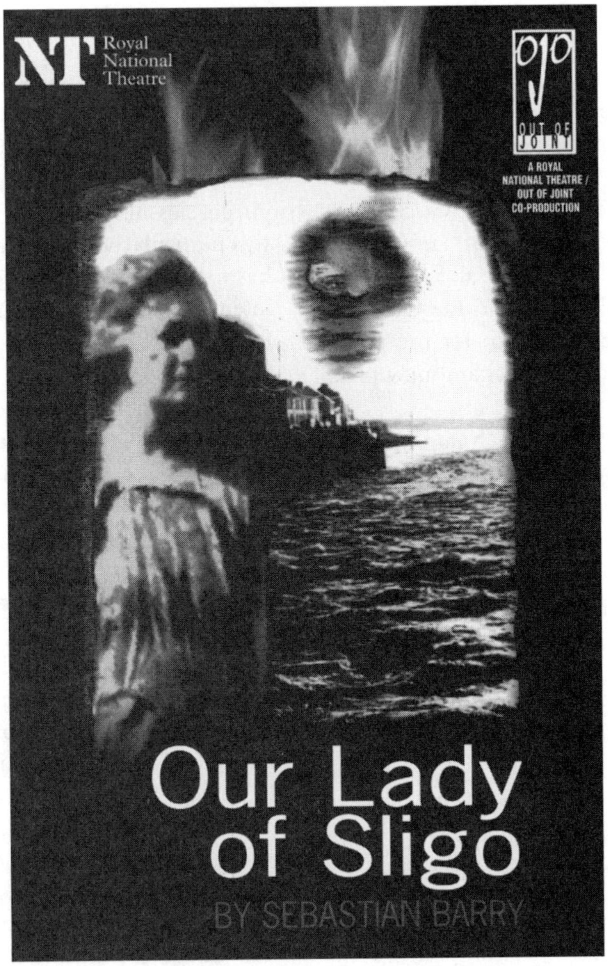

Cover for Barry's 1998 play about his grandmother

finement. In one sense, warder Smith's harsh beatings of Dunne can be seen as a kind of parody of the imposition of law and order of which he had been so proud.

Refusing to be clothed in an asylum suit, Dunne wishes still for a trace of the gold braid that had not been plentiful enough on his dress uniform–a wish the kindly Mrs. O'Dea satisfies with yellow cotton tacking. The power of costume as role is later undercut by a scene in which Smith, feared by Dunne as "Black Jim," appears dressed as Gary Cooper and anoints Dunne's wounds with uncharacteristic kindness. During this episode, Smith reads a long-preserved letter from Dunne's dead son, Willie, which concludes: "I wish to be a more dutiful son, because, Papa in the mire of this wasteland, you stand before my eyes as the finest man I know, and in my dreams you comfort me and keep my spirits lifted." Other scenes include past domestic interaction, such as a moment with a police recruit and Willie singing, or present events, such as the faithful Annie's continued visits, even though her father often mistakes her for his long-missed favorite, Dolly. There is some, perhaps stereotypical, humor in the way in which Annie and Dolly greet their plain sister Maud's suitor, the artistic Matt Kirwin.

The play closes with a moving scene in which Willie, dressed in his World War I uniform, muddy but with a tinge of gold, climbs onto his father's bed while Dunne reminisces about the one moment of mercy he recalls: when his brutal father desisted from beating him for running away to save his pet dog, which had savaged sheep: "And the dog's crime was never spoken of, but that he lived til he died. And I would call that the mercy of fathers, when the love that lies in them deeply like the glittering face a well is betrayed by an emergency, and the child sees at last that it is loved, loved and needed and not to be lived without, and greatly." As Dunne finishes he falls asleep, or perhaps dies, and Willie's ghost lies close to him in the fading light. Such a transcendent moment of forgiveness and reconciliation encapsulates Barry's belief, as stated in an unpublished interview, that "Triumphalism does not produce grace." Reviews of both London productions emphasized the Lear-like quality of Dunne's situation and one critic, Charles Spencer, recognized the language as lyric and luminous prose-poetry (*Telegraph,* 9 June 1995). The play was chosen as the Writers' Guild Best Fringe Play in 1995 and as the Critics' Circle Best Play in 1996, and it was nominated for an Olivier Award (BBC Best Play) in 1995. Barry also won the Ireland Funds Literary Award (1997) and the Christopher Ewart-Biggs Memorial Prize (1996) for the play, which has since been seen in the original and new productions in many countries.

Our Lady of Sligo, which opened in London after preliminary performances in Oxford during the spring of 1998, received generally positive reviews, with particular praise for Sinead Cusack, whose performance as the dying Mai O'Hara captures, according to the critic Michael Billington, both the character's "former impulsive energy" and the sense that "somewhere inside Mai's decaying body lies a potent memory of her reckless, tennis-playing, music-loving younger self." Billington's review for *The Guardian* (8 April 1998) and Susannah Clapp's assessment for *The Observer* (14 April 1998) both emphasized the urgency and the poetic qualities of Barry's writing, though Billington felt that the play does not, "for a largely non-Irish audience, have the public resonance of its prize-winning predecessor." Again the play traces Barry's family history, in this case through an exploration of his grandmother's life as he imagines it to have been. He acknowledges in a note to the play that she was "the darkest person I have written about. . . . a traveller to the heart of personal disaster, a traveller moreover who did not come back." In some ways similar in dramatic structure and strategies to *The Steward of Christendom, Our Lady of Sligo* is less overtly political than its predecessor. Nevertheless, it does examine the plight of the outward-looking Roman Catholic middle classes, who were comfortable enough within the British colonial situation and gradually–as the historian Roy Foster points out in his introduction to the published text–came to occupy positions originally held only by the Protestant Ascendancy class. As Foster suggests and as Barry shows in this play, Irish independence under Eamon de Valera from 1932 in effect wrote out the Catholic bourgeoisie and the Ascendancy from its history. In an interview with John Cunningham for *The Guardian* (25 March 1998) Barry said, "After the civil war, there was a moment full of possibility, when Ireland could have become a European country in an old-fashioned sense, like Monte Carlo. There was a great kind of style in that [middle] class kind of people. De Valera closed all that down when he came into power. . . . he was like a sentimental Stalin."

Ostensibly a tale of Mai's alcoholism, the play shows how small-minded, small-town restrictions–especially during what Barry has called the "suffocating joylessness of de Valera's regime"–heightened the sense of purposelessness that was then endemic in her class and was particularly problematic for women. Thus, the play has a public and historical dimension underpinning the intensely poignant theme of retrospective regret and forgiveness.

The position of the sickbed onstage center at the National Theatre production in the Cottesloe Studio was reminiscent of the setting for *The Steward of Christendom,* as is the somewhat similar way in which Mai's memories of the past intermingle with the present of the play, 1953, when she is under the care of a nursing sister at the Jervis Street Hospital in Dublin and is visited by her husband, Jack, and actress daughter, Joanie. Lighting effects through a large window indicate the passage of time and the blurring of the past and present, the imagined and the real. Also through this window Mai ultimately has a vision of herself as a child and sees her father as she dies. Like *The Steward of Christendom, Our Lady of Sligo* explores the ambivalent relationship between parent and child, both through Mai's problematic interactions with her daughter and Mai's memories of her Dada (father) whose coat is spangled with a slight dusting of silver during his illusory appearances. The image of washing in a basin as a sign of purification and repentance is repeated in Mai's memory of her father washing her when she was a child and in the present when the nurse washes Mai as a patient. In her memories Mai relives her pride in her academic prowess as a student of commerce, her love of music and fashionable American-style clothes, her days with Jack in Nigeria while he worked for the British Colonial Service, and her hatred of Sligo, where she was the first woman to wear trousers. Darker memories outweigh moments of happiness, and the audience pieces together clues about marital tensions, more and more frequent drunkenness, sexual lapses, and growing isolation even within the family, especially after the death of baby Colin–possibly as a result of Mai's drunkenness. Jack has a key speech in act 1: "Ireland, where is that country? Where are those lives that lay in store for us in store like rich warm grain? Mai Kirwin. She never lost that sense of herself as special, particular, legendary." This speech links the elusiveness of national identity and its positive potential with the human will to attempt to hold on to personal identity despite instances of personal folly and selfishness that result in errors, suffering, and alienation from loved ones. Ultimately, Jack comes to a redemptive vision: "just for a moment I had been allotted a different fate and in that moment saw something clearly for the first time. That out of the savage nonsense of our life something might be gleaned. . . . And our children's children might look at our photographs and have some pride in us simply as people that had lived a life on this earth and were to be honoured at least for that."

The poetic language of the play is shot throughout with humor, Mai's violent outbursts, and her lamentations at the indignity of fatal illness. The final interchanges with her family retain an ambiguous edge. As she did at the opening of the play, Mai denies that she is married and does not seem to know her family. Because of the fragmentation of memories and the instability of the different perspectives on her life that reverberate in present-day interactions among family members and the more "everyday" responses of the nursing sister, it is impossible to form a consistent and unambiguous impression of Mai's true identity. The audience does see, framed in the window, Mai's final poignant vision of herself as a child, as she recalls the moment when she named a blue flower for her Dada, and he praised her. Staging the inevitably unstable personal or national identity is central to Sebastian Barry's approach to theater. By 2001 Barry had completed a novel, *Annie Dunne,* and a play, *Hinterland,* for Max Stafford-Clark's company Out of Joint. Barry's *Steward of Christendom,* widely considered a masterpiece, places him as a key figure in the current renaissance of Irish drama. Barry's elliptical approach to history, which celebrates humanity through moments of grace and redemption, has an intensely lyrical, poetic quality that merits status within the Irish canon.

References:

Helen Gilbert and Joanne Thompkins, *Post-colonial Drama: Theory Practice, Politics* (London: Routledge, 1996);

Nicholas Greene, *The Politics of Irish Drama* (Cambridge: Cambridge University Press, 1999), pp. 242–246;

Margaret Llewellyn-Jones, *Contemporary Irish Drama and Cultural Identity,* forthcoming (Bristol: Intellect, 2002);

Christopher Murray, *Twentieth-Century Irish Drama: Mirror Up to Nation* (Manchester: Manchester University Press, 1997).

Papers:

An archive of Sebastian Barry's papers is at the University of Texas at Austin.

Alan Bleasdale

(23 March 1946 -   )

Ros Merkin
Liverpool John Moores University

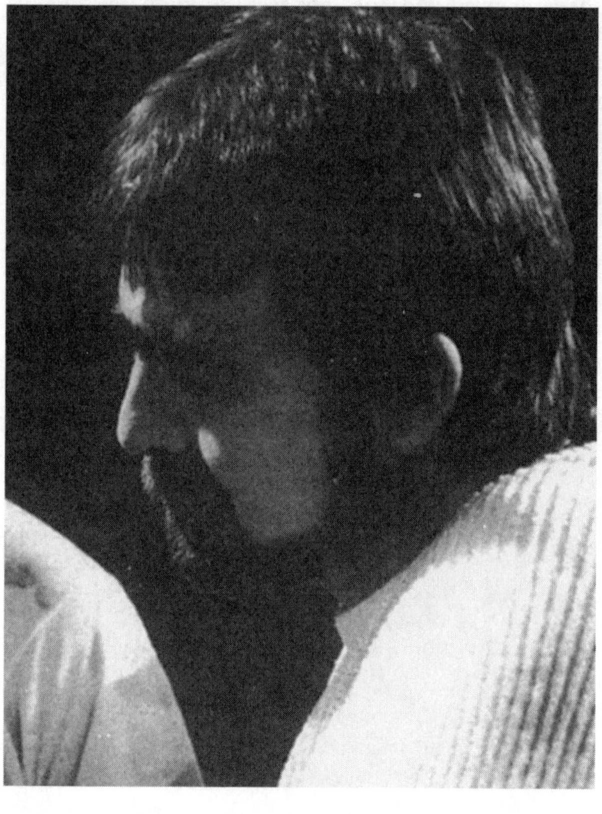

Alan Bleasdale

PLAY PRODUCTIONS: *Fat Harold and the Last 26,* Liverpool, Playhouse Upstairs, 5 April 1975;
The Party's Over, Liverpool, Playhouse Studio, 4 November 1975;
Scully, Liverpool, 1975;
Down the Dock Road, Liverpool, Playhouse, 10 March 1976;
It's a Madhouse, Manchester, Contact Theatre, 21 May 1976;
Should Auld Acquaintance, Manchester, Contact Theatre, 6 November 1976;
Franny Scully's Christmas Stories, by Bleasdale and Kenneth Alan Taylor, Liverpool, 1976;
No More Sitting on the Old School Bench, Manchester, Contact Theatre, 23 November 1977;
Crackers, Leeds, 1978;
Pimples, Manchester, 1978;
Love Is a Many Splendoured Thing, Redditch, 1979;
Having a Ball, Oldham, Coliseum, 15 March 1981; London, Lyric Hammersmith, 8 June 1981; revised, London, 1990;
Are You Lonesome Tonight? Liverpool, Playhouse, 14 May 1985; London, Phoenix, 13 August 1985; San Diego, 1989;
On the Ledge, Nottingham, Playhouse, 23 February 1993; London, National Theatre, 27 April 1993.

BOOKS: *Scully* (London: Hutchinson, 1975);
Who's Been Sleeping in My Bed? (London: Hutchinson, 1977); revised as *Scully and Mooey* (London: Corgi, 1984);
No More Sitting on the Old School Bench (Todmorden: Woodhouse, 1979);
Boys from the Blackstuff: Five Plays for Television (London: Granada, 1985)–comprises "Jobs for the Boys," "Moonlighter," "Shop Thy Neighbour," "Yosser's Story," and "George's Last Ride";
Are You Lonesome Tonight? (London & Boston: Faber & Faber, 1985);
Having a Ball; with, It's a Madhouse (London & Boston: Faber & Faber, 1986);
The Monocled Mutineer, adapted from the book by William Allison and John Fairly (London: Hutchinson, 1986);
No Surrender: A Deadpan Farce (London & Boston: Faber & Faber, 1986);
On the Ledge (London & Boston: Faber & Faber, 1993);
Grievous Bodily Harm (London: Hutchinson, 1999).
Editions: *Scully,* edited by David Self (London: Hutchinson, 1984);
Boys from the Blackstuff, edited by Self (London: Hutchinson, 1985).

PRODUCED SCRIPTS: *The Franny Scully Show,* radio, Radio City, Liverpool, 1975–1979;

"Early to Bed," *Second City First,* television, BBC Two, March 1975;

Dangerous Ambition, television, 1976;

"Scully's New Year's Eve," *Play for Today,* television, 3 January 1978;

Love Is a Many Splendoured Thing, radio, BBC Schools Radio, 3 March 1978,

The Black Stuff, television, BBC Two, 2 January 1980;

The Muscle Market, television, BBC One, 13 January 1981;

Boys from the Blackstuff, television, BBC Two, 5 episodes, 10 October–7 November 1982;

Scully, Channel 4, 1984;

No Surrender: A Deadpan Farce, motion picture, Channel 4 Films, 1985;

The Monocled Mutineer, television, BBC One, 4 episodes, 31 August–21 September 1986;

GBH, television, Channel 4, 7 episodes, 6 June–18 July 1991;

Jake's Progress, television, Channel 4, 6 episodes, October 1995;

Melissa, television, Channel 4, 5 episodes, 11 May–8 June 1997.

OTHER: *Love Is a Many Splendoured Thing,* in *Act 1,* edited by David Self and Ray Speakman (London: Hutchinson, 1979).

In 1982 the British Broadcasting Corporation (BBC) broadcast a series of five television plays by Alan Bleasdale. Titled *Boys from the Blackstuff,* the series proved to be one of the most critically acclaimed of all British television dramas. Its impact was immediate and profound. Joan Bakewell described the series as the greatest achievement of BBC Two, Jonathan Miller equated it with James Joyce's *Ulysses* (1922) as a major twentieth-century work of art, and John McGrath spoke for many when he said: "With *Boys from the Blackstuff,* television drama finally came of age. In its five plays, the realities of being alive in our time are recorded in images that are stronger, more accurate, more memorable and surely longer-lasting than any images so far produced in poetry, novel, cinema or theatre."

The series, which won several awards from the British Academy of Film and Television Arts, certainly emblazoned Bleasdale's name on the consciousness of the nation, capturing the mood of the moment, but the series has also entered the realm of myth and become the yardstick against which all of Bleasdale's subsequent writing is judged. Even if he had written nothing else, Bleasdale would still be regarded as one of the most important British dramatists to have written for the medium of television.

Boys from the Blackstuff not only established Bleasdale as a household name but also displayed many of his main concerns as a writer, concerns to which he has returned time and again. Key among these concerns is a fear of and fascination with insanity–in part a personal fear of going mad and losing control, but also a concern with the mania of what passes for normalcy in the outside world. Unlike his fellow Liverpudlian playwright Willy Russell, who is concerned with "escape and survival," Bleasdale is more interested in those who "stay behind and go mad," as he explained in an interview with Alison Pearson in 1993. He also treats themes of pain and despair, waste and sorrow, the danger of prioritizing ideology over humanity, and the impact of childhood and families. He believes, as he told Dave Hill, that people can be "good and generous and kind"–if only the world would let them. Bleasdale serves up all of these ideas with a taste of absurd, manic comedy and a strong sense of identity as a Liverpool writer. Bleasdale's work, though not directly biographical, comes always from detailed observations of life in his declining city.

Unlike much of his early work, *Boys from the Blackstuff* confirmed for many that Bleasdale was a political writer. Yet, he displays a determination to distance himself from that label. "I'm not a political beast," he told Hugh Herbert in 1991, adding that he did not vote until he was thirty-eight. He does not want to be seen as standing "up on a soapbox" and preaching to people, he explained to Julian Petley in 1987. Indeed, he claims that one of the reasons he killed off Snowy in the first episode was his preaching. *Boys from the Blackstuff* is a critique of what Bleasdale perceives as the overpoliticization of working-class life by some television writers. He is interested in the human face and human implications of politics. He wants his work, as he told Petley, not to say "this or that, but think for yourself." His position is made clear in the words of the headmaster, Jim Nelson, in the 1991 television series, *GBH,* as Nelson stands up to address a Labour Party meeting: "I am here tonight for all those people who refuse to learn about life from manifestos." Bleasdale's political philosophy also appears in *No More Sitting on the Old School Bench* (1979): when a teacher asserts, "As an NUT representative, I find it singularly unfunny," the question comes back, "But what do you find it as a human being?" In Bleasdale's view, "political statements made through human beings are far stronger than polemic."

Bleasdale was born in Liverpool on 23 March 1946. He went to grammar school in Widnes, where he felt like an outsider, a "white negro." He left school to train with the Liverpool Football Club but, rejected as a professional, turned to teaching. He earned his teaching certificate in 1967 from Padgate Teachers Training

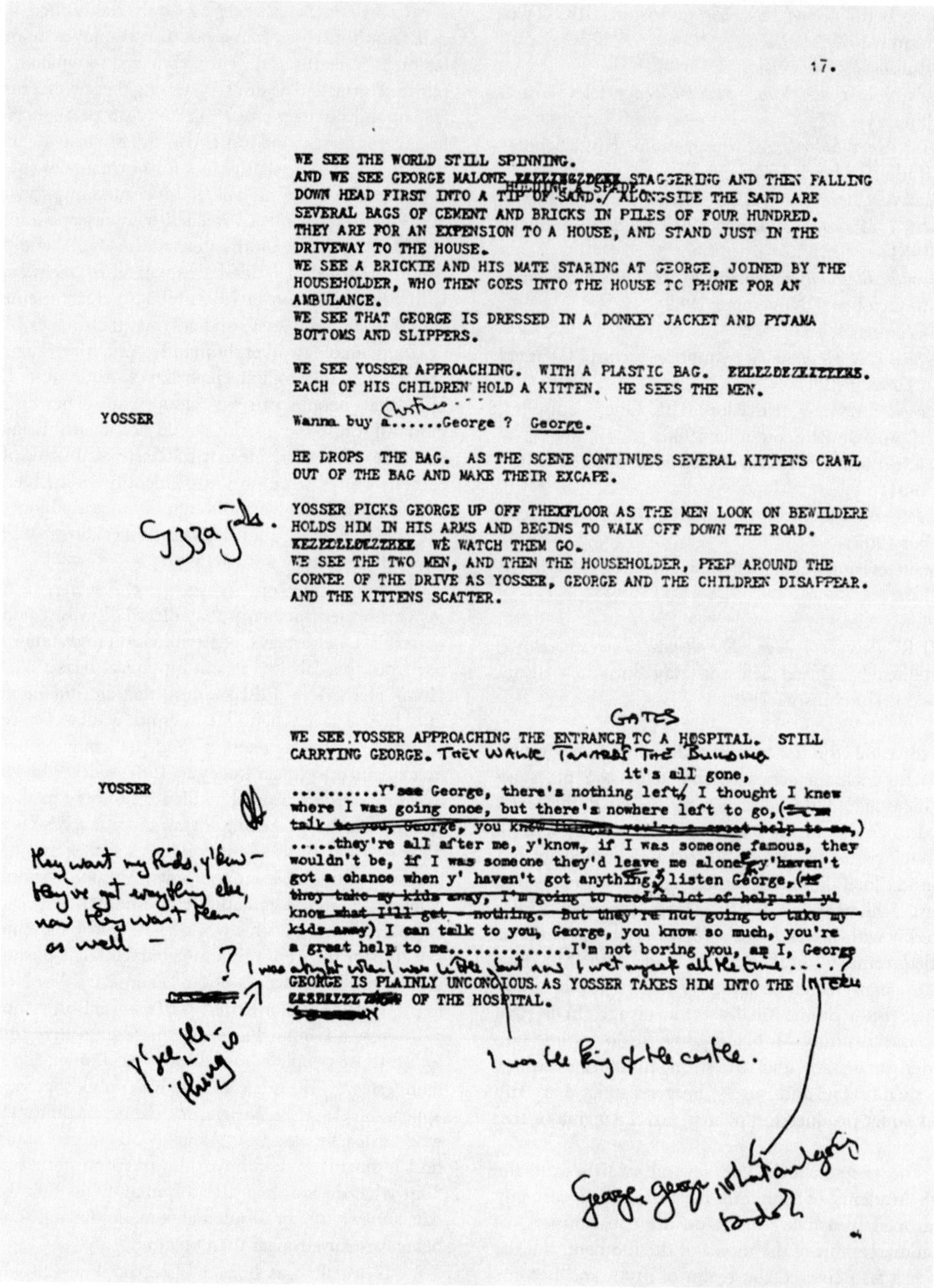

17.

WE SEE THE WORLD STILL SPINNING.
AND WE SEE GEORGE MALONE, HOLDING A SPADE, STAGGERING AND THEN FALLING DOWN HEAD FIRST INTO A TIP OF SAND./ ALONGSIDE THE SAND ARE SEVERAL BAGS OF CEMENT AND BRICKS IN PILES OF FOUR HUNDRED. THEY ARE FOR AN EXPENSION TO A HOUSE, AND STAND JUST IN THE DRIVEWAY TO THE HOUSE.
WE SEE A BRICKIE AND HIS MATE STARING AT GEORGE, JOINED BY THE HOUSEHOLDER, WHO THEN GOES INTO THE HOUSE TO PHONE FOR AN AMBULANCE.
WE SEE THAT GEORGE IS DRESSED IN A DONKEY JACKET AND PYJAMA BOTTOMS AND SLIPPERS.

WE SEE YOSSER APPROACHING. WITH A PLASTIC BAG. EACH OF HIS CHILDREN HOLD A KITTEN. HE SEES THE MEN.

YOSSER Wanna buy a......George ? George.

HE DROPS THE BAG. AS THE SCENE CONTINUES SEVERAL KITTENS CRAWL OUT OF THE BAG AND MAKE THEIR EXCAPE.

YOSSER PICKS GEORGE UP OFF THE FLOOR AS THE MEN LOOK ON BEWILDERE HOLDS HIM IN HIS ARMS AND BEGINS TO WALK OFF DOWN THE ROAD. WE WATCH THEM GO.
WE SEE THE TWO MEN, AND THEN THE HOUSEHOLDER, PEEP AROUND THE CORNER OF THE DRIVE AS YOSSER, GEORGE AND THE CHILDREN DISAPPEAR. AND THE KITTENS SCATTER.

Gizza job.

WE SEE YOSSER APPROACHING THE ENTRANCE GATES TO A HOSPITAL. STILL CARRYING GEORGE. THEY WALK TOWARDS THE BUILDING

YOSSER ....Y'see George, there's nothing left, it's all gone, I thought I knew where I was going once, but there's nowhere left to go, (I can talk to you, George, you know things, you're a great help to me,) .....they're all after me, y'know, if I was someone famous, they wouldn't be, if I was someone they'd leave me alone, y'haven't got a chance when y' haven't got anything, listen George, (if they take my kids away, I'm going to need a lot of help an' y' know what I'll get - nothing. But they're not going to take my kids away) I can talk to you, George, you know so much, you're a great help to me..............I'm not boring you, am I, George I was alright when I was little, but now I wet myself all the time.....?

They want my kids, y'know - they've got everything else, now they want them as well -

GEORGE IS PLAINLY UNCONSCIOUS. AS YOSSER TAKES HIM INTO THE INTERIOR OF THE HOSPITAL.

I was the king of the castle.

George, George, what are y' doing
[illegible]

Revised typescript page for the episode of Bleasdale's 1982 television series Boys from the Blackstuff *that focuses on Yosser Hughes and introduces his catchphrase, "Gizza job" (from Bob Millington and Robin Nelson,* Boys from the Blackstuff, *1986)*

College. His first job was at St. Columbus Secondary Modern School in Huyton, where he worked until 1971. From 1971 to 1974 he taught at King George V School on Gilbert and Ellice Islands and then at Halewood Grange Comprehensive School in Lancashire for one year. Teaching provided the impetus for Bleasdale to start writing. He explained to Pearson that, faced with a class of fifteen-year-olds of "limited abilities" and equipped only with "Janet and John" books, which did not "go down a bomb with lads built like two dockers welded together," he invented Franny Scully, a Scouse tearaway who dreams of playing football for Liverpool. The stories were broadcast on national radio, and *The Franny Scully Show* was a regular feature on the Liverpool commercial radio station between 1975 and 1979. Scully also spawned two novels (1975 and 1977), a stage version toured by the Liverpool Everyman's Vanload troupe (1975), and a television series (1984). In the introduction to the published scripts of the television series (1984) Bleasdale describes the Scully stories as "a morality tale" about "dreams and the danger that they can turn into nightmares." With Scully, Bleasdale demonstrated that his interest lay not just (and, in this instance, not principally) in theater, but that he had the flexibility and the desire to work across multiple media.

Between 1975 and 1978 Bleasdale wrote 7 stage plays, 2 novels, 5 television plays, and 150 radio scripts. Among the plays were *Fat Harold and the Last 26* (1975), drawing on Bleasdale's fleeting experience of working on the buses, and *Down the Dock Road* (1976), based on his experiences as an "in-security" guard on the Birkenhead Docks. These works were followed by *It's a Madhouse* (1976), set in a psychiatric ward, and *No More Sitting on the Old School Bench* (1977), about a down-at-the-heels inner-city school. Later came *Having a Ball* (1981), a madcap farce set in a private clinic and dealing with a jumble of issues, from men's fear of losing their manhood (three of the main characters are waiting for a female doctor to give them vasectomies) to bullying, power, revenge, the state of the health service, and, ultimately, the state of the world. The sense of dislocation in *Having a Ball* is as strong as in any of Bleasdale's later works. Not only are people in the closed world of a private clinic (a parallel to the sealed-off world of a psychiatric ward and the ledge of a later play), they are also struggling to stay afloat. Doreen, the drunken wife of a soldier in the Territorial Army who carries his survival gear with him in a suitcase, cries, "But what is there left? What can we do?" The answer comes back, "Pray? Join the TA? Build a fall-out shelter? Have a vasectomy? March for peace? Buy a machine gun? Collect sleeping tablets so that when the time comes . . . ?" There are more questions than answers. A glimmer of hope–but only a glimmer–is provided by seventy-seven-year-old George, who exhorts the others to "live life to the soddin' full and go screamin' into the hereafter."

What all the plays have in common, apart from their easily discernible connections to Bleasdale's own experiences, is that none of them were first produced in London. Most premiered in the northern cities of Liverpool, Manchester, Leeds, and Oldham; one, *Love Is a Many Splendoured Thing* (1979), was first produced in the west central town of Redditch, near Birmingham. Bleasdale was not perceived as, and did not believe himself to be, a part of the cultural scene of southern England. His work derives from his connections with the northern industrial cities, particularly Liverpool, and was clearly written with that audience in mind.

Boys from the Blackstuff draws from the same root material as the stage plays, depicting the bitterness and despair brought to the lives of five Liverpool men and their families by unemployment. Based on the characters created in Bleasdale's earlier television drama, *The Black Stuff* (1980), the five episodes–each focusing on a different protagonist–follow their struggle to keep their heads above water and to hold on to all that is left to them: the tatters of their self-respect. For Bleasdale, the hero is decent, honest, and placid Chrissie, the common man living an ordinary life until his job is taken away and he is left shipwrecked. For many audience members, however, Yosser Hughes touched a raw nerve. His catchphrases "Gizza job" and "I can do that" reverberated throughout the country, and he became the folk hero for the 1980s. Yet, he is truly a grim and helpless hero. Hughes painfully descends into madness as he loses his job, his wife, his children, his house, his dignity, and his self-respect. He is reduced to head-butting lampposts, elevator walls, confessional boxes, and policemen in a hopeless attempt to articulate his despair and to take away the pain.

Bleasdale offsets the despair with black comedy, reflecting his belief that "life is a farce–an absurd, mad, black farce." The comedy undercuts the emotional intensity of a scene to prevent a descent into melodrama, though Bleasdale is not afraid of emotion. "I go to the theatre and cinema for laughter and tears," he told Alan Franks in 1991, "and I go to my typewriter in the same way."

Boys from the Blackstuff abounds with moments of manic comedy, such as the pub scene at the end of the final episode. In the pub are Ronny Renaldo, whistling "If I Were a Blackbird"; a busboy repeatedly calling out that it is closing time; "Shake-hands" painfully gripping everyone's hands; a pill-popping, alcohol-swigging manager who would shoot himself if he had a gun; and laid-off workers feverishly buying drinks. Such mayhem finds a place in almost everything Bleasdale has

Scene from "Yosser's Story," episode 4 of Boys from the Blackstuff, *with Bernard Hill as Yosser and James Ellis as The Wino*

Scene from "George's Last Ride," the final episode of Boys from the Blackstuff, *in which Chrissie Todd (Michael Nagelis) takes George Malone (Peter Kerrigan) on his last outing, along the dockside of their hometown*

written, from the corridor scene in *Having a Ball* to the New Year's Eve confrontation between Catholic and Protestant pensioners at the Charleston Club in *No Surrender: A Deadpan Farce* (1985).

The ability to laugh in the face of tragedy, however, is not presented as a solution to the problems. Driven to despair by Chrissie's downward slide, Angie, his wife, launches a vitriolic attack on his determination to make a joke of everything, crying, "It's not funny. It's not friggin' funny. I've had enough of that–if you don't laugh, you'll cry–I've heard it for years–this stupid city's full of it." But when she screams at her husband to fight back, she has no idea how he can do so. In the end, for Chrissie there is only the fantasy of escape: as he leaves the pub in the final episode and walks off into the sunset, down a derelict back alley–complete with a partly demolished warehouse bearing the sign "Tate and Lyle. 1922"–all he can say is, "Beam me up Scotty. Beam me up."

The traditional solution, fighting back collectively, no longer seems applicable. Both of the characters who represent that idea die: Snowy leaps from a window, and George Mallone, who in the final episode is still arguing that "those dreams of long ago . . . give me some kind of hope and faith in my class," is left dead and alone in his wheelchair on the derelict dockside. All Bleasdale leaves the characters is the remnants of their humanity and individual identity. Holding on to one's name becomes of paramount importance, most poignantly depicted in Yosser's desperate need to announce to all and sundry that "I am Yosser Hughes." When he finally can only stammer "I'm . . . I'm . . . I'm . . . wet," the audience knows that all hope is gone.

Although most of Bleasdale's popular success has been achieved on the small screen, he has not forsaken the theater. In the mid 1980s he wrote his only work not set in Liverpool and its environs, spurred on by Albert Goldman's unpleasant but widely acclaimed 1981 biography of Elvis Presley. The musical *Are You Lonesome Tonight?* (1985) is Bleasdale's personal vindication of a person he describes as "a real working-class hero, a man of charm, charisma, generosity of spirit . . . someone not quite conceited, unpleasant and knowing enough to survive." The play traces a search for the true Elvis, a nightmarish trip into his soul as, bloated and drug-filled, Presley spends his last night alive trying to "face the facts." He is forced to come to terms with his past by three men, including his former employee and friend, Duke, who are planning to write an exposé that will leave him "bleedin' all over the bookstands of America." In an attempt to keep his self-respect and dignity, he has to get to the truth before they do.

The image of Presley that Bleasdale presents is complex and contradictory. He sways between megalomania and pitiful generosity–at one point he presses a diamond ring into the hand of his bewildered cook. He is riddled with fear and loneliness. He is obsessed with his stillborn twin brother, Jesse, with whom he conducts imaginary conversations and without whom he feels incomplete. He is convinced that if Jesse had lived, things would have been different: Jesse would have handled things better; he would have stood up to the "sharks." The overwhelming image of Presley is as a victim–as much a victim as Yosser Hughes. He is too weak to stand up to the manipulation of men such as Colonel Tom Parker–portrayed in the play as a ventriloquist clutching an Elvis dummy and gloating over the profits he has made. His exploitation by others is coupled with the destructive forces of fame to explain the depths to which such a hero has sunk. In the words of Duke, "What do you give a man who's got everything? All you can give him is more. And more. And more. Until one day . . . he can't take anymore."

Bleasdale was attracted to the idea of writing a television series based on William Allison and John Fairley's book, *The Monocled Mutineer* (1978), because it reexamined history from a different standpoint. He told Petley that "It was the knowledge that the history I'd read for 'O' and 'A' Level was not the history of ordinary people" that fueled his interest in the project. *The Monocled Mutineer* (1986) gave him a chance to look at World War I from the point of view of the ordinary soldiers, "to follow through the implication of that famous remark about the First World War being a case of lions led by donkeys." In the process Bleasdale created a profoundly antiwar work that depicts a deeply class-divided army in which the ordinary soldiers were subjected to brutality in training and then used as cannon fodder by incompetent officers.

The human voice at the heart of Bleasdale's series is Percy Toplis, who was accused of leading a mutiny at Etaples during World War I and was hunted down and killed after the war. The outrage and condemnation from some newspapers showed that Bleasdale had once again touched a raw nerve. The series merited six front-page columns in four days; the most intemperate attack was by Paul Johnson, who, in an article in *The Daily Mail* titled "Morally Bankrupt, Politically Correct," described the series as "another piece of agitprop designed to inflame class hatred and denigrate Britain . . . it [the BBC] not only lies, it lies for the Left. It not only rapes, it rapes for the Revolution." The BBC had left itself open to attack on the question of historical accuracy by changing the billing of the series from "a four-part drama freely based on real events" to "the enthralling true-life story of Percy Toplis." The BBC subsequently apologized to Bleasdale for this distortion.

Scene from the 1985 Phoenix Theatre production of Are You Lonesome Tonight? *in which Simon Bowman plays Elvis Presley, depicted by Bleasdale as "a real working-class hero"*

Among the complaints in the papers was one in *The Daily Mail* that accused Bleasdale of perpetuating the "myth of Percy Toplis as a working-class revolutionary dedicated to overthrowing a widely hated aristocratic establishment." Toplis, however, is at pains to stress that he was no hero; "That's the last thing I am," he tells Woodhall, the man obsessed with capturing him. "Cemeteries are full of heroes." He was not even in the camp when the mutiny started, preferring to spend his time with a woman. Nor does he display any traditionally heroic qualities. Toplis is shown as a trickster, a charlatan, a tearaway, a cynic, a man out for a good time. "What did I do?" he says about the mutiny. "I was just having a laugh." He is a chameleon who changes his name, clothes, and accent at the drop of a hat. He is a consummate confidence man: in one breath–and with real emotion–he convinces the mother of an officer he saw executed for treason that her son died heroically in action; in the next he relieves her of £5. For Toplis, life is about survival. One label he most definitely does not fit is *socialist.* The committed socialist in the series is Charles Strange, who, like the socialists in *Boys from the Blackstuff,* has a hard time and is eventually driven to suicide.

Even though Toplis is not a straightforward hero, he does have a heart; and in the course of events he begins to find himself caring. "I don't know what's got into me today," he says to his fellow mutineers, "I'm feeling all sort of . . . honourable." Visiting Strange after the war and hearing him make a stirring speech, Toplis is moved to tell him, "You were good in there, you know. In fact, you were . . . great. A great man." A second later the spell is broken, and Toplis blackmails Strange into giving him £100. The glimpses of something greater in Toplis are fleeting and also signal his downfall. Caring more–including falling in love with Dorothy, a confidence artist on his own level–leads to his undoing. He can no longer pull the same callous tricks he has in the past, and in the end he is caught by the police and shot on a lonely road near Penrith.

The Monocled Mutineer is not, however, simply another piece of period drama. Bleasdale intended it to have contemporary resonances. Toplis is described as "a hero for our time," his lack of political drive and his desire for a good time reflecting a political apathy Bleasdale saw in the 1980s. "If he were alive now he would continue to be even more fervently apolitical, or possibly even a perfect example of [Norman] Tebbit's philosophy of 'Get on Your Bike,'" Bleasdale told Petley; it is not by accident that Bleasdale shows him cycling to London from Nottingham. There are other contemporary references; parallels are drawn between the spontaneous, disorganized, boisterous, and occasionally brutal nature of the mutiny and events in Liverpool in 1981. "I tried to make it clear that the mutiny, like the Brixton and Toxteth riots, was not politically motivated although it also happened because of politics, because of the condition of the people which is brought on by political factors. Like the rioters of the 1980s, the mutineers had simply had enough of being brutalised and penned up and hit back." Above all, Bleasdale thought that if he got the series right, "I could say something about the bleak times we live in now, that cannon fodder is always cannon fodder, however much you are told that things have changed, be it in the Falklands or on the dole queue."

On the surface, *GBH*–the title derives from the criminal offense of Grievous Bodily Harm–appears to have all the political credentials of Bleasdale's earlier series. The story is about the clash between hard-line Labour council leader Michael Murray and Jim Nelson, the humane, clownish headmaster of a school for special-needs students. Murray seeks revenge on Nelson, who has spoiled his "big day" of shutting down the city in protest of job cuts by crossing a picket line and going in to work. The twist in the tale is that neither Murray nor Nelson are really in control. The strings are being pulled by right-wing infiltrators determined to discredit and dismantle the Left. Murray is shown to be the unknowing puppet of the Right, manipulated by the coolly sensual Barbara–who is later discovered to be the sister of Eileen Critchley, a ghost from Murray's past. It is hard to tell the difference between Right and Left; in the words of Jim Nelson, "Too often lions are led by donkey jackets. Living proof that the further left you go, the more right-wing you become." The working people of the city are shown to be as easily manipulated as their leaders; they are willing pawns in the plans the infiltrators devise, from terrifying the children in the special school to setting fire to the streets in their own city–an image to which Bleasdale later returned in *On the Ledge* (1993). For many the resonances were of Liverpool and, above all, of Labour Party council leader Derek Hatton, and *GBH* was seen as Bleasdale's critique of the Militant-led council of the early 1980s (the Militants were a left-wing faction that was eventually expelled from the ranks of the Labour Party).

Bleasdale, however, points out that *GBH* is not primarily about local-government politics or the nature of socialism, although the latter figures highly in the key confrontation between Murray and Nelson. He argued in the interview with Herbert that "the plot was the external clothing. . . . Underneath it was about what happened to [the actor] Robert Lindsay's character [Michael Murray] when he was a little boy." Murray's childhood was dominated by the twin bullying forces of Eileen Critchley and the headmaster, Mr. Weller, who was given to quoting T. S. Eliot; but a more significant influence seems to be the absence of his father, who died before Murray was born. With this character Bleasdale explores more deeply a theme that has growing significance in his work: the relationship between children and parents and how childhood events influence the adult. Murray is obsessed with being fatherless, a fact that shaped his life even before it started. Murray constantly pesters his mother to tell him what his father was like (he was the workman's friend who tried to change the world from the bottom of Pit Street and in return got a public-housing apartment and an early grave), why he is not there, and what he would have done in his son's position. Murray is equally obsessive about his mother. "What would I do without you? Who else would understand?" he asks her. Later he finds that, indeed, he cannot cope alone.

Murray is revengeful and vindictive, weak and emotionally needy, vain and childish. He is worried about going bald; obsessive about getting revenge against Nelson; tormented by Eileen Critchley's refrain, "You do want to please me, don't you Michael?"; easily manipulated; and infantile in his threats against anyone who disagrees with him. He clings desperately to the idea of being popular and important; in the first episode he tells his brother, "I can never remember a time when I didn't want to be someone. When you're someone, you've got the power to do nearly anything you want." Becoming someone, however, does not mean that he will always be someone; and gradually his life starts to spin out of control, guided by the ever-present Barbara and his own weakness. Murray moves from being an all-powerful council leader with big plans for "his city" to a gibbering, twitching wreck in a hotel, surrounded–and parodied–by a convention of the fans of the television series *Dr. Who* and chased by the ghost of Eileen Critchley.

Murray's downfall is paralleled by the rise of Jim Nelson. An unlikely and unlooked-for hero, Nelson starts the series with severe hypochondria and a fear of going mad. He does, indeed, do some rather odd things, such as standing in a wardrobe in the middle of the night wearing only a white sun hat and a tie, or washing his feet before going to bed in case he dies in his sleep. He has such a fear of crossing bridges that the route to a family holiday has to be meticulously and lengthily planned. Nelson comes back from the brink of insanity to prove himself to be the liberal heart in a heartless world, and he beats Murray in a final showdown at the Labour Club. In this scene Nelson talks about his hatred of bullying and violence, about learning of the need for love and respect from his father, and about the need to have a broad and rounded view of the world. Above all, he makes a plea to "behave with dignity, with honour and . . . without corruption. . . . In the short time we all have, we want to be remembered for the good we have done." For Nelson, socialism is the "redistribution not only of wealth but also of care, concern, equality, decency and belief in humankind." His voice seems to be the voice of the author, who told Hill in 1995 that "since I was a child, all I have ever wanted was to be good and to do good." *GBH* is one of Bleasdale's pleas for all the values for which Jim Nelson stands, and, in this instance, they win the day.

In 1993 Bleasdale wrote "an angry boil of a play," *On the Ledge*. The opening image of two disenfranchised youngsters, one holding the other by the ankles as he leans off the roof and writes the misspelled graffito "ANACHRY RULES" on a boarded-up window in an apartment building, sums up the mood of the piece, as does their cry: "Is this all there fuckin' is?" The play is, in the words of Irving Wardle, "a howl of appalled, uncontrollable rage," a dark look at the despair and self-hatred behind the glib phrase "inner-city dereliction," in which a motley collection of misfits and criminals, the dispossessed and the displaced, cower on the outside ledges of the apartments as those below set fire to the city and to their own homes. There is little plot here beyond Mal's attempt to hold on to the papers that

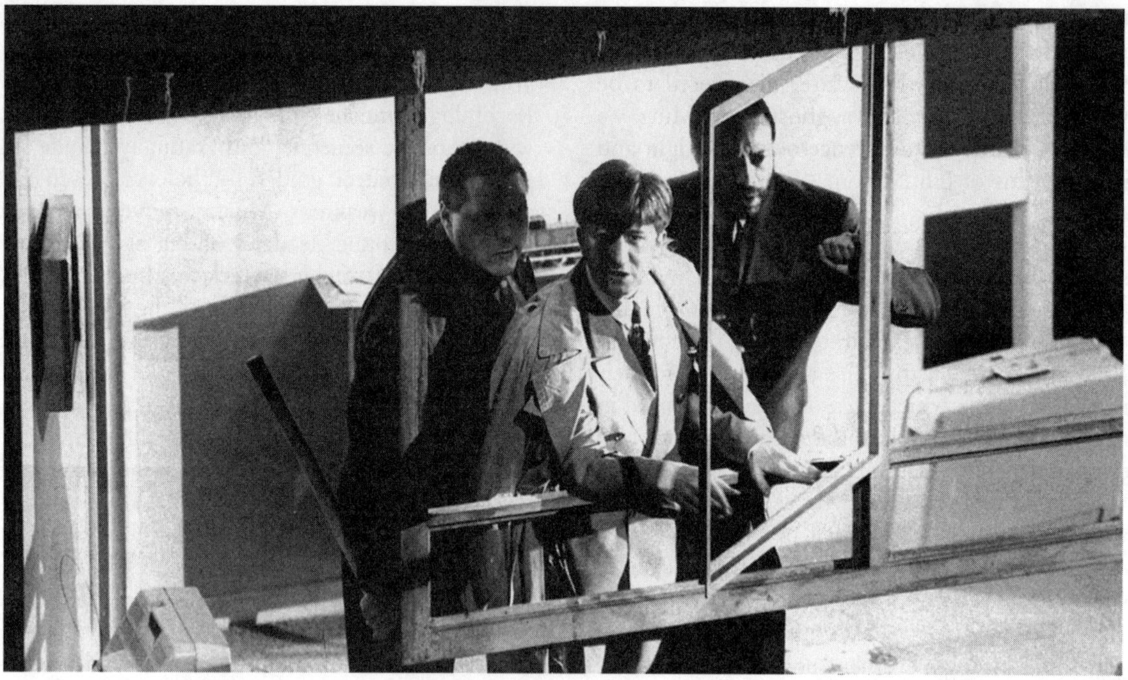

Paul Broughton, Jimmy Mulville, and Alan Igbon in the May 1993 Nottingham Playhouse production of Bleasdale's On the Ledge, *which Irving Wardle called "a howl of appalled, uncontrollable rage"*

prove that her erstwhile boyfriend, Shaun, has been up to no good in the building game. The characters cling to the ledges as the only place of safety, both physically and emotionally, in a world that has gone truly mad and in which, in the words of the fireman sent to the rescue, "the fuckin' community doesn't exist anymore."

The causes of despair are many. The Man on the Ledge, who is intent on suicide though unable to commit it, variously attributes his angst to the decay of moral values, the state of the nation, the prevalence of bad language, and the inevitability of death, a wry comment on Bleasdale's own often-quoted awareness of "the stench of mortality." For fireman Moey, cause for despair comes from the memory of being happy in the past. He tells Mal, "I hate the past–cos I have to live in the present . . . in the past I was happy . . . we thought we stood a chance." For Mal, the representative of liberal goodness, there are two possible causes of such a mess. On one hand, she tells Moey, "it's our fault–it's everybody's fault." Later, Shaun looks down at the burning city and tells her, "Look! Your friends, the deprived and the depraved are fuckin' up again. AGAIN!" In response, she accuses him and everyone who thinks like him. How Shaun thinks becomes clear in his final demonic speech as he burns the incriminating papers in the fire of the city, shouting, "Let them eat stale cake, give them false dawns and broken dreams, shoddy goods and shitty lives, cheap gin and hard drugs. Let despair and squalor and disease be theirs."

Bleasdale's own pessimism is manifest in the play. As in his earlier work, the finger is pointed as much at the working class as at the corrupt councillors and businessmen. Those down below are the real problem. The firefighter decides to stay on the ledge because those on the streets are even crazier, and he dreams of "fuckin' big ovens" with continuously open doors in which to burn a litany of offenders. There is no escape except the ledge, and the ledge makes people isolated observers of the world below. The riot is seen as an act of suicide, not of rebellion. Shaun has come to Liverpool to rebuild the city after earlier riots and has made a fortune out of the poor he was supposed to help. The play shows the frustration and desperation of those at the bottom of the pile, who are trapped in a world from which there seems to be no escape–except to cling to the ledge.

Bleasdale's television series *Jake's Progress* (1995) looks at "how parents screw up their children." Jake is the son of Jamie, an unemployed househusband who cooks pasta, organizes the child care, and was formerly a singer in a rock band that was once fourth on the bill at a concert headlined by Creedence Clearwater Revival. His mother is a hard-pressed National Health Service nurse. Both parents alienate their son, a situation that is perhaps best exemplified when Jake overhears his mother say that the only good thing about her next baby is that he might turn out to be better than Jake. The implication of the story is that the parents' behavior–unwitting or not–and the unusual family structure (father staying at home, mother working) have created a disturbed and disturbing child prepared, with the help of his malevolent imaginary friend, American Jake, to try to hang himself on a clothesline and set fire to his baby brother. The despair, the pain, and the impotence of *Boys from the Blackstuff* and *GBH* are all here, but *Jake's Progress* focuses not on society at large but on its microcosm, a dysfunctional family on the edge of a nervous breakdown. The series points grimly to the seeds of tragedy that potentially lie in all families.

Bleasdale's 1997 television series, *Melissa,* presents a puzzle in more ways than one. A classic murder mystery based on Francis Durbridge's television series of the same title broadcast in 1962, it seems a complete break with Bleasdale's past work. There are no discernible politics in the series, apart from a link to South Africa, and it is set at the opposite end of the social scale from *Boys from the Blackstuff,* amid the "people who smell of money." The audience soon discovers, however, that rather than enjoying the good life, the characters are the "sad and shallow people, the drunks and has-beens," surrounded by blackmail, distrust, and obsession. These characters, who run public-relations companies and drive race cars, have many secrets to hide in safe-deposit boxes, in hat boxes, or simply by remaining silent. They are deeply unhappy, scarred by their past. "There are two things you should never worry about–the past and the inevitable," the journalist Guy Foster is told in the opening episode, an adage disproved by the unfolding plot. Melissa tells Guy, "If we were really clever . . . we'd never get to know each other"; but she cannot escape the inevitable, and by the end of the third episode her past has caused her death.

"I'm a poor orphan," Melissa tells Guy. Left at New Street Station, she was later adopted by foster parents "who were terrible to me." Her real mother, unbeknownst to her, is her boss and friend, Paula, fifteen years old when she gave birth to Melissa. Paula lives with the knowledge that she has wrecked Melissa's life, and that knowledge drives her to murder the foster parents. Guy is as unlikely a hero as Percy Toplis, given to kicking out television screens, computer monitors, and other journalists with ease and frequency; but while Bleasdale sets up the audience to suspect his role in the murders, by the end the viewer and the police are convinced of his goodness. Touches of madness are scattered throughout the script–Rhett Butler dances with the ashes of Scarlett O'Hara to "Save the Last Dance for Me"; the race car driver tries to commit suicide by driving into a brick wall, only to be foiled by the airbag; and the final episode descends into a farcical mesh of fantasy and reality. This episode is full of the key elements of a classic action movie, culminating with a chase on an airport runway and an explosive crash that leaves the villain, Graham Hepburn, dead. In the video Hepburn left for his friends and family to watch while he made his getaway–a slick, stylish production filled with tap dancing, bowler hats, and checkered floors–he explains that he has killed for practice and for money, as a game that was fun while it lasted. *Melissa* is, in part, Bleasdale's contribution to current debates about the effects of on-screen violence.

Bleasdale is concerned with the perfectibility of humankind, with the possibility within people to be good and to live better lives. "It is not predestined," he told Pearson, "that the peasants stay peasants." Yet, such improvement is increasingly hard to find in his work. Instead, the dramas reverberate with defeated aspirations set amid an absurd world, reflecting, above all, an outlook expressed by the comedian Lenny Bruce in one of the only three quotations Bleasdale claims he has memorized in his life: "All my humour is based on destruction and despair. If the whole world was tranquil, without disease and violence, I'd be standing on the breadline, right behind J. Edgar Hoover."

Interviews:

Dave Hill, "Liverpool Echo," *Observer Magazine* (London), 2 February 1986, pp. 36–38;

Julian Petley, "Over the Top," *Sight and Sound,* 56 (Spring 1987): 126–131;

Hugh Herbert, "The Manacled Mutineer," *Guardian* (London), 30 May 1991, p. 22;

Alan Franks, "Black from the Boy's Stuff," *Times Review Supplement* (London), 8 June 1991, p. 19;

Alison Pearson, "First Class to Pity City," *Independent on Sunday* (London), 25 April 1993, pp. 20–23;

Hill, "Son of GBH," *Observer* (London), 8 October 1995, pp. 35–38.

References:

Maggie Brown, "The Worrying Kind," *Guardian* (London), 10 May 1997, pp. 25–28;

Bob Millington and Robin Nelson, *Boys from the Blackstuff: The Making of a Television Drama* (London: Commedia, 1986);

Richard Patterson, ed., *Boys from the Blackstuff* (London: BFI Dossier 20, 1984).

David Campton

(5 June 1924 –)

Jeannie van Rompaey
University of Leicester

PLAY PRODUCTIONS: *Going Home,* Leicester, Vaughan College, 1950;

Honeymoon Express, Leicester, Vaughan College, 1951;

Change Partners, Leicester, Vaughan College, 1952;

Sunshine on the Righteous, Leicester, Little Theatre, Leicester Festival, 27 March 1953;

The Laboratory, Leicester, Little Theatre, 6 March 1954;

Want a Bet? Leicester, Vaughan College, 1954;

Ripple in the Pool, Leicester, Vaughan College, 1955;

The Cactus Garden, Reading, Everyman Theatre, 23 May 1955;

Dragons Are Dangerous, Scarborough, Library Theatre, 28 July 1955;

Idol in the Sky, by Campton and Stephen Joseph, Scarborough, Library Theatre, 2 August 1956;

Memento Mori and *A Smell of Burning,* in *Four Plays of Adventure,* by Campton, Arthur Adamov, and Geoffrey Stephenson, London, Mahatma Gandhi Hall, 5 May 1957;

The Lunatic View: A Comedy of Menace (comprises *A Smell of Burning, Then . . ., Memento Mori,* and *Getting and Spending*), London, Mahatma Gandhi Hall, 25 November 1957; Cambridge, Mass., Poets Theatre, 21 April 1958;

Ring of Roses, Scarborough, Library Theatre, 22 December 1958;

Frankenstein: The Gift of Fire, adapted from the novel *Frankenstein; or, The Modern Prometheus,* by Mary Shelley, Scarborough, Library Theatre, 16 July 1959;

Four Minute Warning (comprises *Little Brother: Little Sister, Mutatis Mutandis, Soldier from the Wars Returning,* and *At Sea*), Newcastle-under-Lyme, Municipal Hall, 30 January 1960;

You, Me and the Gatepost, Nottingham, Old Nottingham Playhouse, July 1960;

A View from the Brink (comprises *Mutatis Mutandis, Out of the Flying Pan,* and *Soldier from the Wars Returning*), Scarborough, Library Theatre, 11 August 1960;

Funeral Dance, Dovercourt, Essex, One-Act Festival, 1960;

Table Talk, in *On the Brighter Side,* by Campton, Brad Ashto, Barry Cryer, Ken Hoare, Johnny Speight, Richard Waring, and Kenneth Williams, London, Phoenix Theatre, 12 April 1961;

Second Post, Nottingham, Old Nottingham Playhouse, 11 July 1961;

Stranger in the Family, Scarborough, Library Theatre, 27 July 1961;

The Boys and the Girls, Scarborough, Library Theatre, 26 December 1961;

Silence on the Battlefield, Dovercourt, Essex, One-Act Festival, 1961;

Incident, Dovercourt, Essex, One-Act Festival, 1962;

Usher, adapted from "The Fall of the House of Usher," by Edgar Allan Poe, Scarborough, Library Theatre, 28 June 1962;

Yer what? Nottingham, New Playhouse, 24 July 1962;

Don't Wait for Me, Ealing [London], Questor's Theatre, May 1963;

Comeback, Scarborough, Library Theatre, 11 July 1963; revised as *Honey I'm Home,* Leatherhead, Leatherhead Theatre, 24 November 1964;

Dead and Alive, Scarborough, Library Theatre, 30 July 1964;

A Point of View, adapted from Campton's radio play *The Manipulator,* 1964; retitled *The Manipulator,* 1968;

Cock and Bull Story, Scarborough, Library Theatre, 29 July 1965;

Split down the Middle, adapted from Campton's radio play, Scarborough, Lower Hall, 13 April 1967;

Two Leaves and a Stalk, adapted from Campton's radio play, Scarborough, Lower Hall, 16 March 1968;

Resting Place, in *Mixed Doubles,* by Campton, Alan Ayckbourn, Harold Pinter, John Bowen, Alun Owen, and four others, London, Comedy Theatre, 9 April 1969;

Time-Sneeze, London, Jeanetta Cochrane Theatre, Young Vic, 7 March 1970;

Wonderchick, Bristol, Bristol University, 11 March 1970;

Now and Then, York, York Theatre Royal, 1970;

The Cagebirds, Hereford, Hereford College of Education, 22 March 1970;

The Right Place, 1970;

David Campton (photograph courtesy of the author)

The Life and Death of Almost Everybody, Ealing [London], Questor's Theatre, 16 April 1970;
Provisioning, London, Little Theatre, 28 July 1971;
Jonah, Chelmsford, Essex, Chelmsford Cathedral, 10 November 1971;
Carmilla, adapted from a story by Joseph Sheridan Le Fanu, Sheffield, Crucible Studio Theatre, 17 June 1972;
Us and Them, 1972;
In Committee, 1972;
Angel Unwilling, adapted from Campton's radio play, 1972;
Relics, Leicester, Oadby Launde Townswomen's Guild, 14 April 1973;
Eskimos, sketch in *Mixed Blessings,* by Campton, Alan Ayckbourn, and James Sanders, Horsham, Capitol Theatre, 12 September 1973;
The End of the Picnic, Vancouver, British Columbia, 1973;
An Outline of History, Bishop Aukland, County Durham, 1974;
George Davenport, the Wigston Highwayman, Countesthorpe, Leicestershire, Countesthorpe College, 13 March 1975;
Everybody's Friend, adapted from Campton's radio play, Leicester, Memorial Hall, Thurcaston, 21 March 1975;
Ragerbo! Peckleton, Leicestershire, Peckleton Village Hall, 1975;
The Do-It-Yourself Frankenstein Outfit, Birmingham, 1975;
Come Back Tomorrow, Leicester, Oadby Launde Townswomen's Guild, 6 April 1976;
Zodiac, music by John Whitworth, Melton Mowbray, The College Theatre, 23 March 1977;

Oh, Yes It Is! Rutland, Braunston Village Hall, 4 November 1977;

After Midnight, before Dawn, Leicester, Wreake Valley School Syston, 7 April 1978;

The Great Little Tilley, Nottingham, Community Theatre, February 1979;

Who Calls? Dublin, Finglas Ladies Club, 1979;

Dark Wings, Leicester, Haymarket Studio, 9 June 1980;

Under the Bush, London, The Three Cups Pub Theatre, 1980;

Attitudes, Stoke-on-Trent, Mitchel Memorial Theatre, 1981;

Star-Station Freedom, Leicester, Phoenix Theatre, 15 April 1981;

Apocalyse Now and Then (comprises *The View from Here* and *Mutatis Mutandis*), Leicester, University Theatre, February 1982;

Olympus, Leicester, Phoenix Theatre, 30 March 1983;

En attendant François, Chelmsford, Essex, 23 March 1984;

But Not Here, Babbington College Theatre, Leicester, 24 March 1984;

Who's Been Sitting in My Chair? Chelmsford, Essex, The Three Cups Pub Theatre, April 1984;

Mrs. Meadowsweet, adapted from Campton's radio play *Mrs. M.,* Arnside Knott W. I. Coronation Hall, Ulverston, Lancashire, 2 March 1985;

Cards, Cups and Crystal Ball, Broadway, Worcestershire, W.I. Theatre Group, 1985;

Singing in the Wilderness, Stoke-on-Trent, Mitchel Memorial Theatre, 1985;

Our Branch in Brussels, Broadway, W.I. Theatre Group, 1985;

Simon Says, Swindon, Swindon Town Hall Studios, Wyvern Theatre, 17 October 1987;

The Spectre Bridegroom, adapted from the play by W. C. Moncrieff, Leicester, Hazel School Theatre, 1987;

A Tinkle of Tiny Bells, Leicester, Babbington College Theatre, 1 April 1988;

The Winter of 1917, Bognor Regis, West Sussex, Royal Hall, 1989;

Can You Hear the Music? Leicester, Babbington College Theatre, April 1989;

Smile, Coleford, The Community Centre, 31 March 1990;

Reserved, London, Old Red Lion, Touch and Go, 15 October 1991;

The Evergreens, Leicester, Babbington College Theatre, 4 April 1992;

Permission to Cry, Leicester, Babbington College Theatre, 7 April 1995.

BOOKS: *Going Home: A Play in One Act* (Manchester: Abel Heywood, 1951);

Honeymoon Express: A Play in One Act (Manchester: Abel Heywood, 1951);

Change Partners: A Comedy in One Act (Manchester: Abel Heywood, 1951);

Sunshine on the Righteous (London: Rylee, 1952);

The Laboratory: A Farce in One Act (London: J. Garnet Miller, 1955);

The Cactus Garden (London: J. Garnet Miller, 1955);

Doctor Alexander (Leicester: Campton, 1956);

Cuckoo Song (Leicester: Campton, 1956);

Little Brother: Little Sister (Leicester: Campton, 1960);

The Lunatic View: A Comedy of Menace (Scarborough: Studio Theatre, 1960);

Four Minute Warning, 4 volumes (Leicester: Campton, 1960)–comprises *Little Brother: Little Sister, Mutatis Mutandis (A Comedy of Menace), Soldier from the Wars Returning,* and *At Sea;*

Funeral Dance (A Play for Women) (London: J. Garnet Miller, 1962);

On Stage: Containing Seventeen Sketches and One Monologue (London: J. Garnet Miller, 1964);

Funeral Dance, in *Six One-Act Comedies for Women,* by Campton, F. E. M. Agnew, Eleanor D. Glaser, Mary Komlosy, Robert G. Newton, and Beatrice M. Plant (London: J. Garnet Miller, 1964), pp. 5–28;

Little Brother: Little Sister; Out of the Flying Pan (London: Methuen, 1966; New York: Dramatists Play Service, 1966);

Two Leaves and a Stalk: A Play for Women in One Act (London: J. Garnet Miller, 1966);

Ladies' Night: Four Plays for Women (London: J. Garnet Miller, 1967; New York: Dramatists Play Service, 1971)–comprises *Two Leaves and a Stalk, Incident, Silence on the Battlefield,* and *The Manipulator;*

Getting and Spending (Leicester: Campton, 1967);

Passport to Florence: A Comedy in Two Acts (London: J. Garnet Miller, 1967);

Roses round the Door and Other Comedies (London: J. Garnet Miller, 1967)–comprises *Roses round the Door, The Cactus Garden,* and *Passport to Florence;*

Silence on the Battlefield: A Tragi-Comedy for Women (London: J. Garnet Miller, 1967);

Incident: A Play for Women in One Act (London: J. Garnet Miller, 1967);

The Manipulator: A Comedy for Women (London: J. Garnet Miller, 1967);

More Sketches (Leicester: Campton, 1967);

The Right Place (Leicester: Campton, 1969);

Where Have All the Ghosts Gone? (Leicester: Campton, 1969);

Laughter and Fear: Nine One-Act Plays, edited by Michael Marland (London: Blackie, 1969)–comprises *Incident, Then. . . ., Memento Mori, The End of the Picnic, The Laboratory, A Point of View, Soldier from the Wars*

Returning, Mutatis Mutandis, and *Where Have All the Ghosts Gone?;*

On Stage Again: Containing Fourteen Sketches and Two Monologues (London: J. Garnet Miller, 1969);

A Smell of Burning, and Then . . .: Two Plays (New York: Dramatists Play Service, 1969);

The Wooden Horse of Troy (London: University of London Press, 1970);

Angel Unwilling (Leicester: Campton, 1971);

The Life and Death of Almost Everybody (Leicester: Campton, 1971; London & New York: S. French, 1971; New York: Dramatists Play Service, 1972);

Jonah (London: J. Garnet Miller, 1972);

The Cagebirds: A Play (Leicester: Campton, 1972; London & New York: S. French, 1976);

Us and Them (Leicester: Campton, 1972; London & New York: S. French, 1977);

Come Back Tomorrow (Leicester: Campton, 1972);

In Committee (Leicester: Campton, 1972);

Now and Then (Leicester: Campton, 1973; London & New York: S. French, 1976);

Carmilla: A Gothic Thriller in Two Acts; Based on a Story by Sheridan Le Fanu (London: J. Garnet Miller, 1973);

Frankenstein: A Gothic Thriller in Two Acts; Based on a Story by Mary Shelley (London: J. Garnet Miller, 1973);

Usher: A Gothic Thriller in Three Acts; Based on a Story by Edgar Allan Poe (London: J. Garnet Miller, 1973);

Relics: A One Act Play for Four Women (London: Evans, 1974);

Time-Sneeze: A Play, foreword by Geoffrey Hodson (London: Eyre Methuen, 1974);

The Boys and the Girls (London: J. Garnett Miller, 1975);

Ten Sketches (London: J. Garnett Miller, 1975);

What Are You Doing Here? (Leicester: Campton, 1976; London & New York: S. French, 1978);

Modern Aesop Stories (Kuala Lumpur, Malaysia: Oxford University Press, 1976);

Oh, Yes It Is (Leicester: Campton, 1977);

One Possessed (Leicester: Campton, 1977);

"Ragerbo!" (Leicester: Campton, 1977);

The Do-It-Yourself Frankenstein Outfit (Leicester: Campton, 1977; London: S. French, 1978);

Zodiac, music by John Whitworth (London: S. French, 1978);

After Midnight, before Dawn: A Play (London: S. French, 1978);

At Sea (Leicester: Campton, 1978);

Parcel: A Play (London: S. French, 1979);

Everybody's Friend: A Play (London: S. French, 1979);

Pieces of Campton: Dialogues (Leicester: Campton, 1979)–comprises *According to the Book, At the Door, Drip, Eskimos, Expectation, Strong Man Act, Sunday Breakfast, Under the Bush,* and *Where Were You Last Winter?;*

Who Calls? A Play (London: S. French, 1980; Chicago: Dramatic Publishing, 1980);

Attitudes (Leicester: Campton, 1980);

Freedom Log (Leicester: Campton, 1980);

Dark Wings (Leicester: Campton, 1981);

Look–Sea; and, Great Whales (Leicester: Campton, 1981);

An Outline of History (Leicester: Campton, 1981);

Who's a Hero, Then? (Leicester: Campton, 1981);

Dead and Alive (London: J. Garnet Miller, 1983);

Two in the Corner (Leicester: Campton, 1983)–comprises *Reserved, En attendant François,* and *Overhearings;*

But Not Here (Leicester: Campton, 1984);

Split down the Middle (Leicester: Campton, 1984);

So Why? (Leicester: Campton, 1984);

Mrs. Meadowsweet: A Play (London & New York: S. French, 1986);

Singing in the Wilderness: A Play (London & New York: S. French, 1986);

Our Branch in Brussels: A Play (London & New York: S. French, 1986);

Cards, Cups, and Crystal Ball (Leicester: Campton, 1986; London & New York: S. French, 1987);

Can You Hear the Music? (London & New York: S. French, 1988);

The Winter of 1917: A Play (London & New York: S. French, 1989);

Smile: A Play for Women (London & New York: S. French, 1990);

Becoming a Playwright (London: Hale, 1992);

Who's Been Sitting in My Chair? (Leicester: Nimbus, 1993);

Provisioning With Eskimos (Leicester: Nimbus, 1993);

The Evergreens: A Play (London & New York: S. French, 1994);

Permission to Cry (London & New York: S. French, 1996).

Collection: *Three Gothic Plays: Frankenstein, Usher, Carmilla* (London: J. Garnet Miller, 1973).

PRODUCED SCRIPTS: *The Laboratory,* television, BBC, 15 September 1955; radio, BBC, 6 January 1960;

One Fight More, by Campton and Stephen Joseph, television, BBC One, 18 December 1956;

Memento Mori, radio, BBC, 8 May 1957;

See What You Think, three episodes, television, BBC One, 1957;

Starr and Company, by Campton, Alan Prior, and others, serial, television, BBC One, 1958;

Funeral Dance, radio, BBC, 2 September 1961;

A Tinkle of Tiny Bells, radio, BBC, 8 March 1962;

Resting Place, radio, BBC, 27 January 1964;

Don't Wait for Me, adapted from Campton's play, radio, BBC, 13 February 1964;

The End of the Picnic, radio, BBC, 16 March 1964;

Alison, radio, BBC, 27 March 1964;

Silence on the Battlefield, radio, BBC, 1 September 1964; television, BBC, 7 October 1967;
The Manipulator, radio, BBC, 24 October 1964;
Stranger in the Family, television, BBC Two, 18 October 1965;
Where Have All the Ghosts Gone? radio, BBC, 1965; television, "Teleplay 68" series, 2 December 1968;
The Fall of the House of Usher, adapted from "The Fall of the House of Usher," by Edgar Allan Poe, television, ITV, 12 February 1966;
Split down the Middle, radio, BBC, 13 November 1966;
Tunnel under the World, television, BBC Two, 1 December 1966;
Someone in the Lift, television, BBC Two, 24 December 1967;
Angel Unwilling, radio, BBC, 1967;
The Missing Jewel, 50 episodes, radio, BBC, 1967;
A Private Place, television, BBC Two, 3 January 1968;
Parcel, radio, BBC, 1968; television, "Teleplay 68" series, Canada, 11 November 1968;
The Triumph of Death, television, BBC Two, 1968;
Where Have All the Ghosts Gone?, BBC Two, "Boy Meets Girl" series, 1968;
Liar, television, BBC Two, 1969;
Time For a Change, television, BBC, 5 May 1969;
Slim John, by Campton, Brian Hayles, Ray Jenkins, and John Wiles, television, 1969;
"Victor," radio, *Inquiry,* BBC Schools Programmes, 1971;
Boo! radio, BBC, 5 January 1971;
"Holiday," radio, *Inquiry,* BBC Schools Programmes, 7 June 1972;
The Bellcrest Story, television, 1972;
People You Meet, television, 1972;
"As Others See Us," radio, *Inquiry,* BBC Schools Programmes, 14 February 1973;
"So You Think You're a Hero?" radio, *Inquiry,* BBC Schools Programmes, 7 November 1973;
Everybody's Friend, radio, BBC, 17 April 1974;
"We Did It For Laughs," radio, *Inquiry,* BBC Schools Programmes, 25 September 1974;
Relics, radio, BBC, 6 January 1975;
"Deep Blue Sea," radio, *Inquiry,* BBC Schools Programmes, 4 June 1975;
"Isle of the Free," radio, *Inquiry,* BBC Schools Programmes, 24 March 1976;
"You Started It," radio, *Inquiry,* BBC Schools Programmes, 5 May 1976;
"Good Money," radio, *Inquiry,* BBC Schools Programmes, 2 February 1977;
"Mental Health," radio, *Inquiry,* BBC Schools Programmes, 28 February 1977;
I'm Sorry, Mrs. Baxter, radio, BBC, 19 March 1977;
One Possessed, radio, BBC, 2 July 1977;
"You're on Your Own," radio, *Inquiry,* BBC Schools Programmes, 21 September 1977;
The Whale Story, radio, *Inquiry,* BBC, 10 May 1978;
Our Friend Bimbo, radio, Denmark, 1978;
"We Know What's Right," radio, *Inquiry,* BBC Schools Programmes, 13 June 1979;
Community, 5 episodes, radio, BBC, 21 and 28 September and 3, 12, and 19 October 1979;
Eskimos, radio, BBC, 27 October 1979;
"Tramps," radio, *Inquiry,* BBC Schools Programmes, 25 May 1980;
"Little Boy Lost," radio, *Inquiry,* BBC Schools Programmes, 4 June 1980;
Three Fairy Tales, radio, Denmark, 1980;
Bang! Wham! radio, Denmark, 1980;
Young Life in England During the Last Four Centuries, radio, Denmark, 1980;
"When the Wells Run Dry," radio, *Inquiry,* BBC Schools Programmes, 16 February 1981;
"Our Crowd," radio, *Inquiry,* BBC Schools Programmes, 4 March 1981;
Peacock Feathers, radio, BBC, 8 December 1982;
"On the Rampage," radio, *Inquiry,* BBC Schools Programmes, 6 May 1983;
"Nice Old Stick Really," radio, *Inquiry,* BBC Schools Programmes, 13 May 1983;
Kahani Apni Apni, 40 episodes, radio, BBC, 1983;
Mrs. M., radio, BBC, 22 February 1984;
Cards, Cups, and Crystal Balls, radio, BBC, 25 March 1987.

OTHER: *Don't Wait for Me,* in *Worth a Hearing: A Collection of Radio Plays,* edited by Alfred Bradley (London & Glasgow: Blackie, 1967), pp. 83–106;
Gulliver in Lilliput: Based on Book One of Gulliver's Travels *by Jonathan Swift* (London: University of London Press, 1970);
Gulliver in the Land of the Giants: Based on Book Two of Gulliver's Travels *by Jonathan Swift* (London: University of London Press, 1970);
The Vampyre: Retold by David Campton; Based on a Story by John Polidori (London: Hutchinson, 1986; New York: Barron's, 1988);
The Spectre Bridegroom: Adapted from the Farce by W. C. Moncrieff (Leicester: Campton, 1987);
Mary Wollstonecraft Shelley, *Frankenstein: Retold by David Campton* (London: Hutchinson, 1987; New York: Barron's, 1988).

David Campton's theatrical career has been long and prolific. Although he has never received the national recognition that some of his contemporaries have enjoyed, his plays have continued to appeal to audiences through a series of changes in theatrical taste. He has won several prizes, including an Arts Council Bursary for playwriting

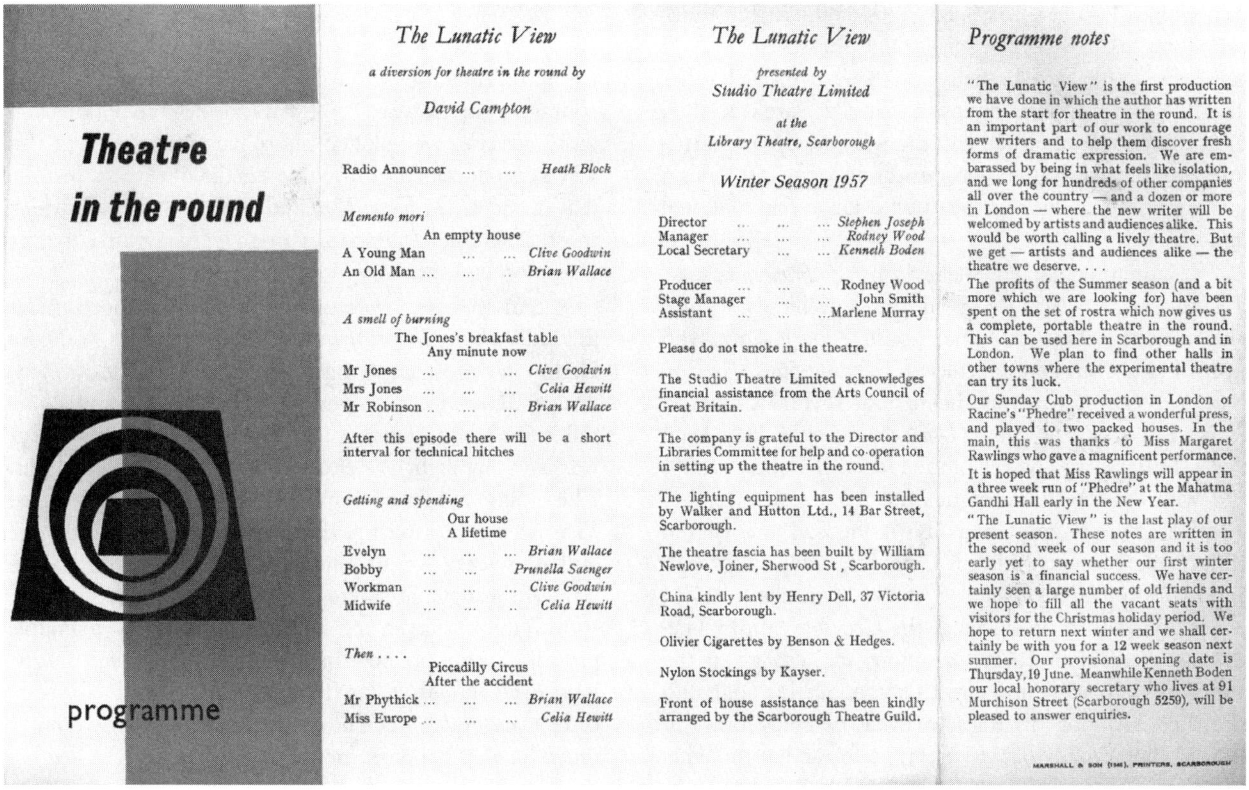
Theatre in the round

programme

The Lunatic View

a diversion for theatre in the round by

David Campton

Radio Announcer ... ... *Heath Block*

Memento mori

An empty house

A Young Man ... ... *Clive Goodwin*
An Old Man ... . *Brian Wallace*

A smell of burning

The Jones's breakfast table
Any minute now

Mr Jones ... ... *Clive Goodwin*
Mrs Jones ... ... *Celia Hewitt*
Mr Robinson .. .. *Brian Wallace*

After this episode there will be a short interval for technical hitches

Getting and spending

Our house
A lifetime

Evelyn ... ... *Brian Wallace*
Bobby ... ... *Prunella Saenger*
Workman ... ... *Clive Goodwin*
Midwife ... . *Celia Hewitt*

Then . . . .

Piccadilly Circus
After the accident

Mr Phythick ... ... *Brian Wallace*
Miss Europe ... ... *Celia Hewitt*

The Lunatic View

presented by
Studio Theatre Limited
at the
Library Theatre, Scarborough

Winter Season 1957

Director ... ... *Stephen Joseph*
Manager ... ... *Rodney Wood*
Local Secretary ... ... *Kenneth Boden*

Producer ... ... Rodney Wood
Stage Manager ... ... John Smith
Assistant ... ...Marlene Murray

Please do not smoke in the theatre.

The Studio Theatre Limited acknowledges financial assistance from the Arts Council of Great Britain.

The company is grateful to the Director and Libraries Committee for help and co-operation in setting up the theatre in the round.

The lighting equipment has been installed by Walker and Hutton Ltd., 14 Bar Street, Scarborough.

The theatre fascia has been built by William Newlove, Joiner, Sherwood St , Scarborough.

China kindly lent by Henry Dell, 37 Victoria Road, Scarborough.

Olivier Cigarettes by Benson & Hedges.

Nylon Stockings by Kayser.

Front of house assistance has been kindly arranged by the Scarborough Theatre Guild.

Programme notes

"The Lunatic View" is the first production we have done in which the author has written from the start for theatre in the round. It is an important part of our work to encourage new writers and to help them discover fresh forms of dramatic expression. We are embarassed by being in what feels like isolation, and we long for hundreds of other companies all over the country — and a dozen or more in London — where the new writer will be welcomed by artists and audiences alike. This would be worth calling a lively theatre. But we get — artists and audiences alike — the theatre we deserve. . . .

The profits of the Summer season (and a bit more which we are looking for) have been spent on the set of rostra which now gives us a complete, portable theatre in the round. This can be used here in Scarborough and in London. We plan to find other halls in other towns where the experimental theatre can try its luck.

Our Sunday Club production in London of Racine's "Phedre" received a wonderful press, and played to two packed houses. In the main, this was thanks to Miss Margaret Rawlings who gave a magnificent performance.

It is hoped that Miss Rawlings will appear in a three week run of "Phedre" at the Mahatma Gandhi Hall early in the New Year.

"The Lunatic View" is the last play of our present season. These notes are written in the second week of our season and it is too early yet to say whether our first winter season is a financial success. We have certainly seen a large number of old friends and we hope to fill all the vacant seats with visitors for the Christmas holiday period. We hope to return next winter and we shall certainly be with you for a 12 week season next summer. Our provisional opening date is Thursday, 19 June. Meanwhile Kenneth Boden our local honorary secretary who lives at 91 Murchison Street (Scarborough 5259), will be pleased to answer enquiries.

Program for a production of Campton's sequence of four short plays in which a sense of the macabre prevails against a background of normality (Collection of David Campton)

in 1957; the British Theatre Association Whitworth Prize for *Everybody's Friend* (1975) in 1975, for *After Midnight, before Dawn* (1978) in 1978, and for *Mrs. Meadowsweet* (1985) in 1985; and the Japan Prize for his radio play "Deep Blue Sea" (1975) in 1977. He has written plays for adults, youths, and children; for professional and amateur groups; and for radio and television both in the United Kingdom and abroad. His work has been presented as frequently in village schools, and college halls as in theaters. He is mainly known for his many well-crafted, imaginative one-act plays and sketches, which are usually satiric in tone; but he has written full-length plays, including adaptations. His prose adaptations for children of works by Aesop, Jonathan Swift, John Polidori, and Mary Wollstonecraft Shelley have also proved popular. His book *Becoming a Playwright* (1992)–where Campton recommends that young playwrights be true to themselves but remember the audience–has become a seminal text for budding dramatists.

Born on 5 June 1924 to David Campton, a hairdresser, and Emily Campton in Leicester, where he still lives, Campton was educated at Wyggeston Grammar School from 1935 to 1941. He worked as a clerk for the Leicester Education Department from 1941 to 1949, with interruptions for service in the Royal Air Force from 1942 to 1945 and in the Fleet Air Arm in 1945–1946. In 1949 he went to work as a clerk for the East Midlands Gas Board. His connection with the amateur theater began with his one-act play *Going Home* in 1950.

In January 1955 Campton met Stephen Joseph at a British Drama League playwriting course; that summer Joseph produced Campton's *Dragons Are Dangerous* at his Library Theatre in Scarborough. This production was the turning point in Campton's career: it led to his parting with the gas board in 1956 and to his break into television. It also marked the beginning of a rewarding association with Joseph and the Library Theatre that lasted until Joseph's death in 1967. Joseph not only directed many of Campton's plays but also offered him inspiration and support. *Then . . .* (1957), for example, was written in response to Joseph's suggestion that, as it was difficult for the audience of a theater-in-the-round production to see the actors' faces, it would be a good idea to write a play in which no faces were seen.

Joseph also suggested that Campton write a piece as "a ballet for the human voice," which resulted in *Out of the Flying Pan* (1960). This cleverly contrived dialogue between two ambassadors consists of distorted diplomatic clichés culled from the English newspapers *The Telegraph* and *The Guardian.* The idioms sound correct but are, in fact, gibberish. The effect is hilarious as the highly satirical subtext is revealed in misquoted phrases such as "I come daring the olive branch" and "we'll truss each other illicitly." The diplomats discuss a treaty, declare war, then meet to discuss a treaty to end the war; the cyclical structure, combined with the nonsensical dialogue, provides a savage, scathing attack on the double- talk of international diplomacy.

Campton adapted Shelley's novel *Frankenstein; or, The Modern Prometheus* (1818) in 1959 specifically to provide a nonspeaking role–the monster–for Joseph, who wanted to act but had difficulty in learning lines. *Frankenstein: The Gift of Fire* was the first of several Campton works in the horror genre. *Usher,* based on Edgar Allan Poe's short story "The Fall of the House of Usher" (1839) and with the actor/playwright Alan Ayckbourn–another member of the Joseph Company–in the lead, followed in 1962. After Joseph's death Campton adapted Joseph Sheridan Le Fanu's vampire story "Carmilla" (1872), which Ayckbourn produced at the Crucible Studio Theatre in Sheffield in 1972. Campton was also given the opportunity to act in and direct plays at Scarborough and elsewhere. Among his roles was that of Petey Boles in Harold Pinter's *The Birthday Party,* performed at the Theatre Centre in Birmingham in January 1959.

Campton's work during the 1950s and 1960s has often been compared with that of Pinter and the exponents of the theater of the absurd, such as Samuel Beckett and Eugène Ionesco. Thematically, the connection can be seen in Campton's portrayal of the absurdity of the human condition and his concern with the politics of power; but he tends to present a more optimistic view of life than the nihilism of Beckett and Ionesco, while the ever-present menace in his plays is, unlike the unstated threat that pervades Pinter's works, readily identifiable as the hydrogen bomb. Campton himself, while admitting similarities of theme and linguistic style, suggests that the likenesses are due to the zeitgeist: the aftermath of World War II, the genuine threat of the bomb, and the breakdown of prewar values. In the play sequence *The Lunatic View: A Comedy of Menace* (1957) a sense of the macabre prevails against a background of normality. In *Memento Mori* a sinister atmosphere is created as a young man seeks to buy a house so that he can hide his murdered wife under the floorboards, but the owner is reluctant to sell because *his* wife is already there. In *A Smell of Burning,* an indictment of British social mores, Mr. and Mrs. Smith argue over domestic details, oblivious to the revolution raging outside. In *Then* . . . the only two people left alive after a nuclear war are a physics teacher and the reigning Miss Europe; they were the only ones to obey the instruction to cover their heads with brown paper bags. They continue to wear the bags, even though doing so means that their love for each other can never be realized. In *Getting and Spending* a couple spend so much time worrying about the upkeep of their house that life passes them by. Campton–like Ionesco, whose work he admires–has the courage to break away from naturalistic conventions and write concise, well-plotted short pieces that express his viewpoint succinctly through comedic devices, especially that of satire. (*Memento Mori* and *A Smell of Burning,* which most resemble Ionesco's work, were written before Campton had seen any of Ionesco's plays.)

Another sequence of short plays, produced under the title *Four Minute Warning* (1960) includes some of Campton's most satisfying work. *Little Brother: Little Sister, Mutatis Mutandis, Soldier from the Wars Returning,* and *At Sea* reflect the fear and menace implicit in the threat of nuclear war and highlight the breakdown of established order. These plays are far from museum pieces in the post–Cold War period, however, as they make a point about the use and abuse of power in general and explore linguistically a type of theater that subverts naturalism. *Mutatis Mutandis* shows the resilience of the human race as a couple proudly take their new baby home, after initial misgivings, even though it has bright green hair, pointed teeth, three eyes, and a tail. The macabre yet optimistic point is that whatever happens, including nuclear war, the need of the human species to reproduce itself will persist: the mutant is "a lovely baby . . . our baby." In *Soldier from the Wars Returning* Campton introduces a precise visual metaphor to demonstrate that the horrors of war affect the perpetrators as well as the victims: as a soldier boasts to a barmaid about the injuries he has inflicted on the enemy, the injuries appear on his own body; he finally limps away, a wreck of his former self. *At Sea* is a theatrical allegory concerning the ineffectiveness of authority and can be considered a pessimistic state-of-the-nation play: a young man tries to persuade the other passengers to save their sinking ship, but, fatally for them, they leave all decisions to the captain, who turns out to be a dummy in uniform.

Little Brother: Little Sister is probably Campton's most successful play to date. The setting is an underground shelter in which Cook seeks to dominate her teenage charges, Sir and Madam. Her apparently benevolent aim is to prevent them from venturing out into the world above, which may still be polluted by radiation from a nuclear war; but it is not difficult to see the parallel between Cook's reluctance to allow the young people to go outside and the reluctance of parents to relinquish control of their offspring. On another level the play can be interpreted as a paradigm of the way a dictatorial regime uses its power to keep the people subservient. Cook wields a giant cleaver and threatens to put the children in the mincer and make them into rissoles (pastry-enclosed croquettes of minced meat or fish, usually fried in deep fat) if they fail to conform to her rules and regulations. To distract Cook from killing his sister, Sir pretends to seduce her by singing the old music-hall love songs that she has taught them; Cook has a heart attack and falls down dead. The brother and sister are then able to go through the door and take their chances in the outside world. The power of the play lies in the contrast of the characters of the gargantuan dictator, Cook, and her innocent charges as, according to Sir, they "grow older every minute" and begin to question her authority. Campton suggests that Cook should be played by a man, which lends both fearsomeness and grotesque comedy to the role. (In the original production at Scarborough, Cook was played by Ayckbourn.) The ingenuity of the piece lies in the way that Cook's dictatorship is based on half-remembered rituals from "the time before," including a mock religious ceremony in which Bible and prayer book have been replaced by snippets of news and clichés from an old newspaper–a comment on the enduring and unstoppable power of the media.

A somewhat diluted version of this element of black comedy continues in many of Campton's one-act plays, including the award-winning *Everybody's Friend* (1975). Although the insights into the oddities of human behavior remain as sharp as before, as the issue of nuclear war became less potent the sense of political commitment ceases to feature so strongly in his work. In *Everybody's Friend* the do-gooder Mrs. Roberts interferes in the lives of almost everybody in her apartment building. Daisy Loxton covets the potted plant belonging to her neighbor, Elsa Furley, and a bitter feud develops between them. In a misguided effort to resolve the problem, Mrs. Roberts throws the plant from the thirteenth-floor balcony. Daisy and Elsa rejoice in a newfound solidarity by throwing Mrs. Roberts after it.

Do-gooders also feature in *Our Branch in Brussels* (1985), set in an unnamed city in the late nineteenth century. Outwardly respectable Mrs. Bee finances a charity for distressed females by transporting the younger, prettier girls to Brussels for prostitution. When her methods are exposed, the ruthless Mrs. Bee laces the drinks of two disapproving committee members and dispatches them to Brussels, as well. These two plays, although ten years apart, are typical of many of the scenarios Campton has used when writing for all-female amateur groups: he often employs a domestic setting, strong female roles, and a well-structured plot with a sting in the tail that verges on farce. In *Funeral Dance* (1960) Edward's common-law wife, Ida, is confronted at his funeral by his real wife, Mildred, who threatens to expose Ida's lack of marital status unless Ida agrees to share her home with Mildred. Ida takes the wind out of Mildred's sails by being the first to break the news to her neighbors–and then surprises Mildred by offering to share her home with Mildred, after all. *Silence on the Battlefield* (1961), written for the

Campton acting in the 1963 Scarborough production of his play Comeback *(photograph courtesy of David Campton)*

same group that presented *Funeral Dance,* also features middle-aged women–in this case, sisters who have lived together all their lives. They love each other but cannot help bickering and fighting. Their short-lived truces offer only brief respites before the next battle commences. *Incident* (1962), a parable about prejudice in which two girls on a walking holiday are turned away from an inn because no one named Smith is to be admitted, was also written for the same group. These well-observed, low-key domestic dramas, which Campton himself admits are "nothing earth-shattering," were the very ones that were accepted for production on radio; *Funeral Dance* was the first to be broadcast. As Campton said in an unpublished interview, "if the W.I.s [Women's Institutes] wanted them, so did the radio."

These "middle-of-the-road" plays have earned Campton his bread and butter, but he has continued to write works that are more innovative and experimental. *Wonderchick* (1970), an allegory about labor relations written for a student group at Bristol University, features an enormous chicken that can sing and dance. Two people find the chicken and exploit it. The chicken rebels, goes on strike, and then begins to exploit them. *The Life and Death of Almost Everybody* (1970), written for the same group but first performed at The Questors' New Play Festival, is about a sweeper (janitor) in a theater who is tempted into creating a world of his own. The sweeper's attempts to keep his characters in order are thwarted by his creations' greed and ambition, aided and abetted by Aunt Harriet, a kind of alter ego who emerges unbidden from the sweeper's subconscious. The work seems to be a self-reflexive piece about playwriting.

Campton's children's play *Time-Sneeze,* in which the hero travels among various places and eras in a time machine, was produced for the Young Vic season at the Jeanetta Cochrane Theatre in 1970, using four stages with the audience standing in the middle. Although the play was scripted for the actors, the children were encouraged to improvise small parts. Apparently the improvisation worked best with private schools that were used to doing this kind of drama and also with the rough East End schools, where the teachers walked around in pairs for protection, as the children were determined to show that they could do as well as the actors.

In Committee (1972), a play that has been frequently produced, is reminiscent of the cliché-ridden gibberish of *Out of the Flying Pan,* but this time it is the jargon of committee meetings that is given the Campton treatment. At an interminable meeting at which no agreement can be reached, the committee members leave the stage one by one and have their places taken by members of the audience.

Campton's plays for the East Midland Arts Touring Company were written to be to adaptable to the type of performance spaces the company might encounter, which meant any place, from prisons to village halls, in which, as Hampton says, "a few actors rub shoulders with a larger number of spectators." A minimum amount of scenery was required. *Ragerbo!* (1975) came into being as the result of a discussion Campton had with the director, Andrew Manley, and the inventiveness of the actors; the audience becomes another collaborator, as asides and ad libs by the actors to the audience are encouraged. The play is a broad comedy with larger-than-life characters and a fair amount of slapstick, embellished with a multitude of disguises. The only scenery is a rack of improbable clothes, plus two signs: "Ladies" and "Gentlemen." The villain undergoes an onstage transformation from a "tatty totter" (a person who collects rubbish and looks through it for anything that might be salable) to a high-ranking police officer, drawing a gasp from the audience at each performance. *Ragerbo!* has a frenetic pantomime quality that generates a great deal of fun.

Campton's plays that are most often produced by amateur groups at festivals are *The Cagebirds* (1970) and *Us and Them* (1972). *The Cagebirds* is popular with both mixed and women's groups, as the birds of the title can be played by either sex. This is a device Campton recommends to would-be playwrights in *Becoming a Playwright.* Characters that can be either gender are more likely to be performed (by amateurs) than if roles limit casting by sex. Each bird has its own song, and, like the dialogue of the diplomats in *Out of the Flying Pan,* the words and phrases do not really make sense. None of the birds listens to the others' songs. When a new wild bird is placed in the cage and suggests that they should escape, unease sets in, and a kind of community feeling is generated as the old residents combine to reject and, finally, to kill her to stop her song forever. Comment is obviously being made on the way people, like the caged birds, prefer to stay in their comfort zones rather than risk change. There is also the suggestion that even seemingly civilized people have the capacity for violence if their way of life is threatened by new ideas, however liberating those ideas might be. *The Cagebirds* can thus be seen as a frightening paradigm of middle-class complacency. In *Us and Them,* written for a youth group, two sets of wanderers looking for a place to settle arrive simultaneously at a fertile spot and divide up the land by building a wall. As the wall is built, block by block, on stage, suspicion and mistrust of "Them" on the other side grows, leading to an explosive confrontation. The visual metaphor of a wall of mistrust is extremely potent.

Runners-up in "the most popular plays for amateurs category" must be *After Midnight, before Dawn* (1978) and *Who Calls?* (1979). The former takes place in a seventeenth-century prison in which six people convicted of witchcraft are tempted to sell their souls to the devil in exchange for escaping the execution that is scheduled for the next morning. The climax involves a scene of ritual menace similar to the one in *The Cagebirds. Who Calls?* is a Victorian ghost story with well-contrasted stock characters. The servants plot the theft of their late mistress's jewelry; but if she is dead, who keeps ringing the upstairs bell?

Of Campton's sketches, *Resting Place*–performed at the Comedy Theatre in London in 1969 as part of *Mixed Doubles,* by Campton, Ayckbourn, Pinter, John Bowen, Alun Owen, and four others–achieves the subtle mixture of comedy and pathos that is associated with much of Campton's work. An old man and woman, resting on a bench in a cemetery, bemoan the fact that when they die they will have to be buried apart. After a while, they decide to go home, counting themselves lucky that they will have kippers for tea. Even the richest man in that graveyard cannot enjoy kippers for tea. *The End of the Picnic,* produced as a radio play in 1964 and on the stage in 1973, is about a younger couple. Since the birth of her son the woman has doted on the boy and ignored her husband. At a family picnic a girl joins them. The two young people wander off; the father watches them through binoculars and sees his son slip an engagement ring on the girl's finger, and he tells his wife. Shocked by this revelation that her son is going to be less dependent on her, she turns to her husband for the first time in years. This delicate little play catches the uneasy relationship of a married couple who have remained together but have been estranged emotionally for years.

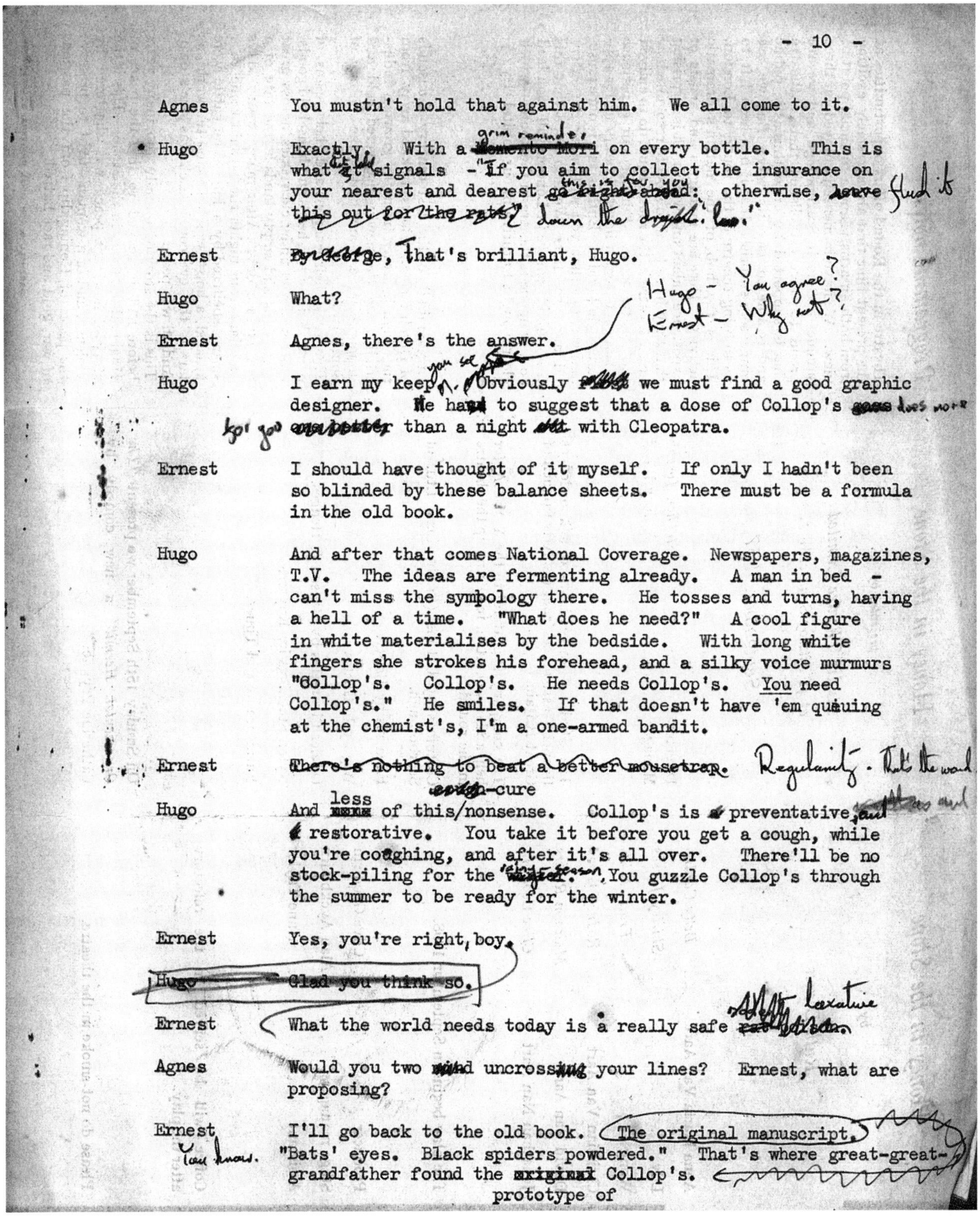

\- 10 -

Agnes You mustn't hold that against him. We all come to it.

Hugo Exactly. With a ~~Memento Mori~~ grim reminder on every bottle. This is what ~~it~~ the label signals - "If you aim to collect the insurance on your nearest and dearest ~~go right ahead~~ this is for you: otherwise, ~~leave this out for the rats~~ flush it down the drain. loo."

Ernest ~~By George~~, That's brilliant, Hugo.

Hugo What?

Hugo - You agree?
Ernest - Why not?

Ernest Agnes, there's the answer.

Hugo I earn my keep, you see. Obviously ~~first~~ we must find a good graphic designer. ~~He~~ ~~has~~ to suggest that a dose of Collop's ~~goes~~ does more for you ~~one better~~ than a night ~~out~~ with Cleopatra.

Ernest I should have thought of it myself. If only I hadn't been so blinded by these balance sheets. There must be a formula in the old book.

Hugo And after that comes National Coverage. Newspapers, magazines, T.V. The ideas are fermenting already. A man in bed - can't miss the symbology there. He tosses and turns, having a hell of a time. "What does he need?" A cool figure in white materialises by the bedside. With long white fingers she strokes his forehead, and a silky voice murmurs "Collop's. Collop's. He needs Collop's. You need Collop's." He smiles. If that doesn't have 'em queuing at the chemist's, I'm a one-armed bandit.

Ernest ~~There's nothing to beat a better mousetrap.~~ Regularity. That's the word.

Hugo And less ~~more~~ of this/~~cough~~-cure nonsense. Collop's is a preventative, as well as a restorative. You take it before you get a cough, while you're coughing, and after it's all over. There'll be no stock-piling for the ~~winter~~ cold season. You guzzle Collop's through the summer to be ready for the winter.

Ernest Yes, you're right, boy.

~~Hugo Glad you think so.~~

Ernest What the world needs today is a really safe ~~rat poison~~ laxative.

Agnes Would you two ~~mind~~ uncross~~ing~~ your lines? Ernest, what are proposing?

Ernest I'll go back to the old book. The original manuscript. You know. "Bats' eyes. Black spiders powdered." That's where great-great-grandfather found the ~~original~~ prototype of Collop's.

Corrected typescript page for Campton's 1964 play Dead and Alive *(Collection of David Campton)*

Of Campton's plays written in the 1980s and 1990s, *Can You Hear the Music?* (1989) is the most frequently performed. It has some similarities to *The Cagebirds;* but instead of birds, the characters are mice who are lured outside by the sweet music of the Pied Piper. It is unclear whether the Piper is the personification of death, but it is doubtful that a better life awaits the mice who leave. *Little Brother: Little Sister, The Cagebirds,* and *Can You Hear the Music?* all pose the question: should one play it safe and keep to the status quo, or be adventurous and take risks? Campton's 1984 radio play *Mrs. M.,* adapted for the stage in 1985 as *Mrs. Meadowsweet,* treats the same theme in a different way. Mrs. Meadowsweet, the owner of a guest house, has the power to blank out her paying guests' unpleasant memories; but in doing so she deprives them of their true selves, so that they become her creatures. A play in which memory is resuscitated for the better is *Smile* (1990), which uses the convention of a family photograph taken in the second half of the nineteenth century as a device to reveal the secret thoughts of each member of the family. Mama, the most reticent of the group and the most accustomed to being ignored, finally faces the truth about the nature of the conception and birth of her twins. She finds herself liberated by this truth, however unpleasant it may be. *The Winter of 1917* (1989) is a ghost play in which characters from the twentieth century enter a large, seemingly deserted country house and find a well-lit room and a roaring fire that gives off no heat. One of the characters, Truepenny, does feel the warmth from the fire as he takes on the persona of a character from another era, the last years of World War I, and engages in a rant against the futility and butchery of war. An abrupt return to the present prevents the development of the argument.

Two of Campton's plays, *The Evergreens* (1992) and *Permission to Cry* (1995), experiment with minimum staging complemented by elaborate lighting and a rich profusion of sound effects. *The Evergreens* is about two elderly characters, known only as Him and Her, who courted in the 1940s but lost contact for thirty years. The rekindling of their love is continually thwarted by misunderstandings and fear of loss of autonomy. The dialogue is sharp-edged and mannered. In contrast, the ending is optimistic and daringly sentimental, as, belatedly, the couple hold hands and join in the community singing of "Side by Side" with other members of the Evergreen Club on their annual outing. *Permission to Cry* deals with the clash between personal and the public personas that so often leads to hypocrisy and grief. Told in a series of flashbacks, the play reveals the feelings of a junior government minister, Julia Gibbon, as she attempts to cope with the loss of her lover, Penelope Wright, an antiestablishment journalist, who was killed accidentally by mounted police at a protest march. Julia is being hounded by a reporter who is looking for a scoop to advance her career. With the spirit of Penelope standing close by, Julia gives a speech in which she asserts that she has nothing to hide in her past. The denial, meant to maintain her public image, opens the floodgates of her grief; she breaks down and asks for "permission to cry."

In the summer of 2001 Samuel French Ltd. was preparing for publication a one-act play Campton had written fifty years previously. Originally titled *Grasshopper Dance* and retitled *Forever Is a Very Long Time,* the play won first prize in the 2001 Leicestershire Playwrights Annual Play Writing Competition. It retells the legend of Tithonus, who is given the gift of immortality without the gift of youth. Eventually, his "sentence" is changed: he is still immortal but becomes a grasshopper–a more agile and carefree being than an elderly man.

David Campton is a remarkably prolific playwright whose subject matter varies from fantasies and ghost stories to keen social commentary. He writes about the seedy and the exotic, the past and the present, the underdog and the bully. His characters are often stereotyped to suit his acerbic, satiric style; yet, his tone can also be whimsical and sentimental. His plays continue to be popular with amateur theatrical groups and radio audiences.

References:

John Bull, *Stage Right: Crisis and Recovery in British Contemporary Mainstream Theatre* (Basingstoke: Macmillan, 1994);

Charles A. Carpenter, *Dramatists and the Bomb: American and British Playwrights Confront the Nuclear Age, 1945–1964* (Westport, Conn. & London: Greenwood Press, 1999);

Christopher Driver, *The Disarmers* (London: Hodder & Stoughton, 1964), pp. 225–227;

Kenneth Pickering, Bill Horrocks, and David Male, *Investigating Drama* (London: Allen & Unwin, 1974), pp. 81–86;

John Russell Taylor, *Anger and After* (London: Methuen, 1962), pp. 181–188;

Irving Wardle, "Comedy of Menace," in *The Encore Reader: A Chronicle of the New Drama,* edited by Charles Marowitz, Tom Milne, and Owen Hale (London: Methuen, 1965), pp. 86–89.

Marina Carr

(17 November 1964 –)

Carole-Anne Upton
University of Hull

PLAY PRODUCTIONS: *Low in the Dark,* Dublin, Project Arts Centre, 24 October 1989;
The Deer's Surrender, Dublin, Andrews Lane Theatre, June 1990;
Ullaloo, Dublin, Peacock Theatre, 19 March 1991;
This Love Thing, Dublin, Project Arts Centre, 1991;
The Mai, Dublin, Peacock Theatre, 5 October 1994;
Portia Coughlan, Dublin, Peacock Theatre, 27 March 1996; New York, The Actor's Free Studio, 1998;
By the Bog of Cats, Dublin Abbey Theatre, 7 October 1998;
On Raftery's Hill, Galway, Town Hall Theatre, 9 May 2000; Washington, D.C., Kennedy Center, June 2000.

BOOKS: *Low in the Dark* in *The Crack in the Emerald–New Irish Plays,* selected and introduced by David Grant (London: Nick Hern, 1990);
The Mai (Oldcastle, County Meath: Gallery, 1995);
Portia Coughlan (London & Boston: Faber & Faber, 1996);
By the Bog of Cats (Oldcastle, County Meath: Gallery, 1998);
On Raftery's Hill (Oldcastle, County Meath: Gallery, 2000).
Collection: *Plays One,* with an introduction by Carr (London: Faber & Faber, 1999).

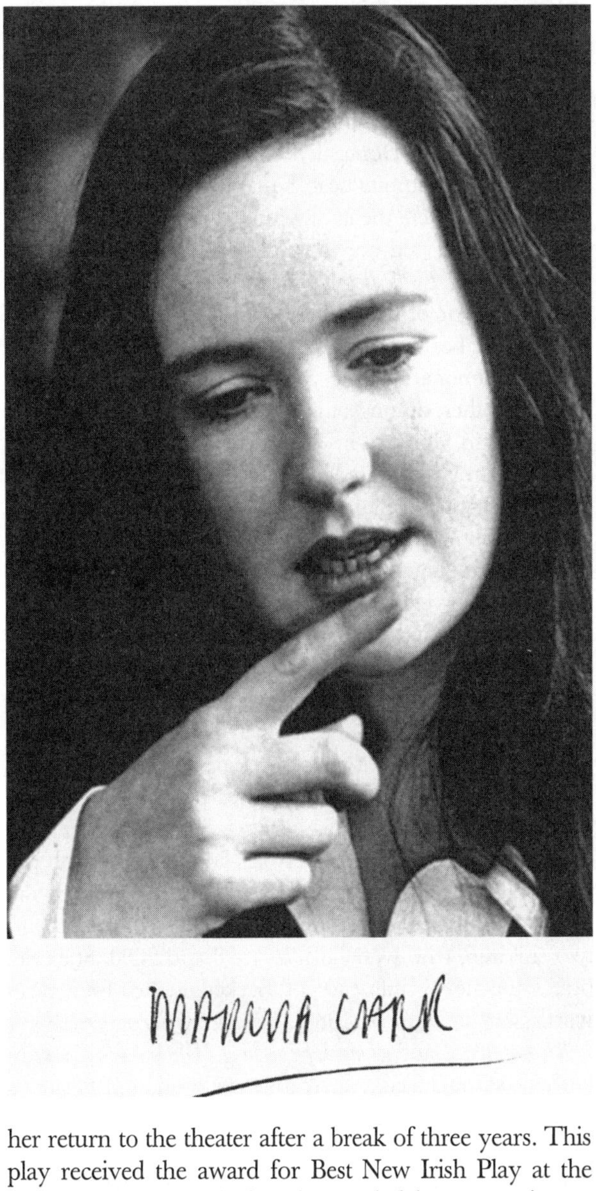

Marina Carr stands at the forefront of a new generation of Irish dramatists whose work has achieved rapid success and much critical acclaim. By the age of thirty-one, she had already completed six plays for the professional theater, including five commissions, with several more under way. Following a period as writer in residence at the National Maternity Hospital, she was appointed Ansbacher Writer-in-Association at the Abbey Theatre in Dublin (1995–1996); Writer in Residence at Trinity College (1998–1999); and writer in residence at Dublin City University (1999–2000). She has been awarded two bursaries in literature by the Arts Council of Ireland and is a member of Aosdána, the Irish government body that provides a lifetime income to artists. Her skills as a dramatist, developed through the radical experimentation of her earlier plays, reached maturity with *The Mai* (1995), marking her return to the theater after a break of three years. This play received the award for Best New Irish Play at the Dublin Theatre Festival and extended her reputation to the London stage and beyond to Europe and the United States. The success of *The Mai* was followed in 1996 with the remarkable *Portia Coughlan,* which won Carr the Susan

Smith Blackburn Prize. *By the Bog of Cats,* presented by the Abbey Theatre at the Dublin Theatre Festival in 1998, was described by David Nowlan, writing in *The Irish Times* (26 September 1998), as "probably Carr's most ambitious play to date." There is a clear development through her writing, from a sparsely theatrical absurdism to the richness of the mythic, which in its contemporary reinstatement of the lyrical and the tragic is no less radical in theatrical terms. Bold and brutal, *On Raftery's Hill* (2000) perhaps maks a change in direction with its more earthbound though hardly realist approach. The critic of *The Irish Times* (11 May 2000) described the production as "a gripping, extraordinary evening of theatre."

The second of six children, Marina Eithne Bridget Carr was born in Dublin on 17 November 1964 to Hugh Carr, a former court clerk from Donegal who had become a prolific playwright and novelist, and Maura Carr, a teacher, also from Donegal. She was reared in the remote and rural Gortnamona near Tullamore in County Offaly. When she was ten, the family moved to the nearby village of Pallas Lake, and her most important pieces–*The Mai, Portia Coughlan, By the Bog of Cats,* and *On Raftery's Hill*–retain a strong flavor of the Irish Midlands in both accent and culture. She began writing plays and sketches while still at the Gortnamona National School, where she was taught by her mother, among others. She went on to attend the Sacred Heart Convent in Tullamore and then to board at Presentation College in Mountmellick. Her mother, who wrote poetry in Irish and played the piano and the violin in the family home, died when Marina was seventeen. In 1987 she graduated with majors in English and philosophy from University College, Dublin (UCD) and wrote her first play for the Abbey, *Ullaloo,* while still a student (although it was not performed until 1991 and was quickly taken off by the director, Garry Hynes). After a year spent teaching and writing in New York City, she returned to enroll for a master's degree focusing on Samuel Beckett at UCD. The thesis was put aside when she began to concentrate on playwriting. She was the first living woman playwright to have a play performed on the main stage of the Abbey, Ireland's National Theatre. She married in 1995 and lives in Dublin with her husband and two children, who were born in 1998 and 2000. She celebrates the heavy influence of Beckett in her four early works, *Low in the Dark* (1989), *The Deer's Surrender* (1990), *Ullaloo* (1991), and *This Love Thing* (1991), which may fairly be summarized as a creative exploration of Beckett's dramatic techniques from a female perspective. *Low in the Dark* was performed at the Project Arts Centre by the ad hoc Crooked Sixpence Theatre Company, marking the debut production of Carr's work on the public stage. An earlier play, *Ullaloo,* was presented in a rehearsed reading with Derek Chapman, Olwen Fouere, and Tom Hickey, at the 1989 Dublin Theatre Festival. The two female and two male characters in *Low in the Dark*–Bender, Binder, Baxter, and Bone–play out grotesque gender roles, mostly revolving around motherhood. Bender produces offspring repeatedly throughout the piece, adding to the million or so she already has. Bone, a male, becomes pregnant, as eventually does Baxter, after worrying that he is barren. Baxter's "pregnancy" at the end of the piece takes the form of a hump on his shoulder/back, the ultimate cliché of grotesque deformation. Binder, a female, tells the audience that babies are always boys, even when they are girls. Later on, Baxter states that babies are always girls. The play is an absurdist exploration of gender constructs, irrespective of biological sex. The characters swap gender roles, assuming the commonplaces of patriarchal order in their playful exchanges–the "men" build walls and work, while the "women" have babies, bake buns, and knit. Masculine and feminine behavior is visually represented in the set, with a bizarre bathroom stage left, and stage right, "the men's space; tyres, rims, unfinished walls and blocks strewn about."

In the absence of plot, the action is held together by a fifth character, the extraordinary figure of Curtains, who is "covered from head to toe in Curtains. Not an inch of her face or body is seen throughout the play." The image of Curtains challenges the representation of woman as a female body under a male gaze. Furthermore, she acts as storyteller, a role traditionally fulfilled in Ireland by an old woman. Her intermittent narrative concerns a man and a woman who pointlessly roam the earth together. In the final section of her story the man and woman realize that "they had never met. And worse still, they never would, they never could, they never can and they never will." The Beckettian aporia is, however, given a further twist, as the female finally takes the lead in this endgame and breaks the gender stalemate:

> One day the man looked out of his window. 'It's time', he said. So he got up on his bicycle and rode all over the earth and he cycled all over the sea. One evening as he was flying over the highways he saw the woman in his path. 'Get out of my road', he yelled, but she would not. 'I've two choices', the man said, 'I can knock her down or I can stop'. He did both. 'You,' she said, 'if you have courage get off your bicycle and come with me.'

With Curtains, Carr wittily asserts the intellectual and emotional status of her female characters and reclaims for women the right to tell their own stories in their own voices on the Irish stage. Evocations of Beckett abound, perhaps most notably, as Anthony Roche points out, in Carr's appropriation of Beckett's well-known answer to the question of why Ireland has produced so many writers: "When you are in the last bloody ditch, there is nothing left but to sing." The couple in Curtains's story encounter a woman singing in a ditch, and another reference makes explicit the significance of gender:

> BINDER: He hinted at desperation sung in ditches.
> BAXTER: She hinted at desperation not sung at all.

What Carr adds to her treasured Beckettian landscape is her own irreverent woman's song, bringing an ironic feminine perspective to an icon of masculine Irish writing. To her Godotesque pastiche of hat-swapping is added a scene of frantic baby-swapping; Vladimir and Estragon seem to merge with Cinderella's ugly stepsisters as Baxter and Bone try to squeeze their feet, not into a boot, as in *Waiting for Godot* (1953), but a pink sock.

Paradoxically, this first public work, in which Carr stakes her claim to be heard on the Irish stage, owes much of its accent to Beckett. *Low in the Dark* received mixed reviews, as did her three other absurdist pieces, *Ullaloo, The Deer's Surrender,* and *This Love Thing,* in all of which Beckett's influence remains strong.

Recognizing the need to develop her craft and discover her own voice, Carr decided to take a break from Dublin, a break that she describes as "my three years in the wilderness." The wilderness she chose was not a geographical wilderness, however, though she did live shortly at Annaghmakerrig in County Monaghan, as well as for a year on the island of Inisnee outside Roundstone, County Galway, where she read the classics and began writing again. She recalled in an interview with Victoria White, "I wanted to learn how to write–I thought the way to start was with the basics. Learn the rules before you break them."

The result of this period away was an immediate success. *The Mai* was presented at the Dublin Festival in 1994, following a commission from the then artistic director of the Abbey, Garry Hynes. The following year the play toured to Glasgow's Mayfest and was later revived in Dublin for a second run at the Abbey. The play marks a distinct turning point in Carr's writing; although a certain existential disquiet still lurks behind the subject of the unfulfilled woman, the dramatic style is rich, lyrical, tragic, and original. The laconic humor of the absurd is replaced with the emotional depth of the mythic.

The play tells the story of Mai, a forty-year-old woman whose husband, Robert, has left her, and whose life is taken up with hoping and waiting for his return. Successful and independent in every sense except for her relationship with Robert, she has built him a house on the shore of Owl Lake, where she sits at the window and watches for him. Robert does indeed return, only to leave her again, a plight that she finds herself unable to bear a second time. Recalling the local legend, in which the mythical Coillte is said to have been drowned in the lake formed by her own tears after being left by her lover Bláth, the story ends with the heartbroken Mai committing suicide in Owl Lake.

The action takes place in 1979 and 1980, with narration in the present by the Mai's daughter, Millie, now thirty, but just sixteen at the time of the tragic events she recalls. A distinctive feature is the presence on stage of four generations of women, including the outrageous Grandma Fraochlán, age one hundred. The three women are complemented by the Mai's two younger sisters, Beck and Connie, and her two elderly aunts, Julie and Agnes. Robert, the husband, is the only man, a weak character surrounded by strong women. The repetitive cycle of destruction, a fundamental premise of much ancient Greek tragedy, is echoed through the reenactment of Celtic legend. The storytelling structure, which illuminates the narration of family histories with strange prophetic dreams and ancient local lore, lifts the drama into a non-naturalistic domain in which past and present, the natural and the supernatural, the mundane and the magical seamlessly coincide.

Grandma Fraochlán, whose mysterious father was never seen again after her conception, remains obsessed with her lost husband, the "nine-fingered fisherman," just as the Mai is obsessed with Robert. The Mai's mother, Ellen, died in childbirth at twenty-seven, or, it is suggested, from a broken spirit, after being abandoned by her own husband. The Mai's daughter, Millie, has a young son by a married man in New York, who refuses to acknowledge paternity. Beck, the Mai's sister, has had a brief and unsuccessful marriage to an Australian. Patterns of behavior and aspiration are repeated across the generations, each woman being haunted by an inherited dream, "a yearning for all that [i]s exotic and unattainable." When their princes fail to materialize, disillusionment is the inevitable consequence.

The women's romanticism is undercut by Julie and Agnes, the two plain and elderly aunts, parochial busybodies advocating respectability and good Catholic values. The two women from "the Connemara click," armed with their fur coats and handbags, present a hilarious satire of family pettiness and materialism, handing out criticism and £20 notes with equal generosity. But even these two are not immune to the allure of romanticism; Julie casually remarks, "it's not fair they should teach us desperation so young or if they do they should never mention hope." The banality of the interfering aunts reveals, by contrast, the emotional integrity of the other women, who refuse to be satisfied with the ordinary. It is worth dreaming of the extraordinary, if only to glimpse the splendor of the impossible. The sensuous Grandma Fraochlán vehemently asserts the transcendent power of love in an absurd universe:

> You're born, you have sex, and then you die. And if you are wan a them lucky few whom the Gods has

Dust jacket, with the actress Olwen Fouere as the title character, for the published version (1995) of Carr's 1994 play about a woman who is deserted by her husband

> blessed, they will send to you a lover with whom you will partake of that most rare and sublime love there is to partake of on this world and lonely planet. I have been one of them priviledged few and I know of no higher love in this world or the next!

With her opium pipe, her mulberry wine, and the giant oar she brings with her as a token of the nine-fingered fisherman, Grandma Fraochlán is the embodiment of the sensuous dreams that both elevate and destroy women such as the Mai. Flaunting her own sensuality, the Mai "plays" her own body with her cello bow in front of Robert, as a taunt. Where Curtains hid her body to avoid the male gaze, the Mai tries to use hers for empowerment.

The part of the magnificent Grandma Fraochlán is written in a dialect suggestive of the Midlands. Juxtaposed with the more standard speech of the younger characters, her way of speaking seems to recall a way of life uncomplicated by the cosmopolitan world of materialism and banality and evokes what John Millington Synge described as the poetic brutality and joy of all that is "superb and wild in reality." The Mai lives and dies with all the dramatic intensity of a tragic heroine, but her restless yearning reflects an emotional reality common to all women who are waiting, as it were, for their prince to come.

Carr's romantic and melancholic emblems are a cello and the geese and swans that inhabit the lake and announce her death. The primeval quality of the symbolism enhances the spiritual and mythic quality of the piece as a whole, which is in stark contrast to her earlier style, although most of the themes recur–an exploration of motherhood and the emotional life of women, an awareness of the futility of existence.

Much of the imagery of *The Mai* is taken up again in Carr's next two plays, *Portia Coughlan* (1996) and *By the Bog of Cats* (1998), which are also set in her familiar landscape of the Midlands. A local landmark in her childhood was Pallas Lake, which is mentioned briefly in *Low in the Dark,* where its mythical associations are lightheartedly sketched: "Pallas Lake, named for Pallas Athene who swam here once." The more sinister Owl Lake of *The Mai* becomes, in *Portia Coughlan,* the Belmont River. Once again it is the locus of tragedy and of legend. The imagery of water in both plays has literal and metaphorical associations. Millie is haunted by it in *The Mai:* "I dream of water all the time. I'm floundering off the shore, or bursting towards the surface for air, or wrestling with a black swan trying to drag me under." She describes Owl Lake as a suffocating caul around her chest. In *Portia Coughlan,* the water again links death and the experience in the womb with another time before and after life, when Portia believes she will be reconciled with her brother, whose singing still calls her to the river.

The central character is haunted by her dead twin, with whom she had shared a profound, if technically incestuous, love and made a pact to be united forever by walking together into the river. At the last moment Portia let go and saved herself, leaving her twin, Gabriel, to drown. Now, some fifteen years later, Portia is thirty years of age, married to Raphael, a lesser angel than her brother, with three children, and still pining inconsolably for her loss. She suggests that their souls were essentially one, and that the twin brother's death deprived her of part of herself. The gender is significant: Carr seems to propose a Jungian theory of the coexistence of masculine and feminine, which coincides with ancient creation myths involving male and female twins.

The play was commissioned for the centenary of the National Maternity Hospital at Holles Street in Dublin, by recruiting one hundred women to donate £50 each toward the cost. Carr ran some workshops with the staff and was given a small room in the hospital in which to write. With its depth of passion and savage beauty, the play was unanimously heralded a remarkable success and later transferred from the Abbey's Peacock Stage to the Royal Court in London.

Once again Carr dares to sing the unsung desperation of women and, more particularly, of mothers, refusing any easy, sentimental celebration of motherhood in her offering for the Maternity Hospital. Like Grandma Fraochlán in *The Mai,* Portia finds herself unable to love her own children because all her passionate energy is consumed in her one true love. The playwright explains in the collection *Range and Reason–Women Playwrights on Playwriting* (1997):

> I don't think the world should assume that we are all natural mothers. . . . You're meant to adore your children at all times, and you're not meant to have a bad thought about them. That's fascism, you know, and it's elevating the child at the expense of the mother. . . . Having said that, I really do believe that children have to be protected. They have to be loved. Somewhere between the two, I think, something needs to be sorted out.

Like her forebears in *The Mai,* Portia yearns to transcend the limits of her petty life and dysfunctional family. She speaks her mind with brutal honesty, facing painful truths and inflicting cruel blows on those around her, particularly her husband, who is utterly devoted but pitifully dull. The irony is that, in a family where every individual bears the scars of physical and emotional deformation from one source or another, the intensity of Portia's obsessive desire for something more wholesome leads to her destruction through insanity and ultimately suicide. The tragedy of her demise is at once shocking and beautiful.

The name of the eponymous heroine comes from the combination of a local surname with the character from *The Merchant of Venice* (who also comes from Belmont and has to choose from a series of lovers). Carr also attributes the origins of the play to a story she once heard in County Offaly about a childhood friend. The third major source of the play is the rough boggy landscape of the Midlands, which Carr describes in an afterword to the published play as "a metaphor for the crossroads between the worlds."

The play is written phonetically in the local dialect, lending a harsh exoticism to the characters whose language swings between the comically forthright and a quasi-mystical lyricism. They are natural storytellers, with Portia telling the prophetic tale of how the Belmont River took its name. When the local community turned against a woman who could predict the future, blaming her for causing the catastrophes she foresaw, and impaled her on a stake, their injustice angered the god of the valley, Bel, who sent a tremendous flood to carry her out to the Atlantic Ocean. Her cries from the river still haunt the valley for those who have the sensibility to hear such things, as did Gabriel, and as does Portia.

Despite the shadowy presence of such supernatural forces, the tragic impulse is still given some genetic source. Again, four generations are represented, with Grandma Fraochlán reincarnated as the viscious yet comic Blaize Scully, Portia's grandmother, whose old age brings with it a refreshing liberation from the constraints of public decency: "An' ah toult you ah spint tha first eigh'y years a' me life howldin' me tongue, fuchin' an' blindin' inta tha pilla. An' Jaysus, if God sees fih ta gimme another eigh'y, tha'll be spint spachin' me mine foul nor fair."

The death notably occurs in the middle of the play, with the final act showing the events leading up to it. Despite this deflation of the ending, Benedict Nightingale in *The Times* commented "*Portia Coughlan* will probably be called melodramatic, but only because we live in an imaginatively timid age and Carr dares a lot." She is indeed an advocate of magic in theater and has expressed regret that the influence of television has reduced everything to the factual and banal.

Carr's 1998 play, *By the Bog of Cats,* revels in dark magic, featuring among its characters a ghost of a murder victim, a ghost fancier and the mysterious omniscient catwoman. Fiercer still than *Portia Coughlan,* designer Monica Frawley, in an interview in *The Irish Times* (26 September 1998), described the play as "Medea in the Midlands." Hester Swane is the woman abandoned by her lover, Carthage Kilbride, who is about to marry into money and respectability, in the person of Caroline Cassidy, the young daughter of a landowning farmer. With Josie, her seven-year-old daughter by Carthage, Hester waits every day for the return of her own mother, who deserted her as a child. The inexorable tragedy unfolds as Hester refuses to leave the bog where she was born, despite a series of warnings that she will not survive the day unless she does so. The audience learns how she once murdered her young brother, Joseph, out of jealousy for her mother's love, and the pattern of violence is ultimately repeated when she disrupts the wedding, sets fire to Carthage's property, and, in a desperate act of defiance, finally cuts her daughter's throat and gouges out her own heart.

The realization that she has failed to avoid repeating the pattern set by her mother, that she has failed to recover from the wounds of her childhood and fulfill her impossible dream, is at least partly what drives Hester to her dreadful fate.

She kills Josie so that the child will not be left to suffer the same lifetime of waiting for a mother who will never return, while others blacken her name with dark stories. The bilious grandmother, Mrs. Kilbride, is a constant reminder that history still repeats itself down the generations. The pattern of violence and loss, however, reverberates through all three families: Caroline Cassidy has no mother, while her father, Xavier, is accused of having killed his own son and let his other daughter die; Carthage Kilbride is said to have helped to kill Hester's brother; even the innocuous neighbor, Monica Murray, bears some responsibility for her own son's death.

Motifs from the previous two plays recur but are used to present an even bleaker picture of a woman's emotional crisis. The cello of *The Mai* becomes a plaintive violin; the remote bog is now frozen beneath ice and snow; the black swan, with whom Hester used to sleep and play as a child, is dead, presaging Hester's own death. The songs of the dead Josie Swane, like those of Gabriel Coughlan, haunt the Bog of Cats. The structure of the play is along classical lines, the action spanning a single day from dawn to dusk. The central wedding scene, full of black comedy and social satire, relieves the doom-laden atmosphere of the first act, before the gruesome ending of the tragedy. The play, under Patrick Mason's direction, was well received at the Dublin Festival in 1998. The only grounds for criticism in *The Irish Times* review were that the dramatic ingredients were "too rich."

On Raftery's Hill opened in Galway in a Druid Theatre production directed by Garry Hynes in May 2000, before transferring to the Royal Court Theatre in London on 29 June. "If Marine Carr's plays have been dark before this, she has descended into hell with *On Raftery's Hill,*" wrote Emer O'Kelly in *The Sunday Independent* (14 May 2000). He continued, "The play is relentless: the flesh crawls, the hairs rise on the back of the neck, the throat closes in panic. And through the seismic horror comes the explosive artistry of the born playwright."

Many of the now familiar themes and motifs are presents again in this play: the all-pervading bleakness of the Midlands landscape, a family in turmoil, the absent mother figure, and the eccentric grandmother reliving the sufferings of her past to the haunting sound of a violin. The play centers on Redmond Raftery, his two daughters, his mother, and his idiot son Ded, who lives in the cowshed. The structure develops by a process of tragic revelation as the audience discovers that Red has abused his elder daughter, who turns out to be the mother of her sister. The play leads relentlessly to the father's destruction of the younger daughter, hitherto relatively unharmed. The whole atmosphere is polluted: festering corpses lie in every field, where Red has shot animals and left them to rot on the land. The magic and lyricism of Carr's earlier plays has been pushed out in this theater of cruelty, which is still a long way removed from documentary realism. Metaphor abounds, but there are no angels in this particular hell. Interviewed by Lyn Gardner in *The Guardian* on 3 July 2000, Hynes explained; "There is a ferocity about the play and subject matter that is not easy. But it's only hard to believe if you don't want to believe it. . . . There has been a stunned quality to the response, and a degree of shock. There is a real need for people to think that people aren't like the family in the play." The play avoids any easy moralizing or sentimentality, which undoubtedly made its general reception more difficult in view of the sensitivity of the subject matter. The critics were enthusiastic; Michael Coveney in the *Daily Mail* (4 July 2000) wrote: "Marina Carr picks up where Eugene O'Neill left off." Luke Glancy in *The Times* (16 May 2000) was full of praise: "the writing throughout stylishly blends urban and Greek myth with tremendous precision, confidently soaring off into stratospheric riffs, then fearlessly tumbling into the pigsty. Carr has never written better dialogue." O'Kelly concluded, "this is a play that howls to be seen; its courage is matched only by its dramatic power."

References:

Eileen Battersby, "Marina of the Midlands," *Irish Times,* 4 May 2000;

Christopher Murray, *Twentieth-Century Irish Drama: Mirror Up to Nation* (Manchester & New York: Manchester University Press, 1997), pp. 235–238;

Clíodhna Ní Anluain, ed., *Reading the Future–Irish Writers in Conversation with Mike Murphy,* introduction by Decland Kiberd (Dublin: Lilliput Press in Association with RTÉ Radio 1, 2000);

Anthony Roche, *Contemporary Irish Drama from Beckett to McGuinness* (Dublin: Gill & Macmillan, 1994), pp. 286–288;

Heidi Stephenson and Natasha Langridge, eds., *Rage and Reason–Women Playwrights on Playwriting* (London: Methuen, 1997): 146–155;

Victoria White, "Twin Speak," *Irish Times* (19 March 1996): 10.

Jim Cartwright

(27 June 1958 -)

Maria M. Delgado
Queen Mary, University of London

PLAY PRODUCTIONS: *Road,* London, Royal Court Theatre Upstairs, 22 March 1986;

Bed, London, Royal National Theatre, Cottesloe Theatre, 8 March 1989;

To, Bolton, Octagon Theatre, 23 August 1989; revised as *Two,* Bolton, Octagon Theatre, 5 September 1989;

Baths, Bolton, Octagon Theatre, August 1990;

Eight Miles High, Bolton, Octagon Theatre, 20 May 1991; revised as *Stone Free,* Bristol, Bristol Theatre Royal, May 1994; revised as *Kiss the Sky,* London, Bush Theatre at the Shepherds Bush Empire, 19 August 1996;

The Rise and Fall of Little Voice, London, Royal National Theatre, Cottesloe Theatre, 16 June 1992;

I Licked a Slag's Deodorant, London, Royal Court Theatre Company at the Ambassadors Theatre, 28 November 1996;

Hard Fruit, London, Royal Court Theatre, 31 March 2000;

Prize Night, Manchester, Royal Exchange Theatre, 27 October 2000.

BOOKS: *Road* (London: Methuen, 1986; revised, 1990);

Bed (London: Methuen, 1991; revised, 1991);

To (London: Methuen, 1991); revised and published with the revised version of *Bed* as *Two and Bed* (London: Methuen, 1994);

The Rise and Fall of Little Voice (London: Methuen, 1992; revised, 1994);

I Licked a Slag's Deodorant (London: Methuen, 1996).

Collections: *Jim Cartwright Plays: 1* (London: Methuen, 1996);

Hard Fruit (London: Methuen, 2000).

PRODUCED SCRIPTS: *Road,* BBC Two, 1987;

Vroom, motion picture, screenplay by Cartwright, Film Four International, 1988;

June, BBC Two, 1990;

Wedded, BBC Two, 1990;

Bed, television, BBC Two, October 1995;

Little Voice, adapted from the play *The Rise and Fall of Little Voice,* motion picture, screenplay by Cartwright and Mark Herman, Scala Productions, 1998.

When the Royal Court Theatre in London programmed Jim Cartwright's *Hard Fruit* for its first production of the 2000–2001 season at its newly refurbished Sloane Square venue, the choice proved Cartwright's rising status in contemporary British theater. Acclaimed by the Royal Court's artistic director, Ian Rickson, as "easily his best play since *Road,*" *Hard Fruit* explores a "hidden world of chest-expanding, middle-aged men who . . . would never have called themselves gay but who have homosexual experiences." The play serves as further confirmation of Cartwright's ability to probe the sociocultural landcapes of Northern England, forging dramatic works that, while rooted in the region's urban environment, can never be simply reduced to that milieu. From the blistering dissection of Prime Minister Margaret Thatcher's England rendered in *Road* (1986)–perhaps the key play of the 1980s in its willingness to move beyond the small-cast, interior-set dramas that dominated the new writing scene at the time–to the imaginative canvases of disenchanted masculinity portrayed in *The Rise and Fall of Little Voice* (1992), *Two* (1989), *Prize Night* (2000), and *Hard Fruit* (2000), Cartwright has reflected the crisis of the moment in the ambitious narratives of his fierce poetic plays.

Cartwright was born on 27 June 1958 in Farnworth, on the edge of Bolton in Lancashire. In an interview in *The Independent* (19 October 1992) he recalled, "My father worked in a factory all his life; my mother read a lot–about six thrillers a week. I went to a secondary modern, a low academic achievement school, a kind of conveyor belt to the factory or, for the girls, the mills. If you were lucky you got a trade, as an engineeer or an electrician." In 1986 he claimed to have read only three books in his life, *The Catcher in the Rye* (1951), *Skinhead* (1982), and *The Life of Buddha.* As he explained to the *Guardian,* "those books contain everything there is to know, I reckon. I'm not very literate me, but why not lib-

Missie Smith, Susan Brown, and Jane Horrocks in the 1987 Royal Court Theatre production of Jim Cartwright's first play, Road

erate theatre from the idea that you have to have a degree or talk posh to be any good in it?" He was fortunate, however, in that some teachers at the school, Harper Green secondary modern, encouraged him to think beyond the confines of such a predetermined future. He started to write poems, although, as he has said, it was the sort of school "where if you came out with an O' level they thought you were a genius." (O' levels were examinations, now replaced, that were required of sixteen-year-olds in England.) The school had a thriving drama department and, while Cartwright recalls visiting his local theater, the Bolton Octagon, only once, to see a play about the Bolton Wanderers football team, he recalls an English teacher reading William Shakespeare's *Richard III* to the class: "it blew me mind."

Leaving school at sixteen, Cartwright was employed in a warehouse "stacking boxes, the ultimate dull job," and found work as an actor. He got a place at drama school but was soon disenchanted and left to work with a friend on performances in people's houses–including a version of Alfred Hitchcock's *Psycho* (1960), which included the famous shower scene in the bathroom. He had started to write pieces of plays and submitted them to the Royal Court Theatre in London, where he was then living; but, disillusioned with acting, he returned to Farnworth hoping, and failing, to find work to subsidize his writing. Signing on as unemployed, he may have lived something of the life that is reflected in *Road.* He married Angela Jones, who worked in the dole office in 1984, and had a child.

Cartwright continued to submit scripts to the Royal Court and, in the mid 1980s, secured a rehearsed reading and a full commission that became *Road,* his first play. The production opened at the Royal Court's Upstairs Theatre in March 1986 before transferring to the main stage. In an interview for *Independent,* Cartwright recalled, "It took them a while, but eventually they did a reading and it went down really well. They were just bits of scenes. They commissioned me to do a play and it took me a while to get it together–not to write it but to get round to doing it. And then suddenly I was a writer, as if it was an accident."

Road went on to win the Samuel Beckett Award (1986), *Drama* magazine award (1986), *Plays and Players Award* (1986), and the George Devine Award (1986). That same year Cartwright became resident writer at the Royal Court, the success of his first play having given him some financial security for the first time.

Produced three times within an eighteen-month period in an exciting promenade production by Simon Curtis, *Road* immediately established Cartwright as a dynamic voice in British theater. The epic structure of the play and its challenging, uncompromising language captures the desperation of a poverty-stricken underclass in Northern Britain. Cartwright's evocation of the activities during an evening on a road in a fictional town ravaged by unemployment serves to restore a transformational sense of theatricality to a stage dominated by realist writers seeking to deliver narrow moralistic verdicts on microcosms of British society. The work also acutely condemns the sociopolitical agenda of Thatcher's Britain without ever once mentioning her name. Through Cartwright's bold, brash, poetic dialect, the contemporary odyssey through a road with no name introduces an array of stunted, impoverished characters seeking short-term relief from their desolation and sense of futility in sex and the bottle. Short, staccato scenes unfold to reveal domestic and public worlds of frightening extremities where the language of the characters is as soiled and unromanticized as the clothes they wear, the food they eat, and the houses they live in. Stark melancholy and robust humor interlock in a poignant elegy to wretched lives in search of elusive comforts. Reflecting and commenting on the squalor and degeneration of their environment, the coexisting narratives of Cartwright's characters serve constantly to evoke both a shattered world of broken dreams and acute social distress, and a reenergized theatrical landscape whose possibilities are constantly being reinvented through a dynamic reworking of audience-performer relationships.

Narrative disorientation is matched in visual and aural terms by constantly shifting locations, multiple areas of focus, intersecting story lines, and a rich montage of sounds (laughter, cries, singing, people passing, and dogs barking) working with the dialogue to create an alternative stage world. Self-pity and dogmatic moralizing are emphatically banished from the stage in an often unsettlingly funny exploration of an urban Britain in which materialistic comforts are few and far between.

Cartwright's second play, *Bed* (1989), commissioned and produced by the Royal National Theatre for the Cottesloe Theatre, also investigates questions of space and surroundings in its lyrical Beckettian exploration of the ravages of time. On a giant thirty-foot bed that dominates the stage, seven elderly individuals occupy a dreamworld that hovers between sleep and waking. Memories and dreams interact with a gentle simplicity as the past is conjured from dark insecure recesses. Once again dispensing with the constraints of plot, *Bed* offers a surrealistic journey into a terrain of painful elegies where nostalgia for a past that might or might not have been punctures the fabric of the text.

Baths, first written for radio and broadcast in 1987, was first staged in a double bill with *Bed* in August 1990 at Bolton's Octagon Theatre. The director, Andrew Hay, was to go on to direct further premiere productions of Cartwright's work while the playwright enjoyed a residency with the theater (1989–1991). With a specially commissioned score by Chris Monks and Akintayo Akinbode, *Baths* evokes dance theater in its refined musicality. Here the rituals of the poolside are wittily deconstructed to provide an amusing examination of the pleasures, delights, and fears of a life spent posturing in search of the body beautiful–a theme he took up again in *Hard Fruit.*

Two, first produced as *To* by Bolton's Octagon Theatre with two high-profile soap-opera stars, John McArdle and Sue Johnstone, consolidated Cartwright's reputation as a poet of the vernacular. His fierce, dramatically exuberant vignettes of personal desolation inhabit an uneasy space between popular and established conventions. The cast of two portray a succession of characters, moving from anguished bickering publicans to the eccentric but always credible clientele who frequent the tired locale. As in *Road* and *Bed* Cartwright demonstrates an uncanny ability to create a world of experiences, pleasures, and fears where the potential of role-playing unlocks an array of possible narrative encounters. The coiling interludes display a dialogic range of veritable skill where the frugality of the recommended decor–mirrored in the play's bleakly suggestive title–encourage a focus on the performers where raucous dramatic exuberance is employed to tremendous visual effect.

In Cartwright's subsequent play, *The Rise and Fall of Little Voice,* written for the versatile actress Jane Horrocks who was also one of the performers in the second production of *Road,* role-play is given pivotal narrative space. Here again the dramatic space of the play rests effortlessly between the genres of soap opera, cabaret, fairy tale, domestic comedy, and social drama. This mixing of genres gives the play its bittersweet tone, allowing comparisons to be drawn with the colorful excesses of Tennessee Williams's work. In slimy third-rate theatrical agent Ray Say and the loud vivacious widow Mari Hoff, Cartwright creates figures both resourcefully attractive and selfishly repellent. Occupying a space that both invokes and acknowledges their textual antecedents, both characters serve as constant reminders of the hard sell of capitalism in its more pathetic manifestations, but they are always governed by a wit and humor that keeps them within the realms of the credible. In the timid, frightened Little Voice who finds solace and comfort in the vinyl recordings of Judy Garland, Shirley Bassey, and Edith Piaf bequeathed to her by her now-dead father, Cartwright offers a beguiling picture of the transition from shy, awkward teenager to resolute young woman. In addition, as with *Road,* the play demonstrates the redemptive potential of music to invigorate lives crushed by the banal forces of poverty and greed.

Praised by Charles Spencer in the *Daily Telegraph* (19 June 1992) for its "knack of combining gritty realism with whimsical echoes of fairytales" and what Nicholas

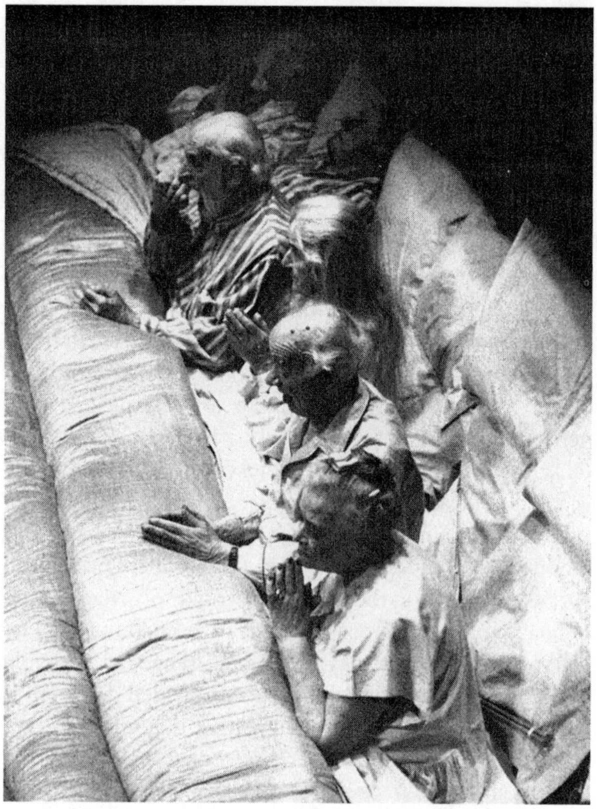

A scene from Cartwright's Bed, *which premiered at the Cottesloe Theatre of the Royal National Theatre on 8 March 1989*

de Jongh in the *Evening Standard* (17 June 1992) calls its "drive, its rough comedy and its emotional power," *The Rise and Fall of Little Voice* enjoyed a conspicuous run at the Cottesloe Theatre before its transfer to the Aldwych Theatre in London's West End. There Alison Steadman's and Jane Horrocks's frenetic performances as the estranged mother and daughter met with widespread critical acclaim. The play won two prestigious awards: the 1992 *Evening Standard* Award for best comedy and the Olivier Award for best comedy in 1993. Cartwright's ability to write strong roles for women, demonstrated in all his work, is here perhaps most evident. Mari Hoff and Little Voice are both a metaphor for the most troubled of mother-daughter relationships and a constant reminder of the ability of women to reinvent themselves within the oppressive constraints of a patriarchal society. In the character of the seedy, sleazy showbiz agent, Ray Say, Cartwright offers a gloriously perceptive vision of a figure desperate to break out of an unsuccessful circuit of tacky local acts, grasping at a final chance of lasting financial success. The appeal of the play rests both in its acknowledgement of its mythical resonances (especially the *Cinderella* narrative) and its dynamic pace and direct, alert language. The play enjoyed a substantial West End run in Sam Mendes's vibrant production and a Broadway opening in a staging by the Chicago-based Steppenwolf Company, directed by Simon Curtis. The play has proved Cartwright's most commercially successful play to date.

Cartwright moved firmly into the domain of musical theater with *Eight Miles High* in 1991 at the Bolton Octagon Theatre, directed by Andy Hay. Later revised as *Stone Free* in 1994 in a production at the Bristol Old Vic, and revived there again in 1996 before touring to the Liverpool Playhouse, the play was received as a nostalgic celebration of the hedonistic open-air festivals of the 1960s. Dependent on audience participation, its humor emanated from the various mind-altering trips suffered by the characters and recounted with languid vigor. The play was also produced at the Sýntiborgar-Leikhúsinv Theater in Iceland in 1996, where it enjoyed a long and successful run. Popular songs from the time are interspersed throughout the sketchy narrative; a traveler returns home to Lancashire where the spirit of San Francisco is infecting his own backyard. As with *Road* and *The Rise and Fall of Little Voice,* music permeates the texture of the work, but the results are never as satisfyingly visceral as in the earlier pieces.

I Licked a Slag's Deodorant (1996), premiered by the Royal Court at the Ambassadors Theatre, is in many ways Cartwright's sparest and most severe play. Two characters simply called Slag and Man meet in a London street. Cartwright provides little information about them. She is a crack addict who feeds her habit through the ill-gotten gains of prostitution. He may or may not be retarded, a loser in search of affection in the aftermath of his mother's death. The play revolves around a series of agonizing monologues conducted by each of the characters in a range of different locales. Each speaks of a life marked by loneliness and grief where brutality reigns in a range of obvious and less apparent manifestations. They drift together, driven by a need for some sort of companionship. As directed by Cartwright on a grimy set by William Dudley, the work is a devastating vision of life on the edge. The terrain of the play is both graphically shocking and devastatingly moving. Its raw evocative language serves as both a lethal weapon and a soothing balm. In the final image the withdrawal chronicled is both the antithesis of the finale of *The Rise and Fall of Little Voice* and a lean antidote to the empty jargon of Hollywood's formulaic handling of the prostitute-client relationship.

The suggestive and even provocative titles of Cartwright's plays have sought to warn the reader/audience of the journey to the shabbier and more bruising corners of contemporary urban life. Like Mark Ravenhill's *Shopping and F***ing* (1996) Cartwright's work has presented, with harrowing intensity, the depraved and degrading lives of a displaced underclass where every utterance questions the vacuous rhetoric of political discourses. Manipulating a range of dramatic genres, Cartwright has established a distinctive voice that, while echoing the theatrical vocabulary of a range of works, perhaps most conspicuously Dylan Thomas's *Under Milk Wood* (1954) and Edward Bond's *Saved* (1965), revels in its own habitation of a sphere of narrative, stylistic, and thematic dislocation.

Hard Fruit, directed by James Macdonald at the Royal Court in 2000, deals with the competitive ethos of male bodybuilding. Cartwright's protagonist, Choke (a brilliant performance by Nicholas Woodeson), believes in stringent self-control, self-restraint, and self-discipline to the point that any degree of vulnerability is seen as weakness. He attempts to convince himself; his neighbor, Mrs. Kooee; and his closest friend, Sump, that he is a machine that cannot break down. His rigid concept of masculinity views illness as an unforgiveable weakness and homosexuality as degrading. Attracted to men, while refusing to label himself gay, he seeks to build the ideal fighting partner, a karate machine that can never let him down. He cowers from human contact ("I never hug. I never touch people, 'cept in a headlock or with a block. I don't know how"), but the occasional collapse of his defenses offers a remarkable insight into a hardened mentality where sexuality has no place. His encounters with the nightclub bouncer Friar Jiggle, the elderly Yack, and the young Silver, whom Yack wants Choke to teach self-defense, situate Choke as a vintage Cartwright character: an individual shaped by his environment who no longer fits into a rapidly changing world but is "always fighting, fighting his true self."

Prize Night, produced at Manchester's Royal Exchange Theatre in 2000, is an autobiographical tale of a northern writer returning to his hometown after years away. Cartwright himself played the role of the local lad coming home for a school prize night. His odyssey through a terrain of memories and reminiscences provides echoes of the fantastical strands of *Road,* but there are also touches of the humor of *Two* in the writer's drinking encounters in his old haunts.

Although Cartwright's voice is particularly theatrical, drawing on and playing with the dangerous proximity of the performer-audience axis, he has also embraced radio, television, and movies to an impressive degree of success. A television production of *Road,* made by Alan Clarke, was first screened in October 1987. The character of Scullery, among others, was omitted, but the idea of the journey through the road was effectively conveyed by a handheld camera filming characters walking through the identical terraced streets where boarded-up windows, scrawny exteriors, and unkempt grass conveyed a landscape of unmitigating bleakness. Empty interiors devoid of comforting furnishings, harsh abrasive lighting, and characters addressing the camera created the aura of a mirage–a world at once removed and yet still painfully recognizable. The peculiar linguistic territory occupied by Cartwright–compact prose governed by the economic syntax of poetry–was complimented by a visual idiom that relentlessly reinforced the dangerous precipice on which the characters exist. Consistently challenging both the mindless (television) and oppressive (surveillance) use habitually made of video, Clarke's rhythmic treatment of *Road* offered a taut drama of tremendous compassion and startling force.

Bed also made the transition from stage to screen in a production adapted and directed for television by Steve Shill. Broadcast in October 1995 as part of the BBC Two *Performance* series, the screen version was given a more tangible location, set both in a hospital and inside the head of a character called the Captain. Once again, the play occupies a fragile space between the real and the imagined, and the irreal atmosphere created in the premiere production was evoked within a magical set that suggests both past and present and accommodates a range of moods and locations.

An earlier television play, *June,* screened in January 1990 on BBC Two, is a compact, delicately crafted monologue exploring some of the preoccupations around emotional suppression and closeted grief which beset a middle-aged woman confronted with a stark reminder of an era where she was made to feel she "was in the movies" and from which she has never fully managed to break free. In Marjorie Yates's brittle performance, *June* provided a nostalgic exploration of a world of buried memories unearthed when she receives a cassette from her wartime lover. Imbued with a thread of yearning for an era long past, *June* drew on motifs which had surfaced in both *Road* and *Bed.* Additionally, the dark humor also gave it something of the feel of Alan Bennett's successful "Talking Head" monologues, which were similarly concerned with women reflecting on lives taken in directions seemingly beyond their control.

Wedded, broadcast as part of a Screenplay Double Bill in August 1990, provided two concurrent monologues delivered by a husband and wife negotiating the breakup of a marriage. Commended by critic Thomas Sutcliffe in the *Independent* (30 August 1990) for its "grasp of the awkward collisions of the mundane and the mythic," the piece articulated the pain of noncommunication, misunderstandings, and unsaid grievances with brutal probity. Moreover, the wife's obsession with Shirley Bassey records suggests a life that finds release and redemption in popular music of the past, something also touched on in *Road* and further developed in *The Rise and Fall of Little Voice.*

Vroom, directed by Beeban Kidron, premiered as the Centrepiece presentation at the 1988 London Film

Sue Johnson and John McArdle in the Bolton Octagon Theatre production of Cartwright's Two *(1989)*

Festival, designed to showcase "a new film of unusual interest by a first-time director." Crucially, the work demonstrated the transfer of Cartwright's dramatic idiom to film. Shot in Accrington, the movie charts the (mis)adventures of close friends, Jake (played by Clive Owen) and Ringe (played by David Thewlis), who escape the doldrums of unemployment and boredom through an American car that evokes a bygone era of wild hedonism and carefree adventure. The arrival of an older woman, Susan (Diana Quick), next door serves to complicate the men's friendship, but the dream to transcend the physical misery of their immediate environment prevails, and the protagonists depart for a new life. Part social drama, part road movie, part romantic comedy, Cartwright's screenplay demonstrates an ability to transcend generic classifications, moving toward fantasy as a strategy for survival–both in filmic and personal terms.

Little Voice, adapted by director Mark Herman, opened the 1998 London Film Festival. With a cast including Michael Caine, Brenda Blethyn, and Ewan McGregor, the motion picture inhabited a landscape that invoked the idiom of *Coronation Street,* the Ealing Comedies, and even the bleaker humor of director Ken Loach. Described by Philip French in the *Observer Review* (8 November 1998) as "rather like *A Taste of Honey* reworked by Donald McGill with the assistance of Dennis Potter," *Little Voice* evoked a magical world of musical transformation where, as in *Road,* characters and audiences alike were transported to a dazzling world of Oz where anything and everything is possible. Jane Horrocks, re-creating the character she had conceived for Sam Mendes's stage production in 1992, offered a startling interpretation of introspective grief and an energizing indication of the power of culture to provide solace, comfort, and verve in the most desperate of circumstances. Through the appropriation of other voices, Little Voice finds her own. Her defiance, compassion, and vigor emerge at the end of the play as a positive strategy for survival in a world of unscrupulous selfishness. *Little Voice,* like *Road,* is testament to Cartwright's belief in the healing qualities of culture in a world where there is little one can be sure of and in which anything and everything can be bought and sold if the price is right. Cartwright's work celebrates the ability to dream, to envisage a better world, and the role of popular culture in facilitating that process. Cartwright provides a stage world devoid of judgments. Reinventing language for the demands of a nation beyond the prosperous Southeast of Thatcher's "classless" England, Cartwright's work occupies an important place in the contemporary British landscape. No other dramatist of his generation has succeeded in forging a dramatic language whose raw energy oscillates so defiantly between magical verse and grim prose. While evoking a tradition that encapsulates Thomas, Williams, Arnold Wesker, and John Osborne, Cartwright has always proved, as Michael Billington has shrewdly observed, "his very own man," a figure who refuses easy categorization. In its pushing of dramatic boundaries and its reenvisaging of the theatrical space, his work has provided to a new generation of dramatists–Mark Ravenhill, Sarah Kane, Martin McDonagh–an example of the defiant potential of the stage to shock, disturb, provoke, and provide a space for dreaming in a society where the pursuit of wealth is all pervasive.

Moreover, in his own recent renegotiation of the roles of dramatist and director, Cartwright has demonstrated an acute understanding of the visceral vocabulary of the stage. In his productions of both *Road* and *I Licked a Slag's Deodorant,* the architectural environments of the Royal Exchange and Ambassadors Theatres were crucially exploited to provide locations of devastating sensorial intensity. The eerily lit, squelching, damp circular set of *I Licked a Slag's Deodorant* was a metaphorical battlefield of relentless gloom and imprisonment, where Polly Hemingway's Slag and Tim Potter's Man confront each other in a series of raw encounters distinguished by what Billington in the *Guardian* (7 December 1996) described as a "sense of sadness and recognition of everybody's crying need for company." In *Road* Laurie Dennett's design emphasized verticality. Characters hung precariously from the gallery and stumbled through the audience evoking images of drunken waywardness. An imaginative use of the public spaces enveloping the auditorium offered raucous, riveting entertainment and a radical sense of theater that exploded the barriers that habitually define and delineate audience and performer spaces. Nothing and no one was safe in a production where the unexpected reared its head to confront an audience denied the safety of the darkened auditorium.

Max Stafford-Clark's decision to tour *Road* as one of the initial productions of his new company, Out of Joint, in 1994 in a proscenium arch production, as well as the reinvention of the play in a range of stagings (traverse, in-the-round, combinations of promenade and seating, in outdoor venues) in Ireland, North America, and beyond, demonstrate its versalitity, resilience, and elasticity. *Road* may have been perceived as the quintessential state-of-the-nation play of the 1980s, but the vibrant stagings it has received in the 1990s confirm it as a poignant reenvisaging of the continuing potential of the theater to rewrite both social and stage history. Rather than fade into obscurity, the play has accomodated a range of powerful readings. Cartwright's subsequent work has drawn on the techniques demonstrated in this first play, listed by Geoff Sadler as "the adroit use of loosely linked episodes and diverse characters . . . familiar Northern social venues–bar, disco, and chip shop, as well as the street itself," while reinventing them for each new piece. Served not only by a superlative group of actors (including Horrocks, Hemingway, and Lesley Sharp), and directors (including Curtis, Hay, and Mendes) who have revelled in the exuberant theatricality of the plays, and more recently by the raw urgency of his own direction, Cartwright exposed the limitations of the dramatic language of playwrights who dominated the English stage in the early 1980s. In so doing he redefined the parameters of theatrical discourse, incorporating a juxtaposition of cabaret, popular music, and stand-up comedy with a poetry which never erases its own roots in the speech patterns of a Northern urban underclass whose resilience, desperation, and endurance, while never romanticized, is compassionately imagined for the stage. His plays are continously in production worldwide and have been translated into more than twenty languages.

Interviews:

Stephen Grant, "On the High Road," *Guardian,* 7 June 1986;

Sid Smith, "Road to Ruin," *Chicago Tribune,* 21 June 1987;

Alex Renton, "Rounded with a Sleep," *Independent,* 8 March 1989;

Charles Spencer, "Northern Lad Makes Very Good," *Daily Telegraph,* 12 October 1992;

David Nathan, "Double Take," *Independent,* 19 October 1992;

Robin Thornber, "Road to Success," *Guardian,* 1 March 1995.

References:

Michael Billington, "Jim Cartwright," in *Contemporary British Dramatists,* edited by K. A. Berney and N. G. Templeton (London: St. James Press, 1994): 119–121;

Ruby Cohn, *Retreats from Realism in Recent English Drama* (Cambridge: Cambridge University Press, 1991), pp. 44–48;

K. A. McLennan, *"Road," Theatre Journal,* 40: 1 (1988): 114–116;

Michael Ratcliffe, *"Road," Drama,* 161 (1986): 35;

Alan Riding, "Creating Angry Art Amid Britain's Plenty," *New York Times* (6 April 1997): 1, 38;

Geoff Sadler, "Road," in *Contemporary British Dramatists,* edited by Berney and Templeton (London: St. James Press, 1994): 805–807;

Anthony Shrubshall, "A Review of *Plays 1* and *I Licked a Slag's Deodorant,*" *Contemporary Theatre Review,* 7: 4 (1998): 125–127.

Agatha Christie

(13 September 1890 – 12 January 1976)

Lucy Kay

Liverpool Hope University College

See also the Christie entries in *DLB 13: British Dramatists Since World War II* and *DLB 77: British Mystery Writers, 1920–1939.*

Agatha Christie (from the Raymond Mander and Joe Mitchenson Theatre Collection)

PLAY PRODUCTIONS: *Black Coffee,* London, Embassy Theatre, 8 December 1930;

Ten Little Niggers, adapted by Christie from her novel, London, St. James's Theatre, 17 November 1943; produced again as *Ten Little Indians,* New York, Broadhurst Theatre, 27 June 1944;

Appointment with Death, adapted by Christie from her 1938 novel, London, Piccadilly Theatre, 31 March 1945;

Murder on the Nile, adapted by Christie from her 1937 novel, *Death on the Nile,* London, Ambassadors Theatre, 19 March 1946; produced again as *Hidden Horizon,* New York, Plymouth Theatre, 19 September 1946;

The Hollow, adapted from Christie's novel, London, Fortune Theatre, 7 June 1951;

The Mousetrap, adapted by Christie from her short story and radio play, *Three Blind Mice* (1947), London, Ambassadors Theatre, 25 November 1952; New York, Maidman Playhouse, 5 November 1960;

Witness for the Prosecution, adapted by Christie from her story, London, Winter Garden Theatre, 28 October 1953; New York, Henry Miller's Theater, 16 December 1954;

Spider's Web, London, Savoy Theatre, 14 December 1954; New York, Lolly's Theatre Club, 15 January 1974;

Towards Zero, adapted by Christie and Gerald Verner from her 1944 novel, London, St. James's Theatre, 4 September 1956;

Verdict, London, Strand Theatre, 22 May 1958;

The Unexpected Guest, London, Duchess Theatre, 12 August 1958;

Go Back for Murder, adapted from Christie's *Five Little Pigs* (1943), London, Duchess Theatre, 23 March 1960;

Rule of Three: Afternoon at the Seaside, The Patient, and *The Rats,* London, Duchess Theatre, 20 December 1962;

Fiddler's Three, Guildford, Yvonne Arnaud Theatre, 1 August 1972;

A Murder Is Announced, adapted by Christie from her 1950 novel, London, Vaudeville Theatre, 21 September 1977;

Akhnaton and Nefertiti, New York, 1979.

BOOKS: *The Mysterious Affair at Styles: A Detective Story* (London & New York: John Lane, 1920);

The Secret Adversary (London & New York: John Lane, 1922; New York: Dodd, Mead, 1922);

The Murder on the Links (London: John Lane, 1923; New York: Dodd, Mead, 1923);

The Man in the Brown Suit (London: John Lane, 1924; New York: Dodd, Mead, 1924);

Poirot Investigates (London: John Lane, 1924; New York: Dodd, Mead, 1925);

The Secret of Chimneys (London: John Lane, 1925; New York: Dodd, Mead, 1925);

The Road of Dreams (London: Bles, 1925); republished as *Poems* (London: Collins, 1973; New York: Dodd, Mead, 1973);

The Murder of Roger Ackroyd (London: Collins, 1926; New York: Dodd, Mead, 1926);

The Under Dog, and Other Stories (London: Dodd, Mead, 1926);

The Big Four (London: Collins, 1927; New York: Dodd, Mead, 1927);

The Mystery of the Blue Train (London: Collins, 1928; New York: Dodd, Mead, 1928);

Partners in Crime (London: Collins, 1929; New York: Dodd, Mead, 1929);

The Seven Dials Mystery (London: Collins, 1929; New York: Dodd, Mead, 1929);

Giant's Bread, as Mary Westmacott (London: Collins, 1930; Garden City, N.Y.: Doubleday, Doran, 1930);

The Murder at the Vicarage (New York: Dodd, Mead, 1930; London: Collins, 1935);

The Mysterious Mr. Quin (London: Collins, 1930; New York: Dodd, Mead, 1930);

The Sittaford Mystery (London: Collins, 1931); republished as *The Murder at Hazelmoor* (New York: Dodd, Mead, 1931);

The Thirteen Problems (London: Collins, 1932); republished as *The Tuesday Club Murders* (New York: Dodd, Mead, 1933); republished as *Miss Marple's Final Cases* (London: Collins, 1972);

Peril at End House (London: Collins, 1932; New York: Dodd, Mead, 1932);

The Hound of Death and Other Stories (London: Odhams, 1933);

Lord Edgeware Dies (London: Collins, 1933); republished as *Thirteen at Dinner* (New York: Dodd, Mead, 1933);

Black Coffee (London: Ashley, 1934; Boston: Baker, 1934);

The Listerdale Mystery and Other Stories (London: Collins, 1934);

Murder in Three Acts (New York: Dodd, Mead, 1934); republished as *Three Act Tragedy* (London: Collins, 1935);

Murder on the Orient Express (London: Collins, 1934); republished as *Murder on the Calais Coach* (New York: Dodd, Mead, 1934);

Parker Pyne Investigates (London: Collins, 1934); republished as *Mr. Parker Pyne, Detective* (New York: Dodd, Mead, 1934);

Unfinished Portrait, as Westmacott (London: Collins, 1934; New York: Doubleday, Doran, 1934);

Why Didn't They Ask Evans? (London: Collins, 1934); republished as *The Boomerang Clue* (New York: Dodd, Mead, 1935);

Death in the Air (New York: Dodd, Mead, 1935); republished as *Death in the Clouds* (London: Collins, 1935);

The A. B. C. Murders: A New Poirot Mystery (London: Collins, 1936; New York: Dodd, Mead, 1936);

Cards on the Table (London: Collins, 1936; New York: Dodd, Mead, 1937);

Murder in Mesopotamia (London: Collins, 1936; New York: Dodd, Mead, 1936);

Murder in the Mews and Other Stories (London: Collins, 1937); republished as *Dead Man's Mirror and Other Stories* (New York: Dodd, Mead, 1937);

Death on the Nile (London: Collins, 1937; New York: Dodd, Mead, 1938);

Dumb Witness (London: Collins, 1937); republished as *Poirot Loses a Client* (New York: Dodd, Mead, 1937);

Appointment with Death (London: Collins, 1938; New York: Dodd, Mead, 1938);

Hercule Poirot's Christmas (London: Collins, 1938); republished as *Murder for Christmas* (New York: Dodd, Mead, 1939); republished as *A Holiday for Murder* (New York: Avon, 1947);

Murder Is Easy (London: Collins, 1939); republished as *Easy to Kill* (New York: Dodd, Mead, 1939);

Ten Little Niggers (London: Collins, 1939); republished as *And Then There Were None* (New York: Dodd, Mead, 1940);

The Regatta Mystery, and Other Stories (New York: Dodd, Mead, 1939);

One, Two, Buckle My Shoe (London: Collins, 1940); republished as *The Patriotic Murders* (New York: Dodd, Mead, 1941);

Sad Cypress (London: Collins, 1940; New York: Dodd, Mead, 1940);

Evil Under the Sun (London: Collins, 1941; New York: Dodd, Mead, 1941);

N or M? (London: Collins, 1941; New York: Dodd, Mead, 1941);
The Body in the Library (London: Collins, 1942; New York: Dodd, Mead, 1942);
The Moving Finger (New York: Dodd, Mead, 1942; London: Collins, 1943);
Five Little Pigs (London: Collins, 1942); republished as *Murder in Retrospect* (New York: Dodd, Mead, 1942);
The Mystery of the Baghdad Chest (London: Bantam, 1943);
The Mystery of the Crime in Cabin 66 (London: Bantam, 1943);
Poirot and the Regatta Mystery (London: Bantam, 1943);
Poirot on Holiday (London: Todd, 1943);
Problem at Pollensa Bay, and The Christmas Adventure (London: Todd, 1943);
The Veiled Lady, and The Mystery of the Baghdad Chest (London: Todd, 1944);
Death Comes as the End (New York: Dodd, Mead, 1944; London: Collins, 1945);
Towards Zero (London: Collins, 1944; New York: Dodd, Mead, 1944);
Absent in the Spring, as Mary Westmacott (London: Collins, 1944; New York: Farrar & Rinehart, 1944);
Ten Little Niggers [play] (London: S. French, 1945); republished as *Ten Little Indians* (New York & London: S. French, 1946);
Sparkling Cyanide (London: Collins, 1945); republished as *Remembered Death* (New York: Dodd, Mead, 1945);
Come, Tell Me How You Live (London: Collins, 1946; New York: Dodd, Mead, 1946);
The Hollow [novel] (London: Collins, 1946; New York: Dodd, Mead, 1946);
Poirot Knows the Murderer (London: Todd, 1946);
Murder on the Nile: A Play in Three Acts (New York: S. French, 1946; London: S. French, 1948);
Come, Tell Me How You Live, as Agatha Christie Mallowan (London: Collins, 1946; New York: Dodd, Mead, 1946);
The Labours of Hercules: Short Stories (London: Collins, 1947); republished as *The Labors of Hercules: New Adventures in Crime by Hercule Poirot* (New York: Dodd, Mead, 1947);
Witness for the Prosecution and Other Stories (New York: Dodd, Mead, 1948);
The Rose and the Yew Tree, as Westmacott (London: Heinemann, 1948; New York: Rinehart, 1948);
Taken at the Flood (London: Collins, 1948); republished as *There Is a Tide* (New York: Dodd, Mead, 1948);
Three Blind Mice and Other Stories (New York: Dodd, Mead, 1948); republished as *The Mousetrap and Other Stories* (New York: Dell, 1949);
Crooked House (London: Collins, 1949; New York: Dodd, Mead, 1949);
A Murder Is Announced (London: Collins, 1950; New York: Dodd, Mead, 1950);
Blood Will Tell (New York: Black, 1951);
They Came to Baghdad (London: Collins, 1951; New York: Dodd, Mead, 1951);
The Under Dog and Other Stories (New York: Dodd, Mead, 1951);
Murder with Mirrors (New York: Dodd, Mead, 1952); republished as *They Do It with Mirrors* (London: Collins, 1952);
The Hollow [play] (London: S. French, 1952; New York: S. French, 1952);
Mrs. McGinty's Dead (London: Collins, 1952; New York: Dodd, Mead, 1952);
A Daughter's a Daughter, as Westmacott (London: Heinemann, 1952);
After the Funeral (London: Collins, 1953); republished as *Funerals Are Fatal* (New York: Dodd, Mead, 1953);
A Pocket Full of Rye (London: Collins, 1953; New York: Dodd, Mead, 1954);
The Mousetrap [play](New York: S. French, 1954; London: S. French, 1954);
Witness for the Prosecution [play] (London: S. French, 1954; New York: S. French, 1954);
Destination Unknown (London: Collins, 1954); republished as *So Many Steps to Death* (New York: Dodd, Mead, 1955);
Hickory, Dickory, Dock (London: Collins, 1955); republished as *Hickory, Dickory, Death* (New York: Dodd, Mead, 1955);
The Burden, as Westmacott (London: Heinemann, 1956);
Dead Man's Folly (London: Collins, 1956; New York: Dodd, Mead, 1956);
Spider's Web (London: S. French, 1956);
4:50 from Paddington (London: Collins, 1957); republished as *What Mrs. McGillicuddy Saw!* (New York: Dodd, Mead, 1957);
Towards Zero [play], by Christie and Gerald Verner (London: S. French, 1957; New York: Dramatists Play Service, 1957);
Ordeal by Innocence (London: Collins, 1958; New York: Dodd, Mead, 1959);
Verdict (London: S. French, 1958);
The Unexpected Guest (London: S. French, 1958);
Cat among the Pigeons (London: Collins, 1959; New York: Dodd, Mead, 1960);
Go Back for Murder (London: S. French, 1960);
The Adventures of the Christmas Pudding, and Selection of Entrées (London: Collins, 1960);
Double Sin, and Other Stories (New York: Dodd, Mead, 1961);
13 for Luck! A Selection of Mystery Stories for Young Readers (New York: Dodd, Mead, 1961; London: Collins, 1966);

The Mirror Crack'd from Side to Side (London: Collins, 1962); republished as *The Mirror Crack'd* (New York: Dodd, Mead, 1963);
Rule of Three: Afternoon at the Seaside, The Patient, The Rats, 3 volumes (London: S. French, 1963);
The Clocks (London: Collins, 1963; New York: Dodd, Mead, 1964);
A Caribbean Mystery (London: Collins, 1964; New York: Dodd, Mead, 1965);
At Bertram's Hotel (London: Collins, 1965; New York: Dodd, Mead, 1965);
Star Over Bethlehem and Other Stories, as Mallowan (London: Collins, 1965; New York: Dodd, Mead, 1965);
Third Girl (London: Collins, 1966; New York: Dodd, Mead, 1967);
Endless Night (London: Collins, 1967; New York: Dodd, Mead, 1968);
By the Pricking of My Thumbs (London: Collins, 1968; New York: Dodd, Mead, 1968);
Hallowe'en Party (London: Collins, 1969; New York: Dodd, Mead, 1969);
Passenger to Frankfurt (London: Collins, 1970; New York: Dodd, Mead, 1970);
The Golden Ball and Other Stories (New York: Dodd, Mead, 1971);
Nemesis (London: Collins, 1971; New York: Dodd, Mead, 1971);
Elephants Can Remember (London: Collins, 1972; New York: Dodd, Mead, 1972);
Akhnaton (London: Collins, 1973; New York: Dodd, Mead, 1973);
Postern of Fate (London: Collins, 1973; New York: Dodd, Mead, 1973);
Hercule Poirot's Early Cases (London: Collins, 1974; New York: Dodd, Mead, 1974);
Curtain: Hercule Poirot's Last Case (London: Collins, 1975; New York: Dodd, Mead, 1975);
Sleeping Murder (London: Collins, 1976; New York: Dodd, Mead, 1976);
An Autobiography (London: Collins, 1977; New York: Dodd, Mead, 1977);
Miss Marple's Final Cases, and Two Other Stories (London: Collins, 1979).

PRODUCED SCRIPT: *Spider's Web,* screenplay by Christie, Eldon Howard, and others, motion picture, Danziger Productions, 1960.

Agatha Christie, crime novelist, playwright, poet, travel and short-story writer, has sold more than one billion copies of her books since 1920 and been translated into more languages than William Shakespeare, second only to the Bible. She also wrote romantic novels under the pseudonym of Mary Westmacott and is considered the most commercially successful woman writer of all time. Her play *The Mousetrap,* playing at theaters in London since 1952, is the longest-running play in the world. In addition, her work has appeared frequently in West End and New York City theaters, is performed widely in repertory companies, and has been adapted for hundreds of radio, screen, and stage productions. The literature available on her life and work is extensive, from armchair companions on her fictional characters, biographies, and autobiographies to more recent academic studies.

Agatha Mary Clarissa Miller was born on 13 September 1890 in Torquay, Devon, the youngest of three children of Frederick Alvah Miller, an American from New York, and Clarissa Boehmer Miller. Her father died when she was a child, and until she was sixteen she was educated at home by her mother. The family often traveled abroad when finances were limited. She attended finishing school in Paris and initially considered a musical career. As a child she read detective novels extensively and improvised mysteries with her sister, Madge. Her childhood dreams were haunted by the image of "The Gunman," pointing to a concern with the violence underlying seemingly "respectable" societies, a theme of many of her later works.

In 1912 Miller became engaged to Archibald Christie; they were married on Christmas Eve, 1914. Christie served as a colonel in the Royal Air Corps, so the couple was separated for most of the war years. Agatha Christie continued to live at Ashfield, her family's Victorian villa in Torquay. She volunteered as a nurse and worked as a pharmaceutical dispenser in local hospitals. Her knowledge of poisons, evident in many of her mysteries, developed through these experiences. After the war, her husband went into business in London, while Christie remained at home with her daughter, Rosalind, born in 1919.

In 1920 Christie's first novel, *The Mysterious Affair at Styles: A Detective Story,* was sent to the publishers who insisted that she rewrite the courtroom ending because of inaccuracies. This work was followed in 1926 by the publication of *The Murder of Roger Ackroyd,* the denouement of which attracted wide critical attention in revealing the narrator as the murderer. Edmund Wilson later criticized the genre as a whole with his controversial article in the *The New Yorker,* "Who Cares Who Killed Roger Ackroyd?" (20 January 1945). Apparently, many people did, and the book even appeared on the shelves of many radical and alternative bookshelves years after its debut. After her mother's death Christie suffered a breakdown, and in December 1926 she disappeared for ten days, attracting great publicity. The breakdown may have been brought on also by her husband's request for a divorce so that he could marry another woman. The Christies were divorced in 1928, and her resultant cynicism can perhaps be identified in the many unsuccessful relationships in her works.

Alibi, Michael Morton's adaptation of *The Murder of Roger Ackroyd,* opened at the Prince of Wales Theatre in London in 1928, with Charles Laughton as Hercule Poirot. Morton replaced the spinster character of Caroline Sheppard, an early prototype of Miss Marple, with a much younger woman–this change proved to be unpopular with Christie who, in her autobiography, expressed a fondness for the character: "She had been my favourite character in the book–an acidulated spinster, full of curiosity, knowing everything, hearing everything: the complete detective service in the home." The 1926 novel had met with a mixed reception–some critics felt that Christie had cheated in her surprise ending, while others saw it as a "stroke of genius." The play was fairly well received and ran for 250 performances before an unsuccessful New York run.

The character of Poirot has since raised some interesting questions about race and the role of the "outsider." Often subjected to racial prejudice, Poirot's "little grey cells" act, not only to solve the obvious crimes, but also to expose collective crimes of institutionalized prejudice and fear of that which is "foreign." The specificity of his Belgian background is also an historical reminder of the role of Belgium during World War I and the low status afforded it by the rest of Europe. The criminal in *Alibi* is a professional representative of British nationalist values and points to a different kind of sickness that needs to be cured.

Francis L. Sullivan played the role of Poirot in the 1930 production of *Black Coffee,* a three-act play that ran for five months at the Embassy Theatre in London. It was later revived and has a long history of repertory success. Sir Claud Amory is murdered, ostensibly for his new atomic formula with the power to kill hundreds of thousands of people. Christie plays with audience prejudice in the names and origins of her characters. Lucia, the half-Italian wife of Amory's son, is likened to Lucretia Borgia. The unexpected arrival of the Italian Dr. Carelli immediately arouses suspicion. The "murder in the dark" convention is exploited here as it is in other plays, for example, *A Murder Is Announced* (1977). The overall tone of the piece is humorous, with false alibis, international spies, and theatrical clichés. Poirot's ventures into psychodrama are naive yet effective, and there are references to hypnosis and the power of auto suggestion, ideas relatively new at the time of writing. The play is set in a library, and the set is dressed precisely to provide clues to the outcome of the mystery. Stereotypes are effectively employed for comic effect,

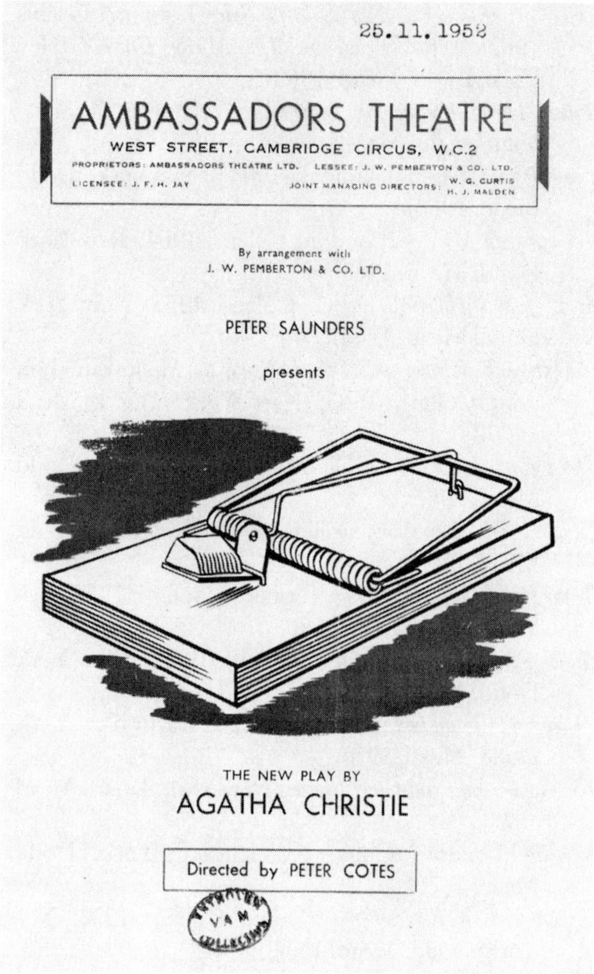

Program cover for the first production of Christie's The Mousetrap, *which became the world's longest continuously running play*

but the underlying critique of scientific knowledge being utilized for capitalist gain and the antihumanitarian effects of such research can be clearly identified, especially in the context of Christie's own wartime experiences. The box of poisons is again an oblique reference to her personal experience as a nurse and pharmacist during the war years, and the theme of entrapment and references to rodents appear frequently in her work. Perhaps *The Mousetrap* is the best known of these, although *Spider's Web* (1954) and *The Rats* (1962) share similar concerns.

In 1930 Christie traveled on the Orient Express to see the excavations at Ur in Turkey. There she met archaeologist Max Mallowan, whom she married the same year. During the 1930s the couple divided their time between their several homes in England and many archaeological expeditions in the Middle East. This period provided Christie with experience of other cultures and a valuable distance from her own British one.

Love from a Stranger (1936) was based on the short story "Philomel Cottage" from *The Listerdale Mystery* (1934). This three-act stage adaptation was not held in high regard by Christie. The play is a study of a serial killer, and the three acts reflect the three stages of the character's decline. When Cecily abandons Nigel, her fiancé of five years, for the charms of Bruce and an idyllic country cottage life, she little realizes the horrors awaiting her in the sinister cellars, her husband's photographic developing room. Tension builds as Cecily uses deceptive means in an attempt to delay her death–the clock striking nine rings out her impending doom. The piece becomes increasingly melodramatic in style, contrasting with the lighthearted and near-farcical opening scenes dominated by the rather ridiculous presence of Auntie Loo-Loo. The play was well received when it opened in 1936, being praised for its manipulation of terror and horror. It ran for 149 performances before transferring to New York for a short run. In 1937 United Artists made a motion picture based on the play with Basil Rathbone and Ann Harding in the leading roles.

During World War II Mallowan served as an intelligence liaison officer in North Africa while Christie remained in London, working again as a volunteer dispenser. Her grandson, Matthew, was born in 1943, and her daughter, Rosalind, married Anthony Hicks after the death in service of her first husband, Hubert Pritchard.

The unfortunately titled *Ten Little Niggers,* another three-act play, opened in 1943 and received enthusiastic criticism as a "kind of theatrical game." After 260 performances at the St. James's Theatre, the show closed temporarily after the theater suffered bomb damage. The play reopened at the Cambridge Theatre. In June 1944 the play, retitled *Ten Little Indians,* opened in New York and ran for 425 performances. It has been revived in many repertory companies, made into a motion picture three times, and continues to be one of her most popular and tense dramas. In many of her plays and novels Christie uses children's rhymes, counting games, and alphabet sequences, uncovering the more-sinister implications of these works. The counting in *Ten Little Niggers* is one of many theatrical devices for the building of suspense. Playing on audience familiarity with the rhyme, Christie empowers the audience and provides clues as to the manner and sequence of the deaths of the victims isolated on Nigger Island, off the coast of Devon. Ten strangers are invited to assemble on the island, where, one by one, they are murdered. The ten China statues on the mantelpiece gradually disappear as the murderer removes one for each of his victims. The manner of their deaths is informed by the nursery rhyme "Ten Little Niggers." The claustrophobic aspects of the play are gradually introduced, providing a sense of slow entrapment. The figures on the mantlepiece reduce, indicating the systematic deaths and certainty of future vengeance. The guilt of the intended victims is clearly announced in the theatrical coup d'état of the voice-over, hinting at a murderous past for each of the assembled victims. In spite of the encroaching doom, Vera Claythorne remains active and intelligent, in contrast to the other characters on the island who are driven to death and despair through fear. Vera, former governess and "good-looking girl of 25," survives the murderer's attempt on her life and marries Philip Lombard. The morality of the censorious Emily, for example, is challenged as she is revealed to be instrumental in the suicide of a young pregnant girl. Emily's antediluvian values are cruel and inhumane.

Vera confronts the murderer and triumphs–in a scene where the concept of justice and its enactment are called into question. The play acts as a metaphor for constricted visions, conservative attitudes and institutionalized violence–and, ultimately, points to the danger in all of these. Although considered problematic for its racist title, the play offers many challenges in terms of class and power, demonstrating the links between privilege and corruption. It also, significantly, hints at the potential murderer in everyone.

Appointment with Death (1945) is an ostensibly comic three-act play set in Jerusalem and Petra, and deals with issues of power in both personal and political terms. Christie utilizes exaggerated portraits of human experience to present tragic themes in a seemingly lighthearted fashion. While on vacation in Jerusalem, Hercule Poirot is drawn into the investigation of the death of the sadistic American widow, Mrs. Boynton, by lethal injection. When a despotic and possessive caricature assumes the role of "summat out of Old Testament"–an ironic comment from Christie on colonizing attitudes–and parodies Middle Eastern culture, the audience is drawn into suspecting everyone, apart from the actual perpetrator of the crime. British party politics, represented by the characters of Lady Westholme (Conservative Party candidate and advocate of women's rights) and Alderman Higgs (Independent candidate)–"a portly, middle-aged man" with a "broad Lancashire accent," are depicted in near cartoon fashion, with ignorance, prejudice, and petty quarrels characterizing both sides. Mrs. Boynton, parodying the Gothic style, signals her own impending death in dressing throughout the play in black, and her domination of the family, her past enjoyment of her work as prison warden, and her sadistic tendencies are more than sufficient motivation for her murder. Issues of freedom and imprisonment are explored throughout the play, and world politics are paralleled with domestic tyranny.

The piece provides a wealth of strong female characters who defy stereotypes. Christie's war experiences are suggested throughout, no more so than in Doctor Theodore Gerard's words: "A man may lay down his life, that is one thing–to be forcibly deprived of it is another. I doubt if that has ever advanced human progress or human happiness." Gerard is a celebrated French authority on schizophrenia. While suffering a malaria attack, he discovers that his hypodermic syringe is missing. Historical and contemporary issues of oppression are set in the context of institutionalized practices and state-condoned acts of violence, whether through family or state.

Christie was never particularly fond of Hercule Poirot and, characteristically, eliminated him from the stage play, possibly because of casting difficulties. *Appointment with Death* opened at the Piccadilly Theatre on 31 March 1945 and ran until the fall. It was made into a motion picture in 1988, with Peter Ustinov in the reinstated Poirot role. At the end of World War II, Mallowan resumed his archaeological work in the Middle East, with Christie often accompanying and directly helping her husband in his work.

Murder on the Nile (1946) was a particular favorite of Christie because of its Egyptian setting and, again, she replaced the Poirot figure of the novel with the character of Canon Pennefather, "the most cynical person I know." When Simon Mostyn rejects his former lover, Jacqueline de Severac, and marries the rich Kay, it seems as though Jacqueline is taking revenge on the married couple by a stalking campaign. When Kay is shot, Canon Pennefather assumes the role of detective and eventually reveals the identity of the murderer. The central concern of the play appears to be the love triangle between Kay, Simon, and Jackie, although in the denouement this focus shifts to a recognition of the capitalist context that provides the motivation for the murder. The act of looking is repeatedly brought to the attention of the audience, and contemporary readings of the play could be informed by a consideration of contemporary theories of "the gaze." Christie reworks the stalker narrative for disturbing effect, thereby challenging gender stereotypes. She also brings class issues to the fore in the amusing contrast between the rich and bigoted Ffoliot Ffoulkes and the "dreadful socialistic young man," Lord Dawlish, alias Smith. The former's racist attitudes are ridiculed by Christie: "I wonder if these Nubian stewards are honest? Their faces are so *very* black," and Dr. Bessner later reinforces the capitalist critique with "but the big man with the cigar, he can rob and cheat and stay inside the law." The play concludes with an astonishing confession from Jackie: "I loved Kay–I know that now," and the killer is persuaded to make a spiritual choice, leaving the play on a cathartic note. Adverse criticism greeted the production in both London and New York, though the 1978 motion picture, with Ustinov as Poirot, proved popular. The potential for visual spectacle in the setting of the play is utilized highly effectively in the motion picture and, in both the stage and motion picture version, the sense of entrapment is provided by the confines of the ship, a microcosm of society and its power relations.

Miss Marple made her first stage appearance in 1949, when Barbara Mullen played this "typical maiden lady living on reduced means in the country" in *Murder at the Vicarage.* Unlike many adaptations of her work, Christie seemed reasonably happy with the two-act stage play by Barbara Toy and Moie Charles, which is based on her 1930 book, *The Murder at the Vicarage.* Set in the country village of St. Mary Mead, the play reveals layers of corruption under the deceptively serene facade of parochial life. Christie's ability to deal with taboo subjects such as adultery and the embezzlement of church funds is apparent, and her characteristic use of humor and irony deflects attention from more serious issues and manipulates the audience into trivializing Marple's detective capabilities. The plot surrounds the death of Colonel Protheroe, whose body is discovered in the study at the vicarage, and the aptly named Inspector Slack is unable to discover the murderer. Marple challenges ratiocinative methodologies and successfully employs her own intuitive ways, drawing on her research into human nature. She occupies a central position in the piece and makes particularly effective use of unexpected entrances–usually through the French windows–that are at once humorous and evidence of her keen intelligence and bold spirit. She offers challenges to prejudices of age and gender. As she states, ironically, to the inspector, "I always find that it is the weaker sex who stand up better in this kind of situation." Griselda, the vicar's wife, rejects her stereotypical female role. She refuses to cook, stating, "I'm sorry, but I'm just not a housekeeper by nature." The play also draws attention to class issues and foregrounds Marple's limited means in the deception of the final scene, a departure from the narrative of the novel. The stage directions are extremely detailed, and Christie presents a parody of English country life, where the most respected members of the community become prime suspects for murder.

In *The Hollow* (1951) Christie provides a cast of strong women, exploring the destructive effects of hero worship and voyeuristic pleasures. Hercule Poirot is invited for Sunday lunch at The Hollow, where Lady Angkatell, an acquaintance from his travels in Baghdad, is entertaining family and friends one late September weekend. On his arrival he finds the guests assembled by the swimming pool, where the body of John Chris-

Christie, with the actors David Horne, Percy Marmount, and D. A. Clark-Smith, at the Winter Garden Theatre during a dress rehearsal for the 1953 production of Christie's Witness for the Prosecution *(photograph by Gerd Treuhaft)*

tow has just been discovered with a fatal shot in the head, having returned from a visit to his former lover, Veronica Cray. Poirot wastes no time in identifying the murderer, despite the wide selection of possible suspects. Henrietta, the sculptor, provides a strong role model of an independent and creative character who has thoroughly "modern" ideas about relationships. Midge Hardcastle, a poor relation who works in a London dress shop, draws attention to the class issues in the play by refusing to accept charity from the wealthy Angkatells–"To show an independent spirit one needs an independent income"–and Gerda, wife of John Christie, is depicted as a rather simple-minded character. She uses the mask of femininity, however, and its associations with stupidity as an empowering device. Likewise, Lucy Angkatell conceals her intelligence and capability behind a flustered exterior and takes great pleasure in the excitement of the murder, inquest, and publicity. Veronica Crane, a shrewd and grasping character and past lover of John Christow, further highlights gender as masquerade in her profession as actor. Christie builds suspense in several ways: the weather deteriorates throughout the play, introducing a thunder- storm in the climactic scene, guns proliferate, and entrances and exits are used effectively to build tension. Props are also used to build the dramatic narrative, and gloves and bags draw attention to the trappings of femininity. Yet, again, Christie replaces the Poirot figure, stating in her autobiography, "he was all wrong there." The play marked the beginning of Christie's relationship with British theater producer Peter Saunders and met with enthusiastic criticism when it opened at the Fortune Theatre.

The opening stage directions for *The Mousetrap* point to a narrative of loss as the stage set reflects "*dwindling resources*" and highlights the decline of the upper classes. Alison Light has rejected claims of Christie's nostalgic tendencies, suggesting, "Hers is not a romantic conservatism, cleaving to the aristocratic as a mark of a better past or a model for the good life. Rather she speaks to a readership reconciled to the present, unfrightened by change and confidently domestic." As the play opens in complete blackout, audience members hear the song "Three Blind Mice." The music fades to a sound track of a whistle, a scream, vocal re-creations of panic and confusion, followed by a silence, interrupted by a documentary-style radio news report. Playing on conventions of suspense, Christie creates immediate excitement, coupled with a sense of pastiche. Giles and Molly Ralston, newlyweds, are the young new proprietors of Monkswell Manor. Shortly after the guests arrive, a record-breaking snowfall isolates the inhabitants from the outside world. Mrs. Boyle is the first victim in the series of murders that follows. Detective-Sergeant Trotter appears on skis at Monkswell Manor and, the audience is led to believe, is set to bring the murderer to justice. As Christopher Wren states, "I adore nursery rhymes, don't you? Always so tragic and *macabre*." The audience is "blinded," like the mice in the nursery rhyme, and the sinister tune hints at the violence to come. The lights come up on the dimly-lit scene of Monkswell Manor, conveniently isolated by the thick snow and its location. Throughout the play Christie signals a concern with sexual politics and representation. Mollie and Giles are struggling to redefine their relationship. Mollie clearly states, "This is a partnership," while Giles refers to her as a "wonderful woman of business." Christie uses prejudice against the camp figure of Wren, who irritates Giles with his rejection of stereotypical gender roles. Christie's sense of humor is apparent in the naming of her characters. The audience feels little sympathy for Mrs. Boyle's death, her name comically suggesting her personality. Trotter, the policeman, is irreverently associated with a pig, and Wren's profession as architect, coupled with his childlike behavior (suggestive of Christopher Robin), are an equal source of amusement. Paravacini's status as 'outsider' and 'foreigner' also draws attention to prejudices of 'otherness' and 'difference' and, ultimately, challenges the audience to rethink its fears and values. Christie uses repetition of words, rhymes, and motifs in the piece to build suspense and enrich the comic texture. Trotter's ridiculously theatrical appearance on skis at the window encourages the audience to laugh at their own reactions and interrupts the trajectory of suspense with his comic entrance. As act 1 draws to a close, Mrs. Boyle is listening to a radio program on "the mechanics of fear," anticipating the blackout and her own murder, parodied by the "gurgles and a scuffle" of the stage directions. Mollie's scream in the darkness mirrors that of the opening, demonstrating Christie's techniques of construction and her understanding of the conventional expectations of the audience.

Act 2 is skillfully structured to bring together all the characters under suspicion. The pace accelerates, moving toward the cliché of the dramatic reconstruction of events, a foiled murder attempt, and revelation of the killer, ironically the conventional upholder of justice. Amusing use is made of crude psychoanalysis, perhaps reflecting Christie's cynicism toward this relatively new science. The piece concludes with a lighthearted scene of domestic bliss, subverted by the revelation that neither Mollie nor Giles know each other's preferences. As Mollie rushes off to rescue her burned pie, the audience is left to question the artificial sense of closure in the piece. Perhaps part of the astonishing success of the play is owing to Christie's obvious pleasure in theatrical forms and her skill in employing these for both comic and serious ends.

Theatre World (February 1954) proclaimed that the latest Christie thriller, *Witness for the Prosecution,* was "now enjoying a brilliant success and all set to restore good fortune to the Winter Garden Theatre." This prediction certainly proved to be true, as the play ran for 468 performances before its successful transfer to the United States. Centered on the trial of Leonard Vole for the murder of Miss Emily French, the play is a stylish courtroom drama with many plot twists and elements of dramatic tension. More seriously, the piece calls into question concepts of justice and moral choices. The opening scene, which gently mocks the authority of judges and the gravitas suggested in the setting–the "*heavy legal volumes*" and "*deed boxes and a litter of documents*"–is quickly undermined by the witty observations of Greta, secretary to Sir Wilfred Robart. The characterizations are skillfully drawn, and the complexity and comic potential of Sir Wilfred Robart's character draws the audience into confronting the same moral challenges as himself. Act 1 concludes with his statement, "Never trust a woman," which cunningly draws the audience into suspecting the entire sex. When his supposed wife, Romaine, gives evidence against him, Sir Wilfred's fears appear to be justified, further reinforced by the news of her duplicity and infidelity from the caricatured character, "Woman." The melodramatic conclusion provides a fitting climax to this fast-moving play where disguise is used extensively to explore issues of identity and provide tension and excitement for the audience.

"Oh, what a tangled web we weave, when first we practise to deceive." Clarissa's quotation aptly describes the confusion caused when she tries to protect her stepdaughter from a murder charge in *Spider's Web* (1954). Unlike the stereotypical wicked stepmother, Clarissa is devoted to Pippa and, unlike that of the mythical Ariadne whose webs are associated with death, Clarissa's metaphorical web of deceit is constructed as a means of protection for her stepdaughter. The tone of this three-act play is highly comical in spite of the more-serious issues of murder, drugs, blackmail, and child abuse. Money proves to be the motivating factor and, again, the most respectable members of society are obliged to collude in deception and question conventional notions of right and wrong. The play

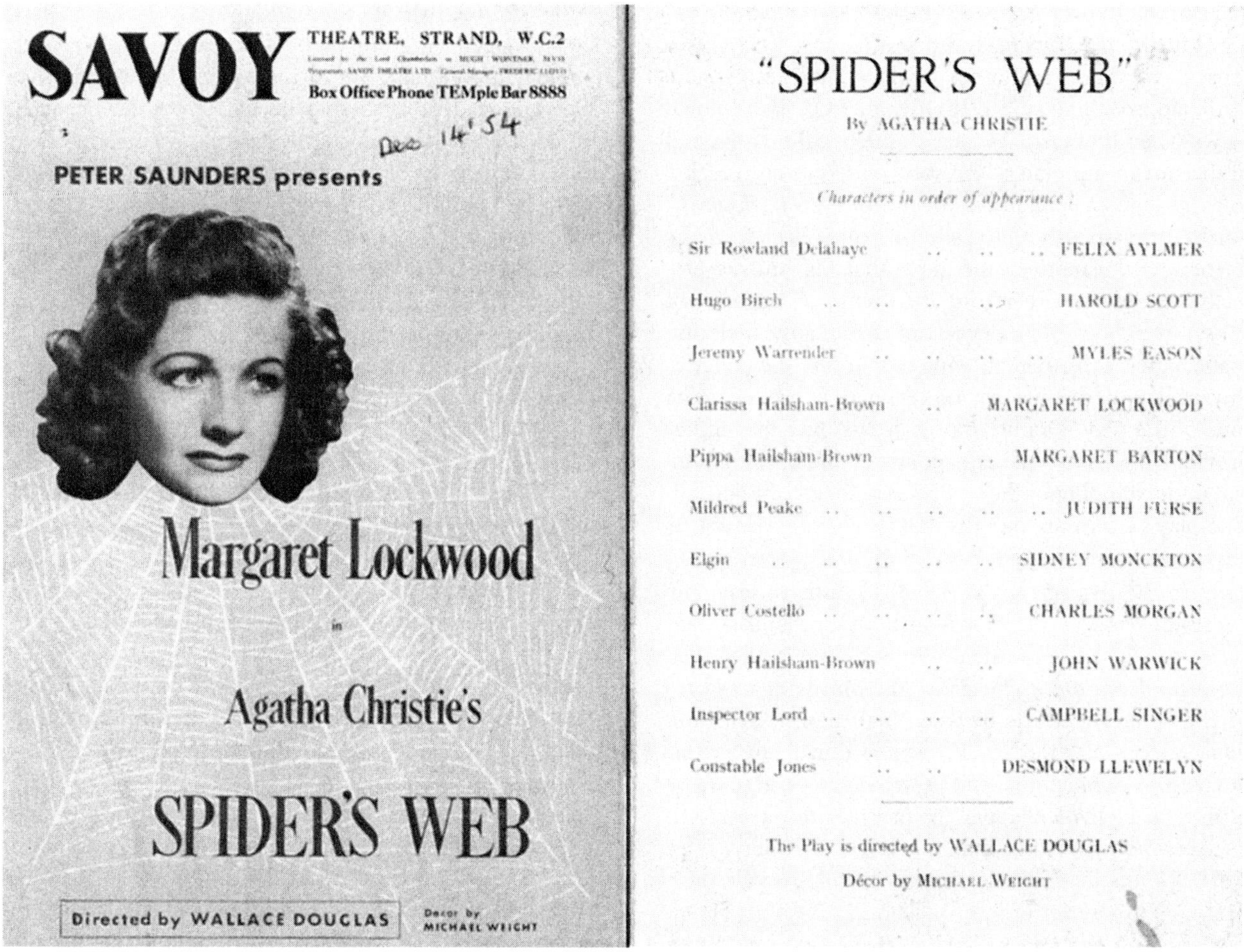
SAVOY
THEATRE, STRAND, W.C.2
Box Office Phone TEMple Bar 8888
Dec 14 '54
PETER SAUNDERS presents
Margaret Lockwood
in
Agatha Christie's
SPIDER'S WEB
Directed by WALLACE DOUGLAS
Decor by MICHAEL WEIGHT
"SPIDER'S WEB"
By AGATHA CHRISTIE
Characters in order of appearance:
Sir Rowland Delahaye .. .. FELIX AYLMER
Hugo Birch .. .. HAROLD SCOTT
Jeremy Warrender .. .. MYLES EASON
Clarissa Hailsham-Brown .. MARGARET LOCKWOOD
Pippa Hailsham-Brown .. .. MARGARET BARTON
Mildred Peake .. .. JUDITH FURSE
Elgin .. .. SIDNEY MONCKTON
Oliver Costello .. .. CHARLES MORGAN
Henry Hailsham-Brown .. .. JOHN WARWICK
Inspector Lord .. .. CAMPBELL SINGER
Constable Jones .. .. DESMOND LLEWELYN
The Play is directed by WALLACE DOUGLAS
Décor by MICHAEL WEIGHT

Program cover and cast list for the first production of Christie's play about a woman who tries to save her stepdaughter from a murder charge

is replete with secrets–secret drawers, secret passages, and an outward veneer of respectability that hides secret histories. In addition, a real-life secret mission of a diplomatic nature is conducted by Henry Hailsham-Brown, Clarissa's husband and a rather bumbling idiot, and suspense is created by his imminent arrival with a top government minister. Miss Peake (alias Mrs. Brown!), described as the "gum-booted Amazonian gardener" by Jan Oxenburg in *The Bedside, Bathtub and Armchair Companion to Agatha Christie,* is a delightfully absurd creation. In removing the corpse using a traditional English "fireman's lift" (throwing the body over her shoulder) and hiding it under her bolster she pushes the boundaries of suspended disbelief to the limits. Extensive use is made of dramatic irony and timing as a futile attempt is made to conceal the body following the unexpected arrival of the police. The role of Clarissa was written especially for Margaret Lockwood, and the play ran for two years at the Savoy Theatre, enjoying favorable reviews. Described by Jan Oxenberg as a "hilarious slapstick of a murder mystery," *Spider's Web* was one of Christie's last great West End stage successes.

When the elderly Lady Tressilian is murdered in *Towards Zero* (1956), suspicion immediately falls on the aptly named Neville Strange. Neville Strange, popular tennis professional, has the rather bizarre idea of inviting to a family meeting at Lady Tressilian's estate, Gull's Point, both his current wife and former wife. When Lady Tressilian is found battered to death with a golf club, Strange, the inheritor of her fortune, is the immediate suspect. Superintendent Battle is called in to solve the crime and soon begins to have his doubts about the obvious suspect. Christie's sense of stagecraft is apparent in the detailed dressing of the set and Kay's melodramatic ripping of the photograph of Strange's previous wife, Audrey, an act observed by Royde. Good dramatic use is made throughout the play of windows which provide opportunities for eavesdropping and unexpected entrances and exits. The murder takes place in a thunderstorm, and the pace of the play is fast with much stage business and heated arguments. The sense of tension is reinforced by the stifling atmosphere of the approaching storm. Royde voices Christie's own views when he says, "As I see it, the murder is the end of the story," and, later, "All sorts of people converging towards a given spot and hour–all going towards zero." Christie reworks the fairy tale of Cinderella when she introduces the motif of the glove that fits Audrey perfectly, leading to her arrest; the theme of entrapment runs throughout. The denouement is highly melodramatic: after a further attempted murder, the killer is thwarted and the pattern of revenge is broken. The tone of the play is rather more serious than that of her previous works and perhaps points to an autobiographical understanding of the sad consequences of rejection. The play ran for six months and received praise for its intricate plotting.

In the two-act *Verdict* (1958) Christie raises some interesting moral questions–such as euthanasia and access to education for the underprivileged–and shifted the focus from the discovery of the murderer to issues of choice and conflicts between high moral ideas and their effects in practice. Professor Karl Hendryk is devoted to scholarship and is reluctant to accept the privileged Helen Rollander for private tutorials. Helen declares her love for him, as does, privately, Lisa Koletzky, his invalid wife Anya's doctor. Anya's murder leads to a series of moral dilemmas for both Hendryk and Koletsky when the latter is arrested for Anya's murder following the death of Helen, the real murderer. Exiled through rather misguided loyalty, Karl is able to continue his research and tutelage while his wife's health rapidly deteriorates. When a new young, rich pupil is unable to gain his affections, she murders his wife, Anya, hoping to remove what she mistakenly believes to be an obstacle to the consummation of their love. After Helen's sudden death, Lisa, a trained physicist, is tried for the murder of Anya and is unexpectedly acquitted. Christie delays the anticipated romantic closure, suggesting a willingness to move away from the formulas of the genre and to experiment with confronting the audience with somewhat different challenges. Although the play contains some elements of suspense–the poison bottle and the shadowy figure of Mrs. Roper–the lighthearted tone of her previous work is replaced by one far more somber in flavor which questions responsibilities and principles. Yet, again, prejudices against foreigners are drawn to the viewer's attention and critiqued. After a disappointing opening night because of a premature final curtain, the play ran for a month with more-favorable reviews.

The Unexpected Guest (1958), a well-crafted two-act play, is set in an isolated house on a foggy November night with the Bristol channel foghorn, with its "melancholy boom," sounding in the distance. Laura Warwick is married to Richard, a former big-game hunter who, after an accident left him wheelchair bound, becomes an alcoholic and a thoroughly unpleasant person. Two years previously he was acquitted of running over a boy when drunk. The boy's father, MacGregor, fakes his own death in Alaska and returns to the house as Michael Starkwedder in order to gain his revenge. The darkness is broken by the approaching car headlights that reveal Laura standing still in the shadows with her husband lying dead at his desk. Starkwedder's knocking at the window completes the near Gothic atmosphere of suspense which is sustained throughout the piece. Christie's sense of fun and irony is disguised by the operations of the genre and the manipulation of audience expectations. The victim of the murder, Richard, is presented in an unsympathetic light–an alcoholic tyrannical figure with a penchant for shooting cats and who kills a child while driving in an inebriated condition. The myth of the "unexpected guest" reminds Laura of her childhood fears, and the play as a whole has a dark and chilling flavor, enhanced by the swirling mists. The sinister cast provides widespread suspicion in their secretive behavior, false alibis, and clandestine liaisons. The nurse, Angell, contradicts his name in his blackmailing activities, and Starkwedder calls into question stereotypical gender traits in his words, "Men are really the sensitive sex. Women are tough." The more serious concern of appropriate care for the mentally ill is an important narrative strand. As Laura makes a fruitless plea for Michael's return at the end of the play, the foghorn is still sounding, providing a bleak postscript to the piece as a whole. The play ran for 604 performances and received high critical acclaim.

Go Back for Murder (1960), an adaptation of *Five Little Pigs,* had a disappointing run of only 31 performances at the Duchess Theatre. Carla Lemarchant's mother died in prison after being convicted of the murder of her father, Amyas Crale. On Carla's twenty-first birthday she reads a note from her mother declaring herself to be innocent of the murder. Carla calls upon Hercule Poirot to identify the real perpetrator of the crime. Christie uses a reconstruction of past events to vindicate Carla's mother, Caroline, of a murder of which she was innocent. The play concludes with a romantic resolution, although Christie incorporates a warning about the consequences of adultery.

The trio of one-act plays, *Rule of Three* (1962), enjoyed slightly better success, although failed to match that of her previous works. *The Rats* is a sinister piece with comic elements as the adulterous couple sit next to a chest containing the body of John, husband of the unfaithful Sandra. Like rats in a trap, the couple are imprisoned with the evidence of their guilt beside them while Alec, in love with Sandra's first husband, frames them for murder. The convoluted plot and dramatic elements–the knocking, the telephone, and the balcony– contribute to the peculiar entertainment provided by the play. At times the tone resembles the work of Harold Pinter, and the play has a developing sense of claustrophobia despite the absurdity of the situation.

Reminiscent of a naughty seaside postcard, *Afternoon at the Seaside* employs caricature and pastiche to mock nostalgic views and attitudes, with many elements of farce and slapstick; a diamond theft plot is interwoven with a romantic one. The character of Percy represents masculinity in crisis, and the policewoman disguised as Beauty is another reminder of gender as performance. There is plenty of stage business in this fast-moving and often hilarious piece. The opening of *The Patient* provides a contrasting clinical tone–the square, plain room is adorned with electrical apparatus, reminiscent of a Heath-Robinson invention, and various medical implements. (The illustrator and inventor William Heath-Robinson [1872–1944] was known for his idiosyncratic inventions and complicated mechanical contraptions.) The buzzer sounds, signaling the start of the experiment–the red light flashes melodramatically and the trappings of horror and torture offer a delightful sense of danger. Motivated by jealousy, Nurse Bond attempts to murder her lover's wife–indeed, marital infidelities abound in the play, providing motivation for the other suspects. The final scene is amusingly melodramatic: the murderer enters in blackout brandishing a syringe, and the supposedly mute patient screams for assistance. Christie plays on the double entendre of the title to provide the audience with the clue to the deception of the piece, and she provides dramatic tension and humor in the parodied spelling scene, more of a seance than a serious medical experiment. In this play, as in the whole trilogy, Christie demonstrates her pleasure in the manipulation of form, style, and genre.

Dulcie Gray played the role of Miss Marple in the Leslie Darbon's adaptation of *A Murder Is Announced* (1977), which ran for 429 performances following Christie's death. When an advertisement for murder appears in the local newspaper on Friday the 13th both curiosity and fear are aroused in the small community of Chipping Cleghorn. Following the second murder, layers of identity are stripped from the characters as the elderly spinster-sleuth Miss Marple and her friend Detective Inspector Dermot Craddock endeavor to ensnare the murderer. Props are again a source of dramatic tension; in this case, a Dresden vase, missing cup, and pearl necklace all assume particular significance. The staging of the charade in the final scene serves to reveal the identity and motivation of the murderer and draws attention to themes of sameness and difference and the dangers of judging by appearance. A sad note is introduced in Miss Blacklock's genuine grief for her friend's death, and the character of Mitzi provides commentary on class and racial prejudice. As she states, "First murder. Now stealing. And why? Because I am a foreigner."

In *Cards on the Table* (1981), adapted by Darbon from Christie's 1936 novel, using a study of the underlying psychology of bridge playing, Ariadne Oliver and Inspector Battle–replacing the Poirot character in the book–discover the murderer of the shrewd and wealthy Mr. Sahaitana, killed with a stiletto heel which, in parodic fashion, points to a female killer, reinforced by the significance of letters and silk stockings. Games are played throughout the piece, both with the audience and within the narrative, and tricks and deception abound. The lighthearted tone of the play, however, masks the underlying greed, violence, and criminality. Female relationships are explored and problematized in the characters of Anne, Rhoda, Mrs. Lorrimer, and Ariadne Oliver, a parody of Christie herself (her works include *The Body in the Study* and *Murder on the Menu*), who identifies the murderer using Marplesque methodology. The play received favorable critical acclaim and ran for six months at the Vaudeville Theatre.

Christie's remarkable success in her books, plays, and movies led to the award of the Commander of the British Empire (C.B.E.) in 1956. In 1971 she was made a Dame of the British Empire. Her last formal appearance was in 1974 at the opening of the movie, *Murder on the Orient Express.* She died at home in Wallingford, Berkshire, in 1976, where she is buried. She gave a detailed account of her life and work in the posthumously published *An Autobiography* (1977).

Although the stage and motion-picture adaptations received a mixed response from Christie–indeed, she wrote several plays specifically for the stage as a result of her dissatisfaction–they still enjoy international success. Frequently praised for her creation of intellectual puzzles and narrative skills, Christie's plays often use humor as a means of misleading the audience and criticizing outer masks of respectability. Her use of parody and irony is extensive and her theatrical crafting skills inform her precise use of timing, sound effects, lighting, entrances, and exits. She has created many familiar and well-loved characters, including Tommy and Tuppence Beresford and Parker Pyne with his supernatural links. The most famous of her creations, however, are the elderly spinster character of Miss Marple and the Belgian sleuth noted for his "little grey cells," Hercule Poirot. Both characters have been played on stage and screen by a range of high-status actors, including Joan Hickson in the British Broadcasting Corporation (BBC) television adaptations and David Suchet in the London Weekend parallel series.

The work of Agatha Christie has been of particular interest to contemporary feminist thought, and her challenges to constructions of class, race, gender, and age have led to a reconsideration of her popularity. Scholars Marion Shaw and Sabine Vanacker suggest that "women domesticated the detective genre and made it into a vehicle for their own ratiocinative and moral capacities. Christie's distinctive contribution to this feminization of the genre was the milieu of apparent ordinariness, the small, unexceptional community which nevertheless harbours a killer."

References:

Earl Bargainnier, *The Gentle Art of Murder: the Detective Fiction of Agatha Christie* (Bowling Green, Ohio: Bowling Green University Popular Press, 1980);

Jen Green, *Reader, I Murdered Him* (London: Women's Press, 1995);

Hubert Gregg, *Christie and All That Mousetrap* (London: Kimber, 1980);

Peter Haining, *Agatha Christie: Murder in Four Acts: A Centenary Celebration of the 'Queen of Crime' on Stage, Film, Radio and TV* (London: Virgin, 1990);

Anne Hart, *The Life and Times of Miss Jane Marple* (London: Sphere, 1991);

Glenwood Irons, ed., *Feminism in Women's Detective Fiction* (Toronto: University of Toronto Press, 1995);

H. R. F. Keating, ed., *Christie: First Lady of Crime* (London: Weidenfeld & Nicolson, 1977);

Kathleen Klein, *The Woman Detective* (Illinois: University of Illinois Press, 1995);

Alison Light, *Forever England: Femininity, Literature and Conservatism Between the Wars* (London: Routledge, 1991);

Janet Morgan, *Agatha Christie: A Biography* (Leicester: Charnwood, 1984);

Glenn Most and William Stowe, eds., *The Poetics of Murder: Detective Fiction and Literary Theory* (San Diego: Harcourt Brace Jovanovich, 1983);

Sally Munt, *Murder by the Book?: Feminism and the Crime Novel* (London: Routledge, 1994);

Charles Osborne, *The Life and Crimes of Agatha Christie* (London: Collins, 1982);

Barbara Rader and Howard Zettler, eds., *The Sleuth and the Scholar: Origins, Evolution, and Current Trends in Detective Fiction* (New York and London: Greenwood Press, 1988);

Robin Winks, ed., *Detective Fiction: A Collection of Critical Essays* (London: Prentice-Hall, 1980).

Noel Coward

(16 December 1899 – 26 March 1973)

Frances Gray
University of Sheffield

See also the Coward entry in *DLB 10: Modern British Dramatists, 1900–1945.*

PLAY PRODUCTIONS: *"I'll Leave It to You,"* Manchester, Gaiety Theatre, 3 May 1920; London, New Theatre, 21 July 1920;

The Better Half, London, Little Theatre, 31 May 1922;

The Young Idea: A Comedy of Youth, Bristol, Prince's Theatre, 25 September 1922; London, Savoy Theatre, 1 February 1923;

London Calling! by Coward and Ronald Jeans, London, Duke of York's Theatre, 4 September 1923;

The Vortex, London, Everyman Theatre, 25 November 1924;

On with the Dance, Manchester, Palace Theatre, 17 March 1925; London, London Pavilion, 30 April 1925;

Fallen Angels, London, Globe Theatre, 21 April 1925;

Hay Fever, London, Ambassadors' Theatre, 6 August 1925; transferred to Criterion Theatre, 7 September 1925;

Easy Virtue, New York, Empire Theatre, 7 December 1925; London: Duke of York's Theatre, 9 June 1926;

The Queen Was in the Parlour, London, St. Martin's Theatre, 24 August 1926; transferred to Duke of York's Theatre, 24 October 1926;

The Rat Trap, London, Everyman Theatre, 18 October 1926;

"This Was a Man," New York, Klaw Theatre, 23 November 1926;

The Marquise, London, Criterion Theatre, 16 February 1927;

Home Chat, London, Duke of York's Theatre, 25 October 1927;

Sirocco, London, Daly's Theatre, 24 November 1927;

This Year of Grace! London, London Pavilion, 28 February 1928;

Bitter Sweet, Manchester, Palace Theatre, 2 July 1929; London, London Pavilion, 12 July 1929;

Noel Coward

Private Lives: An Intimate Comedy, Edinburgh, King's Theatre, 18 August 1930; London, Phoenix Theatre, 24 September 1930;

Some Other Private Lives, London, London Hippodrome, 8 December 1930;

Cavalcade, London, Theatre Royal, Drury Lane, 13 October 1931;

Weatherwise, Malvern, Festival Theatre, 8 September 1932;

Words and Music, London, Adelphi Theatre, 16 September 1932; retitled *Set to Music,* New York, Music Box Theatre, 18 January 1939;

Design for Living, New York, Ethel Barrymore Theatre, 24 January 1933;
Conversation Piece, London, His Majesty's Theatre, 16 January 1934;
Point Valaine, New York, Ethel Barrymore Theatre, 16 January 1935;
Tonight at 8:30, London, Phoenix Theatre, 9 January 1936;
Operette, London, His Majesty's Theatre, 16 March 1938;
Post Mortem, performed by prisoners of war in Oflag VIIB, Eichstatt, Germany, 1940;
Blithe Spirit: An Improbable Farce, London, Piccadilly Theatre, 2 July 1941; transferred to St. James's Theatre, 23 March 1942; transferred to Duchess Theatre, 6 October 1942;
Present Laughter, London, Haymarket Theatre, 29 April 1943;
This Happy Breed, London, Haymarket Theatre, 30 April 1943;
Sigh No More, London, Picadilly Theatre, 22 August 1945;
Pacific 1860: A Musical Romance, London, Theatre Royal, Drury Lane, 19 December 1946;
Peace in Our Time, London, Lyric Theatre, 22 July 1947;
Ace of Clubs, London, Cambridge Theatre, 7 July 1950;
Relative Values: A Light Comedy, London, Savoy Theatre, 28 November 1951;
Quadrille, London, Phoenix Theatre, 12 September 1952;
After the Ball, adapted from Oscar Wilde's *Lady Windermere's Fan,* London, Globe Theatre, 10 June 1954;
South Sea Bubble, London, Lyric Theatre, 25 April 1956;
Nude with Violin, London, Globe Theatre, 7 November 1956;
Look after Lulu! adapted from Georges Feydeau's *Occupe-toi d'Amélie,* New York, Henry Miller Theatre, 3 March 1959;
Waiting in the Wings, London, Duke of York's Theatre, 7 September 1960;
Sail Away, New York, Broadhurst Theatre, 3 October 1961;
The Girl Who Came to Supper, adapted from Terence Rattigan's *The Sleeping Prince,* New York, Broadway Theatre, 8 December 1963;
Suite in Three Keys, London, Queen's Theatre, 14 April 1966;
Semi-Monde, Glasgow Citizens' Theatre, 11 September 1977; Seattle, Ethnic Cultural Theatre, 4 February 2000; London, Lyric Theatre, 14 March 2001.

BOOKS: *"I'll Leave It to You": A Light Comedy in Three Acts* (London & New York: S. French, 1920);
A Withered Nosegay: Imaginary Biographies (London: Christopher's, 1922); enlarged as *Terribly Intimate Portraits* (New York: Boni & Liveright, 1922);
The Rat Trap: A Play in Four Acts, Contemporary British Dramatists, volume 13 (London: Benn, 1924; Boston: Philips, 1924);
The Young Idea: A Comedy in Three Acts (London & New York: S. French, 1924);
Chelsea Buns, as Hernia Whittlebot (London: Hutchinson, 1925);
The Vortex: A Play in Three Acts, Contemporary British Dramatists, volume 19 (London: Benn, 1925; New York: Harper, 1925);
Fallen Angels: A Comedy in Three Acts, Contemporary British Dramatists, volume 25 (London: Benn, 1925; revised edition, New York: S. French, 1958);
Three Plays: The Rat Trap, The Vortex, Fallen Angels; with the Author's Reply to His Critics (London: Benn, 1925);
Hay Fever: A Light Comedy in Three Acts, Contemporary British Dramatists, volume 27 (London: Benn, 1925; New York & London: Harper, 1925; revised edition, New York: S. French, 1927);
Easy Virtue: A Play in Three Acts, Contemporary British Dramatists, volume 26 (London: Benn, 1926; New York & London: Harper, 1926);
The Queen Was in the Parlour: A Romance in Three Acts, Contemporary British Dramatists, volume 50 (London: Benn, 1926);
"This Was a Man": A Comedy in Three Acts (New York & London: Harper, 1926);
The Marquise: A Comedy in Three Acts, Contemporary British Dramatists, volume 53 (London: Benn, 1927);
Home Chat (London: Secker, 1927);
Sirocco (London: Secker, 1927);
The Plays of Noel Coward (Garden City, N.Y.: Doubleday, Doran, 1928)–comprises *Sirocco, Home Chat,* and *The Queen Was in the Parlour;*
Bitter Sweet (London: Secker, 1929);
Bitter Sweet, and Other Plays (Garden City, N.Y.: Doubleday, Doran, 1929)–comprises *Easy Virtue, Hay Fever,* and *Bitter Sweet;*
Private Lives: An Intimate Comedy in Three Acts (London: Heinemann, 1930; Garden City, N.Y.: Doubleday, Doran, 1930);
Collected Sketches and Lyrics (London: Hutchinson, 1931; Garden City, N.Y.: Doubleday, Doran, 1932);
Post-Mortem: A Play in Eight Scenes (London: Heinemann, 1931; New York: Doubleday, Doran, 1931);
Cavalcade (London: Heinemann, 1932; Garden City, N.Y.: Doubleday, Doran, 1933);
Design for Living: A Comedy in Three Acts (London: Heinemann, 1933; Garden City, N.Y.: Doubleday, Doran, 1933);
Play Parade (London: Heinemann, 1933; Garden City, N.Y.: Garden City, 1933)–comprises *Cavalcade, Bitter Sweet, The Vortex, Hay Fever, Design for Living, Private Lives,* and *Post Mortem;*

Conversation Piece (London: Heinemann, 1934; Garden City, N.Y.: Doubleday, Doran, 1934);

Point Valaine: A Play in Three Acts (London: Heinemann, 1935; Garden City, N.Y.: Doubleday, Doran, 1935);

Tonight at 8:30: Plays (3 volumes, London & Toronto: Heinemann, 1936; 1 volume, Garden City, N.Y.: Doubleday, Doran, 1936)–comprises *We Were Dancing, The Astonished Heart, "Red Peppers," Hands across the Sea, Fumed Oak, Shadow Play, Ways and Means, Still Life,* and *Family Album;*

Present Indicative (London & Toronto: Heinemann, 1937; Garden City, N.Y.: Doubleday, Doran, 1937);

Operette (London: Heinemann, 1938);

Second Play Parade (London: Heinemann, 1939; enlarged, 1950)–1939 edition comprises *This Year of Grace!, Words and Music, Operette,* and *Conversation Piece;* 1950 edition adds *Fallen Angels* and *Easy Virtue;*

To Step Aside: Seven Short Stories (London & Toronto: Heinemann, 1939; Garden City, N.Y.: Doubleday, Doran, 1939);

Blithe Spirit: An Improbable Farce in Three Acts (Garden City, N.Y.: Doubleday, Doran, 1941; London: Heinemann, 1942);

Australia Visited, 1940 (London & Toronto: Heinemann, 1941); republished as *His Talks in Australia Broadcast* (Melbourne: Specialty Press, 1941);

Present Laughter: A Light Comedy in Three Acts (London: Heinemann, 1943; Garden City, N.Y.: Doubleday, 1947);

This Happy Breed: A Play in Three Acts (London: Heinemann, 1943; Garden City, N.Y.: Doubleday, Doran, 1947);

Middle East Diary (London & Toronto: Heinemann, 1944; Garden City, N.Y.: Doubleday, Doran, 1944);

Peace in Our Time: A Play in Two Acts and Eight Scenes (London: Heinemann, 1947; Garden City, N.Y.: Doubleday, 1948);

Play Parade, volume 3 (London: Heinemann, 1950)–comprises *The Queen Was in the Parlour, I'll Leave It to You, The Young Idea, Sirocco, The Rat Trap, "This Was a Man," Home Chat,* and *The Marquise;*

Star Quality (London: Heinemann, 1951); republished as *Star Quality: Six Stories* (Garden City, N.Y.: Doubleday, 1951)–comprises "A Richer Dust," "Mr. and Mrs. Edgehill," "Stop Me If You've Heard It," "Ashes of Roses," "This Time To-morrow," and "Star Quality";

Relative Values: A Light Comedy in Three Acts (London: Heinemann, 1952);

Quadrille: A Romantic Comedy in Three Acts (London: Heinemann, 1952; Garden City, N.Y.: Doubleday, 1955);

The Noel Coward Song Book (London: Joseph, 1953; New York: Simon & Schuster, 1953);

Future Indefinite (London: Heinemann, 1954; Garden City, N.Y.: Doubleday, 1954);

Play Parade, volume 4 (London: Heinemann, 1954)–comprises *Tonight at 8:30, Present Laughter,* and *This Happy Breed;*

South Sea Bubble (London: Heinemann, 1956);

Nude with Violin: A Light Comedy in Three Acts (London: Heinemann, 1957; Garden City, N.Y.: Doubleday, 1958);

Play Parade: The Collected Plays of Noel Coward, volume 5 (London: Heinemann, 1958)–comprises *Pacific 1860, "Peace in Our Time," Relative Values, Quadrille,* and *Blithe Spirit;*

Look after Lulu! Based on Occupe-toi d'Amélie by Georges Feydeau (London: Heinemann, 1959);

Pomp and Circumstance (London: Heinemann, 1960; New York: Doubleday, 1960);

Waiting in the Wings: A Play in Three Acts (London: Heinemann, 1960; Garden City, N.Y.: Doubleday, 1961);

Collected Short Stories (London: Heinemann, 1962);

Play Parade, volume 6 (London: Heinemann, 1962)–comprises *Point Valaine, South Sea Bubble, Ace of Clubs, Nude with Violin,* and *Waiting in the Wings;*

Pretty Polly Barlow, and Other Stories (London: Heinemann, 1964); republished as *Pretty Polly, and Other Stories* (Garden City, N.Y.: Doubleday, 1965);

The Lyrics of Noel Coward (London: Heinemann, 1965; Garden City, N.Y.: Doubleday, 1967);

Suite in Three Keys: A Song at Twilight, Shadows of the Evening, Come into the Garden, Maud (London: Heinemann, 1966; New York: Doubleday, 1967);

Bon Voyage and Other Stories (London: Heinemann, 1967; Garden City, N.Y.: Doubleday, 1968);

Not Yet the Dodo and Other Verses (London: Heinemann, 1967; Garden City, N.Y.: Doubleday, 1968);

The Noël Coward Diaries, edited by Graham Payn and Sheridan Morley (London: Weidenfeld & Nicolson, 1982; Boston: Little, Brown, 1982);

The Collected Short Stories, 2 volumes (London: Methuen, 1983, 1985);

Noël Coward: The Complete Lyrics, edited and annotated by Barry Day (Woodstock, N.Y.: Overlook Press, 1998).

Collection: *Plays,* 5 volumes, edited by Raymond Mander and Joe Mitchenson, Methuen Master Playwrights (London: Methuen, 1979)–comprises volume 1, *Hay Fever, The Vortex, Fallen Angels, Easy Virtue;* volume 2, *Private Lives, Bitter Sweet, The Marquise, Post Mortem;* volume 3, *Design for Living, Cavalcade; Conversation Piece;* and *Hands across the Sea, Still Life, Fumed Oak,* from *Tonight at 8:30;* volume 4,

Blithe Spirit; Present Laughter; This Happy Breed; and *Ways and Means, The Astonished Heart, Red Peppers,* from *Tonight at 8.30;* volume 5, *Relative Values, Look after Lulu!, Waiting in the Wings, Suite in Three Keys.*

OTHER: *Spangled Unicorn: A Selection from the Works of Albrecht Drausler, Serge Lliavanov, Janet Urdler, Elihu Dunn, Ada Johnston, Ada Southerby Danks, Tao Lang Pee, E. A. I. Maunders, Crispin Pither, Juana Mandragagita (Translated by Lawton Drift),* edited by Coward (London: Hutchinson, 1932);

"The Boy Actor," in *The New Oxford Book of Twentieth Century Verse,* edited by Philip Larkin (Oxford: Oxford University Press, 1973).

PRODUCED SCRIPTS: *Australia Visited, 1940,* radio, BBC, 1940;

In Which We Serve, motion picture, British Lion/Two Cities Films, 1942;

Brief Encounter, motion picture, adapted by Coward, Anthony Havelock-Allen, Ronald Neame, and David Lean from Coward's play *Still Life,* Cineguild, 1946;

The Astonished Heart, motion picture, adapted by Coward and others from Coward's play, Gainsborough Pictures/Rank/Sidney Box, 1949;

The Kindness of Mrs. Radcliffe, radio, BBC, 1950;

Together with Music, television, CBS, October 1955;

Before the Fringe, scripts by Coward and others, television, 14 episodes, 1967;

Post Mortem, television, BBC Two, 17 September 1968;

"Song at Twilight," *Play for Today,* television, BBC, 1973.

SELECTED PERIODICAL PUBLICATIONS–UNCOLLECTED: "These Old-Fashioned Revolutionaries," *Sunday Times* (London), 15 January 1961;

"The Scratch and Mumble School," *Sunday Times* (London), 22 January 1961;

"Seldom Loved or Envied," *Sunday Times* (London), 29 January 1961.

"For me, the prewar past died on the day Mr. Neville Chamberlain returned with such gay insouciance from Munich," Noel Coward wrote in his diary (26 July 1945). Coward went on to write some twenty plays, a novel, several short stories, and the lyrics and music for many songs after Prime Minister Chamberlain stepped from the airplane with his notorious piece of paper ceding the Sudetenland to Nazi Germany. Coward's knighthood, his work in cabaret, and most of his considered statements about the theater were still to come.

Quintessentially, however, Coward belonged to that "prewar past." Noel Peirce (sometimes spelled *Pierce*) Coward was born on 16 December 1899 in the London suburb of Teddington-on-Thames, Middlesex, to Arthur Sabin Coward, a clerk in a music-publishing firm and a piano salesman, and Agnes Coward, née Veitch. Coward was a professional performer by the age of eleven; as he notes in an autobiographical poem, "The Boy Actor":

> For other boys would be counting the days
> Until end of term and holiday times
> But I was acting in Christmas plays
> While they were taken to pantomimes

He liked, at times, to give the impression that he worked out of economic necessity; and, indeed, his father's failure to cope effectively with the world of work meant that his contribution to the household was more than welcome. It was equally true, however, that he was stagestruck from an early age, and his mother's plea to the magistrates who licensed juvenile performers that he would break down if refused a stage career was not altogether an exaggeration. To both Coward and his mother theatrical eminence meant an opportunity to leave the shabby gentility of the present and recover some of the more-aristocratic connections the family had once enjoyed; but he also had, as a fellow child professional, Micheál Mac Liammóir, recalled in Philip Hoare's *Noel Coward* (1995), a sense that he was "made for" the theater.

Several of Coward's early engagements involved working with the actor-director Charles Hawtrey. Despite his plea to the youngster who dogged his footsteps–"For God's sake, leave me alone!"–Hawtrey became a role model for Coward, who watched and drew conclusions about acting, about plays, and, above all, about comedy, that shaped his whole career. Hawtrey–the original for Lord Goring in Oscar Wilde's *An Ideal Husband* (1895)–had developed a comic style grounded in apparent simplicity. Through elegance, economy, and timing he constructed a series of characters who threw away witty epigrams with languid spontaneity and an air of gentlemanly detachment that created the perfect conditions for another character to deliver a laugh line. While he might seem mannered today, to his contemporaries Hawtrey seemed to have the trick of imitating natural speech and manners. Coward aspired to this simplicity; his light comedy depends less on paradox or epigram than on flippant or casual remarks placed with such perfect precision that they seem almost surreal. His third produced play, *The Young Idea: A Comedy of Youth* (1922), brought the house down with "I lent that woman the top of my Thermos flask and she never returned it. She's shallow, that's what she is, shallow." Alongside this lazy precision, the young Coward, touring in plays such as Brandon Thomas's *Charley's Aunt* (1892) in 1916, developed a sense of structure. When, still in his teens, he had submitted a melodramatic piece titled "The Last Trick" to the producer Gilbert Miller, he was advised that "the construction of a play was at least as important as the foundations of a house"–advice that his own hero Gary Essendine echoes in *Present Laughter* (1943):

> Go and get yourself a job as a butler in a repertory company if they'll have you. Learn from the ground up how plays are constructed and what is actable and what isn't. Then sit down and write at least twenty plays one after the other, and if you manage to get the twenty-first produced for a Sunday Night performance you'll be damned lucky!

The lessons in structure that Coward imbibed were those of the Edwardian "well-made play": the first act opened the story, the second brought the curtain down on an exciting crisis, and the third resolved the crisis–generally by rewarding characters whose behavior conformed to prevalent sexual mores and discomfiting those who undermined those norms. The audience developed considerable expertise in picking up clues from the protagonists' remarks to servants and friends, casual allusions to letters, or other evidence of past indiscretions that were about to disrupt the present lives of the protagonists. The rigidity of the form tended to display the playwright's expertise in managing curtain lines and springing well-prepared surprises rather than the moral or social issues the plot might raise–a fact that George Bernard Shaw used to his advantage in shaping plays such as *Mrs. Warren's Profession* (1902), which conformed to the solid three-act shape and helped to contain the shock of the subject matter. That rigidity provided the backbone for Coward's lightest comedies and ensured the presence of a plot, even a wafer-thin one, that created a sense of action and progress rather than a mere string of witticisms. Even while questioning the codes underlying the plays of his parents' generation, as recalled in his preface to *Second Play Parade* (1939), he saw the value of their shape:

> All of these "drawing-room dramas" dealt with the psychological and social problems of the upper middle classes. The characters in them were, as a general rule, wealthy, well-bred, articulate and motivated by the exigencies of the world to which they belonged. This world was snobbish, conventional, polite, and limited by its own codes and rules of behaviour, and it was the contravention of these codes and rules–to our eyes so foolish and old-fashioned–that supplied the dramatic content. . . . it is easy nowadays to laugh at these vanished moral attitudes, but they were poignant enough in their own time because they were true.

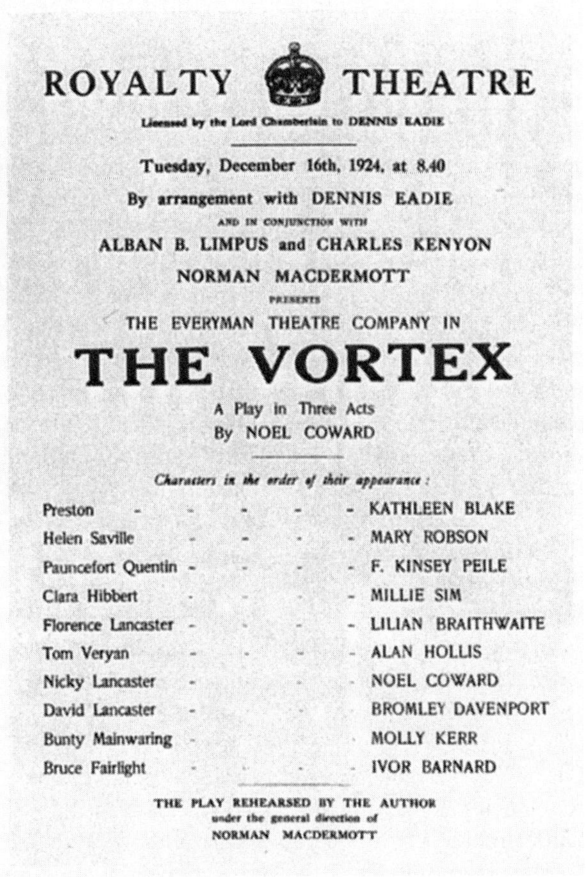

ROYALTY THEATRE

Licensed by the Lord Chamberlain to DENNIS EADIE

Tuesday, December 16th, 1924, at 8.40

By arrangement with DENNIS EADIE

AND IN CONJUNCTION WITH

ALBAN B. LIMPUS and CHARLES KENYON

NORMAN MACDERMOTT

PRESENTS

THE EVERYMAN THEATRE COMPANY IN

THE VORTEX

A Play in Three Acts

By NOEL COWARD

Characters in the order of their appearance:

Preston	KATHLEEN BLAKE
Helen Saville	MARY ROBSON
Pauncefort Quentin	F. KINSEY PEILE
Clara Hibbert	MILLIE SIM
Florence Lancaster	LILIAN BRAITHWAITE
Tom Veryan	ALAN HOLLIS
Nicky Lancaster	NOEL COWARD
David Lancaster	BROMLEY DAVENPORT
Bunty Mainwaring	MOLLY KERR
Bruce Fairlight	IVOR BARNARD

THE PLAY REHEARSED BY THE AUTHOR

under the general direction of

NORMAN MACDERMOTT

Handbill advertising the premiere of Coward's play about a drug addict obsessed with his nymphomaniacal mother

Coward's spectacular early success sprang from his adroitness in mapping the codified values of the form onto a world that was beginning to question them. His apprenticeship came to an end during the years in which England belatedly began to come to terms with the impact of World War I, in which Coward had served in the British Army with the Artists' Rifles regiment (he spent most of his service in the hospital after suffering a concussion in a fall during basic training). After almost a decade of silence, the former soldiers began speaking of their experiences and of returning to a world that failed to offer them a living. Their greatest bitterness was reserved for the generation that had sent them off to fight, and that bitterness percolated down to the generation that had grown up in their shadow. The cult of youth provided Coward, still in his twenties, with a valuable springboard. The young and well-to-do, his natural followers, were politically conservative, but they embraced the new postwar sexual freedom and justified it with airy allusions to Sigmund Freud and repression. Women no longer assumed that their place was in the home; refusing to adopt the decorous clothes and language of their elders, they bobbed their hair, shortened their skirts, and spiced their most mundane conversations with words, such as *divine* and *darling,* that were once reserved for the most solemn occasions. Coward's first major success, *The Vortex* (1924), about a drug addict obsessed with his nymphomaniac mother, seemed tailor-made for this generation and for those who wanted to understand it. The opening of the second act provides a stunning expressionist portrait of the rich and rootless of 1920s society: jazz blares from a gramophone as couple after couple drift, with apparent casualness, past the footlights and deliver acid little fragments of conversations about art, style, music, and sex that etch the social background with instant economy. The disaffected young, already aware in 1924 that their future could hold another war, are the wisest and bitterest:

NICKY It's funny how mother's generation longed to be old when they were young, and we strain every nerve to keep young.

BUNTY That's because we see what's coming so much more clearly.

The affair between Nicky Lancaster's mother and a young man, along with Nicky's nerviness, talent for jazz piano, and addiction to cocaine, offered the 1920s audience an enjoyable shock of recognition: they saw an image of their changing world that was simultaneously exciting and frightening. The frightening aspects were, however, deftly contained by the solid Edwardian structure. The first act introduces the characters and ends with a suspenseful hint that Nicky's fiancée, Bunty, and his mother's lover were once romantically involved. The second act ends with the "strong curtain" essential to every well-made play as Nicky and his mother discover that they have both been betrayed. While Nicky's reaction–launching into madder and madder jazz crescendos on the piano–adds some modern spice, lines such as "You utter cad!" suggest that the play is not going to demand any radical rethinking about the nature of theater. The lord chamberlain, Rowland Thomas Baring, second Earl of Cromer, whose functions included censorship of plays, had his doubts; but Coward saved his play by pointing out that it was really a moral tract. And, indeed, the third act–the confrontation between mother and son that the Edwardians in the audience would have been anticipating all through the intermission–ends with Nicky's drugs and his mother's cosmetics thrown aside and tearful promises from both to amend their lives.

This play is typical of Coward's work: extreme instances of modern manners, both sexual and social, are displayed; the audience feels a thrill that springs from a sense of danger, of living on the edge, but also enjoys the more-comfortable pleasures of moralizing. Coward is their guide in a new world. Not only did he tell a story that fulfilled both needs but, as a performer, he also gave the new image shape. *The Vortex,* as he said, includes "a whacking great part for myself." Nicky Lancaster allowed him to make use of his sexual magnetism: sleek, elegant, and wiry, he radiated a sense of danger; he could slip, without warning, from sophisticated charm to the edge of hysteria. The persona was irresistible. It was also marketable. As *The Vortex* went from low-budget play in a small Hampstead theater to major West End success, recordings of Coward's revue songs brought his style to people who could never afford to see him in the flesh. Songs such as "Parisian Pierrot" and "Poor Little Rich Girl," cited below, offered the same blend of decadence and moralizing:

Cocktails and laughter
But what comes after
Nobody knows. . . .

Coward's trademark dressing gowns sold in large quantities and his high-necked jumpers became de rigeur among would-be imitators. *The Sketch* (29 April 1925) ran a photograph, captioned "Noel the Fortunate," of him sitting in bed in silk pajamas, with cigarette, telephone, and cocktail shaker; it failed to point out that the picture had been taken in the boardinghouse in which Coward still lived with his mother.

By the middle of the decade the familiar Coward mixture dominated the West End. Three plays, all premiering in 1925, provided a characteristic blend: the mildly smutty *Fallen Angels, Hay Fever* (described by Coward at its first curtain call as "clean as a whistle"), and *Easy Virtue,* which received the final accolade for combining topicality and respectability when its opening night was attended by King George V.

In addition to the plays, there were also the revues *On with the Dance* (1925) and *This Year of Grace!* (1928); for the latter the *Observer* (London) review (23 March 1928) consisted of an alphabetical list of superlatives. *This Year of Grace!* enchanted Virginia Woolf, who wrote in a letter to Coward that "some songs struck me on the forehead like a bullet. And what's more I remember them and see them enveloped in atmosphere–works of art, in short."

Coward seemed at this point to have it all: money, fame, and a kind of success of which a bourgeois social climber might dream–the kind that allowed Coward to mix with the titled and to dine at the Savoy and that drew the members of the Bloomsbury Group and T. E. Lawrence and invited comparisons between his work and that of the movers and shakers of literature. Coward, with his gossamer characters who understand, like Sorel in *Hay Fever,* that "we none of us mean anything," evoked

Coward as Elyot Chase and Gertrude Lawrence as Amanda Prynne in the 1930 Phoenix Theatre production of Coward's Private Lives

on stage the same fragmented play of surfaces with which T. S. Eliot and Ezra Pound were experimenting in poetry and the Cubists in art. His was a modernism to which one could dance: Eliot's *The Waste Land* (1922) with jokes and a jazz beat.

Coward's success, however, had another side. He had achieved a precarious balance between creating public taste and pandering to it: if young men of the 1920s wanted to be Noel Coward, they were also capable of stipulating, through the box office, exactly the Noel Coward they wanted to be. *Sirocco* (1927) cast the romantic hero of the decade, Ivor Novello, as a phony and vicious Don Juan; even worse, the young wife he seduces does not return to her sanctimonious husband in a flurry of repentance but sees through the hypocrisy of both of the men in her life and brings down the curtain with the line "I'm free–free for the first time in my life. God help me." While songs such as "Poor Little Rich Girl" allowed the audience to enjoy feeling worldly, they were not prepared to see "romance" so comprehensively undermined: on the opening night people spat at Coward as he left the theater.

The balance was also threatened by the censor, who could not always be evaded with the panache Coward had shown with *The Vortex*. *"This Was a Man"* (1926) was banned in England for a scene in which the hero bursts into laughter when he finds out that his wife is unfaithful; *Home Chat* (1927) was reluctantly passed despite the "characteristic immoral twist" in which an innocent wife plays up to the rumors that cloud her reputation. Both plays, as Coward later admitted, were also poorly made and deserved their unenthusiastic reception.

Semi-Monde, however, was different. Written in 1926, it developed the technique that Coward had pioneered in *The Vortex* of allowing trivial remarks and momentary encounters to form a montage that both encapsulated and commented on well-heeled postwar youth. The entire play is set in the bar of the Paris Ritz, where people meet or avoid one another, gossip, and pass on. In their exchange of casual civilities shifting relationships become apparent, love affairs blossom and die, and innocents are corrupted. It is witty, deft, and, for its time, extraordinarily bold; but because several of the relationships dissected are homosexual, Coward did not submit the play to the lord chamberlain.

Coward spoke bitterly to the American press about the lack of freedom and vitality in the British theater and tried for some years to secure a production of *Semi-Monde* outside England. His failure made clear, perhaps more than any other moment in his early career, how his career would be circumscribed. To read *Semi-Monde* today is to be struck not only by its originality but also by its narrow view of sexual politics. Gay stereotypes abound–quarreling frustrated lesbians, bickering waspish effeminates–and the most sympathetic character finally opts for heterosexuality. Coward only hints, through the mouth of an acid observer who comments that the shrill queens are "not even real of their kind," at the possibility of a homosexual existence like his own, eschewing both scandal and pretense. Censorship ended in Britain in 1968, but *Semi-Monde* remained unperformed until it premiered in Glasgow in 1977. It finally opened in London in 2001.

The *Semi-Monde* affair made it clear that Coward would never be able overtly to explore his most personal concerns, even if he could win over an audience who had already made it clear that they would not unconditionally follow wherever he led. This awareness perhaps prompted Coward's determined drive toward popular success in the 1930s and 1940s; while he could still shock and surprise, he also adroitly adopted new masks to fit the changing times and 1920s cynicism gave way to a desire for reassurance. While the postwar recession dragged on, and the threat of fascism began to loom, the British theater comforted the "age of anxiety" with a diet of thrillers, musical comedies, and costume dramas. Coward anticipated the mood in 1929 with his musical *Bitter Sweet,* an unashamedly sentimental story of the 1890s with a haunting waltz at its heart. Contrasting modern jazz rhythms and sexual selfishness with the courage and chastity of a forbidden Victorian romance, it had an instantaneous effect on fashions not only in music but also in clothes, causing hemlines to drop.

Bitter Sweet largely owed its success to Coward's tunes, and he turned out other romantic, waltz-led confections, such as *Conversation Piece* (1934) and *Operette* (1938), throughout the decade. But *Bitter Sweet* also tapped into another aspect of his image, that of patriot. Much of the excitement it generated stemmed from its overt challenge to the dominance of the American musical: at the beginning and end of the play the heroine, now grown old, sings "I'll See You Again" against a jazz cacophony that symbolizes to her all that is wrong with the new generation–and, by implication, with American music and its values. The British public was able to see its Victorian past in a new way and to celebrate it with a music of its own–or, at least, with music that was unashamedly European. Two years later Coward consolidated this patriotic image with *Cavalcade.*

The box-office potential of *Cavalcade* is best summed up in a telegram from 1931 Coward sent to the impresario C. B. Cochran outlining his staging requirements:

> Part one small interior two departure of troopship three small interior four Mafeking Night in London music hall necessitating pivot stage five exterior front scene Birdcage Walk six Edwardian reception seven Mile End Road full stage but can be opened up gradually and done mostly with lighting part two one White City full set two small interior three Edwardian seaside resort full set bathing machines pierrots etc four *Titanic* small front scene five outbreak of war small interior six Victoria Station in fog full set and lighting effects seven air raid over London principally lighting and sound eight interior opening onto Trafalgar Square Armistice Night full stage and cast part three one General Strike full set two small interior three fashionable night club full set four small interior five impressionistic summary of modern civilisation mostly lights and effects six complete stage with panorama and Union Jack and full cast stop.

He had set out to stretch his own powers as a director, and he succeeded admirably; the spectacular stage pictures planned were all realized, with two exceptions: the General Strike and the air raid.

Cavalcade is the latter-day equivalent of Henrietta Elizabeth Marshall's *Our Island Story: A Child's History of England* (1905): a series of snapshots that, although sometimes tragic in content, illustrate Coward's first-night curtain speech: "It's still a pretty exciting thing to be English." History is domesticated into a saga of two families, the Marryots and their servants, the Bridgeses; the most moving intimate moments are those when the divide between them is momentarily–and artificially–breached. In one scene, for instance, Ellen Bridges confronts her former employer, Lady Marryot, with the news that her daughter, who has "bettered herself" to become a successful singer, is thinking of marrying Lady Marryot's son Joe when he returns from the front. She is met with an icy refusal to discuss the matter and a lament for the old rigid boundaries: "Something seems to have gone out of all of us, and I'm not sure I like what's left." Having constructed a scene in which changing attitudes to money, class, and marriage could have been challenged and debated with no lack of realism, Coward instead has a telegram arrive announcing Joe's death. Lady Marryot faints and is caught by Ellen with the exclamation "Oh my lady," and the boundaries are safely back in place before the audience has had time to take sides. *Cavalcade* provided employment for a large number of actors; typically, Coward ensured that they received more than the rock-bottom entitlement of extras, giving an economic fillip to the pubs and restaurants around Drury Lane. Thus, the play endorsed both the rigidity of the class system and the flexible possibilities of private enterprise. Small wonder that the victory of the "national government" (a coalition of the Conservative and Liberal Parties) two weeks later was attributed to Coward. And, perhaps, small wonder that his glib analysis alienated the intelligentsia who had lionized his revues. "Talk at dinner about . . . Noel Coward," wrote Woolf that same year, as quoted in *The Diary of Virginia Woolf* (1977), "the variety of his gifts: but all out of the 6d box at Woolworth's."

It would be easy to make a case for this view of Coward in the 1930s, the World War II years, and beyond. One could cite the cardboard working-class characters in some of the one-acters that make up *Tonight at 8:30,* the ten-play sequence he wrote for himself and Gertrude Lawrence in 1936 (one of the ten, *Star Chamber,* was omitted from the published version of *Tonight at 8:30* that appeared that same year), or the stiff and awkward attempts to depict middle-class passion in some of the other plays in the sequence, including the most famous, *Still Life,* filmed in 1946 as *Brief Encounter;* or the *Cavalcade* glibness that persists in his other attempts to approach social analysis, the 1942 movie *In Which We Serve* and the play *This Happy Breed* (1943). But to do so would be to offer an unbalanced picture. The Coward of the 1930s and 1940s was also the most innovative comic writer of his time. He was aware that box-office success was not the same as enduring quality; but he also had clear convictions as to where his best work lay. In 1958–not a productive year, yielding little but *Look after Lulu!* (1959), a feeble translation of Georges Feydeau's *Occupe-toi d'Amélie* (1908)–he recorded in the introduction to the fifth volume of his collection *Play Parade* (1933–1962):

> To quote Madame Arcati [the medium in his 1941 play *Blithe Spirit*], "It came to me in a blinding flash" that I had written several important plays–*Hay Fever, Private Lives, Design for Living, Present Laughter* and *Blithe Spirit*. . . . They mirrored, without over-exaggeration, a certain section of the social life of the times and, on re-reading them, I find them both unpretentious and well-constructed.

The comedies share an apparent triviality that is charged and given meaning by a unique erotic energy. All the central characters–especially, perhaps, those Coward wrote for himself to play–refuse to acknowledge any system of beliefs or values:

> AMANDA Darling, I believe you're talking nonsense.
>
> ELYOT So is everyone else in the long run. Let's be superficial and pity the poor philosophers. Let's blow trumpets and squeakers, and enjoy the party as much as we can, like very small, quite idiotic school-children. Let's savour the delight of the moment. Come and kiss me darling, before your body rots, and worms pop in and out of your eye-sockets.

The language may discuss the meaninglessness of life; but it is still bouncy, because there is a commitment within it: not to love–although the fluctuations of passion

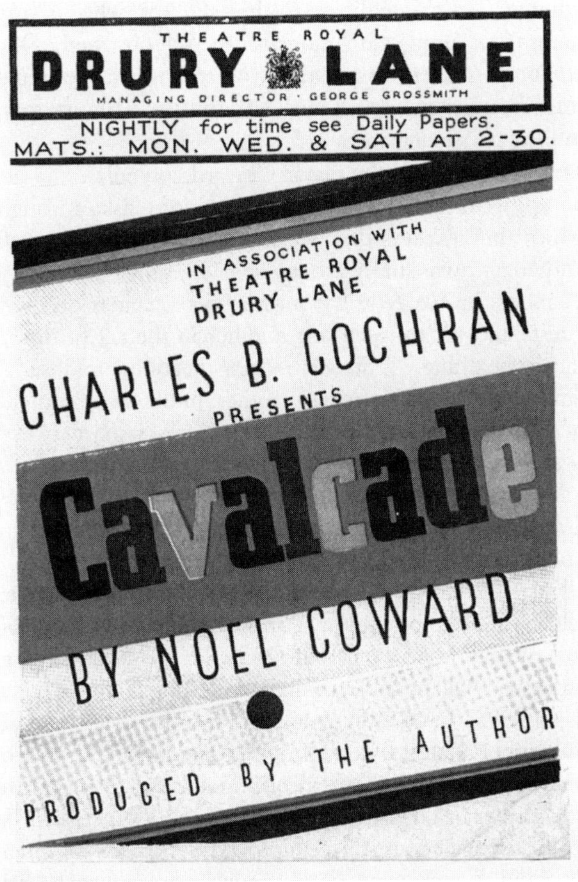

Program cover for the original production of Coward's 1931 play, about the relationship between an aristocratic family and their servants

that make Elyot Chase and Amanda Prynne unable to live together or apart comprise the only real plot of *Private Lives*–but, rather, to style, to the way in which those erotic fluctuations are expressed and acted out. Both *Private Lives* and *Design for Living* (1933) create a kind of hothouse in which the characters seem to have no political or social context–they live in hotels and studios rather than in neighborhoods, and they express no interest in anything but one another. Under these conditions the success of the plays depends on intense teamwork among the leading actors and on the magnetism the actors exert on the audience. Coward devised both plays for specific partnerships–*Private Lives* for himself and Lawrence and *Design for Living* for himself, Alfred Lunt, and Lynn Fontanne–and the intimacy of the original ensemble playing is almost palpable in the text. Cues demand instant response, whether verbal or physical; fantasies and wild improvisations escalate with a speed that reflects an acting partnership nothing can disconcert. The recording Coward made with Lawrence of the best-known scenes from *Private Lives* move at a tremendous speed given that, beneath the banter, the characters are coming to terms with the fact that they are in love. The speed is, perhaps, what attracts the audience to these figures, who, in any naturalistic terms, are monstrously self-obsessed. One responds to them as one does to acrobats on the flying trapeze, more interested in their daring and beauty than in their personalities.

Throughout the major Coward comedies, characters peacock about in a giddy variety of masks through which they express their feelings about desire, betrayal, and their own ability to amuse. The appalling family members in *Hay Fever* try out new personalities on their guests and try to catch one another in the act of doing the same thing. "You were being beautiful and sad," Simon challenges his actress mother, Judith, at a moment of crisis, adding that, in fact, she never was particularly beautiful. She retorts, "Never mind: I made thousands think I was." They communicate in scraps of old melodramas and games that nobody outside the family can understand. The claustrophobia of the closed circle of talent, a consequence of a relentless focus on style, makes, at best, for explosive stage action. The ménage of two men and one woman in *Design for Living* who experiment with all possible combinations but finally decide that they all have to live together, and the household of the author Charles Condomine in *Blithe Spirit,* in which his wives, one living, one dead, trade bitter insults with him and each other, crackle with the energy that springs from a struggle to reconcile desire with the need to find a flip and novel way simultaneously to conceal and express passion–for instance, by vaulting a sofa in *Design for Living* while crying "How do you do?" in Norwegian–rather than lapsing into the literal and trite.

Coward analyzed the process in *Present Laughter,* the comedy he wrote for himself in 1939 (it did not premiere until 1943). Hoping that gathering information for British Intelligence while touring to entertain soldiers during World War II might occupy much of his time (in the end he was not much used, a fact he resented), he shaped the part of Gary Essendine on the assumption that "no matter how long the war lasts it won't affect my suitability for [the] role, since I could play . . . wearing a long white beard." Although *Present Laughter* has a fair quota of love scenes, the focus is on the building and maintenance of the performer/seducer. Gary, a fortyish matinee idol, is not so much a character as a sexy construct that he develops with the help of a faithful army of retainers who are referred to as "The Firm": his agent, his manservant, his secretary, and his former wife. Together they restrain his tendencies to self-dramatization in relationships and divert his charm into the more profitable channel of the theater. When Gary's posturings get the upper hand, they acidly point out the consequences: for example, when he is besieged by an eager young experimental playwright, the secretary, Monica, refuses to cancel the interview: "You were so busy being attractive and unspoiled by your great success that you promised him." The action of the play consists of a series of counterpulls between The Firm, who look after Gary's persona, and those who threaten to consume it.

Present Laughter often approaches farce–characters are pushed into cupboards and hide in the spare room after a night with Gary–but the existential insecurity at the heart of farce is not present in its hero. Gary's situation is potentially tragic, as he loves to demonstrate: "I'm always acting–watching myself go by . . . sometimes I think I'm going mad." Typically, he allows himself to be seduced by Joanna, the wife of his business partner, while they recite the names of London concert halls; it is a bravura erotic sequence that–as The Firm ensure–has no long-term consequences. Thwarted, Joanna gives Gary "a ringing slap across the face"–an action that, in a play without Coward's assured concentration on the theme of performance and its pleasures, might have brought down the curtain. Here, the laughter springs from the fact that Gary is too absorbed in plans for his upcoming tour to notice that he has been struck. Like the majority of Coward's most entertaining characters, he is a monster, but one that the audience refrains from judging because of his charm. And here, for perhaps the first time in Coward's work, is a theory of masks and play that is not wholly pessimistic: Gary's ultimate mask, that of the fearless truth teller who admits that he is always performing, is not, as one might expect, simply the last layer before the emptiness at his center. Rather, it is an expression of the fact that his personality has been handed over to others for safekeeping and that he is confident that they will cherish it.

The public rarely forgave Coward when he failed to come up with a mask to fit the moment. It was perhaps inevitable that in the new postwar realism a playwright who considered his main asset to be "charm" would fall from favor. The early years of the century had provided him with the tools with which to invent himself, and he had helped to invent the 1920s and 1930s. Now he had to come to terms with postwar England, to see the dramatic and social values he had helped to establish questioned, rejected, and, finally, reevaluated. The process was sometimes painful.

The early 1950s seemed promising: Coward's diary for the last week of October 1951 recorded a landslide election victory for Winston Churchill, a cabaret appearance before Princess Margaret, lunch at the Dorchester with "everybody there," and "all London" fighting to get seats for his new play, *Relative Values.* "All London," however, did not include the young, articulate working class that was growing up in the newly formed welfare state and seeking a theater that fulfilled its needs. Even in 1951 a play that derived its laughs from a beloved servant dressing up as one of the family to deceive her upwardly mobile young sister–a play that ends with the line "I drink to the final glorious disintegration of the most unlikely dream that ever troubled the foolish heart of man–Social Equality!"–did nothing to extend Coward's prewar reputation as a multitalented figure with his finger on the contemporary pulse. The year before, his musical *Ace of Clubs* had dealt with the Soho underworld; seeing it alongside Frank Loesser and Abe Burrows's *Guys and Dolls* (1950) confirmed every critical cliché about the superior bite and vitality of American musicals. Meanwhile, Coward was refusing to play the king opposite his old sidekick Lawrence in what later became a major hit of the 1950s, Richard Rogers and Oscar Hammerstein II's *The King and I* (1951); he also turned up his nose at a commission to turn Shaw's play *Pygmalion* (1914) into a musical, leaving the field clear for Alan Jay Lerner and Frederick Loewe to achieve massive success with *My Fair Lady* (1956).

South Sea Bubble both demonstrates and symbolizes the gap that was opening between Coward and the new British theater. He struggled for some years with this light comedy about a tropical island colony, rewriting it after Vivien Leigh initially refused the part of the governor's wife in 1950. When the play finally opened in 1956, the cast received warm reviews; but the timing was ominous. A play in which independence is a bit of a joke, and the "natives" are leadenly patronized (they "weave away and make the most lovely waste-paper baskets and never stop having scads of entrancing children") was still capable of pleasing an audience, and the box-office receipts were healthy enough; but in the year of the Suez crisis the young and theatrically adventurous found more excitement in John Osborne's *Look Back in Anger*.

Coward, aware that the title of his latest volume of autobiography, *Future Indefinite* (1954), had a ring of truth, began to consider the prospect of old age in a theatrical market that had no room for him; he made plans for tax exile, putting his money into a bank account in Bermuda and establishing residence there and in Jamaica. Returning to Europe for the Dublin premiere of his next–admittedly feeble–comedy, *Nude with Violin* (1956), Coward discovered how deeply the public resented him. Newspapers carried cartoons with parodic punch lines such as "This Unhappy Greed," "In Which We Serve (and don't pay tax)," and "Brief Encounter (Catch Me!)." These jibes were all the more barbed because they alluded to works with which Coward had not only gained financial success but had also captured and helped to define certain aspects of the popular imagination. A song from *Ace of Clubs* seemed to symbolize his relationship with both press and public in the 1950s:

When you feel your song is orchestrated wrong
Why should you prolong
Your stay?
When the wind and the weather blow your dreams
sky-high,
Sail away–sail away!

Ronald Lewis as Hali Alani and Vivien Leigh as Lady Alexandra Shotter in the 1956 Lyric Theatre production of Coward's South Sea Bubble

The sense of Coward's work as somehow "orchestrated wrong" persisted for some time and ran deeper than a simple response to the quality of a few plays that were, by his own admission, below par. He had, after all, weathered opening nights in his youth at which disappointed audiences booed and called out "We expected better"; and he had usually (though not necessarily at once) reached the conclusion that he had overvalued his own work. In the 1950s, however, a gulf existed between Coward and the theater in which malice on both sides seemed to feature more prominently than any attempt at real judgment. At the end of the decade he wrote a play about aging, about the theater of his youth, and about the young imposing new values on old performers in a work that is both experiment and farewell: *Waiting in the Wings* (1960), set in an actresses' retirement home. The audience, watching some of the most-loved actresses of the 1920s, such as Marie Lohr and Sybil Thorndike, responded with affection. The reviews, however, ignored the elegiac aspects of the play and treated it as a sign of the senility Coward depicts in one of his characters.

"Timeless, toothless prattle," wrote Robert Muller in the *Daily Mail* (8 September 1960), while Bernard Levin in the *Express* (8 September 1960) pronounced it "so awful as to defy analysis." Coward's diary entries, often cocky in the face of failure, instead evoke the reflective side of the author, wondering "why they hate me so" (11 September 1960). He, in turn, lashed out at the new generation of writers and actors. Taking it for granted that they had no merits of their own, he had lambasted them in private, recording in his diary his response to Shelagh Delaney's *A Taste of Honey* (1958) as "a sordid little play by a squalid little girl" (16 October 1960) and the work of the Actors' Studio as "pretentious balls" (25 May 1958). Now he went public with a series of articles in the *Sunday Times,* admonishing the new generation to "Consider the public. Treat it with tact and courtesy. . . . Coax it, charm it, stimulate it, shock it now and then if you must, make it laugh, make it cry and make it think, but above all, dear pioneers . . . never, never, never bore the living hell out of it."

One possible reason for the mutual animosity was the carefully cultivated media image of the new playwrights as iconoclasts springing from the working class to change a theater to which they owed little. Even the magazine *Woman's Own* (1957) got in on the act with a coy article about what it was like to be married to Osborne. In fact, many of the new playwrights, including Osborne and Harold Pinter, were shaped by their experience as repertory actors, and Coward's treatment of them as inexperienced amateurs did not improve relations.

Coward, although happy in his youth to be seen as "the younger generation knocking on the door of the dustbin"–as quoted by Sir Gerald Du Maurier in James Harding's *Gerald du Maurier* (1989) after seeing *The Vortex*–had nevertheless always identified himself as a product of a theatrical tradition as old as the century. For him, the theater symbolized glamour, opportunities to develop and expand a social circle that read like a page of *The Tatler,* and an outlet for a never-appeased drive toward success. He was not likely ever to question the very need for a theater, as some of the New Wave were to do. Rather, he saw every moment spent there as part of an apprenticeship–not just in playmaking or acting but in the construction of a complex persona.

Coward's greatest success in the 1950s came from a new persona: cabaret artiste in Las Vegas, where he performed his own songs, romantic or ribald, with the same elegant flippancy he had brought to roles such as Elyot and Nicky. Cut loose from plot, his persona was that of the perfect party host: welcoming, unshockable, and witty, a relaxed alternative to the theater of ideas. As the 1960s wore on, however, and the New Wave playwrights, secure in their own theatrical world, no longer felt obliged to define themselves in hostile relation to an older tradition, Coward began to enjoy a revival. A landmark production by James Roose-Evans of *Private Lives* in 1963 moved into the West End to glowing reviews. The vogue for satire, the prevalence of camp in fashion and entertainment, and the preoccupation with style exemplified by slick television shows such as *The Avengers* created a new and sympathetic audience. The major comedies were all televised, and Coward was invited to direct *Hay Fever* at the National Theatre in 1964. As Maggie Smith remarked at the opening, "There seemed to be no generation gap with Noel, he just seemed to leap right into the sixties."

Perhaps the most attractive aspect of Coward's comedy to audiences in this period, in which sexual mores were undergoing major changes, was its androgyny. Experiments such as the National's all-male production of William Shakespeare's *As You Like It,* directed by Clifford Williams and debuting in October 1967, had begun to search for a different kind of theatrical eroticism. In Coward's comedies epithets suggestive of sexual polarization, such as "feminine little creature" and "warring males," are always pejorative. Desire is mediated not through the often wooden romantic clichés of *Brief Encounter* or *Cavalcade,* for which the action grinds to a halt, but through little epiphanies of style that energize it: jokes, improvised fantasies, childish fights, and spontaneous songs immaculately accompanied on the piano, all signifying a sexuality that is not weighed down with gender expectations. Decades before feminism debated these expectations in life and literature, Coward was offering a style of erotic playfulness as an alternative to sexual stereotypes.

"Dad's Renaissance," as Coward called the revival of his career, led him to embark on what he dubbed "a sort of acting-orgy-swansong": *Suite in Three Keys* (1966), a trilogy of plays set in the same Swiss hotel, each containing the requisite "whacking great part" for himself. While two of the plays are fairly undistinguished, *A Song at Twilight* was a remarkable last bow by any standards. It used the devices of the well-made Edwardian play–the surprise curtain at the end of the first act, the compromising letters, the figure from the past–to meditate on the theatrical limitations with which Coward had lived since the banning of *Semi-Monde.* Hugo, an aging writer, is confronted by his former mistress, Carlotta, over a packet of letters: but they are not letters to her. They were written to his male lover, who is dismissed in Hugo's autobiography as "an adequate secretary," and what Carlotta wants is not money but an acknowledgment of Hugo's hypocrisy. Gradually Hugo comes to terms with the fact that his work has been crippled by cowardice, and he reaches an understanding with Carlotta–and also with the wife who has tolerated his lack of love for so long, but whom he now realizes he needs and respects. Coward's makeup in the role suggested that the character was based on W. Somerset Maugham; but it was the poignant self-exploration of his performance that moved the critics, even as they perceived the obvious flaws of the play and wooden attempts to preach. As D. A. N. Jones put it in the *New Statesman* (26 April 1966): "After they've sliced through his pretensions, prejudices and blimperies, he's left wordless at the end, his face working–and I mean working. The hero's a crumpled pierrot, the party's over now; but Noel Coward is in his prime."

Coward's reputation retained its new luster until his death. On his birthday in 1970 a party was given for him by the BBC; and at a lunch at Clarence House, Queen Elizabeth II conferred his long-overdue knighthood. Otherwise, as he typically pointed out, his birthday was uneventful. Also in 1970 he received a special Antoinette Perry (Tony) Award from the League of American Theatres and Producers. In 1972 he received an honorary D.Litt. from the University of Sussex. He died in Jamaica of a heart attack on 26 March 1973 and was buried at Firefly, his Jamaican retreat overlooking the sea. His longtime companion, Graham Payn, and his secretary, Cole Lesley, dressed in white suits and wearing the gold bracelets he gave to those close to him, organized the funeral after drinking a farewell cocktail on the spot chosen for his grave. In 1984 Queen Mother Elizabeth unveiled a memorial in Westminster Abbey that bears the line from the song "If Love Were All" (from *Bitter Sweet*) that sums up his quality: "A Talent to Amuse."

Revivals of Noel Coward plays are frequent, and his place in theater history seems assured. His influence in shaping an elliptical, flip, and poignant style of language has been acknowledged by Pinter and Joe Orton. An album of his songs was recorded in 1999 by a dozen of the most famous names in popular music, including The Pet Shop Boys and Robbie Williams, for AIDS charities, a tribute that reflects his anticipation of the way in which singers such as David Bowie and Madonna have seized the freedom to invent and reinvent personae for themselves. New biographies have appeared in print and on television, discussing more openly the relationship between his own sexuality and the eroticism of his comedy. His lasting memorial consists, however, not just of songs and plays, or even of the records of his own performances, but of a style–a style that, paradoxically, is grounded in the freedom to adopt new masks and endlessly renew itself. As Osborne, once the enemy of all Coward seemed to stand for, put it in Sheridan Morley's *A Talent to Amuse: A Biography of Noel Coward* (1969): "Mr. Coward is his own invention and contribution to this century." Throughout his life Coward invented and reinvented selves that he offered his public. It was a process that ensured his survival during lean times such as the 1950s; but, more important, it was the process itself for which he ultimately will be remembered and respected.

Biographies:

Sheridan Morley, *A Talent to Amuse: A Biography of Noel Coward* (London: Heinemann, 1969; Garden City, N.Y.: Doubleday, 1969; revised edition, London: Joseph, 1985; Boston: Little, Brown, 1985);

Charles Castle, *Noel* (London: W. H. Allen, 1972);

Cole Lesley, *The Life of Noel Coward* (London: Cape, 1976); republished as *Remembered Laughter* (New York: Knopf, 1976);

Frances Gray, *Noel Coward* (Basingstoke: Macmillan, 1987);

Graham Payn and Barry Day, *My Life with Noel Coward* (New York: Applause, 1994);

Joseph Morella and George Mazzei, *Genius and Lust: The Creativity and Sexuality of Cole Porter and Noel Coward* (New York: Carroll & Graf, 1995);

Philip Hoare, *Noel Coward: A Biography* (London: Sinclair-Stevenson, 1995; New York: Simon & Schuster, 1995).

References:

Terry Castle, *Noel Coward and Radclyffe Hall: Kindred Spirits* (New York: Columbia University Press, 1996);

John Lahr, *Coward, the Playwright* (London: Methuen, 1982);

Cole Lesley, Graham Payn, and Sheridan Morley, eds., *Noel Coward and His Friends* (London: Weidenfeld & Nicolson, 1979; New York: Morrow, 1979);

Milton Levin, *Noel Coward* (New York: Twayne, 1968);

Raymond Mander and Joe Mitchenson, *A Theatrical Companion to Coward: A Pictorial Record of the First Performances of the Theatrical Works of Coward* (London: Rockliff, 1957; New York: Macmillan, 1957).

Papers:

Noel Coward's papers are at the University of Birmingham, England.

Sarah Daniels

(21 November 1957 -   )

Pamela Bakker
British Broadcasting Corporation

PLAY PRODUCTIONS: *Penumbra,* Sheffield, Sheffield University Theatre Workshop, 1 July 1981;

Ripen Our Darkness, London, Royal Court Theatre Upstairs, 7 September 1981;

Ma's Flesh Is Grass, Sheffield, Crucible Studio Theatre, 2 November 1981;

Masterpieces, Manchester, Royal Exchange Theatre, 31 May 1983; London, Royal Court Theatre Upstairs, 7 October 1983;

The Devil's Gateway, London, Royal Court Theatre Upstairs, 24 August 1983;

Neaptide, London, Cottesloe Theatre at the National Theatre, 26 June 1986;

Byrthrite, London, Royal Court Theatre Upstairs, 21 November 1986;

The Gut Girls, Deptford, The Albany Empire, 2 November 1988;

Beside Herself, London, Royal Court Theatre, 29 March 1990;

Head-Rot Holiday, London, Clean Break Theatre Company, 13 October 1992;

The Madness of Esme and Shaz, London, Royal Court Theatre Upstairs, 10 February 1994; reading, Los Angeles, Audrey Skirball-Kenis Theatre, October 1993;

Blow Your House Down, Newcastle-upon-Tyne, Live Theatre, 14 February 1995.

BOOKS: *Masterpieces* (London: Methuen, 1984; revised edition, London: Methuen, 1986; Portsmouth, N.H.: HEB, 1991);

Neaptide (London: Methuen, 1986);

Ripen Our Darkness & The Devil's Gateway (London: Methuen, 1986);

Byrthrite (London: Methuen, 1987);

The Gut Girls: A Play (London: Methuen, 1989);

Beside Herself (London: Methuen, 1990; revised, 1991);

Plays: Two (London: Methuen, 1994)–comprises *The Gut Girls, Beside Herself, Head-Rot Holiday,* and *The Madness of Esme and Shaz;*

Come as You Are (Tempe, Ariz.: Dandelion, 2001).

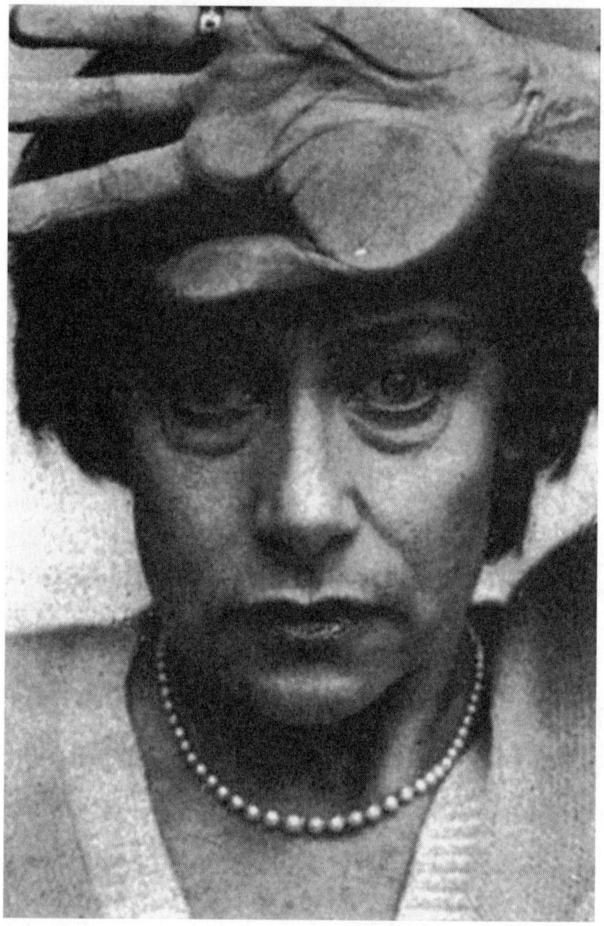

Sarah Daniels, circa 1990

Collection: *Plays: One* (London: Methuen, 1991)–comprises *Ripen Our Darkness, The Devil's Gateway, Masterpieces, Neaptide,* and *Byrthrite.*

PRODUCED SCRIPTS: *Grange Hill,* television, BBC;

Eastenders, television, BBC;

Medics, Granada, series 4 and 5;

Stars, radio, 6 episodes, BBC Radio Five Live, April–May 1992;

Annie on My Mind, radio, BBC Radio Five Live, 12 September 1992;

Friends, radio, BBC Radio Five Live, November 1992;

Purple Side Coasters, radio, BBC Radio 4, 16 November 1995;

Westway, radio, BBC World Service, November 1997.

Since her first two plays were produced in 1981, Sarah Daniels has become one of Britain's leading feminist playwrights. Her success has, however, been tinged by controversy and, often, by extreme critical backlash. Apart from the storm created by certain reviewers following *Masterpieces* (1983) and *Beside Herself* (1990), Carole Woddis's description of the playwright in the *Bloomsbury Theatre Guide* (1988) as "the only radical lesbian feminist to have made it into the mainstream" may help to explain the source of her notoriety. The "lesbian" label does not adequately characterize her work, but, in spite of Trevor R. Griffiths's view that Daniels's radical, as opposed to socialist, feminist stance has made her an "acceptable face of feminism," it is the term *radical* that has done the most harm to her reputation. Both Woddis and Griffiths, although no doubt attempting to endorse Daniels's work, have done her a disservice: by seeing only certain facets of feminism that inform her plays and neglecting others, they, along with many critics, have helped to isolate her work and relegate it not only to an out-of-date brand of feminism but also to one that insufficiently describes it.

While the radical position does surface prominently in some of Daniels's plays, it is a reflection of ideas that were current in society at the time she wrote rather than a deliberate attempt to disseminate a particular brand of feminist theory. She has said, "I don't read a book about some theory and then think, oh, put the theory in the play." In the introduction to *Plays: One* (1991) Daniels tried to quash any process of labeling that might marginalize her work:

> Feminism is now, like panty-girdle, a very embarrassing word. Once seen as liberating, it is now considered to be restrictive, passé, and undesirable to wear. I didn't set out to further the cause of Feminism. However, I am proud if some of my plays have added to its influence.

These words, which to some have denoted a rejection of the term *feminism,* really convey Daniels's uneasiness with the label and the expectations, theatrical or social, that it can create.

Lizbeth Goodman has identified the same sense of uneasiness with the term *feminist theater.* Where there was some agreement on the definition of the term in the 1970s and 1980s, there was "no such agreement in the 1990s. The goal posts have moved. The landscape has changed. . . . There is not one feminism, nor one feminist theatre." Daniels herself has, however, offered an idea of what she would include in her definition of *feminist theater:* "A feminist play is something that isn't just about women, but challenges something to do with patriarchal society, or that actually pushes it one step further and challenges the status quo."

Certainly, the notion of "challenge" has become one of the hallmarks of Daniels's theater. Her plays consistently challenge institutions of male authority over women, and they are, in turn, challenging for audiences to watch. It is this aspect, perhaps, more than any feminist orientation, that has earned Daniels the label of "radical." With subjects that range from lesbian motherhood, pornography, and incest to mental illness, infanticide, and self-harm, the radical nature of these plays lies in their ability to shock audiences by dramatizing issues openly, graphically, and unapologetically. The plays are able equally, however, to make audiences laugh, and this combination of the serious and the comic–or, often, of the absurd–is Daniels's most distinguishing characteristic. Goodman describes Daniels's type of theater as "polemical feminist comic theatre" and suggests that her comedy, like that of Joan Lipkin and Bryony Lavery, plays a strategic role in presenting serious political issues. While many of Daniels's female characters use humor as a political weapon, the humor in her work plays many roles. Ridicule is deployed effectively throughout *Ripen Our Darkness* (1981), for example, to lampoon representatives of oppressive patriarchal institutions; in *The Gut Girls* (1988) the women use wordplay and laughter as antidotes to the bleakness of their work and also as a means of subverting language and, thus, meaning itself; in *Masterpieces* Daniels draws attention to misogynist forms of "humorous" language and the implications they hold for the balance of power between the sexes; and in *The Madness of Esme and Shaz* (1994) much of the humor serves the conventional purpose of promoting audience identification with unorthodox characters. *Ortonesque* is an adjective often applied to Daniels's style, and certainly *black, surreal,* and *irreverent* best describe the type of humor at work in many of her plays, especially the early ones.

While the humor in Daniels's work is one of its greatest strengths, it has also provoked harsh criticism, particularly from male critics. Since much of her drama is concerned with indicting patriarchal institutions, the male representatives of such institutions are harshly attacked, often through humor. Whether figures of ridicule in *Ripen Our Darkness* and *Byrthrite* (1986), the butt of practical jokes in *The Gut Girls* or inadequate, vindictive fools in many of the plays, Daniels's male characters are not known for their sympathetic nature. Male

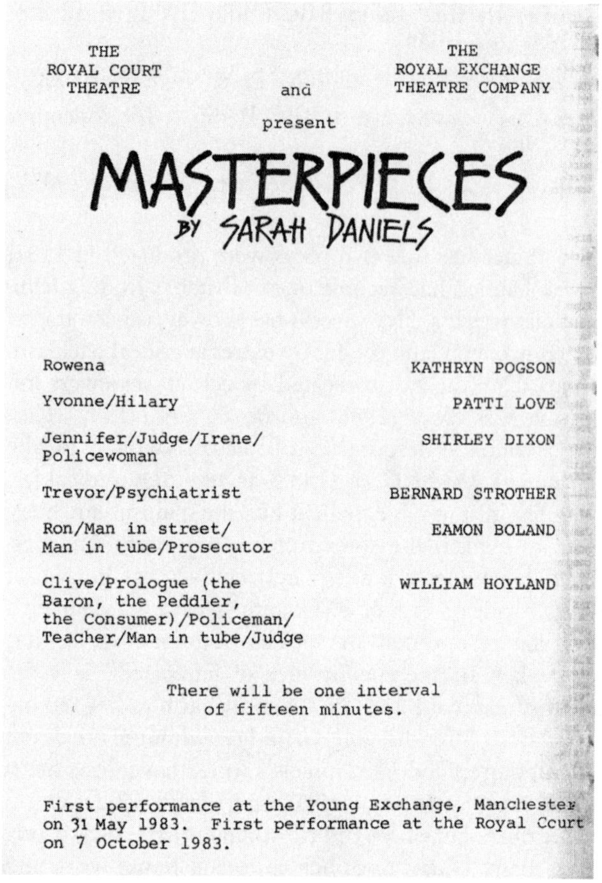

THE ROYAL COURT THEATRE and THE ROYAL EXCHANGE THEATRE COMPANY

present

MASTERPIECES

BY SARAH DANIELS

Rowena	KATHRYN POGSON
Yvonne/Hilary	PATTI LOVE
Jennifer/Judge/Irene/ Policewoman	SHIRLEY DIXON
Trevor/Psychiatrist	BERNARD STROTHER
Ron/Man in street/ Man in tube/Prosecutor	EAMON BOLAND
Clive/Prologue (the Baron, the Peddler, the Consumer)/Policeman/ Teacher/Man in tube/Judge	WILLIAM HOYLAND

There will be one interval of fifteen minutes.

First performance at the Young Exchange, Manchester on 31 May 1983. First performance at the Royal Court on 7 October 1983.

Cover and cast list from the program for the Royal Court Theatre production of Daniels's structurally experiemental play about the violence toward women fueled by the pornography industry

critics, therefore, have often complained of being "excluded" from her dramas. Female critics, on the other hand, have tended to warm to her brand of humor, describing it as "witty," "mordant," and "subversive."

Born on 21 November 1957 in London, Daniels attempted her first play twenty-three years later almost by chance. Bored by the job she held at the time, she responded to an advertisement in *Time Out,* the magazine of the Royal Court Theatre in London, requesting manuscripts by new writers. Encouraged by the Royal Court literary manager's positive response to the play she submitted, she quickly developed several more. Her first two productions were staged in the summer of 1981. *Penumbra* was produced at the University Drama Studio at the University of Sheffield, where she was writer in residence in the English literature department, and *Ripen Our Darkness* premiered at the Royal Court Theatre Upstairs.

Ripen Our Darkness is about the oppression the average woman suffers daily under the patriarchal institutions of society. The action hinges on the raising of one female character's consciousness of this oppression and the various rebellions by which all the women in the play attempt to subvert it or cast it off. Daniels's two main objectives are to lampoon several key patriarchal institutions–marriage, the church, and psychiatry–and to offer strategies for resisting, and alternatives to, these traditional bastions of male control. Most important, throughout the play Daniels emphasizes the political nature of personal relationships and of women's placement within the family. The oft-quoted line of Mary to her husband, "Dear David, your dinner and my head are in the oven," deftly balances a serious indictment of marriage with a decidedly black sense of humor.

Two months after *Ripen Our Darkness* premiered, *Ma's Flesh Is Grass* was produced at the Crucible Studio Theatre. The play exemplifies Daniels's use of black comedy: it opens with Jenny jabbing a fork in her father's cheek as he lies in his coffin in the living room of the family's apartment. Vera's only concern about her daughter's action is that his face not be marked up, "just in case the undertaker wants to go over him again." The audience learns that the father frequently beat and raped both his wife and his daughter, and Daniels consistently juxtaposes mention of such behavior with an equally shocking humor. The father's sister, for example, tells her niece, "Your father, Jennifer dear, was a very moral man. . . . He'd never make love to a stranger."

In May 1983 *Masterpieces* was produced at the Royal Exchange Theatre in Manchester; it transferred to the Royal Court Theatre Upstairs in October and to the main auditorium, the Theatre Downstairs, in January 1984. It is a hard-hitting, issue-based piece of theater. Apart from *Head-Rot Holiday* (1992), it is the only play in which Daniels admits that issues were her starting point: "I felt so strongly about the ideas in the play that, in an attempt to guard against being misunderstood, I censored myself from writing the detail and contradictions which give a character depth," she says in the introduction to *Plays: One*. Whereas her usual approach to writing a play begins with "thinking about it from character," with *Masterpieces* she began with an idea–pornography as violence toward women–and put "a story around that concept." This elevation of an issue over characterization or plot, however, does not make for a dry "play of ideas": *Masterpieces* is imbued with anger–an emotion that is aroused early in the play. Daniels's desire to write about pornography was fueled by anger at its ubiquitous presence in society and at what she saw as the failure of feminism to convey its arguments about the issue to a wide enough audience. Through the theater she hoped to make these issues "accessible in a totally different arena."

Masterpieces is Daniels's most structurally experimental play to date. Every scene and episode is designed to clarify her stance on pornography from a different angle. The play seeks to illustrate and analyze the effects of an industry that, according to Daniels, fuels a continuum of male violence against women. The underlying framework of the play is that of a trial; while the events lead up to a crucial courtroom scene, the trial framework is more figurative than literal. Each scene may be viewed as a witness for the prosecution, placed before the audience as judge. Daniels does not attempt to persuade her audience of the destructive nature of pornography solely through verbal argument but dramatizes the continuum of violence through a wide range of theatrical devices: having actors play more than one character, voice-overs, music, monologue, position freezes, a fragmented time scheme, multiple settings, variations in pacing, and unexpected shifts in atmosphere and action. Tracy C. Davis comments that these devices are designed to promote "stir and debate in spectators."

The level of "stir and debate in spectators" far exceeded the playwright's wildest expectations and has been responsible for much of the opprobrium she has received from the predominantly male critical establishment: "It was a big shock to me when people would come out of the theatre very angry or arguing, or saying it was a load of rubbish." Though it won Daniels the Most Promising Playwright Award from *Drama* magazine in 1983 and is now considered a classic of feminist theater, at its premiere *Masterpieces* aroused more outrage and ridicule than have any of her other works. Missing the point of the play, many reviews took up more space in attacking Daniels as "vitriolic" and an "embittered man-hater" and sympathizing with the "poor" male actors who had to play such "beasts" than in actually discussing the production. Mary Remnant attributes the reaction partly to the fact that Daniels, one of the few British women playwrights to reach mainstream audiences, was addressing a section of the public that was not yet ready to accept a woman writing so politically for the stage. Much of the force of Daniels's plays, including *Masterpieces,* stems from her unwillingness to skirt contentious or painful issues–issues that the majority of the time involve male collusion, whether deliberate or unwitting, in the oppression of women. Many critics have failed to realize that Daniels is not attacking men as individuals but as appendages of institutions of power that seek to subjugate women.

In August 1983 the Royal Court Theatre Upstairs presented *The Devil's Gateway,* which in many ways can be considered a companion piece to *Ripen Our Darkness. The Devil's Gateway,* however, offers a more practical denunciation of patriarchy than the earlier play by bringing in the notion of direct political action. While the action of the play still occurs primarily on the domestic front, the Greenham Common air force base in Berkshire, where women protested against the deployment of American cruise missiles in the 1980s, is a crucial backdrop to the play; images of and messages from Greenham Common are transmitted regularly to the characters through various media sources. These protests carry a greater potential for change than, for example, Mary's "castration" of a cooker in *Ripen Our Darkness;* and while the surreal feminist heaven to which Mary is delivered in that play is presented as an ideal female community as yet unrealized in society, the community of protesters at Greenham Common is perhaps as close as women came to a visibly powerful female "counterworld" in the last half of the twentieth century.

In 1986 *Neaptide* opened at the Cottesloe Theatre at the National Theatre–only the second play by a female playwright to be staged at the prestigious playhouse. Here Daniels's preoccupation with matriarchal alternatives is explored in even greater depth than in

Dinah Stabb as Evelyn and Lizzy McInnerny as Nicola in the Woman's Playhouse Trust and Royal Court 1990 coproduction of Beside Herself *(photograph by Lesley McIntyre)*

The Devil's Gateway. She moves from looking at the need for, and creation of, female counterworlds to testing the actual operation of such counterworlds in society. The matriarchal alliance under examination is an alternative or reconstructed family, a concept also explored in such plays as Michelene Wandor's *AID Thy Neighbour* (1978) and Caryl Churchill's *Cloud Nine* (1979), which satirize the traditional ideal of the nuclear family and posit unorthodox living arrangements among bisexuals, lesbians, and heterosexuals. In *Neaptide* Daniels presents a complete restructuring of the family, wherein women control their own roles and lifestyles. She lays bare the "heterosexism" at the base of Western culture that denies lesbians, particularly lesbian mothers, such control.

Daniels's bringing of lesbianism to the forefront in *Neaptide* is an important step not only in the development of her own writing but also in that of women's theater: Jill Davis points out that Daniels's plays are among the first in print to represent lesbians. *Neaptide,* which, like *Masterpieces,* has the underlying framework of a trial that culminates in a courtroom scene, deals specifically with the issue of child custody for lesbian mothers but also undertakes a broader feminist critique. Goodman sees Claire's lesbianism as a lens through which her situation is focused: "Lesbianism is the example, but prejudice against women is the real issue." This view is supported by the witch-hunt framework of the play.

Daniels's goal in the early to mid 1980s was to bring the voices of contemporary women to the stage; in the latter part of the decade she turned to history's forgotten female voices. *Byrthrite* deals with the torture and killing of "witches" in seventeenth-century England; *The Gut Girls* is set in the slaughterhouses of turn-of-the-twentieth-century Deptford and attempts to paint an historically accurate picture of the ordinary women attempting to break free from physical, social, and economic restraints. Both plays challenge traditional male representations of history by dramatizing aspects of women's lives during particular past eras. In *Byrthrite* Helen asks her husband, the village parson, if she may help him in his recording of the community's history in his diary. The parson's reply is condescending and emphatic: "Don't be foolish, women don't make history." Daniels's choice of the word *make* instead of *write* is important. In one sense the parson is correct: throughout the centuries women have not "made" the wars, revolutions, laws, and institutions that are considered the subject matter of history; nor have they kept the historical records. In another sense, however, the parson is grossly mistaken: both *Byrthrite* and *The Gut Girls* demonstrate not only that women were as crucial in the "making" of history as men but that their urge to record and understand it was equally ambitious.

While *Byrthrite* and *The Gut Girls* are set in different periods and focus on a variety of subjects, they share many features. Each play boasts an abundance of historical detail that delineates the social and economic conditions under which women lived in the era depicted. Certain characters, especially in *The Gut Girls,* are based on actual historical figures. Each play is divided into two parts and follows a chronological time sequence–with the exception of the interpolated songs in *Byrthrite*–and is restricted to a small cast, whose members play two or even three roles. Neither play focuses on a single protagonist but divides its attention among a group of women. The action in both plays is episodic and shifts continually between the individual and collective plights and actions of the women. *Byrthrite* and *The Gut Girls* also share with *Masterpieces* experimental forms and technical devices. The songs in *Byrthrite,* for example, lift the play out of the seventeenth century and draw parallels with modern scientific and technological attitudes toward women's bodies, while in *The Gut Girls* Daniels develops a snapshot approach by successively highlighting and then fading individual or group portraits of characters. Finally, both plays share many thematic concerns, including the reclamation of the lost voices and forgotten deeds of ordinary women, the economic circumscription of women's lives, class conflict, education, women's solidarity and strength, and the power of language and humor. Daniels's goal in both plays is to dramatize women's contributions to the shaping of the movements, events, and ideas of their times.

In the 1990s Daniels narrowed her focus. *Beside Herself, Head-Rot Holiday,* and *The Madness of Esme and Shaz* make central an issue on which she has touched throughout her career: women and insanity. From the psychiatric hounding that results in Mary's suicide in *Ripen Our Darkness* through the labeling of the peace protesters in *The Devil's Gateway* as "mad," Val's depression and nervous breakdown in *Neaptide,* the psychological repercussions of sexual violence against women in *Masterpieces,* and the interpretation of mental illness as witchcraft in *Byrthrite* to the treatment of Priscilla's "female malady" in *The Gut Girls,* the issue of women's madness–or, more often, of women being defined as mad by male society–has been important to Daniels. In the 1990s she examined it from new perspectives and placed it more emphatically center stage.

In *Beside Herself, Head-Rot Holiday,* and *The Madness of Esme and Shaz* Daniels's goals are to render visible the forces that collude to undermine women's sanity and to offer women the opportunity to understand and combat these forces. In each play the sexual abuse of female children or teenagers is presented as a significant factor in precipitating "madness." Daniels also shows how the labeling of women as "mad" by doctors, nurses, lawyers, or social workers can stigmatize them and cause their further oppression.

While the plays have much in common thematically, their stories and styles differ considerably. *Beside Herself* and *The Madness of Esme and Shaz* are what Daniels terms "works of the imagination" incorporating fantasy elements, whereas *Head-Rot Holiday* is a docudrama that deals directly with its issues. *Beside Herself,* the most technically innovative of the three, includes a surrealistic prelude that sets biblical wives in a modern-day supermarket and, later, a physically split protagonist whose ego and superego are played by separate actresses. *Head-Rot Holiday,* which is set entirely in a mental hospital, incorporates the visit of an angel to one of the patients–a surreal incident reminiscent of Mary's ascension to the feminist heaven in *Ripen Our Darkness. The Madness of Esme and Shaz,* the least technically experimental of the plays, offers the broadest range of settings, from a regional secure unit to a Mediterranean cruise liner. *The Madness of Esme and Shaz* is Daniels's first play in which a lesbian relationship is of central rather than peripheral importance to the narrative: the love accidentally discovered by two unlikely women takes them on a journey, both metaphorical and physical, during which they learn to come to terms with and break free from similarly damaged pasts. *Beside Herself* is also a story of a journey, one undertaken reluctantly by a woman who is trying to come to terms with the sexual abuse she suffered at the hands of her father. *Head-Rot Holiday* differs from the other two plays in that its narrative is loosely structured and of secondary importance to the issues it raises. It is an expository piece wherein each scene or episode is designed to illuminate a particular issue facing women who work or are confined in mental hospitals. Like *Masterpieces,* all three plays are shocking and painful to watch. Daniels's style in all of them is confrontational; both characters and audience are forced to face difficult truths about their society. Typical of Daniels, however, is the way in which she weaves, incredibly at times, an enormous amount of humor into such painful subjects. Such deftness at balancing pain with humor has become one of the distinguishing stamps of her work.

Equally characteristic of Daniels is the resilience she has shown in the face of constant vilification of her work by critics. While her plays are not beyond criticism–she fully admits, for example, to overambition and to leaving issues unresolved in her plots–it is apparent that, even by the strictest theatrical standards, she is a playwright more sinned against than sinning. She has continued through the years to extend the perimeters of her dramaturgy and to offer audiences complex theatrical experiences that place the female experience center stage.

In addition to writing for the stage, Daniels also has written for radio and television, including the popular BBC series *Grange Hill* and *Eastenders.* She was writer in residence at the Royal Court Theatre in 1984 and has been a visiting lecturer at universities both in Britain and abroad. Her plays have appeared in Japan, Australia, Canada, Germany, Denmark, and Ireland.

References:

Elaine Aston, "Daniels in the Lion's Den: Sarah Daniels and the British Backlash," *Theatre Journal,* 47 (1995);

Aston, *An Introduction to Feminism and Theatre* (London: Routledge, 1995);

Gayle Austin, *Feminist Theories for Dramatic Criticism* (Ann Arbor: University of Michigan Press, 1990);

Susan Carlson, "Process and Product: Contemporary British Theatre and Its Communities of Women," *Theatre Research International,* 13 (1988);

Carlson, "Self and Sexuality: Contemporary Women Playwrights and the Problem of Sexual Identity," *Journal of Dramatic Theory and Criticism,* 3 (1989);

Carlson, *Women and Comedy: Rewriting the British Theatrical Tradition* (Ann Arbor: University of Michigan Press, 1991);

Sue-Ellen Case, *Feminism and Theatre* (London: Macmillan, 1988);

Case, "The Power of Sex: English Plays by Women, 1958–1988," *New Theatre Quarterly,* 7 (1991);

Case, ed., *Performing Feminisms: Feminist Critical Theory and Theatre* (Baltimore: Johns Hopkins University Press, 1990);

Jill Davis, ed., *Lesbian Plays: Two* (London: Methuen, 1989);

Tracy C. Davis, "*Extremities* and *Masterpieces:* A Feminist Paradigm of Art and Politics," *Modern Drama,* 32 (1989);

Jill Dolan, *The Feminist Spectator as Critic* (Ann Arbor: University of Michigan Research Press, 1988);

Christine Dymkowski, "Breaking the Rules: The Plays of Sarah Daniels," *Contemporary Theatre Review,* 5, no. 1 (1996);

Lesley Ferris, *Acting Women: Images of Women in Theatre* (London: Macmillan, 1990);

Lizbeth Goodman, *Contemporary Feminist Theatres: To Each Her Own* (London: Routledge, 1993);

Goodman, "Theatres of Choice and the Case of 'He's Having Her Baby,'" *New Theatre Quarterly,* 9 (1993);

Trevor R. Griffiths and Carole Woddis, *Bloomsbury Theatre Guide* (London: Bloomsbury, 1988);

Griffiths and Margaret Llewellyn-Jones, eds., *British and Irish Women Dramatists since 1958: A Critical Handbook* (Buckingham: Open University Press, 1993);

Lynda Hart, ed., *Making a Spectacle: Feminist Essays on Contemporary Women's Theatre* (Ann Arbor: University of Michigan Press, 1989);

Graham Holderness, ed., *The Politics of Theatre and Drama* (London: Macmillan, 1992);

Helene Keyssar, *Feminist Theatre* (London: Macmillan, 1984);

Framji Minwalla, "Sarah Daniels: A Woman in the Moon," *Theatre Yale,* 21 (1990);

Mary Remnant, ed., *Plays by Women: Six* (London: Methuen, 1987);

Michelene Wandor, *Carry On, Understudies: Theatre and Sexual Politics* (London: Routledge & Kegan Paul, 1986);

Wandor, *Drama Today: A Critical Guide to British Drama* (London: Longman, 1993);

Wandor, *Look Back in Gender* (London: Methuen, 1987).

Anne Devlin

(13 September 1951 -)

Carole-Anne Upton
University of Hull

PLAY PRODUCTIONS: *Ourselves Alone,* Liverpool, Liverpool Playhouse Studio, 24 October 1985; London, Royal Court Theatre Upstairs, 20 November 1985; Dublin, Dublin Theatre Festival, 1986; Washington, D.C., Arena Stage, 1987;
Mainly after Dark, translation of a play by Arlette Niamand, Edinburgh, Traverse Theatre, 12 August 1986;
Heartlanders, by Devlin, Stephen Bill, and David Edgar, Birmingham, Birmingham Repertory Theatre, 19 October 1989;
After Easter, Stratford-upon-Avon, The Other Place, 18 May 1994; Belfast, Lyric Theatre, November 1994.

Anne Devlin (from the dust jacket for The Way-Paver, *1986)*

BOOKS: *The Way-Paver* (London & Boston: Faber & Faber, 1986);
Ourselves Alone, with The Long March and A Woman Calling (London & Boston: Faber & Faber, 1986);
Heartlanders: A Community Play to Celebrate Birmingham's Centenary, by Devlin, Stephen Bill, and David Edgar (London: Nick Hern, 1989);
After Easter (London: Faber & Faber, 1994; New York: Dramatists Play Service, 1999);
Titanic Town: Based on the Novel by Mary Costello (London: Faber & Faber, 1998).

PRODUCED SCRIPTS: *The Long March,* BBC Radio 4, 8 November 1982;
A Woman Calling, television, BBC Two, 18 April 1984;
The Long March, television, BBC One, 20 November 1984;
Five Notes after a Visit, BBC Radio 4, 1986;
Naming the Names, television, BBC Two, 8 February 1987;
The Venus de Milo Instead, television, BBC One, 9 September 1987;
Naming the Names, BBC Radio 4, 8 December 1987;
The Rainbow, adapted from the novel by D. H. Lawrence, television, BBC One, 3 episodes, 4 December 1988;
First Bite, BBC Radio 4, 1990;
The Uncle from a Miracle, BBC Radio 4, 28 June 1991;
Wuthering Heights, motion picture, adapted from the novel by Emily Brontë, Paramount, 1992;
After Easter, BBC Radio 4, 30 June 1996;
Titanic Town, motion picture, adapted from the novel by Mary Costello, George Faber, and Charlie Pattinson, BBC/British Screen/Company Pictures/Arts Council of Northern Ireland Lottery Fund/Hollywood Partners/Pandora Cinema, 1998;
Vigo, motion picture, by Devlin, Peter Ettedgui, and Julien Temple, based on the play *Love's a Revolution,* adapted by Chris Ward from Paulo Emilio

Salles Gomez's *Jean Vigo,* Impact Pictures/ Nitrate Film, 14 September 1998.

Although Anne Devlin has lived in England since 1984, her Northern Irish background forms the political landscape for her dramatic work. Best known for her two stage plays, *Ourselves Alone* (1985) and *After Easter* (1994), she has also made important contributions to radio and television drama. Her consistent subject is the emotional consequences of the social, religious, and political ideologies by which Northern Irish women are defined. The traditional view of women, upheld by the potent combination of Catholicism and republicanism, maintains a role for them that is passive and largely silent, engaging the iconography of mother or innocent–the Virgin Mary being the ultimate embodiment of both. In exposing the contradictions inherent in these ideological gender roles, Devlin presents a revisionist approach to a patriarchal history that she sees as stifling the female voice.

Although her subject is women in a politicized setting, and her aesthetics are largely in line with feminist precepts–*Ourselves Alone* focuses equally on each of three women in a nonhierarchical structure–her work yields only partially to feminist interpretation. Where the plays might initially seem to be heading toward some kind of agitprop, Devlin ultimately refuses to propose an alternative feminist ideology, instead allowing her characters to find an individual response that is determined by personality and experience, rather than by separatist dogma. Through a deconstruction of the prevailing orthodoxies of Catholic nationalism, her female characters may find self-fulfillment and even solidarity; but the assertion of the individual personality compromises the potential for collective action for social change.

While male adherence to preestablished ideologies is frequently presented as superficial and limiting, the women's counterposition is born of personal experience and is therefore, by contrast, open, subtle, and authentic. Any counterideology, such as feminism, would only replace one political orthodoxy with another. Devlin's female characters are caught in a society whose norms, both past and present, are male-determined. The only escape from such a situation can be found beyond the norm: in the inner, spiritual domain of the individual. Where liberation is achieved, it takes a psychological or even a psychic form, while the social constructs of femininity embedded in Catholicism and republicanism, with which Devlin's women struggle, remain largely intact. Dramatic interest is maintained through an exploration of the complex process of individual self-discovery, which is evolutionary, not revolutionary. In this sense, at least, Devlin's work might be described as realistic, even naturalistic.

Anne Maria Devlin was born in Ireland on 13 September 1951 and brought up in Andersonstown, a Catholic ghetto of West Belfast. Her father, Paddy Devlin, was a socialist politician. She was married on 8 July 1972; no children resulted from the relationship. She taught at Bushmills Comprehensive School in County Antrim from September 1974 to January 1976. Devlin has also taught at Birmingham University until January 1990 and was writer in residence at Lund University in Sweden from March to June 1990. In 1976 Devlin and her husband left Ireland for Freiburg, Germany, where she began to write. The marriage ended in divorce in 1983. In 1982 Devlin was awarded the Hennessy Literary Award for Short Stories for "The Journey to Somewhere Else," which was originally published in *Cosmopolitan* and subsequently published in *The Way-Paver* (1986). Early praise for her writing followed the publication of nine of her short stories in 1986 as *The Way-Paver.* The stories had appeared from 1981 to 1986 in a variety of journals, ranging from *The Irish Press* to *Literary Review* and the Northern Ireland Women's Rights Movement publication, *The Female Line,* which published "Five Notes after a Visit."

Devlin moved to Birmingham, England, with her second husband, producer Chris Parr, in 1984. They had one son, born in October 1984. In 1985 she received the Samuel Beckett Award for Best First Play for TV for her dramas *A Woman Calling* and *The Long March.* Both plays, which were broadcast in 1984, address "the Troubles" from a female perspective. She was made an associate director at the Royal Court Theatre, London, following the success of her play *Ourselves Alone,* which was produced there in November 1985 after premiering in Liverpool the previous month.

In *Ourselves Alone* the sisters Frieda and Josie and their brother's lover, Donna, face the challenges of living on the edge of violence while their men fight in the Irish Republican Army (IRA). The title is a translation of *Sinn Fein,* the name and slogan of the political wing of the IRA, which had recently received voting rights at the time the play was written. It soon becomes clear that Devlin is using the slogan ironically in connection with sexual as well as nationalist politics. The women are left alone while the men are out fighting the cause that claims to embrace all republicans, irrespective of gender. The female isolation that features initially as a negative aspect of the women's lives is, by the end of the play, transformed through female solidarity into a source of emotional strength. The final moments hark back to a time in a shared past when the three women found solidarity and liberation away from men, as Frieda recalls,

> And we sank down into the calm water and tried to catch the phosphorescence on the surface of the waves–it was the first time I'd ever seen it–and the moon was reflected on the sea that night. It was as though we swam in the night sky and cupped the stars between our cool fingers. And then they saw us. First Liam and then John, and my father in a temper because we'd left our swimsuits on the beach. And the shouting and the slapping and the waves breaking over us.

This final image offers a positive vision of women able to celebrate their naked sexuality away from the constraints of masculine definition. The women enjoy the sensuality of the moment until it is shattered by the intrusion of the men, whom they had left "arguing on the beach." Shared female space has to be reclaimed from within the male-dominated environment, and there is only one other scene, earlier in the play, when all three women are allowed to be alone together. Such rare moments are precious, if not altogether harmonious, thus adding to the irony of the title. Most of the time the male/female binary is activated by the intrusion of a male–father, brother, or lover–into the space. The lover is the most significant and frequent intruder.

The younger sister, Frieda, is determined to break away from political affiliations to discover love, claiming "That's the only loyalty I know or care about." She sees her public identity as created out of the masculine history embodied in her brother and father: "When did I ever have a chance to be myself? My father was interned before I was born. My brother's in the Kesh for bank robbery. You mention the name McCoy in this neighbourhood, people start walking away from you backwards." Her frustrated sense of selfhood is expressed through a desire to perform her own revised version of nationalist songs, causing outrage among the IRA men. A further act of rebellion leads her into a disastrous relationship with a member of the Workers' Party. Having been silenced once again, this time by domestic violence rather than ideology, she decides to leave for England, declaring, "I'd rather be lonely than suffocate."

Donna awaits the release from prison of her lover, Liam–Frieda and Josie's brother–for whom she left her husband and child. After being rejected by him, she struggles to bring up their daughter alone amid all the dangerous political activity–including a raid–in the house. The bedroom for her becomes the locus of nightmarish visions, which are also described as "suffocating."

The image of suffocation is central to Devlin's work and recurs frequently in this play and in *After Easter,* as well as in pieces such as the television drama *Naming the Names* (1987). It is an emotional response to crisis, a physicalization of the claustrophobic pressure of masculine definition, often associated with visions or nightmares. In *Ourselves Alone* Donna has visions of the devil that subside during her husband's internment and recommence on Liam's release from jail, when the nighttime anxiety of listening for a raid on the house is resumed. The devil climbs on top of her in a sexually threatening episode and vanishes, albeit temporarily, when she finally finds the voice to ask him to leave her alone. A clear link is established between the presence of her husband, sex, her visions of the devil, and a feeling of suffocation.

Donna's fits of suffocation are explained away as asthma by a male doctor (presumably she does not tell the doctor or anyone about her visions of the devil), just as Greta's psychic experiences in *After Easter* are prosaically ascribed to a psychiatric disorder, and Finn's dreams of strangulation and suffocation in *Naming the Names* are dismissed as epilepsy. Josie, too, has been haunted at night by shadows of male authority, "that dark figure which hovered about the edge of my cot–priest or police I can't tell." And Donna's daughter is already being troubled by "wee dreams." The condition from which such characters suffer is succinctly expressed by Professor Broderick, the fictitious author of *History and Imagination,* in *A Woman Calling:* "our crisis is past, but still we go on dreaming it." The women's selfhood will continue to be stifled by the violent and possessive male down the generations. Even Josie, having tried throughout to escape domination by her father, Malachy, eventually yields to his offer of protection for her and her unborn child, thereby returning to the environment that has imprisoned her identity for most of her life.

Josie is an IRA courier; though technically an agent of terrorism, she remains confined to a traditional female role within the organization and is more a victim than a perpetrator of violence and betrayal. In a particularly poignant scene she describes to her lover, Joe Conran, how she once planted a bomb "to show them I could take the same risks as a man." The bomb failed to explode; since then, she tells him, she has "lost the killing instinct." She goes on: "Now, I tend to think the crushing of a foetus is a tragedy." She is already carrying his child and senses the contradiction inherent in the Orthodox Catholicism of the Republican terrorist: anti-abortionist but pro-violent. Her attempts to challenge the male monopoly on heroics have been thwarted; her aggressive defiance has run its course. By the end of the play, finding herself pregnant, Josie is filled with a humanist desire to create rather than destroy and resigns from the IRA. She embraces motherhood as a promise of happiness, saying: "I'm tired. Tired of this endless night watch. I've been manning the barricades since 'sixty-nine. I'd like to stop for a while, look around me, plant a garden, listen for other sounds; the breathing of a child somewhere outside Andersonstown."

Devlin explained how her own pregnancy influenced the writing of the play: "Mother, or the absence of her, became, in the face of violence, a major force for good. Josie and Frieda have no mother–their friend Donna is a mother substitute. My own personal journey had been toward the maternal."

Josie's return to the fold, under the protection of her father, is not altogether an act of resignation. She adamantly refuses to live the life of her mother, of whom the audience learns little except that she spent most of her time listening for raids and is still present in Josie's dreams. Josie tells Joe how the environment of sectarian violence in which she grew up, like that in which Donna's child is growing up, with the mother keeping night watch, has haunted her whole life: "We grew up by the hearth and slept in cots at the fire. We escaped nothing and nothing escaped us . . . I wish I could go back." Every formative influence in the girls' childhoods seems to have been male, the only female role model being the once-beautiful Auntie Cora, who lost her hands and was left blind, deaf, and dumb at eighteen while doing her "patriotic duty" of female sacrifice: a stock of ammunition she was storing for her brother exploded in her face. In a refutation of the notion of sectarian obligation, Donna later tells Liam that Josie's child "doesn't belong to anyone. It's itself." Josie's desire to leave Andersonstown for an alternative life offers a glimmer of hope for a more peaceful future invested in a generation of children raised without inbred tribal affiliations, born outside "the ranks of the inhuman." The dominant father figure of the past generation will be replaced by the mother of the future, Josie.

The father of Josie's child is Joe Conran, an Anglo-Irish socialist and former British soldier, born of a mixed marriage and himself married to a Catholic from the Bogside. Despite being "cleared" as a volunteer for the IRA by Josie, he shows that his loyalties are divided when he betrays the organization over a shipment of arms. His political betrayal of the republican movement is inseparable from his personal betrayal of Josie. But the inseparability of the political and the personal is dramatized most clearly through the character of Josie. Prior to her affair with Conran, she had had a long and passionate relationship with a republican activist, Cathal O'Donnell. She describes with romantic nostalgia a day they spent together, he teaching her to build barricades, that was soured by the arrival of his wife pushing a pram. Communication throughout their illicit affair seems to have been conducted through subtext at political meetings at "the Club." Josie accuses him of having "put the whole power of this organization between us" when he let her go to return to his pregnant wife.

When Josie first appears, she is waiting for Conran to return to her, yearning for the psychological escape from political and gender roles that sex affords her–"that bed is like a raft and that room is all the world to us." During sex she fantasizes that she is someone else, from another century: "Sometimes I'm a man–his warrior lover, fighting side by side to the death. Sometimes we're not even on the same side." Josie's development through the course of the drama from a woman aspiring to a heroic masculine role to one asserting her own nonviolent humanism is clear in her final rejection of O'Donnell:

> You once told me that to love something was to confer a greater existence on it–you were talking about patriotism–the love of your country. I've only recently realized that you never loved me. You took me. You possessed me. You took my youth and you hid it in a dark corner for a long time. You never draped me with a public celebration. But I'm out of the corner. It's over. The hiding is finished.

Donna, the "woman listening" according to a prefatory author's note, is ultimately reconciled to her situation and decides to stop struggling. The choices of the three women–one to raise a child, another to seek voluntary exile, and the third to accept her life as it is–embody the options available to women in contemporary Ulster. Devlin has stated that the characters "were conceived as a trinity of women–the mother (Donna), the mistress (Josie) and the career woman (Frieda)." There is, she adds, an autobiographical element: "I found the three women representative of the three paths available at different stages of life, my own essentially." The play was written following the breakup of Devlin's first marriage, which left her alone and a frequent returnee to her native Belfast. In allowing each of her female characters to reach her own solution, Devlin sensitively explores an experience of the Troubles that is rarely exposed: that of the women waiting.

Ourselves Alone was greeted with critical acclaim and won Devlin the George Devine Award, the *Irish Post* Award, a *Time Out* Fringe Theatre Award, and the Susan Smith Blackburn Prize for the best play written by a woman, all in 1986. Devlin and her work were also nominated for two Lawrence Olivier Awards that year for Best Newcomer to the Theatre and Best Play, respectively. Most of the critical attention accorded to Devlin remains focused on this first play.

Devlin was a visiting lecturer in playwriting at the University of Birmingham from 1987 to 1989. In the period between her first and second major stage plays she devoted herself mainly to writing radio and television screenplays–most notably *Naming the Names,* which was first broadcast on BBC Two in 1987 and repeated in 1989, winning the Eighth International Celtic Film Festival Best Drama Award for 1988.

Originally written as a short story, *Naming the Names* is about Finn McQuillen, who becomes involved with the son of a Protestant judge only to lure him to his death in an IRA trap. Under interrogation by the security forces, she refuses to identify any other culprits; instead, she repeats a litany of names of Belfast streets that embody a history of male violence, sanctioned and commemorated by the British state. *Naming the Names* exposes the hypocrisy of a selective condemnation of violence by mainstream opinion, which is desensitized to that everyday violence condoned and authorized by the state, either through the "normal" activities of the security forces of the present or the "heroic" military victories of the past.

Devlin wrote a three-part adaptation of D. H. Lawrence's *The Rainbow* (1915) for the BBC in 1988 (it was repeated in 1993), winning the Eleventh International Cable TV ACE Award for Best TV Series 1990. She was a writer in residence at the University of Lund in Sweden in 1990. In 1992 she adapted Emily Brontë's *Wuthering Heights* (1847) for Paramount.

Devlin's second major work for the theater, *After Easter,* opened in May 1994 at the Royal Shakespeare Company's The Other Place in Stratford-upon-Avon, under Michael Attenborough's direction. In *After Easter* she pushes the political context further into the background to explore the Northern Irish female psyche in what she describes in a program note as a "quest play." The play depicts Greta's search for a sense of self, which she finds at the end of a journey that is both physical and metaphysical. Devlin wrote the piece at a time when she, like her central character, had been living in England for some years. The piece skillfully expresses the emotional isolation of the voluntary exile, caught between conflicting desires to be both liberated from and reconciled with the native culture. Perhaps the most remarkable feature of the writing is the sense of unease it establishes, before the ultimate tranquillity of transcendence in the final scene.

Though the conflict within the central character might perhaps be read as a political metaphor for the dual identity–British and Irish–of the people of Northern Ireland, this play focuses even more clearly than *Ourselves Alone* on the psychology and emotional life of its female protagonist. Sectarian ideology is largely embodied in Manus, Greta's brother, who reacts against his communist father by attempting to reclaim his Irish republican heritage. The inadequacies of his political entrenchment are exposed in a farcical scene in

Cover for Devlin's book about three women living on the edge of violence. The title is a loose translation of Sinn Fein.

which he inadvertently brings the security forces charging into the family home and is defended by his mother, while horrific aggression continues to be perpetrated outside. Against a similar backdrop of Northern Irish society to that presented in *Ourselves Alone,* Devlin here explores what she called in a 1994 interview with Jane Coyle "the mystery of the personality."

Thirty-seven-year-old Greta is married to an English Marxist atheist, George, by whom she has eleven-year-old twins and a new baby. Fifteen years previously she had cut herself off from her Irish roots to live in England. Early on in the play, she is being questioned by a Scottish doctor in an English hospital; it appears that she has had some kind of postnatal breakdown. He agrees to let her out for Easter, and she is taken to her sister Helen's London apartment, where she becomes part of another "trinity of women" along with Helen and the third sister, Aoife. When news comes of their father's heart attack, the sisters are obliged to return to their childhood home in Ulster, where Greta must finally confront the deep-rooted anxieties from her past that have haunted her since she left.

Greta has been having visions. Five distinct psychic episodes are described, all inescapably linked–much to Greta's regret–to Catholic iconography. Geraldine Cousin goes so far as to describe her as a "shamanistic Christ figure" in whom birth and death coexist. Like stations of the cross, these visions both punctuate her journey and lead her on toward her ultimate "death" and resurrection. At Helen's apartment a dark figure of woe appears at the end of Greta's bed and screams. It is not a priest or the police this time, as in Josie's memory in *Ourselves Alone,* but something more abstract; Aoife claims that it is a banshee–traditionally a female spirit whose appearance is a portent of death–while the more-modern Helen deems it a projection of Greta's suppressed anger. Greta addresses the figure as "Mother" and describes it as "the whole of Ireland . . . crying out to me." Unsure whether the figure is Christ or the devil, she, speaking to Helen, intuitively knows that the significance is religious and profoundly linked to her Irish roots:

> I mean–why's he picking on me? There's Aoife with her five Catholic children–and her good Catholic marriage. And Mass and Communion at least once a month. And he doesn't pick on her! Or even you, Helen–the way you live. Aoife says you're still lying down before married men.
>
> You'd think you might see the devil in the corner of the room from time to time out of guilt or something. But oh no–he comes tormenting me! Me, I'm not even a Christian. I don't want this–I don't want to be Irish. I'm English, French, German.

It soon transpires that this experience is the latest of many. The vision is followed by physical contractions, interpreted by Greta as the return of the voice that she lost in an earlier vision in preparation for some kind of role that will be bestowed on her. The timing of this event, which comes shortly before the news of her father's heart attack, is significant: this is the voice that calls her back "home" to Mother and to Ireland.

Greta now describes four major psychic experiences from her past. The first took place two years after she left Ireland and represents her "death." While staying in a place that reminded her of the glens of Antrim, she opened her eyes while sleeping to find that the room had disappeared, and she was lying outside under seven stars. With a massive scream, she felt her voice leaving her body and going up into the stars. Shortly afterward, she gave up her job as an art teacher and became pregnant, marking a surrender of the self: to Aoife's remark, "I always thought you threw yourself away," Greta replies, "I had no self to throw away–I died, remember."

Two further episodes involved fire: one in the early hours of Pentecost Sunday, when a flame appeared mysteriously in the curtain, and an earlier incident that coincided with the celebration of the purification of the Virgin Mary (Candlemas), when the flame from a candle lit up Greta's hair and she emitted a strange and beautiful cry, reminiscent of nuns singing. The earliest experience she recounts dates from just before her twenty-fourth birthday and completes the series with a birth narrative. A sleeping bag became the womb, from which she could see two windows, each with a separate view. An old priest, whom she recognized as the devil, was watching her–"I have felt watched all my life," she says. When he tried to smother her with a pillow, she obeyed a kind voice telling her to turn around. Breathing again, she saw a beautiful globe lit up far beneath her, and the voice continued, saying, "Enjoy your fall through space and time." This vision she recognized as her own birth.

In chronological order, the psychic reference points suggest birth, purification, a Pentecostal tongue of fire, and death, followed by the vision of Mother Ireland. The life cycle is profoundly linked with three key aspects of Greta's life: religion, motherhood, and her independent voice. Quite apart from Greta's unwilling vision of purification, the play is littered with references to the Virgin Mary; but these are mostly ironic, as in Greta's flippant response to the psychiatrist when she is asked whether she believes she is the Virgin Mary: "Och, I believe everyone is the Virgin Mary." The parallels between Greta and Mary do not reveal likeness but difference; the religious model of motherhood is presented as reductive and remote from everyday reality.

In her search for a context in which to make sense of her experiences, Greta visits her cousin Elish, the prioress of a convent. Finding that patriarchal Catholic doctrine stands in the way of the spiritual support she seeks from Elish, Greta rejects the invitation to rejoin the Church as one of the Mothers, or what Elish describes as "the real harvesters of souls," and continues her spiritual quest independently of any religious order. The Mother is a fascinating and ambiguous figure whose shadow falls across Greta throughout. A minor incident in the hospital where Greta's father lies dying recalls the ambivalence of Elish's phrase: a pregnant woman appears and dances, while Greta's brother plays "The Harvest Home" on the fiddle. It turns out that the woman is from the "banana ward." Every time she gives birth, her child is taken from her because she is deemed unfit as a parent. The irony of the moment lies in the conjunction of resonances, recalling both

Elish's definition of motherhood through the well-known tune and Greta's situation at the start of the play, when her baby was taken from her while she was in the asylum.

When reports reach the hospital of a sectarian shooting involving nine fatalities, Greta asks, "Is this the Harvest?" The audience recalls Greta's role in summoning the banshee, the harbinger of death, whom she addressed as "Mother" and beseeched not to harm her family. In the opening monologue of the play she recalls how in childhood she would hide in silence while her mother screamed and pounded at her bedroom door. Later she makes a connection with a book her mother was reading at the time, "a cheap pornographic story of incest, the rape of a girl by her father." The motif of sexual jealousy on the part of the mother toward the father-daughter relationship is more fully developed later, when Greta confronts the ghosts of her family origins. Near the end of the play the audience discovers that Greta endured years of drunken beatings from her mother, given and received in the belief that the husband loved his daughter more than he loved his wife. In a scene of black comedy the entire family–Greta; her sisters; their brother, Manus; and their drunken mother, Rose–bicker over whom the husband and father loved the most. The squabble subsides when they take shelter from sectarian violence in the street by squeezing under the table on which the father's body is laid out. Later, alone, Greta is privileged to have an intimate conversation with her dead father before his hand suddenly reaches up from the coffin for her throat. At this moment she realizes her mistake: he did love his wife more than he ever loved his daughter. The tendency of the female family members to define themselves in relation to the male has disrupted the relationship between mother and daughter. Having faced the truth about her past, Greta determines to rid herself of its ghosts and turn her mind to the future.

Returning to London with Helen, Greta comes close to committing suicide but chooses not to follow her father's ashes into the Thames, heeding instead the call of motherhood. The moving final scene finds Greta alone, "at home" for the first time (according to a stage direction), telling a story to her baby. The story is a quasi-mythical tale of origins. A gigantic stag appears to Greta and her mother while they are hunting. The animal is antlered and black, profiled on a high ridge, having leaped through centuries to reach them from the frozen north. Unlike her mother, Greta is not afraid and calmly feeds the hungry beast. She resists its frozen kiss, and eventually the stag's face begins to take on human features. The snows melt, and she climbs on the strong back and flies to the top of the world, to the ultimate source. She tells the child, "and he took me to the place where rivers come from, where you come from . . . and this is my own story."

The stag, with its masculine features, seems to represent the past as it is offered to the women of Northern Ireland. While her mother lived in fear of that past, Greta has now learned to handle it with tenderness, to understand it, and so to come to terms with it. This reconciliation with her past and with the future, in the form of her child, marks the end of Greta's quest for her self and her home. In the final monologue she is at last returned to "the inner room" of her life, from which she has for so long been exiled. This final narration is placed in a traditional Irish setting, with the empty chair positioned near the storyteller. Even though the scene takes place in London–Greta has, indeed, escaped this time–she has found her own voice, which is Irish. In an early exchange Helen had explained that she has nurtured an American accent to replace her Northern Irish one because it is more positively received in England. In a program note Devlin says that if Greta's life is to "become something more truthful than merely an echo of someone else's tongue" she has to "make the transition from the language of the hearth to the language of the heart." Each of her spiritual experiences marks a step along the path to sounding her own authentic voice. In the birth scene she is kept alive by a warm, kind voice when the priest tries to stifle hers with the pillow. The second vision occurs on Pentecost Sunday, the day when the apostles were given "tongues of fire" and "began to speak in other tongues." The Candlemas scene is accompanied by a wordless but beautiful cry from Greta. The death scene is when her voice is altogether lost, only to return in time for her journey back to Ulster.

What happens after Easter is salvation, following death and resurrection. In Devlin's terms, the language of Catholicism is transcended in the liberation of an authentic female voice, imbued with the spirituality of myth and folklore in the Celtic tradition rather than the parroting doctrine of the Church. In the penultimate scene, set on Westminster Bridge, Greta playfully parodies William Wordsworth, replacing the Romanticism of his verse with a gritty reality and finally shouting her exorcism above an apocalyptic crescendo of horses' hooves: "Words! So do I cast out all devils!"

One image of transcendence that recurs throughout the play is associated with light, as a force capable of penetrating even the most apparently solid barriers. Cousin describes how the original set, "partly suggestive of containment–doors, windows, cupboards, a fence, the wall of a bridge–paradoxically revealed the insubstantiality of barriers and boundaries." In this play both physical and psychological barriers are systematically deconstructed to liberate Greta from the historical confines of her culture.

The piece moves easily between the prosaic and the lyrical, the mystical and the banal, with a great deal of wryly observed humor along the way. Still in a predominantly naturalistic mode, *After Easter* is more theatrically daring than *Ourselves Alone,* involving a greater use of symbolism and encompassing a wider stylistic range. The play was well received by critics; they were, however, less unanimous in their praise for *After Easter* than they had been for Devlin's first play, some finding it uneven or unclear. The play was nominated for the Lloyds Playwright of the Year Award for Devlin in 1994, and the text has become a regular feature on British theater studies syllabi.

In placing her emphasis on the emotional contours of the contemporary sociopolitical situation, Devlin has paved the way for a younger generation of Irish playwrights from both north and south, including Christina Reid and Marina Carr, whose transcendence of separatist ideology is effected through the medium of the family. Sean O'Casey is clearly a key predecessor; Devlin's female characters share with Mary Boyle in *Juno and the Paycock* (1924) and Nora Clitheroe in *The Plough and the Stars* (1926) a deep sensitivity to humanist priorities and a capacity to shine light through the vainglorious posturing of the "heroic" male. As Greta says in *After Easter,* "all we have to do is stay alive and tell the truth."

Interview:

Jane Coyle, "Pride of Belfast," *Irish Times,* 2 November 1994, supplement, pp. 2–3.

References:

Geraldine Cousin, *Women in Dramatic Place and Time* (London & New York: Routledge, 1996), pp. 176–178, 187–204;

David Edgar, ed., *State of Play–Playwrights on Playwriting* (London: Faber & Faber, 1999), pp. 96–99;

Susanne Greenhalgh, "The Bomb in the Baby-Carriage: Women and Terrorism in Contemporary Drama," in *Terrorism and Modern Drama,* edited by John Orr and Dragan Klaic (Edinburgh: Edinburgh University Press, 1990), pp. 160–183;

Helen Lojek, "Difference without Indifference: The Drama of Frank McGuinness and Anne Devlin," *Eire,* 25 (Summer 1990): 56–68;

Christopher Murray, *Twentieth-Century Irish Drama–Mirror up to Nation* (Manchester & New York: Manchester University Press, 1997), pp. 193–194;

Anthony Roche, *Contemporary Irish Drama from Beckett to McGuinness* (Dublin: Gill & Macmillan, 1994), pp. 236–241;

Bernice Schrank and William Demastes, *Irish Playwrights, 1880–1995, A Research and Production Sourcebook* (Westport, Conn. & London: Greenwood Press, 1997), pp. 93–96;

Mary Trotter, "Women Playwrights in Northern Ireland" in *The Cambridge Companion to Modern British Women Playwrights,* edited by Elaine Aston and Janelle Reinelt (Cambridge: Cambridge University Press, 2000).

Dic Edwards

(21 January 1953 -)

Anna-Marie Taylor
University of Wales, Swansea

PLAY PRODUCTIONS: *Late City Echo,* Cardiff, Sherman Arena, 10 November 1981;
At the End of the Bay, Cardiff, Sherman Theatre, 23 November 1982;
Canned Goods, Cardiff, Sherman Theatre, 15 November 1983;
Looking for the World, Cardiff, Sherman Theatre, 22 April 1986;
Little Yankee, Milford Haven, Wales, The Torch Theatre, 28 April 1987;
Long to Rain over Us, Leicester, Haymarket Theatre Studio, 15 November 1987;
Doctor of the Americas, London, The Central School of Speech and Drama, 19 April 1988;
Low People, Leicester, Haymarket Theatre Studio, 21 May 1989;
the fourth world, Mold, Wales, Theatre Clwyd, Emlyn Williams Studio, 21 February 1990;
Regan (In the Great Society), Wales Tour, 6 October 1991;
Mother Hubberd, Wales Tour, 3 December 1991;
Casanova Undone, Glasgow, Citizens' Theatre Company, 26 March 1992;
Moon River/The Deal, Wales Tour, Spectacle Theatre Company, November 1992;
The Juniper Tree, Southborough, Kent, Broomhill Opera Company, 18 July 1993;
The Beggar's New Clothes, Southborough, Kent, Broomhill International Opera Festival, 24 July 1993;
The Shakespeare Factory, Wales Tour, Spectacle Theatre Company, September 1993;
Wittgenstein's Daughter, Glasgow, Citizens' Theatre Company, 9 September 1993;
Utah Blue, Cardiff, The Point, 22 February 1995;
David, Wales Tour, Spectacle Theatre Company, February 1996;
Lola Brecht, Aberystwyth, Wales, Castaway Theatre, 23 April 1996;
The Man Who Gave His Foot for Love, Rhondda, Cardiff and Wales Tour, Spectacle Theatre Company, October 1996;

Dic Edwards (photograph by Simon Chapman)

Kid, Wales Tour, Spectacle Theatre Company, October 1997;
Vertigo, Wales Tour, Spectacle Theatre Company, October 1997;
The Freewheelers, Wales Tour, Spectacle Theatre Company, October 1998;

Scene from the 1986 production at the Sherman Theatre in Cardiff, Wales, of Edwards's Looking for the World

Over Milk Wood, Wales Tour, Spectacle Theatre Company, October 1999;

Antigone Now, Wales Tour, October 2000.

BOOKS: *At the End of the Bay* (Lampeter, Wales: Spectrum, 1982);

Low People (Lampeter, Wales: Bardprint, 1989);

the fourth world (Lampeter, Wales: Bardprint, 1990);

Regan (In the Great Society) (Brighton: The Press Gang, 1991);

Three Plays: Casanova Undone, Looking for the World, Long to Rain over Us (London: Oberon, 1992); published as *Casanova Undone and Other Plays* (New York: Theatre Communications Group, 1998);

Wittgenstein's Daughter (London: Oberon, 1993; New York: Theatre Communications Group, 1998);

Utah Blue: Scenes in a Culture of Murder (Cardiff: Made in Wales Stage Company, 1995);

The Shakespeare Factory, Moon River/The Deal, David (Bridgend, Wales: Seren, 1998);

Americana, Utah Blue, Over Milk Wood: Poems (London: Oberon, 2000); republished as *Americana* (New York: Theatre Communications Group, 2001);

Worlds (London: Oberon, 2001)–includes *Lola Brecht, Franco's Bastard,* and *Low People.*

Apart from Dylan Thomas's ubiquitous *Under Milk Wood* (1954), modern Welsh drama has had a low profile in the British theater. Dramatists who write within wider traditions and schools of drama have often been sidestreamed (some may say marginalized) into belonging to what has been constructed as specifically "Welsh" ways of writing. Such was the case with Gwyn Thomas, whose grittily and wittily realistic portrayals of South Wales life of the 1960s and 1970s were rarely seen by critics as being part of a wider, much-celebrated realism in British theater at the time. Ed Thomas has suffered the same fate, and plays such as *House of America* (1998) and *Gas Station Angel* (1998), while sharing the heightened realism of dramatists such as Mark Ravenhill and Sarah Kane, as well as their dissection of the cultural vacuousness of late-twentieth-century Britain, have been reviewed indifferently by London-based critics as being too rhetorical in expression and overtly "Welsh" in their settings.

The uncompromising and darkly poetic work of Dic Edwards, one of Wales's most prolific contemporary dramatists, has undergone a more complex reception than that of Gwyn Thomas and Ed Thomas. Edwards's plays have often eschewed a specifically Welsh locality, with the author seeing his work as belonging to wider European literary and philosophical contexts. In rejecting a specifically Welsh identity for himself as a playwright Edwards has been undercelebrated within Welsh literary circles, where, in view of Wales's own precariousness as a nation, there has been a preoccupation with questions of Welsh ethnic and linguistic identity. The ambition of Edwards's dramatic ideas and his favoring of extended rhetorical speeches have also meant that his plays, while performed throughout Britain, often have been found difficult to assess and categorize by critics. Further problems of categorization have arisen with Edwards's failure to write within a particular genre of drama, as he has written equally disconcerting, issue-based plays for the main stage, for educational theater, and as librettos for operas.

Born 21 January 1953 in Cardiff into a working-class family, Richard Edwards, son of Daniel and Sylvia Edwards, was educated at Whitchurch Grammar School from 1963 to 1969. He left school early and worked as a manual laborer in sawmills and on the construction of dams in Wales. He resumed his education in 1974, studying English and philosophy at St. David's University College, Lampeter, and drama at the master's level at the University of Wales, Cardiff, in 1977–1978. He trained as a teacher at the University of Cambridge in 1978–1979 but left before the end of the course, as he found the academic world of Cambridge stifling. The introspection and snobbery that he detected in Cambridge academic life reappear as dramatic subjects in his 1993 play *Wittgenstein's Daughter.*

After graduation from Lampeter University Edwards worked as a barman in west Wales before embarking on a writing career. His first play, *Late City Echo,* about the Firemen's Strike, was performed in 1981. He has worked as Writer in Residence at Lampeter School, West Wales (1984), at Ysgol Tregybl, Llandeilo (1985); Halfway Primary School, Llanelli (1986); Theatr Clwyd, Mold, North Wales (1989–1990); and at Theatr Powys, Llandrindod Wells (1991-1992). Since 1994 Edwards has worked as a Creative Writing Fellow at St. David's University College, Lampeter and has been a drama tutor at the University of Wales, Aberystwyth, since 1996. His work with school-age children has been continued in his theater in education work. Apart from his brief time in Cambridge and a year in London in the 1970s, Edwards has lived in Wales all his life–first in south Wales and more recently in the rural west Wales towns of Lampeter and Aberaeron. He and his wife, Gwenda, live with his daughter Natalie; his other two children, Amanda and Nicolas, live elsewhere. Although Wales and the intricacies of Welsh identity are rarely explored directly in his work, Edwards is passionate about his country of birth and in public discussion can be vehement and vocal about his nation's strengths and shortcomings.

Edwards has been a prolific dramatist since 1981, but he began writing as a poet, with his first public success on Radio 4 in 1974 on a program titled "Wales, where are your poets?" The poetic impulse has remained in his writing but often has been channeled into heightened, impassioned language that rejects the verisimilitude of naturalistic speech. Edwards's early work, such as *Canned Goods* (1983), *At the End of the Bay* (1982), and *Late City Echo* (1981), reveals the author's commitment to issue-based drama, dealing with the remodeling of Cardiff's Bay and the position of marginalized nations (Poland and Wales) respectively. As the dramatist's work has matured, he has moved increasingly away from realistic external presentation and has tried to give voice to the way that particular behaviors and power relationships arise as a result of socially sanctioned norms of thought. This movement away from social realism to what Edwards has termed "epic journeys of the interior" has inspired several ambitious and remarkable plays that, despite sharing the passionate commitment to the theater's ability to probe the uneasy underbelly of Western civilization (as in the work of writers such as Howard Barker and Edward Bond), have received little critical attention within Wales and the rest of Britain. Indeed, Bond, with whom Edwards has a supportive working relationship, has referred to the Welsh playwright as the most underrecognized dramatist in Britain.

Looking for the World (1986) is set in Greece at the time of the military junta and examines the nature of masculinity in a fascist state through the involvement of a Cardiff-based couple in the brutal murder of a female tramp. Holidaying in a run-down hotel, Paddy, "a socialist . . . a democrat . . . a trade unionist," and Sylvia, his wife, are confronted with the belligerency of the regime and its leaders' necessity to brutalize the sensibilities of male recruits through torture and violence. This process of desensitization is described in the words of the hotel keeper's son: "When it came to be my turn to rush into a cell and kick and punch someone, I'd do it more wholeheartedly. Only when I did it, it would be to a communist . . . beating up a communist gave you a feeling of comradeship . . . as when they left you alone and beat you every few hours, you felt like a stranger in the world."

Left-leaning Paddy, although refusing to believe in such brutality in the cradle of civilization, eventually becomes implicated in a sordid crime, leaving his wife at the end of the drama in tearful panic at the realization that she wants "WAR out of her living room," that the shabby viciousness underpinning the regime has come too close for comfort. Edwards is particularly sympathetic to women's social subjugation and their frustrated knowledge of their powerlessness, and in *Looking for the World* the female characters give voice to the reality of the brutalization

Scene from the 1993 Glasgow Citizens' Theatre Company production of Wittgenstein's Daughter, *in which Edwards explores the nature and power of language*

of their menfolk. Melina, the hotel owner's wife whose once-gentle son has returned to his island home as a desensitized torturer, expresses the way Greek domestic order has broken down in a speech, that is typical of Edwards's heightened, often oratorical use of language:

> I don't understand . . . what's happened to . . . to people? people who give birth to babies and feed them . . . and . . . clothes . . . people who grow the food, make the clothes . . . socks, coats . . . people who look after the babies, the children . . . send them to hospital if they're sick . . . nurses, people who drive the ambulances; people who build the roads to drive the ambulances on . . . people who can show the way the TRUTH people in robes and ceremonies people on thrones churches palaces people in courts in glasses wigs people with knowledge in schools teaching children.

Masculine aggression is depicted in Edwards's next play, *Long to Rain over Us* (1987). The play takes place in a prisoner-of-war camp and again examines the nature of fanatical attachment to nation and to political ideals through contrasting the commitment of a conscientious objector with that of German and Italian prisoners of war and the British colonel in charge of the camp. The close relationship between adherence to particular types of political organization and masculine aggression is further explored in *Regan (In the Great Society)* (1991), one of Edwards's most accessible dramas. Originally commissioned as a protest against Margaret Thatcher's Poll Tax, the play was removed from its immediate political context by Edwards's placing it at the time of the medieval Peasants' Revolt. The destitute Rakestraw family is visited by John Nameless, a representative of a millenarian Great Society, who offers the powerless Rakestraws escape from the burden of taxation through joining his religious order. Narrated at a distance by the ghost of the hunchbacked daughter of the family, Regan, this disturbing play examines the exploitation of the poor through promises of a better life. Possessing little, the Rakestraws condone the sexual exploitation of their daughter by Nameless. In contrast to *Looking for the World,* where brutality is allowed to triumph, however, this play ends on a triumphant note for Regan as she describes how Nameless lost his power over the family through being humiliated sexually by Regan: "I was quite prepared for him to do it. Right in front of them. Because then they would become involved. Then they wouldn't have been able to hide anymore. But I didn't expect that he wouldn't be able to do it! But that's what happened. He couldn't do it! No power. They took his power away. . . . It was brilliant! It was the best day of our lives!"

This awareness that power relationships can be changed and challenged (the most evidently socialist part of Edwards's dramatic writing) is stated explicitly and wittily in *Casanova Undone* (1992), which depicts an aging, impotent Casanova whose sexual exploits have to be carried out by a dildo-wielding assistant. Edwards explores the relationship between master and servant, as well as the congruence between extremes of pleasure and the omnipresence of death in revolutionary times, as in Georg Büchner's *Danton's Death* (1835) and Peter Weiss's *Marat/Sade* (1964). This awareness of extinction is expressed by Casanova:

> When I eat BEEF, as you know, I eat it raw. My white bread soaks up the red blood. When I drink wine, I drink the heaviest blood-red. When I eat cheese, I like best the cheese that's in a state of putrefaction. In my life I live one step away from death.

> One step the wrong way and I'm dead. In the practice of my life I don't fool myself that there's no such thing as death. That's why, when I eat and drink, I eat and drink–as Christ advised–the blood and the body. I despise a person who hides from death. In death I see that life is active because life includes death.

Such philosophical speculation is also present in *Wittgenstein's Daughter,* which follows the trail of Alma, possible daughter of the philosopher Ludwig Wittgenstein, who is searching for her own origins. Pregnant by her French fascist husband, Alma travels to Cambridge to discover that her father's homosexual identity has been concealed from the world, partly through the fiction of his own fathering of her. Edwards positions Alma, with her apprehension of "the uselessness of speaking some things, most things" and her search for personal meaning against the self-confidence of Cambridge. The avowed supremacy of Cambridge is voiced by Wittgenstein's lover, an ancient former boxer: "Cambridge is everything. Cambridge is government. Cambridge is business. Cambridge is science . . . Cambridge is medicine. Ideas about science. Ideas about ideas!" Decidedly antinaturalistic in form (Wittgenstein is a ghost in a cupboard, for example), this lively and confident work attempts to dramatize the manner in which the nature of being is defined through language and the way in which language constricts and limits such definitions. The once-reticent Alma is eventually brought to articulate speech at her father's graveside, for, as she realizes, "It's as if I've learned to speak again! It is so much to do with . . . Talk! . . . But why am I ashamed? Only because I allowed myself to speak *their* words! . . . Everywhere I look there are faces looking at me out of screens saying things to me as though with authority *as though with wisdom* things that are lies!"

Thus, as in *Regan,* Edwards presents an extended argument about the nature of power (here the power of language in circumscribing being) through the inner voyage of a central female character. Similarly, *Lola Brecht* (1996), one of Edwards's most challenging plays in its expression and ideas, charts the journey of "a short and almost fat . . . common woman," who "has been born without destiny," across the violent psychological landscape of Middle Europe. Edwards takes on the task of giving literary expression to the social imagination that could give rise to the atrocities, blind prejudices, and sadistic sexuality that have been part of European history in the twentieth century. This difficult exercise is achieved in this play through the depiction of the brutalization and subjugation of Lola by her overbearing husband as they travel toward Prague in an attempt to locate a political or perhaps religious demagogue. Like Alma in *Wittgenstein's Daughter* and Regan in *Regan,* Lola claims responsibility for her own destiny at the end of the drama, realizing that she has rights and is not completely "without history or destiny" but can claim a place in a wider history rather than be destroyed by the version of history her husband represents.

By way of contrast, in *Utah Blue* (1995) Edwards explores the disturbing inner life of somebody who believes he has been born with a significant destiny, that of murderer Gary Gilmore, whose desire to be executed by firing squad was widely reported in the 1970s. This journalistic cause célèbre is treated, as with earlier plays by the author, in a semigrotesque fashion; with arguments about the nature of self-worth, compassion, and human agency set out mainly as a debate between the extremely articulate, callous, and now-deceased Gilmore and his uncomprehending but humane brother Mikal.

In this play Edwards is particularly skilled in giving voice to the social and religious circumstances that have molded Gilmore's inner life, his lower-class exclusion from the American dream and his Mormon background where, as he admits, death was omnipresent. This antihero's wish to impute autobiographical significance to his life, to have his American moment of fame, is evidenced in his willful call for execution, a kind of self-validation given his poor and unrecognized background. Bond has remarked how Edwards is able to express the complexity of psychological motivation "in a sort of poetic melodrama." But, according to Bond "the melodrama is not expressionistic but analytic." This stratagem can be seen in Gilmore's emphasis on the omnipresence of death in his upbringing:

> When I was a kid, death would whisper in my ear at night. That's how I got to sleep. And as I grew up death would walk with me to school. Yeah! In school I learned with death; in the playground I played with death; when I played hookey, I played hookey with death. Death was in my school bag; in my lunchbox; in my pencil case; with my paint brushes. Death came down the chimney at Christmas and death lit up the Christmas tree.

Edwards risks overblown expression to try to get to the meaning of Gilmore's callous rejection of his religious upbringing. Sometimes, in his frequently wordy work, this impulse to "poetic melodrama" as the playwright gropes and wrestles with meaning can make great demands on the listener, and at times the

Edwards at a workshop for his play Utah Blue *in Aberystwyth, Wales, in 1997 (photograph by Keith Morris)*

complexity of ideas and arguments does not emerge easily.

The playwright has been involved in a long-term theater-in-education literacy project based at Spectacle Theatre in the Rhondda Valley in South Wales. Edwards's involvement with writing for a younger audience has resulted in several plays, such as *Kid* (1997) and *Antigone Now* (2000), that make sophisticated demands on young people's ability to argue and investigate their social reality. Thus, *The Shakespeare Factory* (1993) examines the whole question of literary legacy, and *Over Milk Wood* (1999) is an ambitious dissection of Welsh cultural identity aimed at a teenage audience. The writer himself readily admits to the beneficial effect that writing for this group has had on refining his writing, and that his work has matured even further through engaging with a type of theatrical writing that is sometimes misconstrued as elementary and unsophisticated. Edwards continues to write on increasingly complex ideas. One work is an adaptation of Fyodor Dostoevsky's *The Idiot* (1868) that examines media responses to political refugees.

Letters:

"The Letters of Edward Bond to Dic Edwards," in *State of Play,* edited by Hazel W. Davies (Llandysul: Gomer, 1998), pp. 17–65.

Interviews:

Hazel W. Davies, "Theatre as Forum," *New Welsh Review* (Winter 1995–1996): 77–83;

"A Dereliction of Duty," in *State of Play,* edited by Davies (Llandysul: Gomer, 1998), pp. 82–88.

Reference:

Anna-Marie Taylor, "Looking for the World through the Word: The Social Imagination in Dic Edwards' Drama," in *State of Play,* edited by Hazel W. Davies (Llandysul: Gomer, 1988), pp. 74–81.

T. S. Eliot

(26 September 1888 - 4 January 1965)

Trevor R. Griffiths
University of North London

See also the Eliot entries in *DLB 7: Twentieth-Century American Dramatists; DLB 10: Modern British Dramatists, 1900–1945; DLB 45: American Poets, 1880–1945, First Series;* and *DLB 63: Modern American Critics, 1920–1955.*

PLAY PRODUCTIONS: *Sweeney Agonistes,* Poughkeepsie, N.Y., Vassar Experimental Theatre, 6 May 1933; London, Group Theatre Rooms, 11 November 1934;

The Rock, London, Sadler's Wells Theatre, 28 May 1934;

Murder in the Cathedral, Canterbury Chapter House, 15 June 1935; London, Mercury Theatre, 1 November 1935; New Haven, Yale University Theatre, 20 December 1935; New York, Manhattan Theater, 20 March 1936;

The Family Reunion, London, Westminster Theatre, 21 March 1939; Aurora, N.Y., Wells College, 8 June 1940; New York, Cherry Lane Theatre, 1947;

The Cocktail Party, Edinburgh, Royal Lyceum Theatre, 22 August 1949; New York, Henry Miller's Theater, 21 January 1950; London, New Theatre, 3 May 1950;

The Confidential Clerk, Edinburgh, Royal Lyceum Theatre, 25 August 1953; London, Lyric Theatre, 16 September 1953; New York, Morosco Theatre, 11 February 1954;

The Elder Statesman, Edinburgh, Royal Lyceum Theatre, 24 August 1958; London, Cambridge Theatre, 25 September 1958; Milwaukee, Fred Miller Theater, 27 February 1963.

BOOKS: *Prufrock and Other Observations* (London: The Egoist, 1917);

Ezra Pound: His Metric and Poetry (New York: Knopf, 1918);

Poems (Richmond: Leonard & Virginia Woolf at The Hogarth Press, 1919);

Ara Vos Prec (London: Ovid Press, 1920); republished with one substitution and one title change as *Poems* (New York: Knopf, 1920);

The Sacred Wood: Essays on Poetry and Criticism (London: Methuen, 1920; New York: Knopf, 1921);

The Waste Land (New York: Boni & Liveright, 1922; Richmond: Leonard & Virginia Woolf at The Hogarth Press, 1923);

Homage to John Dryden: Three Essays on Poetry of the Seventeenth Century (London: Leonard & Virginia Woolf at The Hogarth Press, 1924);

Poems 1909–1925 (London: Faber & Gwyer, 1925; New York & Chicago: Harcourt, Brace, 1932);

Journey of the Magi (London: Faber & Gwyer, 1927; New York: Rudge, 1927);

Shakespeare and the Stoicism of Seneca (London: Oxford University Press, 1927);

A Song for Simeon (London: Faber & Gwyer, 1928);

For Lancelot Andrewes: Essays on Style and Order (London: Faber & Gwyer, 1928; Garden City, N.Y.: Doubleday, Doran, 1929);

Dante (London: Faber & Faber, 1929);

Animula (London: Faber & Faber, 1929);

Ash-Wednesday (New York: Fountain Press / London: Faber & Faber, 1930);

Marina (London: Faber & Faber, 1930);

Thoughts After Lambeth (London: Faber & Faber, 1931);

Triumphal March (London: Faber & Faber, 1931);

Charles Whibley: A Memoir (London: Oxford University Press, 1931);

Selected Essays 1917–1932 (London: Faber & Faber, 1932; New York: Harcourt, Brace, 1932);

John Dryden: The Poet, The Dramatist, The Critic (New York: Terence & Elsa Holliday, 1932);

Sweeney Agonistes: Fragments of an Aristophanic Melodrama (London: Faber & Faber, 1932);

The Use of Poetry and The Use of Criticism: Studies in the Relation of Criticism to Poetry in England (London: Faber & Faber, 1933; Cambridge, Mass.: Harvard University Press, 1933);

After Strange Gods: A Primer of Modern Heresy (London: Faber & Faber, 1934; New York: Harcourt, Brace, 1934);

T. S. Eliot at Faber & Faber

The Rock: A Pageant Play (London: Faber & Faber, 1934; New York: Harcourt, Brace, 1934);

Elizabethan Essays (London: Faber & Faber, 1934); republished, with omission of three essays and addition of one, as *Essays on Elizabethan Drama* (New York: Harcourt, Brace, 1956); republished as *Elizabethan Dramatists* (London: Faber & Faber, 1963);

Words for Music (Bryn Mawr, Pa.: Privately printed, 1934);

Murder in the Cathedral, acting edition (Canterbury: H. J. Goulden, 1935); complete edition (London: Faber & Faber, 1935; New York: Harcourt, Brace, 1935);

Two Poems (Cambridge: Cambridge University Press, 1935);

Essays Ancient & Modern (London: Faber & Faber, 1936; New York: Harcourt, Brace, 1936);

Collected Poems 1909–1935 (London: Faber & Faber, 1936; New York: Harcourt, Brace, 1936);

The Family Reunion (London: Faber & Faber, 1939; New York: Harcourt, Brace, 1939);

Old Possum's Book of Practical Cats (London: Faber & Faber, 1939; New York: Harcourt, Brace, 1939);

The Idea of a Christian Society (London: Faber & Faber, 1939; New York: Harcourt, Brace, 1940);

The Waste Land and Other Poems (London: Faber & Faber, 1940; New York: Harcourt, Brace, 1955);

East Coker (London: Faber & Faber, 1940);

Burnt Norton (London: Faber & Faber, 1941);

Points of View, edited by John Hayward (London: Faber & Faber, 1941);

The Dry Salvages (London: Faber & Faber, 1941);

The Classics and the Man of Letters (London, New York & Toronto: Oxford University Press, 1942);

The Music of Poetry (Glasgow: Jackson, Son, Publishers to the University, 1942);

Little Gidding (London: Faber & Faber, 1942);

Four Quartets (New York: Harcourt, Brace, 1943; London: Faber & Faber, 1944);

Reunion by Destruction (London: Pax House, 1943);

What Is a Classic? (London: Faber & Faber, 1945);

Die Einheit der Europäischen Kultur (Berlin: Carl Habel, 1946);

A Practical Possum (Cambridge, Mass.: Harvard Printing Office & Department of Graphic Arts, 1947);

On Poetry (Concord, Mass.: Concord Academy, 1947);

Milton (London: Geoffrey Cumberlege, 1947);

A Sermon (Cambridge: Cambridge University Press, 1948);

Selected Poems (Harmondsworth: Penguin/Faber & Faber, 1948; New York: Harcourt, Brace & World, 1967);

Notes Towards the Definition of Culture (London: Faber & Faber, 1948; New York: Harcourt, Brace, 1949);

From Poe to Valéry (New York: Harcourt, Brace, 1948);

The Undergraduate Poems of T. S. Eliot, unauthorized publication (Cambridge, Mass., 1949);

The Aims of Poetic Drama (London: Poets' Theatre Guild, 1949);

The Cocktail Party (London: Faber & Faber, 1950; New York: Harcourt, Brace, 1950; revised edition, London: Faber & Faber, 1950);

Poems Written in Early Youth (Stockholm: Privately printed, 1950; London: Faber & Faber, 1967; New York: Farrar, Straus & Giroux, 1967);

Poetry and Drama (Cambridge, Mass.: Harvard University Press, 1951; London: Faber & Faber, 1951);

The Film of Murder in the Cathedral, by Eliot and George Hoellering (London: Faber & Faber, 1952; New York: Harcourt, Brace, 1952);

The Value and Use of Cathedrals in England Today (Chichester: Friends of Chichester Cathedral, 1952);

An Address to Members of the London Library (London: London Library, 1952; Providence, R.I.: Providence Athenaeum, 1953);

The Complete Poems and Plays (New York: Harcourt, Brace, 1952);

Selected Prose, edited by Hayward (Melbourne, London & Baltimore: Penguin, 1953);

American Literature and the American Language (St. Louis: Department of English, Washington University, 1953);

The Three Voices of Poetry (Cambridge: Cambridge University Press, 1953; New York: Cambridge University Press, 1954);

The Confidential Clerk (London: Faber & Faber, 1954; New York: Harcourt, Brace, 1954);

Religious Drama: Mediaeval and Modern (New York: House of Books, 1954);

The Cultivation of Christmas Trees (London: Faber & Faber, 1954; New York: Farrar, Straus & Cudahy, 1956);

The Literature of Politics (London: Conservative Political Centre, 1955);

The Frontiers of Criticism (Minneapolis: University of Minnesota Press, 1956);

On Poetry and Poets (London: Faber & Faber, 1957; New York: Farrar, Straus & Cudahy, 1957);

The Elder Statesman (London: Faber & Faber, 1959; New York: Farrar, Straus & Cudahy, 1959);

Geoffrey Faber 1889–1961 (London: Faber & Faber, 1961);

Collected Plays (London: Faber & Faber, 1962);

George Herbert (London: Longmans, Green, 1962);

Collected Poems 1909–1962 (London: Faber & Faber, 1963; New York: Harcourt, Brace & World, 1963);

Knowledge and Experience in the Philosophy of F. H. Bradley (London: Faber & Faber, 1964; New York: Farrar, Straus, 1964);

To Criticize the Critic and Other Writings (London: Faber & Faber, 1965; New York: Farrar, Straus & Giroux, 1965);

The Waste Land: A Facsimile and Transcript of the Original Drafts Including the Annotations of Ezra Pound, edited by Valerie Eliot (London: Faber & Faber, 1971; New York: Harcourt Brace Jovanovich, 1971);

Selected Prose of T. S. Eliot, edited by Frank Kermode (London: Faber, 1975; New York: Harcourt Brace Jovanovich, 1975).

PRODUCED SCRIPT: *Murder in the Cathedral,* by Eliot and George Hoellering, motion picture, Classic, 1952.

T. S. Eliot was one of the most important poets of the Modernist movement and is only secondarily remembered as a playwright. However, his work for the stage constitutes a significant part of his career from the 1930s, and he was a major figure in mid-twentieth-century attempts to reinvigorate the moribund tradition of verse drama–an attempt to reacquaint poetry and drama in ways that look back through the English Romantic period to the Renaissance theater of William Shakespeare and his contemporaries. Nor was his interest in drama a diversion from his central preoccupations as a poet. Throughout his career Eliot was interested in the possibilities of dramatic verse and showed himself adept at both dramatic monologue and dialogue in much of his best poetry, including "The Love Song of J. Alfred Prufrock" (1915), "Portrait of a Lady" (1915), and *The Waste Land* (1922).

His essays on the Elizabethan and Jacobean dramatists also help to contextualize his own poetic-dramatic practice, and he was an acute critic of his own theatrical work. Verse drama in Britain had been unable to break away from the powerful but imperfectly understood verse of the Renaissance dramatists

Robert Speaight (left) as Thomas à Becket in the 1935 premiere in Canterbury of Eliot's Murder in the Cathedral *(photograph by J. W. Deberham; courtesy of the Houghton Library, Harvard University)*

or to create an effective modern dramatic verse. Eliot had learned from the failure of the Romantic and Victorian practitioners of verse drama that pastiche-Renaissance dramatic verse and structure was not the way forward; but, just as crucially, he appears not to have fully understood the expressive possibilities of a theater poetry that lay outside the narrow definitions of language proper, that relied on the total expressive possibilities of the whole theatrical system rather than purely on dramatic language. Eliot found inspiration in existing models, however radically he reworked them, and his theatrical career represents a continuing dialogue between the existing dramatic forms of the conventional theater of his day, the narratives and structures (particularly the chorus) of Greek theater, and the liturgical patterns he derived from his Christian faith.

Thomas Stearns Eliot was born in St. Louis, Missouri, on 26 September 1888, the seventh and final child of Charlotte Champe Stearns Eliot, a schoolteacher and poet, and Henry Ware Eliot, a merchant. From his earliest years he displayed a keen interest in writing, and his first published verses appeared in 1905 in his school magazine, the *Smith Academy Record.* He matriculated at Harvard, where his studies covered both classical and modern European literature, and he published more poetry in the *Harvard Advocate*. Having received his B.A. in 1909, he continued studying for his M.A. at Harvard, taking a year abroad at the Sorbonne in Paris while doing so. After obtaining his M.A. in 1911, he visited London, Munich, and Italy before returning to Harvard to embark on his doctorate.

At the outbreak of war in 1914 Eliot was at Oxford University. In 1915 he met and married his first wife, Vivienne Haigh-Wood, a governess, the same year that his first major poem, "The Love Song of J. Alfred Prufrock," appeared. His first book of poems (*Prufrock and Other Observations*) was published in 1917. He briefly worked as a junior schoolteacher at Highgate before a period working for Lloyds Bank. In 1921 he suffered a nervous breakdown and took leave from Lloyds, and the following year he published his most famous poem, *The Waste Land,* which became a seminal text of urban disintegration. It owes much of its genesis to his own personal state of mind, and much of its shape to the editing of his friend Ezra Pound, another expatriate American. That same year he established the literary magazine *The Criterion.*

He joined what became the influential literary publishing house Faber and Faber as a director in 1925, combining a career as a poet, critic, and dramatist with a working life as a literary editor. He became a British subject and a member of the Church of England in 1927, declaring the following year in his book *For Lancelot Andrewes: Essays on Style and Order* that he was a "classicist in literature, royalist in politics, and anglo-catholic in religion." As his wife's health declined, he renewed an earlier friendship with Emily Hale, a drama teacher.

He turned increasingly to drama in the 1930s, although he continued to write poetry, particularly during World War II, when he wrote three of the *Four Quartets* (1943). After a turbulent marriage he separated from Vivienne in 1932; she died in 1947. He married Valerie Fletcher, his secretary, in 1957.

Eliot's early unfinished dramatic work, *Sweeney Agonistes* (1932), showed the influence of the music hall, with which he was fascinated (he published an essay on the music-hall artist Marie Lloyd in 1923), and of jazz. As early as September 1924, Arnold Bennett wrote in his journal that Eliot had asked his advice about an attempt to "write a drama of modern life (furnished flat sort of people) in a rhythmic prose 'perhaps with certain things in it accentuated by drumbeats.'" The result of this experiment appears to be the two fragments that now constitute *Sweeney Agonistes*–"Fragment of a Prologue" and "Fragment of an Agon"–which were published in *New Criterion* in October 1926 and January 1927 under the title "Wanna Go Home, Baby?" They were published in book form in 1932 as *Sweeney Agonistes: Fragments of an Aristophanic Melodrama,* an erudite but mocking title that demonstrates Eliot's gift for combining apparently disparate cultural traditions. Eliot did not preserve the extra scene he wrote for Hallie Flanagan's production of the fragments at Vassar College in 1933. In "Fragment of a Prologue" two contemporary prostitutes engage in desultory conversation about various clients, do some fortune-telling with cards, and then entertain four visitors. In "Fragment of an Agon" they have been joined by Sweeney and two other men. The small talk continues, punctuated by music-hall-style songs, speculations by Sweeney on "Birth, and copulation, and death," and the male need to "do a girl in." The fragment concludes with a male chorus singing of nightmares and then with knocking on the door.

Although *Sweeney Agonistes* is brief and incomplete, it successfully blends some key influences on Eliot–music hall, light comedy, melodrama, serious thought, and Greek dramatic structure. Sweeney is a character who had already appeared in four of Eliot's poems, in various guises, but always as an *homme moyen sensuel:* in the poem "Sweeney Erect" (1919), for example, Sweeney shaves in a brothel while Doris, who also reappears in the dramatic fragment, deals with another woman's fit. The term "Agonistes" refers both to John Milton's *Samson Agonistes* (1671) and the agon, a key element in Greek tragic drama. Sweeney, unlike Milton's Samson, is an antihero, but he shares Samson's isolation in his inability to communicate, and he exists in a work that attempts to combine elements of the Judeo-Christian tradition with Greek dramatic structure. Eliot's understanding of ancient Greek drama was crucial to his own attempt to rediscover in a contemporary form those elements of religious ritual that the Cambridge anthropologists of the early twentieth century had found in Greek drama. Gilbert Murray had described the agon as a struggle–"the year against its enemy, Light against darkness, Summer against winter"–but Eliot's use of the motif is typically double-edged: the only light embodied by the antihero Sweeney is his knowledge of murder reported in the sensational language of the *News of the World,* while the darkness he struggles against is the philistinism of a London suburb.

The title reference to Aristophanes recalls Francis Cornford, another of the Cambridge anthropologists, who believed that the socially satirical surface of Aristophanic comedy masked an underlying ritual celebration of death and rebirth. Similarly, "melodrama" refers both to the original meaning of the word–a play with music, recalling the idea of a rhythmic prose accentuated by drumbeats–as well as to the more familiar usage to mean a play full of sensational incidents. Eliot himself, in his 4 August 1927 *Times Literary Supplement* (TLS) essay on Wilkie Collins and Charles Dickens, suggested that the difference between melodrama and tragedy was basically the difference between coincidence and fate.

These fragments point both to how Eliot's own dramatic practice evolved and to a missed opportunity. They represent a logical progression from the monologic imagination that had characterized much of Eliot's earlier work and had allowed him to develop a generally acute rendition of certain kinds of speech pattern. They also prefigure much that characterized Eliot's later drama: Sweeney is the man who has seen what other men do not see, the man waiting for a sign, and also the man with an impulse to murder. The theme of the man with greater spiritual insight than the rest of the world is present throughout Eliot's drama, but at this stage he had neither the moral nor the technical solutions to the issues that troubled him. Although *Sweeney Agonistes* is incomplete, in many ways it is Eliot's most successful attempt to blend some key influences into one framework.

When Eliot formally entered the Church of England in 1927 he was willing, like many communist converts of the period, to devote his creative services to the ideology he had embraced. He found this opportunity in *The Rock* (1934), a collaborative Christian historical pageant, which emulated medieval drama in its functional role of expounding doctrine and was part of a fundraising project to build new churches for the new suburbs of London. It brought Eliot together with the theater director E. Martin Browne, another committed Christian, who played a key role in Eliot's development as a dramatist. Browne had been asked to prepare a production as a public demonstration of the aims of the project (pageants were a significant propaganda tool of the period), and he persuaded Eliot to flesh out the scenario. For Eliot the advantages were practical and intellectual: he could make his theatrical debut in the hands of an experienced director who could guide him in the technical matters of stagecraft, and he could write directly in the service of the church. The play was written in sections that could be rehearsed separately by amateur performers from each parish, and Eliot later chose to let the play go out of print.

The Rock was clearly an ephemeral piece designed for a specific function; but it was the first work that Eliot intended for production, significant in that the only poetry in it is assigned to the choruses that link the scenes and provide thematic unity. Eliot was not called upon to differentiate one character from another in his verse, and he said in *The Three Voices of Poetry* (1953) that *The Rock* was simply the poet speaking to the audience, not the poet speaking through his characters. Thus, while the work gave Eliot experience with chorus work, which he used again in *Murder in the Cathedral* (1935) and *The Family Reunion* (1939), it left him with no significant experience of characterization. It also allowed him to use ecclesiastical and ritual elements that arose organically from the subject matter but that posed a more significant challenge in his later, more secular works, in which the relationship between secular action and metaphysical subtext remains problematic.

Eliot's Christianity and his reliance as a writer on existing models played an important role in his development as a dramatist, since his next project was a play based on the life of the martyred archbishop Thomas à Becket. The Canterbury Festival, first held in 1928, had included religious plays staged in the cathedral precincts as a significant element from the beginning, and Eliot accepted a commission to write the 1935 production, which had to be on a religious theme connected with Canterbury. If *Murder in the Cathedral* is recognized as the most successful of Eliot's plays, that recognition encapsulates both the attractions and the problems of verse drama in the twentieth century. As Eliot and his director Browne recognized, its success, like that of *The Rock,* depended on its status as a special case: it was a festival drama that benefited from what would now be called its site-specific connotations; its historical theme, by some kind of implicit analogy with the Renaissance history plays, sanctioned its use of verse; and it addressed an audience who were likely to be receptive to its Christian message.

Since Canterbury Cathedral itself is a monument to the cult of Thomas à Becket, it was not surprising that Eliot should be drawn to the story, even if his play was the third production in a row to deal with the same subject. Eliot chose to concentrate on the martyrdom of Becket rather than on his direct relationship with the king, allowing himself the opportunity to concentrate on the spiritual rather than the political. The theme of the struggle between the values of the world and the transcendent value of religion was one that clearly appealed to a writer who had made a public commitment to religion. Eliot's interest in liturgy, and the fact that the play was to be staged close to the site of Becket's actual martyrdom in the cathedral, ensured that Eliot would adopt liturgical forms to help structure his play. Similarly, his anthropological readings had suggested to him that Greek plays were, in part, celebrations of cults associated with sacred spots that told the story of the cult's origins. This idea of drama as the celebration of a cult tied in neatly with the saint's cult and permitted Eliot to use a distinctive feature of Greek drama, the chorus, which he had already used with some success in *The Rock.*

There was a fashionable theory of the early twentieth century that explained some of Shakespeare's dramaturgy in terms of the writer having included various elements of his plays to appeal to different sections of his audience: clowns for the so-called groundlings, Hamlet's soliloquies for the educated university men; and this theory of the audience appears to have influenced Eliot's dramaturgy. Eliot carefully contrives different groups and different levels of meaning within *Murder in the Cathedral* to appeal to different sections of the audience: church rituals, Greek dramatic conventions, contemporary prose, and the language of the Bible all exist within the same dramatic envelope. Becket himself is the representative of the angels, while the Tempters, externalizations of his own thoughts, are also part of the divine order, representing the diabolical. The function of the Chorus of townswomen is both to represent the "common woman" and to act as an organ of comment on the action, almost as the delegate of the audience. They stand apart from the action, commenting on it and affected by it. They are both the women of Canterbury and representatives of the stream of tourist visitors, both the laypeople of the church and mediators between the action to the audience. They and the Priests share a tendency to fear and to temporizing that makes them closest to the assumed attitudes of the audience. The Knights are compared to beasts, completing Eliot's reproduction of the great chain of being. In the first production the Tempters and the Knights were played by the same group of actors, thus enabling the audience to grasp that the temptations from within have a parallel in the threats from without. This strategy also enhances the force of the Knights' prose address to the audience as a kind of temptation that they have to undergo before they can join in the final chorus of acceptance for Becket's martyrdom. Apart from its ritual and theoretical value, the doubling also served the practical purpose of reducing the number of actors needed.

This deployment of doubling and the stranding of groups of characters allows for the possibility of multiple points of entry for an audience. The skillfulness with which Eliot provides these different viewpoints and entries may account for the popularity of the play beyond its immediate occasion: it is not necessary to be a Christian to find a position within the play that allows access to its debates, although its dramaturgy does discourage identification with some of the positions offered, such as those of the Knights. One of the more innovative moments in the play, for example–when Eliot breaks the medieval frame to allow the Knights to address the audience directly as they attempt to justify their actions in the language of modern politicians–is designed to undercut them.

Eliot had turned his back on the "furnished flat kind of people" of *Sweeney Agonistes* (who found their dramatic voice much later in the work of Harold Pinter), but the initial success of *Murder in the Cathedral* demonstrates its specialized nature. Eliot was an accurate critic of his own achievement: he wrote in *Poetry and Drama* (1951) that "Picturesque period costume renders verse much more acceptable" in the theater, and that "people who go deliberately to a religious play at a religious festival expect to be patiently bored and to satisfy themselves with the feeling that they have done something meritorious. So the path was made easy."

The play was a success, but it was also something of a dead end, since it meant that Eliot would have to find new methods to achieve his goal of reaching a wider audience with a poetic drama that would not be preaching to the converted. One of the key difficulties was in identifying where such an audience might be found: Eliot's theatrical work thus far had been firmly located within a religious tradition addressing the faithful. Although there was what would now be called a "fringe theater" in the 1930s in the form of such projects as the Group Theatre (which staged *Sweeney Agonistes* and the plays of W. H. Auden and Christopher Isherwood), its audience capacities were small and it appealed to another coterie–those committed to radical, usually left-wing, theater. Many left-wing writers, from George Bernard Shaw to Trevor Griffiths, have attempted to subvert theatrical forms from within, using existing generic frameworks as vehicles for nontraditional viewpoints in order to allow audiences easier access to the radical content. Eliot similarly wanted to reach large audiences with his conservative-Christian moral viewpoint, and the only place that could offer such audiences was London's West End theater. However, Eliot's desire to create a verse drama led to a constant tension between the demands of verse and the demands of the kinds of surface subnaturalism that dominated the various theatrical genres he tried to use.

Attempting to present Christian theology in secular terms meant that the relationship between the moral design of Eliot's plays and their actual plots and characterization could sometimes be obscure. This difficulty was compounded by Eliot's choice to explore the relatively unfamiliar Christian path of negative affirmation, in which his protagonists achieve a love of God by what Eliot, following St. John of the Cross, refers to as divesting oneself of the love of created beings. In both *Murder in the Cathedral* and *The Family Reunion,* staged by Browne at the Westminster Theatre in 1939, the protagonists reject earthly happiness in order to pursue a more spiritual quest. The problem, as Eliot himself later saw, is that this path is not a universally practical one, and audiences may admire the martyr (as the members of the Chorus do in *Murder in the Cathedral*) but see no way to emulate him.

In *The Family Reunion* Eliot was trying to broaden his appeal from the Christian coterie audience to a wider social group, using a dramatic verse that related effectively to contemporary speech while deriving his story of sin, expiation, and redemption from the story of Orestes as told in Aeschylus's Oresteian trilogy. In both the ways that the various groups of characters may appeal to an audience and in the conventions and rituals Eliot uses, *The Family Reunion* operates at several different levels. While the title of the play is a conventional one, suggesting the return of outsiders, the revelation of family secrets, and the possibility of telling home truths, it conceals an unconventional story. On the one hand, the play is set in the world of polite society, whose physical location is the drawing room of a country house; on the other, such features as the Eumenides or Furies, the choruses, the lyrical duets, and the soliloquies suggest a completely different set of conventions.

At the level of plot the play works, initially at least, as a conventional mystery: how did protagonist Harry's wife die? Did she fall or was she pushed? The issue is pursued in interviews with the family doctor, the police, and Harry's chauffeur, at the same time Harry appears to be falling for Mary, his cousin. He then sees the Eumenides and leaves the birthday party being held for his aged mother, Amy, which is the ostensible occasion of the family reunion. Amy dies of shock over his departure, leaving Harry's aunt Agatha and Mary walking around the birthday cake muttering verses like a witch's spell. At the second, psychological, level and drawing on the first, there is a different back story: Amy was tied to an unloving husband by whom she had three children; he fell for Agatha, but she rejected him. Mary had been brought up as a possible marriage partner for Harry, but both of them reacted by seeking independence. Harry married a woman his mother hated, and she determined to pretend that nothing had happened, maintaining the house just as it was when he left. She now hopes that his wife's death will bring Harry back as master of the significantly named Wishwood, but when he rejects this idea, she collapses and dies. Agatha has also suffered because her lover, Amy's husband, had planned to murder the pregnant Amy. Agatha had prevented the murder because she felt that she was in some ways the spiritual mother of the unborn child, Harry. She indeed became an adoptive mother to Harry and guides him to what he must do. Psychologically, Harry's problem is that he married to escape the domination of his mother, whom he hates. The offstage marriage was a disaster, both because it was an escape attempt and because he came to hate the

Margaret Leighton, Ian Hunter, Rex Harrison, and director Martin Browne with Eliot at a rehearsal of The Cocktail Party *at the New Theatre in London in 1950 (photograph by Popperfoto)*

mother substitute as much as the mother herself. Although he had suppressed this feeling, he is haunted after his wife's death by a sense of guilt (visualized in the Eumenides). He returns home as part of his attempt to escape guilt, but discovers that his guilt complex stems from his parents' unhappiness and his father's thwarted murder attempt. This realization somehow purges his guilt and allows him to leave, unwittingly killing his mother and thus achieving what his father was unable to do.

The play works to some extent both as psychological drama and as whodunit, revealing characters and situations through some of the traditional machinery of the well-made play. But there is a naturalistic difficulty: it is not really clear that any crime was actually committed, which makes it difficult to see Harry's assumption of the burden of his family's guilt as particularly heroic. Certainly it undercuts the audience's sense of Harry as saint or Christ figure. He is a case study rather than an archetype; despite his willingness to assume the guilt of his tribe, the crimes are potential rather than actual. The process of dealing with guilt may be universal, but the guilt-provoking situation in this case does not, to use Eliot's own terms, provide an adequate "objective correlative" for the guilt. Harry is an elect Christian hero whose heroism is presented through non-Christian means. In the *Oresteia* the analogous situation involves a clear conflict in which the Eumenides are actors in the process; in the modern version they are silent, and their weight has to be carried visually. Perhaps part of the problem is that Eliot has started the process too late in the story; Aeschylus, after all, took three plays to show the murder, the revenge, and the closing of the feud, whereas Eliot tries to do everything in one. Harry's conflict is largely internalized but can seem simply neurotic; there is no externalization as there is with the Tempters in *Murder in the Cathedral,* even though Mary might seem to offer a conventional love interest and therefore a temptation to Harry to find a more mundane salvation. His rejection of Mary and of Amy, jogged by the Eumenides, places him in a curious reversal of the Oedipal situation.

The Orestes story shows a generations-long pattern of vendettas eventually being ended by a reconciling force and the replacement of the Eumenides by the wisdom of Athene. In Christian terms, the story could be read as the replacement of the Old Testament law of an eye for an eye with the reconciliatory wisdom of the Christian gospel. However, as Eliot himself later argued, he did not manage to reconcile the Greek story and the modern Christian reworking effectively: he moved too far away from the original without substituting an effective modern equivalent. The myth was supposed to provide an underlying timelessness, but instead it made the action obscure. The key issue lies in the presentation of the Eumenides, the Furies taken over from Aeschylus but in this play rendered speechless. *The Family Reunion,* which is in many ways Eliot's most successful modern-dress play, particularly in its creation of an effective verse line, uses the wordless presence of the Eumenides to convey significant moral and plot elements that actually need verbal clarification and expansion. A Stockholm production of the play was mounted in 1948 when Eliot received the Nobel Prize for Literature.

During World War II Eliot served as an air-warden and as a fire watcher (from the top of the Faber and Faber office building). Conditions were not favorable for new writing for the theater, and Eliot reverted to nondramatic verse, working on the *Four Quartets.* He returned to drama with *The Cocktail Party,* which was first performed at the 1949 Edinburgh Festival. As the title suggests, the play is set in a fashionable milieu of cocktail parties, gossip, and marital infidelity, and it draws on existing generic expectations, both those of the conventional comedy of manners and those of mystery and resolution. The play starts with a cocktail party given by Lavinia and Peter Chamberlayne, but the hostess is mysteriously absent and an unidentified guest is mysteriously present. These early suggestions that something is wrong at the naturalistic everyday level lead neatly into more metaphysical questions. It emerges that Lavinia has had an affair with Peter Quilpe; Edward has had an affair with Celia Coplestone; and the mysterious guest is Sir Henry Harcourt-Reilly, a psychiatrist and a member of a secret society of moral Guardians. Certain aspects of the play build on familiar elements from Eliot's earlier drama: Celia, like Becket and Harry a member of the spiritually elect, goes to Africa, where she is murdered during a rebellion; Reilly and his fellow Guardians, Julia and Gibbs, are pointers toward salvation, echoing the role of Agatha and Mary in *The Family Reunion* and the Tempters, the Priests, and the Chorus in *Murder in the Cathedral.* There is also an underlying classical framework, the *Alcestis* of Euripides, that underscores Reilly's singing and drunkenness in the first act and a modern libation scene, but the mechanics of Euripides' plot are not the constraint on this play that the *Oresteia* was on *The Family Reunion.* In fact, until Eliot revealed his starting point, no one seems to have recognized it. The play ends with a second cocktail party, which may seem like a return to the beginning but actually serves to show how far the situation has altered: the chaotic kitchen of the first act has been restocked and reorganized as the Chamberlaynes have put their house in order and accepted their destiny. Reilly argues that one must accept the past in order to alter its meaning, and this acceptance is symbolized by the new party which, following the news of Celia's crucifixion, becomes a secular counterpart of the communion service.

The major difference between Eliot's earlier plays and *The Cocktail Party* is in a crucial switch of focus that has made it more popular than any of the other modern-dress plays. Instead of dramatizing Celia's martyrdom and concentrating on the negative affirmation of the Christian vision, Eliot focuses on Edward and Lavinia Chamberlayne. The married couple are the central characters, and they serve as examples of a different, more accessible, Christian tradition, that of affirmation, of recognizing God as not only transcendent but also as present, imperfectly, in all created beings. Whereas Becket's and Harry's way is contemplative, heroic, and monastic, Edward and Lavinia's is active, mundane, and social. They have to learn to love one another, and the audience is able to follow them as they try to apply the meanings of Celia's martyrdom to themselves, allowing the power of the saint's life to transmute their lives rather than trying to emulate the saint. This approach makes the play easier to follow and also more useful as a piece of Christian propaganda, since it allows audiences more points of contact with the central characters, who are, presumably, more like them in their decisions to live in the social world. It is, of course, significant that Reilly is a psychiatrist, a secular equivalent of a priest, since that allows Eliot to introduce

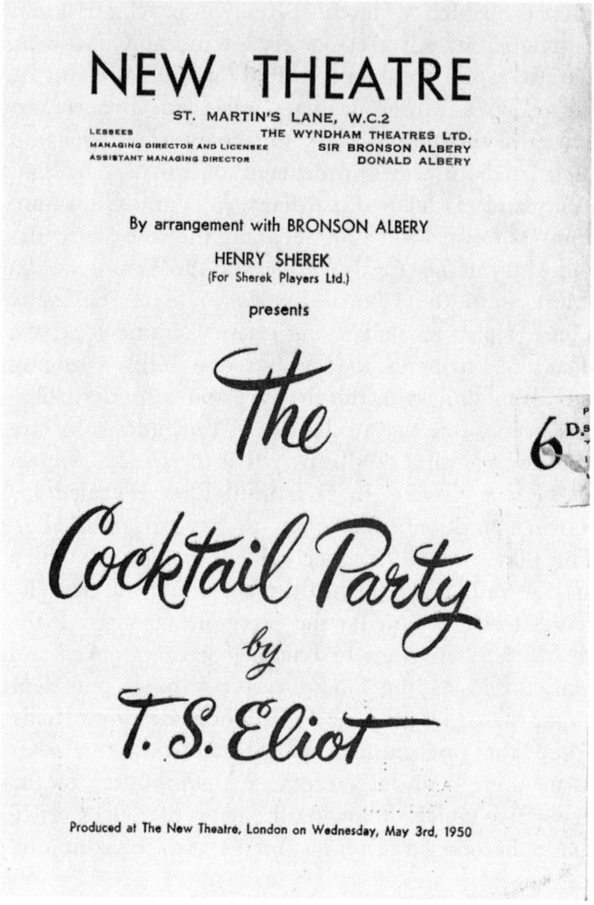
NEW THEATRE
ST. MARTIN'S LANE, W.C.2
LESSEES THE WYNDHAM THEATRES LTD.
MANAGING DIRECTOR AND LICENSEE SIR BRONSON ALBERY
ASSISTANT MANAGING DIRECTOR DONALD ALBERY
By arrangement with BRONSON ALBERY
HENRY SHEREK
(For Sherek Players Ltd.)
presents
The Cocktail Party
by
T. S. Eliot
Produced at The New Theatre, London on Wednesday, May 3rd, 1950

Program cover for the first London production of Eliot's play about marital infidelity, loosely based on Euripides' Alcestis I

complex religious insights in a secular form. Eliot had still not solved all his difficulties in his persistent interrogation of secular dramatic forms in the services of Christianity, however; the secular Guardians remain potentially controversial, since their right to guide the lives of others is not socially sanctioned as a priest's might be. Just as Harry mistakes the Eumenides for devils, so their charges mistake the Guardians for interfering busybodies.

By the time *The Cocktail Party* opened on Broadway in 1950, Eliot had engaged Valerie Fletcher as his secretary at Faber and Faber. Eliot continued to develop his techniques in *The Confidential Clerk* (first staged at the Edinburgh Festival in 1953), in which he abandons the tragic overtones that Celia's martyrdom imparted to *The Cocktail Party* in favor of an action based on a traditional pattern of comic complications centering on a lost and rediscovered baby. The theme is most familiar to modern audiences through Oscar Wilde's *The Importance of Being Earnest* (1895), but Eliot returns to the original lost-baby play, the *Ion* of Euripides, although inevitably there are many overtones of various treatments of the theme. Eliot uses the comic form derived from Euripides and modified in many subsequent treatments as a means of showing his own spiritual interpretations. The theme of a foundling child expresses the Christian implications of a search for identity by showing that self-discovery depends on the discovery of divine parentage. The reversals, recognitions, and reconciliations typical of this type of farce enable Eliot to create situations in which the resolutions are only marginally within the realms of probability but serve also as a dramatic metaphor for God's capacity to move in mysterious ways. Behind the secular quests of fathers for sons and sons and daughters for fathers lies divine love seeking a response in man and revealing the way of reconciliation in Christ.

The play, then, is a comedy of redemption that uses its comedic techniques as a paradigm of the divine. The play is much more integrated in terms of dramatic structure than those that had preceded it, partly because the protagonist's calling has been translated from Harry's existential agony and Celia's martyrdom into a vocation to be a priest, which is perhaps more in keeping with the context, partly because there are no bystanders like the chorus of uncles and aunts in *The Family Reunion,* no busybodies like the Guardians in *The Cocktail Party.* Browne thought that this play had taken Eliot as far toward naturalism as he would want to go, and it has not maintained its place in the repertory.

Eliot's last play, *The Elder Statesman,* was staged in 1958, by which time the parameters of the dramatically possible were expanding under the influence of Samuel Beckett, Bertolt Brecht, Eugene Ionesco, Pinter, and John Osborne. Yet, Eliot remained true to his previous practice, using Sophocles' *Oedipus at Colonus* as a frame to tackle again the themes of guilt and expiation in a contemporary setting. Lord Claverton, the elder statesman of the title, is visited by a man and a woman from his past who remind him of youthful indiscretions that could have blighted his career but were hushed up. Impressed by the mutual love of his daughter and her fiancé, Claverton comes to terms with his guilt and dies contented. However, the protagonist's crimes are not on an Oedipal scale, and his sense of guilt seems disproportionate to his criminality. The moral of the story remains that of the earlier modern-set plays: face yourself as shown in your past and recognize who you are. Alongside the familiar hieratic elements Eliot also introduces the unusual spectacle of young lovers, perhaps reflecting his own newfound marital happiness (he had married Fletcher in 1957); but the language they speak is stilted and at times barely operates at even the functional level of adequate melodrama. *The Elder Statesman* did not transfer to the United States until 1963 and is now largely forgotten.

Eliot was awarded the American Medal of Freedom at a ceremony in the U.S. Embassy in London in 1964. A year later he died in his London home; his ashes were scattered at St. Michael's Church, East Coker.

Whereas *Sweeney Agonistes* demonstrates a haunting unfulfilled potential for the creation of a dramatic form, *Murder in the Cathedral* is a dramatic dead end of another kind. The use of the chorus, the historical subject, and the strong liturgical influence on the structure of the play made it an inappropriate model for development into the serious modern verse drama that Eliot was interested in (although the prose episode of the four Knights attempting to justify their acts offered a potential model of ironic juxtaposition that might have proved fruitful had Eliot been able to pursue it). Instead, he developed in two ways that compromised his aims. Crucially, he was drawn to attempting to address substantial and wider audiences, adopting formal structures derived from West End staples such as the drawing-room comedy, the discussion play, and the thriller, combining these with plots derived from Greek drama and legend with a further Christian layer. The result was always a tension between the various strands that resulted in works of conservative form that sometimes found it difficult to strike an appropriate balance between poetry, plot, character, and moral message. Whereas Eliot's radicalism in poetry had coincided with his youth, his first serious efforts in the theater were the product of his late forties, and he was too conservative and Christian in outlook to find useful models in contemporary avant-garde theater.

The Family Reunion, his second play, includes much of Eliot's most impressive dramatic verse and develops an effective poetic style that allows the middle-class angst of the play to be conveyed well. He did not, however, find a match between his Greek original and the drawing room, because he chose to make the actual crime obscure. *The Cocktail Party* is probably the most popular of Eliot's plays, partly because of his choice to follow the ordinary rather than the exceptional characters, and its influence can be seen in works such as David Hare's *Racing Demon* (1990). *The Cocktail Party,* however, began to thin down Eliot's poetic texture, suggesting that West End conventions were triumphing over Eliot's subversive aims; that verdict was confirmed by *The Confidential Clerk* and *The Elder Statesman,* in which the verse is attenuated to the point of nonexistence.

Eliot may ultimately have failed to create a viable modern verse drama, but since his death he has achieved worldwide theatrical success through *Cats,* Andrew Lloyd Weber's 1981 musical adaptation of his 1939 collection of poems for children, *Old Possum's Book of Practical Cats,* for which, after its Broadway opening in 1982, he received two posthumous Tony awards; and as the antihero of Michael Hastings's 1984 play *Tom and Viv* and the 1995 motion picture based on it, which take as their subject matter Eliot's stormy relationship with his first wife.

Letters:

The Letters of T. S. Eliot, volume 1, edited by Valerie Eliot (San Diego: Harcourt Brace Jovanovich, 1988; London: Faber & Faber, 1988).

Interviews:

John Lehmann, "T. S. Eliot Talks About Himself and the Drive to Create," *New York Times Book Review,* 29 November 1953, pp. 5, 44;

"'The Confidential Clerk' Comments by T. S. Eliot," *New York Herald Tribune,* 7 February 1954, IV: 1;

Donald Hall, "The Art of Poetry, I: T. S. Eliot," *Paris Review,* 21 (Spring–Summer 1959): 47–70;

Leslie Paul, "A Conversation with T. S. Eliot," *Kenyon Review,* 27 (Winter 1964/1965): 11–21.

Bibliographies:

Donald Gallup, *T. S. Eliot: A Bibliography* (London: Faber & Faber, 1969; New York: Harcourt, Brace & World, 1969);

Bradley Gunther, *The Merrill Checklist of T. S. Eliot* (Columbus: Merrill, 1970);

Mildred Martin, *A Half-Century of Eliot Criticism: An Annotated Bibliography of Books and Articles in English, 1916–1965* (Lewisburg, Pa.: Bucknell University Press, 1972);

C. A. Carpenter, "T. S. Eliot as Dramatist: Critical Studies in English, 1933–1975," *Bulletin of Bibliography,* 33 (January 1976): 1–12;

Beatrice Ricks, *T. S. Eliot: A Bibliography of Secondary Works* (Metuchen, N.J.: Scarecrow Press, 1980).

Biographies:

Peter Ackroyd, *T. S. Eliot: A Life* (London: Hamilton, 1984; New York: Simon & Schuster, 1984);

Tony Sharpe, *T. S. Eliot: A Literary Life* (Basingstoke: Macmillan, 1991; New York: St. Martin's Press, 1991);

Lyndall Gordon, *T. S. Eliot: An Imperfect Life* (London: Vintage, 1998; New York: Norton, 1999).

References:

E. Martin Browne, *The Making of T. S. Eliot's Plays* (Cambridge: Cambridge University Press, 1969);

Joseph Chiari, *T. S. Eliot: Poet and Dramatist* (New York: Gordian Press, 1972);

Denis Donoghue, *The Third Voice* (Princeton: Princeton University Press, 1959);

Michael Hastings, *Tom and Viv* (Harmondsworth: Penguin, 1985);

A. P. Hinchliffe, *T. S. Eliot: Plays: A Casebook* (Basingstoke: Macmillan, 1985);

D. E. Jones, *The Plays of T. S. Eliot* (London: Routledge, 1960);

Glenda Leeming, *Poetic Drama* (Basingstoke: Macmillan, 1989);

Randy Malamud, *T. S. Eliot's Drama: A Research and Production Sourcebook* (New York: Greenwood Press, 1992);

Graham Martin, ed., *Eliot in Perspective* (London: Macmillan, 1970);

David A. Moody, ed., *The Cambridge Companion to T. S. Eliot* (Cambridge & New York: Cambridge University Press, 1994);

Kenneth Pickering, *Drama in the Cathedral* (Worthing: Churchman, 1985);

Michael Sidnell, *Dances of Death: The Group Theatre of London in the Thirties* (London: Faber & Faber, 1984);

Carol H. Smith, *T. S. Eliot's Dramatic Theory and Practice* (Princeton: Princeton University Press, 1963);

William Tydeman, *Murder in the Cathedral and The Cocktail Party* (Basingstoke: Macmillan, 1988);

Raymond Williams, *Drama from Ibsen to Brecht* (London: Chatto & Windus, 1968);

Katharine J. Worth, *Revolutions in Modern English Drama* (London: Bell, 1972).

Papers:

Among the most important archives of T. S. Eliot's papers are the Eliot Collection of the Houghton Library, Harvard University (the largest single collection, including the manuscript of *Murder in the Cathedral*); the Hayward Collection of Kings College Library, at Cambridge University (which includes the manuscripts for *The Family Reunion, The Cocktail Party, The Confidential Clerk,* and *The Elder Statesman*); the Henry W. and Albert A. Berg Collection of English and American Literature of the New York Public Library; the T. S. Eliot Collection at the Harry Ransom Humanities Research Center at the University of Texas at Austin; the collection at the Beinecke Rare Book and Manuscript Library, Yale University; and papers at the Princeton University Library.

Seamus Finnegan

(1 March 1949 -   )

Robert Wilcher
University of Birmingham

PLAY PRODUCTIONS: *Laws of God,* London, Half Moon Theatre, 1978;

Race, London, Half Moon Theatre, 1978;

Paddy and Britannia, London, Half Moon Theatre, 1979;

Act of Union, rehearsed reading, London, Institute of Contemporary Arts, June 1980; full production, London, Soho Poly Theatre Club, November 1980;

Soldiers, London, Old Red Lion Theatre Club, 27 October 1981;

James Joyce and the Israelites, London, Lyric Studio Theatre, Hammersmith, 10 March 1982; Tel Aviv, First International Festival of Jewish Theatre, July 1982;

Tout, London, Barbican Theatre, The Pit, 17 January 1984;

North, London, Cockpit Theatre, 22 February 1984;

Beyond a Joke, London, Queen Elizabeth Hall, 21 April 1984;

Mary's Men, London, Drill Hall Theatre, 12 June 1984;

Herself Alone, London, Old Red Lion Theatre Club, 1984;

Gombeen, London, Air Gallery, 9 April 1985;

The Spanish Play, London, The Place, 15 October 1986;

The German Connection, London, Young Vic Theatre, 5 November 1986;

Ghetto, London, Riverside Studios, 11 March 1987;

The Murphy Girls, London, Drill Hall Arts Centre, 2 June 1988;

1916, London, Institute of Contemporary Arts, 11 December 1989;

Mary Maginn, London, Drill Hall Arts Centre, 28 February 1990;

Hypatia, by Finnegan and Miriam Kainy, London, at National Theatre Studio, 1994;

Dead Faces Laugh, London, Old Red Lion Theatre Club, 13 July 1998;

Life after life, London, Old Red Lion Theatre, 15 November 1999; revised, London, Old Red Lion Theatre, 4 April 2000;

Seamus Finnegan (courtesy of Seamus Finnegan)

Maisie, London, Old Red Lion Theatre, 15 November 1999;

Diaspora Jigs, London, Old Red Lion Theatre, 11 May 2001.

BOOKS: *North; also Soldiers, Act of Union, Mary's Men: Four Plays* (London & New York: Boyars, 1987);

The Cemetery of Europe: The Spanish Play, The German Connection, The Murphy Girls: Three Plays (London & New York: Boyars, 1991);

James Joyce and the Israelites; and Dialogues in Exile, Contemporary Theatre Studies, volume 7 (Chur, Switzerland: Harwood Academic, 1995);

It's All Blarney: Four Plays, Contemporary Theatre Studies, volume 8 (Chur, Switzerland: Harwood Academic, 1995)–comprises *Wild Grass, Mary Maginn, It's All Blarney,* and *Comrade Brennan;*

Dead Faces Laugh, introduction by Robert Wilcher, Contemporary Theatre Studies, volume 10 (London: Harwood Academic, 2001).

PRODUCED SCRIPTS: *Doctors' Dilemmas,* television, BBC Two, six drama documentaries, 11, 18, 25 January and 1, 8, 15 February 1983;

The Cemetery of Europe, radio, BBC Radio 3, November 1988.

Seamus Finnegan is from Northern Ireland–more significantly, from Belfast; but his plays have been performed not in Ireland but in London, where most of them have been written. Finnegan is a writer with an ear keenly attuned to the colorful idiom of the Belfast streets and a talent for creating powerful stage images. Since the early 1980s he has built up a distinctive and valuable body of work that includes a variety of theatrical strategies for bridging the gulf of ignorance and indifference that separates the experiences of his characters from the media's simplified images of Northern Ireland.

Unlike the studies of life in rural communities and small towns undertaken by some of his better-known contemporaries on the Irish theatrical scene, most of Finnegan's plays are rooted firmly in the recent history of his native Belfast. His best work combines the desire to communicate to outsiders the daily realities of living in a divided city with a personal quest to understand the complex cultural origins of the bigotries that give Belfast inhabitants their sense of identity. The dramatic tension that makes his explorations of the past and present of the North so compelling derives largely from the need of this voluntary exile to come to terms with his own share in that identity.

Seamus Patrick Finnegan was born on 1 March 1949 to Catholic parents, Billy Finnegan, a bricklayer, and Mary Magee Finnegan in Belfast. He has one sister, Jacinta. He was educated at St. Mary's Irish Christian Brothers Grammar School. His grandfather had been a member of the Irish Volunteers, founded by Patrick Pearse in 1913 to fight for independence from English rule, and in the introduction to *The Cemetery of Europe* (1991) Finnegan describes himself as having been "suckled at the teats of nationalism." He left Belfast in 1971 to take a teacher-training course in the School of Education at Manchester University; in 1974 he moved to London, where he taught for four years at the Jewish Free School. His first sketches were seen at the Half Moon Theatre in London at the end of the 1970s; since 1980 his plays have appeared regularly in small theaters, arts centers, and clubs, many of them directed by Julia Pascal. In 1997 he married Valerie Rose. None of his plays has yet been produced in Ireland or taken up by the commercial theater. As well as writing for the theater, radio, television, and motion pictures, Finnegan has taught at the Spiro Institute for Study of Jewish History and Culture–now the London Jewish Cultural Centre–where he still gives occasional lectures; he also lectures part-time at Southampton Institute of Higher Education.

The first of Finnegan's major plays to be performed was the ironically titled *Act of Union* (1980). The sounds of explosions, gunfire, and sirens provide the backdrop for the opening monologue by Maisie, a middle-aged, working-class Belfast woman. She assumes that her London audience is cut off from the experience of "living here" in the province of Ulster not only by the Irish Sea but also by ignorance and indifference. Addressing them directly, she insists that "Youse people have no idea, y'know." She describes how one of her neighbors was humiliated during a body search at the Queen Street security gates and concludes, "I'm sure it doesn't happen in Oxford Street too often, I can tell you!" Later she relates a recent incident in which an "aul bitch of a Dubliner" refused to serve her in a shop in the Irish capital. Maisie has as little esteem for Southerners–the "gombeen men who'd sold us out time and time again"–as she has for English imperialists. In a final monologue she patiently explains that Catholics and Protestants in Ulster "have more in common than meets the eye" in their hatred of Englishmen and their contempt for the Southern Irish. The "Fighting North" was always different, she claims, "long before there was a Protestant about the place at all."

The rest of the play consists of several narrative strands illustrating what it is like to live in a divided, occupied city and what it means to be Northern. Three scenes set in a docklands public house, run by a Catholic and frequented by Protestant and Catholic members of the Special Branch of the Royal Ulster Constabulary, dramatize the religious inheritance that tears Ulstermen apart and the resentment of intruders that binds them together. Paddy, the landlord, complains about the effects of redevelopment by "the Department of Environment," and the eldest of three policemen is angry that the British army has assumed responsibility for a task that the Royal Ulster Constabulary has been per-

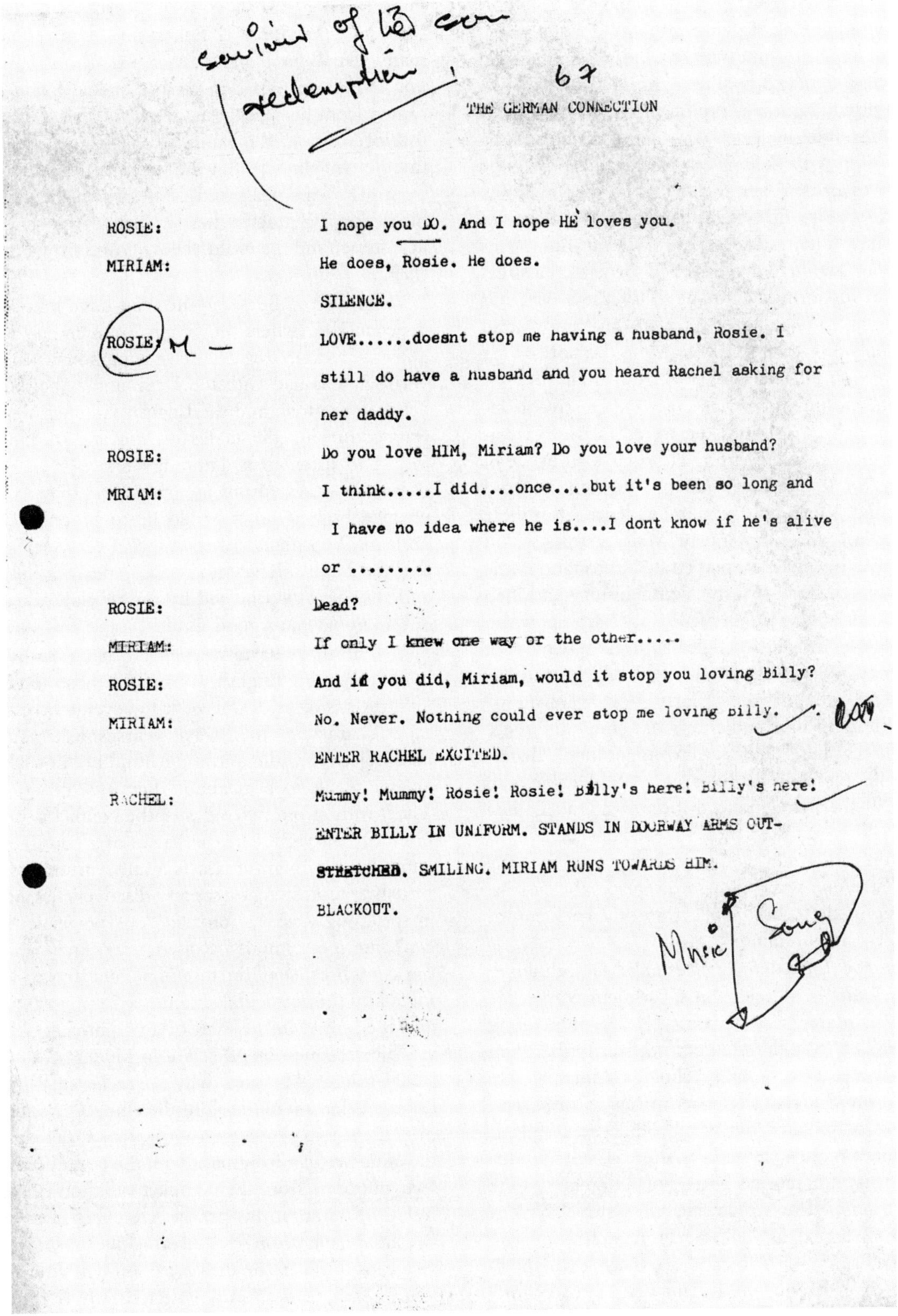

67

THE GERMAN CONNECTION

ROSIE: I hope you DO. And I hope HE loves you.

MIRIAM: He does, Rosie. He does.

SILENCE.

ROSIE: LOVE......doesnt stop me having a husband, Rosie. I still do have a husband and you heard Rachel asking for her daddy.

ROSIE: Do you love HIM, Miriam? Do you love your husband?

MRIAM: I think.....I did....once....but it's been so long and I have no idea where he is....I dont know if he's alive or ....

ROSIE: Dead?

MIRIAM: If only I knew one way or the other.....

ROSIE: And if you did, Miriam, would it stop you loving Billy?

MIRIAM: No. Never. Nothing could ever stop me loving Billy.

ENTER RACHEL EXCITED.

RACHEL: Mummy! Mummy! Rosie! Rosie! Billy's here! Billy's here!

ENTER BILLY IN UNIFORM. STANDS IN DOORWAY ARMS OUT-STRETCHED. SMILING. MIRIAM RUNS TOWARDS HIM.

BLACKOUT.

Annotated typescript page for Finnegan's 1986 play about "shattered men living with shattered dreams" (Collection of Seamus Finnegan) forming for years. Three taped telephone calls followed by improvised scenes of police brutality document the attempts of a solicitor to discover what is happening to a young man detained by the authorities, and in two highly stylized scenes a typical night in Belfast is recounted by four figures lit by spotlights: a nurse, a British soldier, a Protestant cabdriver, and a Catholic who survives an assassination attempt on his way home from a club. The final ingredient in this collage of voices and incidents is a series of comic duologues between Yap, an old man selling newspapers on a street corner, and his former companion, Bucksey, who has been "blown to smithereens by a car bomb" and returns to ply Yap with free whiskey and report on his encounters with St. Peter, the Devil, and God.

In the closing moments Maisie's aggressive assertion of her Belfast identity is answered by an exasperated English voice representing Finnegan's audience of outsiders: "So, that's your solution is it? Fighting. And more fighting. Violence. And more violence." But these are not the last words in the play: Maisie retorts with a reminder of the violence perpetrated throughout the world in the course of British colonial history and then turns to the English soldier singled out by a spotlight. She wonders if he is the one she has seen on television, firing rubber bullets from an armored vehicle; and her final question–"Was yon' a play you were in or what?"–reminds the audience that the difference between "living here" and learning about life in Belfast through the media constitutes an unbridgeable gulf between Northern Ireland and the rest of the United Kingdom. As the ghost of the murdered Special Branch officer put it earlier, how can anyone expect to fight the war in Ulster unless he knows "the place, the people, the geography, the pubs, the alleyways, the back entries of the Northern Irish mind?"

In *Act of Union* Finnegan establishes techniques and themes that he develops in subsequent works. He prefers to explore his subject matter by intercutting voices speaking from different perspectives, rather than by relying on plot or on the psychological interest generated by complex characters. As reviewers of several of his later plays have remarked, Finnegan's style is reminiscent of radio documentary and well suited to his talent for witty and mordant dialogue; and many of the devices he adopts for structuring his material have a strong visual appeal, as well. While the episodic form, use of narrators, and dialectical approach owe something to Bertolt Brecht, the delight Finnegan's characters take in language and anecdote places them firmly in the Irish tradition of John Millington Synge, Sean O'Casey, and Samuel Beckett.

Finnegan's next play, *Soldiers* (1981), is closer to Brechtian epic theater in its historical analysis of the impact of the British army in Northern Ireland since troops first arrived in Belfast in August 1969. Like many details in Finnegan's drama, the shooting of a young man for "carrying 'what looked like a rifle'" is drawn from his memories of life in Belfast. He says in the foreword to the published version of *Soldiers* and three other plays (1987) that he was thinking of a boy from his own street when he described the spot where his fictional character dies, with "the red stain on the kerbstone" and the "wild yellow flowers" of a makeshift shrine.

In *Soldiers* Bucksey and Yap have taken up residence in Hell, where they enjoy an unending supply of poteen. Bucksey regales his companion with a "great yarn" he has had with the Devil about the differences between the Irish and the English–an effective comical way of turning the tables on the audience, which is forced to listen to a damning version of its national character as seen from an Irish viewpoint. "Can you imagine how awful it would be to be one of them?" exclaims Yap, in horrified disbelief. Bucksey's verdict that the English have "no magic" and "are full of class and snobbery" is clinched by the revelation that "they don't know what a good spud is!"

The main narrative burden in *Soldiers* is carried by Marilyn, an English journalist whose reports provide the historical framework for events involving the other characters. For twelve years she has strived to bear objective witness to the truth, but "this is the war no one wants to hear about" because "no one cares." The "truth" from two sides of the conflict is presented primarily through the experiences of a young Irishman and a young Englishman. Ciaran is brutalized by the British peacekeeping forces and discovers during a term in the Long Kesh prison that "our power is that you can't intern our minds." Robert, a Cockney who joined the army because of the lure of adventure and travel, is forced by the accidental shooting of a pregnant woman and the hatred in the eyes of an eight-year-old boy to ask himself questions that are forbidden to the professional soldier: "I mean, why we're here? What we're doing? What's it all for?" In the climactic scenes of the play these two representative figures speak directly to the audience, confronting it with the prejudice that protects outsiders from the complex situation in Northern Ireland. Ciaran, in his prison cell, effects a moment of Brechtian alienation by sneering at those who seek vicarious thrills in the theater: "Come to visit me, have you? Come to spy on a REAL LIVE IRISH 'TERRORIST?'" Robert taunts the spectators with their complacent consumption of secondhand news, neatly packaged by the media: "You've read about it, eh? In newspapers. Books. Seen it all on T.V.?" Then his tone changes from irony to accusation: "But I'm telling you now. . . . Only a squaddie KNOWS what it's like. What it's REALLY like to be in Belfast." By setting these alternative "truths" before the audience, Finnegan exposes the English imagination to some of the fundamental realities of life in Northern Ireland and gives trenchant dramatic expression to his insights into the mental and emotional processes that underpin prejudice and inform conflicting political ideologies.

In 1982, through the good offices of the cultural attaché at the Israeli Embassy in London, Finnegan and Pascal were invited to take their production of *James Joyce and the Israelites* to the first International Festival of Jewish Theatre in Tel Aviv. Since then the playwright has maintained contact with the theatrical community in Israel. Written for the centenary of the birth of the great Irish novelist, *James Joyce and the Israelites* continues Finnegan's experiments with representative characters, extended and parallel story lines broken into discrete episodes, and interludes of commentary. The play also introduces two new themes that are central to much of Finnegan's later drama: the experience of exile and the similarities between the Jews and the Irish in outlook, character, and history.

Sporting a bottle-green waistcoat and seated beneath a Jewish wedding canopy, Joyce presides over the performance, stepping down from time to time to take part in the action or to interrupt a discussion. One series of episodes traces the progress of four generations of a Jewish family from the marriage in 1882 of Nathan and Esther, who have fled to Dublin from pogroms in Lithuania, to 1974, when a second Esther, standing at the grave of her grandparents in a Jewish cemetery in Dublin, surveys the other tombstones: "Some long dead. Others. . . . Emigrated. . . . Like so many Irish before them and after them. All in exile. Forever exiles. While here, remaining, Nadia and Henry. Jews. Now resting under Irish soil." The other narrative line follows Joyce's career as a writer, emphasizing the importance to his art of his relationships with Jews. In one scene he announces his decision to leave Dublin and "become like the Wandering Jew"; in another he discusses the antagonistic claims of politics and literature with a Zionist rabbi. Encounters with Jewish women in Trieste and Zurich provide Joyce with the models for Molly Bloom and Gerty McDowell in *Ulysses* (1922). In 1939 he maintains his stance of public disengagement from politics, complaining that "this damned war is interfering with the world's response to *Finnegans Wake,*" although three offstage voices remind the audience that in real life Joyce helped Jews escape from the Nazis. Toward the end of the play Joyce comes face to face with his greatest creation: Leopold Bloom, the Jewish protagonist of *Ulysses.*

Punctuating these two narratives are conversations between Patrick and Jacob that range over many shared cultural aspects and historical experiences of the Jews and the Irish: the power of ancient tradition over present behavior; attitudes toward sex, family, and religion; the diaspora suffered by both peoples and their subsequent contributions to political and artistic life all over the world; and the "attempts of annihilation made on them," respectively, by the Nazis during World War II and the English during the potato famine of the nineteenth century. Joyce intervenes in each of these scenes to offer his own views, claiming that he himself is both Jewish and Irish and that there is no escape from "the tribe" even in self-imposed exile. At the end, after the great-granddaughter of Esther and Nathan has paid homage to her scattered family, the various strands of the play are woven together as she joins Patrick and Jacob in reciting a litany of Jewish names in response to Joyce's question, "And tell me, does anyone in Dublin read *Ulysses?*"

The reviewer for *The Guardian* (London), Nicholas de Jongh (11 March 1982), described the character of James Joyce as "a dazzling Shavian savant," and the response to Finnegan's 1984 play *North* confirmed the presence of George Bernard Shaw alongside Brecht, Joyce, and O'Casey in his dramatic pedigree. Criticized by B. A. Young in *The Financial Times* (23 February 1984) as "not so much a play as a debate," *North* completes what is essentially a trilogy by returning to the analysis of Northern Ireland begun in *Act of Union* and *Soldiers.* In a carefully articulated structure, three sets of Northern Irish characters pursue courses of action that share a common thematic pattern, each culminating in a revelation about the nature of the cultural inheritance of Ulster. In one narrative strand two Irish Republican Army (IRA) gunmen are spirited away to a safe house in Dublin. They become homesick, however, and while trying to make their way back to Belfast are captured by the Gardai (police), who make it clear that Southern Ireland wants nothing to do with their ideal of "a 32 County Socialist Republic." Incarcerated in Dublin, Liam realizes that Northerners "have no friends and that's true for us Taigs [Catholics] as well as the Prods [Protestants]." In the second narrative thread the Protestant Derek, who goes to London in search of work, has the same epiphany. Shocked by the indiscriminate hostility against the Irish, he gets into a fight and is arrested as a suspected terrorist. An Irish Catholic with whom he finds himself sharing a cell points out that "Loyalist" and "Fenian" are merely "different ways of saying 'PADDY'" on the English side of the Irish Sea. Derek learns the bitter lesson that "what we were LOYAL to . . . doesn't want us . . . despises us."

The third narrative concerns a radical young curate who is reprimanded by his bishop for asserting in a local newspaper that the Catholic Church is "out of step, if not out of sympathy with its flock on the realities of Northern Ireland politics." In the course of a single interview that is shown at intervals during the rest of the play, Father Quinn argues that the Church, which is "but a thin gloss on a Pagan underworld" of ancient mythologies and superstitious practices, will lose its hold on the population if it slavishly supports the English establishment against the nationalist appeal of "Cathleen Ni Houlihan" (the mythical personification of Ireland). The bishop acknowledges that "this province of Ulster has always been troublesomely askew." The priest's insight into the complex culture of the North ties in with Liam's account of the strange mixture of pagan and Christian beliefs in his mother's tales of "holy wells and ancient Mass stones that had once been the graves of Celtic goddesses" and a friend's memories of "being doused in Lourdes water whenever there was thunder and lightning."

Acting as an ignorant chorus to the exposition of these complexities by representatives of the Northern Irish community are two Labour Party members of Parliament in England who advocate a policy of "troops out" and congratulate each other on their anticolonialist stance until a professional historian accuses them of political naiveté and "the worst kind of patronizing liberal guilt." The Englishmen's dialogue is banal and artificial in comparison with the lively idioms and convincing rhythms of the Irish characters' speech.

The Irish gift for idiomatic language, celebratory and abusive by turns, is the lifeblood of *Mary's Men* (1984). Like *Act of Union, Soldiers,* and *North,* it is set in Belfast and draws on the author's boyhood memories: Hoops Maguire is based on the same original as Bucksey, and the material for another character's reminiscences about an artist who sacrificed his genius to the "business of being a 'good' husband and father" was supplied by one of Finnegan's cousins. Unlike the three earlier plays, however, *Mary's Men* is more of an elegy than an argument. Based on Finnegan's experiences as a sixteen-year-old volunteer at a Legion of Mary hostel for the homeless, it is an affectionate portrait of the "down and outs" who nightly seek food, shelter, and nostalgic conversation under the watchful eyes of Cod Alex and his assistant, Hunchback Harry. Instead of the rapid interchange of short scenes found in the earlier plays, the first act is a leisurely introduction to the characters who once cut a figure in the world as a football player, a boxer, an IRA man, and a bank manager with literary and theatrical pretensions. There is a defiant roll call of artists and athletes from Belfast, and the old men painfully revive moments of past glory before their decline into vagrancy. Sentimentality is avoided through the humor of the dialogue, the hint of Surrealism in the white-caked faces and dusty black suits of the six characters, and the skepticism of Hoops Maguire, who dismisses Banker Joe's reverie about his talented cousin as "self-pitying romantic drivel" and pours scorn on his fellow Irishmen as "myth-makers, all of them." In the three scenes of act 2 the men breakfast together before making their way back onto the streets, return in the evening with the news that Hoops has been killed by a car bomb, and take part in a stylized funeral service overseen by Hoops's ghost. Some reviewers interpreted Finnegan's gently ironic tribute to his hometown as a parable of "the Northern condition," one sustained by dreams and rituals and disfigured by violence.

The unpublished *Tout,* performed by the Royal Shakespeare Company in 1984, was commissioned as part of a two-week event marking response to George Orwell's novel *Nineteen Eighty-Four* (1948), and examines issues raised by the trials and activities of "supergrasses" (the equivalent in Northern Irish politics of informers). Reaction to the play provoked Finnegan, as quoted in an article by Elaine Ives-Cameron in *Plays and Players* (May 1984), to comment, "I don't care if audiences agree with my politics so long as my plays stir up energy, make them think."

Gombeen (1985) probes the wound inflicted on the psyche of Northern republicans by the partition of Ireland. The plot revolves around an act of reprisal by two dissidents from Belfast, who kidnap a senior minister from Dublin because his father, a member of the cabinet that negotiated the Treaty of 1922, had been party to the execution of four opponents of the Free State. Critics were dismayed by the dramatist's failure to offer a solution or even a glimmer of hope, and the familiar charge, expressed by Michael Billington in *The Guardian* (London) for 10 April 1985, that the work was "really a lecture in the guise of a play" was repeated.

Finnegan's next project was a trilogy of war plays with the overall title *The Cemetery of Europe.* As the titles of the first two parts–*The Spanish Play* (1986) and *The German Connection* (1986)–suggest, the historical horizons widen to treat the struggle against fascism during the 1930s and 1940s. *The Spanish Play* returns to the episodic structure of epic theater to tell the story of two young working-class recruits from Belfast who join the International Brigade to fight in the Spanish Civil War in 1936. Catholic Billy Robinson and Protestant Tommy Reid become comrades in the service of a cause that transcends their local differences, and other inherited prejudices are challenged by the men and women who join them in the fight against Francisco Franco. In a barn at the foot of the Pyrenees they discard the "tribal allegiance" that made them suspicious

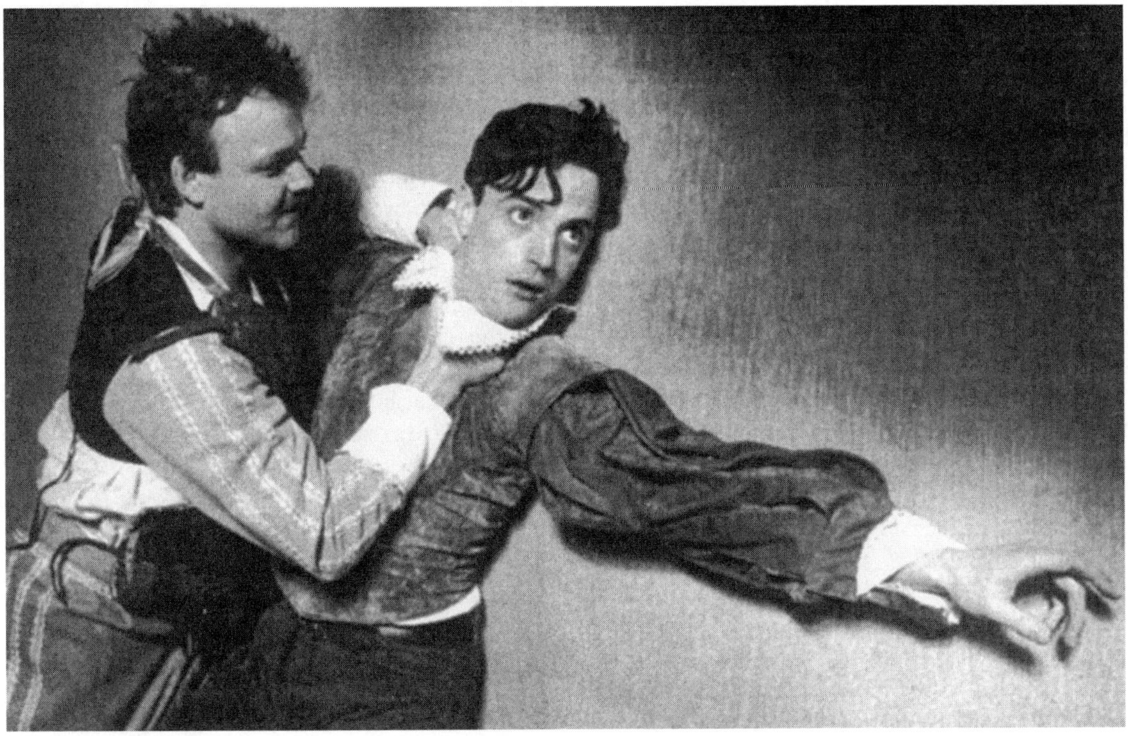

Paul Rhys as Solomon and David Morrissey as Giorgio in the 1987 Riverside Studio production of Finnegan's Ghetto

of the "posh English accents" of a poet from Cambridge and a painter from an upper-middle-class family, and they are given a European perspective on the war against oppression by Sammy, a Cockney Jew whose parents had fled Russia. The horrors of battle and the joys of falling in love–Tommy with the Cambridge painter, Felicity, and Billy with Maria, a Spanish revolutionary–are enacted against a grotesque frieze of dummies that are manipulated to represent a Nazi parade attended by bishops and cardinals, a massacre of peasants by Nationalist (fascist) forces, and a brutal reprisal by the Republicans. The atrocities committed by both sides drive Sammy mad and lead Billy to lose his faith in religion and revolution. Attempting to desert from an army that has betrayed their ideals, the London Jew and the Belfast Catholic are captured by the fascists, who shoot Sammy in the back and subject Billy to torture. This core narrative is punctuated by scenes set in Belfast in which Billy's father, Jimmy, a veteran of the 1916 Easter Rising, sneers at the International Brigade, and two priests take opposite sides, one supporting the antifascist workers' movement in Spain and the other calling for a "Crusade of prayer" against "the scourge of Communism and Anarchism."

The German Connection is set in 1941 in Belfast, where Billy lives in a state of disillusioned apathy and Tommy announces that he is going to enlist in the British army to carry on the struggle for which Felicity sacrificed her life. Jimmy Robinson, unable to see beyond his narrow and embittered nationalism, despises Tommy for running off to "fight for England" like a true Protestant and despises his own son, Billy, for deserting during the Spanish Civil War. Further fuel is added to his bigotry when his wife, Rosie, welcomes into their home two Jewish evacuees from Britain, Miriam Jacobs and her seven-year-old daughter, Rachel. Miriam's husband is a Royal Air Force officer who is missing in action. Love develops between Billy and Miriam in the most naturalistic plot that Finnegan has yet devised. With a strength that recalls O'Casey's Juno Boyle in *Juno and the Paycock* (1924), Rosie copes with her two "shattered men living with shattered dreams," tolerating the drunkenness and blind prejudice of her husband because of the passion that first drew them together amid the dangers of the Irish Civil War and encouraging the relationship between her son and Miriam in the hope that it will mend Billy's spirit, which was broken in Spain. Drawing inspiration from his dead friend Sammy and from Miriam, Billy decides to follow Tommy into the British army, convinced that ideology "is but part of the argument and the cold part at that" and that "to fight for love of someone is the *only* real motivation worth having." When Jimmy sends two thugs to intimidate "that Yiddish hussy who's been fouling my home" and to punish his son for putting on the uniform of his country's enemy, Billy finally rejects the past that has imprisoned his father's mind: "You can keep your little Western Isle. You can keep your dark bog-drenched vision. . . . If this is Ireland I want no part of it." Rosie's dream is now "dead and buried," too, and the play ends with mother and son about to board the ferry for England with Miriam and Rachel, while German warplanes are heard over Belfast.

Before the final part of this trilogy was produced on the radio, Finnegan wrote two plays that deal with two of his principal preoccupations as a dramatist. The first, *Ghetto,* which premiered in 1987 but has never been published, depicts the persecution and betrayal of a Jewish bookseller, his beautiful daughter, and his musically talented son by the Christian community in sixteenth-century Venice. While some reviewers applauded Finnegan's intention of raising timely questions about anti-Semitism and the healing function of art, and many admired the portrayal of the Jewish composer who accepts a commission from the Catholic Church, there was universal condemnation of the melodramatic plot and the archaic fustian of the dialogue.

The second play, *The Murphy Girls* (1988), is set in the contemporary period. The three daughters of Tommy and Nora Murphy have found different ways of escaping from the legacy of Irish history, which still holds their father in thrall with what one of them, Aine, calls "the outmoded ranting slogans of over seventy years ago." The play focuses on Brid, the middle sister, who has left Ireland to teach in London and is "living in sin" there with the grandson of a Jewish immigrant. She returns to visit her family in Belfast and is soon caught up in a wave of nostalgia for the summer of 1968, when she had just finished school and her older sister was at the university. It was "the last summer of innocence," when students were demonstrating throughout Europe and the British army had not yet arrived in Northern Ireland. Brid knows that she is an outsider both in England and in Ireland and that the Belfast she still loves, the Belfast of her childhood memories and the civil rights idealism of her youth, no longer exists. She discovers, however, that even exile cannot preserve her from the hatred and ignorance that continue to dog the relationship between England and Ireland. She is wounded by a sectarian gunman outside a club in Belfast, and when she returns to London, she is picked up by Special Branch officers at Heathrow Airport as a suspected terrorist. In a long reverie Brid remembers how humbled she had been during a visit to Paris, when she and her partner were entertained at lunch by a Jewish couple who had survived the regimes of Adolf Hitler and Joseph Stalin. After all they had been through, they were still interested in other people and still thinking of the future. Later, looking at the marginal position of Ireland and Great Britain–"those two pathetic islands"–on a map of Europe, Brid does not "know whether to weep with impotence and emptiness or cry out in rage and despair."

The final part of Finnegan's second trilogy, a radio play broadcast under the title *The Cemetery of Europe* in November 1988, moves on a generation to tell the story of Benjamin, the illegitimate son of Billy and Miriam, and Aaron, a Hungarian-born Israeli survivor of the Holocaust. When Aaron invites Benjamin to show one of his paintings at an exhibition in Jerusalem, the scene is set for Finnegan to develop his analysis of the conflict between nationalism and internationalism.

In *Mary Maginn* (1990) Finnegan reverts to the documentary style of his earliest work to pay homage to a Belfast woman whose life, presented as a pageant of births, baptisms, weddings, and funerals, is offered as a paradigm of Catholic working-class experience against the background of the history of Northern Ireland. Sidelit, or silhouetted behind four gauze screens, the nationalist leaders Pearse; King George V; British prime ministers Neville Chamberlain, Winston Churchill, and Margaret Thatcher; and Northern Ireland prime minister "Captain" Terence O'Neill chart the course of Irish politics, while the forestage is reserved for the mother, brothers, sister, husband, son, and daughter whose lives and, in some instances, deaths constitute the world of Mary Maginn. Born in 1913, Mary devotes herself to the business of day-to-day survival and regards politics as an external evil only to be acknowledged when it directly threatens her family in the form of Protestant persecution, the British army, or the civil rights activism that draws her children into danger. She dies quietly in bed, beside her husband, in 1986.

Published with *Mary Maginn* in 1995 under the title *It's All Blarney* were the texts of three works in which Finnegan looks further into the processes by which idealism, in the context of Irish and international politics, either gives way to disillusionment or hardens into bigotry. "Wild Grass," commissioned as a *Monday Play* for BBC Radio 4 in 1990 but never broadcast, reworks much of the material used in *Mary Maginn* in a format of flashbacks prompted by the return of Mary's son, Patrick, to Belfast for his mother's funeral, where he quarrels with the other members of his family over his political activities. A two-act play written for the stage but as yet unproduced, *It's All Blarney* pleads for an end to the cycle of violence that is fed by a mind-set that cannot free itself from the past. When an Irish teacher living in London is visited by his older brother, who long ago immigrated to the United States and has been engaged in fund-raising for the IRA, he comes to

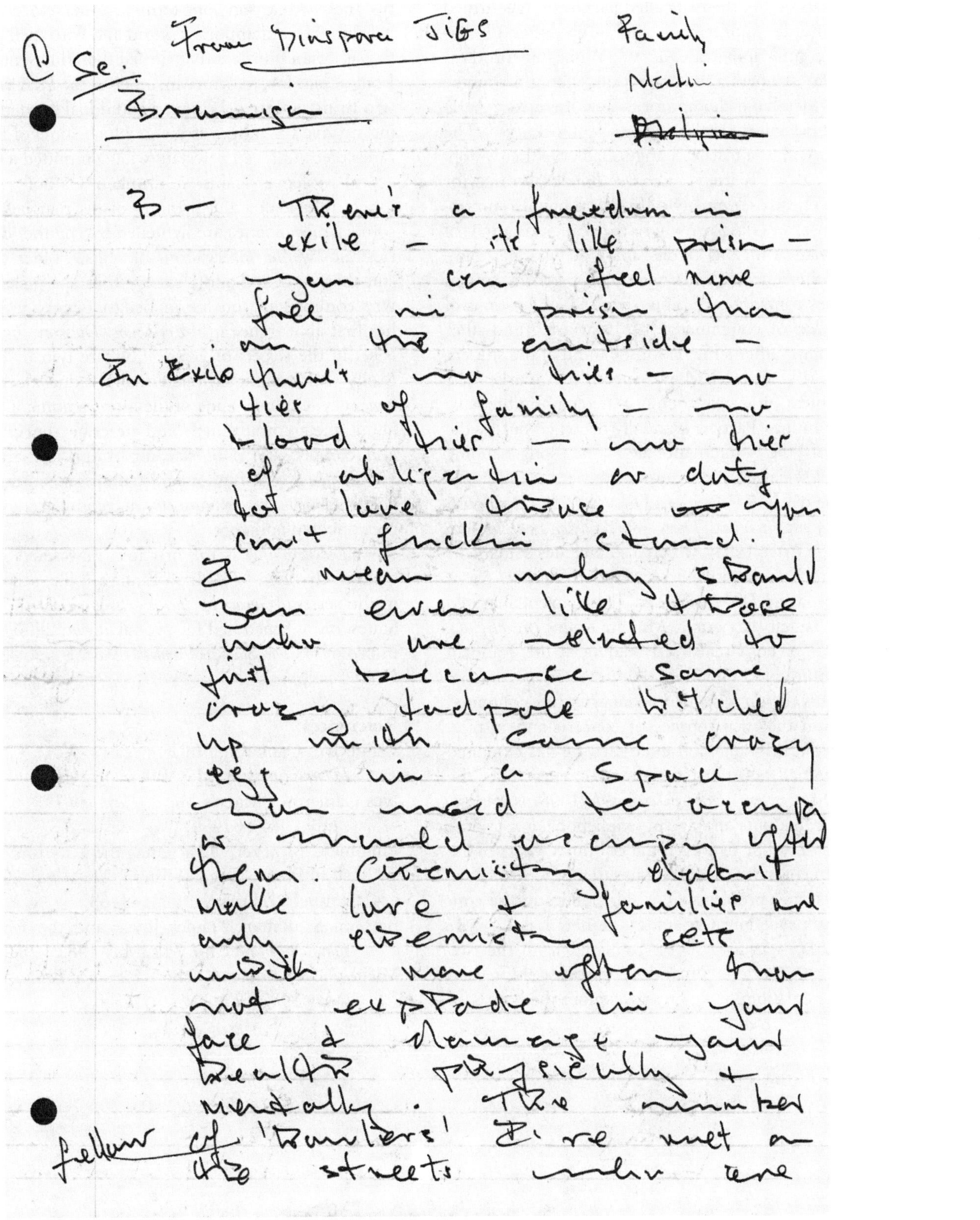

① Sc. From Diaspora JIGS
Family
Nation
~~Religion~~
Birmingham

B — There's a freedom in exile — it's like prison — you can feel more free in prison than on the outside — In Exile there's no ties — no ties of family — no blood ties — no ties of obligation or duty that love [illegible] you can't fuckin stand. I mean why should you even like those who are related to just because some crazy tadpole hitched up with some crazy egg in a space you used to occupy or would occupy after them. Consanguinity doesn't make love & familiar and only consanguinity sets [illegible] which more often than not explode in your face & damage your health physically & mentally. The number of 'brothers' I've met on the streets who are

fellow

Manuscript page for Finnegan's play Diaspora Jigs, *which premiered in 2001 (Collection of Seamus Finnegan)* the realization that their so-called patriotism has turned them both into "monsters . . . full of hatred and bitterness . . . guilt and inadequacy." While the brothers indulge in "slabber" and "empty talk" about a country in which they have chosen not to live, the next generation is being infected with the "ancient sickness." The play ends with the teacher's anguished cry, "Let it stop, now. . . . It's all Blarney!" *Comrade Brennan,* written for the 7:84 Theatre Company of Scotland but also unproduced, is set in Glasgow, where the scattered family of Joe Brennan, a lifelong trades union activist, has gathered for the funeral of his wife. Three generations of Irish exiles confront each other over the implications of the collapse of communism. As Marxist grandfather and capitalist father struggle for the mind of the student Michael, Mikhail Gorbachev's speech that marked the abandonment of Marxist-Leninist ideology by the Russian Communist Party is gradually drowned out by the strains of the "Internationale," the long-standing anthem of socialism and communism.

The diary of Finnegan's January 1993 return visit to Israel forms part of *James Joyce and the Israelites; and Dialogues in Exile* (1995), which also includes statements by six Israeli dramatists and excerpts from their plays. While preparing *Dialogues in Exile* Finnegan collaborated with the Israeli playwright Miriam Kainy on *Hypatia,* which was given a rehearsed reading at the National Theatre Studio in London in 1994.

In his most recent plays Finnegan has continued to draw on the twin sources of concern and inspiration–Northern Ireland and exile–that he has exploited to such varied and satisfying dramatic effect over the course of his career. *Dead Faces Laugh* (1998) is a large-scale piece that puts on stage in semifictional guise some of the major public figures of the last thirty years of the twentieth century in an ambitious attempt to dramatize the deep-seated problems of Ulster politics in the context of the peace initiative under the new Labour government. *Life after life* (2000), conflated from the two one-act plays *Maisie* (1999) and *Life after life* (1999), used intercut dramatic monologues to explore the efforts of two newly released long-term prisoners to cope with "life" in the contemporary world and with their guilt for the sectarian murders that earned them life sentences in Long Kesh. Joe, a former member of the IRA who shot two British soldiers, bears the additional burden of having survived a hunger strike in which some of his comrades died; Billy, a Protestant who committed a random act of violence against a drunken Catholic, faces a lonely future after the breakup of his marriage. Their somber monologues are lightened by childhood memories and by the observations of Maisie, older now but still sharp-tongued and clear-eyed, as she picks up her wry commentary on life in Belfast twenty years after her first appearance in *Act of Union. Diaspora Jigs* (2001) is set in the streets of London, where two Irish exiles, Molly and Brannigan, relate their gradual decline into vagrancy, explode some of the more sentimental myths about their countrymen, and describe the difficulties and compensations of sleeping rough. As always in Finnegan's work, humor and pathos leaven the moral challenge that he extends to the complacency of his metropolitan audience.

Diaspora Jigs is the first in a new series of plays collectively titled "The Irish Empire." The second play in the series, *Waiting for the Angels,* is set in the United States and is scheduled for production in 2002. A work in progress, *The Shamrock and the Stars,* is also set in the United States.

References:

Elaine Ives-Cameron, "In Finnegan's Wake," *Plays and Players,* no. 368 (May 1984): 43;

Ives-Cameron, "Mary's Men," *Plays and Players,* no. 370 (July 1984): 31–32;

Philomena Muinzer, "Evacuating the Museum: the Crisis of Playwriting in Ulster," *New Theatre Quarterly,* 3, no. 9 (February 1987): 44–63;

Barbara Schulman, "James Joyce and the Israelites," *Plays and Players,* no. 344 (May 1982): 28–29;

Michelene Wandor, "Ghetto," *Plays and Players,* no. 404 (May 1987): 22–23.

John Fox

(19 December 1938 -)

Gavin Carver
University of Kent

PLAY PRODUCTIONS: *St. Valentines Firestorm,* Bradford, February 1968;

The Tide Is OK for the 30th, Devon, Instow, July 1968;

The Marriage of Heaven and Hell, by Fox and Boris Howarth, Lancaster, Ashton Memorial, December 1968;

The Cabinet of Dr. Calighari, tour of Yorkshire, January–July 1969;

Naming Ceremony of Daniel Fox, by Fox and Howarth, North York Moors, July 1969;

Earthrise, by Fox, Mike Westbrook, and Cosmic Circus, London, Mermaid Theatre, November 1969; Colchester, University of Essex, May 1970; Exeter, Northcott Theatre, July 1970; Brighton, February 1971; Liverpool, May 1971; Southampton, May 1971; Leeds, July 1971; Lanchester, October 1971;

Circus Time, by Fox, Westbrook, and Cosmic Circus, Bradford, February 1970;

Spring Event, by Fox, Westbrook, and Cosmic Circus, Exeter University, 21 March 1970;

Naming Ceremony of Hannah Fox, by Fox and Westbrook, 1970;

Heptonstall / A.W.A.K.E., Hebden Bridge, May 1970;

Dr. Strangebrew's Diorama, Devon, Instow, August 1970;

Sweet Misery of Life, Harrogate, August 1971; Leith, August 1971; Edinburgh, August 1971;

End of the Summer Garden Party, London, Serpentine Gallery, Hyde Park, August 1971;

Winter Rising, Lanchester Polytechnic, February 1972;

The Travels of Sir Lancelot Quail, Brixton, Surrey Hall, May 1972;

Summer of the Pied Piper / Travels of Lancelot Quail, Burnley, Leith, and Sunderland, August 1972; Somerset, Devon, Cornwall, September 1972;

Beauty and the Beast, Burnley, May 1973;

Ceremony–with fire and ice sculptures, Aberystwyth, Arts Centre, May 1973;

Demon Buskers, Lancashire, August 1973;

Island of the Lost World, by Fox and Howarth, Blackburn, August 1974; revised, Burnley, January–February 1976; Milton Keynes, Leicester, Rennes, La Rochelle, Glasgow, and Barrow in Furness, June–September 1976;

Drowning of the Bottom Hundred, Bangor, Harlech, Aberystwyth, York, January–February 1975;

City of Windmills, Paris, Aubervilliers, May 1975;

Alien, Burnley, July 1975;

Stories for a Winter's Night, by Fox and Howarth, Wath-upon-Dearne, Basildon, Norwich, and Chorley, Winter 1976–1977;

Barrabas, by Fox and Howarth, Burnley, July–October 1977;

When the Pie was Opened, by Fox and Howarth, Welwyn, Digswell Arts Trust, May 1979;

The Garden of Earthly Delights, Liverpool, Crawford Arts Centre, November 1979;

Carnival Night, Ulverston, July 1980;

Eye of the Peacock, Milton Keynes, Merseyside, Renfrew, Fife, Cumbria, and Lancashire, July–September 1980;

A Wedding Ceremony, Little Easton, Essex, October 1980;

Tempest on Snake Island, by Fox and Howarth, Toronto, May 1981;

The Wasteland and the Wagtail, Togamura, Japan, July 1982;

Scarecrow Zoo, Bracknell, October–November 1982;

Raising the "Titanic," by Fox and Adrian Mitchell, music by Luk Mischalle, London, Limehouse docks, August 1983;

Ulverston Charter Week / Lantern Procession, Ulverston, September 1983;

Double or Quit, by Fox, Howarth, and Ian Wedde, North England, February–March 1984;

Tolpuddle Day, Darlington, Arts Centre, May 1984;

Tales for England, Edinburgh, Cumbria, August 1984;

On the Perimeter, by Fox and Sue Gill, tour, February 1985–1988;

Nutcracker, by Fox and Pete Moser, London, Commonwealth Institute, November–December 1985;

False Creek: A Visual Symphony, Vancouver Expo, July 1986;

John Fox (courtesy of John Fox)

The Town Hall Tattoo, Barrow-in-Furness, July 1987;
Lantern Coach: Jack and the Beanstalk, Dumfries and Cumbria, December 1987;
The Lantern Coach: Aladdin, Dumfries and Cumbria, December 1987;
Buffalo Bill's Return, by Fox and Wendy Meadley, Carew Castle, Pembrokeshire, July–August 1988;
Charcoal and Rain, Birmingham, November 1988;
Explorations, Aurillac, France, August 1989;
Discoveries, music by Tim Fleming, Lisbon, September 1989;
Lantern Coach: Robinson Crusoe in Space, Sandwell, December 1989; Tyneside, December 1990;
Britannia's Ragtime Splash, Houston, March 1990;
Shipyard Tales: a tapestry of celebration, conceived by Fox, Barrow-in-Furness, July 1990;
Golden Submarine, Barrow-in-Furness, July 1990;
Lord Dynamite, by Fox and Kevin Fegan, music by Fleming, Barrow-in-Furness, July 1990; outdoor version, London, Newham, July 1991; Totnes, July 1991; Newcastle upon Tyne, July 1991;
Glasgow All Lit Up, Glasgow, October 1990;
Fragile Gift, music by Daniel Fox, Glasgow, 1991;
Lantern Arcade, interactive site-specific installation, music by Daniel Fox, Glasgow, December 1992;
Hollow Ring, by Fox and Moser, tour, North West and South West England, Autumn 1993.

BOOKS: *The Dead Good Funerals Book,* by Fox and Sue Gill (Ulverston: Engineers of the Imagination, 1996);
Ground (Ulverston: Engineers of the Imagination, 1996).

PRODUCED SCRIPTS: *The Original Peter,* by Fox, Mike Westbrook, and Cosmic Circus, television, Arena, BBC-TV, April 1970;
Wings in the Attic, music by Pete Moser, television, Border Television, January 1988;
Piranha Pond, music by Tim Fleming, television, Border Television, January 1990.

OTHER: *The Dead Good Book of Namings and Baby Welcoming Ceremonies,* edited by Fox, Jonathan How, and Sue Gill (Ulverston: Engineers of the Imagination, 1999);

The Dead Good Time Capsule Book, edited by Gill, contributions by Fox (Ulverston: Engineers of the Imagination, 1999).

SELECTED PERIODICAL PUBLICATIONS–UNCOLLECTED: "Theatre to Liberate Fantasies," *Theatre Quarterly,* 2 (October–December 1972);

"The Welfare State: A Guided Tour," *Plays and Players* (July 1973);

"Concerning the Island of the Lost World," *Dartington Theatre Papers,* series 1, no. 2 (1977);

"Pathological Optimists," *Performance,* 4 (December 1979–January 1980);

"Welfare State International: Seventeen Years on the Streets," by Fox and Sue Gill, *Drama Review,* 29 (Fall 1985);

"Hybrid Products," *Performance,* no. 40 (March–April 1986);

"The Flight from Spectacle," *Theatre Forum,* no. 2 (Fall 1992);

"Percy, Ignatz and the Postman," *Mailout* (December 1994–January 1995);

"Theatre Now–The Green Light," *Buzz* (September 1995).

John Fox is best known as cofounder of Welfare State International, one of the most successful "alternative" performance and arts companies to emerge from the late 1960s. Whether one measures success by the level of funding awarded to the company, the quantity of the output, the longevity of the company, critical acclaim, or its impact in its field, Welfare State may arguably be regarded as one of the most exciting performance groups operating out of the mainstream since the 1960s. So deep is the association of Fox with Welfare State it is particularly difficult to discuss the work of Fox without discussing the work of the company. He has been responsible (often in collaboration) for the devising, sometimes the scripting, and usually the direction of a large number of performances and events, ranging from large-scale spectacular celebrations to personal rituals, from community celebrations to environmental installations. As well as being a creator of performance he is also a printmaker, essayist, performer, and poet.

John Fox, son of Horatio, a sea captain and later Member of British Empire, and Lucy (née Hasnip), was born in Hull on 19 December 1938. He studied politics, philosophy, and economics at Oxford, earning a B.A. with honors in 1962. That same year he married Sue Gill, whom he had known since 1955. Fox then turned to fine arts at Newcastle, where he received a B.A. in 1967. A year later his son, Daniel, was born, and in 1971 a daughter, Hannah, was born. Despite this university education, Fox is suspicious of such formalized learning, suggesting in 1972 that the Oxbridge experience "removed so much of one's sensual feelings." Fox has also expressed frustration at the popular and academic interest shown in the history of his work rather than in his present projects and future plans. Welfare State has always intended to create responsive events for a particular place and time, for a social and artistic purpose, rather than work that may be documented as part of a theatrical canon. It is impossible to think of the "text" of the work in the same way that one might consider a typical piece of dramatic literature; the pieces are distinct and ephemeral, seldom published, and conceived as much in terms of their visual, musical, and physical form as they are in terms of dialogue, theme, or plot. Fox may not always write the script itself (if one exists), but the poetic conceptions of the piece and its direction are as much part of the creative totality of the work as any words. "He (John Fox) would administer a general myth, a broad system of religiose symbolism, and within that framework leave people to determine their own gear, word and action." Fox describes the development process variously as being like leading a band, making a painting, or weaving a tapestry, although the term that he regularly applies to the sum of the constituent parts is *poetry.* Many of Fox's pieces exist as part of a larger whole; a single work might be part of a week of events, a year, or even an integral part of a life of work.

The earliest of Fox's performance works were created with an ad hoc group of artists, sometimes including Albert Hunt, with whom Fox and his wife, Sue Gill (who has been a key collaborator throughout their careers), had worked on *The Russian Revolution* in the streets of Bradford, and students from the Bradford College of Art, where Fox was a part-time librarian and lecturer. The first of these, *St. Valentines Firestorm* (1968), sought to re-create the Dresden firebombing in a raid on a public dance in Bradford. Using carnival imagery, sirens, smoke, and performers in airmen's helmets and white coats, the piece allegedly created near panic among its unsuspecting audience. At the time Fox regarded it as morally satisfactory to shock the audience, reminding them of the scale and horror of Dresden; however, Fox later described this event as undesirable "aesthetic fascism" in which the company became part of the problem, not the solution–a position that, in retrospect, he took on much of the early work of Welfare State. *The Tide Is O.K. for the 30th* (1968), an installation and performance on a beach in Devon, was a daylong event with, among many other elements, children's games, the painting of military amphibious landing craft, surreal vignettes of mock officials, faux media teams, the arrival of an actor impersonating Sir Francis

Fox's wife, Sue, dressed to perform in The House That Flew Away, *from his* Island of the Lost World *cycle* *(photograph by Roger Perry)*

Chichester (an adventurer who had sailed around the world in a yacht the year before), and an airdrop of specially written poems. The event finished with an evening of folk songs in a local restaurant, an approach that was later more fully incorporated into the group's repertoire in the form of theatrical barn dances.

After a further project staged in Lancaster, *The Marriage of Heaven and Hell* (1968), a tribute to the poet William Blake that included firelit processions, music, and circus elements, the group formalized as The Welfare State in late 1968 (becoming Welfare State International in 1979), working under Fox's direction and inspiration. Although Fox's work has changed and developed over three decades (most notably in the early 1990s and after 2000), many of the stylistic elements of these early works have remained fairly constant. The pieces are highly visual, informed by carnival, mumming, and other forms of popular theater; they are performed away from conventional theater venues, often outside in streets or parks or on beaches; and audiences are frequently active participants whose contributions might range from assisting the development of the project to joining in a dance at the end. Food, puppets, landscape enhancement, music, and sculpture have all featured consistently in the events. Although one might argue that Fox's work became more refined or sophisticated throughout his career, the early pieces nonetheless illustrate the balance between magical ritual, political satire, and clowning that is present in much of the work that followed. "Their performances were not plays," Fox said, "but epic poems, visual and aural, though virtually without words. They dealt in ritual myth and magic." To describe the visual text is difficult; the work may sometimes look like an animated, postindustrial Hieronymus Bosch painting, a hybrid of pantomime and expressionism, or a symphony of fire, movement, and color.

In the first few years of The Welfare State's existence, Fox was creating work under two banners: events that were more influenced by vernacular art were produced as the work of Welfare State, while events that drew upon more modern technologies such as projection, rock music, and multimedia were devised and produced under the banner of the Cosmic Circus. This loose grouping of artists operated more hierarchically than Welfare State, under the direction of Fox and Mike Westbrook, the latter having particular responsibility for the music. The most frequently performed of the Cosmic Circus events was *Earthrise* (1969), reworked and revived over a period of two years, a complex, multimedia performance that celebrated the potential for creativity in a technological landscape and was inspired by the moon landings. A further work under this banner, *Spring Event* (1970), was "an oblique evocation of the transition from Winter to Spring." The initial scenario for the piece, written by Fox and Westbrook, suggests the form of the event. It starts in darkness and shadow, with empty chairs and silent people in a misty, barren landscape lit with torches and movie clips of the German invasion of Czechoslovakia; sinister creatures (racing cyclists and radio operators) hover in the mist. As the piece develops, life invades the space in several bizarre ways, including a procession of majorettes, a football match, and projections of images of nature. After a battle, including judo, fencing, and a tug-of-war, the invaders claim the space, and a dance follows; the scenario suggests that the audience may participate. The Cosmic Circus operated sporadically but actively until 1972, when Fox left Bradford to take up a post as senior lecturer in fine art at Leeds Polytechnic, but certain elements of the work found their way into Welfare State's later performances.

Probably the most significant work, and certainly the best documented, from the company's earlier years was the ongoing project centering on the life of Lancelot Quail, Fox's hermaphrodite strongman turned working-class hero. After his first appearance in an indoor performance in Brixton, Quail was taken on a month-long tour, *The Travels of Sir Lancelot Quail* (1972), through the West Country from Glastonbury to St. Michael's Mount. Reversing the journeys of Arthur and Joseph of Aramathea, it was billed at the time as the "First Going Away," since "Welfare State could not see that there was anything left to come for, but there were good reasons to leave the barbaric and insensitive culture." The entire month should be viewed as one whole work, rather than the repetition of a single piece, because the traveling–its performances and rituals–was the work. On their journey, which was carried out in procession led by a hearse, the company performed large public celebrations, focused pieces of performance in a circus tent (which local residents also used in a form of creative barter) that responded particularly to the myths and nature of their location, and private rituals undertaken by members of the company only. In the final, extraordinary moments of the journey, members of the company sailed off into the sunset from Marazion (on the far south coast of Cornwall) while a band played on the shore and Hells Angels exploded giant balloons. The company, except Quail, were finally invited on board the submarine HMS *Andrew,* a potent encounter between carnival and military reality.

The journey, which dramatized fiction and myth as much as local history, seemed to propose that folk tale and fable are more responsive and central to culture than radical art; it offered a "relevant and real, if somewhat mystical culture" as a playful cultural paradigm. The whole journey strongly embraced a carnival notion of irreverent humor, reversal, and laughter as an opposition to fixity and authority. As with carnival, however, the bounds between artifice and life were unclear and shifting, offering an alternative to a life of sobriety and rationalization. Also, as with carnival, the liberated time ends, and order is reimposed: in this case Lent arriving in the shape of a submarine (an image of dominant order that emerged in their later work in Barrow-in-Furness). It was, as Mike White wrote in a 1988 *New Theatre Quarterly* article, a burial of naive idealism of the 1960s, pointing out that radical art has to engage with hegemonic reality. The journey (metaphoric and actual) and procession became central to Fox's dramaturgy and appears throughout the company's history. It alludes to carnival and mumming and transforms social space, refusing clear boundaries between what was and was not performance. It puts the performers and the audience in a real space, carrying out a real and dynamic activity (processing, playing, or dancing), energizing the environment; "it takes theatre beyond the proscenium to applied cultural anthropology," as Fox has said. A procession is a jubilant articulation of ownership, demonstrating a right to be on the streets, transforming and subverting the routine of production, consumption, transportation, and habitation; social space is transformed into ritual and ludic space.

In retrospect, Fox has described some of the earlier work as slightly romantic, confrontational, indulgent, and dated, although that does not perhaps do justice to what was achieved. However, it is certainly true that although many of the early projects involved playful parody and humorous, vivid mythological scenarios, there was a clear thread of violence and darkness that emerged in some of the work, such as *St. Valentines Firestorm,* and was perhaps present under the surface of most.

Fox's projects were in general more passionately concerned with the poetic articulation of myths than with overt political opposition. Two connected pieces illustrate this concern well: *Island of the Lost World* (1974 and 1976) and *Stories for a Winter's Night* (1976–1977). These two intimate works were developed with Boris Howarth, then associate director of Welfare State, with whom Fox had worked in creative partnership in 1968–1969 and between 1972 and 1984. Both works were small traveling performances; the former was devised specifically for summer and played in a canvas courtyard, while the latter, for winter, was staged in a wooden hut. Both treated the audience as guests at a storytelling. The first (in its 1976 version) brought ancient and magical tales of demons and spirits, of nature and technology, each a small play in its own right. Simple archetypal stories played with visual ingenuity that offered vignettes of humanity and fables of warning. Some of the plots were taken from ancient sources, while others, such as "The House that Flew Away," came from Fox's original poetic conceptions. *Stories for a Winter's Night* welcomed its audience to an intimate and warm candlelit world in which the tales were both ancient and contemporary, couched in magic, mystery, and comedy. The imagery and stories of both are seemingly timeless, drawing inspiration from folk art, childhood fears, and contemporary news stories. Some of the stories were bleak, some comic, and others warming, offering their audiences something "playful and strange, rich and humane."

Lancelot Quail was reincarnated in an environmental piece in Burnley, *Barrabas* (1977), during which the company lived on-site in caravans, which was their standard mode of operation until setting up a permanent base in 1979. This itinerant lifestyle as a "creative tribe" (even providing its own school for the members' children) had its problems: the company were sometimes regarded negatively by the local community, seen as "freaks who lived on a rubbish dump," and Fox particularly believes that their presence and performances could be alienating rather than inclusive. However, in 1979 Fox moved to Ulverston in Cumbria, a market town only a few miles from Barrow-in-Furness, the site of nuclear submarine shipyards, and a location described by Fox as between Wordsworth and Windscale (a nuclear power station situated nearby). This move inspired and consolidated several changes in the work (although the company did not fully move there until 1983): the projects became more inclusive and open, and as a permanent resident within a community Fox was able to make fuller and more lasting contributions to the space between art and life, participating in extant local events, running workshops, and consulting on personal rituals. The notion of community for Welfare State has never been a buzzword for funding; Fox wholly rejects the notion that he makes "community theatre," though as Jeff Nuttall observed in his *Performance Art: Memoirs* (1979), "living together in creative exchange was as much Foxy's concern as putting on a show for the folks"–a position that is fundamental to many of Fox's projects.

In 1983 Welfare State instigated what became an annual event: the Ulverston Lantern Procession, in which members of the town are invited to make hundreds of paper lanterns, beautiful and ephemeral objects that the company had begun using in their repertoire after a visit to Japan, with further refinements by Alison Jones, once a Welfare State International member. The lanterns are carried through the town on the evening of the procession. As apparently aesthetic and conservative as this event may be, it clearly has a cultural position, identified by Baz Kershaw as subtly oppositional:

> We can read the spread of hand crafting individual and unique lanterns as an implicit comment on the mass-consumerist ethic and commodity standardisation of so-called western developed societies. Or we can interpret the collective celebration of Ulverston as a community as an explicit statement against the individualistic orientation of 1980's neo-conservatism.

A group of people, grown in number from a few hundred to several thousand in the late 1990s, proceed through their town carrying glowing lanterns just a few miles from the Barrow shipyards, one of the most powerful symbols of the state and of authority. But as carnival throughout Britain is not the revolution, perhaps this procession harbors a language of despair as well as celebration. This dialectic is perhaps the essence of carnival, and this tension between cultural optimism and social reality is frequently a conceptual focus for the work. Part of Fox's quest has been to reemphasize the need for carnival contingency and inventiveness, offering to the people, rather than the institutions of state, the means of making cultural artifacts; he will not allow Lent to impose itself for too long or too heavily. After the earlier confrontational pieces, his work has been ambivalently poised between laughter and political critique; in one moment he may create powerfully critical works, only to seemingly undermine his own seriousness in the next. The lantern procession continues and has grown in scale, illustrating perhaps that taking to the streets with music, art, and poetry is a more powerful life force than the vast majority of performances taking place behind the walls of theaters. Lanterns have featured in several other works, most notably the huge community procession in *Glasgow All Lit Up* (1990), a triumphant example of a celebratory reworking of the Glasgow city center.

In the early 1980s Fox made several large-scale works, nationally and internationally. These theatrical performances, often part of larger festivals, were developed for specific locations and importantly involved local participants in their creation and performance. The contents of these pieces were, according to White, "conceived as allegorical models of society at large" and were "essentially rites of fun rather than didactic cosmologies." The most documented of these larger pieces are *Tempest on Snake Island* (1981), *Scarecrow Zoo* (1982), *Raising the "Titanic"* (1983), and later in a similar vein the tour of *Lord Dynamite* (1990). The form of the events ranged from the more focused theatrical environment of *Raising the "Titanic,"* which used portable theater seats for its central performance, to a theatrical journey in *Tempest on Snake Island*. The work *Scarecrow Zoo* provided a week of various activities culminating in a Halloween fire show with "giant puppet politicians arguing over the national cake which duly exploded in their faces." Children rescued the world from the top of a tower of Babel (a recurring image for Fox) in an event that was "an anarchic, cathartic spectacle contained within the strict limits of Halloween, the night of demons." Calendar events such as Halloween have frequently been the inspiration or vehicle for Fox's work, although their initial inclusion in the company's repertoire was brought about, in part, by Howarth.

These theatrical spectacles–now regarded with some suspicion by Fox, who sees them, in part, as a social anaesthetic–all made use of potent and iconoclastic imagery, music, simple story structures, and a high level of audience involvement or community participation. Although each is quite different in its content (since each was designed for a particular context) they all tend to place humanity in tension with the problems (evils) of capitalism and militarism. In *Raising the "Titanic"* Fox used the ship as a metaphor for many of the perceived ills of contemporary culture; the story

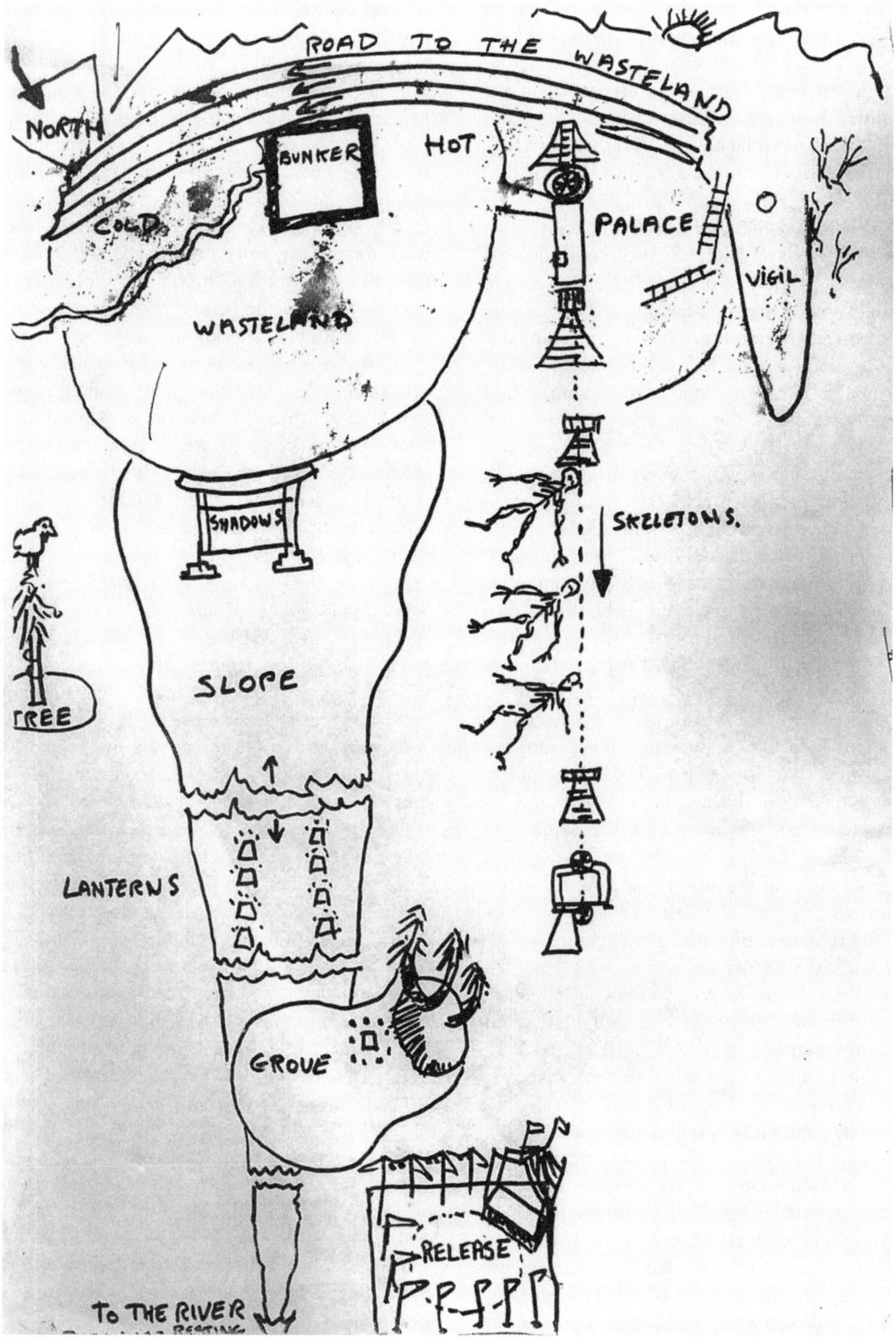

Diagram from the manuscript for Fox's 1982 play The Wasteland and the Wagtail *(courtesy of John Fox)*

draws attention to the stratification of the ship by class and the overindulgent consumption and exploitation undertaken by those in charge while the ship headed to a fate brought about by humanity's arrogance in the face of nature. It was a grotesque, humorous, and highly critical piece of visual and musical theater, which perhaps most clearly acknowledges Fox's debt to Bertolt Brecht.

Commencing in 1983 and continuing, with growing intensity, until 1990, Welfare State directed much of their attention to a variety of projects in Barrow, where a large proportion of the population is economically dependent (directly or indirectly) on the shipyard, which built Trident-class nuclear submarines. Fox saw his involvement in Barrow as an important contribution to local (and national) cultural practices and political debates. This seven-year residency has been well discussed by Kershaw in *The Politics of Performance* (1992). The combination of a protracted interaction with a politically sensitive town and Fox's oppositional politics necessarily created some discomfort. Two of the company's larger projects were seen as provocative and were responded to coolly or negatively; however, the encouragement and support for extant local artists and writers and the celebratory *The Town Hall Tattoo* (1987) were clearly more acceptable. The latter piece celebrated the centenary of the town hall with imagery, pyrotechnics, and processions. The subversion was gentle, fun, but effective; the final flying of Queen Victoria's bloomers off the flag pole ensured that the building and its authority would never be looked at the same way again.

The final event of the seven-year tapestry was a huge performance, *Golden Submarine* (1990), which involved a full repertoire of visual, pyrotechnic, processional, and musical elements and was at heart a pointed satirical attack on the military and industrial establishment. Toward the end of the piece the shipyard sheds are accidentally launched by drunken "Pillars of Society," grotesque puppets of the establishment, revealing a cuckoo (a ravenous exploiter of others' work) on a rotten nest. The piece ends optimistically with the submarine factory transformed into a palace of dreams, as Madonna the cleaning lady, riding an enormous vacuum cleaner, defeats the giant industrialist Shellbent and burns the cuckoo; such images of transformation (visual and social) are common in Fox's work. Kershaw clearly notes the intricate efficacy of this performance, and indeed the whole tapestry. He suggests that on the one hand the piece was simple enough (lacking ideological complexity and argument) to be rejected "by unsympathetic observers and easy to absorb by the powers that be." Kershaw goes on, however, to point out the complex intertextuality that the piece had within the town, and that through local participation and cultural empowerment it represented local voices in raising questions that, while often unspoken, must be central to the town's identity–such as, what would happen if the shipyard closed? In the final analysis this piece, like so much of Fox's work, engages with the heart of the carnival problem. However much one might make radical art, giving voice and cultural empowerment to people who are seldom heard in the discourses of the powerful, it remains the case that such moments are licensed (or at least tolerated), perhaps even evidencing the benign nature of those who wield the power and the checkbooks. Changes do occur, however; perhaps the revolution for which carnival is a rehearsal never takes place, but certainly ripples are set in motion. Participants may not be wholly and instantly changed, but the use to which Fox puts opposition and celebration, social and artistic ritual, is certainly not lost on those who were involved, and the list is long of those who have been "changed" in one way or another by their experiences.

Lord Dynamite, one of the last big performances, was a mythologized biography of Alfred Nobel. Although finally performed as a large-scale, touring, outdoor spectacular opera–with such elements as pyrotechnics, physical performance, large mechanical puppets, and cranes–it was originally written by Fox and Kevin Fegan as a more conventional piece of theater, part of the tapestry of work undertaken in Barrow-in-Furness. The story, told through song and framed by visual performance, explored the contradictions in the life of the man who invented dynamite and initiated the arms race but endowed the Peace Prize. In the final act of the piece a repentant and troubled Nobel, who has seen the violent frenzy of his work and has been counseled by his dead mother and Berthe Kinsky, leader of the European peace movement, founds the prize. He returns to the garden shed that he originally worked from, which, in the last moment of the piece, takes off with Nobel aboard into the night sky and a barrage of fireworks. Nobel has returned to the creativity that inspired his work before it was turned to darker purpose. A review in the *Guardian* (2 July 1992) suggested that although the words were lost in the large arena, the spectacle and the celebratory tingle in the audience were typical of Welfare State's work. This overemphasis on the easy consumption of the spectacle, however, is perhaps what has increasingly turned Fox off to such projects.

The production opened (in its outdoor form) in London for the International Festival of Theatre and then went on tour, a project that nearly broke the company financially and challenged Fox ideologically. While the tour did manage to involve local participants in its various locations, there were several occasions where the performance had to be adapted or canceled because of the requirements of the context. In Totnes, for example, the show had to be rewritten to incorporate Charles Babbage, one of the early pioneers of computers, who had been born to a local family in 1791. In Belfast the show, as originally planned, was canceled because of the proximity of the subject matter to the Troubles. Given the company's accruing deficit and the consumer culture of the early 1990s that celebrated, in Fox's words, "novelty, violence and instant gratification," a culture antithetical to Fox's beliefs, the work had to change direction.

Fox finally seems to find that even these theatrical carnivals, these poetic offerings of alternative life strategies, are flawed; alongside life (and the certainty of death) theater may be seen as a "hollow distraction," and however relevant the theater one is making, it still starts from a basis of art, not life. With this realization in mind, and following an extended trip to Australia (his second antipodean sabbatical), Fox's later projects have been intimately tied up with living, life, and death. Since 1969 he and Welfare State have undertaken betrothal rituals and naming ceremonies for their own children and those of friends (of which there are details in Tony Coult and Baz Kershaw's *Engineers of the Imagination: The Welfare State Handbook,* 1983); and since the early and mid 1990s the investigation of personal rites of passage, especially funerals, has been at the forefront of the work. Fox has hosted seminars and workshops considering the personalization of funerals and published a book on the subject. These events intend to develop rites of passage that are more suited to the individuals involved, using music, poetry, performance, landscape enhancement, and food to provide a relevant and contemporary ceremony to mark moments of particular significance. In keeping with a recurring theme of Fox's work the authorship of culture is placed in the hands of the "folk" rather than the "court." Their approach is practical and poetic, avoiding prescription but rather acting as a catalyst, searching for a spiritual and ritual structure in a secular society: "Remembering that inappropriate ceremonies can be worse than no ceremonies at all we need clear new rites to ground us," Fox explained.

It is perhaps a natural evolution of the work; Fox's concern throughout his creative career has been to place art at the heart of cultural activity, to encourage people to take control of the production and celebration of identity. If people allow their most basic and central personal performances–the rites of passage of naming, betrothal, and death–to be monopolized by distanced institutions, it must be doubly difficult to participate in (and change) less ontological aspects of culture.

In 1993 Fox returned to simple performance and storytelling. *Hollow Ring,* devised and performed with Pete Moser, is "Welfare State in a teaspoon," according to Fox. Utilizing new stories along with traditional tales such as Jacob and Wilhelm Grimm's "The Juniper Tree," the piece provides comic and poetic theatrical parables reflecting on the roots of violence and conflict resolution. Fox calls it a secular prayer, laughter in the face of despair. Using music, lanterns, puppets, paper cuts, shadow screens, and music hall humor, the piece further illustrates on a small scale Fox's delight in mixing the profound with the vernacular. Despite having overseen the production of mammoth, spectacular performances, Fox describes his performance of this work as one of his most nerve-wracking experiences because "there was nothing to hide behind."

Another of Welfare State's projects, Lanternhouse, has been intimately connected with the art of living. With the aid of a Lottery Capital grant they have built a center for celebratory arts, but the building project itself was an artwork, and in the process of its development they undertook exploration into traditional crafts, landscaping, and rituals of the hearth and home. The building is intended to be not only a center for professional creativity and research but also a dynamic part of the local culture and economy, providing a nurturing place for imagination and a site for animated art and performance. On the Welfare State website (http://www.welfare-state.org) the members express their hope that Lanternhouse will be "an inspiration and a hands-on model. A work of art in which the art of work is paramount."

Although framed by a loosely humanist philosophy coupled with a search for secular spiritualism, the work of Welfare State has a clear socialist agenda behind it. Fox particularly deplores mass consumerism, feeling that the commodification of cultural activity robs it of significance and disempowers its users (many projects have utilized industrial waste and sustainable or recyclable resources). The work may usually be packaged with wit and beauty, but at its heart it is a sustained call for people to take responsibility for their cultural production, to utilize myth, poetry, and vernacular participatory art as part of a healing process for society, the ills of which Fox clearly allies to materialism, militarism, and a distancing from nature. Fox's departure from the production of popular large-scale spectacles was in part a response to his perception of the commodification of the work: the events had become spectator sports in a bread-and-circuses society. This paradoxical problem of success has dogged the company throughout much of its existence. In "Theatre Now–The Green Light" (1995) Fox describes a toy dinosaur given to him by his daughter: "Marketable fun, which I am pleased to have, but which has as much to do with real dinosaurs as commodity theatre has to do with the roots of drama."

Fox suggests that he was much influenced by Brecht, and indeed many pieces illustrate stylistic and political parallels. As White observes, Welfare State and Brecht share a common project: "working towards a fuller understanding" of "the most difficult art of all, the great art of living together."

Interviews:

Baz Kershaw, "Between Wordsworth and Windscale," *Performance Magazine,* no. 54 (June–July 1988): 7–12;

David Tushingham, "Exploring to Fulfil a Genuine Need," in *Freedom Machine,* edited by Tushingham (London: Nick Hern, 1996), pp. 33–39.

References:

Peter Ansorge, *Disrupting the Spectacle* (London: Pitman, 1975), pp. 41–42;

Niel Cameron, *Fire on the Water* (Sydney: Currency Press, 1993);

Tony Coult, "The Island of the Lost World," *Plays and Players,* 23 (August 1976): 22–23;

Coult, "Tales for a Winter's Night," *Plays and Players,* 24 (March 1977): 37–38;

Coult and Baz Kershaw, eds., *Engineers of the Imagination: The Welfare State Handbook* (London: Methuen, 1983; revised, 1990);

Ronald L. Grimes, *Beginnings in Ritual Studies* (Columbia: University of South Carolina Press, 1995), pp. 231–252;

Phil Hyde, "Profile: Welfare State," *Performance Magazine,* no. 23 (April–May 1983);

Catherine Itzin, *Stages in the Revolution* (London: Eyre Methuen, 1980), pp. 68–73;

Baz Kershaw, *The Politics of Performance* (London: Routledge, 1992);

Kershaw, "The Politics of Performance in a Postmodern Age," in *Analysing Performance,* edited by Patrick Campbell (Manchester: Manchester University Press, 1996), pp. 133–152;

Katherine Kiddle, *What Shall We Do with the Children?* (Barnstaple: Spindlewood, 1981);

John Lane, *A Snake's Tail Full of Ants* (Totnes: Resurgence, 1996);

Bim Mason, *Street Theatre and Other Outdoor Performance* (London: Routledge, 1992), pp. 123–124, 133–135, 137–138, 147;

Jeff Nuttall, *Performance Art: Memoirs* (London: Calder, 1979), pp. 51, 54, 72–75;

Kenneth Rea, "Welfare State Goes to Africa," *Drama,* no. 2 (1986);

Theodore Shank, "Artistic Commitment is Social Commitment," *Drama Review,* 21 (March 1977);

Shank, ed., *Contemporary British Theatre* (London: Macmillan, 1994), pp. 10–11, 181–182;

Mike White, "Resources on a Journey of Hope: The Work of Welfare State International," *New Theatre Quarterly,* 4 (August 1988).

Papers:

John Fox's papers are in the Bristol University Theatre Collection.

Michael Frayn

(8 September 1933 -)

John Bull
University of Reading

See also the Frayn entries in *DLB 13: British Dramatists Since World War II; DLB 14: British Novelists Since 1960;* and *DLB 194: British Novelists Since 1960, Second Series.*

Michael Frayn (photograph by Mark Gerson)

PLAY PRODUCTIONS: *Zounds!* by Frayn and John Edwards, music by Keith Statham, Cambridge, May 1957;

The Two of Us: Four One-Act Plays for Two Players, London, Garrick Theatre, 30 July 1970;

The Sandboy, London, Greenwich Theatre, 16 September 1971;

Alphabetical Order, London, Hampstead Theatre Club, 11 March 1975; New Haven, Conn., Long Wharf Theater, 8 October 1976;

Donkeys' Years, London, Globe Theatre, 15 July 1976; Brooklyn, New Theater, 12 March 1987;

Clouds, London, Hampstead Theatre Club, 16 August 1976; Dallas, New Arts Theater, 24 August 1985;

Balmoral, Guildford, Yvonne Arnaud Theatre, 20 June 1978; revised as *Liberty Hall,* London, Greenwich Theatre, 24 January 1980; revised as *Balmoral,* Leeds, Playhouse, 29 August 1985; further revised as *Balmoral,* Bristol, Old Vic Theatre, 8 May 1987;

The Cherry Orchard, translation of a play by Anton Chekhov, London, Olivier Theatre at the National Theatre, 3 November 1978;

The Fruits of Enlightenment, translation of a play by Leo Tolstoy, London, Olivier Theatre at the National Theatre, 14 February 1979;

Make and Break, Hammersmith, Lyric Theatre, 18 March 1980; Wilmingham, Playhouse, 28 March 1983;

Noises Off, Hammersmith, Lyric Theatre, 11 February 1982; New York, Brooks Atkinson Theater, 11 December 1983;

Benefactors, London, Vaudeville Theatre, 4 April 1984; New York, 1985; New York, Brooks Atkinson Theater, 22 December 1985;

Number One, translation of a play by Jean Anouilh, Windsor Theatre Royal, 13 April 1984;

Wild Honey, free adaptation of Chekhov's unfinished *Platonov,* London, National Theatre (Lyttleton), 19 July 1984; Los Angeles, Admanson Theater, 9 October 1986;

Three Sisters, translation of a play by Chekhov, Manchester, Royal Exchange Theatre, 11 April 1985;

The Seagull, translation of a play by Chekhov, Watford, Palace Theatre, 7 November 1986;

Exchange, translation of a play by Yuri Trifonov, London, Guildhall School, 1986; first professional production, Southhampton, Nuffield Theatre, 21 November 1989;

Uncle Vanya, translation of a play by Chekhov, London, Vaudeville Theatre, 24 May 1988;

The Sneeze, translation and adaptation of four short plays and four stories by Chekhov, London, Aldwych Theatre, 21 September 1988;

Look Look, produced as *Spettattori,* Rome, 3 January 1989; London, Aldwych Theatre, 30 March 1990;

Here, London, Donmar Warehouse Theatre, 29 July 1993;

Now You Know, adapted by Frayn from his novel, London, Hampstead Theatre, 13 July 1995;

Copenhagen, London, Cottesloe Theatre at the Royal National Theatre, 21 May 1998;

Alarms and Excursions, Guildford, Yvonne Arnaud Theatre, 15 July 1998; London, Gielgud Theatre, 14 September 1998.

BOOKS: *The Day of the Dog* (London: Collins, 1962; Garden City, N.Y.: Doubleday, 1963);

The Book of Fub (London: Collins, 1963); republished as *Never Put off to Gomorrah,* introduction by Walt Kelly (New York: Pantheon, 1964);

On the Outskirts (London: Collins, 1964);

The Tin Men (London: Collins, 1965; Boston: Little, Brown, 1965);

The Russian Interpreter (London: Collins, 1966; New York: Viking, 1966);

At Bay in Gear Street (London: Collins, 1967; Huntington, N.Y.: Fontana, 1967);

Towards the End of the Morning (London: Collins, 1967); republished as *Against Entropy* (New York: Viking, 1967);

A Very Private Life (London: Collins, 1968; New York: Viking, 1968);

The Two of Us (London: Fontana, 1970; London & New York: S. French, 1970);

Sweet Dreams (London: Collins, 1973; New York: Viking, 1974);

Constructions (London: Wildwood, 1974);

Alphabetical Order (London & New York: S. French, 1976);

Clouds (London: Eyre Methuen, 1977; London & New York: S. French, 1977);

Donkeys' Ears (London & New York: S. French, 1977);

Make and Break (London: Eyre Methuen, 1980; London & New York: S. French, 1980);

Noises Off (London: Methuen, 1982; London & New York: S. French, 1982; revised edition, London: Methuen, 1990);

The Original Michael Frayn: Satirical Essays, edited by James Fenton (Edinburgh: Salamander, 1983; London: Methuen, 1990);

Benefactors: A Play in Two Acts (London: Methuen, 1984);

Wild Honey: The Untitled Play, adapted from Anton Chekhov's play (London & New York: Methuen, 1984);

Clockwise: A Screenplay (London: Methuen, 1986);

Balmoral (London: Methuen, 1987);

First and Last (London: Methuen, 1989);

The Sneeze, adapted from plays and stories by Chekhov (London: Metheun, 1989);

The Trick of It (London & New York: Viking, 1989);

Jamie on a Flying Visit; and, Birthday (London: Methuen Drama, 1990);

Listen to This: 21 Short Plays and Sketches (London: Methuen, 1990; Portsmouth, N.H.: HEB, 1990);

Look Look (London: Methuen Drama, 1990; Portsmouth, N.H.: HEB, 1990);

Audience: A Play in One Act, adapted from the play *Look, Look* (London & New York: S. French, 1991);

A Landing on the Sun (London & New York: Viking, 1991);

Now You Know (London: Viking, 1992; New York: Viking, 1993);

Here (London: Methuen, 1993; New York: S. French, 1994);

Now You Know: A Play in Two Acts (London: Methuen Drama, 1995; revised edition, London & New York: S. French, 1996);

Speak after the Beep: Studies in the Art of Communicating with Inanimate and Semi-inanimate Objects (London: Methuen, 1995);

Alarms and Excursions (London: Methuen, 1998);

Copenhagen (London: Methuen, 1998);

Headlong (London: Faber & Faber, 1999; New York: Metropolitan, 1999);

The Additional Michael Frayn (London: Methuen, 2000);

Celia's Secret: An Investigation, by Frayn and David Burke (London: Faber & Faber, 2000); republished as *The Copenhagen Papers: An Intrigue* (New York: Metropolitan, 2001).

Collections: *Plays: One* (London & New York: Methuen, 1985)–comprises *Alphabetical Order, Donkeys' Years, Clouds, Make and Break,* and *Noises Off;*

Plays: Two (London: Methuen, 1991)–comprises *Benefactors, Balmoral,* and *Wild Honey;*

Plays: Three (London: Methuen, 2000)–comprises *Here, Now You Know,* and *La Belle Vivette.*

PRODUCED SCRIPTS: *What the Papers Say,* television, 35 episodes, Granada, 1 March 1962 - 28 January 1966;

Second City Reports, by Frayn and John Bird, television, 6 episodes, Granada, March–May 1964;
"Jamie on a Flying Visit," television, *Wednesday Play,* BBC, 17 January 1968;
One Pair of Eyes, television, BBC, 26 October 1968;
"Birthday," television, BBC, *Wednesday Play,* 12 February 1969;
Beyond a Joke, by Frayn, Bird, and Eleanor Bron, television, 6 episodes, BBC, April–May 1972;
"Laurence Sterne Lived Here," television, *Writers' Houses,* BBC, 9 August 1973;
Imagine a City Called Berlin, television, BBC, 1 March 1975;
Making Faces, television, BBC Two, 6 episodes, 25 September - 30 October 1975;
Vienna: The Mask of Gold, television, BBC Two, 1 May 1977;
Three Streets in the Country, BBC, 2 February 1979;
Donkeys' Years, television, ATV, January 1980;
The Long Straight, television, *Great Railway Journeys of the World,* BBC, 6 November 1980;
Jerusalem, television, BBC, 8 April 1984;
Clockwise, motion picture, Moment Films/Thorn EMI, 1986;
Make and Break, television, BBC Two, 7 June 1987;
First and Last, television, BBC One, 12 December 1989;
Benefactors, television, BBC Two, 23 March 1989;
A Landing on the Sun, television, based on Frayn's novel, BBC, 1994;
Budapest: Written in Water, television, BBC, 22 April 1996;
Remember Me? motion picture, Talisman Productions/ Channel Four Films, 1997.

OTHER: John B. Morton, *The Best of Beachcomber,* selected, with an introduction, by Frayn (London: Heinemann, 1963);
Timothy Birdsall, *Timothy,* edited by Frayn and Bamber Gascoigne (London: Joseph, 1963);
"Festival," in *The Age of Austerity: 1945–1951,* edited by Michael Sissons and Philip French (London: Hodder & Stoughton, 1963), pp. 330–352;
"Australia: The Long Straight," in *Great Railway Journeys of the World* (London: BBC, 1981; New York: Dutton, 1982), pp. 71–95;
Alan Bennett and others, *The Complete Beyond the Fringe,* edited by Roger Wilmut, introduction by Frayn (London: Methuen, 1987).

TRANSLATIONS: Anton Chekhov, *The Cherry Orchard: A Comedy in Four Acts* (London: Eyre Methuen, 1978);
Leo Tolstoy, *The Fruits of Enlightenment* (London: Eyre Methuen, 1979);
Chekhov, *Three Sisters: A Drama in Four Acts* (London: Methuen, 1983);
Jean Anouilh, *Number One* (London: S. French, 1985);
Chekhov, *The Seagull: A Comedy in Four Acts* (London & New York: Methuen, 1986);
Chekhov, *Uncle Vanya: Scenes from Country Life in Four Acts* (London & New York: Methuen, 1987);
Chekhov, *Plays: Chekhov* (London: Methuen, 1988);
Yuri Trifonov, *Exchange* (London: Methuen, 1990).

SELECTED PERIODICAL PUBLICATION–UNCOLLECTED: "The Theatre of Magic," *Observer,* 8 December 1985, pp. 21–22.

In 1998 Michael Frayn had his first original play, *Copenhagen,* staged at the Royal National Theatre on London's south bank. This production was not the first time his work had been seen at the prestigious theater, as several of Frayn's adaptations of the Russian playwright Anton Chekhov's work had preceded *Copenhagen.* It was, however, an acknowledgment of Frayn's status as a major playwright. He is now, along with writers such as Harold Pinter, Tom Stoppard, and Alan Ayckbourn, one of the stalwarts of a new mainstream tradition. Frayn has five *Evening Standard* Awards (1976, 1980, 1982, 1984, and 1998); two Society of West End Theatre Awards (1976 and 1982); and the Olivier Award in 1984. His work is frequently revived in both the professional and the amateur theater and has been performed around the world.

During the 1980s Frayn developed from a minor stage writer to a figure of immense importance. In an *Observer* article (8 December 1985), following the news that *Benefactors* had won the Play of the Year Award from the Society of West End Theatre, Frayn reflected on some of the moments that had given him the most pleasure in the theater. His selection places him securely in a mainstream comic tradition. Included are the end of the first scene of Christopher Hampton's *The Philanthropist* (1970) and the moment when the child unexpectedly gets out of her wheelchair in Peter Nichols's *A Day in the Death of Joe Egg* (1967). "If I had sat in a box at the *Norman Conquests* or *Absurd Person Singular* I should certainly have fallen out of it," Frayn said of Ayckbourn's 1972 and 1973 comedies.

Frayn was born in Mill Hill, in northwest London, on 8 September 1933. His father, Thomas Allen Frayn, was a sales representative for an asbestos company, and his mother, Violet Alice Frayn, née Lawson, had worked as a shop assistant. The family moved to Ewell, Surrey, when Frayn was eighteen months old. He attended Sutton High School and then Kingston Grammar School. On leaving school, he performed his two years' national service in the army from 1952 to 1954, during which he was sent to a Russian interpreters' course at the University of Cambridge before becoming an officer in the intelligence corps. In 1956 he took part in the first student exchange with the Soviet Union and spent a month at Moscow University. On finishing his service, Frayn returned to Cambridge to study philosophy at Emmanuel College. The discipline was dominated at the university by the work of Ludwig Wittgenstein, a formative influence on Frayn.

As a student Frayn contributed humorous articles to the undergraduate newspaper and with John Edwards wrote a revue, *Zounds!,* that was performed by the Cambridge Footlights in 1957, the year of Frayn's graduation. From 1957 to 1962 Frayn worked for the *Manchester Guardian,* first as a reporter and then as a satirical columnist. In 1960 he married Gillian Palmer; they have three daughters. Frayn continued his satirical columns when he moved back to London and worked for *The Observer* from 1962 to 1968. Selections of his columns for the two newspapers were published as *The Day of the Dog* (1962), *The Book of Fub* (1963), *On the Outskirts* (1964), and *At Bay in Gear Street* (1967).

Frayn's first novel, *The Tin Men* (1965), a satire on the failure of mere human beings to rise above the level of computers, is in the satirical mold of his newspaper columns. *The Tin Men* won the Somerset Maugham Award. His second novel, *The Russian Interpreter,* about espionage, won the Hawthornden Prize. Two more satirical novels followed: *Towards the End of the Morning* (1967) and *A Very Private Life* (1968). Television first allowed Frayn to try out his dramatic skills. In 1968 "Jamie on a Flying Visit," a farcical comedy about the collision between the tired inhabitants of a postwar housing estate and a rich visitor from the wife's undergraduate past, was broadcast by the British Broadcasting Corporation (BBC). It and "Birthday" (1969), a story about the overriding imperatives of human reproduction, were produced as part of the *Wednesday Play* series.

The encouragement of the impresario Michael Codron, who later staged many of Frayn's plays and produced his motion picture *Clockwise* (1986), prompted Frayn to try writing for the theater. His first professional theatrical production, four one-act two-actor plays collectively titled *The Two of Us,* opened on 30 July 1970 at the Garrick Theatre in London. It was a modest affair, mainly allowing the two actors, Lynn Redgrave and Richard Brirs, the opportunity to move from one character to another between–and, in the case of *Chinamen,* within–the individual acts. The four pieces are unlinked and are more like revue sketches than sustained dramatic wholes. Together, however, they offer a series of limited perspectives on the mores of the suburban middle class in a way that became increasingly familiar both on stage and on television.

This quality is particularly apparent with the first piece, *Black and Silver,* which is concerned with the problems of taking a baby on a vacation and is straight out of the comedy revue mould. The second, *The New Quixote,* is a study of a burgeoning relationship between a confirmed "bachelor girl" and a young man whom she has invited back to her home, only to find him insinuating his way into staying.

That Frayn's comic investigation of suburban domesticity has its roots in the English absurdist tradition is made clear in the opening lines of *Chinamen,* the title of which is derived from the fact that the husband cannot distinguish among the couples who make up his and his wife's dinner-party acquaintances. As they prepare the dinner table, the husband tries frantically to remember the names of their indistinguishable friends:

> STEPHEN: David and *Laura!* David and *Laura!* David and *Laura . . . ! (He goes out into the living-room as* JO *returns from the kitchen.)*
>
> JO: *John* and Laura! *John* and Laura! For heaven's sake get it straight, Stephen. We've known them for ten years! *(She starts hurriedly distributing soup spoons, as* STEPHEN *hurries back in with another chair.)*
>
> STEPHEN: I can't really tell our friends apart, that's the trouble. John and Laura, John and Laura, John and Laura. . . . They're all exactly the same–same age, same number of children, same sort of job, same income, same opinions. . . . They even look alike! It's like looking at Chinamen. Nicholas and Jay–Simon and Kay–Freddie and Di. . . .

Stephen and Jo end the piece congratulating themselves "that it all went off reasonably well," despite the total havoc the couple has managed to create.

In *Mr. Foot,* the next piece in *The Two of Us,* Frayn looks at a sterile marriage. The husband is enshrined as the upholder of a set of suburban values spoofed in the English absurdist tradition, and the wife, who is the mouthpiece of the satire, is thus separated from those values. She turns first away from and then on the husband by means of a dialogue with an imaginary third person, a man who has come to "take a squint" at the wife to assess her suitability as prop for the husband who is, he assures her, definitely "in line" for a new job. The hints of her involvement with the women's liberation movement are no more convincing than the fantasy she conjures up of running away with the nonexistent investigator, but Frayn does identify her as a woman frustrated with the role of wife and second fiddle. In the wife's role there are hints of a world of tragic waste beneath the comic veneer.

The Two of Us was not a success, despite the audience's warmth toward the dexterity shown by the two actors, and Frayn fared little better with his next play, *The Sandboy* (1971). The central character, Phil Schaffer,

DONKEYS' YEARS

by **MICHAEL FRAYN**

COLLEGE NOTES:—

MR. S. BIRKETT, Head Porter, completes fifty years' service with the College this October .. .. **A. J. BROWN**

C. D. P. B. HEADINGLEY, M.A., M.P., is Parliamentary Under-Secretary of State at the Department of Education and Science .. .. **PETER BARKWORTH**

D. J. BUCKLE, M.B., M.R.C.S., is assistant chief surgeon in the Department of Urology, Royal Wessex Hospital, Southampton .. .. **PETER JEFFREY**

K. SNELL, M.A. is engaged in research in parasitology at British Alkalis (Pharmaceutical Division), Rotherham .. .. .. **ANDREW ROBERTSON**

A. V. QUINE, B.A., is now in the grade of Assistant Secretary at the Department of Education and Science .. .. **JULIAN CURRY**

THE REV. R. D. SAINSBURY, M.A., is Curate-in-Charge of St. Columba's, Small Heath, Birmingham .. .. **HAROLD INNOCENT**

N. O. P. TATE, M.A., has recently published 'The Complete Home Encyclopaedia of Japanese Flower Arrangement' and 'A Boys' and Girls' Guide to Overseas Development' .. .. **JEFFRY WICKHAM**

W. R. TAYLOR, M.A., Ph.D., Research Fellow and College Lecturer in English, has published 'Mythopoeic Structures in the Metonymy of Two Jacobean Children's Rhymes' (*Revue des Etudes Semiologiques*, Toulouse) .. .. **JOHN HARDING**

LADY DRIVER, M.A., The Master's wife (formerly Rosemary Gilbert), has been appointed a member of the Royal Commission on Obesity .. .. **PENELOPE KEITH**

Directed by **MICHAEL RUDMAN**

One of the smaller quadrangles, in one of the lesser Colleges, at one of the older Universities.

The play is in three Acts with ONE INTERVAL of fifteen minutes between Acts II and III.

Cover and cast list from the program for the initial production of Frayn's comedy about a college reunion

is a highly successful early-middle-aged architect: "I have a smugness problem," he declares. A "day-in-the-life" movie is being made for television, and Schaffer expects to be visited by a host of the North London rich, famous, and successful with whom he wishes to be associated. His only visitors, however, are the endlessly quarreling failures, Colin and Sheila, who are locked out of their next-door house. The play is a satire on material success and its trappings and on the media that both creates and records that success. Critics tried hard to find encouraging things to say about it, but the overall reaction was captured well by Michael Billington in *Plays and Players* (November 1970): "While there is no shortage of ideas, there is a surprising lack of theatrical invention."

A sense of waste continually resurfaces in Frayn's plays. It is, however, always at war with an obsession with the mechanics of theater in a way that looks back as much to Luigi Pirandello as it does to the great farceurs. The resultant tension can be seen in *Alphabetical Order* (1975) and *Donkeys' Years* (1976), the plays that really established Frayn as a stage writer. *Alphabetical Order* is set in the library of a small, failing provincial newspaper. A new employee, Leslie, sets out to create a carefully indexed order from the chaos that surrounds her on her arrival. The metaphorical transfer of the order/chaos model to both world events and individual lives works neatly rather than convincingly, and, as a result, the play pulls in two not entirely reconcilable directions. The paper ultimately goes out of business, and the wonderful near ending–wherein the now-unemployed staff vent their feelings by destroying the neatness and precision imposed by Leslie on the clipping library by littering the stage with the jumbled contents of the files–is undercut by Frayn's attempt to draw the thematic threads together for his characters. Leslie, whose attempts to bring order have extended to the troubled lives of her colleagues, is given a final entrance. She is greeted with the hysterical antics of the staff, who are happier with confusion than with her efforts to alleviate it. Told the bad news, she declares that they will continue to bring out the newspaper themselves, a response more dependent on the thematic balance of the play than on any possible psychological or industrial reality. *Alphabetical Order* won Frayn an *Evening Standard* award for Best Comedy of theYear.

In *Donkeys' Years* a collection of people united only in their having received their higher education at an Oxbridge college return to the college for a reunion weekend. As the event gets more and more out of control, the audience observes the characters' lack of development in the intervening years–for instance, status games are still being played between Headingley, an undersecretary in the Department of Education and Science, and Quine, a civil servant in Headingley's department, and the men still play undergraduate pranks on each other. *Donkeys' Years* works better at the level of farce than it does at that of psychological insight.

Among the college inhabitants present to greet the returning graduates are Birkett, the long-employed porter, who remembers them all, and Taylor, a young left-wing don. The program note, which lists the latter's published oeuvre as *Mythopoeic Structures in the Metonymy of Two Jacobean Children's Rhymes,* published by the *Revue des Etudes Semiologuiques,* Toulouse, is evidently meant to be seen as pretentious academic drivel by an audience that, though unversed in semiotics, is still able to recognize the imbalance between children's rhymes and theory. Taylor's work is actually less comic than the more-traditional publications attributed to the visiting Tate, *A Complete Home Encyclopedia of Japanese Flower Arranging* and *A Boy's and Girl's Guide to Overseas Development;* but then, Tate and his companions are depicted as a part of a past, unthreatening world, as characters to be savored in their antics rather than analyzed in their meditations.

The program note about Taylor acts as a cue for the audience to dismiss from its mind the possibility of any meaningful radical critique of the world represented by the visitors. As the play proceeds, Taylor's leftist pretensions are neatly punctured one by one. Birkett's final words–"See you again in another twenty years, Mr. Tate, sir"–leave the hierarchical structure in place, and promise the perpetuation of its absurdities. That the major thrust of the play is farcical should not blind one to the insularity of a world that, though briefly mocked, is never seriously threatened–the one outsider at the party, Snell, is sedated and institutionalized by the end of the play, as is only appropriate for a specter at an exceedingly grubby feast.

One of the most interesting characters in *Donkeys' Years* is Lady Driver, well known to most of the revisiting men from their undergraduate days, who is now the supportive wife of a college master who never appears and is in search of a fresh liaison with an old lover that is always comically prevented. Lady Driver is the necessary prop in a farcical world: the only woman present overnight in an all-male environment, she is hidden, disguised, has attempts made upon her person, is described in the men's old-fashioned argot as a "Popsy," and is finally allowed to escape over the college roofs.

Though the play won the Society of West End Theatre Award for best comedy of the year, Frayn's interest in the mechanics of plot contrivance, not as brilliantly developed as they are in his later work but effective enough, prevents the audience from sympathizing too deeply with the characters. They never take on the kind of empathetic role Frayn appears to want. The confusion of rooms, doors, and clothes is all-important, and the mad excesses of Mr. Snell–aware of all that he had been excluded from as an undergraduate, when he lodged on the other side of the railway station instead of having rooms in college, and all that he has been excluded from since–do nothing to create a bleaker aspect to the piece. He is used simply to add to and confirm the essentially farcical base of the play.

Frayn's next two plays take the tension between theme and stage business in the opposite direction. Both *Clouds* (1976)–originally written (in different form) for and rejected by the BBC–and *Balmoral* (1978; revised as *Liberty Hall* in 1980) push a political context to the fore. Far more simply staged than his later works, which frequently need complicated diagrams for the director, *Clouds* is set in postrevolutionary Cuba. The island is suggested by an empty blue sky and is created according to the varied imaginations of the three visitors who vie to produce the most convincing portrait of life there. A traditional journalist obsessed with facts and a female novelist concerned with feelings and impressions have commissions from rival Sunday newspapers; the third visitor, an American who is fluent in Spanish and plans to write a book, is convinced that he can get nearest to the real Cuba. In reality, each sees only what he or she wants to see, and any meaningful concern with the political dimensions of the plot quickly gives way to an interest in the manipulation by the novelist, Mara–another lone woman, like Lady Driver in *Donkeys' Years*–of the various men, Cuban and non-Cuban, who are united across the political divide in frustrated desire for her. *Clouds* is Frayn's first sustained attempt to allow any real development of insight into character–even if what the audience mostly learns is that the characters do not understand themselves, let alone one another.

The weaker of the two "political" plays, *Balmoral* posits an alternative history in which the Communist Revolution has taken place in Britain rather than in Russia. The royal residence of the title has been converted into a state-run community for writers, offering an austere home for Enid Blyton, Hugh Walpole, Warwick Deeping, and Godfrey Winn as they are visited in 1937 by a journalist from the capitalist Russian press. The journalist has come to interview Walpole, who first disappears–into an overnight shopping line in pursuit of ladies' underwear, it transpires–and then dies. His body is crammed into a trunk, and the dissident servant, McNab, is called upon to play a double part–much of the humor is dependent on the fact that the same actor plays Walpole and McNab–in order for the interview to proceed. The play ends with the journalist finally discovering Walpole in the trunk as he puts another "dead body," an empty whiskey bottle, inside it. Also in 1978 Frayn's first translation of a Chekhov play, *The Cherry Orchard,* opened at the National Theatre in London. Since then he has translated much of the Russian writer's canon. In 1979 he translated Leo Tolstoy's play *The Fruits of Enlightenment.*

Frayn's next original play, *Make and Break,* opened as a tryout at the Lyric Theatre in Hammersmith in March 1980 before moving to the Theatre Royal Haymarket in April. *Make and Break* is set in 1980 on an exhibition stand set up in a hotel suite at an international trade fair in Frankfurt. As the play opens, three salesmen, all of whom work for the same company, are pitching their product to three potential customers. The first salesman, Tom Olley, speaks of nothing but prices and currency conversion tables; the third, Colin Hewlett, of finishings and availability. The other salesman, Frank Prosser, stresses the adaptability of the product:

> Now you want full demountability and you want full recoverability. But you don't want to end up with some kind of temporary accommodation for homeless families. Because you've looked at some of those demountable partitions on the floor down there, and you think a demountable partition's going to look and feel demountable. . . . Well, just forget partitions. Partitions are things that rattle when you slam the door. These are *walls.* This is a wall *system.* Fully demountable, fully adjustable walls combined with a range of fully uniform finishes for your load-bearing elements. Movable solid walls.

The set itself consists of "movable solid walls." The actualization of the product as set reinforces the duality of the product as both solid and endlessly adaptable to the needs of the individual customer and presents a strikingly realized metaphor of Frayn's thematic concern with building and destruction. Furthermore, the farcical potential of a set that allows walls to be turned around on their axes is not lost on Frayn: it gives the audience a wonderfully macabre shock toward the end, when a wall is turned to reveal the dead body of Olley.

The opening dialogue sets the action carefully. Comic only to outsiders (the audience), the language is a part of a recognizable business discourse. The salesman's distaste for a rival product that looks like "temporary accommodation for homeless people" touches on a theme that came to assume major significance as homelessness increased in Britain's major cities in the 1980s and 1990s. Clearly, Frayn's casual introduction of the topic is intended to be received ironically in the context of a trade fair where the leading character, John Garrard, later formulates plans for the production of portable exhibition stands at £20,000 apiece–roughly the price of an average semidetached house in a provincial British city at the time. The opening dialogue is twice briefly interrupted by the sounds of explosions, which are ignored by the characters. It is only when Anni, a German student the salesmen have employed as a temporary assistant, enters that an explanation is offered: "Some people, I suppose, were exploding some things. Some shops, some U-Bahn [subway] station, I don't know." The image of destruction plays an important part in the play. The activities of the terrorists, continually and jokingly related to Anni's political activities by the salesmen, who are unable to distinguish between peaceful and violent oppositional strategies, counter enterprise of building. Olley is reminded that he, too, has been an agent of destruction as a Royal Air Force navigator in the air raids on German cities in World War II, and he is quick to make the connection between the war-time bombs and those of the terrorists: "It looked like the end of the world down there some nights. I thought that was that. . . . Like woodland. Burn it back, and up it comes green next season. Like our walls–it's all demountable. As long as people have still got the ideas in their heads. As long as they've got the skills in their hands."

Only two real alternatives are offered in the play: the world of work and the activities of the terrorist–the one building, if only movable walls, and the other destroying. Frayn's choice of this particular form of construction–as opposed, say, to building houses–is deliberately problematic, but its juxtaposition with the world of the bomber gives even this kind of construction a positive value. The trade stand is not just a microcosm of the world, however; to these men it is their entire world. Even when the born-again Hewlett is prevailed upon to talk about an evangelical meeting he had attended, his colleagues comically translate the account into the terms of their own profession:

PROSSER: They've just had some big do in tents down in Exeter. How many souls did you save down there, Colin?

HEWLETT: I mean we had over a thousand people coming forward.

PROSSER: That firm orders, though, or just enquiries?

Though given outside interests–Prosser, for instance, knows all the opus numbers and keys of Ludwig van Beethoven's entire output but cannot tell which is which–their lives are entirely taken up with the need to sell and to survive in the commercial jungle. Frayn carefully delays the entrance of Garrard, the managing director of the company and the man who will stand as the epitome of the conflicting demands of this world. Prosser anticipates Garrard's arrival: "I'll tell you the first thing he'll do when he walks in here. He'll rearrange that display. Fiddle, fiddle, fiddle, while he goes on about the emptiness of the order book and the price of paper-clips." Garrard is Frayn's most magnificent creation, a frightening figure fueled by the need to sell, unable to rest, constantly planning and scheming–he had hired Prosser, the audience learns, in the waiting room at Golder's Green Crematorium:

PROSSER: Ted Shaw's old pal–Pat McGuire–it was his funeral. They were running ten minutes late.

OLLEY: So naturally, John wondered how to fill in the time.

When Garrard does arrive, a day earlier than expected, the audience is not disappointed. Ignoring the salesmen at first, he carefully opens and shuts the door through which he has entered and calls for a chair, on which he stands to confirm that the hotel in which the trade fair is being held has contracted out to a rival firm. In Garrard's eyes, everyone and everything is a potential customer. In the brisk conversation that follows, Garrard, memorably played in the original production by Leonard Rossiter, moves from his annoyance with the door to the empty order book, his thoughts on the rival trade stands, his plans for expansion into Eastern Europe, and a scheme to market permanent display stands to their competitors. He is only briefly halted by discovering the naked Anni taking a shower in his suite.

From his first entrance Garrard dominates the play. He is one of the great creations of contemporary theater, a monster for whom the other characters feel immense affection, a nightmare embodiment of the world of commerce, a monomaniac whose energy carries an audience along. Garrard's hijacking of the play is vital, turning it from a gentle comedy into a savage, if ambivalent, celebration of the world of trade. He is not all-powerful, and much of his demonic energy is given to planning ways to head off possible disasters; for instance, he does not know whether he will be promoted or fired by the overall director. Garrard is, however, powerful as a stage character in his unswerving certainty that nothing matters outside of his world and that values of commerce transcend everything. Recovered from what he thought was a heart attack, Garrard immediately sets about trying to put a deal together with the former East German doctor who has treated him, easily persuading the physician to use his contacts in the East to get a contract for hospital doors. Presented with the possibility that he might be given control of three more companies, Garrard protests that he could not possibly handle it all–and immediately sets about planning a managerial shuffle. He says he could not live if he could not work, and for once the audience believes him.

One of the more carefully placed ironies in the play is that it is Olley, not Garrard, who is found dead of a heart attack toward the end. The likelihood of Garrard's having a heart attack is planted early in the play and reinforced by the calling of a doctor after he collapses in pain with what, it transpires, is a slipped disc after making love to the secretary, Mrs. Rogers. His sexual encounter with Mrs. Rogers, like everything Garrard does, is driven by curiosity; he is as interested in questioning her about the Buddhism course she has been taking as in actually getting her into bed.

The sheer size of Garrard as a character gives *Make and Break* its strength. He is the model, the other salesmen pale imitations. The characters are victims, certainly, but Frayn is not attempting a radical critique of the overall world in which they live. Frayn makes this point in the introduction to his collection *Plays: One* (1985):

I think *Make and Break* is about how we all compulsively exploit the possibilities of the world around us–about how we eat it–how we *have* to eat it–how we transform it into food and clothes and housing, and of course lay it waste in the process. Is Garrard more monstrous than the rest of us? If he seems so, isn't it because he lacks our saving hypocrisy–because he fails to dissemble the activities that we all have, that we all *must* have if we are to survive? I can't help feeling, too, that if the play is seen as some kind of attack upon business, or industrialism, this is assumed that no one would ever write about these subjects *without* moral condescension of one sort or another. I don't understand why this should be so; it seems to me unbecoming for writers and critics to condescend towards the people who feed and clothe them. It is true that some of the things industry produces are harmful or unnecessary. But Garrard makes walls and doors. Could anyone really think I am advocating a world without walls and doors? All I am trying to show is what they cost.

Frayn followed *Make and Break* with what has proved his most popular play, *Noises Off* (1982). A comedy that depends on its parodic borrowings from the worst traditions of the British farce, it traces progress from the last-minute dress/technical rehearsal and the subsequent run of an awful piece of repertory theatre, *Nothing On,* and the connection between the stage business and the actors' complicatedly interwoven lives. The idea for the play came initially from Frayn's viewing of his own work, *The Two of Us,* from backstage, finding it a more comic experience than observing it from a conventional audience perspective. The three acts move from a front-stage to a backstage perspective in ways that demand utmost dexterity from the technical crew and performers alike, and it was generally received with gales of laughter both in London and on Broadway. Benedict Nightingale thought it "by far the funniest play in London" (*New Statesman,* February 1982), and this view was shared by many critics: "having first parodied a farce, then brilliantly engineered his own, Frayn finally sabotages one. . . . Juggling expertly with its own stock in trade, *Noises Off* is a farce that makes you think as well as laugh," wrote Peter Kemp in *TLS: The Times Literary Supplement* (February 1982).

Act 1 opens with what is apparently a woefully underrehearsed production of a British farce, complete with stock characters and clichéd dialogue. The actors' continual stumbling over their lines is suddenly explained by the intervention of a loud voice from the audience, and the actual audience becomes aware that it is watching a rehearsal supervised by a director whose voice has halted proceedings. In a playfully metatheatrical fashion the chaos and confusions of the play being worked on and later performed, *Nothing On,* mirrors that of the participants, and particularly the director, who is conducting simultaneous affairs with the dumb blonde of the cast and the assistant stage manager (who was employed as a result of her father's firm's sponsorship of the production). The tension between action onstage and off is thus crystallized by the surreptitious relationships between actor and crew, and the result is–chaos overcoming order yet again–a continual disruption of the production despite all the director's best attempts to construct harmony.

The act 1 dress rehearsal, in which everything that could go wrong–fluffed lines, wrongly timed entrances, doors that refuse to open–does go wrong, is followed by a second act in which the audience sees the scene being rehearsed earlier, but now with a supposed audience and from behind the set. This time, events are seen from the perspective of the participants in the production rather than from that of the characters in the production, and the series of emotional crises result in a complete disruption of the proceedings onstage so that the proceedings in *Nothing On* increasingly shrink in importance as far as the theater audience is concerned in comparison to the backstage dramas. The process reaches its culmination when the assistant stage manager, with the exact timing of the most brilliant of farces, announces her pregnancy immediately after the last lines of the scene being performed. The chaos is extended yet further in the final act of *Noises Off,* where–later in the run–the action is again seen from a conventional perspective; and the backstage traumas that had caused continual disruption of the staged action have now infected the entire proceedings. Things onstage stagger from bad to worse–with at one time three comic burglars onstage instead of one–until *Nothing On* finally collapses unfinished, and the curtain is hastily dropped. The chaos of life overcomes all attempts by the play to find shape or meaning. Frayn's ability to weld together the machinery of popular theatrical traditions with rather more intellectual content than the average farce won him an *Evening Standard* award and a Society of West End Theatre Award and has ensured that the play has been regularly revived, by several companies, including the National Theatre and particularly by amateur companies.

Frayn's next play, *Benefactors* (1984), is more somber and more deeply questioning than his earlier works. The action of the play moves from 1968 to 1984. Where time leaps need explanation, Frayn provides asides by the characters to the audience, one of several experimental aspects of the work. *Benefactors* is populated by two married couples, whose personal and public lives become progressively entangled in the fifteen-year narrative span of the play.

David is an architect who has been commissioned by the local government council to design new housing for what is officially called a "twilight-zone." Early in the play the scene is set by Sheila, the wife of Colin, David's friend from undergraduate days:

> Sixty-eight. That was the year. He started on Basuto Road in April, just after Lizzie's birthday. They were such good friends, it was lovely. You felt you could always pop over the road for a chat. I used to go flying over there at all hours. I'd just slip a coat round my shoulders and push the front door open, and–Hoo-hoo! And Jane would be rushing around, doing fifteen things at once, and I'd sit in the kitchen and watch her and I'd think, Oh if only I could be like that! If only I'd got her energy! And the colours of everything in the kitchen were so warm and friendly. And David would come popping in for a moment on the way to one of his sites, and the children were lovely, and they'd all make you feel you belonged there.

Sheila's attraction to her friends' household initially stems from its superiority as a model of organization and effort. As David's plans for the new development assume greater significance, however, Sheila's attraction is transferred to the housing scheme itself. Sheila starts the play infatuated with Jane but then falls in love with David, becoming his secretary and working in his home office. Jane, on the other hand, hates Colin until he comes out in opposition to the redevelopment plan. Jane then arranges funding for the opposition to be organized.

In the beginning David opposes the notion of high-rises; but the conflict between the increasing restrictions on the site and the need to house the maximum number of people increases over the years, and David ends up designing the very thing he had opposed–an outcome that had been predicted all along by Colin. Humanity gives way to an inexorable logic:

> Skyscrapers, Sheila. That's the answer. That's the *only* answer. I've tried every other solution, and it doesn't work. . . . The highest residential buildings in Europe. . . . Because in the end it's not art–it's mathematics. A simple equation. You collect up the terms, you get rid of the brackets, you replace all the a's and b's with the number of three-person households and the length of a coffin and the turning-circle of a corporation refuse vehicle–and there at the bottom of the page on the right-hand side is the answer.

At the beginning of the play Colin refers to the proposed site as Basutoland, and the audience learns that it includes Basuto Road, Bechuana Road, Matabele Road, Machona Road, and Barotse Street. "But when you think how fresh and hopeful that must have sounded once, back in 1890!" David exclaims. His words recall the British colonial past, as do the names of the streets.

Despite her misgivings, Jane is prevailed upon to do a door-to-door survey of the streets in an attempt to find out what the people actually want in their new housing. She protests that she is a social anthropologist, not a social worker, that she is interested in studying people and not in helping them–an attitude that perfectly complements the bureaucratic planner David eventually becomes. The survey is unsuccessful: either nobody is at home or they refuse to answer, and when a door does open in Basutoland, "a black face looks round the door" or a woman indicates that "she can't understand my dialect." Thus, the remnants of Britain's colonial past are actually in the next street; their further development is necessary, as Colin sardonically points out, because "Otherwise the areas where architects and demolition contractors live will start to look a little grey and exhausted again." The lack of human contact, except in the case of Jane and Sheila, is one of Frayn's themes, and the problem is exacerbated when the opposition to the development is taken up by Colin, who moves out of his house–his wife having left him for David–and becomes a squatter on the proposed site.

Eventually the scheme is abandoned; although Colin claims the credit, Frayn makes it clear that the plan was dropped by the council because of economic grounds. The play concludes with summaries of the lives of the four protagonists after the demise of the housing development; there is no political conclusion save Jane's final realization that it is a waste of time to ask people what they want: "I suppose I've changed. I've learnt one thing from working with people anyway: they want to be told what to do." She becomes a community planner.

Benefactors won the *Evening Standard* award for best play of the year, the Society of West End Theatre Award for best play of the year, a Tony nomination for best play, the Lawrence Olivier Award for best play, the Plays and Players Award for best new play, and the New York Drama Critics Circle Award for best new foreign play. Reviewing *Benefactors* in *The Guardian* (5 April 1984), Michael Billington wrote:

> As befits a play about architecture, Michael Frayn's *Benefactors* at the Vaudeville is a brilliant construct. On the ground-floor, it is about a modern master-builder (and the Ibsenite echo is deliberate) who wants to erect tower-blocks for town-planners rather than homes for people. But, on the upper-story, it is a philosophical comedy about good and evil, life and death, liberal tolerance and destructive faith.

One of the themes in *Benefactors* is the conflict between the chaos of personal life and the attempts of systematizers and planners to create and maintain order. Frayn used this theme in 1986 in his first motion picture, *Clockwise,* in which John Cleese plays a secondary-school headmaster vainly trying to keep to the schedule of his time-dominated day in the face of increasingly farcical disorder. Frayn spent much of the 1980s working on translations, including *Number One* (1984), by Jean Anouilh, and three Chekhov pieces–*Three Sisters* (1985), *The Seagull* (1986), and *Uncle Vanya* (1988)–as well as an accclaimed adaptation of Chekhov's first (and untitled) play, *Wild Honey* (1984). In 1989 he wrote another piece for BBC Television, *First and Last,* which won an International Emmy Award.

Frayn's next original stage play, *Look Look,* appeared in 1990. In its structure the play harks back somewhat to the format of *Noises Off,* with the actors playing the audience in the first act and returning to the stage in the second. *Look Look* was not a success; "the play didn't work," said Robert Hewison in *The Sunday Times* (6 May 1990). In 1993 *Here* was staged at the Donmar Warehouse Theatre. A two-actor piece about domestic life, which looks back somewhat awkwardly in its deliberately halting and indecisive dialogue to 1960s English adaptations of absurdism, it was not received much better than *Look Look.* Frayn continued to publish novels, one of which, *Now You Know* (1992), he transformed into a play of the same title in 1995. Frayn and his wife had separated in 1981 and were

SAVOY THEATRE
STRAND WC2

Chairman and Licensee: Sir Hugh Wontner, GBE, CVO
Proprietors: Savoy Theatre Ltd
General Manager: Albert A. Truelove
Secretary: K. P. J. Strange

by arrangement with HUGH WONTNER
MICHAEL CODRON
presents

BENJAMIN WHITROW
PHYLLIDA LAW
ROBERT FLEMYNG
JOHN QUAYLE
GABRIELLE DRAKE
GLYN GRAIN

in

NOISES OFF
A NEW COMEDY by
MICHAEL FRAYN

with
MARY CHILTON ROBERT BATHURST MANDY PERRYMENT

Directed by
MICHAEL BLAKEMORE

Designed by
MICHAEL ANNALS

Lighting by
SPIKE GADEN

Associate Producer
DAVID SUTTON

Noises Off *was first presented, by arrangement with Michael Codron, on Tuesday 23rd February 1982 at the Lyric Theatre, Hammersmith. The production was sponsored by The BOC Group. First performance at the Savoy Theatre on Wednesday 31st March 1982.*

Cover and cast list from the program for a London production of Frayn's most popular play

divorced in 1990; in 1993 he married his longtime partner, Claire Tomalin. The next year he wrote for BBC Television *A Landing on the Sun,* based on his 1991 novel of the same title, which won the *Sunday Express* Book of the Year Award.

In 1998 *Copenhagen* allowed the playwright to make it to the National Theatre at last under his own name, rather than with a translation of Chekhov or Tolstoy. *Copenhagen* deals with the meeting in that city of two erstwhile colleagues and friends, the German physicist Werner Heisenberg and his Danish counterpart, Neils Bohr, in 1941, when Denmark was under German occupation; Bohr's wife, Margarethe, is also present. In the play the impossibility of discovering a single unchallengeable "truth" extends through the scientific experiments and arguments the men discuss to the processes of history, both personal and public. At the center of Frayn's inquiry is the failure of German scientists to deliver an atomic bomb to Adolf Hitler: was the failure the result of Heisenberg's conscious intent, his inability to conceive of the bomb, or the greater zeal of the Jewish physicists who had fled from Hitler's Germany and been recruited into the British and American efforts, as opposed to the German scientists who were torn between patriotism and repugnance at the thought of giving Hitler the ultimate weapon? The play leaves the question open.

When the play opens, all three protagonists are dead; the dialogue moves back and forth between the present and various recoveries of the past. Repetition plays an important part: for example, Heisenberg's arrival in Copenhagen in 1941, which occurs near the beginning of the first act, also closes it. The three characters act both as participants in the debate and as commentators on it. The set at the Cottesloe Theatre was minimalist, putting the stress on the patterns of relationship among the three and on their attempts to uncover–or perhaps to camouflage–the "truth." The constant maneuvering for position on stage, together with an intelligent text that is both serious and witty, brought Frayn back into the ranks of the major playwrights, and the Broadway revival of *Copenhagen* won the Tony Award for best play. Little concession is made to the audience intellectually, as Nightingale noted in *The Times* (London) of 30 May 1998: "No doubt of it, *Copenhagen* is a challenge to those of us whose physics stops short of changing lightbulbs, but it also brims with intellectual excitement. I found it hard-going at times, but exhilarating at others. How often does the theatre deal with science at all?" Like *Clouds, Benefactors,* and, to a lesser extent, *Make and Break, Copenhagen* makes the case for the potential of the mainstream theater to incorporate a drama of serious debate. What Frayn wrote about *Alphabetical Order, Donkeys' Years, Clouds, Make and Break,* and *Noises Off* in the introduction to *Plays: One* also applies to *Copenhagen:* "So far as I can see, all of these plays are attempts to show something about the world, not to change it, or to promote any particular idea of it. That is not to say there are no ideas in them. In fact what they are all about in one way or another (it seems to me) is the way we impose our ideas upon the world around us." Whether the success of *Copenhagen* encourages Michael Frayn to continue with dramatic theater or return to farcical work, as *Alarms and Excursions* (1998) indicates, he has found receptive audiences for both strategies.

Interviews:

John Grigg, "More than a Satirist," *Observer,* 11 June 1967;

Hugh Herbert, "Letters Play," *Guardian,* 11 March 1975, p. 12;

Russell Davies, "Michael Frayn, Witty and Wise," *Observer,* 18 July 1976, p. 8;

Ray Connolly, "Playwrights on Parade," *Sunday Times* (London), 27 January 1980, p. 32;

Craig Raine, "The Quarto Interview," *Quarto,* 4 (March 1980): 3–6;

Pendennis, "Tom Frayn's Son," *Observer,* 27 April 1980, p. 44;

"Why Frayn Went to Mock and Stayed to Pray," *Guardian,* 6 February 1982;

"Mandrake," "Frayn Refrains from the Farce," *Sunday Telegraph,* 11 March 1984;

Benedict Nightingale, "Michael Frayn: the Entertaining Intellect," *New York Times Magazine,* 8 December 1985, pp. 66–68, 125–128, 133;

William A. Henry III, "Tugging at the Old School Ties," *Time* (27 January 1986): 67;

David Kaufman, "The Frayn Refrain," *Horizon,* 29 (January–February 1986): 33–36;

Lesley Thorton, "Funny You Should Say That . . . ," *Observer,* 23 February 1986, pp. 24–26;

Terry Coleman, "Towards the End of Frayn's Morning," *Guardian,* 1 October 1986, p. 6;

Miriam Gross, "A Playwright of Many Parts," *Sunday Telegraph,* 30 November 1986, p. 17;

Mark Lawson, "The Man Who Isn't Ayckbourn," *Independent Magazine,* 17 September 1988, pp. 40–42;

Mick Martin, "A Not So Cosy Bear," *Plays International,* 4 (September 1988): 18;

Lawson, "The Mark of Frayn," *Drama,* 3 (1988): 7–9;

Blake Morrison, "Front Legs and Back Legs," *Observer,* 17 September 1989;

Penny Perrick, "The Adaptability of Michael Frayn," *Sunday Times* (London), 17 September 1989, G8–9;

Heather Neill, "Bleak Comedy of a Changing World," *Times* (London), 24 October 1989, p. 15;

Stephen Pile, "The Other Mr. Frayn," *Daily Telegraph Magazine,* 31 March 1990, pp. 17–21;

Neill, "A Philosopher Speaks," *Times* (London), 17 April 1990, p. 16;

Robert Hewison, "A Last Look," *Sunday Times* (London), 6 May 1990, E1;

John L. DiGaetani, *A Search for a Postmodern Theatre* (New York: Greenwood Press, 1991), pp. 73–81;

Patrick Stoddart, "The Play's Still the Thing," *Times* (London), 8 June 1994, p. 22.

Bibliography:

Malcolm Page, *File on Frayn* (London: Methuen, 1994).

References:

John Bull, *Stage Right: Crisis and Recovery in British Contemporary Mainstream Theatre* (Houndmills: Macmillan, 1994);

Richard Allen Cave, *New British Drama in Performance on the London Stage, 1790–1985* (Gerrards Cross: Colin Smythe, 1987), pp. 61–66, 103–104;

Albert-Reiner Glaap, "Order and Disorder on Stage and in Life: Farce Majeure in Frayn's Plays," in *Studien zur Asthetik des Gegenswartstheaters,* edited by Christian W. Thomsen (Heidelberg: Winter, 1985), pp. 195–208;

Vera Gottlieb, "Why the Farce?" *New Theatre Quarterly,* 7 (August 1991): 217–228;

Christopher Innes, *Modern British Drama 1890–1900* (Cambridge: Cambridge University Press, 1992), pp. 312–324;

Susan Rusinko, *British Drama, 1950 to the Present: A Critical History* (Boston: G. K. Hall/Twayne, 1989), pp. 180–184;

John Frayn Turner, "Desperately Funny," *Plays and Players* (December 1984): 8–10;

Katherine Worth, "Farce and Michael Frayn," *Modern Drama,* 26 (16 March 1983): 47–53.

Shirley Gee

(25 April 1932 -)

Peter Billingham
Bath Spa University College

PLAY PRODUCTIONS: *Typhoid Mary,* London, Barbican Theatre, The Pit, Royal Shakespeare Company, 1983;
Never in My Lifetime, London, Soho Poly Theatre, 1984;
Ask for the Moon, London, Hampstead Theatre, September 1986;
Warrior, Chichester, Minerva Studio, Chichester Festival Theatre, 23 June 1989.

BOOKS: *Ask for the Moon* (London: Faber & Faber, 1987);
Warrior: A Play (London: S. French, 1991);
Never in My Lifetime (London: S. French, 1993; New York: S. French, 1993).

PRODUCED SCRIPTS: *Stones,* radio, BBC Radio 3, 5 November 1974;
The Vet's Daughter, adapted for radio from the novel by Barbara Comyns, BBC Radio 3, 4 April 1976;
Moonshine, radio, BBC Radio 4, 28 February 1977;
Typhoid Mary, radio, BBC Radio 4, 15 January 1979;
Bedrock, radio, BBC Radio 4, 16 August 1979;
Men on White Horses, adapted for radio from the novel by Pamela Haines, BBC Radio 4, 20 October 1980;
Never in My Lifetime, radio, BBC Radio 3 and 4, 23 October 1983;
Long Live the Babe, television, BBC2, 30 August 1985;
Flights, television, BBC2, 1985;
Against the Wind, radio, BBC World Service and BBC Radio 4, 4 December 1988;
The Forsyte Saga, adapted for radio by Gee, David Spenser, and Elspeth Sandys from the novel by John Galsworthy, BBC Radio 4, October 1990.

OTHER: *Typhoid Mary,* in *Best Radio Plays of 1979* (London: Methuen, 1980);
Never in My Lifetime, in *Best Radio Plays of 1983* (London: Methuen, 1984).

Shirley Gee (photograph © Jeremy Grayson)

Shirley Gee is an award-winning dramatist whose writing was effectively ended by the onset of Chronic Fatigue Immune Deficiency Syndrome (CFIDS) in 1988. In the fourteen years prior to that she had achieved several prestigious awards for her plays, especially those written for the radio–ultimately, her favorite medium. Gee needs and deserves to be placed in the wider context of the emergence of feminist women dramatists in the 1970s and 1980s. While her output was inevitably and cruelly limited by her illness, her major works demonstrate a writer of acute sensibility and empathy, especially for her central female characters. These are women struggling against oppressive circumstances, threatening to define them as irredeemably marginalized. Nevertheless, there is a refreshing absence of narrow rhetoric or polemic in her work, and through her distinctive use of a poetic, heightened dialogue she explores characters whose marginalization is paradoxically liberating for them and their voice.

Gee's concern for the outsider owes some of its roots to her father's origins and aspects of her own upbringing. She was born Shirley Thieman in Hampstead, London, on 25 April 1932 to Harry Thieman and Kathleen Tommy Jeffreys Thieman. Her father had been born in England of a German family. He refused to speak German and, never having lived in Germany, considered himself English. At the outbreak of World War I in 1914, he sought to enlist in the British army but was rejected because of his German parentage. This rejection represented a serious blow to his sense of his own identity. Eventually, he was accepted into a regiment that was conscripted from men who had been released from prison and others whose parents were identified as of "alien origin." This regiment was sent to the front but not allowed weapons and was consigned to the most menial tasks, such as digging latrines while also acting as stretcher-bearers.

That experience was deeply traumatic for her father, and Gee has asserted that it left deep emotional and psychological scars within him. That profound sense of the pain and trauma of alienation reemerged when the family moved to Surrey, where they enjoyed the ownership and use of a television set, a relatively rare possession in that period. The local people automatically assumed that the Thieman family were Fifth Columnists, receiving secret messages from the German enemy. Fearing a return of the traumatic consequences associated with the events of 1918, her father sent his wife and daughter to the United States. Within a fortnight of the scare aroused by the prejudiced fears of their neighbors, the family endured the requisitioning of their family home by the army. Shirley Thieman subsequently spent the early war years of World War II as an enforced evacuee with her mother in the United States. Though receiving generosity and hospitality from strangers, many of whom became friends, these experiences of social and personal dislocation, provoked by prejudice and hostility toward the "alien" or outsider, have played a significant role in the exploration of the principal themes within Gee's work. Returning in 1942 to Britain, she was sent to Frensham Heights, a liberal, coeducational boarding school, which she remembers with fond appreciation. Consumed by a passion to become a professional actress, she auditioned for, and was accepted into, the Webber-Douglas Academy of Dramatic Music and Drama in 1950. After successfully completing her training, she went on to work as a professional actress, principally playing weekly repertory on the regional touring circuit. While she was in a touring production of Arthur Miller's *A View from the Bridge* (first performed in 1955), she met another actor in that cast, Donald Gee. Their relationship developed, and on 30 January 1965, they were married. During the early years of bringing up her family, she decided to look for ways of sustaining her interest and involvement in the arts. She enrolled for a daytime adult education class in art appreciation; on one occasion the class was cancelled because of the teacher's absence. Under these seemingly random circumstances, in 1972 Gee joined a creative writing class as an alternative activity. Out of this class came her first play, a drama for radio called *Stones* (1974). Although confessing to little self-confidence in her writing, she was persuaded by her tutor to enter it for the *Radio Times* Drama Bursary Award. To her surprise and pleasure, it was awarded the prize of runner-up and was produced on BBC Radio 3 in 1974. The play was inspired by her walks with her young children to a local Victorian cemetery at the end of the suburban, South London street where they lived: "I used to go around the cemetery quite a bit as it was the nearest green place to take the kids . . . and I used to be very fascinated by the history of the place and the fact that it was very peaceful. At that time there were masses of wild flowers and birds. . . . I was very struck by the contrasts there, these magnificent tombs along with the tiny crosses, and very aware of mortality, when passing the babies' crosses." *Stones,* a poetic drama, is a kind of meditation upon mortality, memory, and the past. It was well received, and its reception led to an immediate invitation from the BBC to write another radio play for them.

Gee still felt herself a novice as a writer and opted for an adaptation (1976) of *The Vet's Daughter* (1959) by Barbara Comyns. Interestingly, the original text is an exploration of a young woman who, it is believed and feared, levitates. This powerful allegory of flight as self-fulfillment and emancipation from the gravitational pull of conventional attitudes fits significantly into the principal themes within Gee's work. After *Moonshine* (1977) came one of Gee's major achievements in her writing for radio, *Typhoid Mary* (1979), which received three prestigious awards–the Giles Cooper Award, the Society of Authors / Pye Award for Best Original Play of 1979, and the Jury's Special Commendation in the Prix Italia. First broadcast in The Monday Play series on BBC Radio 4, *Typhoid Mary* starred Margaret Whiting as Mary and Daniel Massey as Dr. George Soper. The play tells the story of a young Irishwoman, Mary Malone, and begins with Mary as a child in the Ireland of the late nineteenth century. Living in squalid pov-

Playbill for Gee's 1984 play, about the murders of two British soldiers in Northern Ireland (Collection of Shirley Gee)

erty, Mary witnesses–and survives–her family's deaths of typhoid during an epidemic. A passage from the opening scenes captures the dark, vivid, poetic economy of Gee's work at its best. Mary is remembering the death of her baby brother, Michael:

> And they sent the fever cart to us, and they took Michael away. It was dark in the cart, all wood . . . but when I tried to get in with him, to hold him–when I climbed in they flung me to the cobblestones and my mother held me down. And all my screams and all my struggling and all my hate didn't stop the bolt across the wooden door, the driver's whip, the horse's hooves, the neighbours peering through the window cracks, the rain. I stayed there on the cobbles while they rattled him out of my life and into the next world.

Immediately following this harrowing account of infant mortality, the young Mary confides to the Catholic priest: "I hate this place, Father John, and everyone in it. When I'm grown up I'm going to kill them all." These words, uttered in the anger and bewilderment of grief, offer a potentially macabre, prophetic insight into Mary's adult life. Escaping, like so many others, the poverty of her native land, Mary immigrates to the United States.

From this point in the drama the narrative tells of Mary's modest but steady ascent as a cook, first in the diners of the poor West Side of New York to cooking for the prosperous bourgeois families of New England. Even as Mary–through her hard work and tenacity–starts to secure a decent life for herself, however, fever and death begin to shadow her geographical and personal journey toward work and–most crucially–self-respect and independence. Through deftly oblique and carefully revealed connotations, one begins to realize that Mary is either deliberately poisoning those whom she feeds, or, as becomes clear, that she is the immune carrier of typhoid fever. The play cleverly poses the question of whether Mary is an inadvertent, unknowing carrier or a Nemesis incarnating her childhood grief and rage against the world. Consequently, one's empathy and focus is sensitively altered and adjusted as the narrative develops. Mary is eventually tracked down by Dr. Soper, a benevolent epidemiologist. Soper is constructed as a humane and intelligent presence within the play. Nevertheless, despite Mary's protestations that she is not, in any sense, causally responsible for the typhoid fever that follows in her wake, Soper is forced to have her committed to a hospital for tests in her own, and society's, interests.

In an evocative piece of writing at this point in the play Gee conveys, without maudlin sentimentality, Mary's struggle to define herself in the contexts both of her confinement and of the wider world:

> White walls, white sheet, white faced nurses in white masks, all white as a fish's spine. My sepulchre. Through the bars I can see mud. . . . Murky water, dirty sky. At home, the air came clean across the sea. . . . See the stars, Mary, how many millions, and be conscious of how small and insignificant you are. I never liked that. I'm significant to me. Are there more stars in the sky than typhoid germs, I wonder? What am I doing here? Is it my fault that lives fall about me like boulders? Oh God. Let me out, for pity's sake, let me out, damn you all, let me out.

A complex paradox is inherent within Mary's dual identity: the talent and ability that defines and sustains her sense of herself–her cooking–is simultaneously the means by which she contaminates, and even takes, the lives of others. Mary is a finely written and sensitively observed character, embodying some of the implications of late nineteenth-century Darwinian determinism. She is, quite profoundly, an icon of the relationship between environment and individual, explored in terms of gender, class, and the relationship between personal and public histories. Typhoid acts as a malign meta-presence within the play, a signifier of alienation, mortality, and the marginalized. After Mary's initial incarceration, the medical authorities–against Soper's judgment–release her. In the speech that follows her release Mary articulates her determination to maintain her identity, while conveying the problematic nature of destiny or fate that permeates much of Gee's work:

> Lines of my heart, my head, my luck, my life. . . . And here's my destiny. Fate has something up her sleeve for all of us, but she's a special trick for me. They're letting me out tonight. I'll be free. Standing outside . . . steam hissing white from the manhole covers, and all those rich people snapping their way through feasts like barracudas. "Miss Malone, do you solemnly undertake to forego cooking absolutely?" What do they think I'm going to do for God's sake, starve in a land of plenty? I'll change my name, and that'll change my luck. Life would kick you to slats if you let it. But I won't let it.

For Mary, the question of her own survival overrides any sense of the danger and damage that she will take with her. Inevitably, typhoid follows her travels once again, and the authorities, realizing their mistake, ask Soper to find her once more. When he eventually finds her, Mary is exhausted and agrees to a life of solitary, but pleasant, confinement in a bungalow found for her by Soper. Thus, belatedly, she finds some peace and in her final speech asserts that "I've been a bit of a marvel. I've a place in the history books. I've had a destiny. That's more than you can say for some. Isn't it? Isn't it?"

Following *Bedrock* (1979) and her 1980 adaptation of Pamela Haines's *Men on White Horses* (1978), Gee returned to the exploration of women caught in a complex web of personal and public histories and oppressions. In *Never in My Lifetime* (1984) Ireland presents a location and context again, although the setting for this play is contemporary Belfast. Winning the Giles Cooper Award and the Society of Authors / Sony Award in 1983, *Never in My Lifetime* represents Gee's darkest and most pessimistic work, which–as in *Typhoid Mary* and *Ask for the Moon* (1986)–explores characters who struggle to survive against a tide of institutionalized injustice and discrimination. The play investigates, through a nonnaturalistic, episodic structure, the murders of two British soldiers on duty in Northern Ireland. In doing so, it raises important issues of commitment and betrayal in both the personal and the political arenas. The audience is drawn into an environment in which family allegiances and relationships, love, and desire are all savagely compromised and destroyed through the endemic violence of the troubles in Northern Ireland. Tom, a young British soldier, becomes involved in what proves to be a fatal relationship with Tessie, a young, working-class Catholic woman. The pair are talking about her grandfather, who was seriously injured as a younger man in the struggle against the British colonial occupation:

> TOM: What's he on about?
>
> TESSIE: The glorious past. The dirty Brits. Eight hundred years of torment.
>
> TOM: Oh. All that again.
>
> TESSIE: It cheers him up. Stuck in a bed like that.
>
> TOM: Bloody carry on.
>
> TESSIE: He's a right to yell to bit. He lost his foot. Blown off by . . . .
>
> TOM: That's ancient history.
>
> TESSIE: Not to him.
>
> TOM: If you ask me, history's just a list of bloody awful things.
>
> TESSIE: You're right there.

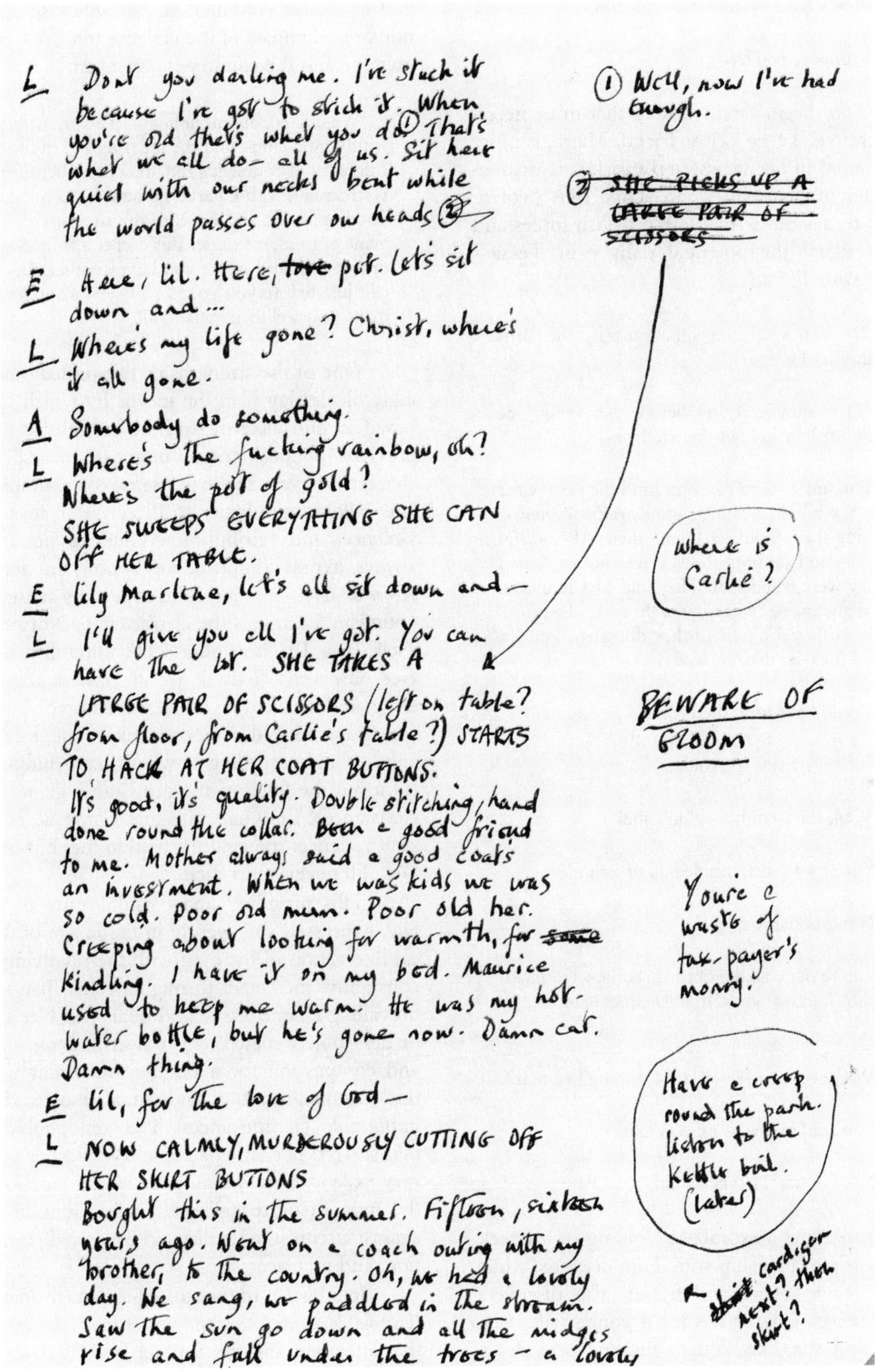

L Don't you darling me. I've stuck it because I've got to stick it. When you're old that's what you do ① That's what we all do – all of us. Sit here quiet with our necks bent while the world passes over our heads ②

E Here, Lil. Here, ~~tore~~ pet. Let's sit down and...

L Where's my life gone? Christ, where's it all gone.

A Somebody do something.

L Where's the fucking rainbow, oh? Where's the pot of gold?

SHE SWEEPS EVERYTHING SHE CAN OFF HER TABLE.

E Lily Marlene, let's all sit down and –

L I'll give you all I've got. You can have the lot. SHE TAKES A LARGE PAIR OF SCISSORS (left on table? from floor, from Carlie's table?) STARTS TO HACK AT HER COAT BUTTONS.

It's good, it's quality. Double stitching, hand done round the collar. Been a good friend to me. Mother always said a good coat's an investment. When we was kids we was so cold. Poor old mum. Poor old her. Creeping about looking for warmth, for ~~some~~ kindling. I have it on my bed. Maurice used to keep me warm. He was my hot-water bottle, but he's gone now. Damn cat. Damn thing.

E Lil, for the love of God –

L NOW CALMLY, MURDEROUSLY CUTTING OFF HER SKIRT BUTTONS

Bought this in the summer. Fifteen, sixteen years ago. Went on a coach outing with my brother, to the country. Oh, we had a lovely day. We sang, we paddled in the stream. Saw the sun go down and all the midges rise and fall under the trees – a lovely

① Well, now I've had enough.

② ~~SHE PICKS UP A LARGE PAIR OF SCISSORS~~

Where is Carlie?

BEWARE OF GLOOM

You're a waste of tax-payer's money.

Have a creep round the park. Listen to the kettle boil. (later)

~~skirt~~ cardigan next? then skirt?

Working manuscript page for Gee's 1986 play, Ask for the Moon *(Collection of Shirley Gee)*

TOM: Half of it's lies. We've got some too.

TESSIE: I suppose you have.

Tessie and Tom begin a relationship that must necessarily be secretive. Tessie's close friend, Maire, is more clearly politicized in her views, and this fact is demonstrated by her involvement as an active IRA "volunteer." Maire recalls the arrival of the British forces and goes on to signal the potential danger in Tessie's involvement with Tom:

MAIRE: Do you remember the morning the Brits came in–another life ago?

TESSIE: That rumble. Long before you could see them. Everyone hanging out the windows.

MAIRE: The sun was red like now, and the sky a clear pink. Over the hill they came, rumble, rattle, battering through with their bulldozers and their APC's and their pigs. On and on until the sky was full of dust. I thought they were wonderful. They had Mrs Finnegan out in the night again. Didn't find a thing. In the morning she found they'd pissed on her doorstep, killed a dog and tied it to her doorknocker.

TESSIE: Could have been the Prods.

MAIRE: She says it was the soldiers.

TESSIE: Well, she would, wouldn't she?

MAIRE: You're very Brit minded all of a sudden.

TESSIE: Not especially.

MAIRE: You're not walking out with some wee squaddie are you? I know your mother lets them in the house.

TESSIE: Whatever makes you think a thing like that?

MAIRE: You couldn't be as mad as that.

TESSIE: No, I'm not. I never would.

Nevertheless, like the inexorable unfolding of a Greek tragedy, Tessie's relationship with Tom deepens, while Charlie, his fellow-soldier and friend, also discovers their deadly secret. Charlie has left a young wife back in England, and she, like Tessie's mother, provides a distancing narrative throughout the play–almost like a Brechtian commentary. Ultimately, Charlie and Tom are lured to their deaths by Tessie and Maire, who, promising a party and sexual favors, lead them into an ambush. Tom is murdered while Charlie is horrifically and critically wounded. In his wife's speech, the full horror and impact of the violence interweaving into her own life and the country is conveyed:

> We talked about holidays, Devon with all those windy little lanes, and the amazing red of the soil. And I thought of course it's red, of course. Because the land is streaming with Charlie's blood. It's coming our way, flooding rivers and beneath the streets, rising through veins of trees, it's under this carpet now and soon we'll drown in it and won't you have another chocolate biscuit just before you go. . . . They were so kind, didn't make you feel their rank at all.

One of the strengths of this difficult and harrowingly bleak play is in the means by which Gee reveals how fear and violence and the unresolved intrusion of previous political crimes permeate all aspects of the characters' lives. There is a sense of an almost arbitrary and callous mundanity to the cycle of fear, prejudice, violence, and retribution. While, to her credit, Gee always avoids simplistic resolutions in her plays, in *Never in My Lifetime* it is hard to see any sense of hope or optimism for any of the characters or Northern Ireland itself. In a 10 November 1998 unpublished interview Gee observed: "I think we all have within us everything, and it's as though you were a revolving crystal or something and the moon strikes one facet of it or another and according to what's happening to you . . . it's again the 'luck of the draw' and, given certain circumstances, I'm quite sure that I have all of the necessary violence, frenzy, fury (within me) but with a bit of luck, I'll never 'meet them.'"

This presiding image and feature of destiny or fate, expressed so cogently in the image of the dialectical interaction of the light with the revolving crystal, is constantly mediated throughout her plays. Another prevailing characteristic and quality of Gee's treatment of her subject matter is a powerful sense of empathy and compassion for a humanity seemingly caught in this Gordian knot of individual choice, desire, and implacable circumstances. The xenophobic prejudice that scarred her father's life and led to her own temporary exile as a child may have left an indelible sense of the individual struggling to define himself or herself against circumstances dictated by prejudice, discrimination, and injustice.

In addition to the subsequent stage adaptations of *Typhoid Mary* in 1983 and *Never in My Lifetime* in 1984–the latter winning the Samuel Beckett Award and the Susan Blackburn Prize–Gee also wrote two plays specifically for the stage. These were *Ask for the Moon* and *Warrior* (1989). *Ask for the Moon* is set in two locations and times, both viewed simultaneously by the audience. The play explores the lives of two sets of women characters. One group–Fanny, Mercy, and Alice–are cottage-workers who make lace in the mid nineteenth century. The other group–Lil, Carlie, and Anwhela–are workers in an inner-city London sweatshop in the present. Gee's play examines, with sensitivity and through carefully delineated characters, the issues arising from these women's lives and, ultimately, the interconnecting links between them. *Ask for the Moon* reveals women who are seeking to survive in the context of oppressive working conditions and poor rates of pay. Lil is an elderly white woman who has worked in the sweatshop all of her life but who now struggles to keep up with the increasing demands of the piecework. Her fellow worker, Carlie, a middle-aged Afro-Caribbean woman, attempts to support Lil, while also seeking to persuade her of the need for unionized representation at work. When Anwhela, a younger Asian woman, arrives as a new employee, Carlie also confronts her with the realities of their position:

> CARLIE: We've got to be paid minimum time rate for God's sake. If we was in a union–it only needs three of us.
>
> LIL: Oh God.
>
> CARLIE: We need some clout. Bang the tins together. So someone'll hear us.
>
> LIL: You won't change a thing.
>
> CARLIE: I can bloody well try.
>
> LIL: I don't want a raise. I'm alright as I am.
>
> ANWHELA: He took me without a card. . . . I must repay him for his kindness.
>
> CARLIE: Kindness! He took you, like Lil, because you're cheap.

Nevertheless, Gee avoids the temptation of defining the sole male character, Eugene–their employer–in simplistic terms. He is portrayed as someone caught up in a social and economic environment in which everyone becomes pressured. Once again, Gee seems to be pitting her characters against a bleak environment of social-Darwinian values and strategies:

> EUGENE: Know what a real competitive wage'd be, Carlie? A Third World wage. I can't do that. There's parts of this city that's Third World enough already. I won't add to it.

He is forced, however, into placing new demands on his workers with which Lil simply cannot keep up with. Accordingly, she finds herself swapping her completed

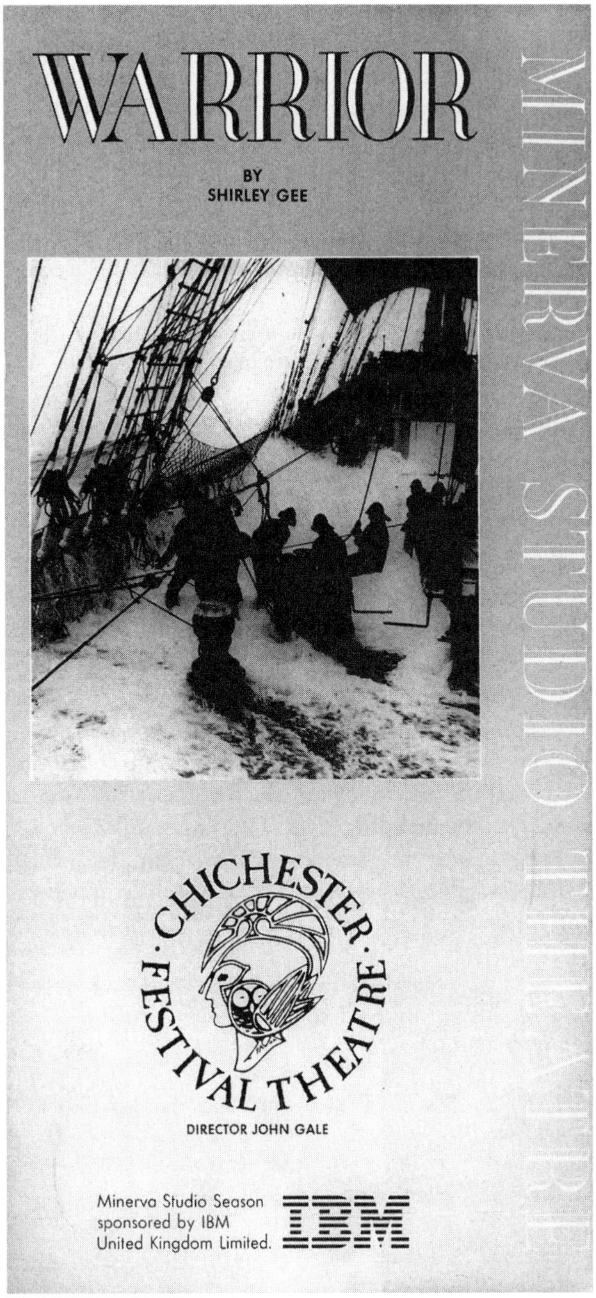

Program cover for Gee's 1989 play, based on the life of an eighteenth-century woman who joined the navy disguised as a man to pursue the husband who had deserted her (Collection of Shirley Gee)

garments with Carlie's in order to escape censure and dismissal. Carlie's discovery of Lil's deception leads to a serious row and a falling-out between the two women. In a piece of dialogue that once again reveals her capacity for a heightened economy of expression, Lil says: "I'm walking down the end of the lane, Carlie. I don't know what's down the bottom but its bloody dark, I tell you. A bloody dark cold wind. With a bit of luck it'll be a long time before you have to look down there. But I haven't got that long. So don't you come in here with your young arm and try to sweep me off the table." After Lil has been dismissed, she finds herself alone in the sweatshop after work hours. There follows a climactic scene featuring Gee's writing at some of its most vividly celebratory. Carlie enters and there is the beginning of a reconciliation between the two women. They begin to heave and throw bales of cloth and garments around the space as if in some Bacchanalian rite:

> CARLIE: (Throwing.) That's for all the kids who've just left school and can't get nothing–
>
> LIL: (Throwing.) All the shabby rags–
>
> CARLIE: All the people stuck in dumps like this–
>
> LIL: (Scattering a pile of bills and leaflets high in the air.) That's for me.
>
> CARLIE: All of us.

The parallel scenes among the lace workers in the previous century are also characterized by women struggling against seemingly overwhelming odds, working long hours in poorly lit, cramped cottages in order to make lace for their employer, Old Fogerty. Vulnerable to having the work taken away from them, the women are thrown into a similar complex web of competition and frustration among themselves:

> MERCY: What are we doing here? The minute that clock strikes Fogerty'll crack his stick down on that door–come on. . . .
>
> FANNY: He's a wicked bastard and one day I'll tell him so.
>
> MERCY: He's all right.
>
> FANNY: He's what?
>
> MERCY: Where'd we be without him, that's the thing. When my family was all took off with fever he could have threw me out, but no.
>
> FANNY: Only because he knew you work like a dog.
>
> MERCY: Do I want to be without my cottage? You want to find yourself without a place to work? Do you? You stitch your lips together, Fan. All right sleeping rough in barns and haystacks, your strength haven't all gone in the lace, but you couldn't work there, could you? Alice's kin haven't an inch to spare between them. So you stitch your lips. We'll just do what he say and what he want. Have it ready, have it right. Now wrap it.

Gee cleverly and carefully explores the making of the lace as a kind of metaphor of both its material means of production and as a transcendent motif of the women's lives. In an important sense, the lace defines them. It is the product of their labor. In and through its production they are validated, and their creativity might even transcend its means of production. This area is clearly problematic, and Gee, to her credit, manages to avoid the pitfalls of sentimentally marginalizing their poverty and hardship. Fanny, who becomes pregnant and faces the possibility of having to kill her child, as she cannot work and care for her child simultaneously, articulates this contradiction between the creativity of their labor and its devastating means of production. In an earlier scene she asserts, "They're mine. I done them. Like a man'll do a painting and be proud, well I done this." In a later scene she claims,

> FANNY: The lace care nothing for nobody.
>
> MERCY: Why should it? We made it and it's beautiful and that's enough.
>
> (Suddenly resolute, FANNY turns back to face them.)
>
> FANNY: Is it? Well, not for me.
>
> (She hands MERCY back the robe, turns to face LIL in the sweatshop.)
>
> I'll have more than lace to remember me by.

The audience realizes that Fanny, who chooses to let her baby live, is, in fact, Lil's great-great-grandmother.

In the final scene Lil is seen sitting absolutely still in full view of the audience but unseen by the others. She has died, and her death acts as a catalyst to bring the women of the past and present together. The one treasured possession that Lil had owned is revealed to have been a portion of the lace that Fanny herself had worked all those years before. Gee powerfully undercuts both the simplistic resolution of agitprop theater and any sense of a comfortable, safe conclusion to these women's lives. As the women begin to sew methodically and silently, Carlie refuses to join them and instead confronts them:

> CARLIE: What are we doing? What the hell are we doing?
>
> (Slowly, during Carlie's speech the women sew less and less, stop and listen.)
>
> This was Lil's. Poor old Lil. So proud. Stitchers right back along her line. And all she's left behind her is a bloody hanky.

(Holding out the lace to the VICTORIANS.)

You put your whole life into a thing and this is all that is left–look at it–Christ! We've got to come out fighting. Swords in both hands. Oh, Lil, why aren't you here? We've got to shout.

MERCY: She can't now.

FANNY: She's too far away.

CARLIE: We've got to shout.

Gee's second play written specifically for the stage, *Warrior* enters new territory in terms of its vivid theatricality. Gee takes a central event from the life of an actual woman, Hannah Snell, who was born in Worcester in 1723, and creates an eclectic, theatrical world of courage, independence, and visionary, apocalyptic horror. Having been left by her husband penniless and with a child to raise, Hannah decides to pursue her errant partner, who has run away to sea and joins the navy disguised as a man. Hannah is susceptible to terrifying prophetic visions that lead to her incarceration in a madhouse:

HANNAH: I cannot. . . . I must. . . . they come into my mind. They say tell about me. Tell when the shadows have lengthened on the grass, when the shadows–NO! The wind lifts the blossom, the wind blows, like it always blows, on all of us.

As Gee says in her author's notes to the published script: "I have pressed Hannah into my service, made her sail my troubled seas. Its a shadow and nightmare shared by many." Hannah's visions are the premonition of nuclear holocaust, and the character, for her author, "Fights on in her war against wars." She and her comrades light up a dark world with their friendship, love, endurance, and courage.

In the intervening dramatic narrative Hannah survives the dangers and horrors of war at sea, proves herself "as a man," and then enters into an arrangement with two of her fellow characters from her nautical adventures, Godbolt and Cuttle. They form a slightly surreal touring concert party and begin to achieve success, until her visions begin to punctuate–and intrude upon–their lively, naively patriotic show. As a male impersonator Hannah becomes a kind of ambiguous, subversive icon–simultaneously titillating and threatening her audience's expectations and perceptions. Subversive elements cannot be permitted to exceed certain boundaries, however, and when her lively "All ye noble British spirits / That amidst dangers glory sought," dissolves into "In the midst of blood and slaughter . . . Blood and slaughter . . . There's blood in the wind. A sea of it . . . ," she is taken to the Madhouse. In the final scene of this extraordinary play of disguise, plays-within-plays, and vivid theatricality, Godbolt and Cuttle arrive to whisk her away from her confinement, to the sea and freedom. Hannah's final lines are "We won't settle for the dark," and these lines close the play.

Throughout her writing, while eschewing easy resolutions, Shirley Gee does not "settle for the dark." Rather, through her compassionate but unflinching exploration of the dark and complex web of humanity, she seeks to expose it to a tentative, fragile light of cautious, but resilient, hope.

Noël Greig

(25 December 1944 –)

Mick Wallis
Loughborough University

Noël Greig (photograph by Peter Czajkowski)

PLAY PRODUCTIONS: *The NAB Show,* by Greig, Steve Gooch, and others, Brighton, The Brighton Combination, May 1970;

Razzle-Dazzle, by Greig and John Turner, Brighton, February 1971;

The Prison Show, Bradford, May 1973;

Dick Rippitdown, Bradford, The General Will, December 1974;

All Het Up, Bradford, The General Will, June 1975;

Present Your Briefs, Sheffield, The General Will, August 1975;

Bring Back the Cat, London, Woolwich Tramshed, December 1975;

Men, by Greig and Don Milligan, Bradford, Bradford Playhouse and Film Theatre, November 1976;

As Time Goes By, by Greig and Drew Griffiths, Nottingham, August 1977; London, Institute of Contemporary Arts, September 1977;

Heroes, by Greig and Turner, London, Albany Empire, December 1977;

The Dear Love of Comrades, London, Oval House Theatre, March 1979; San Francisco, Theatre Rhinoceros, 1982; New York, 1981;

Angels Descend on Paris, London, Albany Empire, March 1980;

Blood Green, by Greig and Angela Stewart Park, London, Albany Empire, October 1980;

Hard Times, adapted from the novel by Charles Dickens, London, Hampstead Theatre, October 1980;

The Gorgeous and the Damned, London, Oval House Theatre, March 1981;

The Barrier, London, Oval House Theatre, October 1983;

Poppies, London, Oval House Theatre, October 1983; produced as *On Parliament Hill,* Sydney, Belvoir Street Theatre, 1985; San Francisco, Theatre Rhinoceros, 1986;

Spinning a Yarn, London, Half Moon Young People's Theatre, October 1984;

Rainbow's Ending, London, Tricycle Theatre, November 1984;

Do We Ever See Grace? London, Tricycle Theatre, September 1985;

Best of Friends, Nottinghamshire, New Perspectives Theatre, October 1985;

Dusty Dreamtime, Liverpool, Merseyside Young People's Theatre, May 1986;

Working Hearts, London, Albany Empire, July 1986;

Laughter from the Other Side, London, Theatre Centre, October 1986;

Whispers in the Dark, London, Theatre Centre, February 1987;

Broken Armour, London, Theatre Centre, February 1988;

Plague of Innocence, Sheffield, Crucible Theatre, February 1988;

The Ministry of Fear, Liverpool, Liverpool Playhouse, July 1988;

Familiar Feelings, London, Theatre Centre, October 1988;

Beauty and the Beast, Taunton, Brewhouse, December 1988;

Paradise Now and Then, London, Drill Hall, October 1989;

The Death of Christopher Marlowe, London, Oval House Theatre, March 1990;

Final Cargo, Sheffield, Major Road at Leadmill, October 1991;

The Good Sisters, translation of a play by Michel Tremblay, Sheffield, Crucible Theatre, October 1991;

Jump the Life to Come, Glasgow, 7:84 Scotland, February 1992;

Dead Heroic, Glasgow, Glasgow Citizens Theatre, February 1992;

The Lie of the Land, London, Theatre Centre, Theatre Center, February 1992;

He Is Ours, Stratford-upon-Avon, Royal Shakespeare Theatre, October 1992;

Dreaming It Up, London, Theatre Centre, December 1992;

The Land of Whispers, London, Theatre Centre, February 1993;

He Is Ours Again, London, Bridge Lane Theatre, November 1993;

Stairway to Heaven, London, St. Anne's Church, Soho, July 1994;

Hood in the Wood, Nottingham, Roundabout Theatre, September 1994;

Help, Loughton, Arts Department, Epping Forest College, December 1994;

Heart of Ice, Nottingham, Nottingham Playhouse, February 1995;

The Gift, Singapore, Theatreworks, June 1995;

Only Children, by Greig and Libby Mason, Winnipeg, Prairie Exchange Theatre, June 1995;

End of Season, Bradford, Alhambra Studio, April 1996;

A Time and a Place, Essex, Copped Hall, June 1996;

Gifts for a Garden, music by Michael Szpakowski, Harlow, Gibberd Garden, June 1997;

Common Heaven, Hemel Hempstead, Old Town Hall, October 1997;

Alice, Nottingham, Nottingham Playhouse, July 1998;

Eye Test, Loughton, Arts Department, Epping Forest College, December 1998;

At Break of Day, Hong Kong, Nomad Theatre, January 2000.

BOOKS: *Two Gay Sweatshop Plays* (London: Gay Men's Press, 1981)–comprises *As Time Goes By* and *The Dear Love of Comrades;*

Poppies (London: Gay Men's Press, 1983);

Do We Ever See Grace? (Cambridge: Cambridge University Press, 1989);

Rainbow's Ending (Cambridge: Cambridge University Press, 1989);

Final Cargo (Walton-on-Thames: Nelson, 1994).

PRODUCED SCRIPT: "Only Connect," by Greig and Drew Griffiths, television, *The Other Side,* BBC Pebble Mill, 1979.

OTHER: "The Body Electric," in *The Left and The Erotic,* edited by Eileen Phillips (London: Lawrence & Wishart, 1983), pp. 113–129;

"Writing in a Context," in *On Gender and Writing,* edited by Michelene Wandor (London: Pandora, 1983), pp. 78–86;

Edward Carpenter, *Selected Writings,* introduction by Greig (London: Gay Men's Press, 1984);

"All Het Up in Bradford," in *Carry On, Understudies: Theatre and Sexual Politics,* by Wandor (London: Routledge & Kegan Paul, 1986), pp. 194–198;

"Codes of Conduct," in *Heterosexuality,* edited by Gillian E. Hanscombe and Martin Humphries (London: Heretic, 1987), pp. 132–136;

"Contact *en* Context, Sportschoenen en Mythen," in *Jeugdtheater in Europa, een overzight,* edited by Henny van Shaik (Utrecht: Katernen Kunsteducatie, 1993);

"Only Connect: *Theater für junge Menschen,*" in *Möglichkeiten der Interkulturellen Ästhetischen Erzeihung in Theorie und Praxis,* edited by Reinhard C. Böhle (Frankfurt am Main: Verlag für Interkulturelle Kommunication, 1993);

Plague of Innocence, in *Gay Plays 5,* edited by Michael Wilcox (London: Methuen Drama, 1994).

SELECTED PERIODICAL PUBLICATIONS–UNCOLLECTED: "Edward Carpenter, 1844–1929," *European Gay Review,* 2 (1987) 75–81;

"Write On," *Guardian* (London), 24 June 1991.

Noël Greig is a prolific writer whose work has only occasionally been seen on the conventional theater circuit. He has worked with many alternative theater organizations and was a leading figure from the beginning in the pioneering company Gay Sweatshop. He was then, and remains, one of the most

Stephen Hatton as George Hukin and Greig as Edward Carpenter in a 1979 production of Greig's The Dear Love of Comrades *(Gay Sweatshop, 1989)*

important dramatic voices in the gay-rights movement.

Noël Anthony Miller Greig was born in Winchester on Christmas Day 1944–hence his given name–to Dorothy (née Hipkin) and Robert Greig. He was educated at Skegness Grammar School and Kings College of the University of London, graduating in 1966 with a B.A. (with Honors) in history. Greig says in "The Body Electric" (1983) that he was "able to jump out of the working class trap I was born into, thanks to the educational advantages of being born in 1944," the year of the education reform act that provided universal free schooling in grammar, secondary, and technical schools in the United Kingdom. In 1967 he worked as a stage manager and actor for various repertory companies in Harrogate and Oldham.

In 1968 Greig and three friends from the university founded the Brighton Combination, in which he worked as actor, director, and writer. The group was named for the synthesis of entertainment forms it furnished for the audience at its Brighton venue, aptly named because of a combination café, dance hall, and arts laboratory that helped inaugurate British community and fringe theater. The Brighton Combination was one of the first of the "alternative" Black-Box Theater spaces in the United Kingdom, alongside the Drury Lane Arts Lab, the Traverse in Edinburgh, and Charles Marovitz's Open Space in London. While its politics were leftist, the Brighton Combination resisted the abstractions and didacticism of the sectarian left.

Concerned that students were coming to dominate their audience, the Brighton Combination left Brighton in 1971 to take its *NAB Show,* named after The National Assistance Board, which Catherine Itzin describes as "a mixture of agit-prop and music-hall" about the social security system, to Claimants Union meetings. (Claimants Unions are organizations of people claiming unemployment or social security benefits.) In 1972 the group founded the Albany Empire in Deptford, a depressed area of South London. Unable to explore questions of sexuality in his work with the company, Greig left the group the year after the move and began a period as a freelance artist. During this time he worked as assistant director at the London opening of Andrew Lloyd Weber and Tim Rice's *Jesus Christ Superstar* and as a director for the Inter-Action community arts center at the Almost Free Theatre on Rupert Street.

In 1973 Greig joined the General Will theater company in Bradford. The work of this group was "good, informative, funny and up to date agitprop" with "an immediate, cartoon-strip flavour, rooted in music-hall knockabout," Greig recalled in "All Het Up in Bradford" (1986). The pursuit of Arts Council funding, however, necessitated planning and bureaucratization, which robbed the group's work of its spontaneity. Also, the company's Marxist ideology was soon rendered irrelevant by the activities of the Bradford Gay Liberation Front, which had a strong working-class base. Greig helped form the Gay Liberation Front Theatre Workshop, for which he wrote the play *All Het Up* to be performed at a 1975 conference on homosexuality and psychiatry. Greig vented his frustration with the narrowness of the politics of the General Will by going on strike in the middle of a performance of David Edgar's *The Dunkirk Spirit* at an International Socialists meeting in July 1975 in Bradford. The ensuing crisis led to lesbians and gays taking control of the company under Greig's leadership, and the General Will began reaching out to youth, ethnic minorities, and women's organizations. Greig wrote *Present Your Briefs* (1975), about gays and the law, and *Men* (1976), a play co-authored with Don Milligan about the conflict between political solidarity and personal sexuality, for the group.

Greig, however, soon found himself subject to criticism and unable to continue working with General Will because of divisions within the gay and lesbian movement. Meanwhile, the tour of *All Het Up* and news of Greig's onstage protest had brought him to the attention of the Gay Sweatshop in London, and in 1977 that organization invited him to collaborate with Drew Griffiths on a play for its men's theater company. *As Time Goes By* (1977) was one of the first full-length plays put on by the Gay Sweatshop. Its thirteen short scenes take the audience through three significant moments in gay history: England at the time of Oscar Wilde's trial for homosexuality in 1896, Berlin under the Nazis in 1929, and New York City just before the 1969 Stonewall Riots, in which the customers of a Greenwich Village gay bar, the Stonewall Inn, fought back against a police raid, leading to several nights of protest and the beginning of the Gay Pride movement. The three sections are linked by cabaret interludes that incorporate popular period songs to comment on the main action.

As Time Goes By opens in 1896 with young Sydney going to work in a gay brothel. His pimp, Hammond, attempts to adapt Christopher Marlowe's homosexual-themed play *Edward II* (1592) to provide entertainment for his aristocratic clients, and his gin-sodden dramatics are a source of comedy; the tone of the play changes, however, when one of the boys steals the day's revenue and the police arrive. The audience's disdain for Hammond is replaced by sympathy when his lover, Arthur, offers to come out of retirement and prostitute himself, and Hammond gratefully accepts. Hammond is interested in money, Arthur in love, while the aristocrat Trevelyan is happy for other gays to be arrested so that authority will be maintained.

The Berlin sequence is set in a gay cabaret club. The communist Hans has to contend with his friends' and his lover's lack of political involvement and with his own awareness that the Left is prepared to use gay-bashing as a political tool. The characters' debate about whether to keep the club open in the face of brutal persecution can be generalized to other oppressive situations.

In the Stonewall segment four characters reveal their feelings in overlapping monologues. A white businessman has been abandoned by his African American lover, who has joined the Black Panther Party; a student wrestles with his relationships with women, the feminist movement, and gay misogyny; a drag queen celebrates Judy Garland as a survivor; and the barman, a draft dodger, says that it is less lonely on his side of the bar. The New York sequence is linked to the Berlin sequence by the entrance of a policeman who has come to arrest any Christopher Street "faggot" he can: he has secreted his badge under his lapel, just as the fascists did their party pins in 1929. Although the play ends with an act of solidarity as the other four characters eject the policeman from the bar, the barman reminds the audience that "the story continues." *As Time Goes By* charts the emergence of a self-valuing gay identity in the face of outside definitions and the individual's internalization of them.

Greig's second Gay Sweatshop play, *The Dear Love of Comrades* (1979), is about the Victorian-era poet Edward Carpenter, whose work was being rediscovered in the late 1970s. A socialist and a homosexual, Carpenter established a utopian community on his seven-acre estate, Millthorpe, near Sheffield. In his introduction to Carpenter's *Selected Writings* (1984) Greig calls Carpenter a representative of that "anarchistic, communitarian, free spirit" that "comes back to us on the great ebb and flow of history . . . in various guises." The play concerns the relationships among Carpenter, his lovers George Adams and George Hukin, and his new lover, the working-class George Merril. The alignment of personality with economic and class ideology is figured most directly in Adams, who attempts to manipulate Merril out of Carpenter's affections, and the audience is invited to dislike him: he sings that he has made "a personal investment / Hope there's interest to claim," and wants the farm to make a profit. Yet, he is the one who points out Carpenter's capacity for compromise and self-deception and the fact that Carpenter's idealism is based on class privilege. Carpenter wants Hukin to leave his workmates for the Millthorpe farm and the bed of his partner, Fanny, for his. When Carpenter calls Fanny Hukin's "wife," Hukin retorts that they are not husband and wife but friends–that they "practise what you preach, and it isn't easy." Carpenter himself does not practice what he preaches: he patronizes Hukin with his writings against jealousy, only to become hopelessly jealous when Merril and Hukin seduce one another. Jealousy draws Carpenter closer to Adams and his destructive manipulations.

Greig most sharply delineates Carpenter's political compromises by contrasting him with the anarchist Fred Charles. At a picnic Charles insists on novel fillings for his sandwiches, while Hukin half-jokingly calls the vegetarian Carpenter "an authoritarian posing as a socialist" for having deliberately left the ham at home. This badinage, along with disputes over the ethics of killing ants, the functions of art, and gentle conflict over whether Charles's anarchism or Carpenter's socialism will emerge victorious, leads up to the climax of the scene: Charles declares that he is leaving the empty talk of Millthorpe for Walsall, where he will find action and the support of other anarchists.

Greig (right) in 1985 with Gay Sweatshop members, all of whom were part of the Times Ten Festival committee (Gay Sweatshop, 1989)

When Charles is arrested on a trumped-up bomb charge, Carpenter forms a defense committee. His management of the situation, however, lacks courage: he instructs Charles's solicitor to enter a guilty plea and negotiate a minimum sentence. Consequently, Charles is sentenced to ten years, though he would gladly have served forty for the sake of exposing police dishonesty. Charles sardonically reports that he recites Carpenter's writings to his working-class cellmate.

Act 1 establishes Carpenter's weaknesses; act 2 accentuates the prejudice surrounding him. In the wake of the Wilde trial Carpenter's publisher refuses to print his *Love's Coming-of-Age* (1896) with its chapter "Homogenic Love." At Adams's prompting, Frank Simpson of the Independent Labour Party comes to Millthorpe to persuade Carpenter to stop speaking out on homosexuality for the sake of the party. In a farcelike scene Carpenter, Adams, Hukin, and Merril are all assembled for Simpson's visit. The visit takes up most of the act but consists of little ostensible action: Simpson witnesses the way they fight and quickly reconcile; he tries to make sense of their roles in conventional gender terms but cannot. Merril and Hukin ultimately cure Carpenter of his possessiveness, and Hukin helps Carpenter to have the courage to "*be* homosexual," rather than merely talk and write about it, and to live openly with Merril.

The Dear Love of Comrades begins and ends with framing scenes in which characters from the play appear alongside the novelist E. M. Forster, who recalls his 1944 broadcast on Carpenter; the audience hears the broadcast on an onstage radio. Forster muses that his own shame had stopped him from mentioning Carpenter's homosexuality and celebrates his coming to self-knowledge when Merril pinched him on the buttock.

Blood Green (1980), which Greig co-authored with Angela Stewart Park, was produced by the men's and women's theaters of Gay Sweatshop. Set in the future, the play deals with genetic engineering, transsexualism, sadomasochism, and violence against women. That year the Arts Council reduced funding, and Gay Sweatshop temporarily ceased production. During the unfunded years Greig served as the administrative director of Gay Sweatshop, and his apartment became the company's office. Meanwhile, he and some other company members founded the New Heart Theatre Company, for which Greig wrote the experimental drama *The Gorgeous and the Damned* (1981).

In 1983 Greig procured Arts Council funding for *Poppies,* which formed the basis of the first Gay Sweatshop tour in three years. The occasion for the writing of the play was the 1983 Gay Campaign for Nuclear Disarmament conference. The one-act piece begins in 1986 on the eve both of Armistice Day, when poppies are worn in remembrance of the war dead, and of a nuclear exchange. Sammy has come to Parliament Hill with his lover, Snow, to bury a box of photographs and letters that he hopes will survive the holocaust and let the future know what ordinary gay men were like in 1986. Now in his sixties, Sammy recalls his love at eighteen for Flag, who joined the air force in 1939. The recollection cues the entrance of Flag and Sammy's own younger self from that time. The two young men debate Sammy's pacifism and Flag's homosexual guilt. Flag died in the war, and Sammy's idealization of him and their romance have contaminated his supposed love for Snow. Class and economic differences in male-male relationships are shown through Snow's insistence that he will not rely on Sammy's wealth and Flag's insistence that he can be knowledgeable without a

Cambridge University education such as Sammy possesses.

To Snow's discomfort, Sammy likes to cruise for anonymous sex. On this occasion he meets an aggressive young man in the bushes who turns out to be Snow's son, Hippo. Hippo cheers the flames below that signify his friends setting on fire the abandoned homes of the rich, and he recounts his own transition from racism to class hatred. He says that Snow's desertion ruined his life and that of his brother, Sal, who is in prison. At the end of the play the three men set off down the hill toward London, picking up Sal on the way, to take possession of the centers of power abandoned by the bunkered politicians and military. The mythical dimension of *Poppies* is further established by the repeated eruption out of the ground of two "Mouldy Heads," choric characters existing between reincarnations who perform clownish routines with ever bigger guns.

Between 1983 and 1986 Greig freelanced as a director and writer for various theatrical groups, including Double Exposure, a mixed company for the disabled, which he cofounded. *Rainbow's Ending* (1984), about the rape of the planet by East and West and the possibilities of popular resistance, was his first play written for performance by children; *Best of Friends* (1985) was the first performed for teenagers; and *Laughter from the Other Side* (1986) was his first play written for schools. Exhausted, Greig suffered a nervous breakdown and left Gay Sweatshop in 1986. He was writer in residence at the Theatre Centre young people's theater in 1986–1987 and has since worked there as a freelance dramaturge. Roughly 75 percent of his work continues to be written for young people, and many of these plays have enjoyed multiple international productions; *Rainbow's Ending* and *Do We Ever See Grace?* (1985), for example, have had more than one hundred productions each.

Plague of Innocence (1988) is set on the eve of 2000, when England, shorn of empire and industrially decayed, has "shrunk to a stained tablecloth" and become a one-party state headed by the Primo, whose Patriotic Television proclaims the New Dawn. In this dystopic fantasy modeled on George Orwell's novel *Nineteen Eighty-Four* (1949) Greig targets Section 28 of the 1987 Local Government Act, which forbade the "promotion" of homosexuality by teachers. The Primo is on his way to the Derbyshire village of Eyam, whose inhabitants in the seventeenth century quarantined themselves and died, rather than risk spreading the bubonic plague. The "great tradition of self-sacrifice" is now emulated in the forcible segregation there of those with HIV; of those at risk for contracting the virus, who are called "Potentials"; and of "Promoters," meaning anyone who is likely to resist the totalitarian state or whose lifestyle deviates from the "Legitimate Family." These outcasts scratch out an existence in the desolate radioactive Gladelands of the north. The Primo is going to Eyam as a publicity stunt, using history as a way of justifying present political actions (much as Margaret Thatcher involved Winston Churchill to justify the Falklands conflict).

Greig's as-yet-unpublished *The Death of Christopher Marlowe* (1990) is a lightly comic piece that plays with history, in part by skewing the names of famous historical figures: Queen Elizabeth I becomes "Eliza," Sir Walter Ralegh is "Rawley," and Sir Francis Walsingham is "Walsing." Each of the two acts flashes back from the Elizabethan dramatist's death in a tavern brawl to his childhood and young adulthood. In the first, Marlowe's sister Anne marries the dour and religious timber merchant Simon, who orders his workman, Peter, to cut down a great oak; Marlowe's other sister, Jennifer, tries to prevent the felling of the tree. Jennifer and Sarah, a healer who lives at the edge of town, imagine a future when all the forests will be replaced by bungalows and highways, and the "metal guts" of trucks will be "gorged with the newest needs and greeds." Sarah advises her that things can be different, and Jennifer hopes for a time when the tree's roots will grow again, "sap flying up to leaves and acorns." Simon later has Sarah burned as a witch.

Jennifer's brother's optimism contrasts with her pessimism: "the world is opening up, and Marlowe's going to ride upon its back," he says. The young "Kit" Marlowe is arrogant, ambitious, romantic, and sexist; he has learned the last quality from his father, John, who beats Jennifer to show that he controls what he owns. When Kit reaches out to say good-bye before leaving for the university, John draws back–then gives him a knife. In this sequence the father is showing love for his son not by embracing him but by offering the tool of his trade: a knife, the thing that will kill Kit. At Cambridge the aspiring playwright readily disowns his craftsman father.

Meanwhile, at court, Queen Eliza is disturbed by science's moving of the earth from the center of the universe, but Rawley assures her that people will always volunteer to be dominated. In an unpublished interview Greig says of this conundrun: "Even when we know we are free of God we'll still be too scared to rid ourselves of God's representative. We need masters." The state will fight competition militarily with oaken battleships, economically with a herring fleet. Immigrants are welcome if they bring wealth; the idle must go to Virginia; heretics will be "scratched."

Handbill for a production of Greig's 1997 play written for teenage actors, about two women living in an area of ethnic cleansing where one was a participant, the other a target

The act ends with Jennifer, resisting Anne's fate, stealing away to France dressed as a man, in search of the fourteenth-century Cathars, "people who saw the soul in every living thing, love in every human embrace. Saw the power of authority as death, freedom from possessions as life." Meanwhile, Peter, dismissed by Simon, heads for the shipyards of London.

In act 1 Marlowe enthused that the public will pay for "blood and death." During act 2 he sees the killing in Ireland, and by the end of the play he hopes that people will be sickened by real and imagined gore and will thereby be purged for a better future. He debates this idea with Rob Poley, the youth who has brought Marlowe into Walsing's secret service by promising him that betraying Catholics will help get his plays performed. In return for not having to inform on his actors, Marlowe is to write plays to teach the English "the pure love of decency, of work, of order." He is killed before he decides.

Physical comedy is included in the play in such incidents as Marlowe and Poley colliding while punting on the River Cam, and a cartoon critique of the production of authoritarian myth is delivered when Eliza insists that she step on Rawley's muddied coat to manufacture "a bit of spectacle and chivalry." The comedy, however, is not warm. While Eliza's coarseness is amusing, it also symbolizes the brutality of the state. While sitting on her "throne" defecating, she demands that cheaper ways be found to kill the Irish. Homosexuality is not depicted in a totally positive light: though partial to men himself, Poley nevertheless doubts that gay soldiers would be able to kill as they should. Peter, trapped by Poley into complaining about the aristocracy, is tortured and crippled. Others in similar situations call "to each other . . . down the centuries." They say that the torture cellars, "still there now, across the world," are built "to prick out thoughts that might distress the dreams of those who plan our future."

Contemplating the forest of masts in the Thames, Poley enthusiastically foresees the river's mouth consuming the world. Jennifer's journey, however, has confirmed her desire for a different future. A woman lover, lying with her beneath the bedcovers "as the milk of morning crept over the room," told her about the suppression of the Cathars. Returning to England, she declares that she has not been to France but has discovered that "there's one country in this world for me. I call it Jennifer." In a final image the fatal wound to Marlowe's eye pours out blood that envelops the whole scene, including Eliza's assembled court. Then an anthem promises that "nature will reveal to us the lesson of her laws / and we will take command of both the consequence and cause."

Greig considers *Common Heaven* (1997), for actors aged nine to thirteen, one of his best plays; it emerged from his workshops with children. The setting is a European border crossing, with a broken bridge to the north and an empty plain to the south, where two women have lived since an ethnic cleansing twelve years previously. Rivka waits for the return of her son, Julius, who was taken from her as an infant on this very spot. The other woman, Gardi, was one of the cleansers; she had hidden Rivka because she knew the woman as one of the colorful characters at a restaurant she used to frequent. She stays out of guilt. A black youth, Teurku, arrives by bicycle from the south, heading for "the land of dumplings," the utopia Julius told him about before Teurku became a boy soldier and killed his former friend. At the end Gardi and Teurku head north, where the boy believes he will find peace; Gardi knows that he will be reviled because of his race. Rivka, though she has heard Teurku's story, continues to wait for her son. The play suggests that there is no "road back" to peace, no way of reversing the wheel of events symbolized by Teurku's bicycle. In Teurku's words, people "must tell the real truth" in order to overcome the trauma of their violent condition and then see where they can go from there.

Greig has worked as a dramaturge for many companies, including Red Ladder, Sheffield Crucible, Theatreworks of Singapore, The Royal Court, Birmingham Repertory Theatre, and 7:84 Scotland. He has taught play writing at various British schools, colleges, and universities, as well in Singapore, Delhi, South Africa, and Winnipeg, and he continues to direct and act.

References:

John M. Clum, *Acting Gay: Homosexuality in Modern Drama* (New York: Columbia University Press, 1992);

Sandy Craig, ed., *Dreams and Deconstructions. Alternative Theatre in Britain* (Ambergate: Amber Lane Press, 1980);

Trevor R. Griffiths and Carole Woddis, eds., *Bloomsbury Theatre Guide,* second edition (London: Bloomsbury, 1991), pp. 147–148;

Catherine Itzin, *Stages in the Revolution: Political Theatre in Britain since 1968* (London: Eyre Methuen, 1980);

Philip Osment, "Finding Room on the Agenda for Love: A History of Gay Sweatshop," in *Gay Sweatshop: Four Plays and a Company,* edited by Osment (London: Methuen, 1989);

Alan Sinfield, *Out on the Stage: Lesbian and Gay Theatre in the Twentieth Century* (New Haven: Yale University Press, 1999).

Trevor Griffiths

(4 April 1935 -   )

Edward Braun
University of Bristol

See also the Griffiths entry in *DLB 13: British Dramatists Since World War II.*

Trevor Griffiths

PLAY PRODUCTIONS: *The Wages of Thin,* Manchester, Stables Theatre Club, 13 November 1969; London, Quipu Basement Theatre, December 1970;

Occupations, Manchester, Stables Theatre Club, 28 October 1970; London, The Place, 13 October 1971;

Poems, London, Quipu Basement Theatre, 29 March 1971;

Apricots, London, Quipu Basement Theatre, 28 June 1971; Edinburgh Festival, Cranston Street Hall, 25 August 1971;

Thermidor, Edinburgh Festival, 7:84 Company, Cranston Street Hall, 25 August 1971;

Sam, Sam, London, Open Space Theatre, 9 February 1972;

Gun, Edinburgh Pool Theatre, Spring 1973;

The Party, London, Old Vic Theatre, 20 December 1973; revised version, National Theatre tour, University of Warwick, 12 November 1974;

The Big House, adapted from Griffiths's radio play, Newcastle upon Tyne, University Theatre, 15 January 1975;

Comedians, Nottingham, Nottingham Playhouse, 20 February 1975; London, Old Vic Theatre, 24 September 1975; London, Wyndham's Theatre, 27 January 1976; revised, University of Chicago, Court Theatre, 16 April 1992;

All Good Men, adapted from Griffiths's television play, London, Young Vic Studio, 13 May 1975;

The Cherry Orchard, adapted from Helen Rappaport's translation of Anton Chekhov's play, Nottingham, Nottingham Playhouse, 10 March 1977;

Deeds, by Griffiths, Howard Brenton, Ken Campbell, and David Hare, Nottingham, Nottingham Playhouse, March 1978;

Oi for England, Royal Court Theatre tour, 12 May 1982;

Real Dreams, Massachusetts, Williamstown Theatre Festival, 8 August 1984; London, Royal Shakespeare Company, The Pit, 30 April 1986;

Piano, London, Cottesloe Theatre, 8 August 1990;

The Gulf between Us, Leeds, West Yorkshire Playhouse, 21 January 1992;

Thatcher's Children, Bristol, Bristol Old Vic Theatre, 19 May 1993;

Who Shall Be Happy . . . ? adapted from Griffiths's television play *Hope in the Year Two,* Belfast, Old Museum Arts Centre, 8 November 1995.

BOOKS: *Tip's Lot* (London: Macmillan, 1972);

Occupations; and The Big House (London: Calder & Boyars, 1972); revised as *Occupations* (London & Boston: Faber & Faber, 1980);

Lay By, by Griffiths, Howard Brenton, Brian Clark, David Hare, Stephen Poliakoff, Hugh Stoddard, and Snoo Wilson (London: Calder & Boyars, 1972);

The Party (London: Faber & Faber, 1974);

Comedians (London: Faber & Faber, 1976; New York: Grove, 1976; revised edition, London: Faber & Faber, 1979);

All Good Men; and Absolute Beginners (London: Faber & Faber, 1977);

Through the Night; and Such Impossibilities (London: Faber & Faber, 1977);

Apricots; and Thermidor (London: Pluto, 1978);

Country: "A Tory Story" (London: Faber & Faber, 1982);

Oi for England (London: Faber & Faber, 1982);

Judgement over the Dead, screenplay from Griffiths's television play *The Last Place on Earth* (London: Verso, 1986);

Real Dreams by Trevor Griffiths and Revolution in Cleveland by Jeremy Pikser (London: Faber & Faber, 1987);

Fatherland (London & Boston: Faber & Faber, 1987);

Piano (London: Faber & Faber, 1990);

The Gulf Between Us; or, The Truth and Other Fictions (London & Boston: Faber & Faber, 1992);

Hope in the Year Two and Thatcher's Children (London & Boston: Faber & Faber, 1994);

Food for Ravens (London: Oberon, 1997);

Who Shall Be Happy . . . ? (New York & London: S. French, 1997).

Collections: *Collected Plays for Television,* introduction by Edward Braun (London & Boston: Faber & Faber, 1988)–comprises *All Good Men, Absolute Beginners, Through the Night, Such Impossibilities, Country: "A Tory Story,"* and *Oi for England;*

Plays One, comprises *Occupations, Comedians, The Party,* and *Real Dreams* (London & Boston: Faber & Faber, 1996).

PRODUCED SCRIPTS: *The Big House,* radio, BBC Radio 4, 10 December 1969;

Jake's Brigade, radio, BBC Radio 4, 11 December 1971;

Adam Smith, as Ben Rae, television, nine of twelve episodes of the series, Granada Television, 23 January–10 April 1972;

The Silver Mask, television, adapted from a short story by Hugh Walpole, London Weekend Television, 15 June 1973;

All Good Men, television, BBC One, 31 January 1974;

Absolute Beginners, television, BBC One, 19 April 1974; television, adapted from the stage play *Occupations,* Granada Television, 1 September 1974;

Don't Make Waves, television, by Griffiths and Snoo Wilson, BBC One, 12 July 1975;

Through the Night, television, BBC One, 2 December 1975;

Bill Brand, television, series in eleven episodes, Thames Television, 7 June–16 August 1976;

Comedians, television, adapted from the stage play, BBC One, 25 October 1979;

Reds, motion picture, Paramount, 1981;

Sons and Lovers, television, seven episodes, adapted from D. H. Lawrence's novel, 14 January–25 February 1981;

The Cherry Orchard, television, adapted from the stage version, BBC One, 13 October 1981;

Country, television, BBC One, 20 October 1981;

Oi for England, television, Central Independent Television, 17 April 1982;

The Last Place on Earth, television, series adapted for television from Roland Huntford's novel *Scott and Amundsen,* in seven episodes, Central Television, February–March 1985; series in six episodes, PBS, October–November 1985;

Fatherland, motion picture, Film 4 / MK2 / Clasart / Kestrel II, 1986;

The Party, television, BBC One, 8 March 1988;

Oeroeg, motion picture, adapted by Griffiths and Jean van de Velde from Hella S. Haasse's novel, 1993;

Hope in the Year Two, television, BBC Two, 11 May 1994;

Food for Ravens, television, BBC Wales, 15 November 1997; BBC Two, 16 November 1997.

OTHER: Anton Pavlovich Chekhov, *The Cherry Orchard,* adapted by Griffiths from Helen Rappaport's translation (London: Pluto, 1978);

D. H. Lawrence, *Sons and Lovers,* screenplay by Griffiths (London: Spokesman, 1982).

SELECTED PERIODICAL PUBLICATIONS–UNCOLLECTED: *Sam, Sam, Plays and Players* (April 1972): 65–79;

Deeds, by Griffiths, Howard Brenton, Ken Campbell, and David Hare, *Plays and Players* (May 1978): 41–50; (June 1978): 43–50.

Of the generation of writers who emerged in Britain during the 1970s broadly sharing a commitment to leftist politics, none has demonstrated such thematic consistency or such coherent and self-aware stylistic development as Trevor Griffiths. Together with such playwrights as David Mercer, Jim Allen, and Dennis Potter, Griffiths was responsible for establishing British television as a dramatic medium in its own right, focusing public attention on the most urgent political issues of the day and frequently provoking controversies that were covered in the news pages of the national press. At the same time, despite his declared preference for television and its capacity to reach a mass audience, his work in the theater has consistently stretched the limits of realism in a search for forms that challenge the audience's sense of present reality, its perception of the past, and the interaction between the two.

Griffiths's recurring concerns as a writer are clearly foreshadowed in his origins and in the formative influences of his early years. He was born in Manchester on 4 April 1935, the second of three children of an Irish mother, Ann Connor Griffiths, and a Welsh father, Ernest Griffiths, who worked as a chemical-process worker in a dye factory. He grew up in Ancoats, a working-class district of East Manchester; at the age of nine he passed the eleven-plus examination and gained entrance as "a scholarship boy" to St. Bede's College, a Catholic grammar school, one of the first generation of children to benefit from the 1944 Education Act, which extended the right of grammar-school education to the working class. In 1952 he went to Manchester University on a state scholarship, graduating three years later with an upper second-class degree in English Language and Literature. National service as an infantryman in the Manchester Regiment, based mostly in his hometown, was followed, as quoted from an interview in *Theatre Quarterly* (Summer 1976), by five years of teaching English and games to "eleven plus failures, sons and daughters of butchers, and local solicitors and whatever" in a private school in Oldham, a few miles from where he was born. In 1960 he married Janice Elaine Stansfield, who came from a militant working-class Labour Party family and worked as a social worker and child-care officer. They subsequently adopted a son and two daughters. In 1961 Griffiths took a job as a liberal studies teacher in a technical college in nearby Stockport, and in 1965 he became a Further Education Officer for the British Broadcasting Corporation (BBC) in Leeds, where he remained for the next seven years.

Soon after leaving the army Griffiths had become involved in the Campaign for Nuclear Disarmament and in the politics of the New Left, absorbing the ideas of such men as E. P. Thompson, Stuart Hall, Perry Anderson, and Raymond Williams. He became chairman of the Manchester Left Club, was briefly a member of the Labour Party, and co-edited and wrote for the left-wing monthly *Labour's Northern Voice*.

Studying English, and particularly Anglo-Saxon and early Middle English, at the university gave Griffiths, as he says in his *Theatre Quarterly* interview, "the feel for language, the sense of the Englishness of language." In his student years he wrote approximately two hundred poems but paid little attention to the theater, which remained completely outside his social frame of reference. When he started to write plays in 1962, he drew entirely on his own experiences of student life, the army, and his relationship with his brother. His third play, the unpublished and unperformed *The Daft Un,* completed in 1966 after he had joined the BBC, was the first in a sequence of "brother plays." He was, according to a 1986 interview with Nicole Boireau, "thrilled by the naturalistic form and the whole way in which you could get quotidian living into frame." What drew him to drama was its "sheer multivalency . . . the fact that you have to occupy so many spaces. It seems to me the best way afforded to us to explore contradictions and dialectic."

As a boy Griffiths had heard the plays of William Shakespeare, Anton Chekhov, and Henrik Ibsen on the radio, relishing "the sense of voices in conflict, of argument, of narrative through argument"; but the movies–mostly Hollywood movies–became his enduring passion. The emancipation of British television drama had begun in 1958 when the Canadian producer Sidney Newman took over the weekly series *Armchair Theatre* and began commissioning plays from new writers that "were going to be about the very people who owned TV sets–which is the working class." The impact on Griffiths of the early television work of Alun Owen, Clive Exton, Henry Livings, and John McGrath was decisive, and his earliest plays were written with television in mind. After joining the BBC, Griffiths tried unsuccessfully to get *The Daft Un* produced. Then, in 1967, he met Tony Garnett, who had recently produced Jim Allen's first two plays and Jeremy Sandford's 1967 *Cathy Come Home* for television. Garnett rejected Griffiths's outline for a play based on an actual case of wrongful suspension for alleged negligence at work in an engineering factory (it was produced subsequently by Alan Ayckbourn for radio in 1969 as *The Big House*) but commissioned a script from Griffiths, recommending that he base it on his experiences as a teacher. The result, completed in May 1968, was *The Love Maniac,* which explored conflicting philosophies of education through the impact of a radical young teacher on a new comprehensive school. Garnett accepted the script for his recently formed company Kestrel Films and contracted to produce it for London Weekend Television. A programming slot could not be found for it, however,

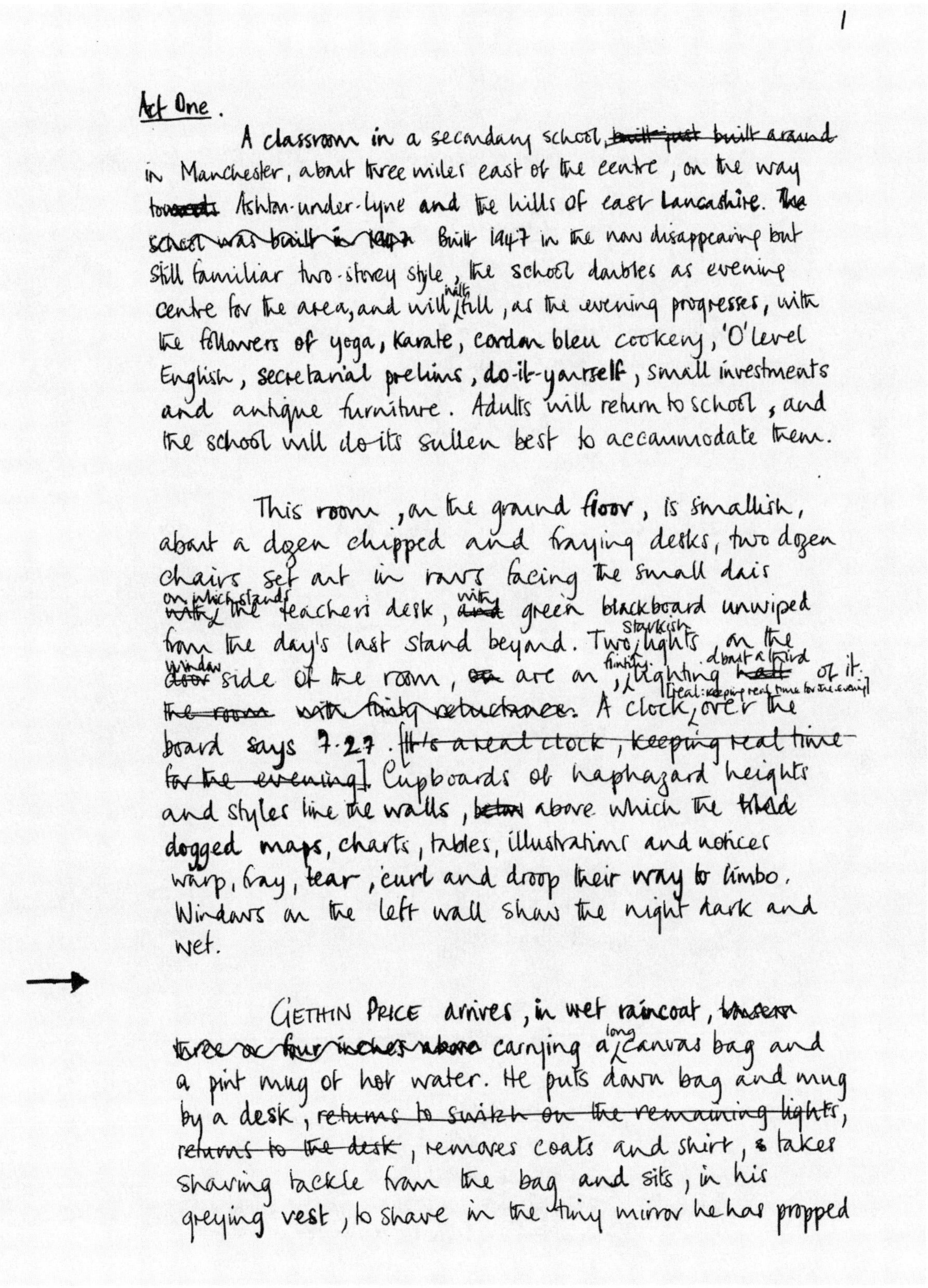
1

Act One.

A classroom in a secondary school, ~~built just built around~~ in Manchester, about three miles east of the centre, on the way ~~towards~~ Ashton-under-Lyne and the hills of east Lancashire. ~~The school was built in 1947~~ Built 1947 in the now disappearing but still familiar two-storey style, the school doubles as evening centre for the area, and will fill, as the evening progresses, with the followers of yoga, karate, cordon bleu cookery, 'O' level English, secretarial prelims, do-it-yourself, small investments and antique furniture. Adults will return to school, and the school will do its sullen best to accommodate them.

This room, on the ground floor, is smallish, about a dozen chipped and fraying desks, two dozen chairs set out in rows facing the small dais ~~with~~ on which stands the teacher's desk, ~~and~~ with green blackboard unwiped from the day's last stand beyond. Two starkish lights, on the window ~~door~~ side of the room, are on, faintly lighting ~~half~~ about a third of it. ~~the room with faint reluctance.~~ A clock, [real: keeping real time for the evening] over the board says 7.27. ~~[It's a real clock, keeping real time for the evening]~~. Cupboards of haphazard heights and styles line the walls, ~~below~~ above which the ~~thick~~ dogged maps, charts, tables, illustrations and notices warp, fray, tear, curl and droop their way to limbo. Windows on the left wall show the night dark and wet.

→ GETHIN PRICE arrives, in wet raincoat, ~~trousers three or four inches above~~ carrying a long canvas bag and a pint mug of hot water. He puts down bag and mug by a desk, ~~returns to switch on the remaining lights, returns to the desk~~, removes coats and shirt, & takes shaving tackle from the bag and sits, in his greying vest, to shave in the tiny mirror he has propped

Recto and verso of the first leaf from the manuscript for Griffiths's 1975 play, Comedians *(Collection of Trevor Griffiths)*

The caretaker finishes, descends, catches sight of Price, almost falls the final step to the floor.

<u>Caretaker</u>
Are you in here?

Price looks round, behind, about, with strange, clown-like timing, the foam gleaming like a mask, brush poised.

<u>Price</u> [finally]
Yeah.

The caretaker sniffs, looks for his clipboard and list of classes; scans it.

<u>Caretaker</u>
I don't see it.

<u>Price</u>
Been ~~here~~ since ~~Septem~~ January.
[Pause] Mr. Waters . . . .

<u>Caretaker</u>
Waters. ~~Oh~~, him. [~~Stu~~ Studying Price at his ablutions]. What is it, Gents' Hairdressing?

<u>Price</u>
Yeah. ~~Someat~~ like that.

<u>Caretaker</u>
I thought you practised on balloons.
I saw it once in a film . . .

He stumps out, carrying the ladder, ~~Price~~ pins Phil Murray to the door as they pass.
~~Yeah, but that was before the raw materials market~~

and the project was abandoned. In 1971 it was produced for radio in a reworked version as *Jake's Brigade.*

Despite these setbacks, Griffiths was able to hire the experienced agent Clive Goodwin, who soon secured a theater production of his next completed work: a one-act play, *The Wages of Thin,* about three men in a public rest room. It was given three late-night performances in November 1969 at the Stables Theatre Club, a ninety-seat venue in Manchester recently established by Granada Television for the development of new writing.

Though presented in the theater, *The Wages of Thin* was originally conceived as a radio play; therefore, the full-length *Sam, Sam,* begun in 1968 but not completed until late the following year, was Griffiths's first genuine stage play. *Sam, Sam,* like *The Daft Un,* drew on his relationship with his brother; but more than that, as he said in "A Play Postscript" when *Sam, Sam* was published in *Plays and Players* (April 1972), the play is "the autobiography, in a broad general way, of perhaps five million people in this society. That's to say, the post-1944 Education Act people, who have moved from working class, social class 5 and 4, through to social class 2, the professional middle class." In act 1, Sam I, an unemployed bricklayer, engages the audience with a savagely funny comic routine, interspersed with altercations with his wife and his mother; a visit to the labor exchange; a brief parody of D. H. Lawrence's 1913 novel, *Sons and Lovers;* and a bitter flashback to his father at the point of death from lung cancer. Act 2 introduces Sam II, a socialist teacher educated into the middle class, as he rehearses a speech on radical educational reform for the annual Labour Party Conference. By contrast, in the naturalistic third act Sam II is seen in vicious marital conflict with his middle-class wife, Patricia, retaliating for her callous humiliation of his mother by insulting her parents when they come for Sunday afternoon drinks. After they leave, the audience realizes that this behavior is a recurrent ritual as Patricia and Sam couple in frenzied sadomasochistic sex, in which she brings him close to climax by scornfully abusing his social inferiority. After Patricia leaves to spend the night with her lover, Sam makes a token attempt at seducing their au pair, then makes a conciliatory phone call to his parents-in-law. The play ends with Sam II saluting his class origins by drinking a toast to the music of the Brighouse and Raistrick Brass Band.

In a prefatory note to the play Griffiths writes, "The brothers Sam are played by the same actor. Since the play describes, in part, the Pyrrhic victory of environment over genes, it is important to sustain this fiction steadily throughout, and especially (however confusing to an audience) the shared use of the single name Sam." This blending of characters is part of Griffiths's overall attempt to match the confusions and contradictions of his subject matter with a formal complexity that both entertains and exercises the spectator.

Sam, Sam was not staged until February 1972, when Charles Marowitz presented it at the Open Space Theatre in London. By that time Griffiths had completed a second full-length play, *Occupations* (1970). Like much of Griffiths's subsequent work, it was rooted in scrupulous historical research–in this instance, into the events of September 1920 when half a million Italian workers occupied their factories, and Italy seemed poised to follow the revolutionary example of Russia. Having discovered the Italian Marxist theoretician Antonio Gramsci from the recent publication in the *New Left Review* of a selection of his articles from *L'Ordine Nuovo* in 1920, Griffiths pursued his research further in Turin and was struck by the obvious parallels between the factory occupations of 1920 and the recent upsurge of industrial militancy and student action in Britain and continental Europe. For him, these events raised fundamental questions concerning the relationship between revolutionary leadership and the rank and file, which are explored in the play through the portrayals of Gramsci, based closely on eyewitness and documentary evidence, and of Kabak, a fictional Bulgarian agent of the Third International who comes to Turin as the occupations start, ostensibly to offer the support of Moscow to the Italian proletariat but primed to negotiate Soviet trade concessions with the Fiat company when the workers' action collapses.

The setting alternates between the intimate space of Kabak's hotel room, dominated by a bed in which his aristocratic Russian mistress is dying of cancer, and the shop floor of the Fiat works–represented, with the aid of slides and sound effects, by the entire theater auditorium–where Gramsci addresses the amassed workforce. The antithesis of Kabak and Gramsci represents the authoritarian and the libertarian impulses in revolutionary politics. Kabak argues, "You cannot *love* an army, comrade. An army is a machine. This one makes revolutions. If it breaks down, you get another one." To which Gramsci responds, "Treat masses as expendable, as fodder, *during* the revolution, you will always treat them thus . . . if you see masses that way, there can be no revolution worth the blood it spills." The words carry a tragic irony in the light of subsequent events in Soviet Russia, but, as Griffiths says in his introduction to the 1980 revision of the play, he wrote *Occupations* equally as "a sort of Jacobinical response to the failure of the '68 revolution in France. *What it asserts* is that courage and optimism do not, of themselves, ensure the success of revolutions, unless they are harnessed, disciplined, tightly organised; in a

Program cover for the second run of Griffiths's play about six students of stand-up comedy who must choose between their teacher's uncompromising precepts and commercial success

word, *led.* And what it *asks* . . . is whether the courage and optimism aren't in some way necessarily damaged, distorted, in that disciplining process."

The characterization in *Occupations* is far removed from agitprop stereotyping, and seductive revolutionary nostalgia and facile optimism are savagely undercut. Faced with defeat, Gramsci seems almost to concede Kabak's position when he says to the defeated Fiat workers: "Revolution is like war: it must be scrupulously prepared by a working-class general staff, as a national war is prepared by the army's general staff." Conversely, Kabak, the ruthless pragmatist, when seen alone in the bleak hotel room with the drugged and sleeping Countess Angelica, affords a glimpse of the price he has paid in human feeling as "he weeps quietly and hopelessly." Valletta, the envoy from Fiat, is "a very fine example of old-style, courteous, bourgeois gentleman; civilized; very cultured; gentle"; he has studied Karl Marx, cherishes visionary plans for free welfare provision for the Fiat workforce, and disdainfully rejects Kabak's attempted bribe. He embodies the fatally underestimated resilience of capitalism as he predicts, "*We* will become the comrades of the future." The text has lost none of its resonance.

Occupations was presented at the Stables Theatre Club in October 1970 and given its London premiere the following year in a production by Buzz Goodbody for the Royal Shakespeare Company at The Place. The Stables production of this teasingly complex play caught the attention of Kenneth Tynan, then literary manager of the National Theatre, resulting in a commission that materialized in 1973 as *The Party.* Meanwhile, by dint of writing by night and working for the BBC by day, Griffiths consolidated his reputation as a writer. His theater work included two one-act plays: *Apricots* (1971), a graphic study of arid sexuality in a failing marriage, and *Thermidor* (1971), a bleak portrayal of betrayed friendship at the time of the Stalin purges, which can almost be read as an epilogue to *Occupations.*

Before leaving the BBC in February 1972 Griffiths, using the pseudonym "Ben Rae" to conceal his moonlighting, wrote fifteen half-hour episodes for *Adam Smith* (1972), a Granada television series about a Church of Scotland minister. Writing for this series was a formative experience for Griffiths in dealing with institutional controls and practices, and it culminated in his removing his pseudonym from the last four submitted scripts in protest at excessive editorial interference. A similar dispute over editorial control led to the cancellation in 1972 of *Such Impossibilities,* Griffiths's television treatment of Tom Mann, the trade-union organizer in the Liverpool transport strike of 1911; the BBC had commissioned the play for the series *The Edwardians.* *Such Impossibilities* was published in book form in 1977.

When first commissioned by the National Theatre, Griffiths was planning to write a play dealing with the Kronstadt rising of the Red Fleet in 1921; but what finally emerged was *The Party.* The action takes place one night in May 1968 at the London home of Joe Shawcross, a Manchester-born television producer; the play is punctuated at intervals by projected television news reports of the violent confrontation in the Latin Quarter in Paris between fifteen thousand student demonstrators and police and Campagnies Republicaines de Securite (CRS) units. The eleven-strong gathering ranges from Andrew Ford, a revisionist Marxist academic and contributor to *New Left Review,* to John Tagg, a veteran Glaswegian working-class Trotskyist leader of the "Revolutionary Socialist Party." As defined by

Shawcross, the aim of the evening is to seek "a genuine socialist analysis of our situation that will give a rational basis for political action beyond the single-issue activities that have kept us fragmented and . . . impotent . . . in the past." The debate is dominated by two twenty-minute speeches, the first by Ford, arguing that the political will of the Western proletariat is exhausted and that alliances should be sought with revolutionary movements in the Third World, to which Tagg responds with growing passion that the fault lies with the false consciousness of the intelligentsia and that the solution is organization, self-sacrifice, and discipline to "build the revolutionary party."

In act 2, after the gathering has broken up in the early hours of Saturday without drawing any conclusions, Joe is left alone with Tagg, who, having contacted his party section in Paris, reveals that it has dissociated itself from what he sees as a brave but ill-conceived romantic venture doomed to betrayal by the French Communist Party and trade-union leadership. Before leaving, Tagg recalls to Joe his one meeting with Leon Trotsky in the 1930s; he then reveals that he is destined to die of cancer before the end of the year, his lifework unrealized. Earlier in the play the evening had been threatened by the drunken interventions of Malcolm Sloman, an old Manchester friend of Joe's and now a successful but self-disgusted television dramatist. At 5:00 A.M. Sloman returns, disheveled from a night spent sleeping in the garden and, recalling his father's employment being terminated at fifty-five after thirty-nine years of service as an electrician, refutes Tagg's analysis, arguing that when the revolution occurs it will come from within the working class itself and without reference to "the authentic voice of Trotsky, or anyone else." Yet, Sloman no more speaks with the authorial voice than does Ford or Tagg. Each represents aspects of the dilemma that the spectator is invited to ponder–along with Joe Shawcross, the "party's" facilitator, himself as impotent politically as he is sexually in his loveless marriage (an aspect excluded from later versions of the play). There are obvious parallels between *The Party* and *Occupations* (the two of which, with the unrealized Kronstadt play, Griffiths has described as a trilogy); equally, an earlier theme is restated in the relationship between Joe and his working-class brother, Eddie, who is in London for a job interview but hopes for a loan from Joe to set up his own backstreet shirt factory. Apprehensive at setting family loyalty above Marxist principles, Joe vacillates but finally agrees to stake this "capitalist enterprise" by giving Eddie the £300 he needs–the only decision that anyone makes in the entire play.

Some months before *The Party* opened, Griffiths was invited at short notice to write a seventy-five-minute piece for the BBC *Play for Today* series. The production budget was limited, allowing for a single multiroom studio set, no filmed inserts, and a maximum of five characters. The script was required within six weeks; but for Griffiths the prospect of the large audience regularly commanded by *Play for Today* was irresistible, particularly as he was anxious to examine the subject of British Labourism at a time when the tide of industrial militancy was running high. By the time *All Good Men* was ready for broadcast in January 1974, the country was in deep crisis: the coal miners' action against the pay policy of the Conservative government was threatening to bring industry to a standstill. Because of power restrictions, a curfew of 10:30 P.M. was imposed on television, so that the running time of the play had to be cut to sixty-three minutes. The text suffered, but the loss was more than outweighed by the added relevance to current industrial and political events that the play now assumed.

All Good Men opens with the preparations for a "hard-core" television interview of Edward Waite, retiring Labour member of Parliament, former cabinet minister and miners' leader, and soon to be elevated to the peerage. On the eve of the interview Waite celebrates his seventy-first birthday with his daughter, Maria, an art teacher in a state comprehensive school; his son, William, a left-wing research postgraduate in politics at Manchester University; and Richard Massingham, a television interviewer. Ostensibly to rehearse the coming interview, William challenges his father to justify the record of the Labour Party in office over the past fifty years. Waite obliges in a flow of impatient rhetoric, a shade too well practiced to be wholly convincing and subtly undercut by inflections and mannerisms that suggest real-life members of the Labour establishment. Yet, the display remains powerful enough to crush William. There are, however, added dramatic tensions in their confrontation: Waite has been seen suffering a mild heart attack a few days earlier, so the viewer knows that he remains in danger of a further collapse; and William is not just any chance left-wing adversary but Waite's own son and a reflection of the young working-class idealist that he himself may once have been.

Goaded by his father's patronizing scorn, William resumes the attack, giving his version of the achievements of the Labour Party–not a social revolution, but "a minimal social adjustment." The debate reaches a climax of acrimony when the son questions the father on the latter's conduct during the General Strike of 1926, thus revealing the true motive behind William's original challenge: in the course of his research he has gained access to confidential files of the Miners' Union that prove that Waite opposed the strike from start to finish and then colluded in pay reductions and dismissals. There is no defense, and Waite can only align himself with the socialist leader Beatrice Webb's view of the General Strike as "a proletarian distemper that had to run its course." Waite announces his acceptance of the peerage and goes to bed, seemingly discredited in the eyes of his son and daughter. Yet, a doubt persists: as Waite has already remarked, William has set up his father's exposure for Massingham's benefit, and now William reveals that he has had photocopies made of the incriminating papers for use in the forthcoming interview. For his part, Massingham has almost certainly planned a hatchet job on Waite; thus, William and Massingham emerge as an unappealing alliance, with William not much redeemed by his contempt for Massingham's phony objectivity, his claim to be "simply the film camera, the tape recorder, the lighting man. . . ."

The closing scene shows the beginning of the interview in the conservatory, with Massingham immediately broaching the question of Waite's view of the General Strike. As Waite starts to reply, his lips move soundlessly, and the image is bright, bleached out, like a pallid waxwork. The camera pulls back to show him alone in a deserted space, draped in his baronet's robes. The credits roll to the strains of "There'll always be an England," as though sounding a requiem for a whole era of Labour government. Once again, Griffiths offers his audience no easy solution: while the play may have exposed the shabby pragmatism of the Labour Party in office, the alternative of high-minded revolutionary zeal, represented by William, has a dogmatic certitude about it that is no closer to working-class humanity. Waite's daughter, Maria, is shrewd, warm, and uncompromised, but she is too peripheral a figure to serve as a political alternative; instead, her character suggests qualities of which her father and her brother have lost sight and offers a critique of both of them.

No less a challenge was presented to the viewer by Griffiths's next work, *Absolute Beginners.* Though commissioned for *Fall of Eagles,* a big-budget BBC One series that was little more than a nostalgic grand tour in thirteen parts of the declining years of remaining autocratic dynasties of Europe, Griffiths's contribution was seen in a different light by the producer, Stuart Burge, who told Griffiths's biographers Mike Poole and John Wyver: "I needed a demonstration somewhere in the series of what was happening in the undergrowth, in the revolutionary world." Televised in April 1974 as episode six in the series, *Absolute Beginners* adheres closely to factual accounts of the London Congress of the Russian Social Democratic Party in 1903, which led to the Bolshevik- Menshevik split. The action centers on Vladimir Ilyich Lenin's ruthless maneuvering to create a single-minded revolutionary vanguard in the face of Vera Zasulich and Yuliy Martov's advocacy of a broad-based party determined by the ideals of human brotherhood. On the sidelines stand Nadezhda Krupskaya, torn between her compassion for Zasulich and her loyalty to Lenin, and the young Trotsky, floridly eloquent and seeking to back the winning side.

Yet, like Griffiths's earlier plays, *Absolute Beginners* presents not simply the contrast between the "hard" Lenin and the "soft" Martov but equally the contrast *within* the Bolshevik leader–the need for political will to be reconciled with human instinct. Thus, Lenin refuses to entertain a grave complaint of personal misconduct against a morally corrupt but politically indispensable agent, and he is seen deliriously fighting the agony of shingles, determined to master his human frailty. The portrayal is far from monolithic: there are moments of intimacy with Krupskaya, when she feeds him bread and milk on his sickbed, tentatively offers herself to him at night, and quietly defies him to console the "distraught and totally destroyed" Zasulich. Finally, after the awkward farewells among the congress delegates at Marx's grave in Highgate Cemetery, Lenin and Krupskaya "turn, walk off towards the gate, two simple bourgeois on a Sunday morning stroll"; the camera cuts abruptly to Czar Nicholas shooting crows at Tsarskoe Selo to the accompaniment of the ominous opening bars of Dmitry Shostakovich's Fourth Symphony.

Comedians (1975), Griffiths's next stage play, had its origin in the long-running Granada Television series *The Comedians,* in which stand-up comics delivered their acts, often racist and sexist, straight to the camera, with laughter dubbed in. This world was one that Griffiths knew well, and in order to confront it with "a saner and more human and more socially-based comedy" he devised the situation of an adult evening class in Manchester run by a veteran comedian, Eddie Walters, now retired, who tells his class, "It's not the jokes. It's what lies behind them. It's the attitude. A real comedian–that's a daring man. He *dares* to see what his listeners shy away from, fear to express." His six pupils find themselves torn between loyalty to Waters's uncompromising precepts and the desire for commercial success as represented by Bert Challenor, a London agent who reminds them, "It's the people who pay the bills. . . . They demand, we supply."

The students' chances of a contract from Challenor hang on their performances at a local club during an intermission in the evening bingo game. Mick Connor remains true to Waters but limps through his confessional Irish Catholic act; Sammy Samuels, a Manchester Jew, loses his courage halfway through and ends by adlibbing a string of antiblack, anti-Irish, and antiwoman gags; the Murray brothers' "ventriloquist" double act falls apart when Ged refuses Phil's prompt to tell an

Adam Kotz as Finn, Richard Platt as Landry, Ian Mercer as Swells, and Neil Pearson as Napper in the April 1982 television production of Griffiths's Oi for England *(photograph © Central Independent Television)*

anti-Pakistani joke; George McBrain from Belfast delivers an irresistible quick-fire performance that exploits every conceivable stereotype. The theater audience finds itself cast as the club members, laughing (or not) at the jokes–forced, in public, to confront their own responses. Finally, Gethin Price, a local truck driver, comes on with a tiny violin and bow. He is wearing "large sullen boots," a battered denim jacket, and Manchester United scarf; "His face has been subtly whitened, to deaden and mask the face. He is half clown, half this year's version of bovver boy. The effect is calculated, eerie, funny and chill." His routine involves a lengthy mime performance culminating in the crushing of his violin under his boot, kung fu exercises, and a lengthy one-way conversation with two life-size dummies dressed as an elegant couple in evening dress. Spurred by their haughty indifference to his jokes and provocations, he pins a flower between the "girl's" breasts, causing blood to ooze down her dress. As he stalks off after this display of icily controlled savagery fueled by class hatred, the bemused club secretary reappears to announce the resumption of bingo.

In the final act, back at the school, Challenor delivers his glib verdicts, awarding contracts to Samuels and McBrain and patronizing homilies to the rest. The group breaks up, leaving Waters and Price to argue about the available options: education or confrontation, gradualism or insurrection, liberal reform or class war–once again, soft or hard. As Griffiths said in a 1976 interview for *Gambit, Comedians* "is not actually a play about politics or political processes, as obviously some of my other plays have been. But of course, it *is* political."

Directed by Richard Eyre, *Comedians* premiered at the Nottingham Playhouse in February 1975, transferring to the National Theatre at the London Old Vic and then to Wyndham's Theatre in the West End. In 1976 it was directed on Broadway by Mike Nichols. Many other productions around the world have followed, including a version for BBC television in 1979, again directed by Eyre. *Comedians* is, without question, Griffiths's most enduringly successful play.

By 1975 Griffiths was recognized as a major force in British theater, but he had long before expressed his preference for television as a dramatic medium. In April 1972, soon after the production of *Sam, Sam,* he said in an interview with *Plays and Players,* "I'm very pessimistic about the theatre. I don't see it as in any way a major form of communicating descriptions or analyses or modifying attitudes. . . . It's in television that I think, as a political writer, I want to be, because very large numbers of people, who are not accessible in any other way, *are* accessible in television." This view was emphatically confirmed by the response to his next play, *Through the Night,* which dealt with the highly sensitive subjects of breast cancer and patient care in hospitals. Shown on BBC One on 2 December 1975, it was seen by an estimated eleven million people and stimulated a correspondence in the newspaper *Sunday People* that totaled more than 1,800 letters in ten days.

In *Through the Night* a young working-class mother, Christine Potts, is admitted to a hospital for a biopsy and, having signed an open consent form, recovers from the operation to find that she has had a cancerous breast amputated. Her fear and confusion are exacerbated by the "old school" surgeon's remoteness and the muttered exchanges with his entourage during the ward round; it takes an unorthodox young resident, Dr. Pearce, to ease her trauma by breaking hospital rules and counseling her in his own room. Explaining the surgeon's remoteness, he says, "for him, you represent a failure, even when the operation is a success. Because each time we use surgery, we fail, medicine fails, the system fails, and he knows it, and he bears the guilt." Pearce goes on to acknowledge, however, that the medical profession too often allows the necessary scientific detachment of its treatment of the patient's parts to extend to its care of the whole patient, leaving him or her adrift in fear and ignorance. Quoting Hippocrates, he says to Christine: "For whoever does not reach the capacity of the common people and fails to make them listen to him, misses his mark. Well, we're all missing the mark, Mrs. Potts. And we need to be told. Not just doctors and nurses, but administrators and office men and boards of management and civil servants and politicians and the whole dank crew that sail this miserable ship through the night." Thus, the broader political implications of the play are indicated, and the continuity with Griffiths's earlier work becomes clear: as Gramsci says in *Occupations,* "love . . . is the correct, the only true dialectical relationship between leaders and led."

Griffiths's next project was the series *Bill Brand,* televised in eleven one-hour episodes by Thames Television from 7 June through 16 August 1976. Tracing the first year in the parliamentary career of a left-wing Labour member of Parliament, the series extended the debate initiated in *All Good Men* between parliamentary Labourism and radical socialism. Brand's struggle to maintain his principles in the face of parliamentary and constituency pressures during his first year at Westminster, while coping with the conflicting demands of his private life–a failing marriage and a mistress who is even more radical than he is–furnished the basis for the series. The crises in which Brand becomes involved closely resembled events of recent history in Britain–or, in some cases, anticipated events yet to happen. In the final episode Brand was still skirmishing with the whip's office and stubbornly invoking the ringing phrases of the party manifesto, which others had conveniently abandoned. Any resolution of his ambivalent position at Westminster would have been a falsification of the uncomfortable real-life truth. *Bill Brand* was shown at the peak time of 9:00 P.M., immediately before the main evening news, and it consistently attracted seven to eight million viewers. Later, it was repeated in the early afternoon, reaching a largely different audience. It remains unequaled as an example of television drama used as a means of extended political debate, surpassing even Jim Allen's controversial *Days of Hope,* which had been televised on BBC One a year earlier.

In May 1977 Griffiths's first wife was killed in an airplane crash. That year Griffiths completed a new idiomatic version of Chekhov's *The Cherry Orchard* (1908) for the Nottingham Playhouse. Griffiths collaborated with Howard Brenton, Ken Campbell, and David Hare to write *Deeds,* a brutal satire of commercial power in modern Britain, which was Eyre's farewell production at the Nottingham Playhouse in April 1978. Later that year Griffiths began work on a television version of D. H. Lawrence's *Sons and Lovers,* which was televised in seven parts on BBC Two in January and February 1981. Meanwhile, Warren Beatty had commissioned him to write a screenplay about the radical journalist John Reed; Beatty both played Reed and directed the movie, *Reds,* which was released in 1981. The script won awards for the best original screenplay from the British Academy of Film and Television Arts (BAFTA) and the Writers Guild of America, as well as an Oscar nomination from the Motion Picture Academy of America.

Up to this point all of Griffiths's scripts for television had been shot either on videotape or on a film/video mix. *Country,* televised as a *Play for Today* in October 1981, was his first work for television conceived for and shot entirely on film, and it involved him in a wholly new area of experience. In a *Radio Times* interview (17–23 October 1981) he said, "When I sat down in 1979 to start a new play for television I asked myself what I had learnt most about in the previous few years. The answer was wealth!" Set over the course of two days in June 1945, as the news comes in of the Labour landslide election victory, *Country* depicts the stupified response of the Carlion brewing dynasty at their annual gathering and the unscrupulous maneuvering that attends the appointment of a new chairman to succeed the aging Sir Frederic. In conscious evocation of the Corleone Mafia family in Francis Ford Coppola's *Godfather* trilogy (1972, 1974, 1990), Carlion is pronounced *Corlion.* Sir Frederic's raffish homosexual son, Philip, effortlessly outflanks the assembled families to seize power, blithely promising to repair his "deficiencies" by acquiring "wife, clubs, clothes" and securing the future of the company by launching bland carbonated beer on an unsuspecting public.

All of Griffiths's earlier television plays used powerful visual imagery but deployed it judiciously to concentrate or to modify verbal meaning; the burden of the debate was carried by the dialogue. But in portraying a class whose forms of communication are oblique and encoded and that seems to lack, as quoted in *Powerplays–Trevor Griffiths in Television* (1982), "any serious ideological thought that needs airing and debating," Griffiths undertook a fundamental stylistic shift. In an interview with Wyver published in *Ah! Mischief–The Writer and Television* (1982) Griffiths said, "I've managed to concentrate meaning visually and gesturally and return to movement. That has been a movement away from the lengthy, articulated ratiocination which is one way, rather a dumb way, of characterising my earlier plays."

The key to the visual style of the movie is Virginia, the renegade elder daughter, who stalks her estranged family with a dispassionate camera. As the shutter clicks, her despised relatives are fixed in black-and-white images–for the pages of the weekly *Picture Post,* the audience later learns–as they return from the latest christening. Similarly, as the camera tracks along the terrace at sherry time, and the microphone picks up disconnected fragments of conversation, both Virginia and the viewer seem to be catching the Carlions unawares. *Country* is punctuated with radio reports of the Tory electoral defeat of July 1945, but Griffiths's eye is fixed equally on the 1980s. The viewer is being warned never to underestimate the resilience of the new pragmatic Toryism, which, like Philip, is totally unconcerned with values and only interested in winning. In the closing scene, as Sir Frederic collapses into senility and the cheery workers celebrate the overthrow of Churchill, the beer they tap is Carlion's, an enduring metaphor for the workers' dependence on the commodity power of capitalism.

Originally, *Country* was conceived as the first of a cycle of six movies under the collective title "Tory Stories," all of which would depict significant events in British postwar history and use beer as a metaphor for the restructuring of British capital. The cost of shooting the entire series on film rendered the project unfeasible, however, and Griffiths reluctantly decided to compress the entire message into the single script.

Country could not have contrasted more abruptly with Griffiths's next play, televised six months later by Central Television. As Stuart Cosgrove wrote in *Screen* (January–February 1983), "*Oi for England* is a three-minute punk single recorded in a garage, set against the multi-track, concept album nuances of *Country.*" Spurred by the inner-city riots in the streets of Britain in the summer of 1981 and by neo-fascist infiltration of rock music, Griffiths wrote *Oi for England* (1982) to challenge the facile media equation of skinhead culture with racism. As a race riot flares in the Moss Side area of Manchester, a novice rock band rehearsing in a cellar is offered its first gig by a British Movement promoter. Finn, Irish by extraction and antifascist by instinct, refuses the offer, and the group breaks up, leaving him and the teenage daughter of their West Indian landlord to protect themselves with previously looted sports padding before they run the gauntlet of rampaging Asians outside. The play concludes powerfully with Finn's systematic destruction of the band's instruments, though his playing on tape of a plangent Irish ballad poses more questions about the influence of his parentage than fifty minutes of screen time could accommodate. A month after the broadcast, localized stage versions of *Oi for England* toured youth clubs and community centers in Greater London and South Yorkshire, marking Griffiths's return to the theater after four years in movies and television.

Two more years elapsed before another stage play, *Real Dreams,* was presented at the Williamstown Theatre Festival in Massachusetts in August 1984. Based on Jeremy Pikser's story "Revolution in Cleveland," which was published together with Griffiths's script in 1987, the play is set in the summer of 1969 and shows a group of young white radicals attempting to give their lives political definition by "bringing the [Vietnam] war home"–specifically, by acting on a command from a revolutionary Cleveland Hispanic organization to burn down a local supermarket on the night of the Fourth of July. The attempt fails because of the farcical ineptitude of the would-be urban guerrillas, and the group fragments; but Griffiths demonstrates the sincerity of their motives and their common purpose with revolutionary movements around the world. In an interview published in *The Guardian* (28 April 1986) he has described the play as an attempt "to recover the sixties from the trashing that the seventies and eighties have given them."

Real Dreams was premiered in Britain in April 1986 by the Royal Shakespeare Company at The Pit, its London studio theater. Also in 1986 Ken Loach's feature movie *Fatherland,* with a script by Griffiths, was released. It follows the progress of a singer who is expelled from East Germany but finds an eager market

Scene from the August 1990 production of Griffiths's Piano *at the Cottesloe Theatre of the Royal National Theatre (photograph by John Hayne)*

for his protest songs in the West. *Fatherland* returns to the theme of the exploitation of art that was central to *Comedians* and *Oi for England,* but it also engages with the evasion and obfuscation that still cloud the history of Nazism.

In February–March 1985 Central Television broadcast Griffiths's seven-part series *The Last Place on Earth.* Based on Roland Huntford's *Scott and Amundsen* (1979), this project set out to contest the myth, enshrined in Charles Frend's reverential movie *Scott of the Antarctic* (1948), that Captain Robert Falcon Scott and not the Norwegian Roald Amundsen and his comrades *morally* won the race to the South Pole in 1911. In an interview with Wyver and Poole, Griffiths described its "real politics" as "the politics of social organization and leadership: collective leadership on the part of Amundsen . . . as against hierarchic, assumptive leadership such as we have today and such as we had then in the British Empire." Ratings for *The Last Place on Earth* were low, but the series stirred up a furious controversy in the press with the custodians of Scott's memory, among them Lord Kennet (Wayland Young) and the directors of the Scott Polar Research Institute and the Royal Geographical Society," contesting Griffiths's version of the historical truth and denying the existence of what he called "unofficial mythography." The dispute was inconclusive, but the immediate effect was to project Huntford's book onto the best-seller list.

In 1990 Griffiths reaffirmed his admiration for Chekhov with *Piano,* a free adaptation for the Royal National Theatre of the screenplay of Nikita Mikhalkov's movie *Unfinished Piece for Mechanical Piano* (1976), which itself was a radical reworking of Chekhov's sprawling apprentice play *Platonov.* In Chekhov's text the process of social breakdown in late-nineteenth-century Russia is conveyed through an overall mood of moral disintegration and, most acutely, through bitter intergenerational hostilities. In the movie Mikhalkov clarifies the sense of breakdown by eliminating the subplots of the play and by stripping away some of the superfluous erotic entanglements. Griffiths's version follows the main story line of the movie, while creating a mise-en-scène that translates the poetry and the incongruity of the original into arresting stage imagery. The date of the action is advanced to the summer of 1904–capturing, in John Peter's words in the preface to the published version (1990), "that eerie, humid moment which precedes the storm of disintegration and defeat." Consistent with this historical repositioning is the far greater prominence given to the "lower orders," correcting what Griffiths perceives as a surprising imbalance in Chekhov's dramatic works: "It's amazing how few peasants there are in Chekhov's plays when they bubble all through his stories." Like Mikhalkov, Griffiths rejects the maverick figure of the horse thief Osip but gives a crucial role to Radish, a character of radical pragmatism derived from the housepainter of the same name in Chekhov's novella *My Life* (1896), and expands the part of the boy Petya into a figure of bright hope who would be more at home in the works of Maksim Gorky than in those of Chekhov.

As well as positioning *Piano* at a specific historic juncture, Griffiths was concerned to give the play a contemporary resonance; referring to Raymond Williams's definition of Chekhov as "the realist of breakdown," in his prefatory note to the published text Griffiths writes, "Should *Piano* prove to be about anything at all, I suspect it may prove, like its illustrious forebears, to be about just this felt sense of breakdown and deadlock; and thus perhaps, in a nicely perverse irony, about what it's like to be living in our own post-capitalist, post-socialist, post-realist, post-modern times." Although Irving Wardle, writing for *The Independent* (12 August 1990), complained that Griffiths "has transformed a tragi-comedy into a vindictive class-war fable," the great majority of critics responded enthusiastically to Howard Davies's production; John Peter wrote in *The Sunday Times* (12 August 1990): "This play is much more than a pastiche: it is a homage to Chekhov and to Russia, and it is animated by the black, clownish humour of the transcendental, surrealist jokers who light up Russian literature from Gogol and Dostoevsky to Chekhov and Nabokov."

During the conservative 1980s the British television and movie industries were largely unreceptive to radical drama. Several projects were commissioned from Griffiths but never realized, and apart from a revised version of *The Party* broadcast on BBC One to mark the twentieth anniversary of the events in Paris of May 1968, nine years elapsed between *The Last Place on Earth* and the next work by Griffiths to be shown on television.

During the run of *Piano* Griffiths began to develop an idea with two actors, Dave Hill and Paul Slack, for a play in which a wall would be built "in real time, on stage, every night." In January 1991, outraged during a visit to the United States by the spectacle of the Gulf War broadcast live on American television, Griffiths returned home resolved that "these guys should be building a wall in the Middle East." The outcome was *The Gulf between Us* (1992), in which a building has been destroyed in an Allied missile attack on a desert shrine in "an un-named country and an un-named city in an un-named war." It transpires that the building housed both a military installation and a crèche, and all the children in the latter were incinerated in the attack. Both sides share the guilt for this atrocity, but the ultimate blame rests with those whose technology boasts the capacity "to tell the time on a child's wristwatch from one hundred miles, the side a woman parts her hair, the stubble on a man's face." These words are spoken by Dr. Aziz, a woman doctor responsible for the crèche, who discovers that the local military neglected to remove the children to safety. Ismail, a young soldier, commands the guards struggling to hold back the children's mothers until the awful truth can be hidden by sealing up the wall. This task is assigned to Billy Ryder, a casually racist English builder who has stayed on through the war, detained by the prospect of a quick fortune and now compelled to work for his exit visa. He is helped, somewhat erratically, by Rafael Finbar O'Toole, an itinerant gilder, and his assistant, Chatterjee, a young Indian laborer from Leeds. The narrative runs from dawn to dusk, from one missile attack to the next, and in the West Yorkshire Playhouse premiere (directed by Griffiths himself) the simulation of total warfare was earsplittingly realistic. The casting of Palestinian actors in the Arab roles also added a dimension of actuality and a moral authority grounded in their experiences in the Middle East. These effects were experienced most acutely when Salwa Nakkarah, as Dr. Aziz, confronted the audience, cradling an incinerated child and demanding to know what prayers they could offer to their God. Yet, the play also includes, according to the program note, "elements that were shimmering and trembling away from *A Thousand and One Nights*." Central to this conceit is the figure of O'Toole, who, while functioning as a character within the play, also stands outside it as "a kind of trans-historical narrator" who miraculously wakes up after being reduced to a heap of smoking rags in the climactic raid. "He's called the Gukha in Arabic," Griffiths said in a 1992 interview with Sarah Hemming. "He is doomed to live forever and keeps coming back. He's like the flea under the king's nightshirt. He's anarchic, anti-authoritarian, devious, cynical and compassionate. . . . And he's the storyteller–he shows you where to look for the next part of the story."

The critical response to *The Gulf between Us* was troubled, even resentful: instead of the rational, dialectical treatment of the conflict that was expected of him, Griffiths had come up with a piece of theater that was by turns violent, visionary, contradictory, and strangely comic. Typical of the predominant reaction was Bene-

Dave Hill as Rafael Finbar O'Toole in the 1992 West Yorkshire Playhouse production of Griffiths's The Gulf between Us *(photograph by Gerry Murray)*

dict Nightingale's comment in *The Times* (23 January 1992): "the piece is more weakened than enriched by Griffiths's attempts to push the proceedings in odd unrealistic directions."

In 1992 Griffiths married Gill Cliff. His next work, *Thatcher's Children,* presented at the Bristol Old Vic in May 1993, was the product of a two-week workshop conducted by the author and the cast of seven young actors. The play charts the progress of seven friends as they come of age in Prime Minister Margaret Thatcher's Britain, from their final year of junior school in 1973 up to New Year's Eve 1999. Separately, they experience the impact of the Youth Opportunities Programme, the Greenham Common protests, the Miners' Strike, the antigay legislation Clause 28, the Poll Tax riots, and the Gulf War. In various ways they are made or broken by the Thatcher years. The fragmentation of community and the replacement of human discourse by the electronic image are paralleled in the stylistic development of the play. After the affectionate comedy of the early scenes Griffiths increasingly uses projected news photographs and voice-overs, and the characters relate their experiences directly to the audience, thereby emphasizing their alienation from each other. An interlude of friendship regained occurs when a reunion is organized by the Sikh Gurvinder, now a wealthy property dealer and drug baron but an outcast from his own family. The idyll soon dissolves: John Major succeeds Thatcher in back-projected images; Tom, the bright boy of the class, participates as a Tornado pilot in the "turkey shoot" of the fleeing Iraqi Revolutionary Guards on the Basra highway in the Gulf War and then takes refuge in traumatized insanity. The two Jamaican sisters, one clever, the other pretty, are reconciled when their mother dies of "coronary infarct. Related factors: racial abuse, precipitating heart failure." But in the closing scene Gurvinder is alone with his computers as the millennium dawns, summoning up virtual-reality figures from a school nativity play–an image of innocent community in bleak contrast to his present state of alienation. The conclusion was too dystopian for most critics, who also castigated the piece for what they saw as its lack of character interaction.

The reception of *Thatcher's Children* was not helped by a production that, in contrast to the powerful realization of *The Gulf between Us,* failed to meet the daunting audio-visual demands of the frequently cinematic script. In an interview in May 1994 Griffiths said, "I write screenplays for the stage and stage plays for the screen." Both descriptions fit his next work, *Hope in the Year Two,* first shown on BBC television in May 1994 and subsequently toured as a stage play, directed by the author, under the title *Who Shall Be Happy . . . ?* (1997). Set on the eve of the execution of the French revolutionary Georges Danton on 16 April 1794–Year Two in the Republican calendar–it constitutes, according to Griffiths's introduction to *Hope in the Year Two and Thatcher's Children* (1994), "a raid on the past, an address to the present and a rejection of the future currently on offer." He applies the description equally to *Thatcher's Children;* but, in fact, it fits most of his plays, which suggest a continuum with an imperfect present and an inauspicious future, an agenda yet to be realized.

Recurrent, too, throughout Griffiths's work is his concern with history–both its making and its subsequent revision. But no previous work had been so intricately self-reflexive in structure, so overtly complicit with its audience, or so purposively histrionic in style as *Hope in the Year Two / Who Shall Be Happy . . . ?* The situation that Griffiths contrives is in itself theatrical: exploiting a rumor that a decoy Danton is imprisoned in the Conciergerie to confuse any rescue attempt, Danton seeks to engineer his escape by pretending to his jailer that he is the counterfeit–an actor who has learned the role of Danton. At one point the audience witnesses the brain-spinning Pirandellian spectacle of Danton playing an actor playing Danton, and playing Jean-Paul Marat and Maximilien Robespierre, as well. The purpose, as Stanton B. Garner Jr. observes, is "not only to theatricalize identity . . . but to reconfigure history itself as an essentially presentational space of gestures and language invested with public recognizability and meaning." Thus, the audience sees the painter Jacques-Louis David's *The Assassination of Marat,* intercut with soldiers from the Marat Company first robbing and then drowning some sixty tethered men, women, and children by scuttling a boat in the Loire, the water closing over the victims' heads as though to conceal the event from history. Pondering this atrocity and the many others in which he was complicit, Danton departs for the guillotine with the question–directed to himself and to the audience–"Who shall be happy, if not everyone?"

In contrast to the incisively intelligent, sinewy Jack Shepherd, who played Danton in the television version, Griffiths found for his stage production a Danton built on a suitably grand scale ("a huge man, big swaggerbelly, great arse," in Danton's own words). As John Peter wrote in *The Sunday Times* (16 June 1996): "Stanley Townsend plays him with an attractive swagger, great intellectual confidence, the rousing sincerity of the demagogue and a voice that broods, caresses, excites and threatens. His performance brilliantly confirms the notion that Danton was the Trotsky of his time."

Since *Who Shall Be Happy . . . ?* Griffiths has divided his time between theater, motion pictures, and television. In November 1997 he made his debut as a television director with *Food for Ravens,* a movie commissioned by BBC Wales to mark the centenary of the birth of Aneurin Bevan, who, as Labour minister of health, was responsible for the creation of the National Health Service in 1948. The play includes a dialogue between past and present, represented by Bevan in Tredegar in 1911, aged thirteen and about to start work in the mine, in conversation with himself in 1960 as he is dying of cancer. In flashback, Bevan appears both as a boy and at defining points in his career, from his support of the miners during the lockout of 1926 to the Labour Party Conference of 1957, when, in his memorable "Naked into the conference chamber" speech, he argued for nuclear disarmament but against unilateralism. While much of *Food for Ravens* is about Bevan's tender relationship with his wife, Jennie Lee, it poses fundamental questions concerning the relationship between personal values and political objectives–questions of acute urgency at a time when the logic of the welfare state was being questioned by a Labour government.

With a compellingly authentic portrayal of Bevan by Brian Cox and strong support from Sinead Cusack as Jennie Lee, Griffiths's lyrical yet incisive production won the Royal Television Society's award as Best Regional Production. Even so, it was televised nationwide on BBC Two the day following its BBC Wales premiere, only after angry protests from Cox and Griffiths in the national press. The corporation's implausible explanations for its belated change of heart, the minimal publicity given to the program, and the late viewing time of 11:15 P.M. tell their own story. In an age when George Faber, the head of single drama for BBC Television, can launch a season by proclaiming, as quoted in *The Observer* (5 March 1995), "There will be a lot more comedy, sex and stars. . . . There will be nothing PC, nothing worthy about *Screen Two* any more," it is no surprise that Trevor Griffiths has turned away from the medium and looked increasingly to the theater for the production of work that continues to be restlessly innovative in form and unswerving in its political engagement.

Interviews:

Merete Bates, "Love and Flannel," *Guardian,* 6 November 1970, p. 8;

Nigel Andrews, "A Play Postscript," *Plays and Players,* 21 (April 1972): 82–83;

Ronald Hayman, "Trevor Griffiths–Attacking from the Inside," *Times* (London), 15 December 1973, p. 9;

Kathleen Tynan, "Party Piece," *Sunday Times* (London), 16 December 1973, pp. 82–87;

Peter Ansorge, "Current Concerns: Interview with Trevor Griffiths and David Hare," *Plays and Players,* 21 (July 1974): 18–22;

Stephen Dixon, "Joking Apart," *Guardian,* 19 February 1975, p. 10;

Jonathan Croall, "From House to Home. Interview with Trevor Griffiths," *Times Educational Supplement,* 25 June 1976, pp. 18–19;

Catherine Itzin and Simon Trussler, "Trevor Griffiths–Transforming the Husk of Capitalism," *Theatre Quarterly,* 22 (Summer 1976): 25–46;

Nigel Thomas, "Trevor and Bill: On Putting Politics Before News at Ten," *Leveller,* November 1976, pp. 12–13;

Pat Silburn, "Gambit Interview: Pat Silburn Talks to Trevor Griffiths," *Gambit,* 8, no. 29 (1976): 30–36;

Alison Summers, "Trevor Griffiths: Politics and Popular Culture," *Canadian Theatre Review,* 27 (Summer 1980): 22–29;

W. Stephen Gilbert, "Closed Circuits," *Guardian Weekend,* 17 October 1981, p. 2;

Adrian Hodges, "The Telephone Calls from Beatty that Changed Two Men's Careers," *Screen International,* 27 February 1982, p. 12;

Paul Tickell, "Reds, White and Blue: The Politics of Colour," *New Musical Express,* 17 April 1982, pp. 24–26;

Mick Eaton, "History to Hollywood," *Screen,* 23 (July–August 1982): 61–70;

John Wyver, "Countering Consent: An Interview with John Wyver," in *Ah! Mischief–The Writer and Television,* edited by Frank Pike (London: Faber & Faber, 1982), pp. 30–40;

Desmond Christy, "Back to the Barricades," *Guardian,* 28 April 1986, p. 11;

Nicole Boireau, "Interview with Trevor Griffiths," *Coup de Théâtre,* 6 (December 1986): 1–29;

Misha Glenny, "Truth Is Otherwise," in Trevor Griffiths, *Judgement over the Dead* (London: Verso, 1986), pp. ix–xlii;

Sarah Hemming, "Caught in the Crossfire," *Independent,* 8 January 1992, p. 17;

Quintin Bradley, "New World Order," *Northern Star,* 9–16 January 1992;

Andrew Billen, "Never Time for Sleeping with the Enemy," *Observer,* 16 May 1993, p. 56;

Andy Lavender, "Lines of Greatest Resistance," *Times* (London), 18 May 1993, p. 33;

Martin Cinnamond, "Of Comedians and *Comedians,*" program for *Comedians,* West Yorkshire Playhouse, 1993;

Clarie Armitstead, "Bloody, unbowed," *Guardian,* 11 May 1994.

References:

Jonathan Bignell, "Trevor Griffiths's Political Theatre: From *Oi for England* to *The Gulf between Us,*" *New Theatre Quarterly,* 37 (February 1994): 49–56;

Edward Braun, "Trevor Griffiths," in *British Television Drama,* edited by George Brandt (Cambridge: Cambridge University Press, 1981), pp. 56–81;

Oscar Lee Brownstein, *Strategies of Drama–The Experience of Form* (New York: Greenwood Press, 1991), pp. 1–24;

John Bull, *New British Political Dramatists* (London: Macmillan, 1984), pp. 118–150;

Michael Davie, "The Truth of Fiction Is Stronger Than the Facts," *Observer,* 24 February 1985, p. 56;

Stanton B. Garner Jr., "*History in the Year Two:* Trevor Griffiths's Danton," *New Theatre Quarterly,* 44 (November 1995): 333–341;

Garner, "Politics over the Gulf: Trevor Griffiths in the Nineties," *Modern Drama,* 39 (Fall 1996): 381–391;

Garner, *Trevor Griffiths: Politics, Drama, History* (Ann Arbor: University of Michigan Press, 1999);

Tom Nairn, "Mucking about with Love and Revolution–Gramsci on Stage at The Place," *7 Days,* 10 November 1971, pp. 18–19;

Mike Poole and John Wyver, *Powerplays–Trevor Griffiths in Television* (London: BFI Books, 1984);

Austin E. Quigley, "Creativity and Commitment in Trevor Griffiths' *Comedians,*" *Modern Drama,* 24 (December 1981): 404–423;

Janelle Reinelt, *After Brecht–British Epic Theater* (Ann Arbor: University of Michigan Press, 1994), pp. 143–175;

"Trevor Griffiths et le théâtre engagé contemporain en Grande-Bretagne," *Coup de Théâtre,* special issue, 6 (December 1986);

John Tulloch, *Television Drama–Agency, Audience and Myth* (London & New York: Routledge, 1990), pp. 89–187, 267–271.

Tony Harrison

(30 April 1937 –)

Steve Nicholson
University of Huddersfield

and

Sara Soncini
University of Milan

See also the Harrison entry in *DLB 40: Poets of Great Britain and Ireland Since 1960.*

Tony Harrison (photograph by Moira Conway)

PLAY PRODUCTIONS: *Aikin Mata,* adapted from Aristophanes' *Lysistrata* by Harrison and James Simmons, Zaria, Nigeria, Ahmadu Bello University, March 1964;

The Misanthrope, adapted from Molière's *Le Misanthrope,* London, Old Vic Theatre, 22 February 1973; Washington, D.C., Kennedy Center, Eisenhower Theatre, 11 February 1975;

Phaedra Britannica, adapted from Jean Racine's *Phèdre,* London, Old Vic Theatre, 9 September 1975; New York, Classic Stage Company Repertory, 14 December 1988;

The Passion, adapted from fourteen plays of the York Mystery Cycle, London, National Theatre, 21 April 1977;

Bow Down, London, National Theatre, 5 July 1977;

The Bartered Bride, adapted from Karel Sabina's libretto for Bedřich Smetana's opera, New York, New York Metropolitan Opera, 25 November 1978;

The Oresteia, adapted from Aeschylus's trilogy, London, National Theatre, 28 November 1981;

The Mysteries, adapted from the York, Wakefield, Chester, and Coventry Cycles, London, National Theatre, 19 January 1985;

Yan Tan Tethera, London, Queen Elizabeth Hall, 5 August 1986;

The Trackers of Oxyrhynchus, Delphi, Greece, ancient stadium of Delphi, 12 July 1988; London, National Theatre, 27 March 1990;

Square Rounds, London, Lyttelton Theatre of the National Theatre, 1 October 1992;

Poetry or Bust, Saltaire, West Yorkshire, Salts Mill, 5 September 1993;

The Kaisers of Carnuntum, Vienna, Carnuntum, 2 and 3 June 1995;

The Labourers of Herakles, Delphi, Greece, ancient stadium of Delphi, 23 August 1995;

The Prince's Play, adapted from Victor Hugo's *Le Roi s'amuse,* London, Olivier, National Theatre, 19 April 1996.

BOOKS: *Earthworks* (Leeds: University of Leeds, 1964);
Aikin Mata, by Harrison and James Simmons (Ibadan, Nigeria: Oxford University Press, 1966);
Newcastle Is Peru (Newcastle upon Tyne: Eagle Press, 1969);
The Loiners (London: London Magazine Editions, 1970);
The Misanthrope (London: Collings, 1973);
Palladas: Poems (London: Anvil Press, 1975);
Phaedra Britannica (London: Collings, 1975);
Bow Down (London: Collings, 1977);
The Passion (London: Collings, 1977);
The Bartered Bride (New York: Schirmer, 1978);
From "The School of Eloquence" and Other Poems (London: Collings, 1978);
Looking Up, by Harrison and Philip Sharpe (West Malvern: Migrant Press, 1979);
The Oresteia (London: Collings, 1981);
Continuous: Fifty Sonnets from "The School of Eloquence" (London: Collings, 1981);
A Kumquat for John Keats (Newcastle upon Tyne: Bloodaxe, 1981);
U. S. Martial (Newcastle upon Tyne: Bloodaxe, 1981);
Selected Poems (Harmondsworth: Viking, 1984; revised and enlarged (London: Penguin, 1987);
The Fire-Gap: A Poem with Two Tails (Newcastle upon Tyne: Bloodaxe, 1985);
v. Tony Harrison (Newcastle upon Tyne: Bloodaxe, 1985; revised and enlarged, 1989);
The Mysteries (London: Faber & Faber, 1985);
Dramatic Verse 1973–1985 (Newcastle upon Tyne: Bloodaxe, 1985); republished as *Theatre Works 1973–1985* (London: Penguin, 1986)–comprises *The Misanthrope, Phaedra Britannica, Bow Down, The Bartered Bride, The Oresteia, Yan Tan Tethera, The Big H,* and *Medea: A Sex-War Opera;*
Ten Sonnets from "The School of Eloquence" (London: Anvil Press, 1987);
Anno 42: Seven New Poems (London: Scargil Press, 1987);
The Mother of the Muses (Cambridge: Rampant Lions Press, 1989);
The Trackers of Oxyrhynchus: The Delphi Text 1988 (London: Faber & Faber, 1990);
v. and Other Poems (New York: Farrar, Straus & Giroux, 1990);
Losing Touch: In Memoriam George Cukor. Died 24.1.83 (Cambridge: Privately Printed at Rampant Lions Press, 1990);
A Cold Coming (Newcastle upon Tyne: Bloodaxe, 1991);
Arctic Paradise and *The Blasphemers' Banquet,* in *Bloodaxe Critical Anthologies 1: Tony Harrison,* edited by Neil Astley (Newcastle upon Tyne: Bloodaxe, 1991);
The Gaze of the Gorgon (Newcastle upon Tyne: Bloodaxe, 1992);
The Common Chorus: A Version of Aristophanes' Lysistrata (London: Faber & Faber, 1992);
Square Rounds (London: Faber & Faber, 1992);
Poetry or Bust (Saltaire, West Yorkshire: Salts Mill, 1993);
Black Daisies for the Bride (London: Faber & Faber, 1993);
A Maybe Day in Kazakhstan (London: Channel 4 Television, 1994);
The Shadow of Hiroshima and Other Film/Poems (London: Faber & Faber, 1995);
Plays Three (London: Faber & Faber, 1996)–comprises *Poetry or Bust, The Kaisers of Carnuntum,* and *The Labourers of Herakles;*
Le Roi s'amuse: The Prince's Play, by Harrison and Victor Hugo (London: Faber & Faber, 1996);
Prometheus (London: Faber & Faber, 1998).
Collections: *Permanently Bard,* edited by Carol Chillington Rutter (Newcastle upon Tyne: Bloodaxe, 1995);
Laureak's Block and Other Poems (Shipton-on-Stour: Privately printed by Celadine / London: Penguin, 2000).

PRODUCED SCRIPTS: *The Blue Bird,* motion picture, lyrics by Harrison, 20th Century-Fox/Lenfilm, 1976;
The Oresteia, television, Channel 4, 9 October 1983;
The Big H, television, with music by Dominic Muldowney, BBC Two, 26 December 1984;
The Mysteries, television, Channel 4, 22 December 1985;
Yan Tan Tethera, television, Channel 4, 19 April 1987;
"Letters in the Rock," television, *Loving Memory,* BBC Two, 16 July 1987;
"Mimmo Perrella Non è Più," television, *Loving Memory,* BBC Two, 23 July 1987;
"The Muffled Bells," television, *Loving Memory,* BBC Two, 30 July 1987;
"Cheating the Void," television, *Loving Memory,* 6 August 1987;
v., television, Channel 4, November 1987;
"The Blasphemers' Banquet," television, *Byline,* BBC One, 31 July 1989;
The Gaze of the Gorgon, television, BBC Two, October 1992;
Black Daisies for the Bride, television, BBC Two, June 1993;
A Maybe Day in Kazakhstan, television, Channel 4, May 1994;
The Shadow of Hiroshima, television, Channel 4, May 1994;
Prometheus, motion picture, Arts Council of England for Channel 4, 1998.

OTHER: Translations in *The Greek Anthology,* edited by Peter Jay (London: Allen Lane, 1973);
Five Modern Poets, edited by Barbara Bleiman (Harlow: Longman, 1993);

Penguin Modern Poets, volume 5 (London: Penguin, 1995).

SELECTED PERIODICAL PUBLICATIONS–UNCOLLECTED: "Two into One: The Beast with Two Backs" and "Grog," *Guardian* (London), 12 January 1994;

"Laureate's Block," *Guardian* (London), 9 February 1999.

Richard Eyre, the former artistic director of the Royal National Theatre, has said of Tony Harrison that his is the "one name that seems to me to justify the claim that there is an unbroken tradition in the British theatre going back to the fifteenth century" (*Tony Harrison: Loiner,* 1997). Harrison's particular strength as a dramatist is his resolute determination to return the poetic voice to the theater, but he returns it in ways that would have seemed quite bewildering to the previous generation who attempted it. Harrison declared in 1987: "Poetry is all I write, whether for books, or readings, or for the National Theatre, or for the opera house and concert hall, or even for TV. All these activities are part of the same quest for a public poetry, though in that word 'public' I would never want to exclude inwardness" (quoted in *Bloodaxe Critical Anthologies 1: Tony Harrison,* 1991). A wide-ranging eclecticism is perhaps the most prominent feature of Harrison's artistic production: in addition to publishing an extensive range of poetry and scripts for stage and screen (both television and motion picture), he has also directed and edited many of his own theater and movie scripts. Yet, Harrison insists that there is an overall identity underlying the different facets of his work and that he writes primarily and essentially as a poet, using different media as appropriate.

Harrison's verse drama is different in kind from, for example, the attempts of T. S. Eliot and Christopher Fry during the first half of the century, which Harrison himself has described as "depressing" and lacking in energy. In his view, poetry should draw attention to the physical quality of the language itself, providing a source of energy and strength and creating "a life support system" that allows an artist to go on speaking in spite of the horrors perpetrated during the twentieth century. Poetry also offers Harrison an all encompassing artistic tool that "can take in the holy and the crude" and that lends itself to the writer's favorite strategy of "contamination," whereby the Yorkshire vernacular is brought into formal metric structures, and elements normally divided between so-called high and low cultures are played off against each other. As Harrison said in a 1992 interview, "my interest as a poet is to use the most 'refined' forms and fill them with a language that has not normally been granted permission to inhabit those forms." Harrison is acutely aware of the ideological and class bias that is manifested within the definitions of "culture" in a society, frequently referring to his own experience at Leeds Grammar School, where he was not permitted to read poetry aloud in English lessons because of his Yorkshire accent. The formal structures of verse, then, constitute the ideal means of expressing the tensions and oppositions that run through contemporary reality, while at the same time enabling the poet to relate dialectically with the language he employs. This dialectic forms a recurrent theme in his openly autobiographical sonnet sequence, *Continuous,* collected in *Continuous: Fifty Sonnets from "The School of Eloquence"* (1981) and is also prominent in the poem *v.* (collected in *v. Tony Harrison,* 1985)–probably Harrison's most widely known work to date, thanks to the extensive media coverage it received following the heated polemic surrounding the television broadcast of Eyre's movie version in 1987.

Harrison was born in Leeds on 30 April 1937 into a working-class family; he was the first child of Harry Harrison, a baker, and Florence Horner Harrison. At the age of eleven, Harrison obtained a scholarship from the local grammar school and later attended Leeds University, where he took an undergraduate degree in Classics and a postgraduate degree in linguistics. On 16 January 1960 he married Rosemarie Crossfield Dietzsch, an artist; they eventually had two children, Jane and Max. In 1962 Harrison moved with his family to Nigeria, spending four years as a lecturer in English at Ahmadu Bello University. He also lived in Prague for a year, teaching at Charles University. In Prague he became aware of the importance, for people living under an oppressive regime, of "reading ancient texts as if they were new," that is, of bending the culture and literature of the past to the expression of new, subversive meanings. He made extensive use of this lesson in his future career as a poet. In 1967 he returned to Britain, where he became the first Northern Arts Literary Fellow, a post he held again in 1976–1977. Since then, Harrison has taken up residence in Newcastle upon Tyne, a refuge to which he continues to retreat in order to work and write, and to escape the more nomadic side of his existence.

In 1969, for instance, a UNESCO fellowship took him to Cuba, Brazil, Senegal, Gambia, and Mozambique. After his second marriage, in 1984, to the soprano Teresa Stratas, the United States became an important reference point, with Harrison dividing his time between Northern Florida, where he composed his bittersweet love poem *A Kumquat for John Keats* (1981), and frequent stays in New York, where he continued a collaboration with the Metropolitan Opera that dates

Program cover for the National Theatre production of Harrison's 1973 adaptation of Molière's Le Misanthrope

from 1970, when he wrote the libretto for Bedřich Smetana's *The Bartered Bride.*

Harrison's life is also punctuated by continuous visits to Greece, which he sees as his spiritual homeland, and throughout the 1970s he devoted much of his energy to producing a new version of Aeschylus's *The Oresteia* for the National Theatre in England. The trilogy, which was directed eventually by Peter Hall in 1981, won Harrison widespread critical acclaim and was accorded the honor, for a foreign production, of being performed in the open-air theater at Epidauros. More recently, the equally ambitious *Prometheus* (1998) project has taken the poet across Eastern Europe and the former Communist countries in a search for postindustrial locations in which to shoot his mythical movie-poem. This challenging enterprise, however, has not prevented him from fulfilling what he deems to be a poet's public role, and the war poems of the 1990s, published in a British newspaper at the time of the Gulf War, and his mission in Bosnia as a war reporter for *The Guardian,* testify to his unwavering commitment to current concerns. When touted as a highly plausible candidate for poet laureate after the death of Ted Hughes, however, Harrison immediately indicated (in verse) the abyss between the public responsibilities incumbent on an artist appointed from within the political and cultural establishment and those that he was willing to define for himself outside the system.

In 1964, while he was at Ahmadu Bello University in Nigeria, Harrison's first collection of poetry, *Earthworks,* was published, and his first theatrical piece was produced. Working with James Simmons, Harrison translated, adapted, and directed *Aikin Mata,* an African version of Aristophanes' *Lysistrata. Aikin Mata* was written for a group of student actors at Ahmadu Bello University who the year before had won first prize at the Ibadan Students' Drama Festival with Wole Soyinka's *The Lion and the Jewel. Lysistrata,* with its comic treatment of the "sex war," seemed a particularly apt text to adapt to a Nigerian context at that time. Also, it allowed a full panoply of music and dance to be introduced directly into the action in ways that seemed to Harrison, as he stated in the preface to the 1966 publication of *Aikin Mata,* to unite the classical and the African traditions of performance: "Masquerades like the Yoruba *Engungun* of Oshogbo with their dual sacred and profane functions as ancestor spirits and as comic entertainers seem closer to Greek Comedy than anything one has in modern Europe." There was considerable opposition to the production because of its outspoken bawdiness, but it played to capacity audiences and found particular favor among the female students.

Harrison did not write for the theater for nearly ten years. During this period he concentrated on his poetic career, having four volumes of verse published. Then, in 1973 his version of Molière's *Le Misanthrope* (1666), which had been specially commissioned, played the National Theatre in London. Although the production was to celebrate the tercentenary of the first production of the play and was originally planned to be played in seventeenth-century dress but with a text in contemporary colloquial English, Harrison transposed the action to 1966 and the "reign" of Charles de Gaulle in France. The inclusion of contemporary material in Harrison's production meant that there was never any real attempt to translate Molière's original text, and Harrison's use of lively and varied rhyming couplets reanimated the play, rescuing it from its museum status as a safely located classic.

The production was immensely popular; it played to packed houses and enjoyed almost universal praise from the critics. Irving Wardle wrote in *The Times* (London) that the production was "as penetrating a re-evaluation of a masterpiece as has yet appeared on this stage" (23 February 1973) while Robert Brustein in *The Observer* (London) called it "the most actable version of Molière I know" (4 March 1973). Unusually, many critics went out of their way to talk about the contribution of the "translator." The reviewer for *TLS: The Times Literary Supplement* (16 March 1973) said, "He isn't the first translator to have rhymed Molière, but the sheer difficulty of the task justifies the praise he has received."

Harrison worked with the heroic couplet form for his next play, *Phaedra Britannica,* a version of Jean Racine's *Phèdre* (1677). Set in nineteenth-century India during the British Raj, Harrison's play was first performed by the National Theatre Company at the Old Vic Theatre in 1975. Although Diana Rigg was widely praised for her enactment of the "Phaedra" figure, the Governor's wife, Harrison said in the preface to the published edition of his adaptation that he was anxious that the play should not become simply an opportunity to display the talents of a single star: "When a play becomes a 'vehicle' only, the greater part of it has died. . . . The way to re-energise *Phedre* . . . is to rediscover a *social* structure which makes the tensions and polarities of the play significant again. To make the roles, neglected for the sake of the "vehicle" role, meaningful again. To grasp the *play* entire."

Harrison's next theatrical piece, *Bow Down* (1977), was a collaboration with the composer Harrison Birtwistle and was a collage of versions of the folk ballad "The Two Sisters." *Bow Down* represented new territory for him technically, but with its emphasis on the emotions and problems of ordinary nonepic people the work can be seen as a part of the writer's refusal to leave behind his own roots. William Mann wrote of it in *The Times* (London) for 6 July 1977, "the tale of the two sisters has become a fuller saga, including a sophisticated but earthy rhymed version of the drowned sister's pillage by the Miller and his licentious varlet . . . and ending with the gruesome fate of the jealous dark sister"; Peter Hayworth in *The Observer* (London) for 10 July 1977 praised Birtwistle's score, saying that it "has a characteristically Northern directness that exactly reflects the text."

While feeling a particular obligation to lend his voice to those who have been silenced or marginalized within history, Harrison is also conscious of his own illegitimacy as their mouthpiece since, as he admits, "I never found a way of using the art I have to speak directly to the people I am writing about." His rewriting of the Medieval Mystery Cycle of plays perhaps typifies the contradiction. This large-scale epic project began in 1977 with *The Passion* and was followed in 1981 by *The Nativity* and in 1985 by *Doomsday,* when the whole three-part event was performed as *The Mysteries* at the National Theatre's Cottesloe Theatre, running from late morning until night. Harrison has recalled his own earlier bewilderment at seeing a production of the York cycle in 1951 in which the principal roles were all taken by actors speaking standard English with a southern or London accent; in *The Mysteries* he set out to redress the balance by having biblical characters speak in Yorkshire dialect and alliterative verse, as well as by introducing modern idiomatic expressions, which brought alive the medieval language with renewed energy. He also determined to echo idioms of medieval staging, not through archaeological or "period" accuracy, but by invoking a contemporary equivalent to the local guilds whose members had created the original production; thus, the actors in the production became construction workers, miners, carpenters, and cleaners–apparently using their skills and tools to make the performance happen. Their joint contribution to what Michael Billington called an "unforgettable piece of communal theatre" is acknowledged in the published text, where they share with the dramatist–an "artisan" among artisans–the credit for the creation of the play. By filtering the medieval text through a twentieth-century consciousness, Harrison is partially able to recapture the fundamental topicality of the mystery plays, in which the retelling of the biblical story was turned into a vehicle for debating contemporary issues and even for voicing social unease–as with the complaints about the hardships of everyday life in the *Second Shepherds' Play.* In the 1984 promenade production spectators found themselves in a dark "Hell" lit by miners' pit helmets, and later saw the devil, a soiled worker, sink into his Hell pit before Jesus Christ's commanding hand. At a time when mine workers were contesting the closure of pits by the Conservative government under Margaret Thatcher, these medieval plays, apparently so remote in time and mood, acquired a renewed impact and relevance in speaking to the present. Yet, the composition of audiences visiting the Royal National Theatre meant that the event was in danger of falling into the trap, identified by John McGrath, of "turning authentic working-class experience into satisfying thrills for the bourgeoisie."

Many of Harrison's theater works have their origins in Greek texts. While acknowledging his own "obsessive concern" with classical drama, Harrison also explains his interest in terms of "a search for a new theatricality and also a way of expressing dissatisfaction with the current theatre," which he sees as too frequently restricted by the confines of inherited naturalistic conventions and newly established television clichés. Within his reworking of the Greek model, Harrison seeks to dislocate audience expectations and assumptions, inviting analysis of the lines of old texts. In his 1981 adaptation of Aeschylus's *Oresteia* for the National Theatre, for example, Greek characters and choruses were played by an all-male cast of masked actors, speaking strongly alliterative verse reminiscent of the Anglo-Saxon tradition and filled with Northern vernacular and intonation. As always in Harrison's adaptations, the relationship between past and present is dynamic, and a principle of "volatility" is employed, whereby a form is haunted by its antecedent or successor; a past situation foreshadows a present one; a mythical character changes into its contemporary counterpart, or vice versa; and narratives move along analogical rather than chronological lines. This juxtaposition of varying spatial and temporal levels results in texts that are inhabited by different voices, and in his appropriations of ancient myths, Harrison ensures that conflicting versions of the same story are narrated. A similar polyphonic principle is apparent within the performance itself, in which the original plurality of languages in Greek drama–word, song, music, dance, and visual poetry–is re-created to guarantee a plurality of perception.

Through such strategies Harrison attempts to fulfill what he deems to be a poet's duty: lending his voice to the inarticulate and to social groups that have been rendered historically and culturally invisible. Often, as with both *The Oresteia* and *Medea: A Sex-War Opera* (1985), the version of the myth that Harrison sets out to recover is one that offers a female perspective that has become hidden or submerged. In his 1985 reworking of the Euripidean tragedy in a libretto commissioned by the New York Metropolitan Opera, which still remains unperformed, for example, the idea of polyphony is given a literal rendering, as previous narrators of Medea's story–from Euripides to George Buchanan, Pierre Corneille, Giovanni Simone Mayr, Luigi Cherubini, Pedro Calderón de la Barca, Francesco Cavalli, and Catulle Mendès–are made to repeat their charges of infanticide, against a female chorus that struggles to reclaim and assert the woman's innocence.

For Harrison, Greek theater also provides a model in terms of processes of theatrical creation. In particular, he has chosen to emulate the practice of writing for a specific team of actors and a single performance to be given at a specific site, arguing that the performance, by adhering to the original ephemeral nature of the theatrical event, enormously increases an audience's attentiveness and participation. Similarly, a play may draw added impact from the topical–and eminently political–connotations of the location for which it is written; for this reason, Harrison, even before his move away from institutional venues toward what he has called the "kamikaze performances" of the 1990s, had determined that his texts should be rewritten for each space in which they were performed. He followed such a pattern, for instance, with *The Trackers of Oxyrhynchus* (1988), his radical adaptation based on the surviving fragments of Sophocles' lost satyr play *Ichneutae,* which Harrison originally created for a single performance at the ancient stadium of Delphi in 1988 and which he significantly altered for its transfer to the Olivier stage at the National Theatre and again for productions at Salts Mill in Saltaire, Yorkshire, and at Art Carnuntum, near Vienna, in 1990.

In re-presenting the satyr play–an integral part of the Greek theatrical experience that remains largely unfamiliar to modern audiences–*The Trackers of Oxy-*

Scene from The Trackers of Oxyrhynchus, *Harrison's radical adaptation based on the surviving fragments of Sophocles' play* Ichneutae *(photograph by Sandra Lousada)*

rhynchus investigates the processes of cultural transmission and their sociopolitical ramifications. The play opens on two Victorian Egyptologists, Grenfell and Hunt, excavating the archaeological site of Oxyrhynchus in a painstaking endeavor to unearth the lost masterpieces of Greek literature. While Grenfell is intent on sorting out heaps of ancient papyri, Apollo manifests himself to the awestruck scholar and orders him to come up with at least one dramatic specimen in which the glorious god of the arts plays the lead. This opening scene marks the transition to Harrison's inset play, as the audience is suddenly ushered into a performance of *Ichneutae,* with Grenfell, possessed by the god, assuming the identity of Apollo, while his colleague is turned into Sophocles' other protagonist, the elderly chief satyr, Silenus. The reenactment of the mythical story of the satyrs' pursuit of Apollo's lost herds runs parallel to the attempted reconstruction of the Sophoclean fragment, with Silenus involving the present-day audience in the search for missing words to fill in the gaps, or "brackets," in the text. Eventually, the trackers reach the cave, where the author of the theft, Hermes, has invented the lyre by craftily turning the guts of the cows into strings. The conclusion shows the symbolic birth of art from nature, with Apollo seizing the sublime instrument from the infant god's hands as compensation and banishing the helpful satyrs from what is now to become the exclusive domain of "high" art.

Through its metatheatrical structure *The Trackers of Oxyrhynchus* manages to involve the contemporary spectators in the quest, urging them to grasp the political implications of the theatrical event. The silencing of the satyrs comes to symbolize the fate of all voices that do not conform to received standards of "art" in a dichotic culture that operates according to socially divisive categories of high and low, elitist and popular, legitimate and illegitimate. In Harrison's play dispossession is shown to result in violence and self-destructiveness: the trackers employed by Apollo are made to represent an embryonic working class and become, in the National Theatre version of the play, both the homeless of the South Bank of London and violent football hooligans who, in destroying the papyrus, obliterate the only extant record of their own cultural heritage. Through Apollo's act of banishing from the shrine of art the presumed coarseness of physicality and of laughter,

Harrison also draws attention to the incomparable loss for culture and society at large that such a division creates–for "Apollonians" of today as well as for "satyrs" of today. By concluding the tragic trilogy on a festive, life-affirming note, Harrison made the satyr play itself testament to the capacity of Greek society for coping with pain or, in Harrison's own words, for "walking through fire still singing." In the century of concentration camps, Hiroshima, and the permanent threat of extinction, the drama, in Harrison's words, "open-eyed about suffering but with a heart still open to celebration," seemed to provide an artistic, and indeed existential, model of paramount importance.

Harrison continued to mine near-contemporary experience with *Square Rounds,* produced in 1992 on the Olivier stage of the National Theatre in London. Set in World War I, the "theatre piece," as the playwright described it in the program, links the inventor of the modern machine-gun, Hiram Maxim, and the producer of poison gas, Fritz Haber. With music by Dominic Muldowney, *Square Rounds* seemed to reviewer Kristy Milne in the *Sunday Telegraph* (4 October 1992) more like a revue than a play: "The comperes are top-hatted scientists. The chorus girls are singing munitions workers. But the star of the show is nitrogen, which human invention has used for both creative and destructive ends."

Harrison's writing does not always originate with a text or narrative, but often derives from an actual space; such is the case with *Poetry or Bust* (1993), a text written to be performed in a former wool combing shed at Salts Mill in West Yorkshire. The play dramatizes the emblematic career of John Nicholson, a former mill worker who became known as the "Airdale bard" and who sold off his talent to powerful patrons and to the London literary market. Through this narrative, Harrison explores personal allegiances in terms of geography, class, and culture, alluding perhaps more explicitly than anywhere else in his work to his own "borderline" social and artistic identity, as he plays on the double possibilities of the term "bust" in identifying the temptation to an artist of forfeiting artistic and personal integrity in the name of posterity, or, as the Muses express the thought in the play, to "chuck away your voice to follow fame."

The Kaisers of Carnuntum, performed in Vienna in 1995 and set in an ancient Roman amphitheater, is another example of Harrison's use of space and location as well as history as key characters in the drama. During the second century A.D. Carnuntum was one of the Roman Empire's frontier posts against German barbarians and the place where the philosopher-emperor Marcus Aurelius wrote his lofty *Meditations,* which earned him the posthumous reputation of a high-minded intellectual. How, then, could history accommodate his violent, riotous, and delinquent son, Commodus? Quite simply: by denying Aurelius's paternity of such a bestial creature and accusing Faustina, the emperor's wife, of having conceived Commodus with a gladiator. In Harrison's play Faustina speaks up against historical falsification, simultaneously and regretfully acknowledging her maternal bonds to the *ur*-hooligan of the classical world and Commodus's undeniably human origins and exposing by this means the common process by which historical transmission denies or sanitizes the troublesome matters of the past: by reclaiming Commodus's right to Carnuntum, amphitheater of today and "place of blood" of yesterday, *The Kaisers of Carnuntum* shows civilization and culture to be inseparable from the bestiality and violence they bring with them. Furthermore, through locating his play in this specific frontier post, Harrison brings contemporary significations into play: once the northern border of the Roman Empire, Carnuntum became, in modern times, the line of demarcation between Western and Eastern Europe and so, once again, between "civilization" and "barbarism"–divisions that necessarily require blurring.

Among Harrison's work of the late 1990s is *The Prince's Play,* an adaptation of Victor Hugo's *Le Roi S'Amuse,* which opened at the Olivier auditorium at the National Theatre in April 1996. This play explores the decline of the monarchy, setting events in Victorian England, which always had parallels with the present crisis of confidence in royalty.

Harrison's television plays for the BBC and for Channel 4 represent a strikingly unusual combination of documentary and metaphor, and they offer a telling demonstration of the capacity of television to provide a space in which, contrary to widespread assumptions, language can be both spoken and heard effectively. According to Harrison, the medium lends itself to poetical use, not least in the way that structural analogies can be identified between the process of film editing and the ways in which poetry organizes word patterns. In 1998 *Prometheus,* his first feature motion picture–which he wrote, directed, and edited–was released. The text, which is entirely in verse, is based on the myth of Prometheus but also narrates the decline of one of the founding myths of contemporary civilization: industrialism.

Interview:

Clive Wilmer, ed., *Poets Talking: The "Poet of the Month" Interviews from BBC Radio 3* (Manchester: Carcanet, 1994).

Bibliography:

John R. Kaiser, ed., *Tony Harrison: A Bibliography 1957–1987* (London: Mansell, 1989).

References:

Gillian Beer, *Open Fields: Science in Cultural Encounter* (Oxford: Clarendon Press, 1996);

Sandie Byrne, *H, v. & O: The Poetry of Tony Harrison* (Manchester: Manchester University Press, 1998);

Byrne, ed., *Tony Harrison: Loiner* (Oxford: Clarendon Press, 1997);

Ruby Cohn, "Digging the Greeks: New Versions of Old Classics," in *Contemporary British Theatre,* edited by Theodore Shank (London: Macmillan, 1994), pp. 41–54;

Neil Corcoran, *English Poetry since 1940* (London: Longman, 1993);

Robert Crawford, *Devolving English Literature* (Oxford: Oxford University Press, 1992);

Romana Huk, "Postmodern Classics: The Verse Drama of Tony Harrison," in *British and Irish Drama since 1960,* edited by James Acheson (Basingstoke: Macmillan, 1992), pp. 202–226;

Joe Kelleher, *Tony Harrison* (Plymouth: Northcote House, 1996);

Marianne McDonald, *Ancient Sun, Modern Light: Greek Drama on the Modern Stage* (New York & Oxford: Columbia University Press, 1992);

Sean O'Brien, *The Deregulated Muse* (Newcastle upon Tyne: Bloodaxe, 1998);

Linden Peach, *Ancestral Lines: Culture and Identity in the Work of Six Contemporary Poets* (Bridgend, Wales: Seren, 1992);

Anthony Rowland, *Tony Harrison and the Holocaust* (Liverpool: Liverpool University Press, 2001);

Carol Chillington Rutter, "Harrison, Herakles, and Wailing Women: 'Labourers' at Delphi," *New Theatre Quarterly,* 13, no. 50 (May 1997): 133–143;

Rutter, "The Poet and the Geldshark," in *Acts of War: The Representation of Military Conflict on the British Stage and Television since 1945,* edited by Tony Howard and John Stokes (Aldershot: Scholar Press, 1996);

Rick Rylance, "Tony Harrison's Languages," in *Contemporary Poetry Meets Modern Theory,* edited by Anthony Easthope and John O. Thompson (New York & London: Harvester Wheatsheaf, 1991);

Michael Schmidt, *Reading Modern Poetry* (London: Routledge, 1989);

Luke Spencer, *The Poetry of Tony Harrison* (London: Harvester Wheatsheaf, 1994);

Oliver Taplin, *Greek Fire* (London: Cape, 1989);

Anthony Thwaite, *Poetry Today: A Critical Guide to British Poetry 1960–1984* (London: Longman, 1985);

Willie Van Peer, ed., *The Taming of the Text: Explorations in Language, Literature and Culture* (London: Routledge, 1988).

Ron Hutchinson

(1947 –)

Michael Mangan
University of Wales, Aberystwyth

PLAY PRODUCTIONS: *Says I, Says He,* Sheffield, Crucible Theatre, 15 November 1977; London, 1978; New York, 1979;
Eejits, London, 1978;
Jews/Arabs, London, 1978;
Anchorman, London, 1979;
Christmas of a Nobody, 1979;
The Irish Play, London, 12 November 1980;
Into Europe, London, 1981;
Risky City, Coventry, Belgrade Theatre, 11 June 1981;
The Dillen, adapted from a book by Angela Hewins, Stratford-upon-Avon, The Other Place, 1983;
Rat in the Skull, London, Royal Court Theatre, 31 August 1984; New York, 1985;
Mary, after the Queen, by Hutchinson and Hewins, Stratford-upon-Avon, The Other Place, 1985;
Curse of the Baskervilles, adapted from Sir Arthur Conan Doyle's novel *The Hound of the Baskervilles,* Plymouth, Theatre Royal, 25 June 1987;
Babbitt: A Marriage, adapted from Sinclair Lewis's novel *Babbitt,* Los Angeles, Mark Taper Forum, 30 August 1987;
Pygmies in the Ruins, Belfast, Lyric Players' Theatre, 7 November 1991; London, Royal Court Theatre, 20 February 1992;
Flight, adapted from Mikhail Bulgakov's play *Beg,* London, Royal National Theatre, 12 February 1997; revised, London, Royal National Theatre, 5 February 1998;
Burning Issues, London, Hampstead Theatre, April 2000;
The Beau, London, Theatre Royal, Haymarket, 24 May 2001.

BOOKS: *Says I, Says He: A Play in Two Acts* (Newark, Del.: Proscenium, 1980);
Rat in the Skull (London: Methuen, 1984; revised edition, London: Methuen / Portsmouth, N.H.: Heinemann, 1995);
Connie (London: Methuen, 1985);
Flight (London: Nick Hern, 1998);
Burning Issues (London: Faber & Faber, 2000);
Beau Brummel (London: Oberon, 2001).

PRODUCED SCRIPTS: *Roaring Boys,* radio, 1977;
Twelve off the Belt, television, 1977;
Murphy Unchained, radio, 1978;
Deasy Desperate, television, 1979;
The Last Window Cleaner, television, 1979;
The Out of Town Boys, television, 1979;
Deasy, television, 1979;
There Must Be a Door, radio, 1979;
The Winkler, television, 1979;
Bull Week, television, 1980;
Motorcade, radio, 1980;
Risky City, radio, BBC, 1981;
Bird of Prey, television, 4 episodes, BBC One, 1982;
Connie, television, 13 episodes, Central Independent Television, 1985;
"The Marksman," television, adapted from a novel by Hugh C. Rae, *Unnatural Causes,* 1987;
Larkin, radio, 1988;
Troopers, radio, 1988;
Dead Man Out, television, 1989;
The Murderers among Us: The Simon Wiesenthal Story, television, 1989;
Perfect Witness, television, HBO, 1989;
Red King, White Knight, television, HBO, 1989;
The Josephine Baker Story, television, HBO, 1991;
Prisoner of Honor, television, HBO, 1991;
Blue Ice, motion picture, Guild / Home Box Office / M&M Productions, 1992;
The Burning Season, television, HBO, 1994;
Against the Wall, television, HBO, 1994;
Fatherland, television, HBO, 1994;
Slave of Dreams, television, Showtime, 1995;
The Tuskegee Airmen, television, HBO, 1995;
The Island of Dr. Moreau, by Hutchinson and Richard Stanley, motion picture, New Line Cinema, 1996.

A submerged but discernible element of autobiography runs through much of Ron Hutchinson's playwriting. This autobiographical dimension is apparent not so much in the specifics of his plays as in the overarching theme of much of his work, which concerns the

Brian Cox as Nelson and Colin Convey as Roche in a scene from the 1984 Royal Court Theatre production of Hutchinson's Rat in the Skull

relationship between England and Ireland, between the present and the past. To characterize him as an Irish playwright, or even as a playwright for whom Ireland is a key topic, is reductive; nonetheless, much of his best work has been written on this theme. His settings have included the dance-hall circuit of the London Irish Ceilidh band in *Eejits* (1978); a run-down Irish club in the English Midlands, which becomes the darkly comic battleground for age-old rivalries and hatreds in *The Irish Play* (1980); the inner-city bleakness of Coventry, recalled in the memories of a dying Irish youth in *Risky City* (1981); and a Paddington police cell in which a suspected member of the Irish Republican Army is being interrogated by a Royal Ulster Constabulary (RUC) inspector in *Rat in the Skull* (1984).

Hutchinson was born in 1947 near Lisburn, County Antrim, Northern Ireland. He moved to Coventry with his parents as a child, and this duality of citizenship gives a particular angle to his writings about England and Ireland. He told Sarah Hemming in a 1992 interview:

> I don't write about Ireland because I have a burning political agenda. I don't have some big belief that I know how to solve the situation or that the solution lies in one thing or the other. No, the reason I write about it is the fact that I feel I was expelled from paradise when I was a child. And that's why I write with passionate feelings and rage and use such stark images–it's the rage of the child who was hurled from paradise and wants to know why. We grew up in a thatched cottage surrounded by green fields. I now know that that paradise was kept aloft by a bitter and twisted thing. I grew up in Antrim in the Protestant heartland and we used to play around the ruins of a house that we called "the Fenian house"–I later found out it was because a Catholic man tried to live there and they'd burnt it. And I now know what all the whisperings I used to hear as a child were about. One of my uncles was shot on the border, and I remember going into Belfast on 12 July [a

> day when marches are held to celebrate a Protestant victory over Catholic troops in 1690]. For me, as a kid, it was a fun day, but now I know it was fuelled by hatred. I suppose my writing comes from the urge to go back and discover that.

After leaving school Hutchinson held a variety of jobs, from gutting fish to working as a clerk in the Ministry of Defense and investigating claims for the Department of Health and Social Security. In 1977 his first play, *Says I, Says He,* was staged at Crucible Theatre in Sheffield; it transferred to London the following year and to New York City the year after that. From 1977 to 1981 his plays were being staged at the rate of about two per year; he also had five works broadcast on British Broadcasting Corporation (BBC) radio and seven on television. In 1978–1979 he was writer in residence at the Royal Shakespeare Company in London.

In 1982 Hutchinson wrote a high-profile television miniseries, *Bird of Prey,* a Hollywood-style political thriller in which an ordinary man is unwillingly caught up in dangerous events involving higher powers beyond his control. Henry Jay, a benignly plodding, stamp-collecting civil servant in the Department of Trade and Industry, is writing an academic report on computer fraud when he stumbles across a massive criminal and political conspiracy. The senior policeman whom he has befriended is murdered, and he meets mysterious and beautiful women, hears strange rumors about a shadowy organization known as *Le Pouvoir* (The Power), and begins to suspect the involvement of personages at high bureaucratic and government levels. When his life and that of his wife become threatened, Henry goes on the offensive, rescues his wife, and unmasks the evildoers.

In 1983 Hutchinson adapted *The Dillen: Memories of a Man of Stratford-upon-Avon* (1981), a relatively unknown book about rural life edited by Angela Hewins from tape-recorded conversations with her husband's grandfather, George Hewins. The play was commissioned by the Royal Shakespeare Company, which performed it in a highly successful promenade production around Stratford-upon-Avon.

The play for which Hutchinson is most likely to be remembered is the startling and powerful *Rat in the Skull,* staged by Max Stafford-Clark at the Royal Court Theatre in 1984. This play stands alongside dramas from the period by writers such as John Arden, Howard Brenton, Brian Friel, Stewart Parker, and David Rudkin who employ the techniques of the theater not merely to portray the conflict between Catholics and Protestants in Northern Ireland but as a tool for understanding it. The setting is a London police station, where Detective Superintendent Harris of the Metropolitan Police has been called in to investigate the assault on a suspected Irish Republican Army (IRA) bomber, Michael Patrick de Valera Demon Bomber Roche (as he repeatedly identifies himself), by Inspector Nelson, a star RUC officer flown in from Belfast to help in the interrogation of Roche. The incident is particularly galling to Harris, since before the assault Roche had almost been persuaded to turn informer. Harris starts by questioning the duty officer, Constable Naylor, who is already in trouble for disobeying a standing order not to leave an RUC officer alone with an IRA suspect. When Naylor casually refers to Roche as "Paddy," Nelson turns on the hapless officer:

> If I hear you refer to this man again as Paddy, well–I'll get annoyed. Understood? . . . Likewise Mickey, taig or Fenian bastard. . . . Even if he *is* a Mickey, taig or Fenian bastard, because each one of those has a shade of meaning a beardless sprig like yourself is not capable of comprehending. Each a particular conjugation in the grammar of hate, as my missus would say. A precise inflection. As she might say.

Much of the pleasure of the work lies in its language–particularly Nelson's speeches, which dominate the first part of the play. His interrogation of Roche is a bravura performance in which he attempts to seduce both the IRA man and the audience, playing parts and shifting roles with a deadly nimbleness. Words–even simple words of insult such as "Paddy" and "taig"–carry weight and are the rightful property only of those whose lived experience has earned them the right to use the expressions. The ignorant Naylor has no such right; nor, by extension, does the audience.

As the interrogation–or "interview," as Nelson insists on calling it–proceeds, the hostility between Nelson and Roche escalates against a backdrop of projected images of Roche's bruised and bleeding face and body. The audience is in no doubt as to where this conflict is leading: the climax will be a brutal assault on the IRA suspect by the RUC officer. And so it is–but it occurs in a quite unexpected way. Far from making Roche the romantically rebellious victim of British/Protestant brutality, the play turns the moment inside out. Attempting to understand Nelson's attack on Roche, Harris grasps for conventionally acceptable motives, such as resentment stemming from Nelson's failed marriage. But by now the audience is beginning to understand the complex interplay of love and hate that has led Nelson to listen to the "rat in the skull." This small voice of doubt drove him to commit the assault, which ended the attempt to "turn" Roche and will lead to the collapse of the prosecution's case, thereby saving Roche's life.

Hutchinson's television miniseries *Connie* (1985) is a family business saga. The title character pioneered a fashion chain in the early 1970s but was outmaneuvered, thrown off the board, and bought out of the firm by her grasping relatives. She went to Greece, where she lived off the proceeds of the sale until the money was gone. Now in her early forties, she has returned to England and wants her old world back. She fights her way back into the firm, pays off some old scores, wins some boardroom battles, and loses others. At the moment of her apparent triumph she loses it all and ends up where she started. The predictability of the plot is offset by the labyrinthine complexity of the relationships among the characters as they continually leap into bed with and betray one another. When the series ends, Connie is leaving the country with her devoted lover; it is clear that before long she will betray him, too. Hutchinson's novelization of *Connie* appeared the same year as the television series.

Also in 1985 Hutchinson collaborated with Hewins on the play *Mary, after the Queen.* In 1987 he adapted Sir Arthur Conan Doyle's classic Sherlock Holmes novel *The Hound of the Baskervilles* (1902) for the stage as *Curse of the Baskervilles.* That same year his adaptation of Sinclair Lewis's novel *Babbit* (1922), titled *Babbit: A Marriage,* was produced in Los Angeles. Hutchinson moved to that city the following year.

Hutchinson's next original piece for the stage, *Pygmies in the Ruins* (1991), features a central character who, like the author, emigrates from Ireland to America. Harry Washburn is a workaholic RUC police photographer in Belfast. The strain of his job leads to a nervous breakdown, and in this half-crazed state he becomes obsessed by the unsolved death of a Dublin servant girl in 1871 after her apparent seduction by a factory owner. The details of the Victorian case merge in his mind with those of the case on which he was working at the time of his breakdown, that of a boy shot to death in his home in Belfast. Is the nineteenth-century case a typically Victorian scandal of sexuality and class oppression? Is the twentieth-century murder really a sectarian killing? These questions are not answered: the boy's killer is not found, and it is not even clear whether the girl was murdered or committed suicide. What does emerge is the darkness at the heart of Belfast past and present–a darkness revealed by Washburn and by his Victorian counterpart, the Dublin physician

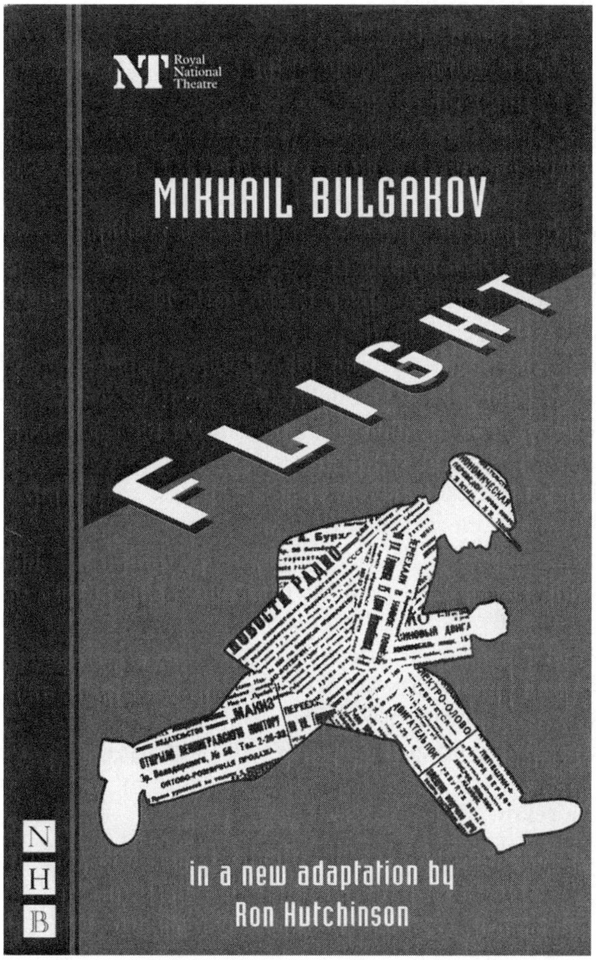

Cover for the published version (1998) of Hutchinson's adaptation of Bulgakov's 1928 play Beg

Dr. Mulcahy, whose inquiries are continually thwarted by the factory owner's family.

The traditional Irish opposition between Dublin and Belfast, between the old-fashioned, down-at-the-heels, stagnant, but civilized South and the energetic, brash, and progressive industrial capitalism of the North, is played out against a pair of investigations that culminate in Washburn's hallucinatory trial at the hands of accusers from both historical periods. "Who are we?" he asks. "Are we the pygmies? Is this done to us or do we do it to ourselves?" Washburn's nightmare state of confusion is a metaphor for the difficulty of finding a solution to the situation in Northern Ireland. At the end of the play Washburn is pulled back from the brink of suicide and decides to immigrate to America. The play suggests that the process that Washburn has passed through is a kind of redemption and that his leaving Belfast is a positive step. Critics, however, have generally seen the ending as a cop-out. *Pygmies in the*

Ruins is an ambitious play that, perhaps, tries to deal with too many issues.

In California, Hutchinson wrote screenplays for television and motion pictures. His credits include some well-respected projects, such as *The Burning Season* (1994), a television movie about the life of the murdered South American activist Chico Mendes, as well as more questionable ones, such as *Prisoner of Honor* (1991), a television movie directed by Ken Russell about Alfred Dreyfus, the nineteenth-century French army officer who was wrongfully convicted of treason, and the motion picture *The Island of Dr. Moreau* (1996), adapted by Hutchinson and Richard Stanley from H. G. Wells's 1896 novel about a mad scientist who transforms animals into human-like creatures. Other television movies, such as the Old Testament-inspired *Slave of Dreams* (1995), produced by Dino de Laurentiis, have been unabashedly commercial projects. As a result, Hutchinson's metamorphosis into Hollywood screenwriter has led to accusations in the United Kingdom that he has sold out or is prostituting his talent. A 1997 interview with Hutchinson in *The Guardian* (London), in fact, is titled "Whoring for Hollywood" and uses phrases such as "the happy hooker" and "turning tricks in Tinseltown."

Yet, Hutchinson has not deserted the theater and is still able to command the biggest stages in the United Kingdom. *Flight* (1997), his adaptation of Mikhail Bulgakov's play *Beg* (1928), was quite well received. Hutchinson says of the work:

> You could put a cast of 300 into this play to get the sheer scale of it. A train comes onto the stage five times as we follow a group of White Russians, fleeing from the horror that was eating them up in their homeland after the revolution. They go to Constantinople, then to Paris and back again. It's a journey from hope to despair, involving great convolutions of the human spirit. Yet Bulgakov could hardly write a line that wasn't wry and funny. It's a defiant laugh in the face of the horror engulfing his world–a new way of writing that blew apart all that Chekhovian wistfulness.

Structured in eight "dreams," *Flight* follows the exiles with a nightmarish comic logic of its own that swings from epic to farce and back again, breaking the rules of stage narrative and offering a huge vision that is both savagely satirical and strangely romantic–a vision that belongs to both Bulgakov and Hutchinson.

Interviews:

Sarah Hemming, "Distant Voices, Full Lives," *Independent* (London), 19 February 1992;

Chris Arnott, "Whoring for Hollywood," *Guardian* (London), 8 January 1997.

Charlotte Keatley

(5 January 1960 -)

Dymphna Callery
University of Wolverhampton

PLAY PRODUCTIONS: *Dressing for Dinner,* Leeds, Workshop Theatre, 24 May 1982;
Underneath the Arndale, Manchester, 14 June 1982;
The Iron Serpent, Leeds, Workshop Theatre, 23 February 1983;
An Armenian Childhood, by Keatley, Pete Brooks, and Steve Schill, Leeds, Workshop Theatre, 4 March 1983;
Powerhouse, 1984;
The Legend of Padgate, Warrington, Cheshire, Padgate Community Arts Centre, 8 June 1986;
My Mother Said I Never Should, Manchester, Contact Theatre, 25 February 1987; London, Royal Court Theatre, 23 February 1989;
Waiting for Martin, Manchester, Palace Theatre, 8 March 1987;
You're a Nuisance Aren't You, in *Fear and Misery in the Third Term,* by Keatley and others, Liverpool, Playhouse Theatre, 21 March 1989; London, Young Vic Theatre, 21 September 1989;
The Singing Ringing Tree, Manchester, Contact Theatre, 1991;
Our Father, 1994;
The Dream of Reason Produces Monsters, Shanghai, Shanghai Academy Theatre, 8 October 1999; Leeds, Workshop Theatre, 18 December 1999.

BOOK: *My Mother Said I Never Should* (London: Methuen, 1988; revised, 1989; revised edition, London: Methuen in association with the Oxford Stage Company, 1997).

PRODUCED SCRIPTS: *Citizens,* radio, by Keatley and others, BBC Radio 4, 1987-1988, 1989-1990;
My Mother Said I Never Should, radio, BBC Radio 4, 28 January 1989;
Badger, television, Granada Television, 31 March 1989;
Falling Slowly, television, Channel 4, 1991;
Is Green the Same for You? radio, BBC Radio 4, 20 July 1992;
North and South, radio, adapted by Keatley from the 1885 novel by Elizabeth Gaskell, 3 episodes, BBC Radio 4, 16-18 July 1997.

Charlotte Keatley's primary contribution to contemporary theater is her highly acclaimed play *My Mother Said I Never Should.* She received the *Manchester Evening News* Best New Play award after the play's initial run in Manchester in 1987, and after its transfer to London in 1989 she won the *Plays and Players* award and shared the prestigious George Devine Award for Best New Playwright. She was nominated for the Laurence Olivier Most Promising Newcomer to British Theatre in 1990. Considered a modern classic, *My Mother Said I Never Should* is one of the most frequently performed plays in Britain; it has been translated into seventeen languages and has been produced in many other countries.

Keatley told Heidi Stephenson and Natasha Langridge in a 1997 interview that she emphasizes the "silent vocabulary" of theater–choreography, lights, gestures, and glances between characters–because "no line of dialogue can carry as many multiple meanings as that moment in the theater when suddenly you see a face, a light, a gesture, a colour, an image, all combined. . . . Those are where the meaning, the storytelling and the impact lie." Her own experience on stage, she said, led her to understand that the essence of acting is using "the whole body to communicate . . . and if someone has you sitting down through most of Act One, well then you've lost half your capacity to express things." Her work exemplifies the shift in contemporary theater from reverence for the literary text to exploiting the visual dimensions and sculptural qualities of theater.

Keatley was born in London on 5 January 1960. Between 1980 and 1986 she worked as a theater critic for the *Yorkshire Post, Times Educational Supplement, Plays and Players, The Glasgow Herald,* and *The Financial Times,* as well as for the BBC Radio arts review program *Kaleidoscope.* Her work served as a thorough education in theater and sharpened her "critical awareness of how and

Charlotte Keatley

why a play works, or doesn't," she told Lizbeth Goodman in 1990.

Keatley won a *Sunday Times* award for acting while studying at Manchester University. She received a B.A. in drama in 1982 and went on to undertake postgraduate work at the University of Leeds. She told Goodman that people in Leeds were "very much orientated towards visual performance theatre. In Manchester, it was more the literary kind of theatre." After working as a performer, designer, director, and writer with the visually based companies Impact Theatre, Rational Theatre, and Hesitate and Demonstrate, she set up her own visually based three-woman company, Royale Ballé.

Keatley's first play with Royale Ballé, the unpublished *Dressing for Dinner,* was performed in Leeds in 1982. Three teenage girls break into an empty house and excavate 1950s-vintage clothes and domestic items from beneath dust covers and behind peeling wallpaper. "Thematically," Keatley told Goodman, "it was about rituals of self-adornment." The play experiments with image, movement, and gesture to explore relationships between women of two generations. Drawing a visual analogy between dressing a woman in the "essential" wardrobe item, the "little black dress," and dressing a fish in aspic, Keatley provokes laughter and then horror to shock the audience into awareness of how women are oppressed by notions of femininity.

Keatley received a master's degree in theater arts from the University of Leeds in 1983. In February of that year her musical *The Iron Serpent* premiered at the Workshop Theatre in Leeds; the following month *An Armenian Childhood,* on which she collaborated with Pete Brooks and Steve Schill, was produced at the same theater. In 1986 she wrote, designed, and directed a musical community play for the townspeople of Padgate, near Warrington. The cast of *The Legend of Padgate* comprised eighty children and adults, some of them costumed as singing hogs, and the set incorporated two hundred paintings by primary-school children and a double-decker bus. Mark Vibrans was the composer and musical director, but Keatley oversaw the whole operation. She told Stephenson and Langridge, "I can't imagine writing plays without having tried all the different components . . . not just acting, directing or design, but trying to sell tickets or make the poster–because it's such a collaborative art form."

Keatley had written the first draft of *My Mother Said I Never Should* in 1985. After several theaters dedicated to "new writing" rejected the work, Brigid Larmour accepted it for the North West Playwrights' Workshop at the Contact Theatre in 1987 and went on to direct it on the main stage. Keatley says in the preface to the 1997 edition of the published text of the play: "It is impossible to convey how important it was to me to have Brigid's absolute faith in the potential of the play during the year and a half before it was staged." She also credits the cast for their contributions to the final script. Since nearly all of the members of the crew were women, she says, "the sense of female magic was extraordinary. . . . We were making this play that was covering things we hadn't been able to say in theatre before."

My Mother Said I Never Should depicts the lives of four women of four generations of the same family–Doris, Margaret, Jackie, and Rosie–from 1923 to 1987, showing the changing cultural expectations of women in the various periods. Asked by Stephenson and Langridge why she chose this particular time span, Keatley replied, "Because these are four generations in which women's lives have changed more radically than ever before." *My Mother Said I Never Should* traces the pattern of conscious and unconscious repetitions in the mother/daughter relationship, showing the denials and silences that dominate it, the ways that maternal and filial love so often become distorted by social pressures, and the constant seesawing between guilt and duty. "I wrote it," Keatley says in the introduction to the 1988 edition of the play, "because I didn't know of any plays about mothers and daughters. I wanted to write about the two-way bond of love and jealousy." As each representative of the successive generations inches toward autonomy, the preceding one hides her true feelings. The play intersperses naturalistic scenes of the women as adults, which carry the narrative line, with five surrealistic, dreamlike scenes–including the opening scene–in which the same characters appear as children, each dressed in a costume appropriate to her era but interacting with the others as though they are all living in the same period. The fragmented time structure of the naturalistic scenes and the timeless child scenes force the audience to piece together the chronology of the four women's lives.

Doris has no choice but to give up her job when she bears Margaret in the 1930s. Her sacrifices to marriage and motherhood go unrewarded when her husband, Jack, cuts her out of his will and leaves everything to their granddaughter, Jackie. Margaret also chooses the role of housewife and mother, and when Jackie has a daughter, Rosie, at eighteen, Margaret raises the child as her own; Rosie grows up believing that Jackie is her older sister rather than her mother. Margaret returns to work for financial reasons when Rosie becomes a teenager; meanwhile, Jackie, with no maternal responsibilities, has forged a dynamic career as an art dealer. Rosie discovers her true parentage when Margaret dies; she then rejects her biological mother, Jackie, and goes to live with Doris, her great-grandmother. In the penultimate scene of the play these two illegitimate daughters form a bond that transcends their age difference and closes the gap between women born at opposite ends of the century.

Although the men in the women's lives do not appear in the play, they are frequently tantalizingly offstage–Jack is mowing the lawn while Doris and Margaret fold laundry; Margaret's son, Ken, is outside in the car when Margaret picks up the baby, Rosie, from Jackie–so that their presence haunts the play, although their views are transmitted through the women. Rosie addresses Jack after his death at the beginning of act 2, when he has left his and Doris's home to Jackie in his will: "I'm not scared of you, Grandad. It's the others who are. You didn't get to me." Jack represents the patriarchal attitudes of a generation raised by Victorian ideology; Rosie represents women who, having grown up in a period when many of those attitudes have been successfully challenged, are reaching out for independence.

This evolution is underlined in the penultimate scene, when Doris demonstrates the new awareness of the world she has acquired through living with Rosie: she takes off her stockings to sun her legs–an act of liberation, for "Jack would never have tolerated this lack of modesty in a woman"–and announces that she told the Animal Liberation man that he was "politically unsound" because his organization uses violence. At eighty-seven, Doris is an example of how age need not hinder personal or political development.

The final scene is set in 1923, with all of the women on stage; Doris is addressing her mother, who has not appeared in the play, thereby emphasizing the sense of a continuing line of mothers and daughters. Doris tells her mother that she has fallen in love with Jack: "I suppose, really and truly, this is the beginning of my life." The audience has just witnessed the same woman at eighty-seven, wearing a pair of trendy sunglasses and announcing that she buys her underwear at Top Shop, a juxtaposition that forces the audience to consider the enormous changes in women's lives during the century.

Keatley does not romanticize the mother-daughter relationship but shows the tensions and unspoken feelings that permeate mothers' attempts to control their daughters and their daughters' resentment of such attempts. Bickering is more evident than love as Doris and Margaret, in particular, try to mold their offspring into socially acceptable women. Jackie even gives her daughter away, choosing to pursue a career and let Margaret raise Rosie. In the children's scenes, the girls readily announce their hatred of their mothers; in the opening scene they propose to kill their "mummies" and suggest methods that include "boiling oil" and a "stake through the heart." A sense of potential cruelty

Shirley Henderson as Rosie and Elizabeth Bradley as Doris in a scene from the 1989 Royal Court Theatre production of Keatley's My Mother Said I Never Should

pervades the play. Keatley observed in the interview with Goodman that "psychological violence" was missing from the 1989 Royal Court production directed by Michael Attenborough: "The Manchester production was more cruel . . . perhaps Mike couldn't bear to allow these women to be so psychologically violent towards each other, so . . . what he transmitted was a less vicious, less specifically female vision of family love and jealousy . . . especially the authority of motherhood, blame-throwing, silent accusations, and expressions of disapproval between mothers and daughters."

The fragmented time structure of the play is not gratuitously chaotic but forces the spectators to search for connections through poetic resonance and implication, rather than direct statement. Keatley told Stephenson and Langridge that her treatment of time in the play was responsible for its rejection by "several experienced" male directors, who said that "it didn't have a structure, and wasn't about anything." In feminist theory this kind of nonlinear or "organic structuralization" is central to the notion of a "female aesthetic," an aesthetic that is claimed to be more readily used and accepted by women. In *Feminist Theatre* Helene Keyssar notes Gertrude Stein's description of her plays as landscapes and suggests that the "concept of a play as a landscape . . . de-emphasises the plot" and "usefully embodies the importance of texture and detail in feminist drama." Texture and detail are paramount in Keatley's play. Clothes and other objects are used in a precise manner–sometimes, as with Doris's 1920s frock, which appears in act 2 and which she wears at the end of the play, and Jackie's 1970s clothes, which Rosie commandeers, to pinpoint an historical period. Sometimes they operate as emotional signifiers, and their reappearance at key moments becomes almost cinematic; Rosie's red baby sock is the most obvious example. Such visual details are part of the nonverbal dimension of theater that Keatley likes to exploit. In the interview with Stephenson and Langridge she described the "object language" as "very ordinary but important" in the play, so that the game of solitaire that Rosie finally wins stands as a symbol of independence. When Rosie wins the game, she has broken "the play's web of guilt, frustration and secrecy."

Keyssar claims that the "diffusion of the playwright's attention among a number of characters" is also crucial to feminist drama, and that the characters are "usually but not exclusively women." In *My Mother Said I Never Should* attention is shared equally among the four characters, and men are absent from the stage. "I had to clear the men offstage to show the power of female expectations: women can be more judgmental of each other than men. I wanted this play to make women angry as well as nourish us," Keatley writes in the introduction to the 1997 edition of the play, leaving no doubt that the differences between women are as vital to her as those between men and women.

Surprisingly few women dramatists have explored the mother-daughter relationship in depth, despite the fact that feminist theory recognizes this relationship as central to questions surrounding female identity. Nancy Friday's groundbreaking *My Mother/My Self: The Daughter's Search for Identity* (1977), for example, maintains that the mother-daughter relationship is the defining one for every woman. Some plays of the 1980s feature but do not focus on the relationship. For example, Louise Page offers insightful perspectives on the relationship between an older mother and daughter in *Salonika* (1983), and in her *Real Estate* (1985) the mother, Gwen, unlike Margaret in Keatley's play, refuses to give up her successful business to look after her daughter's child. Caryl Churchill offers a powerful indictment of abnegated motherhood in *Top Girls* (1982), in which Marlene forges a career in business, leaving her sister, Joyce, to raise her daughter, Angie. Churchill explores the fraught emotions inherent in the mother-daughter bond in *Fen* (1983). Sarah Daniels presents a powerful case for modern lesbian motherhood in *Neaptide* (1982), and many of her plays feature mothers despairing of the feminist tendencies of their daughters. Keatley's play, however, is unusual in charting the relationship over successive generations.

Although *My Mother Said I Never Should* can be categorized as "feminist drama" in Keyssar's terms, it does not advance a feminist agenda; it simply presents family and social pressures through the eyes of women. Keatley, however, acknowledges her position as a representative of her sex. She is willing to carry the banner for women's writing as an essential part of the developments in theater. In her interview with Stephenson and Langridge she recalled confronting Michael Billington, theater critic for *The Guardian,* because he mentions only two plays by a living woman in his 1993 collection of reviews from the previous twenty years, *One Night Stands.* He replied that "everything that didn't seem to be the next real step in culture" had been weeded out. Her response in the interview was that "a book like that, to other people around the world . . . and to people in thirty years' time, says, 'The theatre has been constructed by men, directed by men . . . these are the milestones. These are the representatives of our society.' And that's not actually what's happening in theatre . . . but that's what's written in stone."

Keatley insists that *My Mother Said I Never Should* is a political play, and in the interview with Stephenson and Langridge she quoted the response of Max Stafford-Clark, the key decision maker at the Royal Court Theatre in the 1980s, who "would say, in committees and discussions, 'Look this is a play about society.'" She went on to praise Stafford-Clark, who brought plays by women such Daniels, Page, Churchill, Andrea Dunbar, and Pam Gems to the Royal Court, for his vision in seeing that they were writing "big plays about society and they needed a main stage." Keatley has, however, sometimes been ambivalent about whether *My Mother Said I Never Should* is a feminist play. She told Stephenson and Langridge that feminism is "defined . . . as meaning, 'She doesn't shave her legs. She doesn't like men,'" and that she would not want the play to be "limited to the idea that it's politically, socially angry in the way that 'feminist' has come to mean." Keatley's definition of feminism embraces men: "I think feminism is about the possibility for all of us to change the roles we've been ascribed. Men as well as women," she told Stephenson and Langridge. *My Mother Said I Never Should* is a political play in the sense that four women are observed reacting to the changing values of the twentieth century and to the ideals of each generation: the political is seen through the personal. There is no direct comment in the play on the effects of patriarchal attitudes on women, although in the introduction to the 1997 edition Keatley says that she intended to present the way that women respond to "the expectations of the male society around them, the pressure to be 'good women of their time.'"

The appeal of *My Mother Said I Never Should* lies in its portrayal of ordinary women leading ordinary lives. It is accessible to audiences of a wide range of ages, as women can identify with characters representing their own generation while seeing the development of women in the twentieth century. The play attracts a large audience wherever it is produced, even though people often are not familiar with it. When the play was first performed at the Royal Court, Keatley told Stephenson and Langridge, "no one had heard of me or this play, but it got the most phenomenal advanced bookings." This success may have something to do with the title, which resonates in every woman's head.

My Mother Said I Never Should has rarely been out of production, and Keatley has always been willing to undertake revisions for new productions. The play was originally published by Methuen in 1988 in its New Theatrescripts series, designed for audience members to buy as the program, to coincide with the first London production in early 1989; it was reprinted with revisions in 1988, 1989, and 1990 before being completely revised for the Oxford Stage Company's revival in 1997. The modifications to the stage directions indicate Keatley's concern that the play has sometimes been misinterpreted. She says in the 1997 edition that "there are no cute little girls . . . the children are fearsome and courageous (as children are) and to depict them otherwise in the play or on posters is to misrepresent the adults of whom they are the core." In the original edition she says that the "setting should not be naturalistic" and that "there are no sofas in this play." In the 1997 version she changes the description of the set from "simply a magic place where things can happen" to "simply a magic place where the characters can make contact with the earth," underlining the metaphorical dimension of the piece. In the first edition the play opens with the stage directions "Oldham, Manchester. A patch of wasteground at the end of a terraced street, where children play," which implies a real place; in the 1997 edition it is just "Wasteground, a place where girls come to play." These modifications to the stage environment are meant to capture an elusive sense of place associated with memory rather than the gritty realism of urban wastelands. The time structure is one aspect of the play that has not changed with revisions.

Critics often say that Keatley has not written anything of note since *My Mother Said I Never Should* but has chosen to ride on the reputation of her most successful play. She responds that she is a slow writer and that her material takes considerable time to develop. While Keatley has consistently been labeled a "playwright," she is more accurately described as a theater practitioner who sometimes writes plays. She points out in the introduction to the 1997 revised edition of *My Mother Said I Never Should* that "Playwright has the same word ending as shipwright, wheelwright and cartwright; all ancient crafts," but the assumption that the term implies a writer rather than a craftsperson persists. She spoke with a simple eloquence about the nature of the theater as a language of the unconscious in the interview with Stephenson and Langridge:

> "if you think of the first piece of theater you ever saw . . . your memory is always of an image, or an action, or gesture, and you remember that long, long after the words. . . . Theatre isn't intellectual. You don't need intellectually to understand, analyse or talk about what's happening, and I think between the writer, actor and audience that's understood. . . . an element of a play, once it's enacted on stage, somehow has an energy that's far greater than its apparent, tangible meaning or existence."

Keatley wrote for the long-running radio serial about urban life, *Citizens,* during the 1987–1988 and 1989–1990 seasons. Between 1988 and 1992 she taught playwriting and theater skills at a variety of institutions, including the University of London, the Royal Court Young People's Theatre, the Women's National Touring Theatre, the University of Birmingham, and Vassar College. She has also undertaken projects for deprived areas in Manchester, New York City, and Rajasthan, India. In 1988–1989 she was the Judith E. Wilson Visiting Fellow in English at Cambridge University. In 1989 she adapted *My Mother Said I Never Should* for broadcast on BBC Radio 4; she also wrote *You're a Nuisance Aren't You?* about a woman who loses her son in the Falkland Islands war, as one of the ten short plays in the collaborative anti–Margaret Thatcher work *Fear and Misery in the Third Term* for the Liverpool Playhouse. In 1991 her children's play, *The Singing Ringing Tree,* was produced by the Contact Theatre in Manchester. She collaborated with Dominic Cooke in directing Heathcote Williams's *Autogeddon* (1991), which won a Fringe First award at Edinburgh. Her play *The Dream of Reason Produces Monsters* premiered at the Academy Theatre in Shanghai in 1999. She is currently working on a large-scale play about the eighteenth-century French mathematician Emilie du Châtelet titled *The Genius of Her Sex.* Keatley, who is divorced, has a daughter, Georgia, who was born in 1996.

Interviews:

Lizbeth Goodman, "Art Form or Platform? On Women's Playwriting," *New Theatre Quarterly,* 6 (May 1990): 128–140;

Heidi Stephenson and Natasha Langridge, *Rage and Reason: Women Playwrights on Playwrighting* (London: Methuen, 1997), pp. 71–80.

References:

Nancy Friday, *My Mother/My Self: The Daughter's Search for Identity* (New York: Delacorte, 1977);

Helene Keyssar, *Feminist Theatre: An Introduction to Plays of Contemporary British and American Women* (Basingstoke: Macmillan, 1984).

Barrie Keeffe

(31 October 1945 -)

Ute Berns
Technische Universität Berlin

See also the Keeffe entry in *DLB 13: British Dramatists Since World War II.*

PLAY PRODUCTIONS: *Only a Game,* London, Shaw Theatre, March 1973;

A Certain Vincent, by Keeffe and Jules Croiset, adapted from Vincent van Gogh's letters on tour, Holland, 1974; London, 1975;

Gem, London, Soho Poly Theatre, 7 July 1975;

A Sight of Glory, London, Cockpit Theatre, August 1975;

My Girl: A Love Story, London, Soho Poly Theatre, 15 September 1975; retitled *I Only Want to Be with You,* White Star Theatre, 3 November 1995; revised as *My Girl: A Love Story,* London, Theatre Royal Stratford East, 6 March 1989;

Scribes, Newcastle upon Tyne, Tyneside Theatre Company, October 1975; London, Greenwich Theatre, October 1976; London, Phoenix Theatre, 1977;

Gotcha, London, Soho Poly Theatre, 17 May 1976;

Here Comes the Sun, London, Jeanetta Cochrane Theatre, August 1976;

Abide with Me, London, Soho Poly Theatre, 28 September 1976;

Gimme Shelter: Gem, Gotcha, Getaway, London, Soho Poly Theatre, 31 January 1977; London, Royal Court Theatre, 23 March 1977; New York, Brooklyn Academy of Music, 1978;

A Mad World, My Masters, London, Young Vic Theatre, 1 May 1977;

Up the Truncheon, London, Shaw Theatre, August 1977;

Barbarians: A Trilogy: Killing Time, Abide with Me, In the City, London, Soho Poly Theatre, 28 August 1977; London, Greenwich Theatre, 28 September 1977;

Frozen Assets, London, Warehouse Theatre, 9 January 1978;

Sus, London, Soho Poly Theatre, 18 June 1979; New York, Jean Cocteau Theatre, 1 June 2001;

Bastard Angel, London, Warehouse Theatre, 23 January 1980;

Black Lear, London, Temba Theatre, 1980; revised as *King of England,* London, Theatre Royal, Stratford East, 28 January 1988;

She's So Modern, London, Queen's Theatre, 1980;

Chorus Girls, music by Ray Davies, London, Theatre Royal, Stratford East, 6 April 1981;

A Gentle Spirit, by Keeffe and Croiset, adapted from a story by Fyodor Dostoevsky, on tour, Holland, 1981; London, Shaw Theatre, 4 May 1982;

Better Times, London, Theatre Royal, Stratford East, 31 January 1985;

Not Fade Away, London, Theatre Royal, Stratford East, 12 April 1990;

Wild Justice, London, Theater Royal, Stratford East, 24 May 1990;

Shadows on the Sun, London, Greenwich Playhouse, 2 October 2001.

BOOKS: *Gadabout* (London & Harlow: Longman, 1969);

Gimme Shelter: Gem, Gotcha, Getaway (London: Eyre Methuen, 1977; New York: Grove, 1979);

A Mad World, My Masters (London: Eyre Methuen, 1977; revised, 1980);

Barbarians: A Trilogy Comprising Killing Time, Abide with Me and In the City (London: Eyre Methuen, 1978);

Frozen Assets (London: Eyre Methuen, 1978);

Sus (London: Eyre Methuen, 1979);

Bastard Angel (London: Eyre Methuen, 1980);

No Excuses (London: Methuen, 1983);

The Long Good Friday (London & New York: Methuen, 1984; revised edition, London: Methuen, 1998);

Better Times (London & New York: Methuen, 1985);

King of England & Bastard Angel (London: Methuen, 1988);

My Girl, Frozen Assets (London: Methuen, 1989);

Wild Justice, Not Fade Away, Gimme Shelter: Gem, Gotcha, Getaway (London: Methuen, 1990);

Here Comes the Sun (Cheltenham, U.K.: Thornes, 1991);

Barrie Keeffe (photograph by Nobby Clark)

Barrie Keeffe Plays One: Gimme Shelter-Gem, Gotcha, Getaway, Barbarians: Killing Time, Abide with Me, In the City (London: Methuen, 2001).

PRODUCED SCRIPTS: *The Substitute,* television, Granada Television, June 1972;
Good Old Uncle Jack, radio, BBC, 1975;
Pigeon Skyline, radio, BBC, 1975;
Only a Game, radio, BBC, 1976;
Gotcha, television, BBC, 1977;
Not Quite Cricket, based on Keeffe's *Gem,* television, Thames Television, 1977;
Scribes, television, BBC, 1977;
Self Portrait, radio, BBC, 1977;
Nipper, television, BBC, 1978;
Hanging Around, television, BBC, 1978;
Champions, based on Keeffe's *Abide with Me,* television, Granada Television, 1978;
Heaven Sent, radio, BBC, 1979;
Waterloo Sunset, 1979; revised as *Not Fade Away,* television, BBC, 1980;
The Long Good Friday, motion picture, Black Lion Films, 1980;
No Excuses, based on Keeffe's *Bastard Angel,* television, Central Television, 1983;
King, based on Keeffe's *Black Lear,* television, BBC, 1984;
Paradise, radio, BBC, 1989;
On the Eve of the Millenium, radio, BBC, 2000;
Feng Shui and Me, radio, BBC, 2001.

OTHER: *Here Comes the Sun,* in *Act 3,* edited by David Self and Ray Speakman (London: Hutchinson, 1979), pp. 145–211;
Heaven Sent, in *Best Radio Plays of 1979* (London: Eyre Methuen, 1980), pp. 91–100;
The 1984 Verity Bargate Award Short Plays, edited by Keeffe (London & New York: Methuen, 1985);
The Verity Bargate Award: New Plays 1986, edited by Keeffe (London & New York: Methuen, 1987);
The Verity Bargate Award: New Plays 1987, edited by Keeffe (London: Methuen, 1988);
Verity Bargate: The 1988 Award-Winning Plays, edited by Keeffe (London: Methuen, 1989).

In their 1987 study of post–World War II British drama, Colin Chambers and Mike Prior wrote of playwright Barrie Keeffe: "As a vivid and sharp chronicler of his class, Keeffe is unparalleled." Their assessment highlights the significance of Keeffe's work for the ongoing debate about the "state of the nation" and its values. His plays, which first reached wide audiences during the 1970s, were produced by major English stage companies and complemented by his work for radio, television, and one motion picture. Although many of his plays present dramatic topographies of the East End of London, precise and metaphoric at the same time, revivals and translations into seventeen languages illustrate their transcultural dramatic effectiveness. In his best plays, a strong commitment to social issues, a keen sense of dramatic language and imagery, and a creative awareness of the traditions of the theater find expression.

Barrie Colin Keeffe, the only son of Edward Thomas Keeffe and Constance Marsh Keeffe, was born in East Ham, London, on 31 October 1945 and educated at East Ham Grammar School. His marriage to Dee Truman in 1969 ended in divorce ten years later. He married the writer Verity Bargate in 1981, but she died that same year, leaving him with two stepsons; and in 1983 he married Julia Lindsay, from whom he was divorced in 1993. He lives in Greenwich, south of the Thames in London.

Unlike most of the dramatists that emerged during the same decade, Keeffe did not attend a university. After jobs in a tin factory and as a grave digger, salesman, and freelance journalist, his five years of work (1964–1969) for the East London newspaper *Stratford and Newham Express* became a formative period: he said in an interview with Malcolm Hay that the paper "was busy investigating social injustices, and for me it was a period of finding out about politics: everything I believe in now crystallized then." The political hopes that had been cherished on the theatrical fringe of 1968 passed him by. He had expected major socialist reforms from the Labour Party government that took office in 1964 and remembers "not disillusionment but absolute despair, at the end of it, that so little . . . nothing . . . had changed." He continued to work for a news agency until 1975. Although Keeffe began his writing career with the novel *Gadabout* (1969), his fascination with drama dates from his first school trip to watch a performance by Joan Littlewood's Theatre Workshop at the Theatre Royal, Stratford East. In 1964 he was an actor in that company. For three years he was also an actor-member of the National Youth Theatre, whose director, Michael Croft, later supported the production of Keeffe's first stage play.

Keeffe was dramatist in residence with the Shaw Theatre in London in 1977, under the auspices of the Thames TV Playwright scheme, and also with the Royal Shakespeare Company in 1978. He has been a member of the Council of the National Youth Theatre since 1977, and of the board of directors for the Soho Poly Theatre in London since 1978. Between 1986 and 1991 he was an associate writer for the Theatre Royal, Stratford East. In 1978 he was awarded the French critics' Prix Révélation for his 1976 play *Gotcha,* and in 1982 the Mystery Writers of America Edgar Allan Poe Award for the screenplay of *The Long Good Friday* (1980). He has also directed three of his own pieces: *A Certain Vincent* in 1975, *A Gentle Spirit* in 1981 and 1982, and *My Girl* (1989).

Keeffe views his early plays as "a form of apprenticeship," dismissing the television playscript *The Substitute* (1972) as "a pathetic Cockney *Catcher in the Rye.*" His first performed stage plays venture into sports: *Only a Game* (1973) concerns a soccer star at the end of his career, and *A Sight of Glory* (1975) is about a boxing club in which East End kids find a sense of purpose in a deteriorating neighborhood. It was first produced by the National Youth Theatre of Great Britain. After *A Certain Vincent,* which was an adaptation of Vincent van Gogh's letters, *Scribes* (1975) draws on Keeffe's experience as a journalist and is again set in the East End. Rewritten for television, it won the Thames Television Award.

Keeffe develops a distinctive stance of his own in *My Girl: A Love Story* (1975), a revised version of which received wider attention in 1989. The play is a domestic drama for two actors without any change of set. It recounts the difficult family life of a dedicated social worker named Sam, his wife, Anita, and their young daughter, who live together in a cold and damp flat in Leytonstone. In the second act, the option of an easier existence outside of London has materialized because of Anita's efforts, but the play ends with Sam's thirtieth birthday and the decision left hanging. Sentimental productions easily obscure the precise limits and pressures that bear down on these episodes, which are subtitled "a love story." Sam loses faith in his job, not least because government cuts have reduced social benefits and also have rendered caring-profession salaries insufficient for supporting a family. Similarly, in the pregnant Anita's fight for her husband, love blends into nightmares of abandonment and economic destitution, which reflect her ultimate traditional dependency on the breadwinner. Their despair is evoked in references to a poverty-stricken neighborhood and by the decision of the council to bar the couple's windows–a dramatic symbol for the political answer to local poverty and violence. In this respect the revised version of the play gains additional edge as it is firmly placed in the Margaret Thatcher era. Though the grimness of the story is alleviated by music, humor, and even moments of farce, the strong interdependence between setting and story recalls the drama of "high naturalism," in which, according to Raymond Williams, the physical environment is shown "to soak into the lives" of the characters.

My Girl is a good example of Keeffe's early self-description as a "miniaturist . . . much more interested in the effects of political decisions on people, than in making political decisions." This approach characterizes several of the plays that follow, which present less than a handful of characters in equally few settings. Their dominant naturalistic mode, always sustained by a savage humor, swerves occasionally and to good effect into farce, the absurd, or the grotesque. They dramatize the characters' awareness of their environment in a powerfully colloquial language, which registers their sense perceptions and conveys their bodily presence and interactions with startling immediacy. The usefulness of language as a means of communication between the characters, however, depends on their articulateness, which varies considerably. This also accounts for the relationship between language and violence, presented both as extensions of and substitutes for each other.

The trilogy *Gimme Shelter* (1977), consisting of *Gem* (1975), *Gotcha,* and *Getaway* (1977), marked Keeffe's breakthrough and gave clear shape to his attitude as a dramatist: "I wanted to give a voice to people whose voices aren't heard." *Gem* portrays a group of insurance company employees who are boycotting the firm's annual outing and its cricket match. The protest is initiated by Kev, whose sharp and cynical description of the monotony of his job recalls Jimmy Porter in John Osborne's *Look Back in Anger* (1956). Kev's radical and aggressive rhetoric of class struggle attempts to name the political origins of his situation, but the simple opposition between "us and them" proves inadequate for the different identities and living situations of his colleagues, who eventually drop their resistance and join the festivities. This development from rebellion to acquiescence is corroborated in the last play, *Getaway,* set in the same place a year later, in which Kev and his friends partake in the cricket match. Confronted with the future prospect of the student who works at the firm during vacation, Kev sums up his life as a clerk with the words "enough O-levels . . . to be disillusioned." It is a disenchanted estimate of social mobility, a major topic after World War II.

The core piece, *Gotcha,* has often been performed on its own, although the thematic relations between the three plays are complex. In the contrast to the dramatic framework of *Gem* and *Getaway, Gotcha* begins with an everyday encounter, which then evolves into an image of violent rebellion. David Edgar comments: "I have seen nothing . . . to compare in terms of memorable, (and therefore usable), dramatic power, with . . . the sustained fury of Barrie Keeffe's *Gotcha,* in which a working-class teenager holds three teachers hostage in a school boxroom by threatening to drop a lighted cigarette into a motorcycle petrol tank." The nameless Kid in *Gotcha* is about to leave comprehensive school, which he has experienced as an anonymous mass institution that has reduced him to a cipher and has provided him with a report that precludes any prospects on the job market. By aiming at the teachers' bodies, threatening "blood and bones on the ceiling" and claiming "this is for real," the Kid desperately tries to pierce a public discourse about "equal chances for everyone," which conceals his foreseeable exclusion from any meaningful participation in a society in which work itself has become scarce.

The central image in *Gotcha*–a pupil with a "petrol bomb"–becomes, moreover, a foil for a dramatic analysis of the school normality. With power literally in his hands, the pupil shatters all the institutional and commercial mechanisms on which the teachers, who are for the moment under his control, rely for the routine exercise of their power. This reversal of power relations illustrates how the abuse of institutionalized communication patterns affects the content of what is utterable, enforces specific cultural or class values, and privileges one particular way of speaking while relegating others. In a production in Los Angeles, Kid was successfully cast as a Mexican boy. As Steve Grant remarked, when the central character defies discipline, "the dramatic situation creates just the right amount of intense self-awareness to propel the pent-up rage of the school student, providing an apt and effective correlative for his sudden articulacy." The rigid class boundaries, which apparently dissolve in *Gem* and *Getaway,* are condensed into an insurmountable barrier for the main character in *Gotcha.* Finally, in *Getaway* Kev and Kid meet accidentally but fail to communicate. Kid, disturbed by his stay in a disciplinary institution, tries to salvage an existence from his job as a gardener: "I've changed." The political analysis of these different experiences of loss of self and aspiration, representative of two different generations, is left to the audience.

According to Catherine Itzin, with *Gimme Shelter* Keeffe gained the reputation of a "spokesperson for the dispossessed youth, . . . the unemployed and unemployable," and the trilogy *Barbarians* (1977) continues this theme. The first play, *Killing Time,* introduces Paul and Jan, both white, and Louis, who is black. None of the youths are able to find a proper job after school. They pass the year with petty crimes, except for Louis, who goes on a training course that does not help him either. In *Abide with Me* they have resigned themselves to despised jobs in a tin factory and spend their money supporting the Manchester United team. Finally, in *In the City* Paul marches with the National Front, and the terrified Jan, who has joined the army, will be shipped to Belfast soon. At the annual Notting Hill West Indian carnival they run into Louis, who has moved and found a home in the black community and a job that relates to his training. In a violent eruption of racism and envy Paul beats up his former friend.

The trilogy explores the complex lack of purpose that tends to accompany youth unemployment. The characters' urgent desire "to be part of . . . something" is no longer envisioned as a specific class identity, as for instance in Arnold Wesker's *Roots* (1959). It seems to have turned into a much more existential need "not to be ignored" that may fasten on soccer clubs, church congregations, the National Front, or the army. The plays offer only a minimal narrative and little psychological motivation for the few long monologues directed to the audience. Hence these plays, especially the first two, while quite funny in parts, convey a distinctly Beckettian sense of waiting and repetition in which Paul, momentarily dropping his aggressiveness and self-protective cynicism, can be heard to say "I wish . . . *Pause*. . . . There was something else . . . to mean something." The social parameters of this precarious sense of self are always foregrounded. The huge stadium wall in *Abide with Me,* separating the characters from the action and noise in which they long to partake, serves as an embodiment of the interrelation between social and economic relegation, violence, and racism.

In both trilogies Keeffe's acute sense of spoken language filters into characterizations that combine public discourse and private voices in a multifaceted dramatic language. His young male protagonists repeat and recycle the words of the careers adviser, the mayor's speech, a television series, and various advertisements–all of which depict lifestyles–with ironic or frustrated distance, or with skeptical hope. The dramatized contexts for these speeches and the characters' actual prospects dislocate and undermine these prefabricated dreams. The recognizable multiplicity of languages within a single speaking voice fractures the dramatized subjectivities and precludes any simplified understanding of the characters' authenticity. Yet, language, in the form of an anecdote, also figures as a more communal and self-determined medium. When handled economically, the anecdote successfully incorporates the image of a living oral tradition into the plays. It may nostalgically affirm a collective identity or serve as a confrontational device to shock, and it may even imply an oblique comment on the dramatic narrative as a whole.

Keeffe achieves additional stylistic competence with *A Mad World, My Masters* (1977), which employs a large cast to take a sweeping stride through all social strata. *A Mad World, My Masters,* in which Michael Billington, theater critic for *The Guardian,* saw "the lineaments of a comic classic," was commissioned by Joint Stock, who wanted to make a modern Jacobean play. After one of the company's famous workshops, Keeffe was given ten weeks to write the script, his first comedy. The densely plotted and fast-moving drama features the East London Sprightly clan, set on making money from an insurance company. When the scheme misfires, they swear revenge and find themselves up against a member of the Queen's silver jubilee committee, the tycoon and estate agent Claughton, who has a weakness for young girls and would do anything for a knighthood. The plot is spiced by a constable desperate for a mortgage, a bent doctor, a yellow-press journalist, a trade-union official and his homeless identical twin, a housewife on Valium, and a social worker from the local crisis intervention center. When the action is taken to "Buck House," disguises and misidentifications abound, touching all, including the Queen. The burial of Grandma Sprightly, who is decorated with the epitaph "she tried to take on the upper class, / now the worms are gnawing at her arse" concludes the play.

Unlike Caryl Churchill's *Serious Money* (1987), also modeled on the Jacobean city comedy but confined to the world of high finance, Keeffe's play draws on Thomas Middleton's *A Mad World, My Masters* (circa 1606) for a lower-class vantage point and sets a carnivalesque tone. The mad world drawn in the 1970s relies on cartoon-style characters that are alive with reckless egotism and pursue their obsessions and rapacious moneymaking with zest and ingenuity. This dramatic spirit is fired by racy, gossipy, and outrageously sexist dialogue, complete with witty retorts and considerable situational humor. The art of deceit, cunning, and devious dissimulation, which characterizes the Jacobean view of the laws of the city, finds its analogy in involved cons, which include memorable impersonations of contemporary public figures–various revisions offer a choice between television stars and top politicians. Yet, this satirical topsy-turvy world is not allowed to last. With the help of a sudden twist, the East End tricksters are shown to be out-tricked by the might of the upper class.

In 1978 the Royal Shakespeare Company produced *Frozen Assets*. It tells the story of Buddy, a youngster, who has accidentally killed a ward at a reformatory; Buddy panics and then takes flight. On his picaresque journey he first tries to find shelter with his own family, which is beset with criminal records. An encounter with an aging boxer leads to his meeting the rich face to face, including two politicians. After gaining sufficient insight into the extent of their corruption,

Charlotte Cornwell as Shelley in the Royal Shakespeare Company production of Keeffe's Bastard Angel *at the Warehouse Theatre in London in 1980*

Buddy leaves the country as a stowaway. The play opposes the criminal milieu of organized armed robbery, represented by the gangsters, and the everyday graft of the politicians. It offers no alternative to crime and corruption, but the emphasis is on the lack of proportion in a society that locks up thousands of juvenile delinquents for petty crimes and whose laws value property above anything and protect the rich.

Strictly committed to the boy's perspective, the play retains an episodic and linear plot structure in the manner of a *Stationendrama.* After some bleak though funny encounters in which vividly sketched portraits are drawn almost in passing, the gangsters grow slightly larger than life and offer their moral, "never rob your own class," in genre-specific jargon. In the second act coincidences abound, and the plot seems to head for a Dickensian Christmas tale, including dinner for the "waif," before Buddy escapes. The ship, one of the last to leave the dead docklands, and the notion of the "stowaway passenger" fade into myth. The boxer's last words, celebrating the resilient spirit of the Cockney kids, alienated some reviewers, but the majority appreciated the raw dialogue performed with gusto in comic scenes. Both *A Mad World, My Masters* and *Frozen Assets* were revived in the 1980s in revised versions that strengthened the topical context of the dockland development projects.

The East End underworld that surfaces in these two plays is the main focus in the screenplay of *The Long Good Friday.* In this enormously popular thriller, which was first conceived in 1976 and finally premiered in 1980, Harold Shand (played by Bob Hoskins) is carefully preparing a bent deal in the docklands when his "Corporation" is shocked out of its routine by a series of attacks and explosions. The mysterious origin of these attacks is revealed to be the IRA on a mission of revenge. The different rationalities that rule the profit-oriented criminal corporation and the politically motivated terrorist group, the spiral of violence, and the superior cunning of the American investors are powerful ingredients for this exploration of contemporary issues. Its local and historical specificity invigorated a tried-and-tested Hollywood genre. Around the same time, another nontheatrical venture, Keeffe's radio play *Heaven Sent* (1979), won the Giles Cooper Award.

In *Sus* (1979), a successful short play, Keeffe intervened in a controversy about the rights of the police. The play is set at a police station on the eve of the General Election. A Jamaican named Delroy assumes that he has been arrested "on suspicion," a practice based on a law that was increasingly used in the 1970s to detain people, especially blacks, and repealed in 1981. However, the police charge him with the murder of his wife. After the two detectives, Karn and Wilby, have harassed and beaten Delroy, they learn that the woman died naturally. Several dialogues in this otherwise grittily realistic play border on the absurd, and Karn's Pinteresque monologues add impalpable menace to the concrete threat. In addition, the interrogation is modified by the incoming election results. Initially, this style makes for an almost bantering tone, but by the end of the first act it heightens the sadism that Delroy, who meets the challenge with growing self-awareness, confronts. The detectives, "sick of civil fucking liberties," anticipate a new law-and-order policy backed by the majority and hence drop all caution in releasing their racism. The play was received not only as an indictment of the "sus" law and notorious police practices but also as a dramatic warning of the years to come.

The mood in *Sus* is partly created by the help of music, a device that recurs throughout Keeffe's dramas. From pop songs to rock music and soccer-club anthems to reggae, tunes and lyrics in the plays effortlessly evoke specific cultural contexts. Musical openings, intermissions, and closures focus the emotional atmosphere or punctuate episodic dramatic structures. Nicholas de Jongh, quoted in Hay's article, even claimed that "what Keeffe has tried to do is to supply for the theatre some of the passion and excitement which infuses rock concerts." That may well be true, since rock music as myth and lived reality is both the subject and a vital ingredient of *Bastard Angel* (1980). First performed by the Royal Shakespeare Company, the play revolves around a group called the Angels and their gig in Berlin in January 1980; the beginning of the Angels' show opens the play. The realistic action of the four acts is set in chronological order during the year before, running up to and linked by parts of the concert. After sixteen years in the business, the aging lead singer, Shelley, has kept her hatred of the class system but gained material success at high personal costs in the exploitative system of popular entertainment. As a result, she has lost her belief in what she sings.

This remarkable play achieves an integration of textual, musical, and performance elements that preserves the experience of the emotional force of the music. Its mythical aura as an expression of the youthful rebellion that nourished an entire generation is, however, deconstructed through the text. As Elizabeth Hale Winkler points out in her 1990 study of song in British drama, the narrative of *Bastard Angel* reveals the perceived youthful authenticity of the protagonist as part of a manufactured image, which neither the star herself nor her audience can resist. Skillfully modeled on Anton Chekhov's drama *Platonov* (1923), the play gains additional impact by conveying both a Chekhovian and contemporary sense of lost political hope, anarchic desire, and impasse: "All your energy? And no direction. / That's why. No purpose. That's why . . . I'm in rock' n' roll." History is evoked with critical precision and an irony tinged by nostalgia.

After the satire *She's So Modern* (1980), the musical *Chorus Girls* (1981) draws on a play by Aristophanes and concerns a kidnapped Prince Charles, who has to spend time with the chorus girls beneath a theater stage. Music also plays an important role in the sentimental comedy *Not Fade Away* (1990). It features a rebellious white woman, Grace Webb, who escapes from a senior citizens' center back to Forest Gate, where she assumes the role of both granny and nanny in a black family, until their household is broken up by the police and welfare workers. Much is made of the contrast between the East End that Grace remembers and its contemporary poverty and racism. The old songs with which she entertains her new friends, and her vocabulary of international brotherhood, dating from the communists' agitation against Sir Oswald Ernald Mosley's British Union of Fascists, serve as vivid theatrical markers of historical continuities and change in the East End.

Also set in the black community of the East End, Keeffe's *Black Lear* (1980) was later reworked as *King of England* (1988). It explores the alienation between two generations of West Indian inhabitants: those who immigrated after the war, represented in this play by the tube-train driver Mr. King on the day of his retirement, and their children, represented by Mr. King's two daughters. The father-daughter relationships and the theme of gratitude draw on William Shakespeare's *King Lear,* whose sheer enormity as a tragic source produces interesting intertextual meanings. King Lear's homelessness, after he has been turned out by his daughters, is recast in Mr. King's uncertain sense of belonging. The ingenious translation of Shakespeare's heath into Stratford Shunting Yard, an urban wilderness of signs and directions, serves as a backdrop for the madly incoherent conversation between Mr. King and a fool looking for his whippet.

Better Times (1985) addresses the history of the East End head on. Based on research and many collected memories of local hero George Lansbury, it unfolds the crucial struggle in the early 1920s for an equitable rates system in Poplar, then a London borough ridden with severe poverty and unemployment. Flagrantly challenging the law, the Labour councilors, led by Lansbury, refused to levy the sum due to the London County Councilor and were sent to prison, where they continued to function as a council unit until a compromise was reached six weeks later. The motto of the play, "bad laws should be broken," runs through the dramatized council meetings, the courtroom scene, and the march of the Poplar constituency. Audiences were quick to pick up parallels to contemporary rates issues. Keeffe's close association with the Theatre Royal at Stratford East during the 1980s provided him with a better opportunity than ever to reach an audience of the racially mixed social class he writes about. Some of these later plays are recognizably written for an almost exclusively sympathetic local audience and thus turn into instances of community drama.

Keeffe's play *Wild Justice* (1990) announces his return to the topic of revenge by its title, which refers to Francis Bacon's characterization of revenge "as a kind of wild justice." It recounts the story of a teacher who becomes obsessed with avenging the death of his child, killed as an innocent bystander during a robbery. The father's violent failure to come to terms with his loss ruins his own life and that of his wife, while he tracks down his son's murderer. The prologue, set in a psychiatric ward, introduces the unreliable and paranoid narrator, who discloses the tale in twenty-one flashback scenes. What begins as a quest for revenge made tolerable by the inaction and possible corruption of the police is later morally condemned as male self-satisfaction, which perpetrates violence and precludes the public prosecution that would have satisfied the mother's sense of justice. The attempt to modernize Jacobean revenge plots through a film-noir style that runs counter to the simultaneous explorations of the avenger's state of mind left the reviewers divided. By positing the desire for revenge mainly as a problem of individual psychology, *Wild Justice* differs noticeably from the political emphasis in Keeffe's earlier plays, which reconstructed individual attempts at revenge as "wild" gestures of frustration and rage in a society that is seen to legalize its social injustices.

In all his work so far Keeffe has dramatized the changing and disintegrating fabric of London working-class culture. His plays dissect its sense of history and community, both of which are permeated by unemployment, poverty, racism, and violence. But the dramas also explore how even an enforced geographical and social sense of location can be appropriated as a myth of belonging and turned into a source of identity in a hostile environment. In this respect they differ from, for example, Stephen Poliakoff's plays, in which the young heroes emerge from such postmodern places as video shops, supermarkets, and motorway service stations. The majority of Keeffe's plays draw on modified versions of naturalism, and their strength does not lie in far-reaching political analysis. It consists, rather, of the precise contextualized representation of subjectivities through dramatic language, imagery, and the corporeal presence of the actors, which relocates the fragments of specific public discourses. The most important contribution of Keeffe's work to postwar British drama is that it insists on giving center stage to characters who are barred from social participation and an equal share of material and cultural wealth. Thus, Keeffe dramatically challenges societal and cultural exclusions.

Interview:

John L. DiGaetani, *A Search for a Postmodern Theater: Interviews with Contemporary Playwrights* (New York: Greenwood Press, 1991), pp. 191–199.

References:

Ute Berns, "Political Drama and the Micropolitics of Language," in *Drama and Reality,* Contemporary English Drama in English 3, edited by Bernhard Reitz (Trier: Wiss. Verl. Trier, 1996), pp. 111–123;

Colin Chambers and Mike Prior, "Images of the Working Class," in *Playwrights' Progress: Patterns of Postwar British Drama* (Oxford: Amber Lane Press, 1987), pp. 27–59;

Michael Coren, Theatre Royal: 100 Years of Stratford East (London & New York: Quartet, 1984), pp. 17, 80–81, 83, 92;

Sandy Craig, *Dreams and Deconstructions: Alternative Theatre in Britain* (London: Amber Lane Press, 1980), pp. 41, 113, 142–143, 151, 158;

David Edgar, *The Second Time as Farce: Reflections on the Drama of Mean Times* (London: Lawrence & Wishart, 1988);

Steve Grant, "Voicing the Protest," in *Dreams and Deconstructions: Alternative Theatre in Britain,* edited by Craig (Ambergate: Amber Lane Press, 1980), pp. 116–144;

Malcolm Hay, "Portraits of Angry Young Underdogs: An Assessment of Barrie Keeffe's Plays," *Drama,* 54 (1984): 9–11;

Catherine Itzin, *Stages in the Revolution: Political Theatre in Britain since 1968* (London: Eyre Methuen, 1980), pp. 243–249;

Raymond Williams, "Social Environment: The Case of English Naturalism," in *Problems in Materialism and Culture* (London: Verso, 1980);

Elizabeth Hale Winkler, "The Dominance of Popular Song: Music Hall to Rock" in *The Function of Song in Contemporary British Drama* (Newark: University of Delaware Press, 1990), pp. 208–271.

Hanif Kureishi

(5 December 1954 -)

Linden Peach
Loughborough University

See also the Kureishi entry in *DLB 194: British Novelists Since 1960, Second Series.*

PLAY PRODUCTIONS: *Soaking up the Heat,* London, Royal Court Theatre Upstairs, 1976;

The King and Me, London, Soho Polytechnic Theatre, 7 January 1980;

The Mother Country, London, Riverside Studios, 22 July 1980;

Outskirts: A Play in Twelve Scenes Set over Twelve Years, London, Royal Shakespeare Company Warehouse, 28 April 1981;

Tomorrow–Today! London, Soho Polytechnic Theatre, 8 June 1981;

Borderline, London, Royal Court Theatre, 22 November 1981;

Cinders, adapted from a play by Janusz Glowacki, London, Royal Court Theatre Upstairs, 1981;

Artists and Admirers, translation by Kureishi and David Leveaux of the play by Alexander Ostrovsky, London, Riverside Studios, 26 June 1982; New York, City Stage Repertory Theatre, 1986;

Birds of Passage, London, Hampstead, 15 September 1983;

Mother Courage, adapted from a play by Bertolt Brecht, London, Royal National Theatre, 7 November 1984; revised as *Mother Courage and Her Children,* lyrics by Sue Davis, 1993.

BOOKS: *Borderline* (London: Methuen, 1981);

Birds of Passage (Oxford: Amber Lane, 1983);

Outskirts, The King and Me, and Tomorrow–Today! (London: Calder / New York: Riverrun, 1983);

My Beautiful Laundrette and The Rainbow Sign (London & Boston: Faber & Faber, 1986);

Sammy and Rosie Get Laid: The Script and the Diary (London: Faber & Faber, 1988; New York: Penguin, 1988);

The Buddha of Suburbia (London & Boston: Faber & Faber, 1990);

London Kills Me (London & Boston: Faber & Faber, 1991);

Outskirts and Other Plays (London: Faber & Faber, 1992); republished as *Plays One* (London: Faber & Faber, 1999)–comprises *The King and Me, Outskirts, Borderline,* and *Birds of Passage;*

The Black Album (London: Faber & Faber, 1995; New York: Scribner, 1995);

My Beautiful Laundrette and Other Writings (London: Faber & Faber, 1996)–comprises *My Beautiful Laundrette; The Rainbow Sign; Eight Arms to Hold You; Bradford; Wild Women, Wild Men;* and *Finishing the Job;*

Love in a Blue Time (London: Faber & Faber, 1997; New York: Scribner, 1997);

My Son the Fanatic (London: Faber & Faber, 1997);

Intimacy (London: Faber & Faber, 1998; New York: Scribner, 1999);

Midnight All Day (London: Faber & Faber, 1999);

Sleep with Me (London & New York: Faber & Faber, 1999);

Gabriel's Gift: A Novel (London: Faber & Faber; New York: Scribner, 2001).

Collection: *Intimacy: A Novel and Midnight All Day: Stories* (New York: Scribner, 2001).

PRODUCED SCRIPTS: *You Can't Go Home,* radio, BBC, 1980;

The Trial, radio, based on a novel by Franz Kafka, BBC Radio 3, 1982;

My Beautiful Laundrette, motion picture, Working Title Films/Orion Classics, 1985;

Sammy and Rosie Get Laid, motion picture, Channel 4 Films/Cinecon/Working Title Films, 1988;

London Kills Me, Channel 4 Films/Polygram/Working Title Films, 1991;

The Buddha of Suburbia, television, 4 episodes, BBC, 3 November 1993;

My Son the Fanatic, motion picture, Zephyr Films, 1998.

OTHER: *The Faber Book of Pop,* edited by Kureishi and John Savage (London & Boston: Faber & Faber, 1995).

SELECTED PERIODICAL PUBLICATIONS–UNCOLLECTED: "Alistair Ramgoolam Does Well to Be Uneasy," review of *Digging up the Mountain,* by

Hanif Kureishi (photograph by Melissa Hayden from the dust jacket for Love in a Blue Time, *1997)*

Neil Bissoondath, *New York Times,* 17 August 1986;
"Finishing the Job," *New Statesman and Society,* 1 (28 October 1988): 19–24;
"England, Your England," *New Statesman and Society,* 2 (21 July 1989): 27–29;
"A Long, Cool Glance," *Guardian* (London), 4 November 1989, pp. 15–16;
"Boys Like Us," *Guardian* (London), 2 November 1991, pp. 4–7;
"Wild Women, Wild Men," *Granta,* 39 (Spring 1992): 171–180;
"A Wild Dance to a Dangerous Tune," *Independent on Sunday* (London), 24 May 1992, p. 22.

Hanif Kureishi is one of the best-known British-Asian writers working for the stage and, more recently, for the screen. He has also acquired a reputation for his fiction. As his career has progressed, he has placed an increasing emphasis on his own ethnic background and on the difficulties and the possibilities created by the clash and fusion of cultural and religious traditions.

Kureishi's background has been the subject of controversy, with his mother and sister disputing his versions of it. He was born in London on 5 December 1954 and raised in Bromley, Kent. His mother was English; his father, the son of a doctor, was a lieutenant colonel in the Indian army who immigrated to England after the partition of the Subcontinent in 1947. The father had ambitions as a novelist but failed to obtain a publisher for any of his works.

Kureishi's introduction to the theater came when he was eighteen, when he submitted a short play to the Royal Court Theatre and was invited to meet its literary manager, Donald Howarth. While majoring in philosophy at King's College of the University of London, he worked at the theater selling programs and reading unsolicited scripts for Howarth; he also supported himself by writing pornography under the pseudonym Antonia French. He chose to study philosophy because he believed that the disciplines that were more popular with the students of his day, psychology and sociology, were too crudely scientific in their explanation of human behavior. His antipathy toward the social sciences was no doubt influenced by his predilection for social realism, which was influenced, in turn, by his father's interest in the novel and his own avid reading of French and Russian fiction.

Nineteenth-century European realism and Kureishi's concern as a British-Asian writer with those who are on the margins of society determined the nature of his first significant play, *The King and Me* (1980). It is about a married couple, Bill and Marie, who fill their empty lives with the worship of Elvis Presley; Marie spends every afternoon dancing with Elvis in her imagination. The plot of the play concerns their preparations for an Elvis show, part quiz and part impersonation, in which Bill is to compete to try to win a trip to Memphis for them.

Outskirts: A Play in Twelve Scenes Set over Twelve Years (1981) takes a bleak view of postindustrial Britain. Two friends, Bob and Del, meet regularly–initially as boys–at the "bombsite," an area of wasteland where they talk candidly about their lives and try to buy drugs. They are desperate to leave south London. Bob, unable to obtain employment, has turned to neofascist groups to provide his life with meaning. His mother is waiting at home to beat him with a golf club for doing so; nevertheless, she has his best interests at heart. The same cannot be said for Del's father, who gets vicarious satisfaction from forcing Del to reveal details of his sexual activities with his girlfriend.

Borderline (1981), Kureishi's first significant play written from a British-Asian perspective, concerns two generations of Indian immigrants to Britain. Amjad, a member of the older generation, has suffered racism at the hands of his neighbors, but he holds onto his idealistic fantasies about English justice. He also holds onto traditional Asian culture and wants to marry his daughter, Amina, to a wealthy businessman, Farouk. Another member of the older generation, Anil, complains that "England's a cemetery" and, although he is living with an Englishwoman, alleges that Englishwomen are "stuck-up," "cold," "racist," and "common." Meanwhile, his wife and children are waiting in India for him to send for them. A younger-generation Asian, Ravi, comes to stay with Anil; he believes that he will be able to get rich in England, but one of the first things he notices on his arrival in the country is the dole queue, or welfare line.

Two of the younger-generation characters, Amina and Haroon, are lovers who secretly meet in back of her father's restaurant, in parking lots, and in other out-of-the-way places. In such spaces, with Haroon, Amina can be a different person from the one her father imagines; she can become, in her own words, a "terrible person," candid about sex and employing a frank English vocabulary. Haroon becomes associated in Amina's mind with the risky places where they meet, and it comes as a shock to her when he breaks off their relationship to go to a university outside London because he wants what he had earlier dismissed as "the white lie" and "whitewashed history." After her breakup with Haroon, Amina becomes active in the Asian Youth Front. At the end of the play she urges the Youth Front members to burn down the hall in which the neofascists are meeting.

Kureishi's ethnic background and suburban upbringing in London are reflected in *Birds of Passage* (1983), which concerns the impact of the economic recession on a lower-middle-class family and their friends in Sydenham. The suburbs represent an imagined Englishness that is more real for its inhabitants than are the economic realities of Prime Minister Margaret Thatcher's Britain; as the protagonist, David, a Labour Party councillor, says:

> They're a genuine combination of middle-class and working-class life. Bank clerks, milkmen, civil servants and labourers live side by side with flourishing hedges between them. We have comfortable houses with gardens. We are neither integrated nor alienated. Out here we live in peace, indifferent to the rest of the world. We have no sense of communal existence, but we are tolerant, not cruel. There's a kind of quiet gentle righteousness about the suburbs that I like.

Economic reality is brought home to David by the loss of his job and the failure of his brother and sister-in-law's business. David's daughter, who has a totally different worldview from that of her parents, works as a prostitute to get money to better herself. The most unsympathetic character in the play is David's upwardly mobile former lodger, Asif, an entrepreneur who looks down on the majority of his fellow British Asians: "Most English don't realize that the immigrants who came here are the scum of Pakistan: the sweepers, the peasants, the drivers. They've never seen toilets. They've given us all a bad reputation because they don't know how to behave." Ultimately, David is forced to sell his house to Asif: British imperialism over Asians has symbolically come full circle.

Vincent Ebrahim and Rita Wolff in Kureishi's Borderline *(1981), about two generations of Indian immigrants in Britain*

Characters in Kureishi's later work for the screen–*My Beautiful Laundrette* (1985), *Sammy and Rosie Get Laid* (1988), and *London Kills Me* (1991)–are more independent-minded than in the plays written for the stage, and their social and family circumstances are more complex. In *My Beautiful Laundrette,* for example, Tania is a development of Amina in *Borderline*. She is as sexually assertive as Amina and openly flirts with Johnny, her cousin Omar's white, neofascist gay lover. While Amina escapes the arranged marriage with Farouk through her father's sudden death, Tania runs away. Tania openly acknowledges her father's relationship with Rachel, a white girl, and revels in her mother's disapproval of her flirting with Johnny.

Kureishi's later work for the stage and most of his work for the screen confronts the challenges of the new pluralism. The simple oppositions of Asian/British, traditional/modern, exploiter/exploited, victim/villain, and home/exile become complex and blurred. His works suggest that values have to be worked out through negotiation of the conflicts created by love and desire and by the clash and fusion of cultural and religious traditions.

References:

John Clement Ball, "The Semi-Detached Metropolis: Hanif Kureishi's London," *Ariel: A Review of International English Literature,* 27 (October 1996): 7–27;

Renee R. Curry and Terry L. Allison, eds., *"All Anger and Understanding": Kureishi, Culture and Contemporary Constructions of Rage* (New York: New York University Press, 1996);

Felicity Hands, "How British Are the Asians?" *Wasafiri Magazine,* 21 (1995): 9–13;

Seema Jeena, "From Victims to Survivors: The Anti-Hero and Narrative Strategy in Asian Immigrant Writing," *Wasafiri Magazine,* 17 (1993): 3–6;

Suzie MacKenzie, "All For Love," *Guardian Weekend* (London), 2 May 1998, pp. 24–28;

Nahem Yousaf, "Hanif Kureishi and 'the Brown Man's Burden,'" *Critical Survey,* 8 (1996): 14–25.

Sharman Macdonald

(8 February 1951 –)

Dymphna Callery
University of Wolverhampton

PLAY PRODUCTIONS: *When I Was a Girl, I Used to Scream and Shout,* London, Bush Theatre, 12 November 1984; California, Costa Mesa, 1989;
The Brave, London, Bush Theatre, 1 June 1988; New York, Atlantic Theater, 13 July 1999;
When We Were Women, London, Cottesloe Studio, National Theatre, 15 September 1988;
All Things Nice, London, Royal Court Theatre, 4 January 1991;
Shades, Woking, New Victoria Theatre, 16 June 1992; London, Albery Theatre, 23 July 1992; Florida, Florida Shakespeare Festival, 1994;
The Winter Guest, Leeds, West Yorkshire Playhouse, 23 January 1995; London, Almeida Theatre, 9 March 1995;
The Borders of Paradise, London, Watford Palace, 16 March 1995;
Sea Urchins, Dundee, Dundee Repertory Theatre, 20 May 1998; Glasgow, Tron Theatre, 17 June 1998;
Hey Persephone, libretto by Macdonald, music by Deirdre Gribben, Suffolk, Aldeburgh Festival, June 1998; London, Almeida Theatre, 1 July 1998.

Sharman Macdonald (photograph by Ivan Kynel; from the dust jacket for Sharman Macdonald: Plays One, *1995)*

BOOKS: *When I Was a Girl, I Used to Scream and Shout* (London & Boston: Faber & Faber, 1985);
The Beast (London: Collins, 1986);
Night, Night (London: Collins, 1988);
When I Was a Girl, I Used to Scream and Shout, with When We Were Women, and The Brave (London & Boston: Faber & Faber, 1990);
All Things Nice (London & Boston: Faber & Faber, 1991);
Shades (London & Boston: Faber & Faber, 1992);
Sharman Macdonald: Plays One (London & Boston: Faber & Faber, 1995)–comprises *When I Was a Girl, I Used to Scream and Shout, When We Were Women, The Winter Guest,* and *Borders of Paradise;*
The Winter Guest: Screenplay, by Macdonald and Alan Rickman (London & Boston: Faber & Faber, 1997);
Sea Urchins (London & Boston: Faber & Faber, 1998);
After Juliet (Cheltenham: Thornes, 2000; London & Boston: Faber & Faber, 2001).

PRODUCED SCRIPTS: *Mindscape,* television, BBC Scotland, 1987;
Wild Flowers, television, Channel 4, 1989;
Sea Urchins, radio, BBC Radio 3, 1996;
The Winter Guest, motion picture, Fine Line Features, 1997;
The Music Practice, television, BBC Two, 1998.

Sharman Macdonald is an important part of the theatrical renaissance that started in Scotland in the 1980s. Her work puts strong emphasis on the personally felt experience, and she was immediately successful with her first performed play, *When I Was a Girl, I Used to Scream and Shout.* This play opened at a fringe venue in London, the Bush Theatre, in 1984, and then transferred for a long run in the West End, initially starring Julie Walters. Nothing Macdonald has done since has quite matched this early success, and at various times she has announced that she will not work for the theater anymore. Indeed, before her next play was produced in 1989, she had two novels published, *The Beast* (1986) and *Night, Night* (1988). She has continued to work as a playwright, and her first play is now established as a modern classic and frequently revived. Macdonald is not a writer who tackles issues; in her plays, social concerns become those of the individual in particular circumstances, not an opportunity for debate. Her work does not conform to the notion that argument is at the center of theater, for her theater is about texture, relationships, idiom, and the poetics of action. Sympathy and emotional truth, old-fashioned concepts that owe much to the naturalism of Anton Chekhov and August Strindberg, pervade her work, along with a rueful eye for the comic in everyday situations. She asserts that when she worked as an actress it was never the applause that she liked but the laughter; and as a writer watching her own work in performance, she told Heidi Stephenson and Natasha Langridge in an interview published in 1997, "the joy is in the laughter." She offers a humorously humane voice in a cynical age.

Sharman Stewart Macdonald was born in Glasgow on 8 February 1951, the only daughter of an engineer, Joseph Henry Hosgood Macdonald, and a secretary, Janet Rowart Williams. She moved to Ayrshire from Glasgow at age ten, and in 1965 she moved to Edinburgh, where she later attended Edinburgh University, acting in the drama society and working as a go-go dancer and postal worker to pay her fees at drama school. After graduating, she worked as an actress, including a stint with John McGrath's 7:84 Theatre Company, then moved to London with her husband, Will Knightley, also an actor, whom she married on 29 August 1976. She has lived there ever since, although her Scottish roots are evident in the settings of her plays, from provincial West Coast towns to urban Glasgow, and in the predominance of Scottish characters; "I think I live a little in Scotland," she said in the 1997 interview. Her plays are marked by a distinctive and rhythmic use of language, rooted in an acute ear for dialogue. She is an astute observer, possessing a Chekhovian feel for the emotional undercurrents of existence and a similar, but more heightened, sense of comedy. She has made the territory of adolescence her own, as well as offering powerful and painful insights into the mother-daughter bond.

Writing had been a dream for Macdonald since childhood, but she told Stephenson and Langridge that although she had always written, her work had "always been prose and it had always been very bad poetry." She began exploring dialogue as an actress, killing time in rehearsal rooms: she entertained herself by improvising characters and writing down what came out, and her dialogue bears the refreshing vitality of an actor-dramatist. At home with a baby, her son, Caleb, born in 1979, she wrote *When I Was a Girl, I Used to Scream and Shout,* which she sent to the Bush Theatre under a pseudonym. It was read initially by Alan Rickman and was then produced to critical acclaim; it went on to storm the Edinburgh International Festival and returned for a long run in the West End. This play won the *Evening Standard* Most Promising Playwright Award and the Thames Television Playwright Award, which gave Macdonald the post of writer in residence at the Bush Theatre (1984–1985). On a personal front this success brought enough temporary financial stability to have another child, a daughter named Keira, born in 1985–who, Macdonald wrote in the introduction to her 1995 volume of plays, "still calls herself the Bush baby." At this point Macdonald gave up acting to concentrate on writing, despite the fact that she says the family was living on bread and lentils. She has since written eight more plays, two novels (the first of which was nominated for the Booker Prize), four screenplays, and an opera libretto.

The Bush Theatre is tiny, and its smallness is perfect for the nuances of intimate naturalistic work; yet, its designers also have a reputation for dealing with complex ideas in simple ways. Robin Don's set for *When I Was a Girl, I Used to Scream and Shout* created a brilliantly lifelike rendition of a rocky shore, which also becomes Fiona's childhood home as the play swings across time, from 1983 to 1955 and the 1960s. Tensions between Fiona and Morag, her mother, bubble to the surface in the summer heat. Their relationship involves resentment on both sides, as Morag's biting tongue and Fiona's emotional coolness veil their unwillingness to forgive each other for the events of the past: Fiona got pregnant at fifteen to interfere with Morag's plan to move to the Middle East with a new man and leave her daughter behind. The play shifts seamlessly between their bickering in the present and enactments of key moments in Fiona's childhood and adolescence, when prepubescent sexual games with her friend Vari prefaced her fumbling and messy seduction of her boyfriend, Ewan. The emotional truth in Macdonald's portrayals of the love/hate relationship of mother and daughter, together with her unerring, candid revelations of female sexual awakening, earned high praise from critics.

Michael Coveney in *The Financial Times* (13 November 1984) described Macdonald's writing as "not exactly feminist but intriguingly feminine," for although the play is clearly woman-centered, it does not foreground gender as an issue. Macdonald loathed the sense of righteousness attached to radical feminism in the early 1980s, and her purpose was to explore what she calls the "corners" of the gender debate. Like Charlotte Keatley's *My Mother Said I Never Should* (1987), Macdonald's debut play has been described as an exploration of the sexual repression passed down from mother to daughter. However, Macdonald explains that the impetus for the scenes between Vari and Fiona came from overhearing her son talking about "willy games" with his friend, and that she sees Morag and Fiona as repressing each other. Appalled when people felt she had not been fair to Morag, she wrote Morag's background into her next play, *When We Were Women* (1988). She maintains a more personal than political version of feminism, refusing to divide the sexes or the world into "good" and "bad." She is more concerned with exploring the complexities of human relationships, and does so with a compassion that recognizes the suffering inherent in the realization of one's imperfections.

Much of Macdonald's subsequent work is seeded in her first play: mother-daughter relationships and the peculiar rites of adolescence feature in all her work, and the shore is a dominant setting. But the heritage is sometimes more specific; she explained in her 1995 introduction that she wrote *When We Were Women* "to knit into the youth of Fiona's mother's generation," and *All Things Nice* (1991) extends the generations to examine the grandmother-grandaughter relationship. She told Stephenson and Langridge, "It was a 'what if?' It feeds back to *When I Was a Girl*. . . . If Morag *had* gone abroad what would have happened?" While Macdonald does not repeat herself, she clearly reworks ideas in new contexts and plows similar ground so that there is a strong correspondence between themes, characters, and settings. The beach is featured in three major plays as a place where the elements meet and where the private lives and personal intimacies of relationships are played out in dialogue that would not be out of place within the confines of domestic interiors, but that takes on a new magnitude in this setting. Similarities between characters are apparent in the insights she offers on adolescents of both sexes, the way the ever shifting toughness and tenderness of Morag surfaces in Elspeth in *The Winter Guest* (1995), and more concretely in two old biddies from that play, with their love of cremations and cream teas; they had appeared in her television movie *Wild Flowers* (1989), and she "couldn't let go of them." These correspondences may be what makes her work distinctive, but it is easy to make too much of that aspect and to lose sight of the way in which she deals with human frailty and fallibility; for human failure to meet ideals or expectations is at the core of her work. This concern is evident in the nonjudgmental way characters are portrayed in *When We Were Women,* Macdonald's third play.

Reviewers often point out the absence of grown-up men in Macdonald's work, for husbands and fathers have either died or left in most plays; yet, in *When We Were Women* she writes for two adult men. The mother-daughter relationship is present, but this time there is a father, Alec, and a sailor called Mackenzie. Alec and Maggie wait for news of their two sons, away fighting in World War II. Alec drinks, and Maggie dilutes the whiskey with syrup of figs. He knows she does it but never confronts her. She indulges his drinking and hides the bills and the degree to which they are in debt. A portrait of an enduring marriage emerges as they watch the abortive relationship developing between their daughter, Isla, and Mackenzie. Isla marries him and, once pregnant, learns he is a bigamist. Maggie rejects her grandchild, forcing Isla to choose adoption, a decision less grounded in puritanical retribution than a middle-aged woman's plea to be freed from the demands of children. Macdonald's refusal to judge is evident. There is no judgment of Mackenzie either; his bigamy is a fact of life rather than a moral dilemma, a choice made as much through despair born from wartime experience as from promiscuity. His wife, Cath, could take her revenge by putting him in jail, but instead he is recalled to active service. Lyn Gardner, reviewing the play for *City Limits* (22 September 1988), found the play "top heavy with narrative," which may be attributed to its premature arrival on stage as a stand-in for a production of *The Father* at the Cottesloe in 1988, when it was still a work in progress. In June of that year, Macdonald's only attempt at a more plot-driven play, *The Brave,* was staged at the Bush Theatre. Set in Algeria, *The Brave* tells the story of a thirty-something Scottish woman and her sister attempting to bury a Moroccan she has killed in self-defense. The attempts to remain in a period setting and to move away from Scotland met with only limited success.

With *All Things Nice* (commissioned and directed by Max Stafford-Clark in 1991 at the Royal Court Theatre), Macdonald returns to Scotland, where fifteen-year-old Moira stays with Gran and their paying guest, the bedridden Captain, in a Glasgow tenement, while her mother, Rose, writes to her from an "ex-pat" colony of oil-company wives in the Middle East. The play

Maurice Roeves as Jamie and Kate Lynn-Evans as Susan in the 1988 Bush Theatre production of Macdonald's The Brave *(Collection of Bush Theatre Company)*

inhabits both worlds simultaneously; while Rose turns to other men and drink as her marriage crumbles, her daughter negotiates the tricky and bewildering adult world, where some men are flashers, others slobber and try to touch her, and one lends her his leather jacket. Moira learns about life via her friend Linda, in much the same earthy and comic way that Fiona was educated by Vari, and she discovers through Joe more wholesome male affection than the Captain's. There are similarities in theme and tone to *When I Was a Girl, I Used to Scream and Shout;* however, Moira's slow passage to maturity is observed in more conventional chronological terms. Although the play is set in the city, many stage directions place the girls standing by windows, presenting them simultaneously as onlookers and girls on the brink of life.

Shades followed in 1992, directed by Simon Callow and opening in Woking before transferring to the West End, where it was billed as "Pauline Collins in *Shades, a love story.*" This foray into commercialism put immense pressure on the piece, as it is essentially a chamber work, and Macdonald found the experience traumatic enough to announce her retirement from theater writing just before the opening. Once more the work is set in Glasgow, but in the 1950s; and the central relationship is not mother and daughter, although that features briefly, but mother and son–a delicate exploration of the depths and superficialities of the bond between the widowed Pearl and her prepubescent son, Alan, which, at times, borders on the incestuous. Alan is a sensitive ten-year-old who plays a recalcitrant kid, sulky schoolboy, and potential lover while observing Pearl's preparations for a night out with a new man, Callum. Apart from one short section when his grandmother Violet arrives to look after Alan, the stage is occupied only by Pearl and Alan in act 1. The opportunity to explore the relationship between Violet and Alan when Pearl goes out is missed, and Violet consequently comes across as Macdonald's most heartless of mothers. In act 2 Pearl's evening out with Callum ends with him backing off from commitment when he realizes the love she still bears for her dead husband, and she returns home to change the sheets Alan has wet.

Despite the richness of characterization, there is something about the shape of this play that feels forced, if not unbalanced. Perhaps the fact that act 1 is literally twice the length of act 2 has something to do with this problem. Unlike Macdonald's other plays, it has disturbing undertones which are never really addressed. The apparent resolution, that Pearl will overcome her fear of growing older and letting go of Alan, is not sufficiently weighted to be totally convincing. And the audience never discovers why Pearl's husband died. Her resentment at his death has something to do with the suddenness and the undignified manner of it–"If I was going to die I'd do it properly. Not go half-cock. Toes in the air. Trousers round my knees on the bathroom floor. At thirty-five years old"–but no other information is forthcoming.

Macdonald creates vibrant and vital women characters in middle and older age. She told Stephenson and Langridge that Rose and Pearl, Morag and Elspeth have "a kind of drag-queen quality . . . taken from women I knew when I was young," women of the 1950s who kept high standards of housework as well as personal grooming (painted nails and stilettos) while holding down a job, women who "never ever thought there was any need for a feminist movement at all. My mother scorned it because she was the power, as my grandmother had been before her." Macdonald claims that her own feminism comes from her fear that she cannot live up to their expectations. She does not debate the typical issues of feminism in her plays. She paints instead a series of portraits of daughters who cannot live up to their mothers, women who fail to meet ideals whether they are set by men or feminism. Often, too, the women are beset by a hunger for male approval. Their lack of anger is striking in relation to the work of Macdonald's contemporaries, those heartfelt 1980s plays by Sarah Daniels and Caryl Churchill that logged women's appeal for equality; yet, her experimentation with form has clear resonances with Gertrude Stein's view of women's plays as "landscapes" and places her work in the domain of women's writing.

Macdonald's plays are notable for their lack of plot, and are character-driven rather than narrative-driven. Their poetic structure invariably straddles two acts with divisions to mark shifts in time or location rather than separate scenes. These shifts move back and forth across years in the earlier work, but the later plays, including the libretto for *Hey Persephone* (1998), all use the convention of a continuous flow of action over one day broken only by shifts in location. Her stage directions are remarkable for the way in which they convey an atmospheric essence in a highly condensed manner; for example, the opening of *Borders of Paradise* (1995) reads simply "*Torchlight. Sound of surf.*" The lyrical quality of her work has prompted reviewers to use words such as "elliptical," "atmospheric," and "evocative" when describing her effects. A judicial use of music and sound, a painterly use of light, and an attention to detail in terms of objects all contribute to these effects, so that her plays project themselves impressionistically and imagistically.

Family and friends are important factors in Macdonald's output. A remark by a female friend sparked *When I Was a Girl, I Used to Scream and Shout,* and Macdonald says of her mother: "she ought to be paid royalties. Not that I've ever put her on the stage; just some of the things she's said . . . and I've borrowed her extraordinary vitality." Her husband bought her a typewriter when she first wanted to write and offered criticism on her early drafts of *When I Was a Girl, I Used to Scream and Shout;* she has also remained friends with Rickman, who later became instrumental in the genesis of *The Winter Guest.* In her 1995 introduction she says "without Will, without Alan, *When I Was a Girl, I Used to Scream and Shout* and *The Winter Guest* wouldn't exist in the form they do." Her office door stays open because she likes the way that things coming in from outside feed the work: "plays come out of life after all . . . what I put on the stage never happened in fact but it all comes from somewhere in life . . . I just edit it."

The lifelike sense in which things connect through echoes and resemblance as opposed to the contrivances of plot distinguishes *The Winter Guest,* her most highly praised play since her debut. The play had a joint production between the West Yorkshire Playhouse and the Almeida, premiering in Leeds before transferring to London. Both northern and southern sensibilities were in agreement about the subtle power of the play, and many reviews refer to it in terms of its poetic tonal qualities. In 1995 theater critics had been assaulted by a new wave of confrontational writing; for example, Sarah Kane's *Blasted,* which heralded the beginnings of a new "brat-pack" producing work that focused on violence and sexual shocks. Macdonald's play offered a humane and gentle contrast.

The play was commissioned by Rickman and Ruby Wax via their company, Raw Produce, an unusual and radical example of artists investing in each other. Macdonald explains in her 1995 introduction that Rickman had heard the actress Lindsay Duncan talking to Macdonald over supper: "The stories she told of her mother's illness fascinated Alan . . . strange what makes a play happen." The play is dedicated to Duncan's mother. Rickman directed the stage play and went on to co-write the screenplay and direct the motion picture. It was the first time Macdonald had been portrayed as a subject by a writer, and Rickman was closely involved in the development of the script, writing long letters in response to each draft. These letters were, says Macdonald, "indecipherable," but the laborious process of trying to work out what he'd written paid dividends in the necessarily slow and methodical way she was forced to work on redrafting. She pays credit to him in the program for the Almeida production: "he never identified a problem, just implied it, so I was given the safety net to go on being risky."

There is no plot in *The Winter Guest.* The action is structured around a morning and an afternoon in which the characters barely interconnect beyond the pairings initially set up: a mother and daughter, an adolescent son and a girl, two younger boys truanting on the beach, and two old biddies obsessed with the latest burial. Again, traces of autobiography are apparent: when Stephenson and Langridge asked why she wrote a play with death as a kind of present reality for all the characters, Macdonald replied, "because I was living amongst it. We'd been living with old people very present . . . so the generations had been dancing around me and that was necessarily reflected . . . I just wanted to juxtapose, I wanted them all there, because that's what it is, that's life."

Irving Wardle in *The Independent* (29 January 1995) described *The Winter Guest* as a piece "in which the seven ages of man converge in a moment of frozen time." Nothing much happens. The son, Alex, tentatively approaches adolescent love in an attempt to exorcise the ghost of his father; the two old women plan their next funeral outing; and the truant boys light a fire on the beach, spread Deep Heat on their genitalia, and find an abandoned kitten. Meanwhile, Elspeth tries to persuade her grieving daughter not to emigrate. All are poised uncertainly between past and future, and that is what connects them. The symphonic patterning provides tonal contrasts that in turn offer layers of meaning beyond surface reality.

In screen form, *The Winter Guest* retains much of the atmosphere of the stage play. Robin Don had designed a remarkable set that allowed action to take place simultaneously on the icy beach and the promenade and inside the house, but the impossibility of achieving this simultaneity on film drove Macdonald to despair in attempting to transpose the stage play into a screenplay. Yet, oddly, she had written the stage play as an experiment with movie structure, thinking that she might not be invited to write for the screen again after completing *Wild Flowers*. The screen version of *The Winter Guest* shows an admirable refusal to alter the poetic structure of the stage play and develop it in terms of plot.

Commissioned by Lou Stein as his swan song as artistic director at the Watford Palace, *The Borders of Paradise* may have suffered critically by being staged almost concurrently with *The Winter Guest,* and Macdonald says she "hasn't finished with it yet." Stein relates in the program notes how it began with a conversation about a closely bonded group of boys: "Sharman wanted to write a play about youth's arrogance and vulnerability." In this play there are only adolescents, no adults. Having a fifteen-year-old son gave Macdonald a perspective on contemporary adolescence, and new insight into the experience for boys. The setting is once again the beach, though this time it is high summer in the West Country, where the surf rolls in and the girls park high on a cliff above in order to watch the boys on their surfboards. It is the first dialogue piece Macdonald has written using British dialect, except for the two girls, who are Scottish. In *Sea Urchins* (1998), too, although the setting is the holiday coast of Wales and several characters are English, the central character, Rena, is Scottish. Macdonald told Stephenson and Langridge: "the Scottish voice entrances me . . . there's an emotional availability within it that I can't let go of. I think it's the way I'll always express myself." And in *Hey Persephone* she comes back again to urban Glasgow and the mother-daughter bond with a reworking of the Demeter myth. This work is Macdonald's first opera libretto and the first time she has written so predominantly in verse, capitalizing on her feel for rhythm in language and her ability to write economic, condensed dialogue. Her next project is a screenplay for a movie concerning an Englishwoman who visits Genoa in 1961.

After Juliet (2000), written for the BT National Connections scheme, was developed from an idea by Macdonald's daughter, Keira, who wanted to know about Rosaline, Romeo's first love in Shakespeare's play. The play is written in loose verse and looks at what happened after the deaths of Romeo and Juliet. Produced all over England in 1999 by young people's theater groups, colleges, and schools, the play has since been produced in Australia, Canada, Italy, and the United States. Furhter, three productions of the play have come to the Royal National Theatre; in July 2001, an Italian production of the play came to the Cottesloe. Translated into Italian, *After Juliet* has been adapted into, as Macdonald says in an unpublished interview, a "wonderfully physical production" by director Barbara Nativi.

Interview:

Heidi Stephenson and Natasha Langridge, *Rage and Reason: Women Playwrights on Playwriting* (London: Methuen, 1997).

Tom Mac Intyre

(10 October 1931 –)

Bernadette Sweeney
University of Dublin

PLAY PRODUCTIONS: *Eye-Winker, Tom-Tinker,* Dublin, Peacock Theatre, 7 August 1972;
The Old Firm, Dublin, Project Arts Centre, 25 September 1975;
Jack Be Nimble, Dublin, Peacock Theatre, 10 August 1976;
Find the Lady, Dublin, Peacock Theatre, 9 May 1977;
Deers Crossing, Oberlin, Ohio, Oberlin College, Spring 1978;
Doobally/Black Way, Le Ranelagh, Paris, Calck Hook Dance Theatre, April 1979; Dublin, Edmund Burke Theatre, Trinity College, 8 October 1979;
The Great Hunger, Dublin, Peacock Theatre, 9 May 1983; Edinburgh, Assembly Rooms, Edinburgh Festival, 11–16 August 1986;
The Bearded Lady, Dublin, Peacock Theatre, 10 September 1984;
Rise Up Lovely Sweeney, Dublin, Peacock Theatre, 9 September 1985;
Dance for Your Daddy, Dublin, Peacock Theatre, 2 March 1987;
Snow White, Dublin, Peacock Theatre, 27 June 1988;
Ariane and Blue Beard, libretto by Mac Intyre, Leeds, Grand Theatre, 17 September 1990;
Kitty O'Shea, Dublin, Peacock Theatre, 8 October 1990;
Go On Red, Galway, Punchbag Theatre Company, 14 February 1991–comprises *Fine Day for a Hunt, Foggy Hair and Green Eyes,* and *Jack Be Nimble;*
The Mankeeper, Limerick, Midas Theatre-in-Education Company, Mary Immaculate College, 30 September 1991;
Fine Day for a Hunt, Galway, Punchbag Theatre Company, 16 July 1992;
Chickadee, Waterford, Red Kettle Theatre Company, 18 May 1993;
Foggy Hair and Green Eyes, Dublin, Project Arts Centre Production, Clarence Hotel, 4 October 1993;
Sheep's Milk on the Boil, Dublin, Peacock Theatre, 17 February 1994;
Good Evening, Mr Collins, Dublin, Peacock Theatre, 11 October 1995;

Tom Mac Intyre (photograph by Bill Doyle; from the dust jacket for The Word for Yes: New and Selected Stories, *1991)*

You Must Tell the Bees, Cork, Firkin Crane Arts Centre, 26 September 1996;
The Chirpaun, Dublin, Peacock Theatre, 3 December 1997;
Caoineadh Airt Uí Laoghaire, Galway, 16 April 1998;
Cúirt an Mheán Oíche, Galway, 19 November 1999;
The Gallant John-Joe, Culdoff, McRory's Hotel, 23 January 2001.

BOOKS: *The Charollais* (Dublin: Dedalus, 1969);
Dance the Dance (London: Faber & Faber, 1970);

Through the Bridewell Gate: A Diary of the Dublin Arms Trial (London: Faber & Faber, 1971);
Blood Relations: Versions of Gaelic Poems of the 17th and 18th Centuries (Dublin: New Writers' Press, 1972);
The Harper's Turn (Dublin: Gallery, 1982);
I Bailed Out at Ardee (Dublin: Dedalus, 1987);
The Great Hunger: Poem into Play, by Mac Intyre and Patrick Kavanagh (Mullingar, County Westmeath: Lilliput, 1988);
Fleurs-du-Lit (Dublin: Dedalus, 1990);
The Word for Yes: New and Selected Stories (Oldcastle, County Meath: Gallery, 1991);
A Glance Will Tell You and a Dream Confirm (Dublin: Dedalus, 1994);
Ag Caint Leis an mBanríon (Baile Atha Cliath: Coiscéim, 1997);
Cúirt an mHeán Oíche (Baile Atha Cliath: Coiscéim, 1999);
Silenas na gCat (Baile Atha Cliath: Coiscéim, 1999);
Caoineadh Airt Uí Laoghaire (Baile Atha Cliath: Coiscéim, 1999);
Stories of the Wandering Moon (Dublin: Lilliput, 2000).

OTHER: Pádraic Ó Conaire, "The Woman on Whom God Laid His Hand," translated by Mac Intyre, in *The Finest Stories of Pádraic Ó Conaire* (Swords, County Dublin: Poolbeg, 1982), pp. 11–24;
Sheep's Milk on the Boil, in *New Plays from the Abbey Theatre,* edited, with an introduction, by Christopher Fitz-Simon and Sanford Sternlicht (Syracuse, N.Y.: Syracuse University Press, 1996), pp. 71–110;
Good Evening, Mr Collins, in *The Dazzling Dark: New Irish Plays,* selected, with an introduction, by Frank McGuinness (London: Faber & Faber, 1996).

PRODUCED SCRIPTS: *The Visitant,* radio, RTE Radio, 22 October 1980;
Painted Out, television, RTE, 1981;
Green Sky over White Bend, radio, BBC Radio 4, 28 September 1982;
The Mirror, radio, RTE Radio, 1 January 1983;
Grace Notes, radio, RTE Radio, 13 November 1983;
Fine Day for a Hunt, radio, RTE Radio, 24 November 1985;
The Mankeeper, radio, BBC Radio 3, 29 October 1988;
Stirabout, radio, BBC Radio 3, 12 November 1988;
Scruples, television, RTE, 8 June, 15 June, 22 June 1989;
Willy Wynne Con Motto, radio, BBC Radio 4, 27 September 1989;
Fine Day for a Hunt, radio, BBC Radio 3, 11 November 1989;
Rise Up Lovely Sweeney, radio, *Drama Now,* BBC Radio 3, 13 November 1991;
Rise Up Lovely Sweeney, RTE Radio, 16 February 1993.

SELECTED PERIODICAL PUBLICATIONS–UNCOLLECTED: "Snow White: Rehearsal Script One," *Krino,* 5 (Spring 1988): 51–56;
"No Young Bums: Why Don't Young People Go to the Theatre?" *Irish Stage and Screen,* 1 (March 1989): 26.

Tom Mac Intyre has been a vibrant presence in Irish theater since the early 1970s. In a country that treasures its literary tradition, particularly in the theater, Mac Intyre has brought an element of play and of risk to the stage that has profoundly influenced recent theatrical developments. He has worked consistently and has had many of his plays produced at the Peacock Theatre, the smaller stage of the National Theatre Society, as opposed to the larger Abbey Theatre. Despite having worked within the establishment, however, Mac Intyre is a controversial figure who has somehow managed to remain outside the dominant discourse.

Born in Cavan on 10 October 1931, Mac Intyre, whose parents were teachers, studied English literature at University College Dublin and worked in the United States periodically from the mid 1960s until 1980. While in New York in the early 1970s he was deeply influenced by the developments in dance theater, and his subsequent work throughout the 1970s and 1980s sought to marry his facility with words with a theater of image, where his presence in the rehearsal process was central. Mac Intyre began to establish himself as a writer in the early 1970s: his first novel, *The Charollais,* was published by Dedalus Press in 1969; his first volume of poetry, *Dance the Dance,* was published by Faber and Faber in 1970; *Through the Bridewell Gate: A Diary of the Dublin Arms Trial,* was published by Faber and Faber in 1971; and a volume of Mac Intyre's verse translations, *Blood Relations: Versions of Gaelic Poems of the 17th and 18th Centuries,* was published by New Writers' Press in 1972. Such diverse interests also came to include theater, where he could combine language with the immediacy of movement, the potential of which he had come to appreciate in the work of choreographers Martha Graham, Pina Bauch, and Merce Cunningham.

On 7 August 1972 Mac Intyre's *Eye-Winker, Tom-Tinker,* a two-act political play set in Dublin in "the modern era," was staged at the Peacock Theatre and directed by Lelia Doolan. His second play, *The Old Firm,* was produced at the Project Arts Centre in September 1975, and in August 1976 *Jack Be Nimble,* advertised as "a new mime play by Tom Mac Intyre," was staged as a Peacock Workshop production, directed by Patrick Mason. Another Peacock Workshop production, *Find the Lady,* followed in May 1977; based on the legend of Salome, the play was also directed by Mason. This association with Mason, who had initially joined the Abbey as a voice coach in 1972, later proved fruitful for both playwright and director.

In 1978 Mac Intyre spent time working at Oberlin College in Ohio, collaborating with students and director Wendy Shankin on *Deers Crossing,* produced in the spring of that year. The Calck Hook Dance Theatre developed out of this project, and later in 1978 Mac Intyre was awarded a bursary by An Chomhairle Ealaíon (the Arts Council of Ireland), which enabled him to work with Calck Hook in Paris. Mac Intyre's *Doobally/Black Way* was produced by Calck Hook at Le Ranelagh in Paris in April 1979 and was well received by critics and the public. In October, *Doobally/Black Way* was staged at the Edmund Burke Theatre in Trinity College as part of the Dublin Theatre Festival. Reactions to the play in Dublin differed greatly from those of the Parisian audience, however, and on the second night of the run the performance was interrupted as irate members of the audience were removed by police. This controversy did not generate a bigger audience for the play; neither did its success in Paris endear Dublin audiences to it. Mac Intyre's experimentation with form and his determination to explore alternative options for Irish theater were, if anything, reinforced by this experience, however, as his stage adaptation of *The Great Hunger* proved four years later.

Tom Hickey in the 1983 Abbey Theatre production of Mac Intyre's The Great Hunger

The Great Hunger, Patrick Kavanagh's 1942 poem, was shaped into a play by Mac Intyre in collaboration with Mason and actor Tom Hickey in 1983. To take an established work by a poet such as Kavanagh and transfer it to the stage was in itself risky, but the creative nature of its staging further identifies *The Great Hunger* as a landmark in Irish theater history. Mac Intyre's decision to rework one of the most celebrated of modern Irish poems was seen by some as foolish, if not irreverent. The original script comprises a selection of lines and images taken from the poem and reordered by the playwright. The language Mac Intyre used was sparse, and during the subsequent collaborative rehearsal process with Mason and the actors, including Hickey as the central character, Patrick Maguire, the physical nature of the piece became apparent.

Early reactions to Mac Intyre's adaptation were guarded, and some reviewers believed that the playwright would have been better served by a more rigid adherence to the text, staged in a more conventional way. The 1983 production of the play was a departure from the theatrical practices in Ireland at that time, as the poem was a departure from conventional poetry when it was published in 1942. Maguire, the beleaguered small farmer of *The Great Hunger,* is a lonely, frustrated man living under the tyranny of the Catholic Church, the land, and, perhaps most interesting, his mother. Kavanagh uses Maguire's mother to explore the combination of circumstances that have left Maguire trapped. His life is shown to be stunted by her control, but by drawing her as embittered and defensive Kavanagh indicates that her life, too, is frustrated and defined by a cruel ideal. The land, which provides Maguire's livelihood, offers little comfort. His life is an endless round of drudgery; the presence of fertility in nature joins with the presence of his mother to emphasize his impotent, God-fearing existence.

Just as Kavanagh had dismantled the prevalent image of idyllic rural life, Mac Intyre used *The Great Hunger* to challenge the prevalent image of Irish theater in the 1980s. He chose a vibrant, physical form of theater to act as a vehicle for Kavanagh's masterpiece. The press release issued by the National Theatre prior to the opening of the play in 1983 described the poem as having "evoked a unique and highly individualistic response from the playwright." Mac Intyre created a nonlinear, image-driven text (described by the playwright as a score), which evidences not only his "individualistic response" to Kavanagh's poem but also the playwright's exposure to the work of dance-theater practitioners such as Meredith Monk and his discovery, as quoted by Mary Harron for *The Observer* (30 November 1986) of what he described as "a gloriously contemporary idiom . . . the fragmentation of narrative, the power of the image, the poetry of movement–these elements had an ability to reach the audience, to burn in a way that traditional narrative couldn't."

The language of the performance score was taken directly from the poem, but through rhythm and chant the lines became a fluid, living part of the process rather than a faithful recitation of Kavanagh's work. These rhythms were developed for the production during the collaborative rehearsal period. Mac Intyre's constant presence facilitated the reworking of *The Great Hunger* both during the original run and to a greater extent for the subsequent production at the Edinburgh Festival in 1986. The 1986 production of the play differed considerably from the earlier one: there was less reliance on the sound track and more on the actors, and certain elements of the script were reworked or replaced. Discussions were held after the previews of the 1983 production in the Peacock Theatre, when Mac Intyre and Mason had the opportunity to assess the audiences' reactions to the play. This direct contact with the audience following an indirect theatrical appeal to their senses through sound, image, and movement gave an added dimension to the organic nature of the piece.

The audience was a real part of this endeavor. The choice of Kavanagh's poem was an initial play upon the general social frame of reference of the Peacock Theatre audience, who were sufficiently distanced from the nationalist image making of the 1940s to recognize it for what it was. Also, the audience of the 1980s recognized Kavanagh as an acknowledged and respected figure in Irish literature. Thus, Mac Intyre's play both included the intellectual expectations of the audience in the process and worked against them. Mac Intyre's aim was to connect with the audience on another level. He believed, as quoted by Kathryn Holmquist, that "The immediacy of the pictorial, of the imagistic, by contrast with the verbal, relates essentially to what we call sensory impact: you *look,* you *see.* In the verbal theatre, the energy hasn't got that directness." Mason was also committed to the search for a means of communicating with an audience that would challenge any preconceived notions of theater. *The Great Hunger* reaches its audience through the staging of movement, image, and association.

Maguire's life is depicted onstage in a space defined by a high farm gate upstage center, a tabernacle downstage right, and a wooden effigy representing "The Mother" downstage left. From the beginning the audience is confronted by these three central forces on Maguire's life. The presence of the Mother on stage as an inanimate object resonates throughout the play. The decision to "cast" the Mother thus was made by Mac Intyre at the outset. The object cleverly evokes the unfeeling, driven character of Kavanagh's poem, who is sketched as a seated woman. The Mother represents onstage the far-from-cozy domestic hearth. Maguire literally runs in circles around the Mother in scene 3 as he struggles to remove a cloth cover from the effigy. In scene 8 he poignantly strives to speak to her as he gently wipes her rigid face. The scene ends with Maguire slowly beating the unyielding breast of the effigy, encapsulating both his need for his mother and his frustration with her, without his speaking a word. The other women characters–Maguire's embittered sister, Mary-Anne; the sexually vibrant neighbor Agnes; and an innocent "Schoolgirl"–each offer insights into the frustrated potential of women in Kavanagh's rural Ireland.

The Church is represented both by the tabernacle and an actor playing "The Priest," who is seen at various points throughout the play performing card tricks. The device of the Priest as illusionist neatly underlines his motivations: he does not deal with the real needs and concerns of his congregation but works to suppress and distort them. The Church confronts the exuberance of nature in scene 5. The characters brandish branches of greenery as they move about the stage with abandon. Their individual reactions to the greenery give the audience a succinct measure of their attitudes to life. Agnes lies down and strokes her body sensually with her branch, while Maguire chooses one of the biggest branches and moves about the space ecstatically until his sister takes the branch from him and gives him a smaller one instead. As they dance wildly to the surging music, the Priest enters, dressed in his vestments. They all stop abruptly, put aside the fertile greenery, and kneel in regimented order before him, all joy suppressed.

The repetitive, backbreaking nature of working the land is highlighted in scene 2 when neighbors Maguire, Malone, and Joe are seen picking potatoes. With the deliberation of dancers each actor moves down the neatly ordered potato drills. Rhythmically delivered lines from the poem, interrupted and overlapping as they gain momentum, are punctuated by the sound of potatoes landing in metal buckets. Scene 9 is an energetic representation of plowing. As Maguire leads Malone and Joe, who are now acting as horses, the three women and Packy–a young, almost otherworldly character–add to the general confusion, two of the women flapping white cloths to suggest wheeling seagulls. The scene collapses in laughter; then, Maguire moves to the gate upstage and tellingly kicks it as he repeats savagely: "It's not a bit funny. Not a bit funny . . . not a bit funny."

In Mac Intyre's play Maguire is all too aware of his failure as he literally hits out against those controlling forces. Such a physical interpretation of Kavanagh's poem, which attempts to grasp all that the stage medium has to offer, was condemned by some, who felt that the form of the play had proven to be a poor vehicle for a poem of such literary weight. In 1988 the National Theatre toured Russia for the first time with *The Great Hunger* and a production of John B. Keane's *The Field* (1965), directed by

Ben Barnes. The decision to bring *The Great Hunger* was unpopular with many who believed that traditional Abbey fare would be more suitable for the debut of the National Theatre in Russia. Others believed that any success enjoyed by the play was ultimately because of the caliber of its source material. *The Great Hunger* also toured London in 1986, Paris in 1987, and the United States in 1988. Kavanagh's genius was revealed in *The Great Hunger* through his fearless undermining of the preoccupations of the day. By shaping the play in such an uncompromising way he remained true to the iconoclastic nature of Kavanagh's poem; in their staging, the playwright, director, and actors worked together to bring a broader awareness of theater to Irish audiences.

As *The Great Hunger* toured throughout the mid 1980s, the collaborators continued to produce innovative work for the Peacock stage. Their 1984 production, *The Bearded Lady,* was a theatrical exploration of the mind of Jonathan Swift. Mac Intyre interpreted Swift through the author's own work, depicting him as Gulliver in the land of the Houyhnhnms and the Yahoos. The male Houyhnhnms and the female Yahoos are effectively portrayed–the rational Houyhnhnms as horses on high platform hoofs, the Yahoos as wild and primitive monkeys. Each group moved accordingly in the Peacock Theatre production, as directed by Vincent O'Neill, who also played the Master Houyhnhnm. Critical reaction favored the performance of the piece over its text, but the collaborators furthered their explorations of the potentials of physical theater in this vivid production with Hickey as the conflicted Swift.

Rise Up Lovely Sweeney, the third collaborative production of Mac Intyre, Mason, and Hickey, was staged in September 1985. The play was a modern interpretation of the mythical story of Sweeney, *Buile Shuibhne,* who was cursed to wander Ireland as a bird. The myth has been explored by many, including Seamus Heaney in *Sweeney Astray* (1983), but Mac Intyre uses a modern idiom. Sweeney is politicized, a man on the run in contemporary Ireland. Again Hickey portrays a man with a damaged psyche, but the theatricality of the piece showed that Mason, Mac Intyre, and Hickey were not simply revisiting old territory but developing their work in an organic and challenging way. The design by Bronwen Casson created a clinical but disjointed environment where Sweeney realized the ambiguous anxieties of the age in a contemporary, broken Ireland. The "mad" Sweeney could be in an asylum or a hospital–the setting is clinical but not realistic or definitive in its location–but healing remains elusive. Mac Intyre's concern for the "hurt mind," as noted by Dermot Healy in his program notes for *Rise Up Lovely Sweeney,* quoting Sweeney–"I'm talking of the hurt mind, hurt mind in wait and knowing as the hurt mind knows"–can be recognized as central to his plays of this period.

Dance for Your Daddy was produced 2 March 1987. In *The Great Hunger* Maguire's relationship with his mother was central; in the latter play the playwright examines the relationship between father and daughter. In the original production Hickey played Daddy/Elderly Roué and Joan Sheehy played Daughter/Dark Daughter–the "hurt minds" in this case are the split or damaged psyches of the main characters. Snatches of dialogue in Irish, French, and English were combined in movement and dance with other stage languages in a way that had become synonymous with Mason's direction and the rehearsal process of the group. Other performances such as Vincent O'Neill as Homme Fatal/Dirty Old Man and Bríd Ní Neachtain as Wife/Liz Taylor highlighted the role of gender in society and the role-playing of the individual within that society. In *Dance for Your Daddy* father and daughter are seen struggling to redefine their relationship.

On 27 June 1988 the final play of the collaboration was staged. Mac Intyre's *Snow White* was directed by Mason and starred Hickey as the seventh dwarf, Sheehy as Rose Red, and Michele Forbes as Snow White. The absence of other actors who had performed in earlier plays and the participation of a new stage designer, Monica Frawley, signaled a change in direction for Mac Intyre. In *Snow White* the relationship of mother and daughter is central and, unlike in *The Great Hunger,* the mother is portrayed by an actor. Reminiscent of the Mother in *The Great Hunger,* however, is the presence of a dressmaker's dummy, and Snow White's interaction with it illustrates her perceived lack of physical affection. Mac Intyre uses the Grimm's fairy tale, as told by the seventh dwarf in the prologue, as a point of departure from which he considers issues of recrimination and loss. By using a multitude of references and images Mac Intyre examines another injury to the hurt mind.

Kitty O'Shea was Mac Intyre's first play to be produced at the Peacock after *Snow White.* Mac Intyre has referred to the "conservatism" of *Kitty O'Shea* as representing a new beginning for him. The play was directed by Ben Barnes and opened on 8 October 1990. With its dense language, *Kitty O'Shea* examines the fate of a woman who played a pivotal role in Irish history, having been credited with the downfall of Charles Stewart Parnell. Mac Intyre concentrates on O'Shea and her experience; the form of the play, with its monologues and memories, contrasts her attitude toward life with that of her daughter, Norah, and forces the women to reevaluate their own self-images.

In the early 1990s Mac Intyre worked with the recently formed Galway company Punchbag, who produced three of his one-act plays under the title *Go On Red* (1991); one of these one-acts, *Fine Day for a Hunt,* was produced separately by Punchbag the following year. Mac Intyre had a difficult working relationship with Punchbag,

Program cover for the first production of Mac Intyre's 1995 play, starring Karen Ardiff and Bryan F. O'Byrne (photograph by Amelia Stein; courtesy of Abbey Theatre)

however; in 1993 he and Hickey reworked another of the one-acts, *Foggy Hair and Green Eyes,* and presented it to a limited audience of ten people at the Clarence Hotel as a Project Arts Centre production for the Dublin Theatre Festival. Mac Intyre and Hickey had worked together earlier in 1993 on *Chickadee,* which Hickey directed for the Red Kettle Theatre Company of Waterford. Described on 19 May 1993 by an *Irish Times* reviewer, David Nowlan, as a play that "lies mid way between the lucid and the opaque," *Chickadee* is an unerring exploration of male sexuality through the relationship between the middle-aged Hubert and his young lover, Julie.

In 1991 Mac Intyre adapted his short story "The Mankeeper" for a theater-in-education project produced by Midas Theatre, a company set up under the auspices of Mary Immaculate College in Limerick. *The Mankeeper* was performed by professional actors, directed by Paul Brennan, and toured primary schools around Limerick city and county.

Mac Intyre returned to the National Theatre in 1994 with a production of *Sheep's Milk on the Boil,* which opened on 17 February. Elements of the collaboration of the 1980s were present: having successfully directed *Chickadee,* Hickey was once again working with Mac Intyre in the role of director; Mason, although not directly involved, was by this time artistic director of the Abbey. Mac Intyre identifies *Sheep's Milk on the Boil* as the beginning of his recent phase of work (including the successful 1995 production *Good Evening, Mr Collins*), which fuses the physicality of the earlier work with a poetic but at times prosaic use of language, an incisive and richly funny combination reflecting what the playwright referred to as "a new excitement with the verbal in the theatre."

Good Evening, Mr Collins was directed by Kathy McArdle and staged at the Peacock Theatre as part of the 1995 Dublin Theatre Festival. A rich and irreverent exploration of the life of Michael Collins (played by Brian F. O'Byrne in the first production and Seán Rocks in the 1996 revival and national tour), the play combines dark comedy with an affection for its central character. Collins is depicted as a man of love and loyalty both personal and political. Shades of Mac Intyre's earlier work are present in the form of the play and also in the character of Collins, portrayed as another of Mac Intyre's hurt minds, an all-too-knowing victim.

Mac Intyre shows a biting political awareness in his portrayal of Eamon De Valera, a national figure who became, as the playwright Marina Carr noted in the program for the 1995 production, "the Court Jester who has his eye on the throne." De Valera assumes many guises in the course of the play. As a schoolteacher in cap and gown in scene 4, he addresses the audience directly as if he were speaking to a class, then instructs Collins on the work of Niccolò Machiavelli. As a concert pianist in scene 5 of act 2, he plays music by Frédéric François Chopin throughout a scene in which Collins expresses foreboding; then, after Collins leaves the stage, De Valera rises and accepts the applause of his rapturous public.

The audience is given theatrical insight into Collins through the women in his life, Moya Llewellyn-Davies, Kitty Kiernan, and Hazel Lavery, played in the original production by the same actor, Karen Ardiff. While confusing at times, this casting decision underlines Collins's reputation as a ladies' man while drawing attention to the role of women in the history of state politics. Mac Intyre developed a textured language of Irish, English, and local idiom for the play to identify each character and to play with notions of Irishness. Collins speaks plainly but tells of disturbing dreams that resonate with the audience's knowledge of the circumstances of the character's death. In act 1, scene 6, Collins sits alone at a table, writing by candlelight. The intimacy of the scene grows as he speaks of his childhood and tells how he fell through a trapdoor as a child but was saved by "a lap of hay." He recalls telling that story previously and how the listener had wished that the lap of hay "always be there" for him. This evocative blessing is immediately challenged as Collins is confronted by a vision of De Valera, Kitty Kiernan, and the English army captain, taunting him as they move about the stage.

In *Good Evening, Mr Collins* Mac Intyre presents his audience with an irreverent version of history, by turns hilarious, contentious, and playful. The theatricality of the play was noted favorably by commentators, but its success with critics and audiences implies a level of awareness that was fostered by Mac Intyre's earlier work. The comedy and subversiveness of the piece owe much to the many and varied references with which the audience could identify, but underneath was a softness toward Collins and what Mac Intyre described in an afterword for *The Dazzling Dark: New Irish Plays* (1996) as "the man's courage, laughter, his fallible longings." The play was reworked and revived in 1996 at the Peacock Theatre before a successful national tour.

Mac Intyre again utilized dance in *You Must Tell the Bees,* devised by the playwright in collaboration with the Irish Modern Dance Theatre, known for its creative choreography and staging; the play was first performed in the Firkin Crane Arts Centre, Cork, on 26 September 1996. Although Mac Intyre's work was noted by this point for his use of image and movement onstage, his use of dance as the creative point of departure relates directly back to his work with the Calck Hook Dance Theatre in Paris in the late 1970s. Identified by its collaborators as "a dance theatre work," *You Must Tell the Bees* was choreographed by John Scott, with music composed by Rossa Ó Snodaigh. The piece is loosely based on Mac Intyre's poem "Widda," in which a beekeeper's widow tries to come to terms with her husband's death. The imagery of bees and honey and of capture and release are central, with the dancers embodying the widow's memories. The play also includes poetry and fragments of dialogue spoken by the dancers. The dancers remained more comfortable with the language of movement rather than the word in performance, but in its collaboration with as image- conscious a playwright as Mac Intyre the company brought an awareness of the body to the stage that is often marginalized in Irish theater. *You Must Tell the Bees* toured Ireland throughout September and October 1996; it was then performed at the Peacock Theatre as part of the Dublin Theatre Festival and was well received. Mac Intyre's use of language and poetry is balanced by an appreciation of the visual, which places him outside the literary Irish theater tradition; *You Must Tell the Bees* is a rich and evocative testimony to the playwright's vision.

The emergence of Mac Intyre as an innovative playwright with a deep commitment to the process of creation of a play did not signal a lack of interest in other literary genres. *The Harper's Turn,* a collection of short stories, was published in 1982, and another collection, *The Word for Yes: New and Collected Stories,* in 1991. He also published poetry collections, including *I Bailed Out at Ardee* (1987), *Fleurs-du-Lit* (1990), *A Glance Will Tell You and a Dream Confirm* (1994), and the Irish-language volume *Ag Caint Leis an mBanríon* (1997). Mac Intyre became a member of Aosdana, the affiliation of Irish artists, writers, and composers, in 1981. He has also written articles, screenplays, and a libretto for Opera North. There have also been radio productions of Mac Intyre's short stories and plays, including two versions of *Rise Up Lovely Sweeney,* in 1991 and 1993.

Mac Intyre's work and influence as a playwright has developed throughout his career. An early appreciation of modern dance and movement inspired his vision of a physical theater of image. As poet, novelist, and short-story writer, Mac Intyre demonstrates an extraordinary command of language, and he has combined this quality with his interest in physical expression to produce some of the most challenging works of Irish theater. These plays have not always been successful; some, such as *Doobally/Black Way,* have antagonized audience members, while others, such as *Snow White,* have been considered too abstract. The importance of Mac Intyre's contribution was encapsulated by the reaction to *The Great Hunger,* however, especially national and international reactions to the reworked version of the play in 1986. The response highlighted not only international attitudes to Irish theater, but also the reluctance of some Irish theater practitioners to challenge those attitudes. With the end of the Mason-Mac Intyre-Hickey collaboration, which also included designer Bronwen Casson and a core group of actors, Mac Intyre's work took a new direction. His plays of the late 1980s and early 1990s represent a distancing on the part of the playwright from some of the extremes explored by the collaboration. By the mid 1990s, however, Mac Intyre's work had found a balance; word and image worked together with the playwright's imagination and sense of play. Mac Intyre's influence can be found in the work of other emerging playwrights, including Michael Harding and Marina Carr.

An overview of Tom Mac Intyre's production history suggests that the National Theatre has offered him uncommon support. His work defies categorization, however; he writes with what fellow playwright Marina Carr describes, as quoted in the program for *Good Evening, Mr Collins,* "the Bandit Pen." The risks he has taken have not always been successful, but he continues to take them nonetheless. Mac Intyre's presence within the Irish theater tradition challenges actors and audience alike to allow themselves to experience all the potentials of theater.

References:

Mairead Byrne, "To Harvest. Two Men, A Poem, A Play. A Meeting Under Fire," *In Dublin* (6 May 1983);

Michael Etherton, "Patrick Mason at the Abbey: Theatre of the Image," in his *Contemporary Irish Dramatists* (Basingstoke: Macmillan Education, 1989), pp. 45–47;

Paul Hadfield and Lynda Henderson, "Plays in Performance: Ireland," *Drama: The Quarterly Review* (Autumn 1983): 45–46;

Dermot Healy, "Let the Hare Sit," *Theatre Ireland,* 11 (Autumn 1985): 9–10;

Katherine Holmquist, "In the Beginning Was the Image," *Theatre Ireland,* 6 (April–June 1984): 150–152;

Seamus Hosey, "The Abbey in Russia," *Theatre Ireland,* 15 (May–August 1988): 14–17;

Brendan Kennelly, "The Great Hunger for Experiment," *Sunday Tribune,* 20 September 1988, p. 21;

Helen Meany, "The Magic of Dissonance," *Irish Times* [Dublin Theatre Festival Supplement], 24 September 1996;

Deirdre Mulrooney, "Tom Mac Intyre's Text-ure," in *Theatre Stuff: Critical Essays on Contemporary Irish Theatre,* edited by Eamonn Jordan (Dublin: Carysfort, 2000), pp. 187–193;

Christopher Murray, "The Avant-garde," in his *Twentieth Century Irish Drama: Mirror Up to Nation* (Manchester, U.K. & New York: Manchester University Press, 1997), pp. 231–238;

Murray, "The State of Play: Irish Theatre in the 'Nineties," in *The State of Play: Irish Theatre in the 'Nineties,* edited by Eberhard Bort (Trier, Germany: Wissenschaftlicher Verlag Trier, 1996), pp. 9–23;

Fintan O'Toole, "Tom Mac Intyre Taking Away the Safety Net," *Sunday Tribune* [*Arts Tribune* supplement], 8 May 1983, p. 7.

Tony Marchant

(11 July 1959 -)

Peter Billingham

PLAY PRODUCTIONS: *Remember Me?* London, Theatre Royal, Stratford East, December 1980;
London Calling, London, Theatre Royal, Stratford East, June 1981;
Dealt With, London, Theatre Royal, Stratford East, June 1981;
Thick as Thieves, London, Theatre Royal, Stratford East, 11 November 1981;
Stiff, London, Soho Poly Theatre, November 1981;
Raspberry, Edinburgh, Edinburgh Festival, 30 August 1982; London, Soho Poly Theatre, 14 September 1982;
The Lucky Ones, London, Theatre Royal, Stratford East, 19 October 1982;
Welcome Home, Hemel Hempstead, Old Town Hall Arts Centre, 8 February 1983; London, Royal Court Theatre Upstairs, 16 March 1983;
Lazy Days Ltd., London, Theatre Royal, Stratford East, 1985;
The Attractions, London, Soho Poly Theatre, 13 July 1987;
Speculators, London, Barbican Theatre, The Pit, 9 December 1987;
The Fund Raisers, London, Finborough Theatre, July 1997.

Tony Marchant

BOOKS: *Thick as Thieves: Two Plays* (London: Methuen, 1982);
Welcome Home; Raspberry; The Lucky Ones: Three Plays (London: Methuen, 1983);
The Attractions (Oxford: Amber Lane Press, 1988);
Speculators (Oxford: Amber Lane Press, 1988).

PRODUCED SCRIPTS: *Raspberry,* television, BBC, 1983;
Reservations, television, BBC, 1984;
The Moneymen, television, London Weekend Television, 1986;
Death of a Son, television, BBC, 1987;
This Year's Model, television, 1988;
The Attractions, adapted from Marchant's stage play, television, BBC, 1989;
Take Me Home, television, BBC One, 1989;
Goodbye Cruel World, television, BBC, 1992;
Into the Fire, television, BBC One, 1995;
Holding On, television, BBC Two, November 1997;
Different for Girls, motion picture, BBC, 1998;

Great Expectations, adapted from the Charles Dickens novel, television, BBC Two, 12 April 1999;
Bad Blood, television, Carleton, 18 April 1999;
Kid in the Corner, television, Channel 4/Tiger Aspect, 24 November 1999;
Never Never, television, BBC, 4 November 2000.

OTHER: Poems in *No Dawn in Poplar* (London: Tower Hamlets Arts Project, 1980).

Tony Marchant's early work, which depicted the lives of the disenfranchised young in London's urban underclass, excited audiences and critics alike. Plays such as *The Lucky Ones* (1982), for which he received the Most Promising Playwright award from *Drama* magazine, characterize the vibrancy and promise of his early writing. This promise has been developed and fulfilled most completely in his work for television, dating back to the popular and critically acclaimed *Take Me Home* (1989).

Marchant received the Royal Television Society Writers Award/Best Drama Serial Award and the British Academy of Film and Television Arts's Best Drama Serial Award for *Holding On* (1997). This eight-part dramatization of lives in contemporary London places him in a line of left-wing dramatists for British television that includes Dennis Potter, David Mercer, and John McGrath.

Marchant was born into a working-class family in East London on 11 July 1959. He is married and has three sons. After winning a scholarship, Marchant attended a Catholic grammar school, necessitating a daily bus journey from his home in London's East End to the school in prosperous Blackheath in South London. This geographical journey might be seen as a prototype of the metaphorical journeys so central to much of Marchant's best work. These journeys delineate a dialectial tension between a character's working-class origins and the contrasting, bourgeois milieu into which that character moves. Such a move might be afforded, for example, by educational opportunity, career ambition, or–in the case of characters such as Shaun and Gary in *Holding On*–undisclosed personal traumas. The inherent struggles and contradictions for the individual who migrates across borders of class, environment, and ethnicity, for example, are crucial and pervading themes in all of Marchant's major works.

Marchant began to write around 1976, and he acknowledges the influence of the early punk era. More formal early influences included Barrie Keeffe's 1976 play *Gotcha* (televised in 1977) and Steven Berkoff's *Greek* (1979). Keeffe's play convinced Marchant that it was possible to write with passion and intelligence about working-class life, in a way that respected the class environment, while tackling the issues of disempowerment, disillusionment, and inner-city alienation. The exciting tactile physicality of Berkoff's performance language impressed Marchant, who realized that such work could reach a mass audience and attract serious–if controversial–critical attention. The two productions convinced Marchant that television and theater writing offered him the most potent and effective means of self-expression.

Marchant's first published work appeared in *No Dawn in Poplar* (1980), an anthology of poems published by the Tower Hamlets Arts Project, a local community press in the area of East London where he was born and grew up. The project was connected with the Worker Writers of Great Britain. Following the inspiration engendered by his encounters with the work of Keeffe and Berkoff, Marchant's first stage play, *Remember Me?* (1980), defined his future career development and established some of the abiding concerns of his later work. The play deals with two disenfranchised youths who break into their old school to steal back from a system that has marginalized and neglected them. The Theatre Royal, Stratford, in East London had opened a studio theater in the same year and met with Marchant after receiving his unsolicited script. Adrian Shergold, who later directed other work by Marchant, including the award-winning *The Lucky Ones* and the multi-award-winning *Holding On,* directed *Remember Me?* This significant relationship with the Theatre Royal expressed the interrelationship between Marchant and his working-class environment.

The Theatre Royal, renowned as the former base for Joan Littlewood's Theatre Workshop, continued to have a mission–reflected in its artistic policy–to produce plays by working-class writers for working-class audiences drawn from the surrounding East End location. In an unpublished interview Marchant recalled his father and friends coming to the 1981 premieres of *London Calling* and *Dealt With,* double billed as *Thick as Thieves,* with the same expectations that they would have brought to their regular visits to boxing bouts in the East End.

The early plays, from *London Calling* to *The Lucky Ones* and *Welcome Home* (1983), all feature individual male characters who are frequently damaged or compromised by their working-class roots. Within this genre the principal character type is the articulate but angry and confused young man, such as Paul in *London Calling* and Goldy in *Welcome Home.* These characters are imbued with a powerful, articulate awareness conveyed without condescension or idealization and expressed in a recognizable and authentic working-class idiom. Paul's vision of the freedom of dolphins swimming through the former dock waters is a potent meta-

Tilly Voshburg and Marion Bailey in the SoHo Poly Theatre production of Raspberry, *which premiered on 14 September 1982*

phor of his yearning for liberation and self-realization, feelings that are savagely undermined by his experience of the deprivations of late-capitalist, inner-city existence. The title of the play is taken from The Clash's definitive 1979 punk album, indicative of that counterculture with which Marchant identified.

Welcome Home deals with a group of young British soldiers returning to Britain after the Falklands War. They are back to officiate at the funeral of a comrade who died in that conflict. The dark irony inherent in the title of the play is carried throughout by Marchant's dialogue, which is characteristically uncompromising. More than in any of his other early work, the language embodies the ways in which the characters' physical and ideological environment brutalizes them. Another feature of these early plays is the dialectical clash between characters such as Goldy and those such as Sharp, whose aggressive, reactionary views are affirmed and celebrated by the dominant ideology of their times, during Margaret Thatcher's administration. Goldy, by contrast, becomes profoundly unsure about the values and base of that culture. In the final scene of the play Goldy has to risk his life to disarm the dysfunctional Polo, a younger soldier who has succumbed to post-traumatic stress. As he disarms Polo, Goldy says to the others: "he's trembling, like a little dog. . . . And I'm hugging him cos I want to . . . he might need it . . . he don't get his dignity from being ready to put the boot in and have a war with anyone who upsets him. No one does." In a play written during times of violent civil unrest, epitomized by race riots in Brixton, Toxteth, and elsewhere, Sharp expresses the threat of potential right-wing military intervention in British domestic affairs: "Some people think we should be doing something more useful . . . it's not as if this country is without its problems. . . . and the police can't always cope can they? . . . out of their depth in Brixton, Bristol, Liverpool . . . There's a growing feeling that we can sort out the problems. . . . Because we've proved ourselves."

By contrast, *The Lucky Ones* represents Marchant's first obvious use of a sharply ironic and satirical humor. The title itself carries a satiric edge, as it describes the young people employed as low-ranking civil service staff in a time of growing unemployment. Played by Phil Daniels (who went on to play the role of Gary Rickey in *Holding On*), protagonist Dave is a working-class character who sees through the transparency of the attempts of the status quo to motivate and control the staff. Dave's response is to resist taking the system, or its strategies, too seriously; his character is conveyed through his opening speech: "D'you want to hear a bit of philosophy? Why is it . . . that you can never get a bit of chocolate out of a vending machine? . . . I've seen people . . . slumped and sobbing beside vending machines. . . . Life is like a vending machine I reckon–out of order but with no sign up to warn you." Dave's principal adversary is Lawrence, a timeserving, middle-management civil servant who is responsible for the department where Dave and his acquiescent colleagues work. Lawrence, a comically developed character like Bendall in the earlier *Dealt With,* epitomizes and espouses the doctrine of "compliant acquiescence equals job security and–limited–advancement." In scene 6 of the play, Marchant cleverly uses the character to define the sometimes self-serving, smug ideology of that era:

> Let me put your freedom of choice into perspective. I was talking about this being England, 1982. Last week, personnel had 250 applications for two vacant clerical posts they advertised . . . you're what's known as the lucky ones. . . . Only fools would want to do something that might jeopardise their tenuous grip . . . and find themselves stranded in an ocean of . . . unemployment. . . . Let me know when you've seen the light. Cheers.

At the climax of the play there is a conflict focused on Lawrence's insistence that the clerks fulfill a double role as unpaid waiters and waitresses at a ceremony to commemorate the retirement of a senior figure. Dave seeks to lead a resistance to this routine exploitation but finds himself torn by the implications of Lawrence's realpolitik. Dave, who arrives at the function in a bar steward's uniform, seems to have capitulated. At the opening of scene 8, however, he emerges in the basement, having absconded with the retirement gift of a carriage clock. The gift is a perfect symbol for the reward of a timeserving and timekeeping orthodoxy. Following a final confrontation between Lawrence and Dave, the erstwhile rebel hands the clock over to his superior and loses his job. Where victory lies is unclear at the end of the play. Debbie–sufficiently inspired by Dave's actions–returns the humiliation inflicted upon them by suddenly removing Lawrence's wig. At times the author's political considerations intervene rather too much in the farcical, satirical dynamics of the play. Lawrence's character, for example, tends toward stereotype. Nevertheless, the character of Dave represented a new direction for Marchant, and he served as a subversive countersign, predating the character of Gary Rickey some fifteen years later in *Holding On.*

Raspberry (1982) is the only Marchant play in which the characters are exclusively female. Set in the maternity ward of a National Health Service hospital, this one-act play sensitively explores the growing friendship between two working-class women, both patients in the ward. Chris is an older woman in her thirties, and Eileen is seventeen. Chris is there to give birth, while Eileen is awaiting an abortion. With affection but without sentimentality, Marchant carefully delineates their increasing sense of mutual support and understanding. Chris and her husband had been trying unsuccessfully for a baby; she later reveals that she had an abortion in a private clinic when she was younger, suggesting a possibly tragic interconnection between the two events. In the final scene, Chris recounts an incident to Eileen:

> There's a young boy lives on our estate. He's a spastic, wears callipers. . . . the other kids . . . called him Raspberry. You know, raspberry ripple-cripple. One day, he turned round, stuck his tongue out and blew one. 'There's a raspberry', he said. . . . That's bottle, that's being strong. . . . All I know is you're in here, your boyfriend doesn't have to be. I'm in here, my husband ain't. . . . It's like having stones thrown at you–like the cripple boy. Like a raspberry. But we blow 'em as well, right, and stick up for ourselves.

These working-class characters are imbued with an emerging articulate sense of their own lives and of those reactionary social structures and attitudes that seek to repress and dictate to them. In these early plays Marchant is finding and defining his own "voice" while continuing to negotiate that journey from his working-class origins in Tower Hamlets to prosperous Blackheath.

Take Me Home established Marchant's credentials and stature as a major television dramatist. Consisting of three one-hour episodes, the series was broadcast in 1989 on BBC One in a late-evening time slot. It attracted critical acclaim and an unexpectedly high viewership of twelve million, making it an enormous success. The drama is set in one of the burgeoning "new towns" of the period and was actually filmed in Telford (although other new developments such as Milton Keynes had also been considered). Within this bleak, artificially constructed environment, a narrative unfolds centering upon the unlikely development of an affair between Tom, a middle-aged, working-class taxi driver, and Kathy, a young professional woman married to the "upwardly mobile" Martin. The young couple has been relocated through Martin's job as a computer programmer with INFOCO, a multinational Japanese information-systems corporation. The state of continual building evident in the environment of the new town captures and conveys the constructedness of the characters' lives and their postmodern alienation.

The dialogue in *Take Me Home* explores new areas of understatement and economy, in which subtext and oblique allusion begin to replace some of the relative certainties of the plays of the earlier period. Tom is trapped in a loveless routine of a marriage to

Liz, who finds work as a catering assistant at INFOCO. The predictability of their relationship is indicated through this dialogue of economy and depressing banality when, as they go to do their regular weekly supermarket shopping, Liz responds to Tom's "Did you do a list?" with "I don't have to, I know what we want." However, Tom's relationship with the younger Kathy develops precisely because he loses the lifelong certainty of "what we/he wants." The unlikely friendship begins when Tom picks up Kathy, a distressed and tearful "fare" (customer), and ultimately develops into a sexual relationship.

Kathy has uneasily agreed to Martin's demand that she abort their baby in the interests of their material security and advancement. Martin is a younger and potentially more successful variant of Bendal and Lawrence from the earlier plays. His character verges on stereotype in comparison with the intricately developed and textured characters of Tom, Kathy, and Liz. Nevertheless, he is as constructed by the values and strategies of the Thatcher era as the environment in which he and Kathy now find themselves. In episode 1 he refers to the unborn baby as "an accident . . . mistake . . . someone else in our house. It might even finish us before we've even begun."

Tom picks up Kathy in his cab when Martin fails to meet her at the clinic. They drive out to a park on the edge of town, where Kathy seeks Tom's advice and friendship. The location for what proves to be the initial stage in their future relationship is significant, as is the name of the minicab firm for which Tom works: "Frontier." Only at the edge, margins, or frontiers of their respective life experiences are they able to meet, relate, and engage in a critique of each other's lives. The sense of post-Romantic ennui and longing–developed in later Marchant works–is deftly communicated through the musical signatures given to Tom and Kathy: the pained emotionalism of Dusty Springfield ballads of lost love and rejection, and the melodic but socially aware lyrics of Deacon Blue (a Glasgow-based band that enjoyed a growing, if marginal, following at that time), respectively. Marchant skillfully uses understated dialogue between the two characters when they meet in the park. When Kathy initially tries to defend to Tom her decision to have the abortion, she says: "I don't know what I'm doing in this town. . . . I did it for us [her and Martin], for our happiness." Tom answers with the residual bitterness of a middle-aged man who has experienced redundancy at work and at home: "Well, this town's not all easy parking and badminton." When Kathy chides him by saying "You're just old fashioned," he remarks with irony and wisdom borne out of life's disappointments: "So? Look what 'modern's' done to you?" Underlying these tentative negotiations is a latent, mutual sexual attraction and overpowering personal need. Kathy observes: "People don't just lie back now and accept fate, you make your own luck," and the relationship moves inexorably into the potent but dangerous waters of sexuality.

They arrange secret liaisons, but inevitably the tensions of class and gender expectations undermine their liberating passion, as their partners also begin to suspect the unpinning of their own domestic agendas. A complex web of personal and public duplicity, as well as intimate and social betrayal, propels the four principal characters into a dangerous acceleration of fractured desire, loss, and revenge. One memorable image is of Tom–distraught beyond help at Kathy's apparent rejection of him–slumped, drunk, at an automatic teller machine in the Muzak-drenched shopping mall. Jeering teenage boys complete his descent into abject loss and suffering. This powerful image predates what is a central motif in *Holding On:* the "redemptive journey" of the character who, in seeking to escape the past, embarks on a transgressive journey that leads to personal suffering with wider social and public consequences.

Even as Tom and Kathy find a mutual reconciliation, the prospect of a new life together is ultimately–and painfully–destroyed by Tom's inability to leave his wife, Liz, at the climactic moment. In a scene of pathos and emotional loss, Tom's taxi is shown in the rain-drenched early hours approaching the soulless city center, where Kathy waits for him. The audience sees–from Kathy's disbelieving point of view–Tom arriving not alone but with Liz in the passenger seat of his taxi. This penultimate and climactic scene in episode 3 encodes powerful themes, such as the latent power of sexual desire and attraction to transcend, if temporarily, frontiers of class and age. The scene also signals the emasculating power of the past, which is meaningful only in terms of acknowledgment of the certainties of class with its resonant, traditional, unquestioning values.

The final scene of the series shows Tom taking Kathy, who is unlikely to ever return, to the railway station. The formalities of small talk are finally overtaken by an image of an anguished Tom watching the train carry away both Kathy and his hope of a liberated future. *Take Me Home* is a powerful piece and remains, along with *Holding On,* one of the major dramatic achievements of Marchant's career and of contemporary British television. As a cultural barometer of the late Thatcher period, it had a profoundly residual impact that can still be felt. In terms of the transference and development of wider political concerns into the context of individual sensibilities and lives, *Take Me Home* demonstrates an important stage in the development and maturing of Marchant's dramatic voice and technique. Marchant successfully presented leftist critique and analysis in the format of a drama that found great popular acclaim. He achieved this combination through his use of setting, the quality of the characterization and dialogue, and an intuitive recognition of the zeitgeist of the late 1980s.

Marchant endeavored to achieve a similar evocation of contemporary life in the series *Holding On,* broadcast in eight one-hour episodes on BBC Two in the autumn of 1997. *Holding On* is kaleidoscopic in structure and multi-ethnic and multivocal in its interweaving of narratives within contemporary London existence. The dominant themes in the drama are the binary oppositions enclosure/disclosure, private/public, as well as personal/political. The central character is Shaun, who starts out as a conscientious and hardworking investigator for the Inland Revenue (the British income-tax agency). Shaun's role as an investigator carries a dual significance: not only does he seek to investigate and prosecute the institutionalized injustices of the City represented by the corrupt businessman Werner, but Shaun's own character is investigated by Marchant as it is undermined by his escape from the demands and commitments of a traumatic past.

Shaun's descent into a personal hell is broadly similar to that of Tom's in *Take Me Home.* In execution and detail, however, Shaun's descent is more complex, representing even more of an achievement of plotting and characterization. Shaun becomes aware of the tragic and senseless murder of Sally, a clerical worker, by Alan, a paranoid schizophrenic. From the moment in episode 2 when he reads about the murder, Shaun's behavior begins to change drastically.

He negotiates a massive bribe to enable the subject of his investigation, Werner, and Werner's associates to avoid prosecution. He then betrays his wife by having an affair with Tina, a young woman who works in a travel agency. Shaun's public and personal betrayals have consequences that return to haunt him. As the authorities discover his criminal activities, and his wife becomes aware of the relationship with Tina, he plummets into the underclass of the marginalized inner city. Having provoked a savage beating upon himself in a crowded London bar, Shaun, bloodied and destitute, eventually arrives at the house of Annie, the mother of Alan, Sally's murderer. In this scene at the end of the penultimate episode, the audience discovers that Annie is also Shaun's mother. Oppressed by the demands and obligations of having to help care for Alan, Shaun ran away from home without warning or any contact thereafter. As he and Annie begin the slow, painful process of reconciliation, Shaun is able to begin to readdress his relationships with Alan and Vicki. Central to Marchant's authorial strategy is the conviction that both the private/public and the personal/political binaries are Möbius-strip indicators of contemporary life at the close of the twentieth century.

Another significant character who is obliged to confront his past in order to live fully in the present is Gary Rickey, a working-class restaurant critic. Gary, a fashionable food critic, is bulimic. This condition is in a complex web of connections with Gary's own revulsion and discomfort with his class origins. Privileged with direct address to the camera, Gary serves as a potent channel for Marchant's use of sharp satire and humor to comment upon the political and cultural expediencies and vanities of the age. A post-Thatcher "Basildon Man"–albeit from Billericay–Gary embodies the consumer ethic of unrestrained monetarism, asserting: "Culture? I eat it. Art? I want it on my plate."

Gary represents the linear development of Dave from *The Lucky Ones,* the skeptical, brashly masculine, working-class character caught between opposition to reactionary values and a pragmatic recognition of their enduring intrusion in social and political life. Through his bulimia he eventually loses his lucrative and well-paid job as a food critic. He begins the painful process of confronting and reconciling himself to his past through a chance meeting with a young Asian soccer reporter, Karen. Gary's return to his earlier work as a soccer reporter and his relationship with Karen offer some of the few surer grounds for optimism in the drama.

In episode 4 there is a good example of Marchant's use of Gary to disclose the inherent contradictions and hypocrisy of a governing culture in which, to use Marchant's own words in an unpublished interview everyone is "busy marketing their finer feelings. . . . it's just a brand, a copyright." This sequence also offers an important insight into the way in which the episodic structuring of the narrative enables different characters and narratives within the piece to interact and interconnect. The scene is in a restaurant where Gary is entertaining a New Labour apparatchik who agonizes over the "moral" implications of her expensive meal. Simultaneously, using Gary and Shaun passing one another in the restaurant as a visual narrative device, the camera comes across Shaun and Tina. The camera then pans up from the taxi in which Gary and his dinner companion travel back to his flat and enters the interior domestic world of Zahid and Helen.

Zahid is a young professional Asian working as Shaun's junior assistant on the Werner case. Frustrated and suspicious because Shaun seems to be operating independently and outside procedures, Zahid becomes the agent of the disclosure of Shaun's public and private deception. There is an inherent subtext of self-interest, as Zahid stands to gain a promotion for his crucial role

Perry Benson as Mr. Lawrence, Kim Taylforth as Debbie, and Phi Daniels as Tim in the Stratford East production of The Lucky Ones *in 1982*

in Shaun's downfall and arrest. Zahid and Helen also seek to negotiate their relationship in response to the pressures they both face in the context of Zahid's family background. When a frustrated Helen tells him that he cannot live two lives, Zahid retorts angrily: "That's bollocks, I've been living two, three lives all my life." These sentiments reflect abiding conflicts of integrity, loyalty, commitment and ambition that appear again throughout *Holding On:* there is a constant clamor between the demands, for example, of ethnicity, personal desire, and ambition.

These issues interweave through the narratives of Florrie, an Afro-Caribbean mother, and Chris, her son, whose senseless murder by a white middle-aged cab driver, Bernard, carries powerful and tragic overtones of the controversial Stephen Lawrence case, in which the failure of the police properly to investigate and prosecute the racially motivated killers of the black youth exposed deeply rooted institutional racism in the British legal system. Following Chris's death, Florrie and her daughter, Janet–supported eventually by Marcus, Chris's business partner in Massive FM, an underground radio station–embark upon a campaign for justice following the derisory two-year sentence handed out to Bernard. Ultimately, the complications of growing political awareness and compromised personal relationships drives Marcus, high on crack cocaine, to a suicide attempt. Florrie talks him out of it and begins completion of the cycle of grief, bitterness, and reconciliation. The tragedy of Chris's death is remembered and sustained in the hope of both personal reconciliations and a public/political conviction: "Our message is that a black life is not expendable. . . . We refuse to be guilty of the crime of being black."

In an eight-minute sequence at the end of the final episode Marchant employs the use of a bleak, darkly comic, travelogue-style voice-over from the recuperating Gary to serve as counterpoint to the panoramic view of life in London that *Holding On* constitutes. All of the principal narratives are referred to in this sequence, with Gary's breezy counterpoint acting as a kind of alienation device in terms of the human narratives that are presented. For most of the characters, there is evidence of hard-won hope for the future, although the tragedies of the deaths of Sally and Chris are a constant presence. In this final sequence Bernard, consumed by guilt, remorse, and rejection, commits suicide by throwing himself off a bridge over the Thames. As Bernard jumps, Gary comments reassuringly that "London's emergency services are the best in the world."

Holding On remains Marchant's most ambitious and successful work to date. The drama reveals his continued exploration of issues and themes that were embryonic in his earliest works for the stage. The personal and political agendas that are the central and distinguishing characteristic of his writing are brought into clear focus. Marchant has never engaged in simplistic agitprop in his work, even in the early dramas driven most fully by a passionate outrage at social and political oppressions and their human cost. Despite its considerable qualities and achievements, *Holding On* did not fare as well as *Take Me Home* in terms of audience figures, averaging only one to two and a half million viewers per episode. The lower figures can be explained in part by the proximity of the series scheduling to the sudden and unexpected death of Princess Diana. As David Snodin, the producer of both *Take Me Home* and *Holding On,* has since observed: "*Holding On* came out two days after her funeral, and most people were 'televisioned out' by then." Snodin went on to say that "nobody wanted to feel that London was a bad place" at that time.

Tony Marchant occupies an important role in contemporary British television drama as a writer of distinctive skill who informs his work with a passionate, questioning, and leftist humanism. This combination brings to his work a hard-won and measured optimism. Reflecting on the personal and political ethic that has characterized much of his work, Marchant commented in an unpublished interview: "The abiding theme of *Holding On* is about how we construct a society, and that's really about recognising mutuality and reciprocity, connectedness and the realisation that we don't go on our personal journeys in complete isolation or in a vacuum."

References:

Peter Billinghamm, "Holding On: Signs of the City. The Notion of the 'Redemptive Journey' in the Television Plays of Tony Marchant," in *On the Boundary: Turning Points in TV Drama, 1965–2000,* edited by Jonathan Bignell, Stephen Lacey, and Madeleine MacMurraugh-Kavanagh (Basingstoke: Macmillan, 1999);

John Dugdale, "No Cheeky Chappies, East End Villains or Docklands 'Glamour': Can This Really Be London? *EastEnders* Must Be in a Right Two-and-Eight. The BBC's Newest Drama Series Aims to Show What the Capital's Really Like," *Guardian* (London), 1 September 1997, II: 14–16;

John Lahr, "Young Turks of the Theatre: Playwrights Andrea Dunbar and Tony Marchant," *New Society* (4 November 1982): 220–221;

Cordell Marks, "How I Created *Holding On*'s Shaun," *Radio Times* (4–10 October 1997).

Frank McGuinness

(29 July 1953 -)

Ben Francombe
University College Bretton Hall

PLAY PRODUCTIONS: *The Factory Girls,* Dublin, Peacock Theatre, 11 March 1982; London, 1988;
Borderlands, Dublin, 8 February 1984;
Observe the Sons of Ulster Marching towards the Somme, Dublin, Peacock Theatre, 18 February 1985; London, Hampstead Theatre, July 1986; Boston, 1988;
Baglady, Dublin, Peacock Theatre, 5 March 1985; London, 1988; Springfield, Conn., 1988; produced as *Ladybag,* Dublin, Damer Hall, 23 September 1985;
Gatherers, Dublin, 29 September 1985;
Innocence: The Life and Death of Michelangelo Merisi Caravaggio, Dublin, Gate Theatre, 7 October 1986;
Yerma, adapted from Federico García Lorca's 1934 play, translated by Deirdre Ni Ceallaigh, Dublin, Peacock Theatre, 29 April 1987;
Rosmersholm, adapted from Henrik Ibsen's 1886 play, translated by Anne and Karin Bamborough, London, National Theatre, 1 May 1987;
Times in It, Dublin, Peacock Theatre, 10 May 1988;
Carthaginians, Dublin, Peacock Theatre, 21 September 1988; London, Hampstead Theatre, 1989; Williamstown, New York, 1991;
Peer Gynt, adapted from Ibsen's 1867 play, translated by Anne Bamborough, Dublin, Gate Theatre, 4 October 1988;
Mary and Lizzie, London, Barbican Theatre, The Pit, 27 September 1989;
Beautiful British Justice, in *Fears and Miseries of the Third Term,* Liverpool, 1989; London, 1989;
Three Sisters, adapted from Anton Chekhov's *Tri sestry* (1901), translated by Rose Cullen, Dublin, Gate Theatre, 28 March 1990; London, Royal Court Theatre, 1990;
The Bread Man, Dublin, Gate Theatre, 2 October 1990;
The House of Bernarda Alba, adapted from Lorca's *La casa de Bernarda Alba* (1944), translated by Ni Ceallaigh, Belfast, Lyric Theatre, July 1991;
The Threepenny Opera, adapted from Bertolt Brecht's *Die Dreigroschenoper* (1928), translated by Constance Hayes, Dublin, Gate Theatre, 9 July 1991;

Frank McGuinness (from the program for The Bread Man, *1990)*

Someone Who'll Watch over Me, London, Hampstead Theatre, 10 July 1992; New York, Booth Theatre, 1992;
The Stronger, translated from August Strindberg's *Fordringsägare* (1889), Dublin, Project, 8 February 1993;
The Man with the Flower in His Mouth, adapted from Luigi Pirandello's 1930 play, Dublin, Project, 8 February 1993;
The Bird Sanctuary, Dublin, Abbey Theatre, Spring 1994;
Hedda Gabler, adapted from Ibsen's 1890 play, New York, Roundabout Theatre, 1994;

Uncle Vanya, adapted from Chekhov's *Dyadya Vanya* (1897), Derry, The Guildhall, 20 February 1995;

The Caucasian Chalk Circle, adapted from Brecht's 1948 play, London, Cottesloe Theatre at the Royal National Theatre, 21 April 1997;

A Doll's House, adapted from Ibsen's *Et dukkehjem* (1879), London, West End, 1997;

Electra, adapted from Sophocles' play, London, Donmar Warehouse Theatre, 1997;

Mutabilitie, London, Royal National Theatre, 1997;

Dolly West's Kitchen, Dublin, Abbey Theatre, 1999; London, Old Vic Theatre, 2000;

The Storm, adapted from Alexander Ostrovsky's 1860 play, London, Almeida Theatre, 1999;

Miss Julie, translated from Strindberg's *Fröken Julie* (1888), London, Haymarket Theatre, 29 February 2000.

BOOKS: *The Factory Girls* (Dublin: Monarch Line, 1982; revised edition, Dublin: Wolfhound, 1988);

Observe the Sons of Ulster Marching towards the Somme (London: Faber & Faber, 1986);

Innocence: The Life and Death of Michelangelo Merisi Caravaggio (London & Boston: Faber & Faber, 1987);

Carthaginians and Baglady (London & Boston: Faber & Faber, 1988);

Mary and Lizzie (London: Faber & Faber, 1989);

Someone Who'll Watch over Me (London & Boston: Faber & Faber, 1992);

Booterstown (Oldcastle, Ireland: Gallery, 1994);

Mutabilitie (London: Faber & Faber, 1997);

Dolly West's Kitchen (London: Faber & Faber, 1999);

The Sea with No Ships (Oldcastle, Ireland: Gallery, 1999).

Collection: *Plays One* (London: Faber & Faber, 1996)–comprises *The Factory Girls; Observe the Sons of Ulster Marching towards the Somme; Innocence; Carthaginians;* and *Baglady.*

PRODUCED SCRIPTS: *Scout,* television, BBC Northern Ireland, 1987;

The Hen House, television, BBC Northern Ireland, 1989.

OTHER: *Borderlands,* in *TEAM Theatre Presents Three TEAM Plays,* edited by Martin Drury (Dublin: Wolfhound, 1988);

The Dazzling Dark, edited by McGuinness (London: Faber & Faber, 1996);

Henrik Ibsen, *A Doll's House,* adapted by McGuinness from a translation by Charlotte Barslund (London: Faber & Faber, 1996);

Sophocles, *Electra,* adapted by McGuinness (London: S. French, 1997);

Henrik Ibsen's Peer Gynt, adapted by McGuinness from a translation by Anne Bamborough (London: Faber & Faber, 1990);

Anton Chekhov, *Three Sisters,* adapted by McGuiness from a translation by Rose Cullen (London & Boston: Faber & Faber, 1990);

August Strindberg, *Miss Julie and The Stronger,* adapted by McGuinness (London: Faber & Faber, 2000).

Frank McGuinness is one of the leading Irish dramatists of his generation. His work reflects an Ireland that evolved in the 1980s, a decade in that country when, in the words of Fintan O'Toole, "impermanence became absolute, when the attempt to construct a realm of symbols and images and values that would be unchanging came into ever sharper conflict with a shifting, divided and contradictory reality." McGuinness takes the self-doubt that informed cultural debate in the 1960s and 1970s–the "I don't know, I-I-I don't know" that closes Brian Friel's *Philadelphia, Here I Come!* (1964)–and edges it toward a harder, broader perspective that interfaces history with the present, the positive with the negative, and society with the personal. McGuinness acknowledges–almost celebrates–conflict in his society, forcing the realization that harmony, peace, and stability can never precede the acceptance and, ultimately, the celebration of difference. Eamonn Jordan chose the title of scene 4 of McGuinness's play *Mary and Lizzie* (1989), "The Feast of Famine," as the title for his study of McGuinness's work. For Jordan this title "captures the confluence of positive, negative and contradictory forces" that is prevalent in McGuinness's work. This title, in turn, reflects a changing cultural identity in Ireland: the growing acceptance of objective analysis of the past, rather than the neurotic manipulation of history to suit a defined, isolationist society.

As a united Irishman (both Irish citizen and Ulsterman) McGuinness has the ability to step over the limitations and definitions of the border and examine personal tragedy and individual struggle irrespective of sides. McGuinness's leading characters–Pyper in *Observe the Sons of Ulster Marching towards the Somme* (1985), Caravaggio in *Innocence: The Life and Death of Michelangelo Merisi Caravaggio* (1986), and Dido in *Carthaginians* (1988)–are all removed from, and yet inextricably linked to, the community or culture that forms the context of the play. The isolation and the frustrated entrapment felt by these characters within a defining and at times brutally dogmatic context leads to the discovery of a deeper conflict, that of the personal.

Such an attempt to find a unifying definition for McGuinness's work, however, does not do justice to the prolific and diverse nature of his writing career.

McGuinness has continued with an academic career as well, and he has shown an academic's commitment to the broad perspective and to experimenting with a wide selection of dramatic styles, forms, and contexts. He has risen to the challenge of dramatic translation, drawing out a particularly Irish intensity to the works of such twentieth-century theatrical giants as Federico García Lorca, Anton Chekhov, and Bertolt Brecht. He has worked on large-scale and small-scale projects, attempting present-day social realism and historical expressionism. He has worked for theaters throughout Ireland and in Britain while remaining linked to the Abbey Theatre, Dublin. He has met with success and accepted criticism, and he has continued to find fresh ideas and new momentum.

McGuinness was born in Buncrana, County Donegal, on 29 July 1953. His parents, Patrick and Celine (O'Donnell) McGuinness, were a breadman and factory worker, respectively. He attended Carndonagh College, Donegal, from 1966 to 1971 and then went to the University College of Dublin, where he graduated in 1976 with a B.A. and M.Phil in medieval studies. The next year he became a lecturer at the University of Ulster, Coleraine. In 1979 he left and worked for a year at University College, Dublin.

McGuinness's first professional play evolved out of a writing workshop he attended in Galway in 1980. The workshop was presided over by Patrick Mason, who at the time was a staff director for the Abbey Theatre. *The Factory Girls* was premiered by the Peacock Theatre Dublin, the studio theater for the Abbey, in 1982.

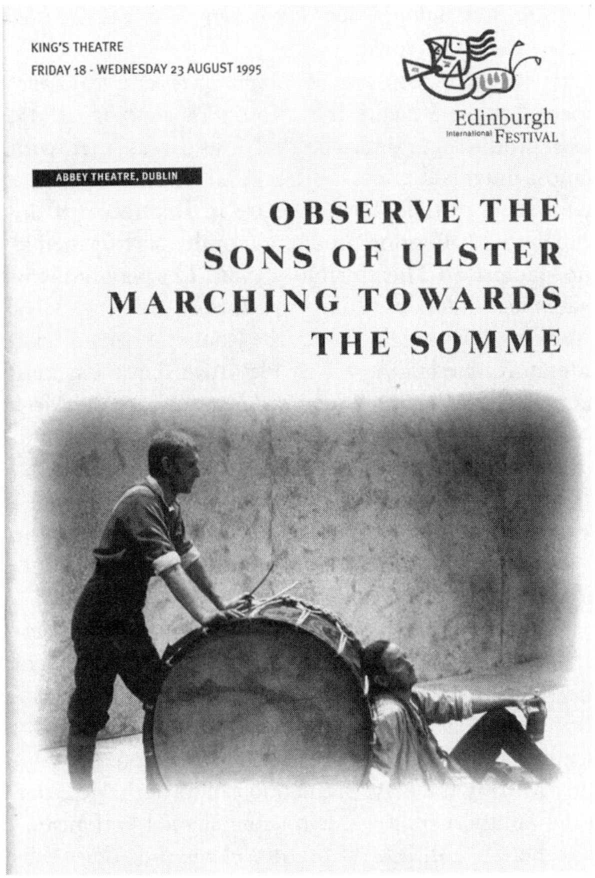

KING'S THEATRE
FRIDAY 18 - WEDNESDAY 23 AUGUST 1995
Edinburgh
International FESTIVAL
ABBEY THEATRE, DUBLIN
OBSERVE THE SONS OF ULSTER MARCHING TOWARDS THE SOMME

Program cover for McGuinness's play about eight Ulster Protestants fighting together in World War I (Collection of Frank McGuinness)

In his introduction to the collection *Plays One* (1996) McGuinness explains that his intention with *The Factory Girls* was "to write a play that celebrated the working-class culture of women in the part of Donegal I grew up in." *The Factory Girls* is a naturalistic play but not one "squarely within the literary tradition of Irish theatre," as Ray Comiskey suggests. Rather, *The Factory Girls* fits within the tradition of the social-realist community drama that had evolved in both Britain and Ireland in the 1970s. Its situation and central issues of exploitation and disenfranchisement of women within the working environment have strong parallels with Sarah Daniels's later community play *Gut Girls* (1988).

The play introduces five different women united first by their grudging tolerance of the extreme economic pressures that undermine the quality of their work, but ultimately by their refusal to accept the demands of their employers for redundancies and new working practices. The play shows the hopelessness of the industrial structures and conditions of rural Ireland in the early 1980s. Central to this situation is the hierarchy that dominates the working life of the factory, with a young, inexperienced manager and a complacent male union representative, who both refuse to acknowledge or respect the demands and needs of the women and ultimately underestimate the women's self-respect and unifying determination. Not realizing the pressures already on the women, the management imposes impossible new working practices. With no other option open to them, the women decide to occupy the manager's office in protest; yet, this joyous statement of resistance is slowly undermined by the inevitable suspicion of the Donegal community and the growing doubts of the vulnerable and isolated women.

The great strength of the play is the direct, combative dialogue drawn from personal insight. The celebratory nature of the play is never allowed to lapse into romantic myth. There is a real sense of inexperience, however, in the structuring of the climax, which falls into a confused transition of the balance of power within the group and weakens the theatrical impact. As a first play, *The Factory Girls* is naturalistic, personal, sincere, straightforward, and rough around the edges. Though McGuinness demonstrated his competence as a writer, few thought that *The Factory Girls* was the precursor to a masterpiece.

Observe the Sons of Ulster Marching towards the Somme opened at the Peacock Theatre on 18 February 1985. The production, directed by Mason, was met with almost universal critical acclaim and transferred to the main stage of the Abbey Theatre in December of the same year. A London production of the play opened at the Hampstead Theatre in July 1986. The play has won many accolades, including the *Evening Standard* Most Promising Playwright award, the Rooney Prize for Irish Literature, the Harvey's Best Play Award, the Cheltenham Literary Prize, the *Plays and Players* award for Most Promising Playwright, the London Fringe Award, and perhaps most significantly, the Ewart-Biggs Peace Prize. In 1994, coinciding with the Republican and Loyalist cease-fires of that year, the play was revived at the Abbey under Mason's direction and again won international acclaim.

Observe the Sons of Ulster Marching towards the Somme stands out as one of the most important Irish plays of the 1980s. On one level the play embraces the conciliatory spirit that had started to infiltrate the seemingly deadlocked conflict in the North. According to Christopher Murray the play "seemed to call forth the generosity of Southerners towards much-maligned Unionism," and there is a direct, celebratory element to *Observe the Sons of Ulster Marching towards the Somme* that calls for acknowledgment of the strong historical and cultural tradition of the Ulster Protestants. Indeed, the actual historical context of the play–the Battle of the Somme during World War I, in the critical year of 1916–shows how McGuinness was determined to force acknowledgment of a plural history in Ireland. McGuinness has talked of his "extreme anger" on discovery of the dissipation of the Loyalist Regiment, the Thirty-sixth Division, in the carnage of this infamous battle and of the fact that this strand of Irish history had been kept from him and the rest of Catholic Ireland. As Charles Hunter reported in *The Irish Times* (15 February 1985), McGuinness believes that if the knowledge of the parallel, historical turning points of 1916 had been shared then, it could have led to "an imaginative understanding of why people were behaving the way they did."

There is a deeper, darker level to *Observe the Sons of Ulster Marching towards the Somme,* one that draws the audience away from social, historical, and political statements on the concept of Irishness and toward a more personal, emotional, and universal examination of human nature. Ultimately, in *Observe the Sons of Ulster Marching towards the Somme* the history is that of personal memory. Unifying mythology sits uncomfortably alongside–and at times, conflicts with–personal life experience. Rather like the five women in *The Factory Girls,* the eight men at the Somme unite ultimately through their commitment to each other as individuals, rather than through their Ulster inheritance. As one of the men, Crawford, says for all of them, "I'm a soldier that risks his neck for no cause other than the men he's fighting with"–not for God, not for King and Empire, and not for Ulster. The tragedy of this philosophy lies in the fact that it takes the brutal horror of their experiences in Flanders and the brave acceptance of death to draw this personal and individual consciousness out of the mire of predefined identity.

The inevitability of this inglorious Road to Damascus is revealed from the start. In "Remembrance," the first of four parts within the play, the audience discovers Pyper, a lonely, present-day survivor, who delivers a guilt-ridden, angry affirmation of his debt to "the irreplaceable ones" whom he left behind on the battlefield. Pyper stands alone as Ulster stands alone; and as he grows older and gets closer to death, he begins to expose the terrible emotional conflict between personal sacrifice and political posturing:

> We claimed we would die for each other in battle. To fulfil that claim we marched into the battle that killed us all. That is not loyalty. That is not love. That is hate. Deepest hate. Hate for one's self. We wished ourselves to die and in doing so we let others die to satisfy our blood lust.

Thus, to Pyper at least, "Ulster lies in rubble" and the "temple of the Lord is darkness," and so he calls on his ghostly comrades and the ghost of his former self to "dance in the deserted temple of the Lord" and to relive their experiences of coming to terms with their own mortality.

In the second part, "Initiation," the volunteers meet for the first time in the makeshift barracks of a training camp. The dramatic contrast between this act, with its straightforward series of introductions, and the preceding bitterness and lonely anguish could not be greater and serves to strengthen the tragedy of eventual and inevitable disillusionment. The men show a seemingly innocuous pride in the geographical distinctions of background: from Enniskillen and Tyrone, from Coleraine and Derry, and from Belfast. Their polite interest in, or jovial contempt for, their new comrades' townships, professions, and pastimes seems nothing more than good humor and up-front posturing. Throughout, there is an absolute presumption of Protestant unanimity that leads to a gradual freeing of language and the more direct expression of opinions. The strength of this uniting force is demonstrated beyond all doubt by their blind commitment to the war they are going to fight: "my country's at war," and they go "for the glory of his majesty the King and his people." Doubt has no place in this barracks. The younger Pyper, determinedly on the outside of this group, raises one small, ironic voice in conflict to the received dogma. He is at war "because I'm dying anyway. I want it over quickly." Pyper's individualist pronouncements are seen as just that–individual, the words of a joker or "rare buckcat." His suggestion that "we could end up dying for each other" is frankly amazing and repulsive to the others with their higher, grander beliefs.

The transformation between this part and the third part, "Pairing," which takes place in Ulster during their first period of leave, is stark and portentous. In the time lapse between the two acts partnerships have formed, the embryos of which were seen in the previous act, and the public and political posturing has been eroded and replaced by a personal and emotional self-consciousness brought on by the realities of this war. The stage is divided into four areas. Within four separate locations McGuinness skillfully links four isolated conversations that expose a growing and painful doubt, borne out by the memories of the horrors of France and through the emotional discoveries that envelop the conversations. Of the four conversations two dominate: one through the drama of actions, the other through the drama of words.

Craig has brought Pyper home to Boa Island on Lough Erne. Dominating the island and the conversation between the two is a series of stone carvings. These sexually ambiguous stone figures draw out much in Pyper's troubled young mind. At first he sees them as symbols of his Protestant ancestors–the Protestant Gods–that he has reacted against. The metaphor of sculpting drawn out by Craig's insistence that Pyper "carves" him in a way that is "beyond language" takes them from the "stone" of rigid dogma to the "flesh" of human contact by way of their clear sexual unification. The liberation of the sexual act is far from clear, however, as it merely brings Pyper into sharper realization of the false nature of his earlier escape from Ulster and the great Unionist leader Edward Carson. He has been drawn into the world of Craig who, himself, is trapped by his Protestant identity. Craig tells Pyper that "Carson is asking you to dance in the temple of the Lord," and Pyper is ready.

The most dramatic confrontation with reality, however, is left to Anderson and McIlwaine, the raucous pairing from the shipyards of Belfast. Their Orange (Protestant) credentials, laid out bluntly in the meetings previously, are further demonstrated by their determination to march alone, save for a bottle of Bushmills whiskey and a traditional Lambeg drum, to "the Field"–destination of the annual "Twelfth" parade of

Rosalean Linehan in a scene from the Abbey Theatre production of McGuinness's Carthaginians, *which premiered on 21 September 1988 (photograph by Fergus Bourke)*

the Orange Order (commemorating the victory of Protestant William III over the Catholic James II). The Twelfth of July, however, has passed, and the field is deserted. Isolated and lonely, they start to lose heart. McIlwaine explains, "it's no good here on your own. No good without speakers. No good without bands." McIlwaine takes these drunken ramblings onto a darker plain: he hits the drum, and the sound reminds him of the ill-fated *Titanic* hitting the Lagan River when she was launched. Anderson sees the warning signs–"We weren't to blame. No matter what they say"–but McIlwaine has drawn an ominous parallel: "The war's cursed. It's good for nothing. A waste of time. We won't survive. . . . The war is our punishment." Attempting to drag McIlwaine out of his guilt-ridden thoughts, Anderson says, "There's more than Belfast in this war," though McIlwaine quickly continues, "but Belfast will be lost in this war. The whole of Ulster will be lost." Alarmed, Anderson forces McIlwaine to the drum and demands he play loudly with his fists. The sound, drowning out the doubts, brings the lights up on all areas: the drumming and the speech making that Anderson belatedly attempts, speaks to all the volunteers. Anderson, attempting to capture the rhetoric of glorious commemoration, gradually comes to realize the stark message in that rhetoric:

> The Boyne is not a river of water. It is a river of blood. The blood that flows through our veins, . . . And this blood will not be drained into the sewers of an Irish republic. . . . We will fight it as we have fought in other centuries to answer our King's call. . . . And our men will follow that call to freedom. They will fight for it. They will kill for it. They will die for it. . . . Die, die, die.

Suddenly Anderson realizes their fate. All eight volunteers are trapped in the destiny of the Protestant people of Ulster. They stand alone–united, but alone–against the forces of history, proud but helpless against the inevitable outcomes of Home Rule (the movement for internal autonomy for Ireland) and of the war they now see as their personal undoing.

In many ways the revelations within this play are now complete. The final act, "Bonding," has a wider significance: a drawing of the audience into a sympathetic acknowledgment of tragic inevitability. The symbols displayed in this act–the reenactment of the sham Battle of Scarva, the Last Prayer, and the final exchange of Orange sashes–only serve to accentuate the feelings of rhetorical impotence set against the now-clear agenda of historical inevitability. The most poignant moment comes by way of Pyper's affirmation of his Ulsterman's soul, a conversion that comes too late. Speaking of the odor coming from the Somme, he announces: "It smells like home. It's bringing us home. We're not in France. We're home. We're on our own territory. We're fighting for home." The rhetoric no longer has resonance. While Pyper has finally gained his Unionist credentials, the others are weary with the burden of theirs. Craig retorts, "It's too late to tell us what we're fighting for. We know where we are. We know what we're to do. And we know what we're doing it for. . . . You won't save us. You won't save yourself."

Despite this blunt rejection there is a positive tinge in Pyper's Unionist embrace, for with this belated confirmation comes the final and genuine unification of this small group of men. McGuinness, in the process, carefully directs his audience toward acceptance of Pyper and his comrades; the audience is pleased when Pyper finally agrees to wear a sash in battle.

What is so strong in *Observe the Sons of Ulster Marching towards the Somme* is the way that McGuinness has blended naturalism and expressionism, or more accurately, a strong narrative with symbolic significance. The identification and exploitation of this historical moment and the shifting emotional force behind the shifting political perceptions is central to the power of the play. While McGuinness has thus far failed to repeat the theatrical strength of *Observe the Sons of Ulster Marching towards the Somme,* he has, in three of his four major plays since, made a conscious attempt to develop a clear expressionistic style.

In *Innocence,* directed by Mason at the Gate Theatre, Dublin, in 1986, McGuinness attempts to repeat the expressionistic exploitation of the historical, focusing this time on the life of the Italian post-Renaissance painter Michelangelo Merisi Caravaggio. Again, McGuinness explores the interface of glory and celebration with the cruel, darker world of personal entrapment, in the process drawing the spectator through the blunt and violent world of patronage and prostitution.

There is much of Pyper in McGuinness's Caravaggio: both are artists struggling to come to terms with their own world. The difference is that Pyper's deliberations on personal pressures prevent him from continuing his work. Caravaggio, on the other hand, is prolific–a man touched with a tragic genius–precisely because of his sense of his own damnation. The "Feast of Famine" is clear: the expression of beauty through the rough, dark world of Rome. "Life" and "Death," which serve as titles for each act, represent the light he sees and paints, and the dark he imagines, the desire for truth and painting "as God intended the eyes to see" and the reminder of "unpleasant truths" as his benefactor, the Cardinal, suggests. Caravaggio embraces the idea that he is "chosen, not commissioned," yet, he sees being chosen as entrapment, dragging him toward inner darkness. The painful meeting with his brother makes him confront the desperate belief that he paints the truth. The brother attacks Caravaggio's work and says, "you paint like a drunkard sees. Badly. It's as if you're asleep. All in the dark." The brother underlines observations made by both Lena, Caravaggio's erstwhile model and companion, and the Cardinal. Caravaggio's vision seems distorted to these people. The Cardinal remarks, "God saw good and evil. You saw evil." At the heart of Caravaggio's religious observance, therefore, is guilt and deep frustration at never being able to reach the spiritual totality of religious expectation.

McGuinness's Caravaggio is a deeply human person, entrapped not by the weakness of the flesh but by the belief that these "weaknesses" have entrapped him. His homosexuality, an example to him of his own transgression, is to McGuinness almost incidental, just one part of a hugely complex personality. With this essential compassion McGuinness draws the audience out of historical reflection toward a clear modern parable: an indirect challenge to the moral, social, and political intransigence that had dominated the demanding Free-State identity, but was by 1986 beginning to crack.

In this way *Innocence* is a clear companion to *Observe the Sons of Ulster Marching towards the Somme:* a celebration of the complex individual, confronted by a

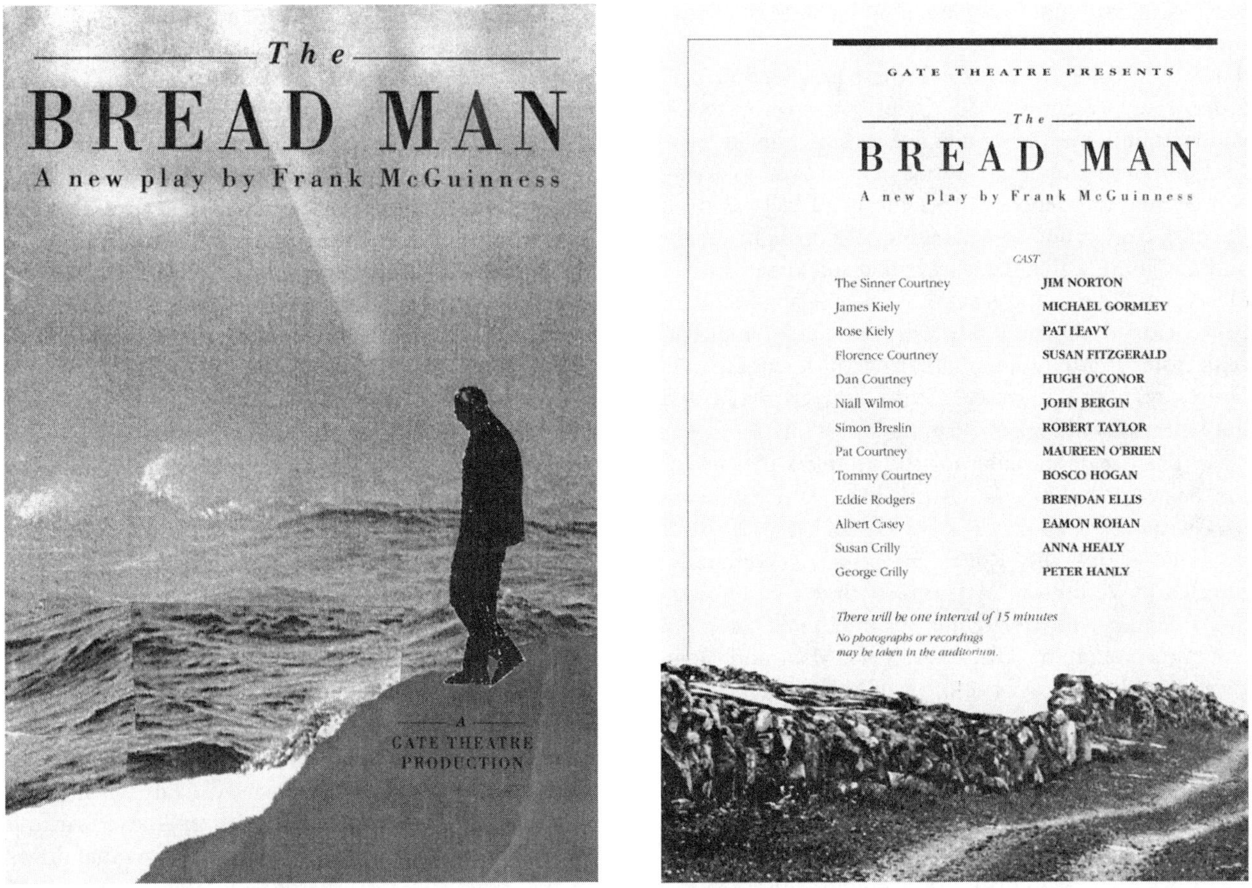

Program cover and cast list for McGuinness's 1990 play (Collection of Frank McGuinness)

crude presumptive reality. In this world of blunt and direct symbolism, however, McGuinness could not hope to repeat the profoundly moving revelations of his previous play. *Innocence* lacks the genuinely demanding experience of the profoundly personal examination of cultural and political taboos and falls into the self-conscious examination of themes using a crude, sexual world as diluted analogy. Nonetheless, *Innocence* stands as a useful staging post in McGuinness's journey to discover an expressionistic form that adds a symbolic overlay to a naturalistic base.

McGuinness's expressionist experiments are given firmer context within his 1988 play *Carthaginians*. The play was originally written for Field Day Theatre Company, the Derry-based, predominately Nationalist, theater group, but ultimately premiered at the Abbey under the direction of Sarah Pia Anderson.

Carthaginians works as a Northern-Catholic companion to *Observe the Sons of Ulster Marching towards the Somme*. The focus again is on an isolated group of individuals in crisis, who are removed from a community and its defined structures. Three women and three men are camping in a cemetery in Derry City waiting for the dead to rise. More deliberate than that of the Protestant soldiers, the group's isolation is a self-imposition that stands as a stubborn, but inevitable, response to what James Liddy has called "a culture tragically frozen in permanent present." The testament to the war-weary Catholic population of Northern Ireland is clear: through the characters' storytelling, the analogy of Virgil's Dido and Aeneas draws parallels between the destruction of Carthage by Rome and that of Derry by the British Army on Bloody Sunday in 1972. Indeed, McGuinness strengthens the link between the two through the introduction of a seventh character, Dido, a "patriot and poof," a distorted "queen" of this distorted Carthage. McGuinness again uses a homosexual character not to draw out a particular issue, but as a control to the isolation of the graveside dwellers. As he stands starkly alongside the others, prepared to perform the normal chores, Dido's personal isolation serves as a justification for the group's seemingly strange rejection of the turbulent normality beyond the gates.

The cathartic experience of playing out the ridiculous and the trivial, through the modern-day ritual of the general knowledge quiz and the enthusiastic enactment of a burlesque play on Bloody Sunday, draws these characters out of their personal preoccupations. There is nothing strange about these people, united in a distorted present day. As the play moves on to the climactic Sunday–the moment of resurrection–the victims of that fateful Derry Sunday are evoked as a way of releasing the people of this corner of Ireland from the dark, guilty, and static memory. As the light breaks and birdsong begins, Dido says that it is time to leave Derry, to "love it and leave it." Once again McGuinness demands a fresh start, dragging a moment of Irish history into a calm and balanced present day. As Dido says, "how's Derry? Surviving. Carthage will not be destroyed."

The act of speaking for the voiceless that lies at the heart of *Carthaginians* is taken to its extreme in McGuinness's 1989 play *Mary and Lizzie,* first performed in London by the Royal Shakespeare Company, directed by Anderson. McGuinness draws on two historical figures who are no more than footnotes in someone else's biography. Two Irish sisters, Mary and Lizzie Burns, are known to have lived with Friedrich Engels and guided him through the working-class districts of Manchester. This fact is all that is known of Mary and Lizzie; they are voiceless and faceless. Their contribution to the most important philosophical debate of the nineteenth century is undefined in such an extreme way as to leave them in an historical purgatory, neither fully historical nor fully mythical. McGuinness exploits this anomaly by taking the sisters on a journey through various locations that are both mythical and historical, constructing a surreal dream play that allows them to use their floating status as a counterpoint to the repression and discontent of the other characters in the play.

First, there are the women within the "City of Women," unmarried mothers abandoned by English soldiers and rejected by their own community. Mary and Lizzie feel attracted by the women's suspension from defined lifestyle but find no salvation in their violent hatred. Nor do they find salvation in the false seduction of "Mother Ireland'" or her son, the "Magical Priest," who represents the "killing combination" of Protestantism and Catholicism. Mary and Lizzie escape out of the mythical restrictions of Ireland into the clearer historical restrictions of Victorian England, meeting the Queen Victoria herself, a petulant, selfish, pantomiming dame who shows little interest in charitable governance. Finally, they move to Manchester and to Engels who, when first discovered, is enjoying a period of rest and relaxation in bed with Karl Marx. In spite of this dalliance, it becomes clear that both men lack the sexual openness and emotional courage that have become central to the characters of Mary and Lizzie. Through Engels's inability to confront his own sense of the "dark" when shown the "dangerous poor," his account of the Manchester poor is exposed as detached and meaningless as Mary sneers, "Change the world, eh? Change yourself first. Mr. Engels is afraid of the dark."

Throughout these episodes a virtue is made of the sisters' dreamlike status, their ability to move from location to location and from theatrical style to theatrical style, detached from the situations that have cast restrictions on others, yet able to draw out a particular celebratory joy within the tragedy. This play shows McGuinness at his most provocative and contradictory, drawing out high theater from moments of harsh conflict. Scene 4, "The Feast of Famine," forms the heart of *Mary and Lizzie* and stands at the heart of McGuinness's work: a ballad-singing pig describes a ritual celebration of the central evocative moment in Irish history. The scene is a complete exploitation of theatrical convention for the purposes of breaking down received assumptions and bringing forward wider symbolic and personal resonance: the voiceless finding a voice.

Mary and Lizzie stands as a climax in McGuinness's most overt expressionistic experiments. His next major play, *Someone Who'll Watch over Me,* which premiered in 1992 at the Hampstead Theatre in London under the direction of Robin Lefevre, is a return to a clearer narrative- and character-based drama that draws on the experiences of Western hostages in Lebanon. Because of the international issues the play raised, *Someone Who'll Watch over Me* was an outstanding success, transferring first to the West End and then to Broadway, where it was nominated for a Tony Award. For the critics the play was a return to the form of *Observe the Sons of Ulster Marching towards the Somme.* There is a neatness to the structure in the nationalities of the three main characters: an Irishman, an Englishman, and an American. The narrative is driven by the kind of dialogue familiar to those who have read the autobiographies of real-life hostages such as Brian Keenan, who offers a passionate introduction to the published script. On first inspection it appears that McGuinness has rejected expressionist messages and replaced them with direct, blunt, even crude representation. There are stereotypes at work here: the American, Adam, is physical and competitive, brash and vain; Edward, the Irishman, is talkative and loud, loves the horses and the drink; the "Brit," Michael, is foolish and pompous, sexually repressed, and educated, but not about Irish history. On the first level of insight–the insight of captivity–these stereotypes serve McGuinness well. Each hostage deals with confinement in predictable ways: Adam keeps fit, Edward escapes into his imagination, and Michael attempts to keep a stiff upper lip. The inevitable conflict among these characteristics forms a natural entertainment, both for the audience and for the characters themselves. Like the graveside dwellers in *Carthaginians,* Adam, Edward, and Michael relieve the tedium of waiting by playing games; and in this play the games are drawn from the characters' own understanding of their defined identities. The central game, selecting quite different, treasured memories, is a simple confirmation of separateness: they each have different and predictable tastes in music, literature, and movies. In the separateness, however, there is celebration. The reaching out for popular culture–the desire to remember what has personal meaning regardless of social and ordered significance–draws the stereotypes away from reactionary divisions.

In the face of the blunt uniformity of their situation–chained together, representative "Western" pawns in a harsh game of political and religious posturing–the hostages triumph in their differences. In the acknowledgment of difference McGuinness takes his characters through the sniping separation of early conversation to a point where they show genuine love and compassion.

Someone Who'll Watch over Me is blunt and at times crude. The situation that surrounds the characters is a cruel one, but McGuinness struggles through to discover a rich sense of shared human need. The final interaction between the Irishman and the Englishman, in which Edward initiates an act recounted earlier by Michael, by combing his hair, is a gesture of remarkable tenderness at the moment of ultimate separation.

McGuinness always looks for the tenderness behind the conflict, the celebration within the difference, or the feast of the famine. His plays are, like all great Irish literature, universal while remaining strongly locked within the mood of a nation. McGuinness uses the darkness of defined identity as a starting point for positive examination of the personal and spiritual. McGuinness, writing about Keenan's memoir of captivity, *An Evil Cradling* (1992), could be writing about his own work when he states, "from this horror has come something wonderful."

References:

Richard Allan Cave and Martin McLoone, "J'Accuse: A Study of *Mary and Lizzie* and *The Hen House,*" *Theatre Ireland* (December 1989): 56–82;

Ray Comiskey, "Frank McGuinness: A New Breed of Irish Playwright," *Irish Times,* 2 May 1987;

Brian Cosgrove, "Orpheus Descending: Frank McGuinness's *Someone Who'll Watch over Me,*" *Irish Literary Review: A Journal of Irish Studies,* 23 (Autumn/Winter 1993): 197–201;

Michael Etherton, "Dublin and Belfast: Frank McGuinness, *Observe the Sons of Ulster Marching towards the Somme,*" in his *Contemporary Irish Dramatists* (Basingstoke: Macmillan, 1989), pp. 47–51;

Claire Gleitman, "'Like Father, Like Son': *Someone Who'll Watch over Me* and the Geopolitical Family Drama," *Eire Ireland* (Spring/Summer 1996): 78–88;

Jennifer Johnston, Paul Arthur, and Lynda Henderson, "The Bread Man," *Theatre Ireland* (Winter 1990/1991): 35–39;

Eamonn Jordan, *The Feast of Famine: The Plays of Frank McGuinness* (Berne: Peter Lang, 1997);

James Liddy, "Voices in the Irish Cities of the Dead: Melodrama and Dissent in Frank McGuinness's *Carthaginians,*" *Irish University Review,* 25 (Autumn/Winter, 1995);

Helen Lojek, "Differences without Indifference: The Drama of Frank McGuinness and Anne Devlin," *Eire Ireland* (Summer 1990): 56–68;

Lojek, "Watching over Frank McGuinness' Stereotypes," *Modern Drama,* 38 (Fall 1995): 348–361;

Christopher Murray, "'A Modern Ecstasy': Playing the North," in his *Twentieth-Century Irish Drama: Mirror Up to Nation* (Manchester: Manchester University Press, 1997), pp. 187–222;

Fintan O'Toole, *A Mass for Jesse James: A Journey through 1980's Ireland* (Dublin: Raven Arts, 1990);

O'Toole, "'You Don't Think I'm as Stupid as Yeats, Do You?'" *Irish Times,* 24 September 1988;

Anthony Roche, "Northern Irish Drama: Imagining Alternatives," in his *Contemporary Irish Drama: From Beckett to McGuinness* (Dublin: Gill & Macmillan, 1994), pp. 216–277;

Victoria White, "Someone to Watch over Him?" *Theatre Ireland* (Summer 1993): 22–24;

Angela Wilcox, "'The Temple of the Lord Is Ransacked,'" *Theatre Ireland* (Winter 1984/1985): 87–89.

Papers:

A collection of Frank McGuinness's manuscripts is at the National Library of Ireland.

John Mortimer

(21 April 1923 –)

Richard Foulkes
University of Leicester

See also the Mortimer entry in *DLB 13: British Dramatists Since World War II.*

John Mortimer (photograph by Julian Calder)

PLAY PRODUCTIONS: *The Dock Brief* and *What Shall We Tell Caroline?* London, Lyric Opera House, Hammersmith, 9 April 1958; London, Garrick Theatre, 20 May 1958;

I Spy, Salisbury, Salisbury Playhouse, 16 March 1959;

Triangle, Cleaning up Justice, and *Collector's Peace Conference,* in *One to Another,* by Mortimer, Harold Pinter, and N. F. Simpson, Hammersmith, Lyric Theatre, July 1959;

The Wrong Side of the Park, London, Cambridge Theatre, 3 February 1960;

Lunch Hour, Salisbury, Salisbury Playhouse, 20 June 1960; London, Criterion Theatre, 13 February 1961;

Collect Your Hand Baggage, London, London Academy of Music and Dramatic Art, December 1961;

One over the Eight, includes sketches by Mortimer, music by Lionel Bart, London, 1961;

Two Stars for Comfort, London, Garrick Theatre, 2 April 1962;

Changing Gear, includes sketches by Mortimer, Lionel Bart, 1965;

A Flea in Her Ear, translated from Georges Feydeau's *La Puce à l'oreille,* London, National Theatre at the Old Vic, 8 February 1966;

The Judge, Hamburg, Deutsches Schauspielhaus, 29 January 1967; London, Cambridge Theatre, 1 March 1967;

Home, ballet scenario by Mortimer, London, 1968;

Cat among the Pigeons, translated from Feydeau's *Un Fil à la patte,* London, Prince of Wales Theatre, 15 April 1969;

Come as You Are, London, New Theatre, 27 January 1970–comprises *Mill Hill, Bermondsey, Gloucester Road,* and *Marble Arch;*

A Voyage round My Father, London, Greenwich Theatre, 25 November 1970; London, Haymarket Theatre, 4 August 1971; Oxford, The Playhouse, 2 May 1995;

The Captain of Köpenick, translated from Carl Zuckmayer's *Der Hauptmann von Köpenick,* London, National Theatre at the Old Vic, 9 March 1971;

I, Claudius, adapted from Robert Graves's *I, Claudius* and *Claudius the God and His Wife Messalina,* London, Queen's Theatre, 11 July 1972;

Collaborators, London, Duchess Theatre, 18 April 1973;

Heaven and Hell, London, Greenwich Theatre, 28 May 1976–comprises *The Fear of Heaven* and *The Prince of Darkness;*

The Lady from Maxim's, translated from the Feydeau's *La Dame de chez Maxim,* London, National Theatre, 18 October 1977;

A Little Hotel on the Side, translated from Feydeau and Maurice Desvallières's *L'Hôtel du Libre-Echange,* London, National Theatre, 9 August 1985;

Die Fledermaus, translated from Carl Haffner and Richard Genée's libretto, London, Royal Opera House, 9 January 1989;

When That I Was, Ottawa, 1992;

A Christmas Carol, adapted from Charles Dickens's novel, London, Royal Shakespeare Company at the Barbican Theatre, 28 November 1994;

Naked Justice, Leeds, West Yorkshire Playhouse, 26 January 2001.

BOOKS: *Charade* (London: Bodley Head, 1947);

Rumming Park (London: Bodley Head, 1948);

Answer Yes or No (London: Bodley Head, 1950); republished as *The Silver Hook* (New York: Morrow, 1950);

Like Men Betrayed (London: Collins, 1953; Philadelphia: Lippincott, 1953);

The Narrowing Stream (London: Collins, 1954; New York: Viking, 1989);

Three Winters (London: Collins, 1956);

With Love and Lizards, by Mortimer and Penelope Mortimer (London: Joseph, 1957);

Three Plays (London: Elek, 1958; New York: Grove, 1962)–comprises *The Dock Brief, What Shall We Tell Caroline?* and *I Spy;*

One to Another (London: S. French, 1960);

The Wrong Side of the Park (London: Heinemann, 1960);

Lunch Hour and Other Plays (London: Methuen, 1960)–comprises *Lunch Hour, Collect Your Hand Baggage, David and Broccoli,* and *Call Me a Liar;*

Two Stars for Comfort (London: Methuen, 1962);

The Judge (London: Methuen, 1967);

Come as You Are (London: Methuen, 1971)–comprises *Mill Hill, Bermondsey, Gloucester Road,* and *Marble Arch;*

A Voyage round My Father (London: Methuen, 1971);

Collaborators (London: Eyre Methuen, 1973; London & New York: S. French, 1973);

Knightsbridge (London & New York: S. French, 1973);

Will Shakespeare (London: Hodder & Stoughton, 1977); republished as *William Shakespeare: The Untold Story* (New York: Delacorte, 1977);

The Bells of Hell (London & New York: S. French, 1978);

The Fear of Heaven (London & New York: S. French, 1978);

Rumpole of the Bailey (Harmondsworth & New York: Penguin, 1978);

The Trials of Rumpole (Harmondsworth & New York: Penguin, 1979);

Rumpole's Return (London: Penguin, 1980);

Regina v. Rumpole: Rumpole for the Defence, and Rumpole's Return (London: Allen Lane, 1981);

Clinging to the Wreckage: A Part of Life (London: Weidenfield & Nicholson, 1982; New Haven: Ticknor & Fields, 1982);

In Character (London: Allen Lane, 1983);

Rumpole and the Golden Thread (Harmondsworth & New York: Penguin, 1983);

The Liberty of the Citizen, by Mortimer, Franklin Thomas, and Lord Hunt of Tanworth (London & New York: Granada, 1983);

Edwin and Other Plays (London: Penguin 1984)–comprises *Bermondsey, Marble Arch, The Fear of Heaven, The Prince of Darkness,* and *Edwin;*

Paradise Postponed (London & New York: Viking, 1985);

Character Parts (London: Viking, 1986; Harmondsworth & New York: Penguin, 1986);

Rumpole's Last Case (Harmondsworth & New York: Penguin, 1987);

Summer's Lease (London & New York: Viking, 1988);

Rumpole and the Age of Miracles (London & New York: Penguin, 1988);

Rumpole à la Carte (London: Viking / New York: Penguin, 1990);

Titmuss Regained (London & New York: Viking, 1990);

Dunster (London & New York: Viking, 1992);

Rumpole on Trial (London & New York: Viking, 1992);

The Best of Rumpole (London & New York: Viking, 1993);

Murderers and Other Friends: Another Part of Life (London & New York: Viking, 1994);

Thou Shalt Not Kill, by Mortimer and others (Sutton, Surrey: Severn House, 1994);

Under the Hammer (London: Penguin, 1994);

Rumpole and the Angel of Death (London & New York: Viking, 1995);

Felix in the Underworld (London & New York: Viking, 1997);

The Sound of Trumpets (London: Viking, 1998);

The Summer of a Dormouse (London: Viking, 2000).

Collections: *The First Rumpole Omnibus* (London: Penguin, 1983)–comprises *Rumpole of the Bailey, The Trials of Rumpole,* and *Rumpole's Return;*

The Second Rumpole Omnibus (London: Penguin, 1987)–comprises *Rumpole for the Defence, Rumpole and the Golden Thread,* and *Rumpole's Last Case;*

The Rapstone Chronicles: Paradise Postponed and Titmuss Regained (London: Viking, 1991);

The Third Rumpole Anthology (London: Viking, 1997)–includes *Rumpole à la Carte, Rumpole on Trial,* and *Rumpole and the Angel of Death.*

PRODUCED SCRIPTS: *Like Men Betrayed,* radio, BBC, 1955;

No Hero, radio, BBC, 1955;

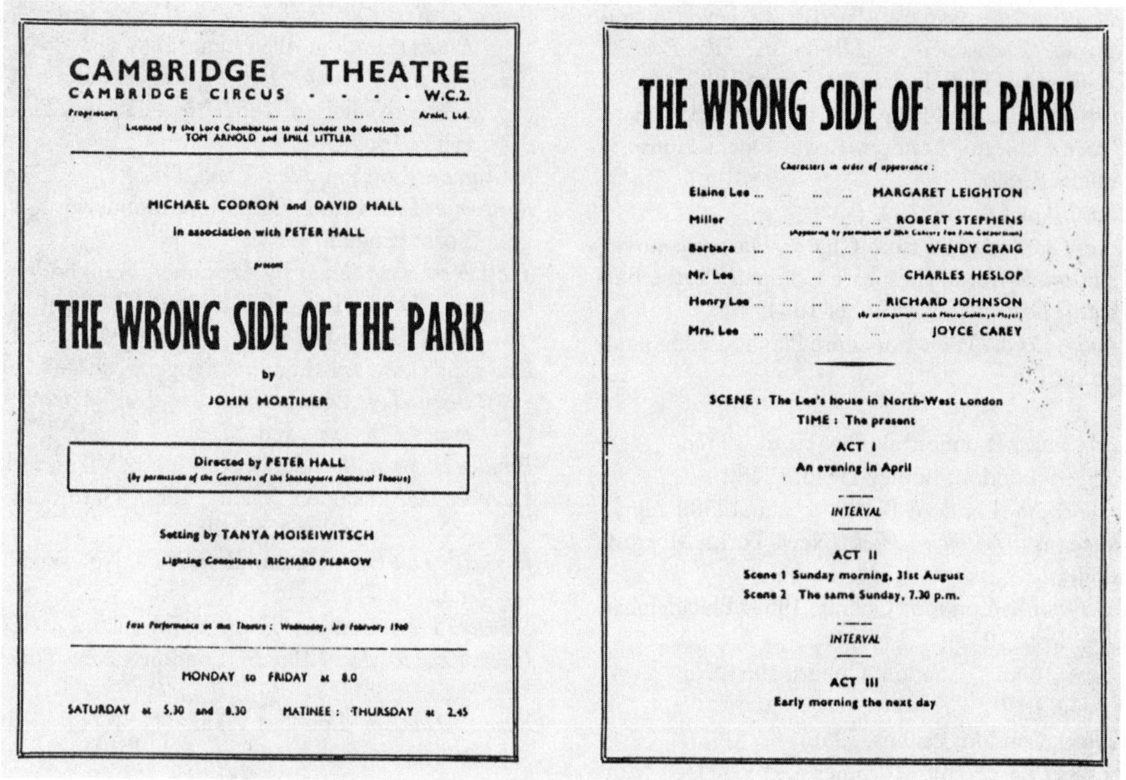
CAMBRIDGE THEATRE
CAMBRIDGE CIRCUS . . . . W.C.2.
TOM ARNOLD and EMILE LITTLER
MICHAEL CODRON and DAVID HALL
in association with PETER HALL
present
THE WRONG SIDE OF THE PARK
by
JOHN MORTIMER
Directed by PETER HALL
Setting by TANYA MOISEIWITSCH
Lighting Consultant: RICHARD PILBROW
MONDAY to FRIDAY at 8.0
SATURDAY at 5.30 and 8.30 MATINEE: THURSDAY at 2.45

THE WRONG SIDE OF THE PARK
Elaine Lee ... MARGARET LEIGHTON
Miller ... ROBERT STEPHENS
Barbara ... WENDY CRAIG
Mr. Lee ... CHARLES HESLOP
Henry Lee ... RICHARD JOHNSON
Mrs. Lee ... JOYCE CAREY
SCENE: The Lee's house in North-West London
TIME: The present
ACT I
An evening in April
INTERVAL
ACT II
Scene 1 Sunday morning, 31st August
Scene 2 The same Sunday, 7.30 p.m.
INTERVAL
ACT III
Early morning the next day

Program title page and cast list for the 1960 play in which Mortimer said he wrote "a big, operatic and extended part for an actress"

The Dock Brief, radio, BBC Third Programme, 12 May 1957;
The Dock Brief, television, BBC, 16 September 1957;
I Spy, radio, BBC Third Programme, 19 November 1957;
I Spy, television, BBC, 28 January 1958;
Call Me a Liar, television, BBC, 22 April 1958;
Three Winters, radio, BBC, 1958;
Ferry to Hong Kong, motion picture, screenplay by Lewis Gilbert and Vernon Harris, additional dialogue by Mortimer, 1959;
David and Broccoli, television, BBC, 26 January 1960;
Lunch Hour, radio, BBC Third Programme, 25 June 1960;
The Innocents, motion picture, adapted by Truman Capote and William Archibald from Henry James's novel *The Turn of the Screw,* additional scenes and dialogue by Mortimer, 20th Century-Fox/Achilles, 1961;
The Encyclopedist, television, BBC, 1961;
Guns of Darkness, motion picture, adapted from Francis Clifford's novel *Act of Mercy,* Warner Bros., 1962;
I Thank a Fool, motion picture, adapted by Mortimer and Karl Turnberg from Audrey Erskine-Lindop's novel, Eaton/MGM, 1962;
Lunch Hour, motion picture, London Films, 1962;
Collect Your Hand Baggage, television, Anglian Television, 29 August 1963;
The Running Man, motion picture, adapted from Shelley Smith's novel *The Ballad of the Running Man,* Peet Productions, 1963;
A Voyage round My Father, radio, BBC Third Programme, 1963;
Bunny Lake Is Missing, motion picture, adapted by Mortimer and Penelope Mortimer from Evelyn Piper's novel, Columbia/Wheel Productions, 1964;
Personality Split, radio, BBC, 1964;
Education of an Englishman, radio, BBC, 1964;
A Rare Device, radio, BBC, 1965;
A Choice of Kings, television, Associated Rediffusion, 1966;
The Exploding Azalea, television, Thames Television, 1966;
The Head Waiter, television, BBC, 1966;
The Other Side, television, BBC, 1967;
Hughie, television, 1967;
A Flea in Her Ear, motion picture, adapted from Georges Feydeau's *La Puce à l'oreille,* 20th Century-Fox, 1968;
Desmond, television, BBC, 1968;
Infidelity Took Place, television, BBC, 1968;

A Voyage round My Father, television, BBC, 1969;
John and Mary, adapted from Mervyn Jones's novel, motion picture, 20th Century-Fox, 1969;
Married Alive, television, 1970;
Swiss Cottage, television, BBC, 1972;
Knightsbridge, television, BBC, 1972;
Rumpole of the Bailey, television, BBC and Thames Television, 1975, 1978, 1979, 1987, 1988;
A Little off the Edgware Road, The Blue Film, The Destructors, The Case for the Defence, Chagrin in Three Parts, The Invisible Japanese Gentleman, Special Duties and *Mortmain,* television, adapted from short stories by Graham Greene, Thames Television, 1975–1976;
Mr Luby's Fear of Heaven, radio, BBC, 1976;
Will Shakespeare, television, 1978;
Rumpole's Return, television, 1980;
Unity, television, adapted from David Pryce-Jones's book *Unity Mitford,* 1981;
Brideshead Revisited, television, adapted from Evelyn Waugh's novel, Granada Television, 1981;
Edwin, radio, 1982;
The Ebony Tower, television, adapted from the story by John Fowles, Granada Television, 1984;
Paradise Postponed, television, Thames Television, 1986;
Rumpole, radio, 1988;
Glasnost, radio, 1988;
Summer's Lease, television, Thames Television, 1989;
The Waiting Room, television, 1989;
Titmuss Regained, television, 1991;
Under the Hammer, television, 1994;
Cider with Rosie, television, 1998;
Tea with Mussolini, motion picture, Cattleya, 1999;
Don Quixote, television, adapted from the novel by Miguel de Cervantes, Turner Network Television, 2000.

OTHER: Georges Feydeau, *A Flea in Her Ear,* translated by Mortimer (London & New York: S. French, 1968);
A Choice of Kings, in *Playbill Three,* edited by Alan Durband (London: Hutchinson, 1969);
Feydeau, *Cat among the Pigeons,* translated by Mortimer (London: S. French, 1970);
Carl Zuckmayer, *The Captain of Köpenick,* translated by Mortimer (London: Methuen, 1971);
Desmond, in *The Best Short Plays, 1971,* edited by Stanley Richards (New York: Avon, 1971);
Feydeau, *The Lady from Maxim's,* translated by Mortimer (London: Heinemann, 1977);
Harry Hodge and James H. Hodge, *Famous Trials,* introduction by Mortimer (London: Viking, 1984);
Feydeau, *Three Boulevard Farces,* translated, with an introduction, by Mortimer (Harmondsworth, U.K. & New York: Penguin, 1985)–comprises *A Flea in Her Ear, The Lady from Maxim's,* and *A Little Hotel on the Side;*
Die Fledermaus; or, the Bat's Revenge, translated by Mortimer, libretto by Carl Haffner and Richard Genée, based on *Le Réveillon,* by Henri Meilhac and Ludovic Halévy (London: Viking, 1989);
Edward Marjoribanks, *Famous Trials of Marshall Hall,* introduction by Mortimer (London: Penguin, 1989);
Great Law and Order Stories, edited by Mortimer (London: Penguin, 1990);
The Oxford Book of Villains, edited by Mortimer (Oxford, U.K. & New York: Oxford University Press, 1992);
Great Law and Order Stories, edited, with an introduction, by Mortimer (New York: Norton, 1992);
Charles Dickens's A Christmas Carol, adapted by Mortimer (London & New York: S. French, 1995).

SELECTED PERIODICAL PUBLICATION–UNCOLLECTED: "I, Claudius," *Plays and Players,* 19 (September 1972): i–xvi.

John Mortimer has had an unusually wide range of parallel careers. A successful career at the bar was initially accompanied by his emergence as a novelist. Briefly associated by critics as a part of the "new wave" that included writers such as Harold Pinter in the late 1950s, he was expected by some to become a major force as a writer for the stage. Although many of his stage plays have merited revival, he has become best known as a writer for television–particularly as the creator of the lovable, eccentric lawyer Rumpole of the Bailey. Through his career he has concentrated on what he finds most fascinating, the comic examination of the idiosyncracies and foibles of humankind.

John Clifford Mortimer was born on 21 April 1923. The only child of barrister Clifford Mortimer and his wife, Kathleen, he received an upbringing that equipped him not only for what he described in *Clinging to the Wreckage: A Part of Life* (1982) as his "predetermined path" as an advocate, but also for his other vocation as dramatist and author. Whether or not there was an element of the tyrannical in the clapping with which his father, by then blind, received the young Mortimer's solo performance of William Shakespeare's *Hamlet* (circa 1600–1601), for the aspiring "little eyas" it was an enterprise of great pitch and moment.

The butt for Clifford Mortimer's inexhaustible stream of Shakespeare quotations, often applied with a degree of ingenuity worthy of their begetter, John Mortimer regularly accompanied his parents to the Shakespeare Memorial Theatre in Stratford-upon-Avon, where, perhaps compensating for his late arrival in the

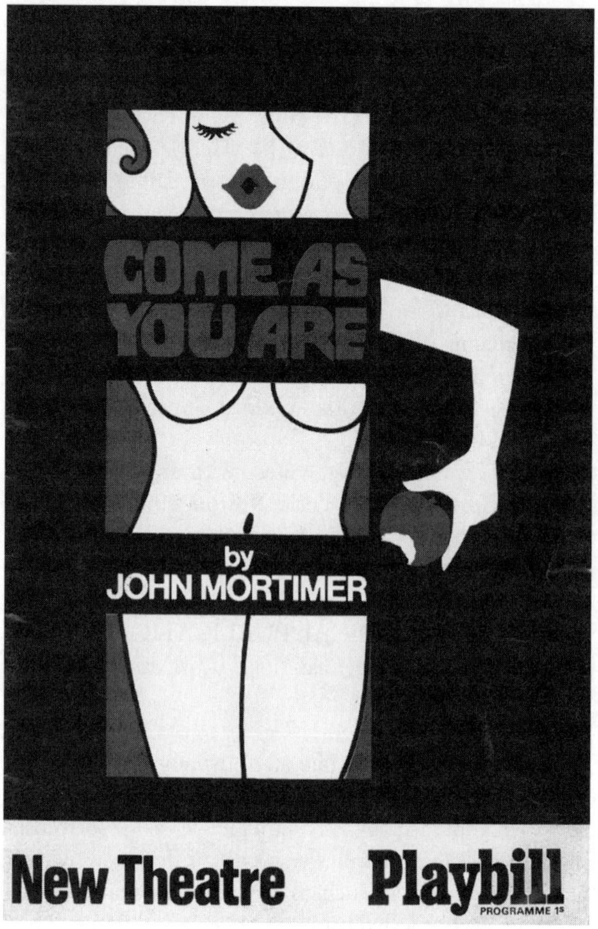

Program cover for the 1970 London production of Mortimer's four short plays, Mill Hill, Bermondsey, Gloucester Road, *and* Marble Arch

front row of the stalls, the elder Mortimer would deliver the lines a few seconds before the actors. Other diversions included pantomime in Brighton, performances of the Crazy Gang comedy troupe, and West End shows. In Bill Mann, his contemporary at the Dragon preparatory school and later music critic for *The Times,* Mortimer found a kindred spirit with whom he wrote and performed plays during vacations and shared honors in school productions. In their last year Mann played Bunthorne in a production of William S. Gilbert and Arthur Sullivan's *Patience* (1881) and Mortimer, the title role in Shakespeare's *Richard II* (circa 1595).

While at Harrow School, from 1937 to 1940, Mortimer fell under the spell of George Gordon, Lord Byron and W. H. Auden, formed "a one-boy communist cell" (as he recalled in *Clinging to the Wreckage*) and some lasting friendships–Sandy Wilson was a contemporary–and decided, to his father's disdainful incredulity, to become a writer. When it came to university, however, Clifford Mortimer brooked no dissent; Mortimer studied law at Brasenose College, Oxford, though as an undergraduate he met poets John Heath-Stubbs, Stephen Spender, and Dylan Thomas and published his own efforts in *Cherwell,* a university literary magazine. A period as fourth assistant film director for the Crown Film Unit proved to be only a temporary diversion from his "predetermined path" leading to the bar, to which he was called in 1946. His marriage in 1949 to Penelope Dimont, already a published novelist, provided him with a ready-made family, to which the couple made two additions. The earning power of a young barrister proving to be unequal to the demands of his expanding family, Mortimer pursued his career as a novelist, which had begun in 1947 with *Charade,* producing a further five novels between 1948 and 1956. In 1956 Mortimer was introduced to Nesta Pain, a BBC Radio producer, who asked him to write a play for her. The result was *The Dock Brief,* (1957) which in due course became a television play (1957), a stage play (1958), and a motion picture (1962) starring Peter Sellers.

The title of the play was taken from the then legal practice of unrepresented criminal defendants picking a barrister from the group gathered in the court for that purpose. Inevitably such barristers were the dross of their profession. Mortimer creates a colossus of professional incompetence in Morgenhall, "an aged barrister with the appearance of a dusty vulture," and pairs him with a pathetically inept client, Fowle, who candidly admits to murdering his wife. With Pain's help Mortimer exploited the freedom of radio–disembodied voices unattached to a realistic set–to work "at a new level of reality, one that was approximately two feet above the ground," as he put it in *Clinging to the Wreckage.* This quality enabled Mortimer to explore what he described as "the interaction between reality and illusion, circumstance pulling against fantasy," as John Russell Taylor quoted him in *Anger and After* (1969). Thus, Morgenhall (the first of many Mortimer characters known only by his surname, in this case ironically echoing the celebrated advocate Sir Edward Marshall Hall) speaks elaborately and verbosely, mingling Latin tags with schoolboy slang ("I've always been mustard keen on my work") and archaic quaintness ("a mean sneeping wind"). Mortimer introduces into the relationship between Morgenhall and Fowle the first of the inversions that recur throughout his plays by making the barrister the more dependent of the two: "Remember the hopes I've pinned on you," he tells Fowle. Mortimer also deploys what became another favorite device–that of role-playing–as Fowle enacts judge, witness, and juryman. The denouement, in which the case against Fowle is dropped because of Morgenhall's incompetence and the barrister is dissuaded from attempting suicide by the prospect of defending Fowle's future "trivial offences," clearly resides in a realm of fantasy in which murder and professional incompetence are treated as endearing eccentricities.

At producer Michael Codron's suggestion, Mortimer wrote *What Shall We Tell Caroline?* as a companion piece for *The Dock Brief.* In this second play he leaves the confines of the prison cell for the living room of the Loudons of Highland Close School in "Coldsands," a room with three doors and tall French windows. Arthur Loudon, the irascible headmaster; his wife, Lily, whom he calls by her childhood nickname "Bin"; and his "tall, debonair and gay" assistant, Tony Peters, are locked inescapably in a triangular relationship based on the illusion that Arthur is indifferent to Bin and Tony is in love with her. Although this illusion is exposed–Arthur can only express his love through anger and Tony holds no torch for Lily–the ménage à trois is reconstituted at the end of the play, as the best and only modus vivendi for its three constituents. In the meantime the Loudons have celebrated their daughter Caroline's eighteenth birthday with rituals unchanged since her early teens, and only Tony, whom she passionately embraces at the end of the first scene, realizes that she is now a woman. In making Caroline wordless in the first scene Mortimer demonstrates the power of silence (it prompts a long account of her life from Bin), and her brief announcement in the second scene of her departure for London shows the effect of Arthur and Bin's fantasy on their daughter, who takes her flight into reality. In *What Shall We Tell Caroline?* Mortimer produces a variation on the illusion-reality theme and introduces the triangular configuration (always two men and one woman) that is a staple ingredient of much of his work.

In *I Spy,* first a radio play on BBC Third Programme in 1957 and eventually produced for the stage in 1959, Mortimer revisits Coldsands to evoke a world of seaside nostalgia in which Mrs. Morgan finds happiness with Mr. Frute, a private detective whom her husband has employed to establish marital misconduct, of which she to that point has been guiltless. Though the mutual joyousness of the lead characters forestalls criticism of the circular neatness with which the play ends, Mortimer seems to indicate in *I Spy* that he considered the clever conclusion at the curtain, which was de rigueur for revue sketches such as the four he contributed to *One to Another* (1960), less appropriate for longer works.

With *The Wrong Side of the Park,* first performed at Cambridge Theatre on 3 February 1960 under the direction of Peter Hall, Mortimer set himself the challenge of writing a full-length stage play with "a big, operatic and extended part for an actress," as he noted in the preface to the published play. A decaying Victorian house in northwest London accommodates Elaine and Henry Lee, his elderly parents and her pregnant younger sister; but, far from being overcrowded, there is room for a lodger, Miller, the namesake of the disgraced doctor in Terence Rattigan's *The Deep Blue Sea* (1952). By means of his skillful deployment of the necessarily complex set, his facility with dialogue, and some role-playing episodes, Mortimer fills out his three acts; the substance of the play, however, is Elaine's fantasy that her first marriage was a success and her second a failure, whereas the reverse is really the case. Elaine takes flight but returns, in an ending that Mortimer only finalized after two weeks of performances.

If *The Wrong Side of the Park* seems to hark back to the work of fellow Harrovian Rattigan, *Call Me a Liar,* which was first produced for BBC Television on 22 April 1958, locates Mortimer in the milieu that Harold Pinter explored in his *The Birthday Party* of the same year, of dingy boardinghouses and landladies preoccupied with their lodgers' appetite for breakfast cereal. The world of illusion, complete with wife and children, that Sammy Noles has created for himself, initially to forestall sympathy for the loss of his real family in a Nazi bombing raid, threatens to prevent him from furthering a relationship with a German girl with whom he shares an attraction. Whereas Pinter might leave the dividing line between truth and illusion blurred, Mortimer does not flinch from a happy ending in which the girl (the first of many unnamed characters) prevails upon Sammy to stay with her in his newly rediscovered reality.

Lunch Hour (1960) illustrates the hazards of the opposite approach. Dispensing entirely with names, Mortimer shows a man and woman entering a bedroom in a shabby hotel near King's Cross station. To legitimize their presence there, the man has told the manager that he and the woman are married, a subterfuge into which she enters with excessive zeal, berating her "husband" for dragging her and their three children all the way from Scarborough on a bitterly cold day "to scurry off to a small hotel in King's Cross" and for dumping the children with an aunt. By means of inversion and role-playing, fantasy has so vanquished reality that *Lunch Hour* ends with the man lamenting, "We never took off our overcoats!"

Collect Your Hand Baggage is an enigmatic little piece, "written with another larger play [*Two Stars for Comfort*] in mind," as the author noted in the introduction to *Lunch Hour and Other Plays* (1960), in which the play appears. The principal character, Crispin–"a middle-aged Bohemian"–is given to frequenting London Airport nocturnally with a group of much younger friends (suitable parts for the students at the London Academy of Music and Dramatic Art, where the play was first performed in 1961). They rally round his efforts to raise the price of a ticket to Paris to accompany his landlady's daughter there, but it transpires that her rendezvous is not with

Glenda Jackson as Katherine and John Wood as Henry in the 1973 Duchess Theatre production of Mortimer's Collaborators *(courtesy of John Haynes)*

him but with another man. The element of surprise is scarcely adequate even for a piece of this modest length.

No less curious, but rather more successful in the telling, is *David and Broccoli* (first produced for BBC television on 26 January 1960), which traverses the private school where David is a pupil and the private hotel where he lives with his father. The unathletic David fears and loathes the slow-witted physical education instructor, "Broccoli" Smith, who, he discovers, has a naive passion for the occult. In the contest between youthful intellect and mature brawn David convinces Broccoli that the end of the world will occur on the following Thursday (in Mortimer's writing everything happens on a Thursday). As a result Broccoli disrupts an awards ceremony at the school with the news that the world has not ended and is consequently dismissed from his job. This time the world of fantasy has been manipulated by the world of reality, in which Broccoli goes off to face an uncertain future and David betrays no concern or regret for what he has done.

Two Stars for Comfort, which, like *Collect Your Hand Baggage,* had its origins in an unpublished novel, is set in the riverside hotel of Sam Turner, a character on the grand scale, played in its original 1962 production at the Garrick Theatre by Trevor Howard, returning to the stage after eight years in movies. In *Clinging to the Wreckage* Mortimer describes Turner as "a man who always told people what he thought they wanted to hear," but beneath his charm and affability he is disintegrating because of loneliness and doubt. A group of young people similar to those in *Collect Your Hand Baggage* descend on Sam's hotel, where they encounter an old retainer, Drake; a gaggle of stereotyped regulars; and Sam's wife, who is about to leave on her annual visit to relatives in Ruislip (Mortimer, as ever, is deliberate in his choice of place-names: Ruislip is an unappealing London suburb that is totally inappropriate for a holiday) while the regatta is on. All is not well this year, however: a rival hotel has wrested control of the events from Sam; his annual flirtation with Ann Martin, a marginal member of the young crowd, takes a more serious turn; and his wife threatens divorce. The action is filled out with some theatrical turns: Sam performs "Stars Fell on Alabama" and several drum solos and gives a virtuoso display of the techniques of his former profession (the law) when he turns the tables on a prudish colonel who complains about a woman exposing herself to him by making the colonel appear to be a voyeur. Perhaps in a nod to the play within a play in *Hamlet,* the climax takes the form of a performance in which the young people, displaying a level of tactlessness worthy of the prince of Denmark, act out Sam's involvement with Ann. The tension builds between Sam's indulgence of the performance and Ann's demands that he stop it. Eventually the play is halted by her mounting hysteria, but Sam pays the price of his refusal to cut the fantasy short by forfeiting his relationship with Ann.

Mortimer's next production was *A Flea in Her Ear* (1966), a translation of Georges Feydeau's *La Puce à l'oreille* (1909), followed by another full-scale play, *The Judge,* which, after its ill-received premiere in Hamburg, opened in the West End, at Cambridge Theatre on 1 March 1967, with Patrick Wymark as the unnamed judge. With *The Judge* Mortimer learned the freer use of the stage that he developed further in *A Voyage round My Father.* Thus, the two acts consist of seventeen scenes, and both the judge and his marshal, Trapp, address the audience directly. They also take part in a game of legal cross-examination reminiscent of those in *The Dock Brief.* It gradually emerges that the judge, at the end of his career, has returned to his hometown seeking judgment for some past misdemeanor involving the young Serena, who now runs an antique shop as the front for a rather amateurish brothel. The stage is peopled with Mortimer's customary range of attendant characters, but the spotlight remains firmly on the judge. Uncharacteristically resisting the temptation to give clear explanations, Mortimer maintains mystery bordering on obscurity to the end, but he does not quite succeed in finding the right level of reality on which to explore the potentially grand theme and ultimate inversion of the judge seeking his own judgment.

In contrast, Mortimer's next West End offering, *Come as You Are*–which premiered at the New Theatre in London on 27 January 1970–consists of four short plays, of which he wrote in the introduction to the 1971 published version: "Needless to say, a half-hour play is exactly twice as hard to do as one which lasts an hour." Each of the plays is set in a different part of London; the most successful of them is *Bermondsey,* which takes place in a public house, the Cricketers, in which the contrast between the appearance and the reality of a triangular relationship is explored. The relationship between the landlord, Bob Purvis, and his former army comrade Pip is revealed early on as homosexual; Bob's wife Iris's awareness of, and indeed collusion with, the bond between the two men only gradually becomes apparent, however, when she and Pip form an alliance to scare off the young barmaid Rosemary, with whom Bob is considering running off to some fantasy riverside inn. The play ends with Rosemary vanquished and the reconstituted trio singing "The Holly and the Ivy" around the piano.

"Gloucester Road," in which Mike and Bunny Thompson share their maisonette with former Royal Air Force pilot and used-car salesman Tony Delgardo, replicates *What Shall We Tell Caroline?* with the trio returning to their consoling fantasies after the brief incursion of hippie Clare Dobson as the occupant of their rented room. *Mill Hill* features Denise Blundell and her prospective lover, dentist Peter Trilby, who can only have sex when he is dressed as Sir Walter Ralegh and his partner as Queen Elizabeth. This proclivity leads to a typical Mortimer role-playing episode, which is followed by an equally typical inversion when Denise's husband, Roy–also a dentist–arrives unexpectedly and takes over as Ralegh, dispatching Peter to collect the Blundells' son, Gerald, from school. In *Marble Arch,* in which a fading movie star attempts to dispose of her apparently dead lover, Mortimer shows that, perhaps in the process of translating Feydeau, he had picked up some of the techniques of farce. *Come as You Are* exhibits many Mortimer traits to best advantage: variations on the theme of illusion and reality; triangular relationships; role-playing; symbolic place-names; and what Michael Billington in *Plays and Players* (March 1970) termed "anecdotal tidiness."

Originally written for radio in 1963, *A Voyage round My Father* was subsequently rewritten for and performed on television and the stage and adapted as a motion picture. Many of its incidents are also recounted in Mortimer's memoir *Clinging to the Wreckage.* In *Plays and Players* (January 1971) Robin Waterhouse, reviewing the first stage production–which premiered at the Greenwich Theatre in London on 25 November 1970–found the script "disappointingly thin" and "lean"; but Billington, in the October 1971 issue of *Plays and Players,* hailed the West End production at Haymarket Theatre as the rare exception to the rule that "Any work that started its life on television normally suffers when transferred to the stage." The success of the play lay principally in its episodic form, which had become acceptable in the theater during the single decade since Mortimer made his first essay at a full-length stage play with the naturalism of *The Wrong Side of the Park.* Thus, held together by the central character of the father and with the son as narrator of, as well as participant in, the action, the play consists of a sequence of brief episodes or sketches: childhood theatricals; the prep-school headmaster's dire warnings about "unsolicited cake"; the lesbians Miss Cox and Miss Baker; Father's dazzling courtroom performance; the movie set, with the electrician's recurrent, innuendo-laden inquiry "Seen the King last night?"; Father's discouraging interview with his prospective daughter-in-law, Elizabeth; the son's success as a dramatist; and his father's death. Throughout, the father's blindness is never openly acknowledged, and mere reality is triumphantly vanquished by illusion. The role of the father has attracted a succession of eminent actors: Mark Dignam, Michael Redgrave, Laurence Olivier, Robert Lang, and Alec Guinness; Guinness observed of the play in *Plays and Players* (September 1971): "The characters are very lightly sketched in and I think you can't be too realistic about the performance."

Collaborators, which premiered at the Duchess Theatre on 18 April 1973, amounts to a reversion to the past in terms of its period (late 1950s) and the prevailing naturalism of its two-act structure. The arrival of American movie producer Sam Brown in the professional and then personal lives of Henry and Katherine Winter creates a typical Mortimer triangle. His invitation to the couple to collaborate on a movie script based on their own lives gives one sense to the title of the play; as personal relationships develop among the trio, another sense, of collaborating as deserting an established alliance to form a new one with an enemy, is added. Many familiar devices are deployed: Henry's exaggerated infidelity, place-names used for comic effect, rhetorical use of brand names, courtroom reenactment, sexual inversion, and song-and-dance routines (in this case based on those of Fred Astaire and Ginger Rogers); but drama had advanced rapidly in the previous fifteen to twenty years, and comparisons with Edward Albee, Pinter, and even Neil Simon were not to Mortimer's advantage. *Collaborators* was Mortimer's last full-length original work for the theater until the premiere of *Naked Justice* in 2001, though he produced adaptations and translations in the interim.

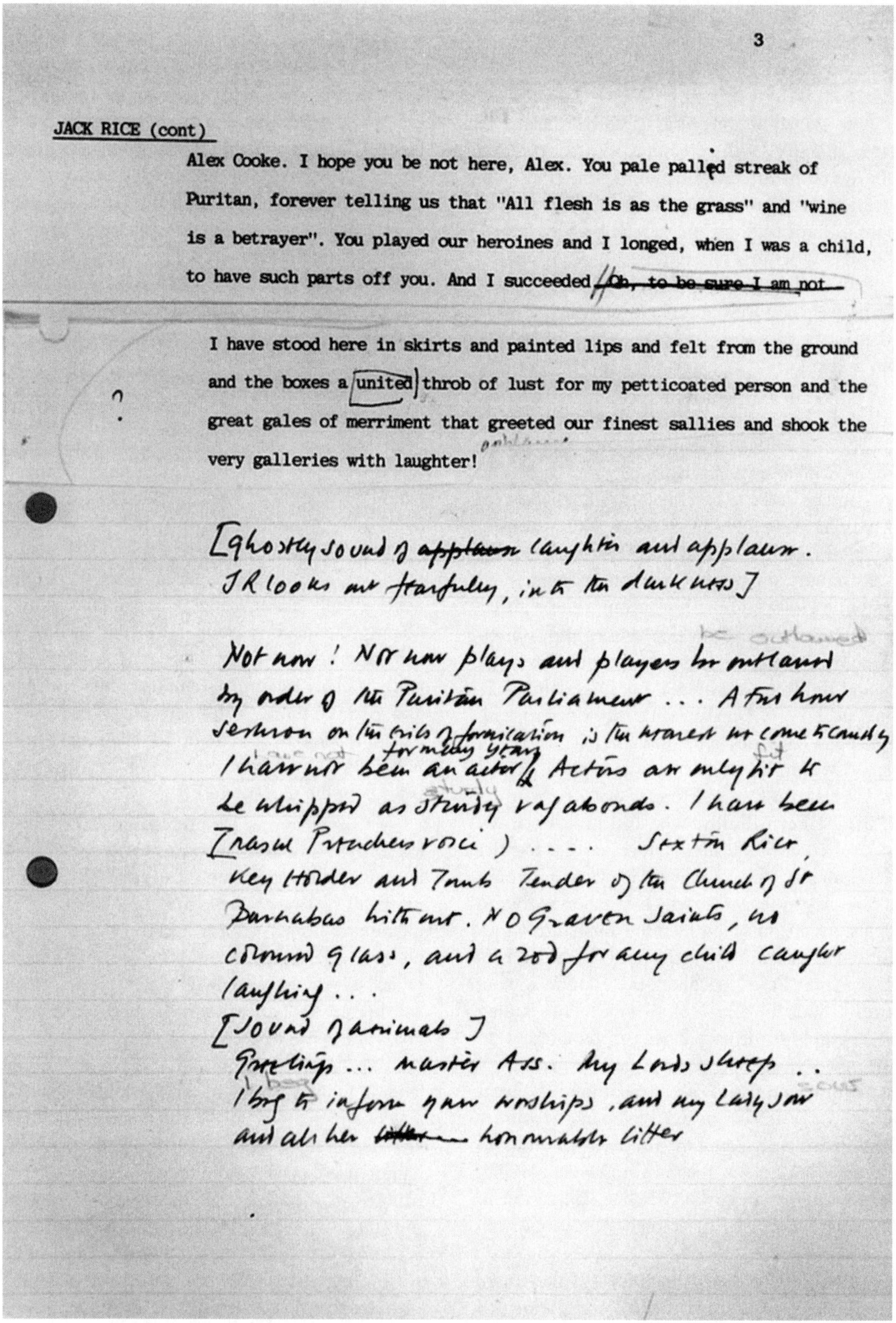

3

JACK RICE (cont)

Alex Cooke. I hope you be not here, Alex. You pale palled streak of Puritan, forever telling us that "All flesh is as the grass" and "wine is a betrayer". You played our heroines and I longed, when I was a child, to have such parts off you. And I succeeded // ~~Oh, to be sure I am not~~

I have stood here in skirts and painted lips and felt from the ground and the boxes a united throb of lust for my petticoated person and the great gales of merriment that greeted our finest sallies and shook the very galleries with laughter!

[Ghostly sound of ~~applause~~ laughter and applause.
JR looks out fearfully, into the darkness]

Not now! Not now plays and players be outlawed by order of the Puritan Parliament ... A two hour sermon on the evils of fornication is the nearest we come to comedy. I have not been an actor for many years. Actors are only fit to be whipped as sturdy vagabonds. I have been [nasal Preacher's voice] .... Sexton Rice, Key Holder and Tomb Tender of the Church of St Barnabas Within. No Graven Saints, no coloured glass, and a rod for any child caught laughing...

[Sound of animals]

Greetings ... master Ass. My Lord's sheep .. I beg to inform your worships, and my Lady Sow and all her ~~litter~~ honourable litter

Page from a draft for Mortimer's 1992 play, When That I Was *(Collection of John Mortimer)*

Heaven and Hell, which premiered at the Greenwich Theatre on 28 May 1976, was adapted from Mortimer's 1976 radio play *Mr Luby's Fear of Heaven;* the play is set in a Tuscan hospital, where an inversion takes place between a young Italian poet, Lewis Luby, and the prosaic Tommy Fletcher from Humberside, who has actually run a gamut of sexual experiences that Luby can only imagine. A companion piece, *The Prince of Darkness,* combines a consideration of the place of miracles in the Anglican Church, brand-name consumerism, and revue-style humor.

In *Edwin,* a radio play first broadcast on 16 October 1982, the title character may or may not be the son of Sir Fennimore and Lady Truscott. Sir Fennimore, a retired judge, seems to relish the suspicion that the boy's father is longtime family friend Tom Marjoriebanks, a latter-day version of Tony Peters from *What Shall We Tell Caroline?* Whereas Pinter might leave the characters' and the audience's desire for verification unfulfilled, Mortimer cannot resist the neatness of the revue-sketch ending with a concluding hint that it is the gardener, Cattermole, with whom Lady Truscott has been conducting a lengthy liaison.

Although Mortimer's main professional interest as a lawyer was divorce, he held the opinion, as he expressed in *Clinging to the Wreckage,* that "Love affairs aren't much of a subject for drama, really." In his preface to *Three Boulevard Farces* (1985), the collected edition of his translations of Feydeau's comedies, Mortimer observes that "The advent of the permissive society, were it ever to come about, would make the continuance of farce writing impossible." Mortimer was considered by some to have offered significant encouragement to the permissiveness of society: he led the defense when Penguin Books was tried in 1960 under obscenity laws for publishing an unexpurgated edition of D. H. Lawrence's *Lady Chatterley's Lover* (1928).

This social shift did not, however, negate the appeal of classic period farce, as Kenneth Tynan, literary manager of the National Theatre and himself a leading advocate of permissiveness, realized when he invited Mortimer to translate Feydeau's *La Puce à l'oreille.* Tynan's other inspiration was to engage a French director, Jacques Charon, who instilled a genuine Gallic style in his English cast. The key to the success of the play is that throughout the abundant improbabilities of the plot–a cleft palate, a bogus love letter, a pair of scarlet suspenders, a set for act 1 with nine points of exit, and a disappearing bed–the characters never waver in their conviction that they are engaged in serious business. In farce Mortimer found ample scope to explore the interaction between reality and illusion that had fascinated him from his early days as a dramatist.

The success of *A Flea in Her Ear* upon its initial production led to further Feydeau translations. A West End production of *Cat among the Pigeons,* adapted from *Un Fil à la patte* (1894), premiered at the Prince of Wales Theatre on 15 April 1969, with Charon directing a cast in which Richard Briers, in particular, displayed controlled frenzy and sophisticated quick thinking to a degree rarely evident in English farce.

The National Theatre returned to Feydeau in 1977 with *The Lady from Maxim's,* Mortimer's translation of *La Dame de chez Maxim* (1899), the tale of a Moulin Rouge dancer known as the Shrimp, who, mistaken for the respectable Madame Petypon, encounters several of her admirers during a visit to the Chateau du Grélé in Touraine. The Shrimp's unconventionally crude language provided a particular challenge for Mortimer as translator, since it is based on the slang of her current milieu rather than her social or geographical background. Mortimer's effective rendering of the Shrimp's stock greeting to men–"Eh, allez donc, c'est pas mon pere?"–as "Come on darling, how's your father?" was well served by her accompanying action of whipping a gartered leg over the back of a chair, but less so by her Cockney accent, which inevitably carried associations of George Bernard Shaw's *Pygmalion* (1913), as does the transformation of the street cleaner into a dustman.

On 9 August 1985 the National Theatre, of which Mortimer was a board member from 1968 until 1988, produced *A Little Hotel on the Side* (adapted from Feydeau and Maurice Desvallières's *L'Hôtel du Libre-Echange,* 1894) on the vast Olivier stage, which provided generous space for the elaborate sets, in particular that for the Free Trade Hotel, whither most of the characters repair in the second act. Again Mortimer displayed great ingenuity in finding equivalents for double entendres and wordplay, with Mathieu's climate-induced speech impediment providing notable opportunities. Mortimer's other excursion into translation is his adaptation of Carl Zuckmayer's farce *The Captain of Köpenick* (originally *Der Hauptmann von Köpenick,* 1931), which premiered at the National Theatre at the Old Vic on 9 March 1971 with Paul Scofield in the title role.

Mortimer's adaptation of Robert Graves's novels *I, Claudius* and *Claudius the God and His Wife Messalina* (both 1934) was originally intended for the motion-picture screen, but as the prospects for the movie receded director Tony Richardson decided to transpose it to the stage, casting David Warner in the title role at the head of a large cast. *I, Claudius* premiered at the Queen's Theatre on 11 July 1972. For Mortimer, who proclaimed that "The more actors you have, and the more things that are going on, the easier it is," the size of the cast, at least, was a welcome prospect. Drawing on his schoolboy classics and his experience of translating Feydeau, Mortimer opted for a conversational style, as he told *Plays and Players* in August 1972: "You must believe that what you are hearing is what you would hear if you were in Rome, alive today but somehow transported back in time, and you could understand everything that was going on. But there mustn't be suddenly something which jars you out of that and into another world." As in *A Voyage round My Father,* he furthers the action through the seamless flow of incidents rather than separate scenes and makes the protagonist, in this case Claudius, the narrator as well. The pace of the play becomes hectic: Claudius's one true love, Camilla, is introduced, proposed to, and dispatched in breathtaking succession, and his wife, Messalina, progresses rapidly from virgin to brothel habitué. The material also gives Mortimer the opportunity to mine one of his favorite themes, as indicated by Claudius's outburst at the destruction of his illusions about Messalina–"Damn all truth-tellers!"

Mortimer had no hand in the subsequent successful television adaptation of the Graves novels, but he worked increasingly in that medium, adapting his own novels, including *Summer's Lease* in 1989, and other people's (the best known being his 1981 adaptation of Evelyn Waugh's 1945 novel *Brideshead Revisited*) and writing original scripts, most notably for episodes of the various *Rumpole* series. The style of television, with its building up a picture through a series of short snapshots rather than a portrait in depth, suited Mortimer.

On 28 November 1994 Mortimer returned to the theater with an adaptation of Charles Dickens's *A Christmas Carol* for the Royal Shakespeare Company at the Barbican Theatre. Mortimer's version, in two acts of twelve and fifteen scenes respectively, shows the same technical fluency as *Voyage round My Father* and *I, Claudius,* and though critics traced his use of a participant narrator to David Edgar's 1982 adaptation of Dickens's *Nicholas Nickleby* (1838–1839), Mortimer could point to his previous use of the device in his earlier plays. The affinity between Dickens's language and Mortimer's is illustrated by the shared vocabulary of Scrooge and, for example, Morgenhall from *Dock Brief,* and by Mortimer's ability to write pastiche Dickens, as in his lines for the specters Ignorance and Want. The world of *A Christmas Carol,* in which fantasy and reality and Christmases past, present, and future converge, provided an opportunity for Mortimer to explore some of his favorite themes. Whereas Mortimer's own creations are obliged to choose between illusion and reality, Scrooge is spared any such dilemma, being allowed to return from the spirit realm and bring that experience to bear on the real world. Mortimer effects this fantasy process with such skill as to disarm the incredulous.

Although in the late 1950s Mortimer was grouped with the Royal Court generation of avant-garde dramatists and appeared on the front cover of the September–October 1958 issue of *Encore* alongside Arnold Wesker and Pinter, his natural milieu was the declining middle classes rather than the emergent working class; further, his distinctive, Dickensian or Betjemanesque style gave him the potential for truly popular appeal, which no other member of that peer group possessed. Mortimer became the chairman of the Royal Court Theatre in 1990 and thus was instrumental in steering the company through the closing years of the twentieth century.

With his second wife, also named Penelope, by whom he has two daughters, Mortimer still lives in the memory-laden house that his father built near Henley-on-Thames and in which scenes from the 1982 television version of *A Voyage round My Father* with Laurence Olivier were shot. In 1997 Mortimer published another novel, *Felix in the Underworld,* and *Tea with Mussolini,* with his screenplay based on the childhood experiences of director Franco Zeffirelli, was produced in 1999. He has also worked on an unproduced screenplay based on Jessica Mitford's 1990 autobiography, *Hons and Rebels.* In 1998 Mortimer was knighted. In 2001 his first full-length original play in more than twenty years, *Naked Justice,* about an apparently illiterate black teenager accused of murdering his mother's drug-dealing lover, was produced. Benedict Nightingale's review in *The Times* (London) for 3 February 2001 was typical of the critical response: "It's a characteristically warm, goodhearted, likeable piece, and it has a strong, neat plot with a nice unsettling twist at the end, but it needs work if it's to make the hoped-for trip from Leeds to London." It never did.

Reference:

John Russell Taylor, *Anger and After,* revised edition (London: Methuen, 1969), pp. 214–226.

Papers:

Collections of John Mortimer's manuscripts are at Boston University and the University of California, Los Angeles.

Peter Nichols

(31 July 1927 -)

John Bull
University of Reading

See also the Nichols entry in *DLB 13: British Dramatists Since World War II.*

Peter Nichols (photograph by Tom Miller)

PLAY PRODUCTIONS: *The Hooded Terror,* adapted from Nichols's television play, Bristol, Bristol Old Vic Theatre, 1964;

A Day in the Death of Joe Egg, Glasgow, Glasgow Citizens Theatre, 1967; London, Comedy Theatre, 20 July 1967; New York, Brooks Atkinson Theatre, 1 February 1968;

The National Health, or Nurse Norton's Affair, London, Old Vic Theatre, 16 October 1969; New York, 10 October 1974;

Forget-Me-Not Lane, London, Greenwich Theatre, 1 April 1971;

Neither Up nor Down, London, Almost Free Theatre, 1972;

Chez Nous, London, Globe Theatre, 6 February 1974;

The Freeway, London, Old Vic Theatre, 2 October 1974;

Harding's Luck, adapted from the novel by Edith Nesbit, London, Greenwich Theatre, 26 December 1974;

Privates on Parade: A Play with Songs in Two Acts, London, Aldwych Theatre, 17 February 1977;

Born in the Gardens, Bristol, Theatre Royal, 29 August 1979;

Passion Play, London, Aldwych Theatre, 13 January 1981;

Poppy, music by Monty Norman, London, Barbican Theatre, 5 October 1982;

A Piece of My Mind, London, Apollo Theatre, 1 April 1987;

So Long Life, Bath, Theatre Royal, 29 August 2001.

BOOKS: *A Day in the Death of Joe Egg: A Play* (London: Faber & Faber, 1967); republished as *Joe Egg* (New York: Grove, 1967);

The National Health, or Nurse Norton's Affair: A Play in Two Acts (London: Faber & Faber, 1970; New York: Grove, 1970);

Forget-Me-Not Lane: Humorous, Serious and Dramatic Selections (London: Faber & Faber, 1971; New York: S. French, 1972);

Chez Nous: A Domestic Comedy in Two Acts (London: Faber & Faber, 1974);

The Freeway (London: Faber & Faber, 1975);

Privates on Parade: A Play with Songs in Two Acts (London: Faber & Faber, 1977);

Born in the Gardens: A Play in Two Acts (London: Faber & Faber, 1980);

Passion Play (London: Methuen, 1981);

Poppy, music by Monty Norman (London: Methuen, 1982; revised and enlarged, London: S. French, 1991);

Handmade Films Presents: Privates on Parade (London: W. H. Allen, 1983);

Feeling You're Behind: An Autobiography (London: Weidenfeld & Nicolson, 1984);

La Notte Comincia Ancora una Volta: Atti del Convegno Fabrizio Ruffo fra Storia ed Immaginario: San Lucido 27–28 luglio 1984, by Nichols and others (Cosenza: Effesette, 1985);

A Piece of My Mind (London: Methuen, 1987);

Blue Murder: A Play or Two (London: Methuen, 1996);

Diaries: 1967–1977 (London: Nick Hern, 2000);

Show of Strength Theatre Company Presents: So Long Life (London: Nick Hern, 2000).

Collection: *Plays* (London: Methuen, 1987); revised and enlarged as *Nichols Plays,* 2 volumes (London: Methuen, 1991)–comprises in volume 1, *A Day in the Death of Joe Egg, The National Health, Forget-Me-Not Lane, Hearts and Flowers,* and *The Freeway;* in volume 2, *Chez Nous, Privates On Parade, Born in the Gardens, Passion Play,* and *Poppy.*

PRODUCED SCRIPTS: *A Walk on the Grass,* television, BBC One, 1959;

Promenade, television, Granada, 1959;

Ben Spray, television, Granada, 1961; revised, television, London Weekend, 1972;

The Reception, television, Granada, 1961;

The Big Boys, television, BBC, 1961;

The Continuity Man, television, BBC One, 1963;

Ben Again, television, Granada, 1963;

The Heart of the Country, television, ATV, 1963;

The Hooded Terror, television, ATV, 1963;

The Brick Umbrella, television, ATV, 1964;

When the Wind Blows, television, ATV, 1965;

Catch Us If You Can, motion picture, Anglo-Amalgamated Productions/Bruton Film Productions, 1965; released in the United States as *Having a Wild Weekend,* distributed by Warner Bros., 1965;

Georgy Girl, motion picture, adapted from the novel by Margaret Forster, screenplay by Nichols and Forster, Columbia/Everglades, 1967;

Daddy Kiss It Better, television, Yorkshire, 1968;

The Gorge, television, BBC One, 1968;

"Majesty," television, adapted from the short story by F. Scott Fitzgerald, *The Jazz Age,* BBC Two, 1968;

"Winner Takes All," television, adapted from the short story by Evelyn Waugh, *The Jazz Age,* BBC Two, 1968;

Hearts and Flowers, television, BBC One, 1970;

A Day in the Death of Joe Egg, motion picture, adapted from Nichols's play, Domino, 1972;

The National Health, motion picture, adapted from Nichols's play, Columbia, 1972;

The Common, television, BBC One, 1973;

Forget-Me-Not Lane, television, BBC One, 1975.

OTHER: *Promenade,* in *Six Granada Plays* (London: Faber & Faber, 1960);

Ben Spray, in *New Granada Plays* (London: Faber & Faber, 1961), pp. 185–222;

The Gorge, in *The Television Dramatist: Plays by Leo Lehman, Peter Nichols, John Bowen, Jack Rosenthal, Dennis Potter,* edited by Robert Muller (London: Elek, 1973), pp. 71–148;

Hearts and Flowers, in *The Television Play,* edited by Robin Wade (London: BBC, 1976).

SELECTED PERIODICAL PUBLICATION–UNCOLLECTED: "The Rime of the Ancient Dramatist," *Observer* (London), 23 January 1993.

Peter Nichols is one of many recent dramatists for whose work the developing medium of television was a major catalyst. His television career started in 1959 with *A Walk on the Grass* and *Promenade.* His first stage production, *The Hooded Terror* (1964)–concerned with the violence to be found in the apparently secure familial context–was first seen as a televised play a year earlier. *The Continuity Man,* an account of a generational battle in a family that Nichols had received an Arts Council bursary to create as a stage play, was turned into a television script instead and screened in 1963. Nichols found acceptance as a stage writer with *A Day in the Death of Joe Egg* (1967) but continued to write television scripts such as *Daddy Kiss It Better* (1968), *The Gorge* (1968), *Hearts and Flowers* (1970), and *The Common* (1973), all of which dissect the anxieties of family life.

Television encouraged and nurtured the naturalism that has become associated with Nichols's work. As Brian Miller observes:

> His television plays are assumed to come straight and undistilled from his own life. Perhaps it is his concentration upon family and domestic subjects, the parallels to be drawn between characters in different plays, the high degree of naturalism in the dialogue and ease of characterisation suggesting "slice of life" that reinforce this view. Nichols isn't, some might say, a true dramatist at all, but a human tape-recorder, albeit a highly accurate and selective one.

Although Miller goes on to argue that Nichols's television plays are actually skillfully constructed, with considerable emphasis on form, it is true that his television plays place a heavy premium on naturalism and involve reworking of apparently biographical material. Nichols offers his audience a series of inventories of marriage and the family that are by no means separated from wider social contexts but in which the personal and the domestic are always strongly emphasized. Furthermore, the social contexts, particularly in the early

-13-

BRI: No, Mum.

SHE: Seeing Jesus?

BRI: ~~No, Mum. You misunderstand. This was~~ On top of the Electricity Building.

SHE: (RELIEVED) Oh. That's alright. ~~then. Thought for a second she was off her chump.~~

~~BRI:~~ ~~Think~~ Thought she was off her chump, ~~Mum?~~

~~SHE:~~ ~~Just~~ for a second, Dad.

BRI: No, Mum she's ~~clever, Mum.~~ doing well they say.

SHE: DaddY's pleased you're trying, love. What with your eleven-plus on the way.

BRI: You want to get to a decent school, don't you?

SHE: ~~She knows, don't you?~~ I don't want to be shunted into some secondary modern slum, she says — KISSING HER. BRI GETS UP, RUMMAGES IN THE ~~SATCHEL.~~ GRIP.

BRI: ~~Otherwise you'll get shunted into a secondary modern slum - perhaps even~~ like the one where Daddy teaches -

SHE: ~~And~~ Share a crowded room with forty or fifty council-house types and blackies.

BRI: ~~And surely to God you've had encough of that at the~~ I've had enough of them, she says, at the Spastics(Nursery.

~~EVA~~ JOE: A-a-a-h.

SHE: ~~S&&~~ I'm trying my best, she says.

BRI: That's alright then. Here's a note from Mrs - um -

SHE: A school report, Dad.

BRI: Yea. (READS) 'Thank you for the present for Colin's birthday.' Which is Colin?

SHE: Little boy ~~&&£&£&&&£&&£&&&~~ who had meningitis.

BRI: One who never stops whimpering?

SHE: That's him. I sent a cuddly bunny.

Revised typescript page from A Day in the Death of Joe Egg *(Collection of Peter Nichols)*

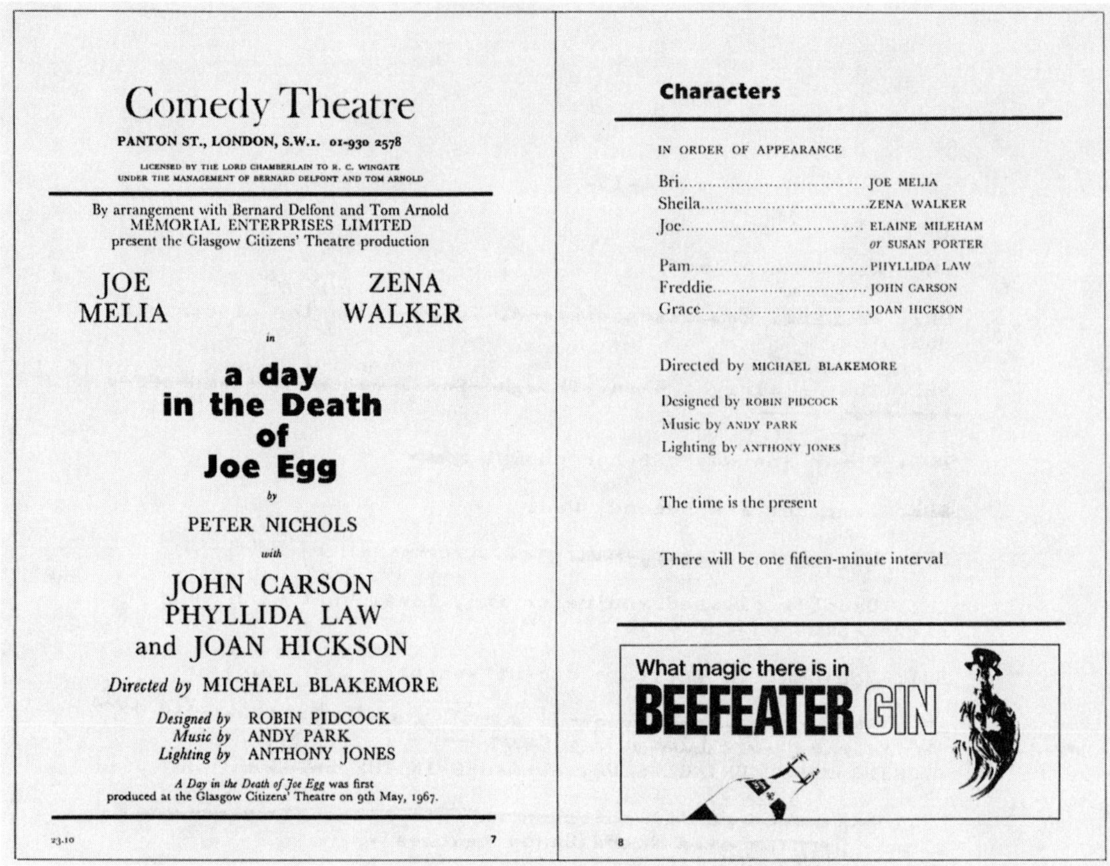

Comedy Theatre

PANTON ST., LONDON, S.W.1. 01-930 2578

LICENSED BY THE LORD CHAMBERLAIN TO R. C. WINGATE
UNDER THE MANAGEMENT OF BERNARD DELFONT AND TOM ARNOLD

By arrangement with Bernard Delfont and Tom Arnold
MEMORIAL ENTERPRISES LIMITED
present the Glasgow Citizens' Theatre production

JOE MELIA ZENA WALKER

in

a day in the Death of Joe Egg

by

PETER NICHOLS

with

JOHN CARSON
PHYLLIDA LAW
and JOAN HICKSON

Directed by MICHAEL BLAKEMORE

Designed by ROBIN PIDCOCK
Music by ANDY PARK
Lighting by ANTHONY JONES

A Day in the Death of Joe Egg was first produced at the Glasgow Citizens' Theatre on 9th May, 1967.

23.10 7

Characters

IN ORDER OF APPEARANCE

Bri........JOE MELIA
Sheila........ZENA WALKER
Joe........ELAINE MILEHAM *or* SUSAN PORTER
Pam........PHYLLIDA LAW
Freddie........JOHN CARSON
Grace........JOAN HICKSON

Directed by MICHAEL BLAKEMORE

Designed by ROBIN PIDCOCK
Music by ANDY PARK
Lighting by ANTHONY JONES

The time is the present

There will be one fifteen-minute interval

8

Program title page and cast list for the London production of Nichols's play about a young couple struggling to raise a severely brain-damaged child

work when Nichols was not yet a full-time writer, lean heavily on his own experiences.

Peter Richards Nichols was born on 31 July 1927 to Richard George and Violet Annie Poole Nicholas. He attended Bristol Grammar School from 1936 to 1944, then performed his compulsory national service in the Royal Air Force. He was a student at the Bristol Old Vic Theatre School from 1948 to 1950, then acted in provincial repertory theater, television, and motion pictures for five years. He studied at Trent Park Teachers' Training College from 1955 to 1957 and taught school until 1959. His television plays *Ben Spray* (1961) and *The Big Boys* (1961) draw on his time as a teacher. In 1959 he married Thelma Reed. The couple had four children, including Abigail, who suffered from spastic paralysis until her death in May 1971 and provided the inspiration for *A Day in the Death of Joe Egg*. Virtually everything he has ever written appears to draw heavily on his own life. Michael Coveney wrote in the *Financial Times* (2 April 1987): "No playwright since [Eugene] O'Neill and [Luigi] Pirandello has been more overtly autobiographical than Nichols. Even the unhappy Pirandello disguised his private life in few discreet veils."

Nichols first experimented with the mixture of social realism and fantasy that became his trademark in the television play *The Reception* (1961). He reduces the simple events of a wedding reception to farce in a way that frequently pulls the action away from the then-expected television mode of naturalism and toward the surreal.

In 1965 *When the Wind Blows,* another drama of marital breakdown, was broadcast by ATV. That same year Nichols completed his first motion-picture screenplay, *Catch Us If You Can* (released in the United States as *Having a Wild Weekend*). A somewhat flimsy attempt to present something of the aura of the "swinging London" of the 1960s, the movie featured the Dave Clark Five in a vain attempt to continue where the Beatles had left off in Richard Lester's *A Hard Day's Night* (1964). *Catch Us If You Can,* however, provided Nichols with enough money to allow him to take a year off from his television work and write a stage play dealing with a subject that was more intensely personal than anything he had done previously.

A Day in the Death of Joe Egg is a dark comedy about a young couple, Bri and Sheila, struggling to bring up a severely brain-damaged child. From the start the work announces that it is a stage play as Bri, a teacher, addresses the audience as if it is his class at school. He scolds them for their lack of concentration and threatens to keep them in detention:

> Another word and you'll all be here till five o'clock. Nothing to me, is it? I've got all the time in the world. (*Moves across without taking his eyes off them.*) I didn't even get to the end of the corridor before there was such a din all the other teachers started opening their doors as much as to say what the hell's going on there's SOMEBODY TALKING NOW! (*Pauses, stares again, like someone facing a mad dog.*) Who was it? You? You, Mister Man? . . . I did not *accuse* you, I *asked* you. Someone in the back row?

All of the characters speak directly to the audience at various points in the play. Sheila's mother, for example, explains why she has popped in, adopting the kind of comic confessional mode that soon became the trademark of the playwright Alan Bennett: "on Tuesday Mrs. Parry and I make a habit of meeting for the pictures if there's anything nice . . . don't laugh, will you, but they reduce the price for old-age pensioners . . . Anyway last week Mrs. Parry rang and said . . . she had to stay in for a vacuum." Elsewhere, direct address is used in a more serious mode to allow the characters to express their true thoughts. Much of the action involves Sheila and Bri acting out a variety of scenarios and offering imaginary responses from the point of view of the nonspeaking child, whom they have nicknamed "Joe Egg." After they comically reenact a series of cameos from Joe's short life, Sheila addresses the audience on her feelings about her child. After a lighting change signifying a move from an already qualified naturalism, Joe, who is paralyzed, comes impossibly skipping onto the stage. Sheila then announces the intermission: "Ladies and gentlemen, there will now be an interval. Afterwards the ordinary play, with which we began the performance, will continue."

Much of the audience interest and involvement with what might otherwise have seemed merely sentimental comes from this continual shifting between theatrical modes. As Irving Wardle remarks:

> What the play confirms is that it is still possible for a dramatist to know who he is talking to. Peter Nichols has observed the speech habits, social attitudes, and ideological confusions of the British sixties, and on his stage presents our own image. This is not avant-garde writing: it is addressed to the general civic conscience, and it endows the random audience with the sense of a common human bond.

A Day in the Death of Joe Egg shared the John Whiting Award for best play of the year and won the *Evening Standard* Play of the Year Award. The play ran for four months in London and was successfully remounted in New York.

Willingness to experiment with the parameters of naturalism has characterized all Nichols's efforts for the stage. His next play, *The National Health, or Nurse Norton's Affair* (1969), moves between the main plot, which concerns the attempts of the inhabitants of a male hospital ward to create individual identities for themselves in a world of homogenizing institutionalization, and a parody of television soap operas that use hospitals primarily as locations for romances between nurses and doctors. The play derived in part from Nichols's own experience of hospitalization. The play, which won the *Evening Standard* Play of the Year Award, was originally conceived for television, but broadcasting companies refused to accept it.

Nichols's next play is his supreme achievement on stage to date. *Forget-Me-Not Lane* was produced at the Greenwich Theatre in 1971, televised by the BBC in 1975, and revived at the same theater in 1990. Nichols's experimental use of stage space was a major contribution to the theater that went unrecognized at the time. Reviewing the revival of the play in the *Independent on Sunday* (25 March 1990), Wardle praised Nichols for his use of techniques that were innovative in 1971:

> Memory, as Nichols presents it, is Pandora's box. Open it, and you lose control of the contents. Novelists know all about this. To show it on stage required a new technique, which Nichols supplied by combining direct narration with remembered scenes, all located in a continuous psychological present. For audiences primed on the flashback, it came as a stunning insight when the remembered characters started talking back to the hero–"I'm part of your mental landscape for ever, duckie,"–until he is left screaming at them to leave him alone.

This continual and fluid movement back and forth though history allows an intense analysis of the influence of family–for both good and ill–over the life of the individual. The play operates almost on the level of a publicly rehearsed drama-therapy project, though Nichols's dramatic craftsmanship is always present not only to shape the piece but also to display that shaping to the audience. In the second act, for instance, the father, Charles–who is actually dead and being remembered–plays his new set of mail-order records, much to the chagrin of his wife, Amy, who can think of other things on which to spend the money. The son, Frank, trying to intervene, moves himself into another time and is immediately moved again by his wife, Ursula:

AMY: Only last week I asked for the money for a spring outfit and he said we couldn't run to it. As though he hasn't got enough records banging away all day and night.
FRANK: Why don't you take some interest in his music? Isn't that one of your common interests?
CHARLES: You hold your tongue, Sonny Jim.
FRANK: Sonny Jim? I'm nearly forty. A middle-aged man with three whopping kids.
URSULA: No, at this time you were nearly thirty and Matthew hadn't been born.
FRANK: Oh, Christ!

Nichols's intricate tracing of the tangled relationship between father and son is unmatched on the modern stage. Toward the end of *Forget-Me-Not Lane* Frank asks his mother to recall a variety show they attended in 1940. Instantly, as always, the scene moves smoothly into a dramatization of the event; but this time it has been carefully prepared for. The significance of the variety acts in the lives of mother, father, and son has been an integral part not only in the remembered history of their relationship but also in the very way in which the play is structured. These particular performers, Mr. Magic and Miss 1940, have already been introduced. Charles's noisy opposition to Mr. Magic's smutty jokes is not intended to serve as an instant explanation of anything but, rather, comes as the culmination of a series of "recalls" that stress the complexity, not the simplicity, of the event's psychological effect.

In his later plays Nichols continues to present versions of his own life but with a new element of self-reflective irony that the character Queenie in *Born in the Gardens* (1979) describes as the peculiarly English disease. While *Forget-Me-Not Lane* is a savagely comic examination of Nichols's roots, in his subsequent work he moves on to consider not where he had come from but where he had arrived and, more disturbingly, where he was going. Nichols was a successful playwright with access to worlds unknown by the characters of *Forget-Me-Not Lane*. In the introduction to *Plays* (1987) Nichols writes that that play was created in a "detached Victorian house beside Blackheath in South East London" bought with the royalties from the Broadway run of *A Day in the Death of Joe Egg*. From this point onward the characters in his domestic plays become increasingly upwardly mobile. By 1974 the action in *Chez Nous* has moved to a writer's rebuilt retreat in France, and the characters' speech has acquired a knowing wit. As Nichols's own financial and social status rose, so did those of his characters.

The Freeway (1974) is set in a slightly future time in which all political parties promise the freedom of all citizens to drive a car and in which all social programs have been sacrificed to the cause of making the country a gigantic freeway. The entire play takes place in a traffic jam caused by the combined efforts of the Scrubbers–an "anti-motor group whose avowed aim is to paralyse the Freeway"–and a strike by the Wreckers and Breakers Union. The newly appointed Minister for Movement is unable to do anything about moving the traffic in an England that has symbolically and in reality come to a standstill, caught between mindless Luddites and a parody of the worst of the trade union movement.

The distaste exhibited in the play for what is represented by the automobile–despoliation of the countryside, the deterioriation of urban life, and the diversion of public spending from social services to highway construction–is unequivocal. Nichols takes many characteristic swipes at the absurdities and casual brutalities of the contemporary world. For instance, although the traffic is stalled in the middle of what is left of rural England, virtually no remnants of traditional country life are left. There are no animals in the fields, only dairy complexes in distant sheds, and the only nonhuman sounds heard are those of the hungry guard dogs patrolling the wire fences to contain the would-be travelers within the bounds of the freeway and frighten potential thieves as the situation becomes a struggle for simple survival. An American describes how children are brought to see chickens–"the old-fashioned kind with the beaks left on"–at British Columbia county fairs, and May, one of the inhabitants of the motor home that dominates the set, responds, "That's nice, keeping up the old ways."

Nichols's point of view seems to be expressed by Wally, a vaguely anarchist figure who has left the car factory in protest at the inhumanity of the production line:

WALLY: I watched them greedy bastards run the world. And I watched them turn the rest into greedy bastards too. Like a plague it's been, except not with rats but money.
EVELYN: If it's a plague, there's nothing to be done then, is there?
WALLY: Quit running. Make it work, wherever you happen to be.

In 1977 Nichols achieved a major hit with *Privates on Parade,* which received the Society of West End Theatre Award as comedy of the year and comedy performance of the year, and Dennis Quilley and Nigel Hawthorne received awards as actor of the year in supporting roles. The play is concerned with attempts by a British army entertainment troupe to perform in Singapore and Malaya during the "Emergency" of the early 1950s. The setting allows Nichols to address issues of class and race without becoming didactic. The

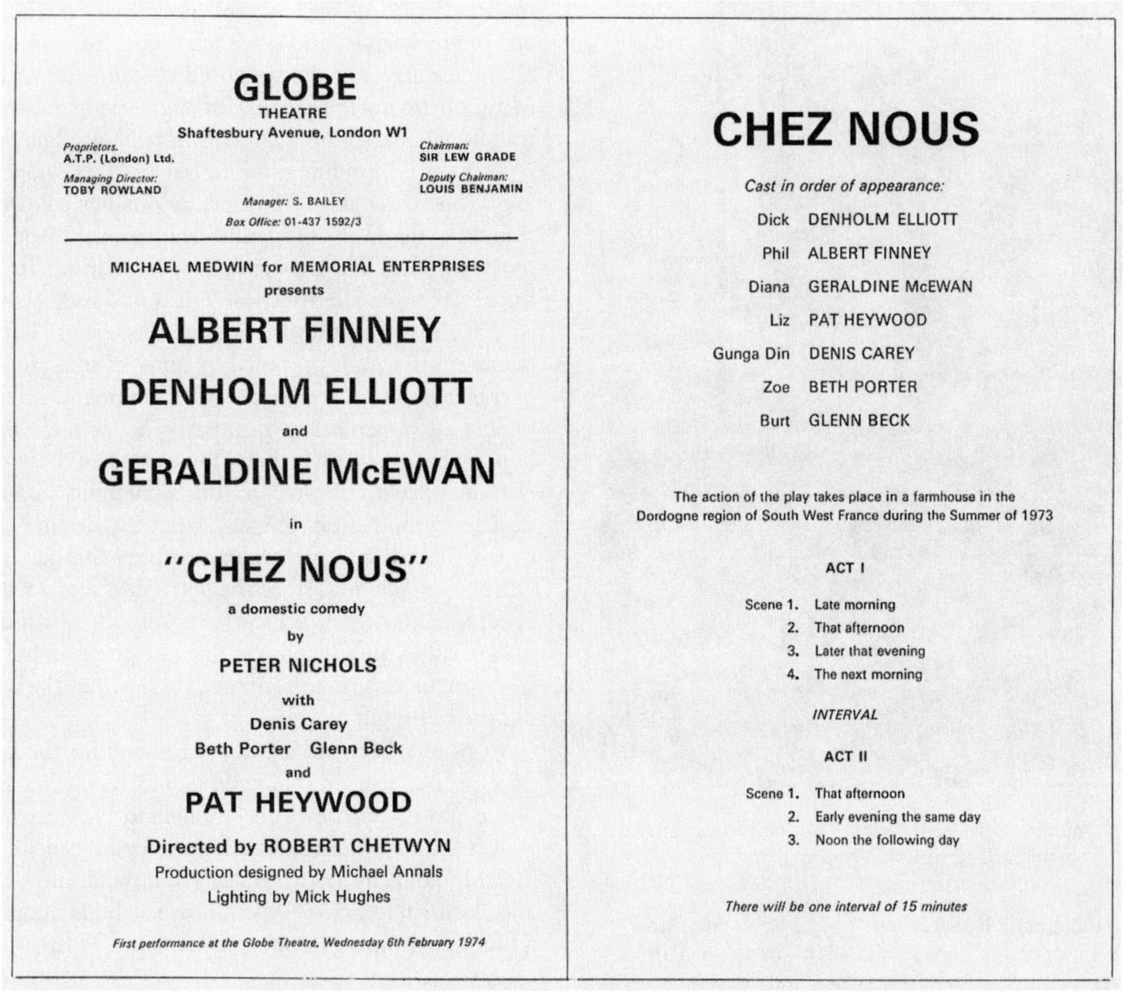

GLOBE
THEATRE
Shaftesbury Avenue, London W1

Proprietors. A.T.P. (London) Ltd.
Managing Director: TOBY ROWLAND
Chairman: SIR LEW GRADE
Deputy Chairman: LOUIS BENJAMIN
Manager: S. BAILEY
Box Office: 01-437 1592/3

MICHAEL MEDWIN for MEMORIAL ENTERPRISES
presents

ALBERT FINNEY
DENHOLM ELLIOTT
and
GERALDINE McEWAN
in
"CHEZ NOUS"
a domestic comedy
by
PETER NICHOLS
with
Denis Carey
Beth Porter Glenn Beck
and
PAT HEYWOOD

Directed by ROBERT CHETWYN
Production designed by Michael Annals
Lighting by Mick Hughes

First performance at the Globe Theatre, Wednesday 6th February 1974

CHEZ NOUS

Cast in order of appearance:

Dick	DENHOLM ELLIOTT
Phil	ALBERT FINNEY
Diana	GERALDINE McEWAN
Liz	PAT HEYWOOD
Gunga Din	DENIS CAREY
Zoe	BETH PORTER
Burt	GLENN BECK

The action of the play takes place in a farmhouse in the Dordogne region of South West France during the Summer of 1973

ACT I

Scene 1. Late morning
2. That afternoon
3. Later that evening
4. The next morning

INTERVAL

ACT II

Scene 1. That afternoon
2. Early evening the same day
3. Noon the following day

There will be one interval of 15 minutes

Program title page and cast list for one of Nichols's three plays produced in 1974

tone is set in the opening as the army-hardened Corporal Len Bonny greets the newly arrived private Steve Flowers:

> STEVE: Anyone home? Hullo?
> LEN: Where d'you fucking come from?
> STEVE: Bukit Timah, Sarge. Up the Bukit Timah Road.
> LEN: I don't mean where d'you fucking come from in Singapore? I mean what you doing creeping in here like a fucking mouse?
> STEVE: Come to get my arrival chitty cleared.

This form of address is contrasted to that deployed by the highest-ranking officer in the play, Major Giles Flack, who gives a caricature of an invitation to the ranks: "I want to take this last opportunity of inviting you to drop in for tea if you find yourself in Berkshire. Nothing remarkable, of course, only a simple seventeenth-century mill house, typical of hundreds throughout the length and breadth of England. No very brilliant company either–only my wife and the Labradors."

Much of the appeal of *Privates on Parade* undoubtedly came from the memories of some spectators of their own army experiences under the then-abandoned system of compulsory national service. The ability of the play to make audiences laugh assured a long West End run, and *Privates on Parade* proved to be, along with *A Day in the Death of Joe Egg,* one of the two most commercially successful plays of Nichols's career.

Nichols's willingness to mix mainstream populism with acerbic social commentary is demonstrated in his 1979 play, *Born in the Gardens.* Queenie, who has been living in the United States, talks with her brother, Hedley, about her impressions on returning to England. The state of the theater soon enters the discussion, and Queenie is less than complimentary:

> QUEENIE: Knock it off, Hed. I know England . . . The irony, the privacy, the quote-unquote eccentricity. Over there you hear so often about the wonderful British theeyater you almost come to believe it so last night

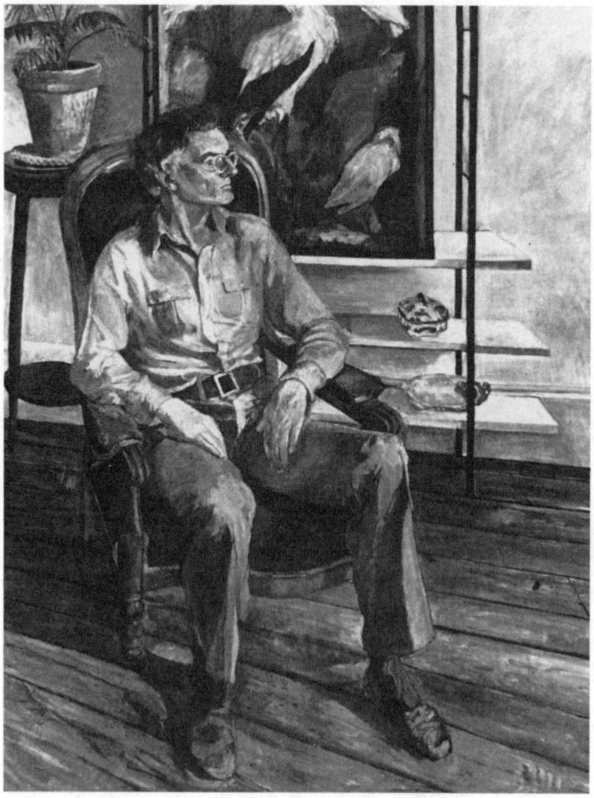

Portrait of Nichols by his wife, Thelma (from his Feeling You're Behind: An Autobiography, *1984)*

I went to a play. Irony. Sooner or later, no matter how the writer tries to slice it, the actors finish in a row delivering quote-unquote witty lines, and discussing the state of the nation. No conflict, no action, no resolution, no hope. Everybody goes home depressed out of their skulls.
HEDLEY: I'd have thought the West End theatre was the last place to look for an awareness of change.

Born in the Gardens seeks to take the pulse of the British nation at a momentous juncture: the play was ready to go into production at the time of the May 1979 election that brought victory to Margaret Thatcher and led to a succession of Conservative administrations. It opened in Bristol in August and transferred to the Globe in London in 1980. Although the play ostensibly deals with the events surrounding the funeral of a husband and father, Nichols also seeks to address the larger social and political context.

The action takes place in a rambling, rundown mock Tudor mansion bordered on one side by squatters and by a Chinese household on the other. It is inhabited by the recently widowed Maud and her son Mo, a dealer in genteel nineteenth-century pornography and a lover of traditional jazz. These uneasy leftovers of a past world are unsuccessfully dealing with a modern world of microwaves, deep freezes, dishwashers, dimmer lights, and color television. Surrounded by all the trappings of the supposed consumerist paradise, Mo mourns for the passing of the 78 rpm record; his traditional jazz is now stocked under "Nostalgia" at the record store–"anything before last week is under Nostalgia," he complains. Maud abandons her color television set in favor of a black-and-white model ("She never took to colour. The people didn't look natural," according to Mo) that she watches with the sound turned off so that she can talk to the faces on the screen. The electronic equipment is provided by another son, Hedley, a backbench Labour member of Parliament. Maud is unable to remember which party he belongs to and hopes that now that his Conservatives have been elected he will be able to do something about the decline of the nation. She attributes the decline chiefly to the influx of foreigners represented for her by the "Sambo" at the local store she patronizes along with the supermarkets where she buys mammoth quantities of instant soups and Tampaxes that she places in her deep freeze in an attempt to convince Hedley that she is making use of his gift.

Maud, Mo, and Hedley are joined for the funeral by Queenie, who has adopted California as her home. She is paying for her visit to England with a commission from an American newspaper for an article, "The Sick Men of Europe," with visits to Ireland, Italy, Spain, and Portugal to follow. Asked how she finds things after a fourteen-month gap, she responds:

No, nothing's changed. Not the little gardens as you come in at Heathrow, nor the little garden sheds, nor the chimneys stacked on the little houses. And however homesick you may have felt out there in the *real* world, you could suddenly scream. The airport staff huddle in truculent groups like working men from a *Punch* cartoon debating the earliest moment they can decently take their tea-break. No one moves, except after reference to some petty set of ideological quibbles based on a Labour Party mythology about the bad old days. And everything's so small–it's Dinkytown . . . No, nothing's changed, there isn't room. And because of that it's all getting steadily worse.

The zoological garden in Bristol, where the play is set and where it was originally produced, housed a gorilla that was supposedly the oldest in captivity. Albert, whose name recalls that of Queen Victoria's consort, was "born in the gardens." This theoretically "wild" animal would symbolically oppose the world of civilization and the electronic gadgetry of the new Garden of Eden, but he was caged and contained from birth. Indeed, Albert is now dead, safely stuffed and on exhibition in a museum for gawking tourists. Hedley

Anton Rodgers, Benjamin Whitrow, Louise Jameson, Billie Whitelaw, and Eileen Atkins in Nichols's Passion Play, *which premiered 13 January 1981 at the Aldwych Theatre (photograph by Catherine Ashmone; Zoe Dominic Studios)*

imagines that the same thing could happen to all of England in the near future: "Mock-ups of all the sights at the airport. A huge Disneyland with a monorail to take you straight from your plane to Buckingham Palace, the Tower, *The Mousetrap,* the Waxworks, a typical English pub, et cetera, finishing with the biggest Y-front shop in the world and this would lead you back to the departure lounge without having to go to London at all." None of the characters contemplates the possibility of change, other than for the worst.

Maud and Mo also see themselves as "born in the garden," but their vision of Eden is one of impossible nostalgia. The mock-Tudor house with pretensions to antiquity that is continually given modern additions by Hedley becomes symbolic of the state of the country. Queenie, the convert to the ideology of the New World, brings the recurring imagery of "heaven," "garden," and "paradise" into the sharpest focus:

> Merrie England! A fake-Tudor mansion with a lot of modern equipment no one knows how to operate or repair. The telly is the best in the world–even if the sound doesn't work–the corner shop is run by an African Asian, the post office by a Sikh, the doctor's from Hong-Kong and the natives are all unemployed.

Hedley and Queenie plan to sell the house at a profit and place Maud and Mo in a modern duplex near London–the pragmatic English politician and the American entrepreneur symbolically selling off the country for what it will yield. Hedley returns to the demands of his wife and his mistress, while Queenie gives an outline of her "Sick Men of Europe" over a transatlantic telephone line to a lover who, she becomes aware, is already entertaining an alternative bedmate.

In the last scene Mo and Maud are alone again; the guests have departed, and the coffin that dominated the room at the outset has finally been removed. Nothing has really changed in their lives or in the state of the nation, and nothing is ever going to change. A Conservative administration has taken over from a Labour one, but these two Beckett-like characters, living in their mutually re-created pasts, continue their dialogue as before. Mo plays his old jazz records, and Hedley, instead of installing the pair in a new house, has settled on the installation of a waste-disposal unit. This bleak vision welcomes the brave new world of free enterprise.

Nichols entered the 1980s with a play that set out to examine the lives of the newly enriched of the early Thatcher years. *Passion Play* (1981) is about James, a wealthy art dealer and restorer; his adulterous relationship with Kate, who, at twenty-five, is half James's age; and the effect the affair has on his previously unthreatened marriage with Eleanor, a woman whom, it is revealed, he hardly knows. The main force of the play lies in the interplay among the characters, exchanges in which wit always threatens to give way to real emotion. The results are some wonderfully comic moments, perhaps the most successful being Eleanor and James's acceptance of the idea of a ménage à trois with Kate, who has actually come to tell them about a new lover she has met on an airplane.

The play depends heavily on the cleverness of the dialogue, but, as always, Nichols uses theatrical devices to surprise the audience. James's problem is that he wants to have the best of both worlds: to keep his happy marriage and, at the same time, maintain his relationship with his mistress. He also has a sense that he has somehow lost out; the lack of inhibition displayed by Kate is a continual reminder of all the things that he never did when he was young. To bring these ideas home to the audience Nichols introduces two alter-ego figures, Jim and Nell, who occupy the stage at the same time as James and Eleanor and debate with their "real" counterparts. In the second act the four take part in a complicated argument:

> ELEANOR: If you think it's only your poor old cock she's after, you're flattering yourself.
> JIM: *gives her a glass of water.*
> NELL: She wants to take you away from me.
> JAMES: I don't think we can ever know with her. She belongs to another generation–free of convention, independent–
> NELL: Hah!
> JAMES: One of the people men of my age wanted to create.
> JIM: Yes, the freedom we advocated is the air they breathe.
> NELL: (*to* JIM) Her independence is based on daddy's tax-dodge trusts.
> JAMES: She parks on double yellow lines, she walks straight to the head of queues, she grabs what's going–
> ELEANOR: In other words, disregards the morality you've always lived by.
> JAMES: I've been very moral, yes.
> ELEANOR: So go to her. What's keeping you here?
> JIM: You!
> NELL: An old flavour?
> JIM: (*indicating the room*) This!
> NELL: A prison?
> JIM: (*to* NELL) We need her, Eleanor. She can save us.
> NELL: You can't have both.
> JIM: Why not?

The other side of adultery is increasingly shown as the play develops. It is a side Eleanor is told about at the beginning of the play by Agnes, the former wife of Kate's now-dead lover, when Agnes informs her of Kate's new liasion with James. Later, Nell talks to Agnes about the specialist her husband has prescribed for her emotional problems after the revelation of his adultery:

> NELL: I thought I was going mad. They told me it was a symptom of the menopause.
> AGNES: Who did?
> NELL: The doctors.
> AGNES: All men?
> NELL: Yes.
> AGNES: They're everywhere.

Agnes tells Nell that the doctor to whom she has been sent is the same one Agnes's husband recommended for her when she found out about his affair: "Their old chum Michael at the Middlesex sends all the psychologically battered wives to him. It's part of the male conspiracy."

The play has two endings that are staged simultaneously, one involving the real characters, the other the alter egos. A Christmas party is about to begin at James and Eleanor's house. Eleanor and Nell separate for the first time, the wife to get ready for the party, the alter ego, now acting independently, to plan a parting. James welcomes guests, while, unseen by the others, Jim and Kate embark on yet another sexual encounter. Nell leaves by the front door, opting for her own life outside of marriage in a way that Eleanor still cannot. The last words of the play are given to Eleanor, still keeping up appearances and wishing everyone "Happy Christmas."

Nichols's next work, *Poppy* (1982), is a lavishly produced knockabout pantomime dealing with the opium trade between Britain and China. Using many of the devices of early-1970s agitprop theater, the play concludes with an attempt at contemporary relevance as Queen Victoria is transformed into Elizabeth II and Dick Whittington into a modern city gentleman for the final curtain call.

Poppy was successfully transferred from the Barbican Centre to the West End, even as *Passion Play* was being revived. Nevertheless, dispirited by a series of struggles with theatrical managements and directors, Nichols announced his disillusionment with the theater in *Plays and Players* (June 1984): "The theatre has lost her bloom, and her wizened features are raddled under the rouge." He abandoned playwriting to retire to the country, where he unsuccessfully attempted to write a novel.

Nichols resumed his theater career with *A Piece of My Mind,* a comedy about the early success and later decline into unpopularity and silence of Ted Forrest, a playwright who, like Nichols at the time, is in his fifties. The play grew out of Nichols's dissatisfaction with his status as a mainstream writer, which he discussed in the January 1987 issue of *Plays and Players:*

> I've been asking myself the question: if I could write without thinking all the time about the potential effect

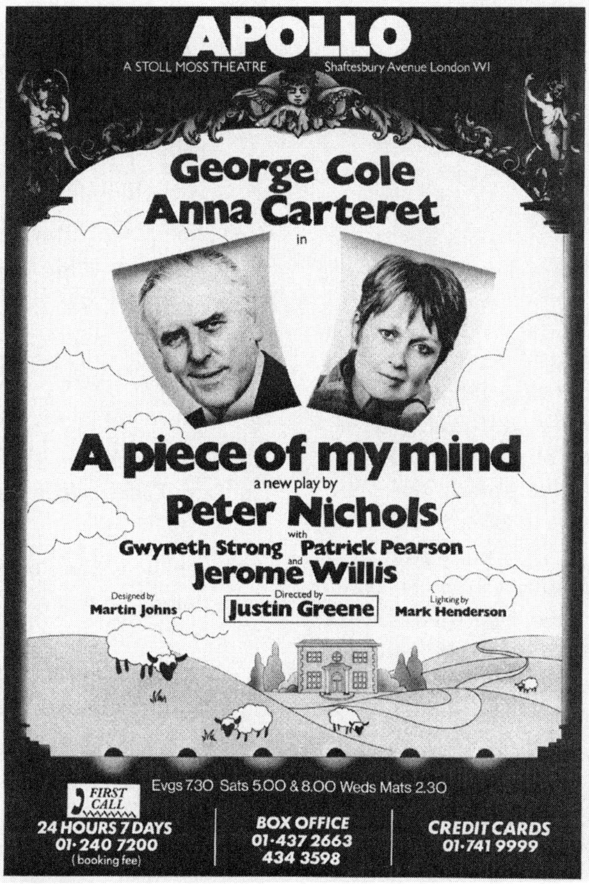

Advertisement for Nichols's 1987 play, produced five years after his previous play

> and appeal of a play, without thinking about all the commercial aspects and all those things you have to think about as a pro, would that mean I could free myself to start thinking and writing in a new way? Could I retreat from being a very public sort of playwright into something more irresponsible?

A Piece of My Mind takes Nichols back to his dramatic roots as a writer influenced by the first wave of absurdism, a point made sardonically by an actor character who is temporarily playing a critic and commenting on Forrest's unhappy relationship with his agent: "The scene where he batters his agent to death in her office aims to be Absurdist but manages to be merely absurd." The play, full of jokes borrowed from playwrights such as Pirandello, Oscar Wilde, and Samuel Beckett, seeks to place Nichols as a playwright. In act 1, Forrest is questioned by a female character, Mai:

> Do you see your plays as advocating revolution like those of David Mercer, Edward Bond, Trevor Griffiths, David Edgar, John McGrath, Margaretta D'Arcey . . . Willy Russell, Caryl Churchill, Howard Barker, David Hare, Howard Brenton . . . or do you see them as supporting the status quo like those of Alan Bennett, John Osborne, Robert Bolt, Michael Frayn, Julian Mitchell, Tom Stoppard, Christopher Hampton . . . John Mortimer, Simon Gray, Peter Shaffer, Charles Wood, Peter Nichols . . . ?

Nichols is expressing his resentment of the fact that theater audiences find his work unthreatening and wishing that he had been a different kind of writer.

By 1993 Nichols felt neglected as a playwright. In January of that year *The Observer* published his parody of Samuel Taylor Coleridge's ballad *The Rime of the Ancient Mariner,* "The Rime of the Ancient Dramatist": "An aged playwright accosteth the Artistic Director of the National Theatre, Richard Eyre, seizing his chance to chide him on the rejection of all he hath submitted, so that his plays hath not been seen on the South Bank since the days of Olde Vic." In the poem Nichols accosts Eyre, demanding to know why, in view of his track record, his new works are not being put on at the National Theatre. Eyre's attempts to shake him off are futile:

"These antique tales I know full well.
Spare me the rest!" quoth Eyre.
"If I won't put your new stuff on,
Why don't you try elsewhere?"

"Where else *is* there for large-scale plays?"
Cries th'embittered hack;
"Does all this work mean nothing,
My record on the track?

"What say you to a revival then?
D'you want to see me beg?
You've done old Bonds and Priestley,
So how about 'Joe Egg'?"

To date, nothing has come of the plea, although 1993 did bring a revival of *A Day in the Death of Joe Egg* at the King's Head Theatre. The critic Robert Butler was not alone in welcoming the return of the play. In the *Independent on Sunday* (13 June 1993) he remarked: "The first shock in *A Day in the Death of Joe Egg* comes from the programme. It is 22 years since Peter Nichols' play about a couple with a severely handicapped child was seen in London. Don't ask why. . . . *Joe Egg* is unlike any play I've seen; concerns about whether it's dated fade next to the claims that can now be made for it." *Passion Play* was revived in 2000.

Interview:

Ronald Hayman, "Interview," in *Playback 2* (London: Davis-Poynter, 1973).

References:

James Allister, "All Passion Spent," *Plays and Players* (June 1984);

Richard Foulkes, "'The Cure is Removal of Guilt': Faith, Fidelity and Fertility in the Plays of Peter Nichols," *Modern Drama,* 29 (1986): 207–215;

Malcolm Hay, "Piece of Mind," *Plays and Players* (January 1987);

Oleg Kerensky, *The New British Drama* (London: Hamilton, 1980);

Brian Miller, "Peter Nichols," in *British Television Drama,* edited by George W. Brandt (Cambridge: Cambridge University Press, 1981), pp. 110–136;

Andrew Parkin, *File on Nichols* (London: Methuen, 1993);

June Schluter, "Adultery Is Next to Godliness: Dramatic Juxtaposition in Peter Nichols' *Passion Play,*" in *Modern British Dramatists: New Perspectives,* edited by John Russell Brown (Englewood Cliffs, N.J. & London: Prentice-Hall, 1984);

John Russell Taylor, *The Second Wave: British Drama of the Sixties* (London: Methuen, 1971), pp. 16–35;

Irving Wardle, "A Second Shot at Life," *Independent on Sunday,* 25 March 1990.

Stewart Parker

(20 October 1941 – 2 November 1988)

Elmer Andrews
University of Ulster

PLAY PRODUCTIONS: *Spokesong,* music by Jimmy Kennedy, lyrics by Parker, Dublin, John Player Theatre, 6 October 1975; New Haven, Conn., Long Wharf Theatre, 1978;
The Actress and the Bishop, London, King's Head Theatre, 1976;
Catchpenny Twist, Dublin, Peacock Theatre, 25 August 1977;
Kingdom Come, music by Shaun Davey, London, King's Head Theatre, 1978;
Nightshade, Dublin, Peacock Theatre, 9 October 1980;
Tall Girls Have Everything, Louisville, Kentucky, Actors' Theatre, 1980;
Pratt's Fall, Glasgow, Tron Theatre, 8 January 1982;
Northern Star, Belfast, Lyric Theatre, 7 November 1984;
Heavenly Bodies, Birmingham, Birmingham Repertory Theatre, 21 April 1986;
Pentecost, Londonderry, Guildhall, 23 September 1987.

BOOKS: *The Casualty's Meditation* (Belfast: Festival Publications, Queen's University of Belfast, 1967);
Maw: A Journey (Belfast: Festival Publications, Queen's University of Belfast, 1968);
Spokesong (London: S. French, 1979);
Catchpenny Twist (Loughcrew, Ireland: Gallery, 1980); republished as *Catchpenny Twist: A Charade in Two Acts* (New York & London: S. French, 1984);
Nightshade (Dublin: Co-Op, 1980);
Dramatis Personae: A Lecture Dedicated to the Memory of John Malone (Belfast: John Malone Memorial Committee, 1986);
Three Plays for Ireland (London: Oberon, 1989)–comprises *Northern Star, Heavenly Bodies,* and *Pentecost.*

PRODUCED SCRIPTS: *Speaking of Red Indians,* radio, 1967;
Minnie and Maisie and Lily Freed, radio, 1970;
Requiem, radio, 1973;
The Iceberg, radio, BBC, 1975;
I'm a Dreamer, Montreal, radio, 1976;
Catchpenny Twist, television, BBC, 1977;

Stewart Parker (from the program for Spokesong*)*

I'm a Dreamer, Montreal, television, BBC, 1979;
The Kamikaze Ground Staff Reunion Dinner, radio, BBC, 1980;
Iris in the Traffic, Ruby in the Rain, television, BBC, 1981;
Joyce in June, television, BBC, 1981;
The Kamikaze Ground Staff Reunion Dinner, television, 1981;
Blue Money, television, BBC, 1985;
Radio Pictures, television, BBC, 1985;
The Traveller, radio, BBC, 1985;
Lost Belongings, television, BBC, 1987.

Stewart Parker loved theatricality. In *Dramatis Personae: A Lecture Dedicated to the Memory of John Malone* (1986) Parker outlines his ideas about theater and play. Play, he said, when it is freed from the connotations of frivolity and infantilism, is no mere diversion or idle escapism. "Play is how we experiment, imagine, invent, and move forward," he wrote. "Play is above all how we enjoy the earth and celebrate our life upon it." The irrational nature of play affirms indeterminacy and individual freedom. For Parker play is the antithesis of nihilism and despair. He refers to Samuel Beckett's grim world, where human dignity, the illusion of meaning, and the possibility of authenticity and responsibility have all been stripped away, but where play is the one thing left to mark the characters' humanity.

Parker refused, however, to abandon the humanist agenda with its faith in mind and man. Man is still in charge of his destiny. Man is not the victim of an indifferent universe but a self-created victim of his own illusions. A viable response is still possible. Change, not resignation, is the keystone of his aesthetic. Play is more than the minimalist assertion of humanity, more than a way of whiling away the time, more than meaningless games and automatic speech to fill the waiting. Beckett's characters are beyond the scope of meaningful choice or action, reduced to passive victims. Parker affirmed a fundamentally optimistic and positive view of man's potential. His concept of play is more truly existential than Beckett's, for while Beckett forms an abstract concept of man's nature and role and presents it in its original conceptual form, individualizing it only slightly, Parker presents characters whose actions and situations are in process.

Parker saw theater as the chief cultural means that could help people review and refashion their given reality. He believed theater to be a potentially dynamic force in society, a medium political by its nature, a laboratory in which new ideas may be tried out and repressed forces in consciousness and the culture may be given a voice. Through play people can explore convictions and dismantle and refashion received identities. Parker's kind of play is an essentially "protestant" vocation–protestant in the root sense of the word, opposing itself to congealed meanings and refusing to be locked into orthodoxy. Art, Parker believed, "amplifies and distorts, seeking to alter perceptions to a purpose." Play must take over from politics, for in his view the politicians had failed the people by keeping them incarcerated in outworn, dangerous myths. It is up to the playwrights, Parker insisted, to open up new possibilities. "If ever a time and place cried out for the solace and rigour and passionate rejoinder of great drama," he wrote, "it is here and now. There is a whole culture to be achieved. The politicians, visionless to a man, are withdrawing into their sectarian stockades. It falls to the artists to construct a working model of wholeness." This "working model of wholeness" has eluded Irish dramatists, Parker believed, because of their past-oriented habit of mind. The time had come "to cease the task of picking over the entrails of the past, and begin to hint at a vision of the future." With this productive, dynamic, forward-looking concept of play, Parker found common ground with Bertolt Brecht. He shares Brecht's desire to change the world but resists the dogmatic, authoritative, hectoring mentality, which he saw as characterizing much of post-Brechtian, committed theater. Brecht is exemplary in his concern to make learning pleasurable. Parker champions a concept of theater that "will be neither didactic nor absurdist. It will aim to inspire rather than to instruct, to offer ideas and attitudes in a spirit of critical inquiry . . . and by means of this, above all, to assert the primacy of the play-impulse over the deathwish."

James Stewart Parker was born on 20 October 1941 in East Belfast. His parents, George Herbert, a tailor's cutter, and Isabel (née Lynas) Parker, were Unionist working-class people. Stewart Parker was educated at Ashfield Boys' Secondary School. According to his schoolmate Terence Brown, in "Let's Go to Graceland: The Drama of Stewart Parker" (1991), even as a young adolescent Parker "had a sense of style, carried himself with the genial authority of the man who knew his own mind. Stewart was a performer, who brought personal panache, a sense of music's freedom from the immediate tediums of life in a rather grim place, along with a ready wit and a warm disposition."

In 1959 Parker entered Queen's University Belfast to study English. During his years at university he suffered from bone cancer, which necessitated the amputation of a leg. In an article in the *Sunday Independent* (6 November 1988) Seamus Heaney recalled the time Parker, encumbered by his artificial leg made of aluminum, stood and read aloud his poems to Philip Hobsbaum's "Group":

> In spite of this, he lurched formally and significantly to his feet, a move which in retrospect gains great symbolic power. It was a signal of personal victory, of the triumph of artistic utterance over demeaning circumstances, of the possibility of genial spirits in the face of destructive events. As such it had a meaning not only for himself but for the imaginative and spiritual life of Northern Ireland as a whole over the two decades that were to come. . . . He stood for that victory over the negative aspects of Ulster experience which everyone wants to believe is possible.

Parker graduated with a B.A. in 1964, married Kate Ireland on 26 August, and began teaching English at Hamilton College, in Clinton, New York. In 1966 he was awarded his M.A. in poetic drama from Queen's University of Belfast, and in 1967 he began a two-year teaching stint at Cornell University. That same year he published a pamphlet of poems in the Belfast Festival

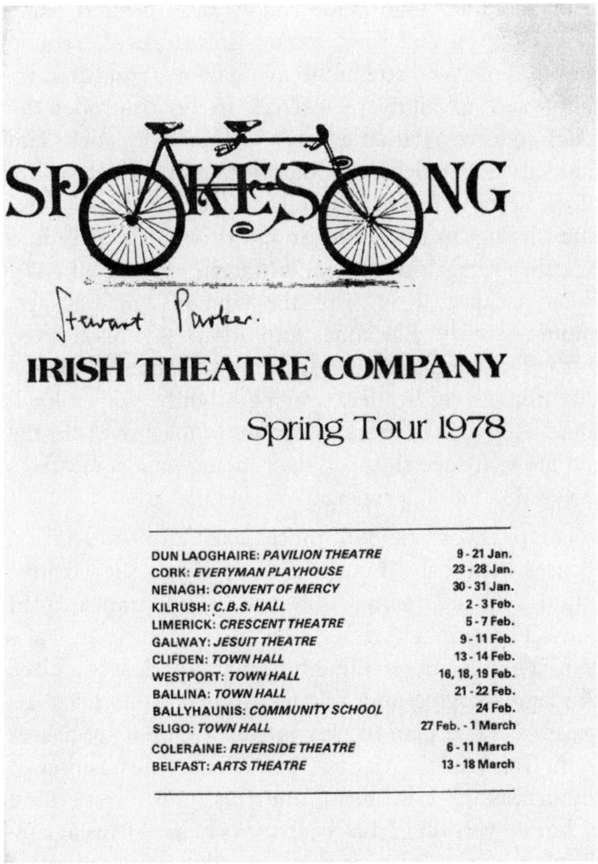

SPOKESONG

Stewart Parker.

IRISH THEATRE COMPANY

Spring Tour 1978

DUN LAOGHAIRE: *PAVILION THEATRE*	9 - 21 Jan.
CORK: *EVERYMAN PLAYHOUSE*	23 - 28 Jan.
NENAGH: *CONVENT OF MERCY*	30 - 31 Jan.
KILRUSH: *C.B.S. HALL*	2 - 3 Feb.
LIMERICK: *CRESCENT THEATRE*	5 - 7 Feb.
GALWAY: *JESUIT THEATRE*	9 - 11 Feb.
CLIFDEN: *TOWN HALL*	13 - 14 Feb.
WESTPORT: *TOWN HALL*	16, 18, 19 Feb.
BALLINA: *TOWN HALL*	21 - 22 Feb.
BALLYHAUNIS: *COMMUNITY SCHOOL*	24 Feb.
SLIGO: *TOWN HALL*	27 Feb. - 1 March
COLERAINE: *RIVERSIDE THEATRE*	6 - 11 March
BELFAST: *ARTS THEATRE*	13 - 18 March

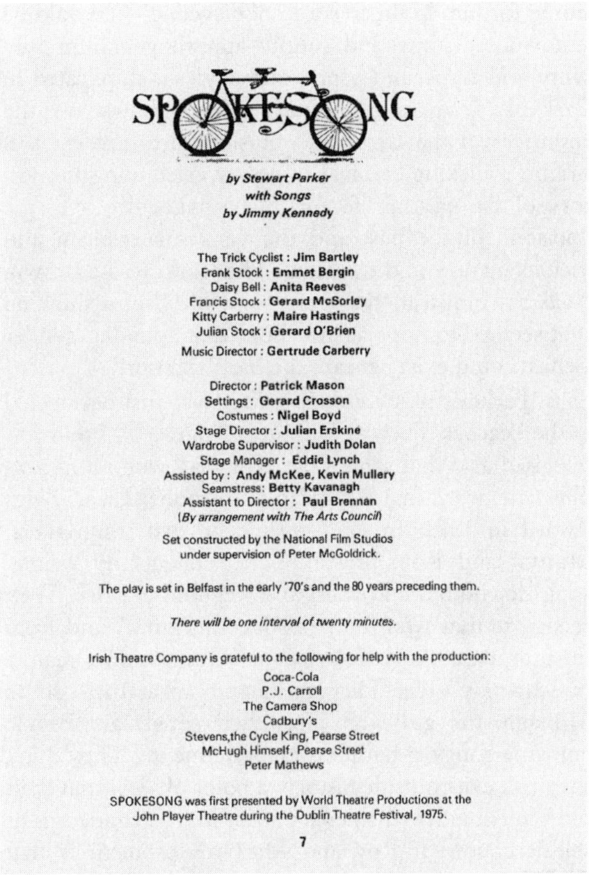

SPOKESONG

by Stewart Parker
with Songs
by Jimmy Kennedy

The Trick Cyclist : **Jim Bartley**
Frank Stock : **Emmet Bergin**
Daisy Bell : **Anita Reeves**
Francis Stock : **Gerard McSorley**
Kitty Carberry : **Maire Hastings**
Julian Stock : **Gerard O'Brien**

Music Director : **Gertrude Carberry**

Director : **Patrick Mason**
Settings : **Gerard Crosson**
Costumes : **Nigel Boyd**
Stage Director : **Julian Erskine**
Wardrobe Supervisor : **Judith Dolan**
Stage Manager : **Eddie Lynch**
Assisted by : **Andy McKee, Kevin Mullery**
Seamstress: **Betty Kavanagh**
Assistant to Director : **Paul Brennan**
(*By arrangement with The Arts Council*)

Set constructed by the National Film Studios under supervision of Peter McGoldrick.

The play is set in Belfast in the early '70's and the 80 years preceding them.

There will be one interval of twenty minutes.

Irish Theatre Company is grateful to the following for help with the production:

Coca-Cola
P.J. Carroll
The Camera Shop
Cadbury's
Stevens,the Cycle King, Pearse Street
McHugh Himself, Pearse Street
Peter Mathews

SPOKESONG was first presented by World Theatre Productions at the John Player Theatre during the Dublin Theatre Festival, 1975.

7

Program cover and cast list for Parker's first stage play, signed by the author

Poets' Series, *The Casualty's Meditation* (1967), in which he explored in a positive way his experience of suffering from cancer and losing his leg.

After spending five years in the United States, Parker returned to Belfast in 1969 to devote himself to writing. He moved to Edinburgh in 1978, but Ulster was never far from his mind. In the preface to his last major work, *Lost Belongings* (1987), a six-part television drama, he writes, "I can freely own up that the audience with which I was first and foremost concerned in everything I have ever written was my own people, the people of Northern Ireland, Ulster, the Six Counties, Lilliput, a place so fundamentally factional that it can't even agree on a name for itself."

Though his reputation rests mainly on his stage plays, Parker also wrote for radio and television. Among his radio plays, the best are *The Iceberg* (1975), about the sinking of the *Titanic,* and *The Kamikaze Ground Staff Reunion Dinner* (1980), which was also adapted for BBC television and was winner of the 1980 Giles Cooper Award and nominated for the Italia Prize. His television plays include *I'm a Dreamer, Montreal* (1979), winner of the Christopher Ewart-Biggs Memorial Prize; *Iris in the Traffic, Ruby in the Rain* (1981); *Joyce in June* (1981); *Radio Pictures* (1985); *Blue Money* (1985), winner of the Grand Prix of the Banff International Television Film Festival; and *Lost Belongings,* a Thames Television six-part version of the Irish legend of Deirdre, in which Deirdre represents the sensitive artist, the life force, and the spirit of hope and resilience in the face of rapacious cruelty and apocalyptic destructiveness.

Parker's first stage play was *Spokesong,* the big hit of the 1975 Dublin Theatre Festival. From Dublin it transferred to London, where the play won him an *Evening Standard* award, and then to Broadway. The protagonist is Frank Stock, owner of a bicycle shop, a man of individual conscience, animated by a dream of a more vital, natural life. Frank agitates for outlawing the motor car and rediscovering the virtues of bicycling. His master plan is for fifty thousand free bicycles to be distributed around the center of Belfast. Frank is trapped and besieged in his shop, beset by the city planners on one side and by bombers and racketeers on the other. The central dramatic tension is between what a man feels life ought to be and the thwarting, hostile reality of what is. Frank's irrepressible joy of life, epitomized for him in the freedom of bicycling–"it would be funny and sunny and simply appealing and prettily witty and zippy and peppy and gay!"–is duplicated in Parker's dramatic technique, which draws on the resources of the circus and music hall to present this bright, rollicking carnival of a play celebrating the victory of the natural life and man's ingenuity over the "poison" of the past and the venal materialism and vicious bigotry of the present. The work, wrote Brown, "was a whimsical, charming piece of wishful thinking that seemed to hope against hope that a kinder, gentler Belfast could exist beneath the hard exterior."

Parker's play *Catchpenny Twist* was first performed at the Peacock Theatre, Dublin in August 1977 and was televised also that same year. The play won an *Evening Standard* award in 1977 and a Christopher Ewart-Biggs Award in 1979. In *Catchpenny Twist* two songwriters, Martyn and Roy, prostitute their talents by writing songs for both the Loyalist and Republican sides. They recognize that what they produce is "gunk" and from time to time they wish for something more than a "catchpenny" life. They rationalize what they do to Monagh, the girl who sings their songs, as "People enjoying songs, a harmless entertainment." They think they can exist outside history, a point of view that their old acquaintance, the fierce patriot Marie, condemns as self-deception. If Roy and Martyn's problem is that they have distanced themselves too much from the past, Marie's problem is that she has not distanced herself enough. Quick to criticize Roy and Martyn's ideological illusion, Marie cannot see her own failings–that she is incarcerated in historical prejudice and tribal bigotry and has surrendered individuality and human freedom to the service of the cause. Parker presents her through a humorless, theoretical language stripped of individual personality, charged with rhetoric and laden with cliché. In contrast to the fossilized Marie, the three central characters, Martyn, Roy, and Monagh, are given an attractively vigorous speech, with a sharp, ironic edge and surreal humor. None of these characters, however, have much depth. They are mere music-hall caricatures.

The play has a highly fragmented, episodic structure, one usually associated with movie and television drama scripts. The dialogue is liberally interspersed with musical turns. Music in the play is a means employed by the opposing factions to deepen rather than transcend discord and division. The three central characters represent a fluid, unsettled, Protean identity, though they are the only characters with names, the others being designated simply as Man, Woman, and Girl. In having some of the actors play a variety of roles, Parker foregrounds the constructed, Brechtian nature of his presentation: identity is chosen and constructed rather than being simply received and fixed. With Martyn and Roy, Parker dramatizes the condition of those who attempt to avoid choice and responsibility and to allow themselves to be controlled by external forces. Parker exacts a high price for such "bad faith" by having Roy and Martyn caught in the crossfire of the sectarian feuding in Ulster. He ends the play by intensifying his satiric thrust and driving the play into macabre surrealism. Roy and Martyn are sent a mysterious package. Roy "rips the tape off the package. Simultaneously–Blackout. Explosion. A noisy drum intro. The band strikes up. A red spot comes on. Showing Monagh on her feet, smiling brightly, with a hand mike. Roy and Martyn's seats are toppled over. In the red glow, we see them on their knees, hands and faces covered in blood, groping about blindly."

Nightshade (1980), much like *Catchpenny Twist,* focuses on those who abuse and pervert the creative impulse for their own selfish material and unprincipled ends. The main character, Quinn, is a mortician/magician. The set, representing his funeral parlor, is a place of magic. Staging and lighting "should be as magic as possible." The kind of play in which Quinn specializes is the mechanical routine–the "efficient disposition of the deceased." His funeral undertaking is only a more elaborate version of the cheap tricks he performs at children's parties. Quinn is devoted to the obliteration of human feeling, especially grief. His business is designed to aestheticize death so that the grieving can be excused their grief and relieved of their humanity. He aims to satisfy the demand for painless loss and efficiency. He meets people's need not to have to feel deeply or confront the reality of death. The mystery of death is turned into big business. Quinn's showmanship is duplicated in Parker's theatricality, but there is the crucial difference of intentions between Quinn the magician, who gives illusion that has the appearance of truth, and Parker, who gives the truth in the pleasant disguise of illusion.

Nightshade is a confused plethora of actions and motifs that are only loosely related. Parker describes the action as "fast and continuous, a constant traffic, the fitful opening and closing of possibilities." The play aspires to the condition of dream. Expressionistic staging techniques are used to intercut different planes of action and different points in time. Parker displays a boldly experimental sense of theater and stage spectacle; a penchant for witty, absurdist dialogue; a love of the irreverent and shocking; and a pervasive comic insouciance. Characters have little more depth or complexity than that of cartoon figures. The action tends toward comic fantasy and incorporates elements of vaudeville and the surreal. The play, with its anarchic playfulness and self-indulgent lyricism, fails to generate any real tension or emotion.

Pratt's Fall was first performed at the Tron Theatre in Glasgow in 1982. The play tells of the unscrupulous Mahoney, who, refusing to be locked into the given as if it were the natural order of things, wants to change the world. He sets out to persuade the audience that the United States was discovered by the ninth-century monks of Ardfert. Mahoney's intentions are admirable. He wants to reactivate man's spirituality in a materialistic world and believes that the miracle of faith that impelled St. Brendan and the early missionary adventurers who sailed the Atlantic is exemplary. With Mahoney, Parker extends his investigation of the ludic impulse, which began with Frank Stock and continues through Martyn and Roy and then Quinn. Mahoney combines Frank's spiritual idealism with Quinn's cheap trickery. In his characterization of Mahoney, Parker blurs the line between the shaman and the sham–the two faces of the poet. The play insists that belief, however empowering or reassuring, must pay its dues to fact.

Appearing around the same time as Brian Friel's *Translations* (1981), *Pratt's Fall* also is concerned with maps and mapping. Both plays emphasize that available meanings depend on what language or what map is shared in the first place. Maps constitute knowledge, but they also distort it. "As you know," says Godfrey, the geographer in *Pratt's Fall,* "a completely accurate map of the world is impossible." Committing oneself to a certain set of premises is also to commit oneself to a certain set of distortions: "Every method of projection incurs a different form of distortion." Sign systems, such as languages and maps, are the ideological products of a particular history. Mahoney wants to rewrite history with the aid of a bogus map. His map represents an individual's quixotic effort to assert Celtic faith and spirituality against the constraining English rule of reason personified by Victoria Pratt, the English cartographer, who is described as "the most loyal subject of the secular realm," and who has the task of evaluating Mahoney's eccentric claims.

Parker is as critical of Victoria's rationalism as he is of Mahoney's spiritualism. Her comic fall comes from her not knowing the limitations of the rational ideal. In the end she is forced to acknowledge to Mahoney: "I do realise that you were right of course. Beliefs govern the world not facts. Facts are as neutral as bullets, and as plentiful." *Pratt's Fall* prefigures the central preoccupations of Parker's mature drama and points to what authentic play might be: the challenge of creatively transforming the past in order to open up new horizons of possibility in the future, and the need for dialectical relationship between imagination and

Program cover for Parker's play about people who pervert the creative impulse for selfish purposes

reason, the ideal and the real, in a common project of universal liberation.

Parker's view of history is dramatized in the last three major stage plays he wrote. *Northern Star,* first performed in the Lyric Players' Theatre in Belfast on 7 November 1984; *Heavenly Bodies,* first performed in the Birmingham Repertory Theatre on 21 April 1984; and *Pentecost,* first performed in the Guildhall in Derry by the Field Day Theatre Company on 23 September 1987, all demonstrate the characteristic qualities and preoccupations of his drama–his positive outlook, his faith in man, the power of play, and his irrepressible carnival spirit and love of theatricality. The three plays, offered as a trilogy, were published in 1989 under the title *Three Plays for Ireland.*

In Ireland the burden of history weighs heavily. Traditionally, Irish literature, like Irish life, has been haunted by the past. The Gothic tradition has especially strong roots in the Irish imagination–as, for example, in the works of Bram Stoker, Sheridan LeFanu, and Charles Robert Maturin; in John Banville's haunted houses; and in Heaney's whispering landscapes–and all three of Parker's history plays are haunted by ghosts as well. The Phantom Bride in *Northern Star* is the silent, voracious, territorial numen–in the tradition of Mother Ireland, Kathleen Ni Houlihan, and the Shan Van Vocht–who demands nothing less than blood sacrifice from her Irish sons. The Phantom Fiddler in *Heavenly Bodies* is an elegiac shade of the days of the Great Famine, a symbol of Irish disinheritance, dispossession, and disillusion. Lily Matthews in *Pentecost* is the guilt-ridden, repressed, life-denying ghost of Protestant Ulster. As Parker remarks in his introduction to the three plays, "Ancestral voices prophesy and bicker, and the ghosts of your own time and birthplace wrestle and dance, in any place you choose to write–but most obviously when it actually is a history play."

In each play he focuses on characters "drawn from the marginalia of the historical record": Henry Joy McCracken, who was a minor figure in the 1798 rebellion in Ireland; Don Boucicault, who was a major force in Victorian theater but has subsequently been considered marginal; and a nondescript quartet of ordinary people caught in the crossfire of the Troubles in Belfast in 1974. Through these characters Parker examines both the vexed question of Irish identity and the perennial tension that exists between the individual and the "forces of the age." He wants to examine the possibility of dealing with the past without being trapped in it or transfixed by it. People cannot escape the past, but perhaps it can be used selectively and creatively rather than accepted blindly and unquestioningly.

In *Northern Star* Parker takes as his subject the activity of the United Irishmen between 1791 and 1798, and his central character is the Presbyterian cotton manufacturer, McCracken, a revolutionary idealist seeking the republican brotherhood of man. The play presents McCracken's thoughts on the eve of his execution after the failure of the 1798 rebellion. McCracken, the man with an Enlightenment vision of uniting Protestant and Catholic, in actuality establishes the tradition of republicanism that divided Protestants and Catholics more deeply than ever and laid the foundation for modern-day violence in Ulster. A republican inspired by the revolutions in France and the United States, he creates a situation that leads to the consolidation of the link between Ireland and Britain through the Act of Union in 1801. The play is set in the "Continuous Past." McCracken repeatedly addresses the "Citizens of Belfast," present as well as past. Parker dramatizes the story of the United Irishmen in terms of the "Seven Ages of Man," and each of these distinct, preordained ages are played in a pastiche of a different Irish playwright. Thus, the Age of Innocence is conveyed in the lighthearted, satirical style of Richard Brinsley Sheridan and Oliver Goldsmith; the Age of Idealism is represented in terms of Boucicault's melodramatic extravagance; the Age of Cleverness is presented in the style of Oscar Wilde; the Age of Dialectics in the manner of George Bernard Shaw; the Age of Heroism through John Millington Synge's highly charged poetic language; the Age of Compromise through the florid rhetoric of Sean O'Casey; and the Age of Knowledge in the style of Brendan Behan and Beckett.

Throughout the play McCracken sees himself as an actor on the stage of history, playing a predetermined role. He is obsessed with a destructive fatalism. Act 1 ends with the spectral appearance of the Phantom Bride, who holds him in her deadly thrall: "She kisses him, and then, with a predatory leap, clamps her bare legs round his waist and her arms round his neck." McCracken is the traditional patriot son and lover ordained for martyrdom. Parker dramatizes his failure to break free of the fetters of the past, his failure to improvise a fate for himself other than that assigned him by the traditional mythology of Irish patriotism and republican blood sacrifice. He ends act 1 with the stage directions: "The moon goes behind a cloud. Darkness." No "northern star" lights this firmament. Trapped in the past, unable to accomplish the necessary metamorphosis either in himself or in his people, wedded to failure and despair, McCracken is identified as being as much of a ghost as the Phantom Bride. Ghosts, says Parker in his introduction, are "uncompleted souls." McCracken has not wholly moved out of myth into history, from romance to reality. As his mistress and mother of his child, Mary Bodle, says to him, "I won't fornicate with a ghost–with a man in a dead-cart. The country's full of them. I want the man I loved, Harry. The man who gave me that child." The play ends with McCracken himself placing the noose round his neck. All he can speak of is death, disillusionment, lost opportunity, stillbirth, and entrapment in life-denying roles. Jimmy Hope, in fact, represents the hope of the future. The "future ghost of Jimmy Hope enters" and reiterates his commitment to an independent republic formed out of a united laboring class in opposition to a corrupt and repressive system. McCracken acknowledges that "the steadfast light, the real Northern Star [is] him. Not me." Parker does little, however, with the character of Jimmy Hope, who consequently remains a merely symbolic personage, incorporated into the play to reassure the audience that all is not lost and that the spirit of equality, liberty, and fraternity lives.

The positive values that Parker suggests to his audience are actually represented in the formal means he employs. While dramatizing the traditional republican view of history as continuous, cyclical, and locked within a determinate pattern, Parker includes another

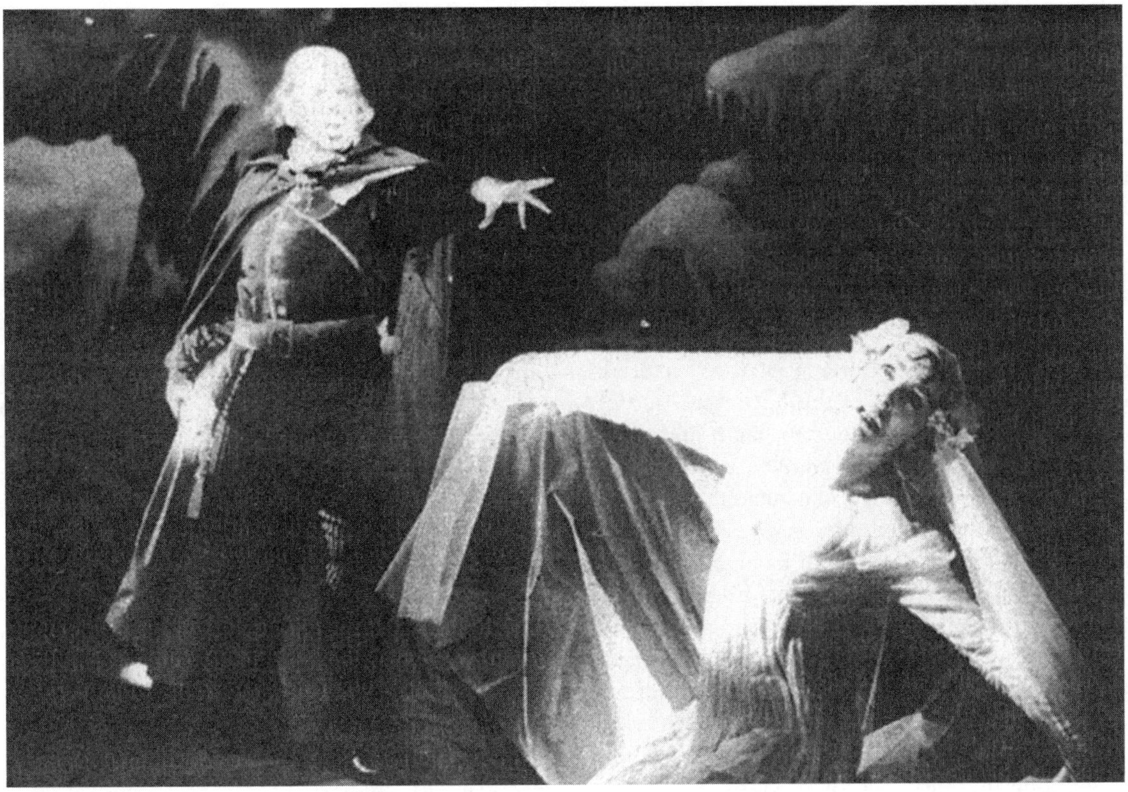

Timothy Spall and Marie Francis in a scene from the 1986 Birmingham Repertory Theatre production of Parker's Heavenly Bodies

view of history as a plethora of discourses, idioms, themes, and conventions. Parker's technique is essentially "estranging," challenging the audience to see how their world is constructed out of pre-existing codes and discourses. The play is an experiment in reworking established patterns and discourses and adapting them to new purposes. Parker is engaged in a process of translation that acknowledges the importance of the past but recognizes the need continually to reorder it. The form of Parker's play demonstrates the possibility of using the past creatively, rather than merely accepting it passively and fatalistically, as McCracken does. Through this form he shows that there are many ways of representing and understanding the world and that people need not become trapped in any one of them. *Northern Star* represents Parker's attempt to evolve new "forms of inclusiveness." The moment of history that he presents coexists with all the other moments, and the play is an echo chamber of ghostly voices all clamoring for attention. In showing McCracken's lack of faith, his demoralization and Beckettian bleakness, in revealing his death wish and martyr complex, Parker shows a man who has failed to shake himself free of the traditional Irish pathology of failure, the old romance of defeat. McCracken has lost the capacity for play. Parker's own elaborate, multi-idiomatic style suggests the desired wholeness and freedom. Blending actuality, memory, and fantasy, using techniques from August Strindberg and the German expressionists and from Eugene O'Neill and Arthur Miller, Parker moves easily between different periods, languages, and levels of reality, breaking down conventionalized modes of perception and figuration and developing Brechtian effects of alienation to shock the audience out of "the same old roles."

The second of Parker's trilogy of history plays, *Heavenly Bodies,* takes as its subject the playwright, adapter, actor, director, and manager Dionysus Lardner Boucicault, a prolific of Irish dramatists with about two hundred pieces to his credit, the most impressive practitioner of the comedy of wit between George Farquhar and Goldsmith in the eighteenth century and Oscar Wilde's *The Importance of Being Earnest* in 1895, an expert in stage mechanics and stage management, and the "cleverest, most theatrically inventive English-speaking playwright of his age," according to Andrew Parkin in "Metaphor as Dramatic Structure in Some Plays of Stewart Parker" (1986). Parker recognized in Boucicault "an ancestral voice" crying out to be reclaimed, as he observes in the program notes for the original production. "It was not merely his equivocal Irishness. There were more specific traits that struck a chord, scepticism, a convivial pessimism, a shameless theatricalism. He was a maverick foraging in the badlands between high art and vulgar entertainment. His plays veered from the sadly ridiculous to the gloriously ridiculous, with a very occasional tincture of the sublime." Moreover, Boucicault was the perfect subject for a study of "the struggle between the individual will and the forces of the Age in which it operates." In Boucicault, Parker saw "the larger melodrama of the Victorian world." The values inherent in the Victorian "age of steam," Parker believed, "continue to haunt and meddle with our own world, having enjoyed a whole new resurgence in the course of the Thatcherite eighties." Boucicault was of particular interest because he was both a product of his age and one of its bitterest critics, simultaneously inside and outside the English mainstream. He is an image of the deeply divided individual, unable to transcend the conflicts that tear him apart, as deeply disabled as McCracken was by the forces of his time. Boucicault is the artist who submits to "market forces" and English expectations, yet retains an ambition to continue the great line of serious Irish drama coming down from Farquhar, Goldsmith, William Congreve, and Sheridan. Parker emphasizes Boucicault's commercialism and sentimentality, his infidelity and egotism, his philandering and profligacy, but also celebrates his love of theatricality and his tenacious, indomitable spirit. Boucicault is most attractive in his resistance to the old romance of failure and victimhood: "there is no shred of virtue in being a victim–history disables all of us, in whatever fashion, it's the use to which we put our disabilities, that's virtue–not how much we suffer them–it's how we act upon them."

Heavenly Bodies exhibits a similar technical adventurousness and self-conscious theatricality as found in *Northern Star.* Both plays feature deeply divided characters, either broken or denied wholeness by the forces of the age. Both plays tell the story of their central character in a series of flashbacks, amplified in Boucicault's case by excerpts from his own plays, which are cast in a variety of styles–comedy of manners, farce, melodrama. In the voice of Myles na Coppaleen, "lovable rascal and comic hero" of *The Colleen Bawn* (1860), Boucicault ingratiates himself with Queen Victoria. At the end of Parker's play Boucicault assumes the role of Conn in the wake scene from *The Shaughraun* (1874). Earlier in *Heavenly Bodies* he takes on the role of Alan Raby from his own play *The Vampire* (1852), assuming the vampire's sinister power in his relationships with his first two wives. He is a consistently comic character, never more so than at the end when his ascent to heaven is unceremoniously–and hilariously–aborted. The scientific age ultimately lets him down–literally–and he is left stranded onstage with no "exit line" to take him off. His bed ascends toward heaven. Music and singing build to a climax. A starlit backdrop sparkles, and "Suddenly water starts cascading down on the catafalque. Boucicault sits up smartly–he is getting drenched. The music and heavenly choir stop abruptly . . . The star and all the other lights flash, crackle, fuse and expire. Circus music. Blackout."

Boucicault is a symbol of modern man, his identity dispersed across a range of roles. *Heavenly Bodies,* like Parker's other plays, foregrounds its own theatricality. History is performance, character an amalgam of roles, speech is endlessly allusive, the play a palimpsest of prior texts. Parker's insistence on the multiplicity of the self, his continual shifting between Boucicault's life and his art, his fluid handling of time and place, past and present, and his loose episodic structure might suggest merely fragmentation and discontinuity. The techniques of pastiche and collage that he employs, however, are an attempt to find a form of wholeness, at least at the formal and stylistic level of his representation.

In the third play, *Pentecost,* he moves toward an affirmation of the "workable model of wholeness" at the level of explicit content as well as formally and stylistically. Where in *Northern Star* and *Heavenly Bodies* Parker used a large cast and a loose, kaleidoscopic structure that ranges freely in space and time, in *Pentecost* he focuses on four main characters and concentrates the action in one setting, the "downstairs back part of a respectable working-class 'parlour house.'" There is some shifting between different levels of reality, although not so extravagantly as in the first two plays. The ghost of Lily Matthews, the fiercely Protestant former occupant of the house, shares the same stage space as the other characters and interacts passionately with one of them. The time is 1974, at the height of the Troubles, in the middle of the Ulster workers' strike called by Protestant loyalists in opposition to the power-sharing executive proposed by the British government. Like McCracken's hideout or Boucicault's stage, the house is a kind of sanctuary in the midst of the storm, for the audience is kept constantly aware that in the streets outside, law and order have broken down and rival mobs are running riot. The four characters who converge in the house are all dislocated and disoriented, reeling from the traumas and failures of their personal lives, which mirror the larger social breakdown. Marion has not been able to come to terms with the death of her child, Christopher, but now, having shed husband and home, she wants to make a new start in life, though she does not know how. Lenny, her estranged husband, has been a feckless, irresponsible individual who has lived in a state of "suspended animation" since Marion left. Now he agrees to sell Marion the house, which had been left to him on the death of a great-aunt. Ruth is a "refugee" from domestic violence, in flight from her sadistic policeman husband. Peter is an old buddy of Lenny's, an aimless, cynical dropout just returned from England. These characters are the walking wounded, and the play is concerned with the process of their possible redemption.

Using a form of heightened realism, Parker brings these four characters vividly alive, giving them a flexible, idiomatic speech and developing a loose, drifting structure of action. He also keeps the audience aware of larger implications, investing the realistic substance of the play with various kinds of symbolic nuance. The boldest device he uses is the ghost of Lily Matthews. Parker wants the audience to see that Marion parallels and completes Lily's life story. She repeatedly identifies with the ghost, though she is Catholic and Lily is emphatically Protestant. Both Marion and Lily lost children when they were thirty-three years old, the age at which Jesus was crucified. With the help of Lily's secret letters and diary, Marion sets out to uncover Lily's past. Lily resents Marion's interrogation as much as Ruth resents Marion's efforts to make her face the reality of her marriage. The play does not underestimate the difficulty of honest self-confrontation. Marion gradually forces Lily to confront her past, her affair with the English airman, the momentary freedom and flight she enjoyed with him, the child she had by him, and her abandonment of it so that she could keep up the appearance of a respectable, devoted wife. The forces of the age have made a victim of Lily, forcing her into denial of her past and her own sensual life. As she listens, Marion is determined that she will not repeat Lily's mistake and turn her own life into a perpetual crucifixion. She ultimately finds the strength to affirm life, hope, and find a beneficent purpose in life. The new recognitions that Marion ultimately achieves by the end of the play are the product of her encounter with her ghostly predecessor. She believes that it would be wrong simply to re-create the past, which is what she had thought of doing by turning the house over to the National Trust and having it preserved as a museum piece. Instead, she decides that she will fix it up, live in it once it has been renovated, and use it for her own purposes. "What this house needs most," she finally decides, "is air and light."

The ghosts in the first two history plays–the Phantom Bride and the Phantom Fiddler–are not negotiable. They are nonspeaking parts. Silent, marginal, repressed figures though they may be, they exert a powerful influence over the protagonists in both plays, the Phantom Bride ultimately betraying McCracken to his death and the Phantom Fiddler standing as an image of home, nation, the past, and conscience that haunts Boucicault to his death. The main difference with the ghost in *Pentecost* is that Marion speaks and interacts with it, and out of the relationship that develops between Lily and Marion, the former is finally able to rest in peace and the latter attains a new kind of visionary seeing. In *Pentecost* Parker centers the exchange between past and present. He insists that there must be communication and negotiation with the past, otherwise it remains a merely oppressive, lumpen presence in people's lives, forbidding, unyielding, and misunderstood. The past must be wrested from mythology, given a human form, and returned to real life so that it can be dealt with as part of the continuous dialectics of historical process. By persevering in her relationship with the recalcitrant Lily, Marion ultimately wins through to the salving, solving awareness of the transcendent unity of all life.

Stephen Rae as Lenny Harrigan in the Field Day Theatre Company touring production of Parker's Pentecost

Another nonnaturalistic device that Parker uses to generate new recognitions is the orchestration of a series of monologues, which carry the audience, in a rising tide of emotion and rhythmic intensity, toward Marion's culminating and concluding insights. Like Beckett's characters, Parker's urge each other to keep talking, to keep contributing to the process that may lead to clarification and closure. Peter's story of the attempt to solve the problem of the Troubles by dumping LSD in the Belfast city reservoir, so that the entire citizenry would be transformed into "spaced-out contemplatives," is comically absurd, but the language he uses–"visionary," "beatific," "messianic impulse," "holy trinity of the new age, father, son and holy ghost," "redemption," "simple transcendental gesture"–suggests an underlying serious religious quest. Ruth's story is a recitation of the biblical account of Pentecost. All these stories, including Lily's story of her experience of love with the English airman, express the longing to move beyond the constraints of the contingent world, to extend perception and attain visionary seeing, to escape from the structures of rationalized, routinized consciousness.

Finally, there is Marion's story. Referring to Lily's wasted life, Marion enunciates a vision of wholeness in which she comes to terms with death and loss and affirms the oneness of all life. She urges recognition of the Christ within. Insisting that salvation has nothing to do with the churches, she emphasizes the need for people to take responsibility for their own lives. Like Lily, Marion has denied life and therefore denied herself and Christ. The play ultimately returns the audience to the individual, the "Christ in ourselves" as the source of regeneration and change–change from within rather than from without. Through Marion, Parker evangelizes for an end to "the sacrilege on life," for a vigilant, creative use of the past so that humanity can transcend the destructive myths and stereotypes that have imprisoned it for so long. She affirms life over death and proposes a view of the past as "creditor" rather than "master"–that is, something from which the people can take rather than something that takes them. The final cure lies not in political action but in a fundamental engagement, which alone can give change a moral as well as a sociological dimension. The play ends on a note of newfound harmony. The bickering and hostility stop. Lenny reaches out to touch Marion, then joins Peter for a soulful rendition of "O for a Closer Walk with Thee," while Ruth symbolically throws open the windows of the house.

The story of Pentecost, a favorite text of evangelical Protestantism, is humanistically refurbished to express the playwright's faith in the basic goodness of the human heart, which must be encouraged to extend itself, to find the resources to resist the deadening routines of habit and prejudice, and to realize its full potential. The biblical tale also is used to express faith in the original religious function of the theater, in its visionary capability and Pentecostal fire, against the contemporary annihilating suspicion of the word. The ending, however, is tentative, cautious, and ambiguous. Parker's model of wholeness is present as an ideal rather than convincingly embodied in action.

Stewart Parker died on 2 November 1988 from cancer, at the age of forty-seven. *Pentecost* was revived after his death at Andrew's Lane, Dublin, in July 1996; *Northern Star* was revived by Rough Magic under the direction of Parker's niece Lynne Parker at the Dublin Theatre Festival in October 1997.

References:

Elmer Andrews, "The Will to Freedom: Politics and Play in the Theatre of Stewart Parker," in *Irish Writers and Politics,* edited by Okifumi Komesu and Masaru Sekine (Gerrards Cross: Colin Smythe, 1990);

Terence Brown, "Let's Go to Graceland: The Drama of Stewart Parker," in *Studies on the Contemporary Irish Theatre: Actes du Colloque de Caen, 11–12 Janvier 1991,* edited by Jacqueline Genet and Elisabeth Hellegouarc'h (Caen: University of Caen, 1991), pp. 21–35;

Michael Etherton, *Contemporary Irish Dramatists* (Basingstoke / Macmillan, 1989), pp. 15–25;

Claudia W. Harris, "From Pastness to Wholeness: Stewart Parker's Reinventing Theatre," Contemporary Irish Drama Special Issue, *Colby Quarterly,* edited by Anthony Roche, 27 (1991): 233–241;

Andrew Parkin, "Metaphor as Dramatic Structure in Some Plays of Stewart Parker," in *Irish Writers and the Theatre,* edited by Masaru Sekine (Gerrards Cross: Colin Smythe, 1986), pp. 135–150;

Anthony Roche, "Northern Irish Drama: Imagining Alternatives," in *Contemporary Irish Drama from Beckett to McGuiness* (Dublin: Gill & Macmillan, 1995), pp. 216–278.

David Storey

(13 July 1933 –   )

Robert Wilcher
University of Birmingham

See also the Storey entries in *DLB 13: British Dramatists Since World War II; DLB 14: British Novelists Since 1960;* and *DLB 207: British Novelists Since 1960, Third Series.*

PLAY PRODUCTIONS: *The Restoration of Arnold Middleton,* Edinburgh, Traverse Theatre, 22 November 1966; London, Royal Court Theatre, 4 July 1967;

In Celebration, London, Royal Court Theatre, 22 April 1969; Washington, D.C., Arena Stage Company, June 1974;

The Contractor, London, Royal Court Theatre, 20 October 1969; New Haven, Connecticut, Long Wharf Theatre, December 1971;

Home, London, Royal Court Theatre, 17 June 1970; New York, Morosco Theater, 17 November 1970;

The Changing Room, London, Royal Court Theatre, 9 November 1971; New Haven, Connecticut, Long Wharf Theatre, December 1972;

Cromwell, London, Royal Court Theatre, 15 August 1973;

The Farm, London, Royal Court Theatre, 26 September 1973; New York, Circle Repertory Company, 10 October 1976;

Life Class, London, Royal Court Theatre, 9 April 1974; New York, Manhattan Theatre Club, December 1975;

Mother's Day, London, Royal Court Theatre, 22 September 1976;

Sisters, Manchester, Royal Exchange Theatre, 12 September 1978;

Early Days, Brighton, 31 March 1980; London, Cottesloe Theatre at the National Theatre, 22 April 1980; Washington, D.C., Eisenhower Theatre of the Kennedy Center, June 1981;

Phoenix, Ealing, Questors Theatre, 7 April 1984;

The March on Russia, London, Lyttleton Theatre at the National Theatre, 6 April 1989; Cleveland, Play House, April 1990;

Stages, London, Cottesloe Theatre at the National Theatre, 12 November 1992.

David Storey (from the dust jacket for Storey: Plays: One, *1992)*

BOOKS: *This Sporting Life* (London: Longmans, 1960; New York: Macmillan, 1960);

Flight into Camden (London: Longmans, 1960; New York: Macmillan, 1961);

Radcliffe (London: Longmans, 1963; New York: Coward-McCann, 1964);

The Restoration of Arnold Middleton: A Play in Three Acts (London: Cape, 1967; London & New York: S. French, 1968);

In Celebration (London: Cape, 1969; New York: Grove, 1969);

The Contractor (London: Cape, 1970; New York: Random House, 1970);

Home (London: Cape, 1970; New York: Random House, 1971);

The Changing Room (London: Cape, 1972; New York: Random House, 1973);

Pasmore (London: Longman, 1972; New York: Dutton, 1974);

Cromwell (London: Cape, 1973);
Edward, drawings by Donald Parker (London: Allen Lane, 1973);
The Farm (London: Cape, 1973; New York: S. French, 1974);
A Temporary Life (London: Allen Lane, 1973; New York: Dutton, 1974);
Life Class (London: Cape, 1975);
Saville (London: Cape, 1976; New York: Harper & Row, 1977);
Home, The Changing Room, Mother's Day (Harmondsworth, U.K.: Penguin, 1978);
Early Days, Sisters, Life Class (Harmondsworth, U.K.: Penguin, 1980);
A Prodigal Child (London: Cape, 1982; New York: Dutton, 1982);
Present Times (London: Cape, 1984);
The March on Russia (London & New York: S. French, 1989);
Storey's Lives: Poems 1951–1991 (London: Cape, 1992);
Storey: Plays: One (London: Methuen, 1992)–comprises *The Contractor, Home, Stages,* and *Caring;*
A Serious Man (London: Cape, 1998).

PRODUCED SCRIPTS: *This Sporting Life,* motion picture, Independent Artists/Rank, 1963;
Home, television, National Education Television USA, BBC, 1973;
Grace, television, adapted from a story by James Joyce, 1974;
In Celebration, motion picture, American Film Theatre, 1974;
Early Days, London Weekend Television, 1981;
The Contractor, television, BBC Two, 23 April 1989.

David Storey was first known as a novelist belonging to a movement of Northern realist writers, including Alan Sillitoe and Stan Barstow, that began in the first furor over John Osborne's *Look Back in Anger* (1956) and the creation of the "angry young man" syndrome. Storey won early acclaim; his first novel, *This Sporting Life* (1960), won the Macmillan Fiction Prize, and his second, *Flight into Camden* (1960), won the John Llewellyn Rhys Memorial Prize and the Somerset Maugham Award. *This Sporting Life* became an important element in the new wave of British cinema in the early 1960s, and its powerful treatment of the Rugby League proved popular. His early work is frequently concerned with the generational gap between educated, upwardly aspiring children and their working-class parents and articulates well the change in the social composition of the country. His work for the stage initially bears a clear relationship to the territory explored in his novels and usually is concerned with the struggles of the individual in a meticulously realized social context.

David Malcolm Storey, the third son of Frank, a coal miner, and Lily Cartwright Storey, was born in Wakefield, Yorkshire, on 13 July 1933. David Storey attended Queen Elizabeth Grammar School in Wakefield from 1943 to 1951 and then entered Wakefield School of Art in 1951. At first he was drawn toward painting, and to help finance his way through the local art college he signed a contract in 1952 as a professional rugby league footballer with Leeds. When he won a scholarship to study at the Slade School of Fine Art in London in 1953, he was still bound by this contract and for some time was obliged to return to Yorkshire every weekend to play rugby. In a talk for British Broadcasting Corporation (BBC) radio in 1963, he described his regular train journeys north from an artistic life in the capital to take part in "an extremely hard game" that was "almost an extension of the experience that a man undergoes in digging coal underground." The consequent sense of duality–of being "continually torn between the two extremes of my experience, the physical and the spiritual"–runs through much of his literary work. His sense of duality also manifests itself as guilt about the rejection of a code that values physical work above mental work and as the consciousness of a split between "a masculine temperament" that he associated with the industrial north and "a woman's sensibility and responses" that he discovered in "the intuitive, poetic and perhaps precious world to which I felt I had escaped."

Storey graduated from the Slade with a diploma in fine arts. In 1956 he married Barbara Rudd Hamilton, with whom he had two sons and two daughters. He also was released from his fourteen-year rugby contract that same year. Storey began working as a substitute teacher in the gritty East End area of London in 1957; the experience was not a good one, and Storey became depressed. Discouraged because *This Sporting Life* had not yet been accepted for publication, he wrote in 1959 the first draft of a play titled "To Die with the Philistines," into which he poured his feelings of frustration and despair. The publication of three prizewinning novels–*This Sporting Life,* which received the Macmillan Prize; *Flight into Camden,* winner of the Rhys Memorial Award; and *Radcliffe* (1963), which won the Somerset Maugham Award–meant that the script was put aside, until Lindsay Anderson showed an interest in it when he was directing the motion picture of *This Sporting Life* in 1963. A production by the English Stage Company came to nothing, but Gordon McDougall, when an assistant at the Royal Court Theatre, had read "To Die with the Philistines" and brought the work to Traverse in Edinburgh in 1966. The play was staged at the

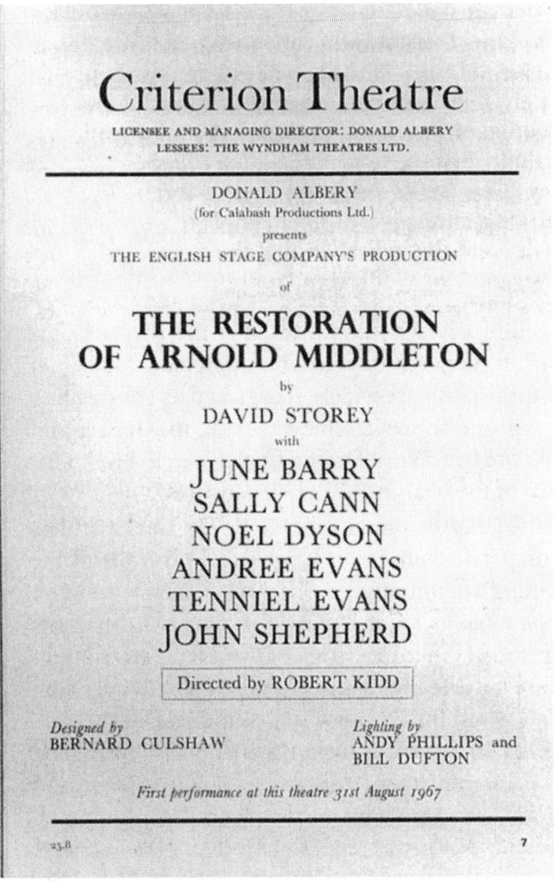
Criterion Theatre

LICENSEE AND MANAGING DIRECTOR: DONALD ALBERY
LESSEES: THE WYNDHAM THEATRES LTD.

DONALD ALBERY
(for Calabash Productions Ltd.)
presents
THE ENGLISH STAGE COMPANY'S PRODUCTION
of

THE RESTORATION
OF ARNOLD MIDDLETON

by
DAVID STOREY
with

JUNE BARRY
SALLY CANN
NOEL DYSON
ANDREE EVANS
TENNIEL EVANS
JOHN SHEPHERD

Directed by ROBERT KIDD

Designed by
BERNARD CULSHAW

Lighting by
ANDY PHILLIPS and
BILL DUFTON

First performance at this theatre 31st August 1967

7

Program cover and title page for Storey's first play, about a history teacher edging toward a mental breakdown

Traverse in a revised version as *The Restoration of Arnold Middleton.* In the following year the play was directed by Robert Kidd for the English Stage Company and subsequently transferred to the Criterion Theatre in West End. The success of the play with critics was sealed by Storey's winning the *Evening Standard* award for the most promising playwright of the year.

The title character is a history teacher whose eccentric behavior is partly a cover for the irritations that beset him in his professsional and domestic lives and partly a result of some deeper disturbance that is edging him toward a mental breakdown. At school he is directing the production of a play about Robin Hood, who embodies Arnold's own sense of being always "on the outside of things . . . disenfranchised, dispossessed." At home he infuriates his wife by filling the house with historical bric-a-brac, so that she feels she is stuck "among his trophies." Reviewers complained that the causes of Arnold's incipient madness are not made clear: on the one hand, his attraction toward his mother-in-law and estrangement from his own parents hint at problems seated in the psychology of the individual; on the other hand, his symptoms are reminiscent of the existential anguish expressed in absurdist drama of the period. The strengths of the play lie in the verbal energy of the text and in the power of its dramatic climaxes, in one of which the mother-in-law reveals that she has had a sexual encounter with Arnold at the end of a drunken evening. Arnold's cathartic return to sanity in the closing moments–in place of the original ending, in which he committed suicide–sounds a theme that recurs in many of Storey's later plays: life becomes tolerable not by pretending to solve intractable problems or trying to forget ancient hurts, but by learning to live with them. As Arnold tells his family and friends, the scars inflicted by experience cannot be eradicated or ignored. "They inhabit the skin," he says. "They grow there after a while like natural features. . . . Remove them–and you remove life itself."

As a painter and novelist Storey had hitherto shown little interest in drama. He told Brendan Hennessy that he had to overcome "a kind of built-in proletarian distrust" of the theater and recalls in the introduction to *Plays: One* (1992) that he had seen few plays, since a childhood exposure to William Shakespeare's *Hamlet* (circa 1600) at the Grand Theatre in Leeds had put him off by its ridiculous pretense that what was on the stage was real. Stimulated by the performance of his first play, however, he diverted his creative energies into a spate of dramatic works, none of which took more than five days to complete. *The Contractor* (1969) was written first, drawing upon *Radcliffe,* followed by *In Celebration* (1969), *Home* (1970), *The Changing Room* (1971), *Cromwell* (1973), and *The Farm* (1973), all of which were produced at the Royal Court and all but *Cromwell* directed by Anderson. The first four of these plays are widely recognized as constituting Storey's most distinctive achievement in the theater and won him the New York Drama Critics Circle Award for best play of the year in 1971, 1973, and 1974.

In Celebration, produced before *The Contractor,* has been compared with D. H. Lawrence's portraits of life in a mining community. In the play a family reunion triggers an explosion of resentment over past betrayals and injustices. The three sons of a miner, returning to Yorkshire to celebrate their parents' fortieth wedding anniversary, gradually reveal the emptiness of the professional roles to which their education has consigned them. When the father reminds them that he spent half his life "making sure none of you went down that pit," the eldest, Andrew, replies bitterly, "I've always thought, you know, coal-mining was one of the few things I could really do. . . . And yet, the one thing in life from which I'm actually excluded."

The plot centers on Andrew's anger at the parental "good intentions" that have robbed all three sons of purpose and identity. He feels especially vengeful toward the socially pretentious mother, who has never forgiven her husband for the premarital pregnancy that condemned her to the existence of a miner's wife. The memory of that first child, Jamey, who died at the age of seven, haunts the family. The youngest son, Steven, teetering on the verge of mental collapse, has nightmares in which he sees Jamey pleading to be absolved from the guilt of his conception. Andrew has come home determined to destroy both his father's self-deceiving vision of the "good life" he has spent with "a good woman" and his mother's complacent belief in the success of her sons. He seems particularly anxious to enlist Steven as an ally in his campaign of vengeance. In an impassioned indictment he tries to make his father face the fact that his sons are "less than nothing . . . has-beens, wash-outs . . . a pathetic vision of a better life." The old man scarcely takes in what is being said and can only think of protecting his wife from Andrew's vindictiveness. Everything seems to be set for an Ibsen-like shattering of the elder Shaws' comforting fantasies, but Storey fashions his climax instead out of a cryptic exchange in which Steven warns Andrew not to disturb their mother's peace of mind: "I don't want you doing any damage here." The play ends on a quiet note; the sons depart, and their parents resume the routines of daily life with the illusions that have sustained them for more than forty years still intact.

The quality of understatement, which is reminiscent of the subtextual method and elegiac mood of Anton Chekhov, was developed in *The Contractor* into what Storey described in an interview with Peter Ansorge in *Plays and Players* (September 1973) as "poetic naturalism." The resulting dialogue has been compared with that of Harold Pinter in its sensitivity to the fragmentary rhythms of everyday speech and its avoidance of the explicit. *The Contractor* also establishes a structural pattern for Storey's drama, in which a public event takes place offstage in the interval between acts: in this play it is a wedding, in *In Celebration* it is the Shaws' anniversary dinner, in *The Changing Room* it is a rugby match, and in *Cromwell* it is an unidentified battle. What the audience sees onstage is the carrying through of a process peripheral to this event, which often involves the assembling of a group of people for a specific purpose and their dispersal once it has been accomplished. The marriage of Ewbank's daughter in *The Contractor* brings together not only three generations of his family but also the disparate body of workmen who erect a marquee in act 1, decorate it with muslin and ribbons in act 2, and dismantle it in act 3 after the wedding reception has taken place. The essential action of the play, the wedding, which has metaphorical resonance rather than narrative dynamic, is summed up in the instructions given by Ewbank, a prosperous tenting contractor, to the workforce that has gathered on his lawn: "Get it up. Get it finished. And get away." The hired laborers go about their task while joking, teasing each other, and bickering among themselves; the common purpose of raising and lowering the vast canvas structure enables them to transcend the inadequacies of their private lives.

The fragile and temporary community constituted by Ewbank's work crew is set against the disintegration of his own family. His daughter is marrying "a bloody aristocrat" who earns nothing but contempt from the self-made man. Ewbank's son, who has been to university, has no interest in taking over the family business, although he shows a genuine pride in his father's craftsmanship and seems anxious to prove something by persistently offering to lend a hand in erecting the tent. Old Ewbank, the grandfather, pathetically adrift in a world of machines, wanders in and out, accosting anyone who will listen to him: "Here. Now there's a bit of rope I made. . . . A hand-made rope is a bit of the past." Ewbank himself is acutely aware that time is running out for his own generation. His repeated comments about the wedding of his only daughter and the tent he has lovingly prepared for the occasion, such as "I shall never do it again. I shan't. Never . . . ," "It'll not happen again, you know . . . ," and "Come today. Gone tomorrow," become a litany of regret for a world that is passing. In the final moments, when the canvas has been packed away and the workmen have departed, he stands disconsolately beside his wife looking down at the view: "You'd think you'd have something to show for it, wouldn't you. After all this time. . . . I don't know. . . . What's to become of us, you reckon?"

Storey sets out to create a mood rather than develop a plot or pursue a thesis in *Home*. Both *The Contractor* and *Home* have been related to the loss of the British Empire or–the dramatist's own suggestion about the dismantling of the tent–"the decline and fading-away of a capitalist society." But in the same passage (quoted by Russell Taylor), he adds that it should not be confined by any one interpretation and declares that a play "lives for me almost in the measure that it escapes and refuses definition." Of all Storey's plays *Home* is the one that expresses most poignantly the experience of disorientation and loss. For Jack and Harry, inmates of an asylum for the mentally ill, the past "doesn't bear thinking about," although they spend their time doing little else. As they pursue various conversational gambits, delicately skirting subjects too painful to contemplate, they occasionally let slip hints of their terrible feeling of isolation and of their nostalgia for an irrecoverable world in which they once had a part to play.

In his closest approach to Samuel Beckett, Storey goes beyond the "poetic naturalism" of *The Contractor* in the "more overtly stylistic" art of *Home* and distills many of his central themes into the muted music of duets and quartets scored for the contrasting voices of its four principal characters. The well-dressed Harry and "slightly more dandyish" Jack have an air of faded gentility, with their clipped phrases and out-of-date idioms–"By jove," "Apple a day," "Best foot forward"; the conversation of the coarser Kathleen and Marjorie, a pair of working-class Cockneys, revolves around the physical aspects of life–"Pull your skirt down, girl," "Took out all me teeth," "What've we got for lunch?" Whereas the tactful evasions of the men in the opening dialogue leave the audience unsure about the circumstances of their acquaintance, the bluntness of the women dispels any doubt about the nature of the place that is now "home" to all four of them–"Don't want me to escape," "Not like the last one I was in," "What you put away for, then?" By the end of act 1 tentative new relationships have been formed and, as Kathleen takes Harry's arm and Marjorie takes Jack's, they arrange to meet at the same spot after lunch for a "little chat." In the course of act 2 the doomed negotiations across the frontiers of class, education, and sensibility break down and the two women go off, stoically resigned to the failure of their attempt to "make something." Harry and Jack resume their contemplation of the glorious past of "this little island" in which they no longer feel at home–"Empire the like of which no one has ever seen," "Shan't see its like," "The sun has set." A note of deeper, more generalized despair is sounded as the light fades and they begin to weep quietly together: "Shouldn't wonder He's disappointed." (*Looks up.*) "Oh, yes." "Heart-break." "Oh, yes." "Same mistake . . . Won't make it twice." "Oh, no." "Once over. Never again."

John Gielgud and Ralph Richardson on the cover of the program for the 1970 New York production of Storey's play about four people in an asylum for the mentally ill

The Changing Room premiered in 1971. The play is set in a rugby team's locker room, and the audience sees the players before the match, at half-time, and just after they have won. The motley individuals who arrive one by one from separate backgrounds are transformed into a team by the time they line up in their numbered shirts at the end of the first act. Class tensions and personal antagonisms are put aside as they prepare to face an ordeal that will make severe demands upon their combined resources of courage, stamina, and determination. An elegiac note is sounded by Owens, the captain, when the rest of the team have changed and gone home–"Aye. One more season, I think. I'm finished. . . . Been here, tha knows, a bit too long."

Storey was an associate artistic director at the Royal Court Theatre from 1972 to 1974, and his plays continued to be produced at regular intervals there until 1976. During this time he was still pursuing his parallel career as a novelist. *Pasmore* was published in 1972 and won the Geoffrey Faber Memorial Prize in 1973. *A Temporary Life* was also published in that year. The cultural climate was altering, however, just as Storey was achieving critical and box-office success with his quiet, theatrical studies in the human need for communion and permanence in the face of social fragmentation and change. Storey told Ansorge that *Cromwell,* which closed after a short run in 1973 and did not transfer to the West End, "took shape" in the winter of 1968–1969, "when Vietnam and Northern Ireland were at their heights"; and in the light of Storey's critical remarks about "the new group of Cambridge playwrights like Howard Brenton and David Hare," *Cromwell* can be taken as his response to both the inevitable impingement of the public upon the private world and the aggressively political drama that rose to prominence in the early 1970s.

Locating his dramatization of the problems of commitment in what is suggested to be Cromwellian Ireland, he follows the fortunes of a group of men who answer a summons to enlist on the Catholic side in a civil war. Cromwell is the Godot of a play in which the ideological and military struggle between scarcely distinguishable armies becomes a metaphor for the absurdity of the human predicament in its political dimension. Never making an appearance and never named directly, Cromwell is "the Big One" who determines the fate of those caught in a conflict beyond their power to control or understand. Proctor, who claims to have caught a glimpse of him once "passing between the trees," believes that "without ideals no man can live"; Morgan, a pragmatist, switches his allegiance to the winning side, gains promotion in the Protestant army, and is slain by Proctor as a turncoat; and Logan and O'Halloran, two itinerant Irish laborers, holding aloof from service to any cause except self-preservation, provide a sceptical commentary on the activities of the armed "idealists and opportunists" who leave destruction in their wake. *Cromwell* is emphatically not an attempt to intervene in the debate about Vietnam or Northern Ireland. Rather, by choosing an historical setting and adopting a heightened prose that tends to fall into the rhythms of blank verse, Storey evokes, in essentially poetic and symbolic terms, the moral and practical dilemma of those who are wary of the destructive potential of idealism but who nevertheless feel with Proctor that they "must have goals, and ways and means . . . if men are victims what value are the things they struggle to?"

In *The Farm,* produced later in 1973, Storey returns to more familiar territory with a portrait of a dysfunctional family that inhabits an isolated Yorkshire farmhouse. Most of the Slattery clan are still living at home. Slattery himself, in an advanced state of alcoholism at the age of sixty-five, never tires of reiterating that work is "the only bloody thing that's real" and that he has spent his life "sweating i' the bloody fields." The three daughters are all childless, much to the disgust of their father, who believes that the main function of a woman is "to have babbies when she's young" and hates "to see something going to rot." Mrs. Slattery tries to police her husband's drinking when she is at home but spends much of her time attending adult evening classes, where she is being taught sociology by men who, in Slattery's opinion, have "learnt nowt but what they've read inside a book." Arthur, the twenty-one-year-old son, is the only member of the family who has managed to escape the ancient farm. The house itself is, indeed, much more than a simple, naturalistic set in which Storey can exhibit the jibes, quarrels, and outbursts of anger or despair that make up the daily routine of the Slatterys. One daughter sees the house as "one huge, corporeal mass . . . a sort of animal with seven heads"; another says that living in the farmhouse is "like being inside a person." As the play proceeds it becomes evident that they are trapped on the farm like "detritus from the past," bound together by a sterile habit of mutual contempt, incapable of making the kinds of positive choices that came under scrutiny in *Cromwell.* A minimal plot is supplied by a visit from Arthur, who turns up in the middle of the night to announce that he is engaged to a divorced woman twice his age and intends to bring her home to meet the family. His announcement sparks more than one tirade from his father about a life wasted "composing bloody sonnets" and a growing excitement among the women, which is felt to be shared by the house itself: "I can feel the vibrancy running through the building." The anticipated visit is canceled, however–another of Storey's deliberate anticlimaxes–and Arthur prepares to turn his back on his father for good: "I don't know why I troubled even to think of coming back."

Storey's next play, in which he turned the spotlight directly on his own theatrical practice, can be seen as the summation of his seven years of activity at the Royal Court. The dramatist who had been alienated as a child by the patent sham of *Hamlet* had made his own plays out of slices of life in which his human subjects were observed coping–or failing to cope–with personal crises and social relationships in the various contexts of home, workplace, sports club, and mental institution. In *Life Class,* produced in 1974, he found a provocative emblem of his own craft in the situation of a group of students gathered around the nude figure of a woman in a classroom of an art college. Storey teases his spectators with an image that makes the distinction between reality and artistic imitation ambivalent: the model is both an object to be regarded dispassionately as the material from which the students are supposed to create art and a real woman capable of distracting the students' attention by the sexual appeal of her unclothed body. Allott, the teacher, offers his pupils a view of art that reflects Storey's personal approach to the theater. Allott claims to be no longer satisified with the traditional conception of art as "a residual occupation," which leaves behind "certain elements of its activity . . . stone, paint, canvas." For him the process is more important than the product, and the process can neither be assigned a meaning nor distinguished from life itself: "we, elements as it were of a work ourselves, partake of existence . . . simply by being what we are . . . expressions of a certain time and place, and class . . . defying . . . hope . . . defying anguish . . . defying, even, definition . . . All around us . . . our rocky ball . . . hurtling through time . . . Singing . . . to no one's tune at all."

In the evanescent art of theater Storey had contrived to combine the local and the universal aspects of human existence as he had observed it in characters representative of his own "time and place"–facing the void of ultimate meaninglessness with humor and resignation, while learning to live with the more individual scars left by the wounds sustained in the domestic, social, and political battles of day-to-day living. An art that will not go beyond observation and commit itself to a point of view, however, is open to the same objection that led Proctor to insist that men must have goals if they are to be more than victims. Storey gives dramatic expression to this dilemma, inherent in Allott's principle that "only the disinterested person . . . sees what's truly there," when one of the students sexually assaults Stella, the model, and the teacher stands quietly by, watching this demonstration of the theory that he has expounded earlier: "our meeting here today . . . the feelings and intuitions expressed by all of us inside this room . . . are in effect the creation–the re-creation–of the artist." Even though the rape proves to have been

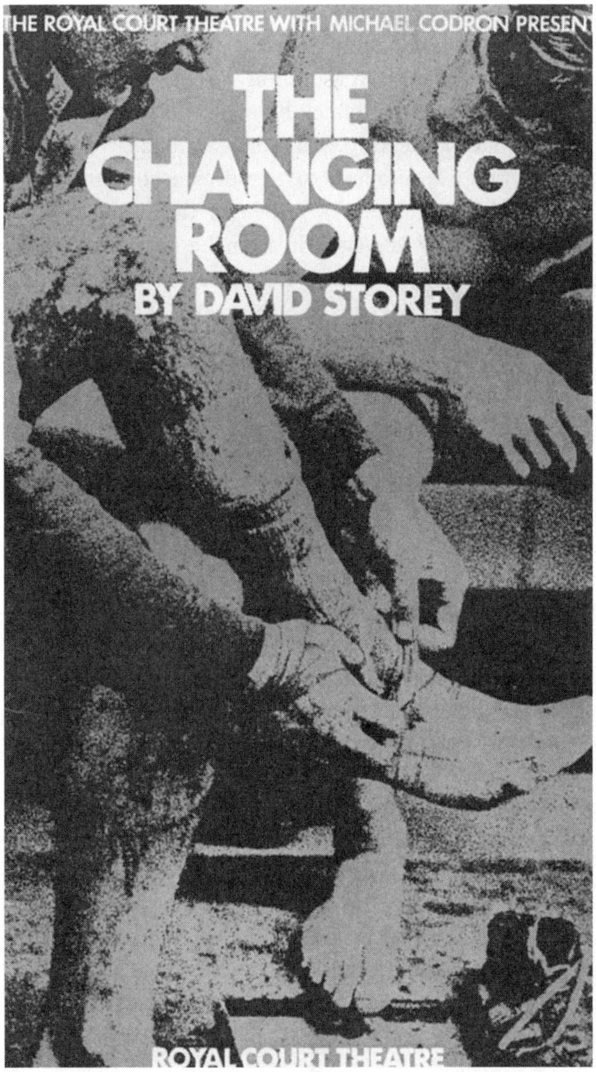

Program cover for the London production of Storey's 1971 play, which went on to win the New York Drama Critics Circle Award

only simulated as a joke–again blurring the boundary between life and art for the audience–the bewildered accusation of one of the female students remains valid: "How could you! Let him do it, sir!" By abdicating moral responsibility in the real world, in which Stella was apparently being violated as a human being, Allott has forfeited the respect of his students in the life class, where Stella functions only as a human form.

There has been a marked decline in Storey's theatrical career since the mid 1970s. The unpublished "Night," which deals with a group of actors preparing to perform a play, was withdrawn from the Edinburgh Festival while still in rehearsal in 1975. In the following year *Mother's Day,* a black farce in the manner of Joe Orton, was unfavorably received by reviewers and audiences alike and was the last of Storey's plays to be produced under the auspices of the Royal Court, until the revival of *The Changing Room* in 1996. He received much more positive recognition for his novel *Saville,* published in 1976, for which he was awarded the prestigious Booker Prize. *Sisters,* in which a mentally unstable woman, after the failure of her dreams of fame and glamor, desperately seeks refuge in the home of her younger sister, was staged in Manchester in 1978 and did not warrant a transfer to London. *Early Days* (1980), Storey's first work for the National Theatre, was designed as a vehicle for the veteran actor Sir Ralph Richardson. In his compassionate and often funny portrait of Kitchen, a senile politician whose hopes of the highest office were dashed by one unwise speech, Storey explores both the freedom from the "strait-jacket" of respectability and responsibility that comes with old age and the fear of impending death that sends the mind back to "those early times" when it received its first impressions of loss and isolation. Storey published his novels *A Prodigal Child* in 1982 and *Present Times* in 1984. *Phoenix,* after an amateur premiere by the Questors of Ealing in 1984, was given ten performances by a professional touring company in the provinces the following year. The action took place on the stage of a northern theater that was about to be demolished, where the artistic director–the son of a miner–had specialized in putting on realistic plays about working-class life, until he had been forced to bow to the demand for politically committed drama. Storey, who has frequently drawn material for plays not only from his own life but also from his earlier writing, recycled parts of *Present Times* in both *Life Class* and *Phoenix.*

The production of *The March on Russia* (1989), his second work for the National Theatre, was either welcomed or dismissed by reviewers as a reprise of his 1972 novel, *Pasmore,* and of *In Celebration* but was clearly notable for reuniting Storey with Anderson and designer Jocelyn Herbert, whose naturalistic sets had been a hallmark of the Royal Court during Storey's heyday. The octogenarian Pasmores, played by Bill Owen and Constance Chapman (who had taken the roles of Mr. and Mrs. Shaw in 1969) are visited by their three children on the occasion of their sixtieth wedding anniversary. Twenty years on, the old couple's children are still wrestling with their own problems, but the dramatic focus has shifted to the miner and his wife, now living in a retirement bungalow in an anonymous seaside town. As some of the reviews acknowledged, the play is primarily not a pessimistic analysis of the "state of England" but a compassionate and witty celebration of the grit, dignity, and humor with which the elderly Pasmores accept each other's foibles, their displacement from a familiar environment, and the oblivion that will soon overtake them.

A collection of Storey's plays was published in *Plays: One*–including *Stages,* directed by Anderson for the National Theatre in 1992, and the as yet unproduced *Caring.* In the former a novelist-painter is visited in the aftermath of a nervous breakdown by a series of women who set off reveries about his working- class past in Yorkshire, his early struggles as an artist in London, and his passionate affair with his mother-in-law. The critics judged the piece more a poem than a play, beautifully evoking the pleasures and pains of memory but lacking in dramatic urgency. *Caring* is a two-hander about an aging theatrical couple, whose lifelong habit of role-playing on and off the stage has blurred their ability to distinguish between fact and fantasy.

When *The Changing Room* was included in the season of Royal Court Classics in 1996, the "quietly implicit" quality of this example of Storey's theatrical art at its near best caused some reviewers to wonder why it had seemed so impressive in 1971. Some, seeing it for the first time, paid tribute to "the integrity that comes from honest observation" and the "unforced tenderness" with which this "humane and eloquent" Yorkshireman had placed before them "the shifting moods of everyday experience."

Interviews:

"Journey through a Tunnel," *Listener* (1 August 1963): 159–161;

Brendan Hennessy, "David Storey Interviewed by Brendan Hennessy," *Transatlantic Review,* 33–34 (1969): 5–11;

Ronald Hayman, "Conversation with David Storey," *Drama,* 99 (Winter 1970): 47–53; reprinted in his *Playback* (New York: Horizon, 1974), pp. 7–20;

Glenn Loney, "Shop Talk with a British Playwright: David Storey Discusses *Home* and Other Scripts," *Dramatists Guild Quarterly,* 8 (Spring 1971): 27–30;

Peter Ansorge, "The Theatre of Life: David Storey," *Plays and Players* (September 1973): 32–36;

Victor Sage, "David Storey in Conversation," *New Review* (October 1976): 63–65;

"Working with Lindsay," in *At the Royal Court: 25 Years of the English Stage Company,* edited by Richard Findlater (New York: Grove, 1981), pp. 110–115.

References:

Charles A. Carpenter, "Bond, Shaffer, Stoppard, Storey: An International Checklist of Commentary," *Modern Drama,* 24 (1981): 546–556;

Richard Allen Cave, *New British Drama in Performance on the London Stage: 1970 to 1985* (Gerrards Cross: Colin Smythe, 1987), pp. 133–168;

Ruby Cohn, *Retreats from Realism in Recent English Drama* (Cambridge: Cambridge University Press, 1991), pp. 35–41, 185–188;

Richard Dutton, *Modern Tragicomedy and the British Tradition: Beckett, Pinter, Stoppard, Albee and Storey* (Brighton: Harvester, 1986);

William J. Free, "The Ironic Anger of David Storey," *Modern Drama,* 16 (1973): 306–317;

Free and Lynn Page Whittaker, "The Intrusion Plot in David Storey's Plays," *Papers on Language and Literature,* 17 (1982): 151–165;

William Hutchings, *The Plays of David Storey: A Thematic Study* (Carbondale: Southern Illinois University Press, 1988);

Hutchings, "David Storey," in *British Playwrights, 1956–1995: A Research and Production Sourcebook,* edited by William W. Demastes (Westport, Conn.: Greenwood Press, 1996), pp. 382–398;

Hutchings, ed., *David Storey: A Casebook* (New York: Garland, 1992);

Steven Joyce, "A Study in Dramatic Dialogue: A Structural Approach to David Storey's *Home,*" *Theatre Annual,* 38 (1983): 65–81;

Albert E. Kalson, "Insanity and the Rational Man in the Plays of David Storey," *Modern Drama,* 19 (1976): 111–128;

Oleg Kerensky, *The New British Drama: Fourteen Playwrights since Osborne and Pinter* (London: Hamish Hamilton, 1977);

Herbert Liebman, *The Dramatic Art of David Storey: The Journey of a Playwright* (Westport, Conn.: Greenwood Press, 1996);

Maria Margaroni, "Storey's 'Snare of Doubling,'" *Modern Drama,* 39 (1996): 507–517;

Barbara Olsson, "Alienation in Storey and Chekhov: A Reassessment of *In Celebration* and *The Farm,*" *Yearbook of Studies in English Language and Literature,* 80 (1986): 119–133;

Malcolm Pittock, "David Storey's *Phoenix:* A Dream of Leaving," *English Studies,* 71 (1990): 410–425;

Pittock, "Storey's Portrayal of Old Age: *The March on Russia,*" *Neophilologus,* 78 (1994): 329–341;

Geoff Pywell, "The Idea of Place in *The Contractor,*" *Journal of Dramatic Theory and Criticism,* 5 (1990): 69–79;

Austin E. Quigley, "The Emblematic Structure and Setting of David Storey's Plays," *Modern Drama,* 22 (1979): 259–276;

Phyllis R. Randall, "Division and Unity in David Storey," in *Essays on Contemporary British Drama,* edited by Hedwig Bock and Albert Wertheim (Munich: Hueber, 1981), pp. 253–266;

Janelle Reinelt, "The Central Event in David Storey's Plays," *Theatre Journal,* 31 (1979): 210–220;

Philip Roberts, "David Storey's *The Changing Room,*" in *The Royal Court Theatre 1965–1972* (London: Routledge & Kegan Paul, 1986), pp. 107–120;

Carol Rosen, "Symbolic Naturalism in David Storey's *Home,*" *Modern Drama,* 22 (1979): 277–289;

Susan Rusinko, *British Drama, 1950 to the Present: A Critical History* (Boston: Twayne, 1989), pp. 112–120;

Rakesh H. Solomon, "Man as Working Animal: Work, Class and Identity in the Plays of David Storey," *Forum for Modern Language Studies,* 30 (1994): 193–203;

John J. Stinson, "Dualism and Paradox in the 'Puritan' Plays of David Storey," *Modern Drama,* 20 (1977): 131–143;

John Russell Taylor, *The Second Wave: British Drama for the Seventies* (London: Methuen, 1971), pp. 141–154.

George Tabori

(24 May 1914 -   )

Antje Diedrich
Liverpool John Moores University

PLAY PRODUCTIONS: *Flight into Egypt,* New York, Music Box, 18 March 1952;

The Emperor's Clothes, New York, Ethel Barrymore Theater, 23 February 1953;

Miss Julie / The Stronger, translated from August Strindberg's *Fröken Julie* (1888) and *Fordringsägare* (1889), New York, Phoenix Theater, 1956;

Brou Ha Ha, London, Aldwych Theatre, 27 August 1958;

Brecht on Brecht: An Improvisation, New York, Theatre de Lys, 14 November 1961;

The Resistible Rise of Arturo Ui: A Gangster Spectacle, translated from Bertolt Brecht's *Der aufhaltsame Aufstieg des Arturo Ui* (1957), music by Hans Dieter Hosalla, New York, Lynn-Fontaine Theater, 1963;

Mother Courage, translated from Brecht's *Mutter Courage und ihre Kinder* (1939), Washington, Arena Theater, 1963;

Andorra, translated from Max Frisch's 1961 play, New York, Brook Atkinson Theater, 1963;

The Guns of Carrar, translated from Brecht's *Die Gewehre der Frau Carrar* (1937), New York, Theatre de Lys, 1968;

The Cannibals, New York, American Place Theater, 17 October 1968; Berlin, Schiller-Theater, Werkstatt; 13 December 1969;

The Niggerlovers: The Demonstration and *Man and Dog,* with music by Richard Peaslee, New York, Orpheum Theater, 1 October 1969;

Pinkville, with music by Stanley Walden, New York, American Place Theater, 17 March 1971; Berlin, Dreieinigkeitskirche, 19 August 1971;

Clowns, Tübingen, Germany; Zimmertheater, 8 May 1972;

Sigmunds Freude, adapted from transcripts by Frederick Solomon Perls, Bremen, Bremer Theater, 28 November 1975;

Talk Show, Bremen, Theater der Freien Hansestadt, 23 October 1976;

Changes, Munich, 1976;

George Tabori

The 25th Hour, Haarlem, Netherlands; Centrum, 10 February 1977; Düsseldorf, Schauspielhaus, Fabrikhalle Lentjeswerke, 20 September 1992;

Verwandlungen, adapted from Franz Kafka's "Die Verwandlung" (1937), Munich, Kammerspiele Werkraumtheater, 23 February 1977;

Die Hungerkünstler, adapted from Kafka's "Ein Hungerkünstler" (1938), Bremen, Theater der Freien Hansestadt, 10 June 1977;

Ich wollte meine Tochter läge tot zu meinen Füßen und hätte die Juwelen in den Ohren: Improvisationen über Shakespeare's Shylock, adapted from William Shakespeare's *The Merchant of Venice* (circa 1596–1597), Munich, Kammerspiele, Keller in der Knöbelstraße, 19 November 1978;

My Mother's Courage, Munich, Kammerspiele, Theater in der Reitmoorstraße, 17 May 1979;

The Voyeur, Berlin, Theatertreffen, Spiegelzelt, 15 May 1982;

Jubilee, Bochum, Schauspielhaus, Kammerspiele, Foyer, 30 January 1983;

Waiting for Godot, adapted from Samuel Beckett's 1952 play, Munich, Kammerspiele, Werkraum, 4 January 1984;

Peepshow, Bochum, Schauspielhaus Kammerspiele, 6 April 1984;

M, adapted from Euripides' *Medea* (431 B.C.), Munich, Kammerspiele Werkraumtheater, 3 January 1985;

Mein Kampf: Farce, Vienna, Akademietheater, 6 May 1987;

Masada, adapted by Tabori and Ursula Voss from Flavius Josephus's *Jewish War* (79–81), Graz, Austria, Steirischer Herbst, 25 October 1988;

Weisman and Copperface: A Jewish Western, Vienna, Akademietheater, 23 March 1990;

Babylon-Blues, Vienna, Burgtheater, 12 April 1991;

Goldberg Variations, Vienna, Akademietheater, 22 June 1991;

Nathans Tod, adapted from Gotthold Ephraim Lessing's *Nathan der Weise* (1779), Wolfenbüttel, Lessingtheater, 14 November 1991;

Unruhige Träume, from Kafka's "Die Verwandlung" (1937), Vienna, Burgtheater Probebühne, 29 April 1992;

Der Grossinquisitor, adapted from Fyodor Dostoevsky's *Bratya Karamazovy* (1879–1880), Munich, Residenztheater, 29 January 1993;

Requiem for a Spy, Vienna, Akademietheater, 17 June 1993;

Rosa Luxemburg–Red Roses for You, libretto by Tabori, dance theater by Johan Kresnik, Berlin, Volksbühne, 29 October 1993;

Exit; Don in Heaven; The Mass-Murderess and Her Friends, Vienna, Akademietheater, 11 June 1995;

The Ballad of the Breaded Veal Cutlet, Vienna, Akademietheater, 29 March 1996;

The Last Night in September, Vienna, Akademietheater, 10 January 1997;

Purgatorium, Vienna, Akademietheater, 29 May 1999;

The Brecht File, Berlin, Berliner Ensemble, 9 January 2000.

BOOKS: *Beneath the Stone the Scorpion* (London & New York: Boardman, 1945);

Companions of the Left Hand (London & New York: Boardman, 1946);

Original Sin (London: Boardman, 1947; Boston: Houghton Mifflin: 1947);

The Caravan Passes (London & New York: Boardman, 1951);

The Emperor's Clothes: A Domestic Comedy in Three Acts (New York: S. French, 1953);

Flight into Egypt: Play in Three Acts (New York: Dramatists' Play Service, 1953);

The Journey: A Confession (New York: Bantam, 1958; revised edition, London: Transworld, 1959);

The Good One (New York: Permabooks, 1960);

Brecht on Brecht: An Improvisation (New York: S. French, 1967);

Erzählungen, translated by Ursula Grützmacher-Tabori and Peter Sandberg (Munich & Vienna: Hanser, 1981);

Unterammergau, oder, Die guten Deutschen, translated by Grützmacher-Tabori (Frankfurt: Suhrkamp, 1981);

Spiele: Peepshow, Pinkville, Jubiläum, translated by Grützmacher-Tabori (Cologne: Prometh, 1984);

Betrachtungen über das Feigenblatt: ein Handbuch für Verliebte und Verrückte, translated by Grützmacher-Tabori (Munich & Vienna: Hanser, 1991);

Editions and Collections: *Theaterstücke,* 2 volumes (Munich & Vienna: Hanser, 1994).

PRODUCED SCRIPTS: *I Confess,* motion picture, adapted by Tabori and William Archibald III from Paul Anthelme's *Nos Deux Consciences* (1902), Warner Bros., 1953;

The Young Lovers, motion picture, by Tabori and Robin Estridge, Pacemaker, 1954;

The Journey, motion picture, M-G-M, 1959;

No Exit, motion picture, adapted from Jean-Paul Sartre's 1944 play *Huis Clos,* Zenith International, 1962;

Secret Ceremony, motion picture, by Tabori and Marco Deneri, World Film Services/Universal, 1968;

Parades, motion picture, Cinerama, 1972;

Insomnia, television, Sender Freies Berlin, 1974;

Weisman and Copperface: A Jewish Western, radio, Norddeutscher Rundfunk, 1978;

The 25th Hour, radio, RIAS Berlin, 1978;

White Christmas, television, Zweites Deutsches Fernsehen, 1979;

My Mother's Courage, radio, RIAS Berlin/Norddeutscher Rundfunk/Süddeutscher Rundfunk, 1979;

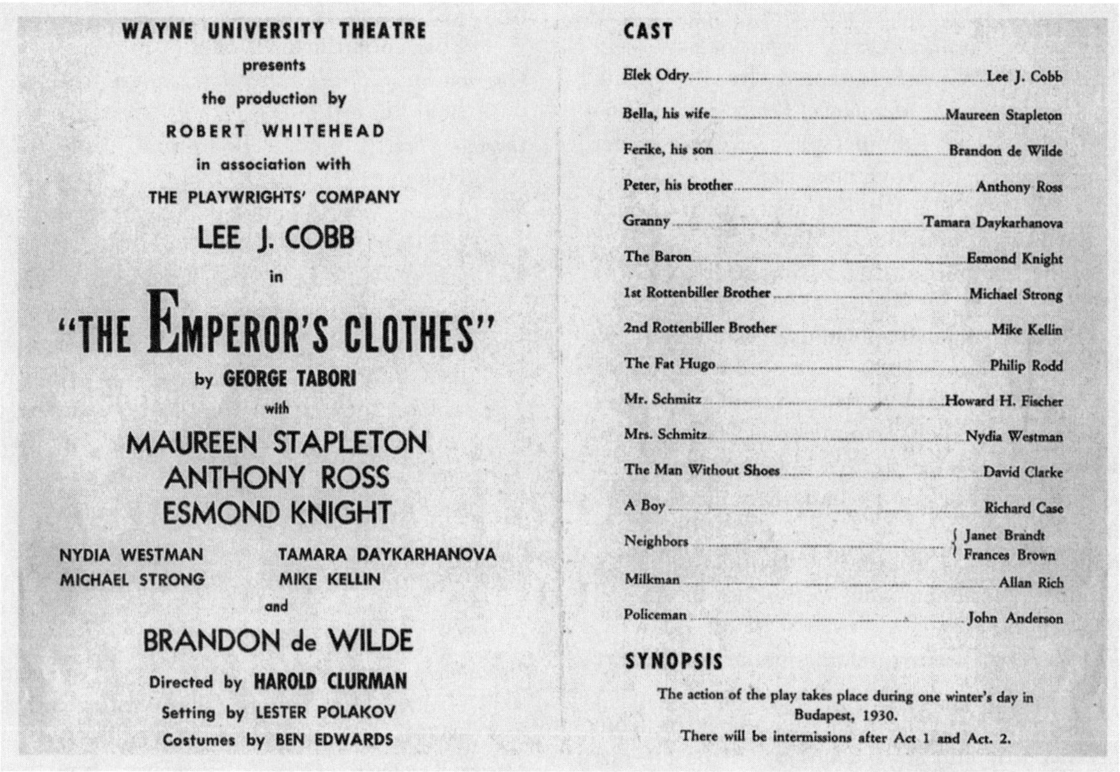

WAYNE UNIVERSITY THEATRE
presents
the production by
ROBERT WHITEHEAD
in association with
THE PLAYWRIGHTS' COMPANY
LEE J. COBB
in
"THE EMPEROR'S CLOTHES"
by GEORGE TABORI
with
MAUREEN STAPLETON
ANTHONY ROSS
ESMOND KNIGHT
NYDIA WESTMAN TAMARA DAYKARHANOVA
MICHAEL STRONG MIKE KELLIN
and
BRANDON de WILDE
Directed by HAROLD CLURMAN
Setting by LESTER POLAKOV
Costumes by BEN EDWARDS

CAST

Elek Odry	Lee J. Cobb
Bella, his wife	Maureen Stapleton
Ferike, his son	Brandon de Wilde
Peter, his brother	Anthony Ross
Granny	Tamara Daykarhanova
The Baron	Esmond Knight
1st Rottenbiller Brother	Michael Strong
2nd Rottenbiller Brother	Mike Kellin
The Fat Hugo	Philip Rodd
Mr. Schmitz	Howard H. Fischer
Mrs. Schmitz	Nydia Westman
The Man Without Shoes	David Clarke
A Boy	Richard Case
Neighbors	Janet Brandt Frances Brown
Milkman	Allan Rich
Policeman	John Anderson

SYNOPSIS

The action of the play takes place during one winter's day in Budapest, 1930.
There will be intermissions after Act 1 and Act. 2.

Program title page and cast list for a touring production of Tabori's second play

The Voyeur, radio, RIAS Berlin/Norddeutscher Rundfunk/Süddeutscher Rundfunk, 1981;

Sigmunds Freude, radio, RIAS Berlin, 1983;

Jubilee, radio, RIAS Berlin/Bayerischer Rundfunk, 1983;

First Night, Last Night, radio, RIAS Berlin/Norddeutscher Rundfunk, 1986;

Insomnia, radio, RIAS Berlin/Bayerischer Rundfunk, 1986;

Mein Kampf, radio, RIAS Berlin/Österreichischer Rundfunk/Süddeutscher Rundfunk/Bayerischer Rundfunk, 1988;

How to Be Happy without Overexerting Oneself, radio, RIAS Berlin/Südwestfunk, 1991;

Requiem for a Spy, radio, Mitteldeutscher Rundfunk/DS-Kultur/Südwestfunk, 1993;

Der Großinquisitor, radio, Mitteldeutscher Rundfunk/Hessischer Rundfunk, 1994.

OTHER: "Holy Night," in *Voyage: An Anthology of Selected Stories,* edited by Denys Val Baker (London: Sylvan, 1945);

The Cannibals, in *The American Place Theatre: Plays,* edited by Richard Schotter (New York: Dell, 1973);

Meine Kämpf, translated by Grützmacher-Tabori, in *DramaContemporary: Germany: Plays by Botho Strauss, George Tabori, Georg Seidel, Klaus Pohl, Tankred Dorst, Elfriede Jelinek, Heiner Müller,* edited by Carl Weber (Baltimore: Johns Hopkins University Press, 1996).

SELECTED PERIODICAL PUBLICATION–UNCOLLECTED: "Hamlet in Blue," *Theatre Quarterly,* 20 (1975/1976).

George Tabori not only embodies the rare combination of playwright, director, and occasional actor, but, as German theater critic Peter von Becker points out in *Materials for the Film "Tabori Theater Theater Tabori"* (1991), he is also one of the last witnesses "from the generation of emigrants between 1933 and 1945, of the connection between overseas exile and the central European cultural tradition." His life as an emigrant made him understand that every "human being is different," and that to categorize human beings according to race or nationality is to objectify individuals and thereby smooth the path to their destruction. Of the many plays Tabori has written, those dealing with the Holocaust and questions of Jewish identity are the most acclaimed and have earned him many literary prizes and awards. Tabori's voice is distinct in the German-speaking theater landscape, an eclectic mixture of black humor with tragedy, of Judeo-Christian mythology with historical fact, of banality and vulgarity with human greatness. One of his legacies as a playwright lies in his attempt to contribute to a truly felt reconciliation between Germans and Jews. Konrad P. Liessmann appropriately called him a "reconciliation artist" who surely deserves to flourish outside the German-speaking theater.

Although Tabori gained British citizenship in 1941 and adopted English as his language, he has always been more of a cosmopolitan, a migrant who has lived and worked in nineteen different countries throughout his life. He certainly would not align himself with any nationality. As quoted by Jörg W. Gronius and Wendy Kässens in *Tabori* (1989), he has asserted that "My home is the stage, my bed, and books."

Tabori was born 24 May 1914 in Budapest–at the time still part of the Hapsburg Empire–to Cornelius Tabori, a Jewish journalist and left-wing intellectual, and his wife, Elsa. Tabori's upbringing was nonreligious, and he often states that he only became aware that he was a Jew with the rise of fascism in Germany and Hungary. After the *matura* in 1932 he started an apprenticeship in a hotel in Berlin, where he witnessed Adolf Hitler's seizure of power in January 1933. He returned to Hungary in May but spent another three months in Germany in 1934, working in a Dresden hotel. In 1935 he followed his brother Paul to London, where Tabori worked as a tourist guide and as a translator for a Hungarian news agency. After visiting Budapest for Christmas in 1939 he had problems returning to Britain and so took on work there as a foreign correspondent for several newspapers. His time in Budapest marked the beginning of an odyssey around the Balkans and the Mediterranean that took him to Sofia, Istanbul, Jerusalem (where he married Hannah Freund in 1941), and Cairo. Tabori joined the British army as an intelligence officer during his travels. In 1943 he returned to London, where he worked in the Hungarian Department of the British Broadcasting Corporation (BBC). While in Jerusalem, Tabori had begun writing his first novel, *Beneath the Stone the Scorpion,* in English. The novel was published in Great Britain and the United States in 1945 and was followed by *Companions of the Left Hand* in 1946. During the war Tabori's father and several members of his family were murdered in German extermination camps.

Tabori moved to Hollywood in 1947 to work as a scriptwriter at M-G-M and later for Warner Bros. for directors such as Alfred Hitchcock, Anthony Asquith, Anatole Litvak, and Joseph Losey. Tabori described his stay there as "the worst time" of his life. Embarrassment over his work in motion pictures led him to withdraw his name from some of the scripts he wrote. He was dissatisfied with the lack of artistic autonomy under the "salad-system," in which several writers work on the same script, and the increasing pressures of anticommunist sentiment in Hollywood. Tabori moved to New York in 1950, where he lived and worked mainly as a scriptwriter and translator for the next twenty-one years. Shortly after moving to New York, Tabori divorced Freund.

Tabori early in his career, circa 1950

Tabori encountered Bertolt Brecht while in Hollywood and was inspired to write for the theater. His

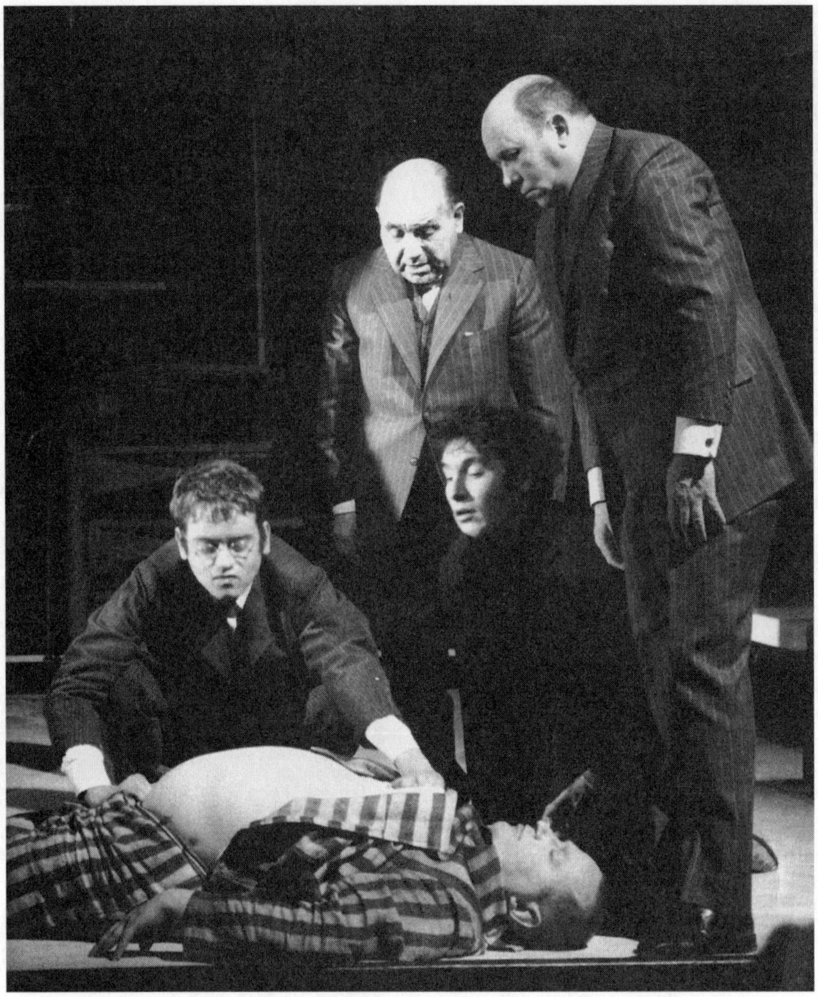

Scene from The Cannibals, *Tabori's unconventional treatment of the Holocaust that marked a turning point in his career*

first two plays, *Flight into Egypt* and *The Emperor's Clothes,* were produced on Broadway in 1952 and 1953, respectively. They are written in naturalistic mode (with detailed stage directions) and are tragic, almost melodramatic in tone. *Flight into Egypt* deals with a Viennese family's futile attempt to obtain American visas from Egypt after World War II and ends with the sick father committing suicide. *The Emperor's Clothes,* set in Budapest in 1930, is based on an autobiographical incident. A young boy, disappointed by his father's compromise of his political beliefs for the sake of finding work as a teacher, boasts to his friends that his father is a hero engaged in secret revolutionary activity. The father is arrested and regains his son's adoration by admitting to the charges brought against him. Tabori's next original play was completely different in style: *Brou Ha Ha* is a political satire about colonialism, international policies, and the Cold War, set in an imaginary sultanate in the Persian Gulf. The play premiered in London in 1958.

During the 1950s and 1960s Tabori was an observer at Lee Strasberg's Actors' Studio through Swedish actress Viveca Lindfors, whom he married in 1953. Lindfors had the idea of devising a Brecht collage. *Brecht on Brecht: An Improvisation,* a compilation of various Brecht texts, most of which were translated by Tabori, premiered in 1961 in New York and was so successful that it ran for several years. Throughout the 1960s Tabori also translated *The Resistible Rise of Arturo Ui: A Gangster Spectacle* (1963), *Mother Courage* (1963), *The Guns of Carrar* (1968)–which he codirected with Marty Fried at Castleton State College in Vermont in 1967–and Max Frisch's *Andorra* (1963). In 1966 Lindfors and Tabori founded their own company, the Strolling Players, with which they successfully toured *Brecht on Brecht.* The same year Tabori became the

Tabori at his writing desk

artistic director of the Berkshire Theatre Festival in Stockbridge, Massachusetts, and in 1969 *The Niggerlovers: The Demonstration* and *Man and Dog* premiered in New York. Each of the two short plays addresses racial conflict and the increasing polarization of black people and white liberals. With *The Niggerlovers* Tabori began exploring what later became one of his trademarks, the almost subversive blending of serious issues with jokes.

This blending of tragedy with laughter flourished in *The Cannibals,* which Tabori codirected with Fried at the American Place Theater in New York in 1968. The play received a mixed reception in New York, but his "black mass" about Auschwitz caused controversy at the Schillertheater premiere in West Berlin the following year. *The Cannibals* marked a turning point in Tabori's career as a theater artist. He once stated in a television interview that he has rewritten the same play ever since. In later plays he explores the major thematic and formal characteristics of his playwriting introduced in *The Cannibals* from different perspectives, adding new facets and placing different emphases in form and content. *The Cannibals* is the first of Tabori's plays in which the Holocaust comes to the fore. The controversial reception the play received in West Germany was a result of Tabori's unconventional way of dealing with this sensitive historical matter.

The play is set in Auschwitz. A group of concentration camp inmates kill one of their fellow prisoners in a fight over a piece of bread that he had been hiding from them. Almost starved to death, they decide to eat his corpse, despite the declared opposition of the central character, Uncle (an alter ego of Tabori's father). As the meat is cooking on the stove, the inmates pass time by telling and role-playing stories, indulging in fantasies about food and sex, acting out moments from their past, and imagining a possible future. These activities culminate in an argument between Uncle, who accepts his suffering as God given and argues that the only form of resistance is to behave totally unlike the victimizers, and Klaub, who believes in survival by any means. Annoyed by the discussion, the inmates remember how Uncle foiled an escape attempt on the train to Auschwitz because the plot involved murdering the guards. They blame him for their situation; role playing turns into real violence when the victims become victimizers. The camp commander, Schrekinger, raids the shack, discovers the meat, and orders the inmates to eat it. Most refuse and are immediately sent to the gas chamber. Only two obey; they survive.

The Cannibals is, strictly speaking, not about Auschwitz but about the difficulty, even impossibility, of remembering Auschwitz. In the course of the play the actors step out of character several times and address the audience directly. The action of the play gradually reveals that the characters seen on stage are not the actual inmates, but their sons and the two survivors, who together are reenacting the events. Tabori's use of this Brechtian device takes the play out of the frame of realism or documentary drama and creates a representation of the process of memory instead. The sons take on the roles of their fathers as a means of understanding and coming to terms with what happened to the fathers. One of Tabori's recurring themes is the question of how to deal with memory and how to become free of traumatic memories of the past. His plays suggest that memory cannot be reduced to facts but needs to be embodied and experienced in the present. The theater is an ideal place to do so for actors and audience alike.

In his attempt to revive the past Tabori refuses piety, pity, sentimentality, and a "mythologization of Auschwitz." He also undercuts any simplistic categorization of victims and perpetrators into good and bad. The inmates are by no means dignified heroes. Before Tabori celebrates their resistance at the end of the play, he shows them in all their humanity: he exposes their fears, their cowardice, their aggressiveness, their brutality, and their vulgarity. Tabori is not afraid to violate taboos and to juxtapose the profane and the sublime as the two extreme ends of the spectrum of human life.

Tabori believes that theater is a healing art, fulfilling its therapeutic function by appealing first of all to the affective dispositions of the mind. Theater should address what is embarrassing and what is repressed from individual and collective consciousness. Theater should serve the members of the audience as a means of self-realization. Therefore, Tabori's "theater of embarrassment" makes extensive use of black humor: for him jokes are rooted in catastrophe, and he regards humor–under the banner of Jewish tradition–as a means of survival in dark times. Writing *The Cannibals* was a therapeutic act for Tabori, a way of coming to terms with his father's death in Auschwitz.

Tabori divorced Lindfors in 1970. As a result of the controversial success of *The Cannibals,* he was again invited to Berlin in 1971 to direct his play *Pinkville,* a critical revue on the Vietnam War modeled on Brecht's *Mann ist Mann* (1926). His work on the play marked the beginning of a late career as a theater director. A year later at the Zimmertheater in Tübingen he premiered *Clowns,* a farce with surreal elements that deals with the decline of the American way of life as represented by a family in New York. In 1975 Tabori mounted a production in Bremen titled *Sigmunds Freude* (James' Joys), for which he used transcripts of Gestalt therapeutic sessions led by Frederick Solomon Perls. Tabori wanted to investigate the interrelation between theater and psychotherapy. *Sigmunds Freude* was the first of many adaptations of nondramatic texts for the stage.

Tabori had distinguished himself as a director through his actor-centered approach. He had worked as a freelance director in Hamburg, Bonn, and Bremen, and from 1976 to 1978 developed and expanded his ideas during a two-year experiment at the Bremen Theatre Laboratory. There he investigated the nature of the relationship between actor and role. Tabori's collaborative approach to the work and his ethos as a practitioner show the influence of Jerzey Grotowski, the Open Theater, and the Living Theater. Tabori's eclectic working method, however, is most informed by the methods of Gestalt therapy and Strasberg, placing particular emphasis on the use of sense and affective memory and the actor's presence.

In 1976 Tabori presented *Talk Show* with his "laboratory" actors. The play is set in a sanatorium in Beverly Hills and addresses the patients' problems in coming to terms with illness, the process of aging, and death in an environment that is mainly concerned with eternal youth. Tabori wrote the first draft of the play, then developed and rewrote the work throughout the rehearsal process, a practice he maintained throughout his career. In general Tabori's writing is strongly informed by his theater practice and vice versa. His playful, open-ended rehearsal style, based on improvisation, is inscribed in the many role plays in which his dramatic characters engage.

Tabori directed an adaptation of Franz Kafka's "Die Verwandlung" (The Metamorphosis, 1937) at the Kammerspiele in Munich in early 1977. *Verwandlungen* (Metamorphoses) intertwines passages from Kafka with the play-within-a-play situation of a director and a group of actors rehearsing Kafka's work. In June of that same year Tabori staged an adaptation of Kafka's "Ein Hungerkünstler" (A Hunger Artist, 1938), titled *Die Hungerkünstler* (Hunger Artists), for which his laboratory actors underwent a period of more than thirty days of fasting.

After the premature end of the theater laboratory because of a change in theater management, Tabori became director in residence at the Munich Kammerspiele for the 1978–1979 season. His first production was an adaptation of Shakespeare's *The Merchant of Venice* (circa 1596–1597). With *Ich wollte meine Tochter läge tot zu meinen Füßen und hätte die Juwelen in den Ohren: Improvisationen über Shakespeare's Shylock* (I Would My Daughter Were Dead at My Foot, and the Jewels in Her Ear: Improvisations on Shakespeare's Shylock, 1978), Tabori returned to his engagement with the Holocaust on stage. Scenes from the play were interwoven with

Scenes from the 1987 production of Mein Kampf: Farce, *the theological work that established Tabori as a leading contemporary German-language playwright*

Ignaz Kirchner and Gunter Einbrodt in Mein Kampf: Farce

references to anti-Semitism and the Holocaust, as well as Jewish history and religion.

My Mother's Courage, staged in Munich in 1979, is a companion piece to *The Cannibals.* The play describes the survival of Tabori's mother, Elsa, who was already on one of the many death trains to Auschwitz when she managed to persuade a German officer to send her back to Budapest. In *My Mother's Courage* the epic element is even more predominant than in *The Cannibals.* The character of the son narrates the story to the audience as his mother reenacts the events and approves or disapproves of his version and the poetic liberties he takes.

After *My Mother's Courage* Tabori was able to reunite most of the members of the Bremen Theater Laboratory group for several productions. The group had tried to survive as an independent theater company with almost no funding, however, and was forced at last to dissolve because of financial difficulties. Their last project was the premiere of Tabori's *The Voyeur* in 1982, a play that had originally been part of *The Niggerlovers.*

In 1983 Tabori started rehearsing *Jubilee* at the Schauspielhaus Bochum. *Jubilee* was written to commemorate the fiftieth anniversary of Hitler's seizure of power. The idea for the play came from Brecht's daughter Hanne Hiob, who also provided Tabori with her collection of documentary material on Nazi crimes, neo-Nazi activities, and Jewish jokes. The play premiered in January 1983. *Jubilee* is a montage of scenes set in a Jewish graveyard. The dead, in various stages of decay, are condemned to remember and to reenact traumatic moments of the past while being confronted with the harassment and the defilement of their graves by neo-Nazis in the present. The play is a powerful metaphor for the idea that the memory of the victims still haunts the world, especially in the face of rising neo-Nazism. It earned Tabori the Mühlheimer Dramatikerpreis, an annual award for new German playwriting.

Tabori returned to Bochum to direct *Peepshow* (1984), about a man with an eternal Oedipus complex. In 1984 he also put on an adaptation of Samuel Beckett's *Waiting for Godot* (1952) at the Munich Kammerspiele. His successful staging of the play earned him the position of director in residence. Tabori fulfilled only two years of his four-year contract before moving on to the Circle, a small theater in Vienna, where he served as artistic director and theater manager in 1987. He hoped to establish a model similar to that of the Bremen Theater Laboratory. The first four years of his stay in Vienna mark one of the most productive and successful phases of his life. With the 1987 premiere of the "theological farce" *Mein Kampf* at the Akademietheater, the second house of the Burgtheater in Vienna, he was recognized as one of the leading playwrights of the German-speaking theater.

Many of the themes of *The Cannibals* recur in *Mein Kampf,* but with an interesting twist: The focus shifts from the victim to the oppressor, and the play is set before the Holocaust rather than after. *Mein Kampf* deals with a fictitious encounter between the young Hitler and the Jew Shlomo Herzl, a book peddler, in a "flophouse" in Vienna in the first decade of the twentieth century. The narrative, based on a short story by the same name, is built on a few facts from Hitler's autobiography. Tabori develops the historical into a crude, surreal fantasy–a "directed dream," as he called it in Palm and Voss. Hitler has come to Vienna in order to undergo an entrance exam at the Academy of Fine Arts. Shlomo Herzl quickly develops an affection for the young country bumpkin, who is moody, messy and unable to look after himself. He begins to take care of Hitler, who demonstrates ingratitude in anti-Semitic rages and takes advantage of Herzl's kindheartedness. To Lobkowitz–a kosher cook who believes that he is God–Herzl's love borders on masochism. Herzl even saves Hitler from the clutches of Frau Death, who visits the flophouse looking for Hitler. In the final act, Hitler, who has gone into politics, returns to look for the manuscript of a book Shlomo was working on, titled *Mein Kampf,* to ensure the elimination of any discrediting passages. His companion, Himmlischst, kills Herzl's beloved hen, Mitzi, and cooks it in a blood sauce. Herzl comments: "If you start burning birds, you'll end up burning people." Frau Death arrives to pick up Hitler and warns Herzl of the atrocities to come.

Mein Kampf is another powerful and disturbing attempt to demythologize history by putting the Führer on stage. Tabori shows the criminal before the crime, thus not only poking fun at Hitler's megalomania but also establishing an emotional link to him as a human being. The play implies the simultaneously simplistic and daring hypothesis that Hitler's evil was rooted in his inability to feel and to love. Therefore, Herzl cares for him. At the same time the play indirectly questions whether Herzl's altruism has done much good to the world. Some critics suggest that the relationship between Hitler and Herzl represents the dialectics of an unholy alliance between victim and perpetrator: neither can assume his role without the other. In the opinion of German Jewish critic Thomas Rothschild, *Mein Kampf* reveals "that Jews define themselves against Hitler . . . that to the present day they are fatally dependent on him, that . . . talking about Jews is almost impossible without the consciousness of Auschwitz." He warns that "a group, which constantly understands itself and allows itself to be understood as victims, loses the sovereignty and self-determination which distinguish human beings from objects that can be manipulated."

Tabori in 1992 at the vandalized Berlin memorial to Bertolt Brecht, whose work Tabori adapted in the 1960s

The engagement in the play with the Nazi past found particular resonance at the time because of Kurt Waldheim, former secretary general of the United Nations, who had been elected as president of Austria despite the fact that incriminating information about his role as an officer in the German army during World War II had come to light. The consequence was that *Mein Kampf* was perceived as a political response to the Waldheim affair, and other Tabori productions at the Circle were seen as challenges to Catholic, conservative Austria. *Masada,* based on Flavius Josephus's account of the Jewish war against the Romans in the first century, received a staged reading in November 1988 in commemoration of the fiftieth anniversary of the *Reichskristallnacht,* the so-called Night of Broken Glass in 1938 when Nazis led a pogrom against Jewish communities in Germany and Austria. Tabori developed the script with his dramaturge, Ursula Voss.

In spring 1990 Tabori premiered his next play, *Weisman and Copperface: A Jewish Western,* at the Akademietheater. The play focuses on problems of identity and satirizes the lack of solidarity among oppressed groups. Weisman and his daughter Ruthie, who is disabled, lose their way in the American desert, where they encounter Copperface, a Native American. Whereas Weisman regards himself as Jewish and assumes the role of the eternal victim, Copperface suffers from a confusion with regard to his cultural identity, no longer knowing who or what he is, which results in aggressively racist behavior. The play culminates in a showdown in which the two protagonists engage in a grotesque verbal competition about who is the more disadvantaged in life and society, with Ruthie as the winner's trophy. Weisman finally has to admit to and accept his own fascist potential. *Weisman and Copperface* earned Tabori the Mühlheimer Dramatikerpreis for the second time.

In the summer of 1990 Tabori had to abandon the Circle because of financial difficulties. Because of his success as a playwright he continued developing his playwriting practice at the Burgtheater and the Akademietheater. In 1991 he premiered *Babylon-Blues,* a sequence of unrelated scenes exploring the nature of happiness, followed by another considerable success with *Goldberg Variations,* in which the biblical history of the world is represented as a theater rehearsal. The megalomaniacal theater director, Mr. Jay, is mounting a new production based on the Holy Scripture. The play presents the Creation, the Garden of Eden, the story of Cain and Abel, Abraham, Jonah, Moses, up to the Crucifixion of Christ. Jay's ambitious plans are constantly thwarted by his collaborators. Technical

Scene from the 1993 production of Tabori's Requiem for a Spy *(from* George Tabori, *1994)*

breakdowns as well as the moods and complaints of actors and technicians stir up all sorts of problems. With *Goldberg Variations* Tabori finds a theatrical metaphor for his belief that God is nothing but a projection of human longing for perfection. Like the biblical God, Mr. Jay does not take the fallibility of human beings into account. Humanity is unable to comply with Mr. Jay's rules and commands because failure and moral imperfection are unavoidable characteristics of the human condition. Happiness is to be found in an acceptance of failure and moral imperfection rather than in the aspiration to perfection. In Andrea Welker's *George Tabori: Dem Gedächtnis, der Trauer und dem Lachen gewidmet. Portraits* (1994), Tabori states that perfection is "blasphemy."

For the next two years Tabori worked predominantly on adaptations. In autumn 1991 he staged an adaptation of Gotthold Ephraim Lessing's play *Nathan der Weise* (Nathan the Wise, 1779) for the Residenztheater in Munich. *Nathans Tod* (Nathan's Death) is a critical reworking of Lessing's optimistic Enlightenment drama on religious tolerance, through the lens of the twentieth century. In 1992 Tabori staged another adaptation of Kafka's "The Metamorphosis," with the title *Unruhige Träume* (Troubled Dreams), at the Burgtheater. In 1993 Tabori produced a new play for the Residenztheater in Munich. The unsuccessful *Der Grossinquisitor* (The Grand Inquisitor), loosely based on an episode from Fyodor Dostoevsky's novel *Bratya Karamazovy* (The Brothers Karamazov, 1879–1880), explores the relationship between two brothers and a prostitute. This production was followed by *Requiem for a Spy* (1993)–a comic espionage drama about treason, truth, and lies–and a libretto for Johan Kresnik's dance theater piece, *Rosa Luxemburg–Red Roses for You,* on German revolutionary Rosa Luxemburg, which premiered at the Volksbühne in Berlin in 1993. *Requiem for a Spy* was also Tabori's last great success as a playwright. In several interviews in the early 1990s Tabori, after having suffered a stroke and a failed eye operation, stated that he was trying to come to terms with his age and with the fact that he was approaching death. Several of his next projects engaged with the subject. In 1992 he staged *The 25th Hour,* a play about illness and death that he had written more than twenty years previously. In 1996 he staged three short plays–*Exit, Don in Heaven,* and *The Mass-Murderess and Her Friends*–which explore death by suicide, old age, and execution in humorous ways.

Tabori's next play, *The Ballad of the Breaded Veal Cutlet* (1996), came closest to his previous successes. After his retirement gourmet critic Alfons Morgenstern, a Viennese Jew, develops persecution mania and believes that the SS, the Nazi security force, is after him. He can overcome this delusion only by visiting his family grave for the first time and by genuinely mourning the victims of the Third Reich. *The Last Night in September,* another series of three short plays, opened in early 1997. Two years later Tabori directed *Purgatorium,* the first play he wrote in German.

When Claus Peymann, the artistic director of the Burgtheater, left at the end of the 1998–1999 season to take over directorship of the Berliner Ensemble, the eighty-five-year-old Tabori moved with him. In January 2000 Tabori staged a new play, *The Brecht File,* based on actual files the Federal Bureau of Investigation (FBI) kept on the German writer and on the interrogation of Brecht before the House of Un-American Activities Committee. In this play one of the two FBI agents who shadow Brecht becomes the playwright's disciple.

References:

Hans-Peter Bayerdörfer and Jörg Schönert, eds., *Theater gegen das Vergessen: Bühnenarbeit und Drama bei George Tabori* (Tübingen: Niemeyer, 1997);

Peter von Becker, *Materials for the Film "Tabori Theater Theater Tabori"* (Munich: Goethe Institute, 1991);

Anat Feinberg-Jütte, "'The Task Is Not to Reproduce the External Form, but to Find the Subtext': George Tabori's Productions of Samuel Beckett's Texts," *Journal of Beckett Studies,* 1–2 (1992): 95–115;

J. A. Garforth, "George Tabori's Bare Essentials–A Perspective on Beckett Staging in Germany," *Forum Modernes Theater,* 9 (1994): 59–75;

Jörg W. Gronius and Wendy Kässens, eds., *Tabori* (Frankfurt am Main: Athenäum, 1989);

Leah Hadomi, *Dramatic Metaphors of Fascism and Antifascism* (Tübingen: Niemeyer, 1996), pp. 3–6;

Hadomi, "The Historical and the Mythical in Tabori's Plays," *Forum Modernes Theater,* 8 (1993);

Gungula Ohngemach, *George Tabori* (Frankfurt am Main: Fischer, 1989);

Peter Radtke, *M wie Tabori: Erfahrungen eines behinderten Schauspielers* (Zurich: Pendo, 1987);

H. Regitz and Ivo Ismael, "The Concept, Keep on Making Mistakes. George Tabori and Ivo Ismael Working Together at the Oper, Leipzig," *Ballett International,* 2 (1995): 16–17;

Thomas Rothschild, "Judische Anarchisten, Nitizen zu George Tabori und Thomas Brasch," *Neue Gesellschaft/Frankfurter Hefte,* 3(1990): 259;

Andrea Welker, ed., *George Tabori: Dem Gedächtnis, der Trauer und dem Lachen gewidmet. Portraits* (Vienna: Bibliothek der Provinz, 1994);

Welker and Tina Berger, eds., *George Tabori: Ich wollte meine Tochter läge tot zu meinen Füßen und hätte die Juwelen in den Ohren* (Munich: Hanser, 1979).

Gwyn Thomas

(6 July 1913 - 14 April 1981)

Chris Hopkins
Sheffield Hallam University

See also the Thomas entry in *DLB 15: British Novelists, 1930–1959.*

PLAY PRODUCTIONS: *The Keep,* London, Royal Court Theatre, 7 August 1960;
Loud Organs, Blackpool, Grand Theatre, 22 October 1962;
Jackie the Jumper, London, Royal Court Theatre, 1 February 1963;
Sap, Cardiff, Sherman Theatre, 12 November 1974;
The Breakers, Cardiff, Sherman Theatre, 16 November 1976.

BOOKS: *Where Did I Put My Pity? Folk Tales from the Modern Welsh* (London: Progress, 1946);
The Alone to the Alone (London: Nicholson & Watson, 1947); republished as *Venus for the Voters* (Boston: Little, Brown, 1948);
All Things Betray Thee (London: Joseph, 1949); republished as *Leaves in the Wind* (Boston: Little, Brown, 1949);
The World Cannot Hear You: A Comedy of Ancient Desires (London: Gollancz, 1951);
Now Lead Us Home (London: Gollancz, 1952);
A Frost on My Frolic (London: Gollancz, 1953);
The Stranger at My Side (London: Gollancz, 1954);
A Point of Order (London: Gollancz, 1956);
Gazooka and Other Stories (London: Gollancz, 1957);
The Love Man (London: Gollancz, 1958);
Ring Delirium 123 (London: Gollancz, 1960);
The Keep (London: Elek, 1962);
Gwyn Thomas: Three Plays, edited by Michael Parnell (Bridgend: Seren, 1962)–comprises *The Keep, Jackie the Jumper,* and *Loud Organs;*
A Welsh Eye (London: Hutchinson, 1964);
A Hatful of Humours (London: Schoolmaster, 1965);
A Few Selected Exits (London: Hutchinson, 1968);
The Lust Lobby: Stories (London: Hutchinson, 1971);
The Sky of Our Lives: Three Novellas (London: Hutchinson, 1972);

Gwyn Thomas (Collection of Sherman Theatre, Cardiff)

The Subsidence Factor: The Annual Gwyn Jones Lecture (Cardiff: University College Cardiff Press, 1979);
Ellis Wynne (Cardiff: University of Wales Press, 1984);
Selected Short Stories (Bridgend: Poetry Wales, 1984);
High on Hope: Extracts from the Western Mail Articles, edited by Jeffrey Robinson and Brian McCann (Cowbridge: Brown, 1985);
Sorrow for Thy Sons (London: Lawrence & Wishart, 1986);

Meadow Prospect Revisited, edited by Parnell (Bridgend: Seren, 1992).

OTHER: *The Dark Philosophers,* in *Triad One,* edited by Jack Ainstrop (London: Dobson, 1946);

The Loot, in *Eight Plays: Book 2,* edited by Malcolm Stuart Fellows (London: Cassell, 1965).

PRODUCED SCRIPTS: *Gazooka (A Rhondda Reminiscence),* radio, BBC Welsh Home Service, 11 January 1952; BBC Third Programme, 2 January 1953;

The Orpheans, radio, BBC Welsh Home Service, 2 September 1952; revised as *The Singers of Meadow Prospect,* BBC Welsh Home Service, 9 April 1954;

Forenoon, radio, BBC North of England Home Service, 25 January 1953;

Festival, radio, BBC Welsh Home Service, 9 April 1953;

Our Outings, radio, BBC Welsh Home Service, 27 October 1953;

The Deep Sweet Roots, radio, BBC Home Service, 12 November 1953;

Vive l'Oompa, radio, BBC Third Programme, August 1955;

Up the Handling Code, radio, BBC Welsh Home Service, 15 November 1955;

To This One Place, radio, BBC Welsh Home Service, 26 November 1956;

Merlin's Brow, radio, BBC Welsh Home Service, 18 October 1957;

The Long Run, radio, BBC Welsh Home Service, 17 July 1958;

The Slip, television, BBC One, 14 October 1962;

The Walk Out, radio, BBC Third Programme, 7 March 1963;

The Dig, television, BBC One, 24 October 1963;

The Entrance, radio, BBC Light Programme, 29 April 1964;

The Keep, television, BBC One, 6 May 1964;

The Alderman, radio, BBC Home Service, 17 January 1966;

The Giving Time, radio, BBC Radio 4, 19 December 1968;

He Knows, He Knows, radio, BBC Radio 4, 3 August 1972;

Up and Under, television, BBC One, 3 March 1973;

The Worriers, radio, BBC Radio 4, 22 August 1974;

Adelphi Terrace, television, BBC Two, 7 August 1975;

The Long Lesson, radio, BBC Radio Wales, 17 March 1978.

Gwyn Thomas was an extraordinarily prolific and inventive writer across a range of genres. In some respects, theater may not have been his ideal form in that his interest in plot, development, and conventional dramaturgy was always less than his interest in dialogue almost as an end in itself (it may well be that his extensive work on radio drama was more suited to his talents). Moreover, his experience of theater was plagued by misfortunes over which he had no control and that lessened the impact and reputation he might have had. Nevertheless, he was a distinctive playwright who played a part in the innovations that happened in British theater in the 1960s, as well as being an important, if not always universally welcomed, contributor to postwar debates about Welsh national identity.

Thomas was born in Cymmer, Porth, a coal-mining area in the Rhondda valley in South Wales, on 6 July 1913. He was the youngest of twelve children. His father, Walter Thomas, was a coal miner with a fondness for books, but he was rarely in regular employment and neglected his family. His mother, Ziphorah Davies Thomas, came from a family where music and reading were important. She died, however, in 1919, when Gwyn was six years old. He was thereafter brought up mainly by his sister Nana, who was seventeen when their mother died.

Thomas did well at school, inspired partly by the successes there of his eldest brother, Walter. From Rhondda County School he won a scholarship to St. Edmund Hall, Oxford, to read French and Spanish. He found Oxford deeply alienating and was completely unable to adjust to the difference in social milieu from that of his upbringing, as well as being held back by his acute poverty. He wrote in his autobiography, *A Few Selected Exits* (1968), that "had I been a Venusian I would not have made smaller contact with the place." He spent some time in Madrid as part of his course, where he was impressed by the atmosphere of Spain but suffered from ill health and a shortage of money. Nevertheless, he completed his degree in 1934.

He at once moved back to his native Rhondda, but employment prospects were not good–the region was officially classified a "distressed area" during the 1930s. He was more or less unemployed for six years, until 1940, although he did some lecturing for the Workers Educational Association in Glamorgan. During this period he also tried to write and publish fiction, but without success. He married his wife, Lyn, in 1938. After briefly working in Manchester as an education officer, he gained a teaching post at Cardigan Grammar School in 1940, moving to a similar school at Barry in Glamorgan in 1942. He continued to write while teaching, completing at least three novels by the end of World War II.

In 1945 Lyn Thomas sent off three complete typescripts of novels to three different publishers. Each was accepted, and Thomas's reputation as an idiosyn-

St. Edmund Hall, Oxford. Thomas's room is on the top left.

cratic and original novelist was established. From then until 1962 Thomas maintained both his teaching post and a prolific writing output. In 1950 Thomas's reputation, and his friendship with the writer Glyn Jones and the radio producer Elwyn Evans, led to his being invited to contribute to a radio broadcast in "Why I Write," a series on the BBC Welsh Home Service. This broadcast was his first active involvement with radio, a medium that he thereafter enjoyed and frequently contributed to in various forms, including interviews and other entertainments, as well as original radio plays (fourteen of these were produced by the BBC between 1952 and 1974). His radio dramas as well as his general reputation may have been responsible for first bringing him to the attention of the theater world. Thomas did not conceive of himself as a playwright initially.

In 1956 George Devine, artistic director of the Royal Court Theatre in London, invited Thomas to lunch to discuss the possibility of Thomas writing a play for the Royal Court. This invitation was part of a general policy on Devine's part to give writers not principally known for drama the opportunity to write original work for the theater. Thomas was fond of the theater but had doubts about his own ability to write for it, particularly since his novels had often been criticized for inattention to construction and plot and he had no experience of writing for the stage. Devine persuaded Thomas that the Royal Court could offer technical advice on dramaturgy, and he became intrigued by the possibility.

His doubts seemed at first to be confirmed by his unsuccessful attempts at playwriting, with the difficulty compounded by a lack of time–he now had more writing commitments than he could comfortably meet. Though he made starts on plays between 1956 and 1958, he was not sufficiently satisfied with a play to finish it for production until 1960. His first play, *The Keep* (1960), is, like virtually all of Thomas's writing, set in South Wales, with a specific date of 1954. It has autobiographical elements, with references to his own family life in the 1930s. The play concerns the Morton family, which comprises a father, a daughter, and five brothers. The mother, Dinah May, apparently went to the United States and died in an accident there some years before. The father, Ben, is the head of the family in name but is ineffectual. The daughter, Miriam, takes on all the actual labor of looking after the men, while the eldest brother, Constantine (usually referred to as "Con"), assumes authority in the family as he becomes successful at work and in local society.

Despite this appearance of a mutually supportive family bound together by loss, there is in fact an atmosphere of appalling strain, boredom, and claustrophobia in the house, which forms the main setting of the play. The title suggests a defensive structure against the outside world, but, as becomes clear, the keep also houses a prison. The other brothers–Alvin, Oswald, Russ, and Wallace–feel increasingly trapped by Con's power and, indeed, by the image of a close family that binds them all to the house and prevents them from leaving for an independent adult life elsewhere. The author's introduction to *The Keep* makes its focus on the family clear: "Some families burst apart like bombs and never again achieve unity. Others grow circular, deep like old ponds. The family in this play . . . are like that." The brothers represent various facets of South Welsh life and a range of different class positions: Alvin is a tinplate worker, Oswald a railway ticket clerk (and incompetent choral conductor), Russ a teacher, Wallace a doctor, and Con has just achieved his ambition of becoming town clerk. Ben, the father, at some point in the past left his family "for a brief escape into a pasture of sensual liberty," as Thomas describes it in his useful introduction, and is now fixated on that lapse with a "self-lacerating piety." Finally, Dinah May, despite her absence from the stage, exerts a powerful presence for every member of the household.

All of these characters are fixed in the past, with the apparent exception of Con, who constantly plays on that past to maintain the immobility of the family inside the "keep." In fact, though, despite his apparent ability to make progress through his scheming and manipulation, he is also motivated wholly by an inability to move on from the past or to allow the rest of the family to "betray" itself by doing so. During the play the other four brothers rebel against Con's authority and announce their plans to escape:

> *Con:* And do you know what I was always afraid of? . . . That you'd all be waiting to tell me that you were going, or even that you were already gone. The house empty and Mam betrayed. . . .
> *Russ:* What we said wasn't a joke, Con. We're on our way.
> *Wallace:* Pretoria.
> *Oswald:* Swindon.
> *Alvin:* Birmingham.
> *Russ:* London.

Like the three sisters in Anton Chekhov's *Tri sestry* (1901), however, they never do leave. At the end of the play Ben reveals that Dinah May did not die in the United States years ago but had been living with another man until her death in the previous spring. The whole basis of the Mortons' family life has been a lie. The family seems to stand for a bleak vision of post–World War II Wales itself–trapped within myths of piety and obsessed by the past, there seems little possibility of development. "We are dead," says Ben at the end of the play. "Silence. Silence." Nevertheless, the play in performance proves extremely funny, for the characters are blessed with a verbal dexterity with which to meet their actual immobility.

The Keep has little action and no variety of scene: when events occur, they happen offstage and are merely reported. Instead, Thomas relies on speech as the principal dramatic instrument–a general characteristic of his plays. As the critic Ian Michael has suggested, this static quality increases appropriately the claustrophobic feeling of *The Keep*. Critic Michael Parnell said about the play that it seems "to find its level somewhere between drawing-room comedy and kitchen sink domestic tragedy."

On the first night of its tryout production at the Royal Court, the theater was flooded by a freak storm and the performance had to be postponed. A second attempt the following Sunday, 7 August 1960, was a success, however. Invited critics reacted favorably, and Devine decided to proceed with a full-scale production at the Royal Court. Thomas made some revisions after the tryout version, cutting some dialogue. The production went ahead in November 1961 and was mainly well received and favorably reviewed. Several reviewers noted the comic exuberance of the play. Some expressed minor doubts about the lack of action and the reliance on dialogue, while one took this line further to complain of "an overweight of wit." Performances were well attended from the first night on, and attendance was boosted by a televised performance. A second run followed at the slightly larger Piccadilly Theatre, with smaller audiences than was hoped for. As a further sign of success, the play was selected by the critic J. C. Trewin for publication in the 1961 edition of his *Plays of the Year* anthology.

Overall, Thomas's first play was a positive experience both for him and for Devine, who was keen that Thomas should write another play for him soon. Thomas set to work on *Jackie the Jumper* (1963). He was also approached at the same time by a producer called Richard Rhys, who asked him to write a play with music, which became *Loud Organs* (1962). Thomas had other work in hand, however, including journalistic commitments and offers of commissions for both books and movie scripts. He began to realize that he would have difficulty completing all of these pieces of work, and in 1962 made the decision (with some anxiety) to resign from his teaching post and become a full-time writer.

Loud Organs was completed in 1962, slightly before *Jackie the Jumper*. In discussing the idea of a play with music, Rhys and Thomas had come up with the idea of setting it in Tiger Bay, the run-down dock area of Cardiff. Thomas's inspiration for the play was an actual event in another part of the city, Butetown–the reopening of a disused chapel as a nightclub. One of the two main characters is a former boxing manager, Theophilus Wffie Morgan, who is also the owner of the Cot Club and Bingo Hall, a wholesale fruit and vegetable seller, and a pimp. He dominates most of the rest of the cast, most of whom are his underlings in the club. These include the head waiter, Nymrod Pym, a minister who has been expelled from his chapel because of his alcoholism, and three trios: three former boxers turned waiters, three men (Glyn, Bryn, and Wyn) who have come to watch a rugby match, and three hostesses at the club. The other main character, Jim Bumford, is a stranger to the club, brought there by Glyn, Bryn, and Wyn. Jim, who gives evasive and troubled answers, usually suggesting a response in a context beyond that imagined by the questioner, is a mystery.

From his first entrance Wffie views Jim with "the most profound and bristling suspicion." The three rugby spectators vouch for him, but they are never sober and are satisfied that they met him in a pub. Jim's answers do little to reduce Wffie's suspicions:

> *Bryn:* No, I can tell you're upright. *(He examines Jim's hand.)* And clean work, too.
> *Wffie:* They are the really dirty sort. You'll see. What have you worked at? What's your tool?
> *Jim:* The sad thought.
> *Wffie:* Another slippery bastard. . . . What's your business?
> *Jim:* Nothing fixed. Kind of research.

Loud Organs develops mainly through a repetition of these kinds of mysterious challenges to Wffie's authority, a muted conflict that is never clearly resolved. As so often in Thomas's drama, plot development is not the main point. Instead the play is interested in a witty but uncomfortable dialogue between Wffie and Jim, punctuated by songs and by the reactions of the "the people"–the three trios. It main theme, related to that in *The Keep,* is the state of modern Welsh society. Both *The Keep* and *Loud Organs* have a single static set that is a microcosm of Wales; but where the earlier play is intensely concerned with the grip of the past on the present, *Loud Organs* is dominated by a sense that there is only a rootless, hedonistic present that offers little opportunity for insight into the real conditions of life.

Thomas circa 1955, when he began writing for radio (photograph by Lyn Thomas)

Thus the three trios often form a chorus representing the views of ordinary people. Though often amusingly expressed, and with a sense of the attractions of the pleasures on offer, there is a considerable cynicism and anxiety in the play about the lack of any sense of reality beyond the immediate:

> *Eirlys:* Do you go through life with one woman, one shape, in your mind?
> *All the boys:* Many women, many shapes.
> *Mollie:* Have your dreams ever caught up with the facts?
> *All the boys:* No. Very easy to miss, dreams. Like buses.
> *Mollie:* What are the facts?
> *Bryn:* No idea.
> *Glyn:* We've never had a clear view of the facts.
> *Wyn:* If we see them coming, we duck.

Jim suggests the limitations of these kinds of view and the exploitative role of Wffie but offers no strong views on how to replace them with something better.

Loud Organs was given two provincial tryouts but was not well received on either occasion, partly because of problems with the musical aspect of the play. Though Thomas had envisaged a play with three musicians (playing guitars plus a drum kit) to accompany the songs and provide background music, the tryouts used, against his wishes, a larger orchestra. Consequently, there were evident technical problems as the actors failed to hear their cues, and the words of the songs became inaudible. Another problem may have been a

Publicity photo for the 1961 production of The Keep, *Thomas's first play (Collection of Royal Court Theatre, London)*

less than enthusiastic reception from some Welsh audiences of Thomas's harsh satire on several markers of Welsh national identity and pride, including attacks on rugby as an opiate of the masses.

Despite this particular disappointment, Thomas remained interested in writing for the theater. His next play, *Jackie the Jumper,* resembles *Loud Organs* in that it abandons any pretense of realism for a more experimental kind of theater, which allows for an intense but flexible use of music and highly crafted dialogue. *Jackie the Jumper* differs from the earlier plays in that it is set in the past, but as he had previously, Thomas uses this setting to suggest wider mythic resonances beyond the specific. The play is based on the riots that took place in Merthyr in the 1830s and on their leader, Dic Penderyn (a Welsh folk hero whom Thomas had already written about in his 1949 novel, *All Things Betray Thee*). In his preface to the play, "After the Chip-Shop," Thomas discusses the influence on the play of his "life-long addiction to grand opera" and his experience as stage manager of amateur productions of melodramas: "So, with that background, it was inevitable that I should edge my way back to melodrama, but melodrama invested with a kind of verbal dignity and a range of ideas that would have stood Todd, the demon, on his ear and reaching for the brush to stop my mouth with lather." The play, Thomas continued, is about the struggle between the rebel Jackie and his uncle "Resurrection" Rees, a preacher, against the background of "the early struggles of a society tormented and besmirched by the eruption of the great iron-furnaces and the descent of the great puritanical vetoes."

The struggle between immediate pleasure and higher purposes, which is important in *Loud Organs,* can be seen again in *Jackie the Jumper,* but in the latter play the seizing of pleasure is portrayed as an act of rebellion rather than of conformity. Jackie the Jumper is a rebel against religion, industrialization, and joyless work–perhaps Thomas's nineteenth-century agrarian version of a 1960s radical: "let's wipe away this pox of smoke and toil and get back to the laughter that must once have been the King-thing on this earth," he advocates. When asked where he has been, he answers, "Over a lot of mountains, down a lot of valleys, asking people why they were knitting inch-thick shrouds for themselves, giving up the art of loving." Jackie is a shadowy figure, constantly talked about until he materializes and inspires real life within the South Welsh, who have been repressed since "the preachers and the iron hit them."

That Reverend Rees is Jackie's uncle is significant to the play; Thomas portrays repression and rebellion as near relations. Neither side seems able to win a final victory, and both are able to sway the people with their rhetoric (though the sympathies of the play always seem weighted toward Jackie's rebellion). In this sense, though the play might seem a highly political one, it has little faith in political progress–Jackie says he has "tried to interpret the dreams of people who didn't even know they were asleep." At times the play has an almost absurdist sense of life as a circular plot without the real possibility of change, though the mere possibility of refusing to conform always remains important. Thus, in one reply to his uncle, Jackie strikes a note evocative of Samuel Beckett, perhaps directly influenced by *Waiting for Godot* (1953):

> *Rev. Rees:* You are the sacramental victim, the expendable pagan. You have no root here. Your passing would provoke tears but no fists. . . .
> *Jackie:* We are rarely more than a light flickering between two identities. I could have spoken all the words he spoke. And he, I suppose could have doubled for me. We inhabit a procession of wombs that grow darker, and we avoid the one authentic birth by acts of clownish mischance. Straighten your legs, Jackie, and get out of this.

The play ends on a related and ambiguous note–the last lines can be read either to mean that Jackie will be caught and hung by the soldiers, or that he will escape and live to fight another day.

Jackie the Jumper had its premiere at the Royal Court on 1 February 1963, and had a moderately favorable critical reception. It was not a success in terms of attracting an audience, however, though this lack of attendance may have been partly a result of the harsh winter at the time of the opening of the play. The production closed by the end of the month.

The Keep, Loud Organs, and *Jackie the Jumper* are Thomas's major plays in terms of their public impact. He also wrote three further stage plays, however: *The Loot* (1965), written for performance at a school; *Sap* (1974); and *The Breakers* (1976). *Sap* was a further development of the kind of fantastical musical theater that Thomas had developed in his *Loud Organs* and *Jackie the Jumper*. He had the original idea for the piece in 1962: it was to be set during World War I, focusing particularly on the Welsh experience of the war and using popular songs from the era, as well as dance and innovative staging, to construct an ironic but moving critique of the emotional climate of the Great War. Thomas made considerable progress with this idea, signing a contract for it to be produced at the Theatre Royal at Stratford East and delivering an outline and a list of the songs to be used, in 1963. There seemed to be little progress on the appearance of a production, however. Then the musical *Oh! What a Lovely War,* billed as "conceived and directed by Joan Littlewood," had its extremely successful premiere at the Theatre Royal on 19 March 1963. Like Thomas's plan for *Sap, Oh! What a Lovely War* juxtaposes the cheerful songs of the era with the horrors of war. Thomas was disappointed by what appeared to be an obvious case of plagiarism, especially since it seemed to vindicate his idea that fantastical musical theater could win popular acclaim. Rather than take any action, however, he put his own work on *Sap* away in a drawer. In 1974 he returned to the project, at the suggestion of the Welsh Drama Company, who produced *Sap* at the Sherman Theatre in Cardiff to good reviews.

Thomas wrote one further theater play, *The Breakers,* also for the Welsh Drama Company, which premiered at the Sherman Theatre on 16 November 1976. The three acts of the play are set one hundred years apart, in 1776, 1876, and 1976. *The Breakers* follows the Welsh Bowen family's fortunes and experiences of liberty and oppression in Pennsylvania in the eighteenth and nineteenth centuries and in their ancestral homeland in the twentieth century. Though the Bowens are well-off middle-class professionals in South Wales in the 1970s, they are not content, and at the end of the play they are looking for suitable places to emigrate to. The play continues Thomas's obsessive exploration of entrapment, both material and spiritual.

Biography:

Michael Parnell, *Laughter from the Dark: A Life of Gwyn Thomas* (London: Murray, 1989).

References:

Howard Fast, *Literature and Reality* (New York: International Publishers, 1950), pp. 67–77;

Glyn Jones, *The Dragon Has Two Tongues* (London: Dent, 1968), pp. 107–123;

Ian Michael, *Gwyn Thomas* (Cardiff: University of Wales Press, 1977).

Books for Further Reading

Acheson, James, ed. *British and Irish Drama since 1960.* Basingstoke: Macmillan, 1992; New York: St. Martin's Press, 1993.

Adams, David. *Stage Welsh.* Llandysul: Gomer, 1996.

Allsop, Kenneth. *The Angry Decade: A Survey of the Cultural Revolt of the Nineteen-Fifties.* London: Owen, 1958.

Anderson, Michael. *Anger and Detachment: A Study of Arden, Osborne and Pinter.* London: Pitman, 1976.

Ansorge, Peter. *Disrupting the Spectacle: Five Years of Experimental and Fringe Theatre in Britain.* London: Pitman, 1975.

Arden, John. *To Present the Pretence: Essays on the Theatre and its Public.* London: Eyre Methuen, 1977.

Armstrong, William, ed. *Experimental Drama.* London: G. Bell, 1963.

Barnes, Philip. *A Companion to Post-War British Theatre.* London: Croom Helm, 1986.

Bell, Sam Hanna. *The Theatre in Ulster: A Survey of the Dramatic Movement in Ulster from 1902 to the Present Day.* Dublin: Gill & Macmillan, 1972.

Bigsby, C. W. E. *Contemporary English Drama.* Stratford-upon-Avon Studies, no. 19. London: Arnold, 1981.

Billington, Michael. *One Night Stands: A Critic's View of Modern British Theatre.* London: Hern, 1994.

Black, Kitty. *Upper Circle: A Theatricle Chronicle.* London: Methuen, 1984.

Bock, Hedwig, and Albert Wertheim, eds. *Essays on Contemporary British Drama.* Munich: Hueber, 1981.

Brandt, George W. *British Television Drama.* Cambridge: Cambridge University Press, 1981.

Brown, Ivor. *Theatre 1954–5.* London: Max Reinhardt, 1955.

Brown. *Theatre 1955–6.* London: Max Reinhardt, 1956.

Brown, John Russell, ed. *Modern British Dramatists.* Englewood Cliffs, N.J.: Prentice-Hall, 1984.

Browne, Terry. *Playwrights' Theatre: The English Stage Company at the Royal Court Theatre.* London: Pitman, 1975.

Bull, John. *New British Political Dramatists.* Basingstoke: Macmillan, 1984.

Bull, *Stage Right: Crisis and Recovery in British Contemporary Mainstream Theatre.* Houndsmills: Macmillan, 1994.

Calder, Angus. *The People's War.* London: Cape, 1969.

Cameron, Alasdair, ed. *Scot-Free: New Scottish Plays.* London: Hern, 1990.

Cave, Richard. *New British Drama in Performance on the London Stage: 1970–1985.* Gerrards Cross: Smythe, 1987.

Chambers, Colin. *Other Spaces: New Theatre and the RSC.* London: Eyre Methuen, 1980.

Chambers. *Peggy: The Life of Margaret Ramsay.* London: Methuen, 1998.

Chambers and Mike Prior, *Playwrights' Progress: Patterns of Post-War British Drama.* Oxford: Amber Lane, 1987.

Cohn, Ruby. *Retreats from Realism in Recent English Drama.* Cambridge: Cambridge University Press, 1991.

Coveney, Michael. *The Citz: Twenty-One Years of the Glasgow Citizens Theatre.* London: Hern, 1990.

Cowell, Raymond. *Twelve Modern Dramatists.* Oxford: Pergamon, 1967.

Craig, Sandy, ed. *Dreams and Deconstructions: Alternative Theatre in Britain.* Ambergate: Amber Lane, 1980.

Daubeny, Peter. *My World of Theatre.* London: Cape, 1971.

Davies, Andrew. *Other Theatres: The Development of Alternative and Experimental Theatre in Britain.* Basingstoke: Macmillan, 1987.

Doty, Gresdna, and Billy Harbin, eds. *Inside the Royal Court Theatre 1956–81.* Baton Rouge & London: Louisiana State University Press, 1990.

Duff, Charles. *The Lost Summer: The Heyday of the West End Theatre.* London: Hern, 1995.

Edgar, David. *The Second Time as Farce: Reflections on the Drama of Mean Times.* London: Lawrence & Wishart, 1988.

Edwardes, Pamela, ed. *Frontline Intelligence I: New Plays for the Nineties.* London: Methuen Drama, 1993–comprises April de Angelis, *Hush;* Declan Hughes, *Digging for Fire;* Judith Johnson, *Somewhere;* Edward Thomas, *East from the Gantry.*

Edwardes, ed. *Frontline Intelligence II: New Plays for the Nineties.* London: Methuen Drama, 1994–comprises Karen Hope, *Foreign Lands;* Sarah Kane, *Blasted;* David Spencer, *Hurricane Roses;* Rod Williams, *The Life of the World to Come.*

Elsom, John. *Post-War British Theatre.* London: Routledge & Kegan Paul, 1976.

Elsom, ed. *Post-War British Theatre Criticism.* London: Routledge, 1981.

Esslin, Martin. *Brief Chronicles: Essays on Modern Theatre.* London: Temple Smith, 1970.

Esslin. *The Theatre of the Absurd.* Garden City, N.Y.: Doubleday, 1961.

Etherton, Michael. *Contemporary Irish Dramatists.* Basingstoke: Macmillan, 1989.

Fay, Gerard. *The Abbey Theatre.* London: Hollis & Carter, 1958.

Findlater, Richard. *Banned!: A Review of Theatrical Censorship in Britain.* London: MacGibbon & Kee, 1967.

Findlater, *The Unholy Trade.* London: Gollancz, 1952.

Findlater, ed. *At the Royal Court: Twenty-Five Years of the English Stage Company.* Ambergate: Amber Lane, 1981.

Findlay, Bill, ed. *A History of Scottish Theatre.* Edinburgh: Polygon, 1998.

Fitz-Simon, Christopher. *The Irish Theatre.* London: Thames & Hudson, 1983.

Genet, Jacqueline, and Cave, eds. *Perspectives on Irish Drama and Theatre.* Gerards Cross: Smythe, 1990.

Goodman, Lizbeth. *Contemporary Feminist Theatres: To Each Her Own.* London: Routledge, 1993.

Goorney, Howard. *The Theatre Workshop Story.* London: Eyre Methuen, 1981.

Griffiths, Trevor, and Margaret Llewellyn-Jones, eds. *British and Irish Women Dramatists Since 1958: A Critical Handbook.* Buckingham: Open University Press, 1993.

Harrington, John, ed. *Modern Irish Drama.* New York & London: Norton, 1991.

Hart, Lynda, ed. *Making a Spectacle: Feminist Essays on Contemporary Women's Theatre.* Ann Arbor: University of Michigan Press, 1989.

Harwood, Kate, ed. *First Run: New Plays by New Writers.* London: Hern, 1989–comprises Simon Donald, *Prickly Heat;* Paul Godfrey, *Inventing a New Colour;* Clare McIntyre, *Low Level Panic;* Winsome Pinnock, *Leave Taking;* Billy Roche, *A Handful of Stars.*

Hayman, Ronald. *British Theatre Since 1955: A Reassessment.* Oxford: Oxford University Press, 1979.

Hayman. *The Set Up: An Anatomy of the English Theatre Today.* London: Methuen, 1969.

Haynes, Jim. *Thanks for Coming!* London: Faber & Faber, 1984.

Herbert, A. P. *No Fine on Fun: The Comical History of the Entertainments Duty.* London: Methuen, 1957.

Hinchliffe, A. P. *British Theatre 1950–70.* Oxford: Blackwell, 1974.

Hobson, Harold. *Theatre in Britain: A Personal View.* Oxford: Phaidon, 1984.

Huggett, Richard. *Binkie Beaumont: Eminence Grise of the West End Theatre 1933–1973.* London: Hodder & Stoughton, 1989.

Hunt, Albert. *Hopes for Great Happenings.* London: Eyre Methuen, 1976.

Hunt, Hugh, Kenneth Richards, and John Russell Taylor, eds. *The Revels History of Drama in English,* volume 7. London: Eyre Methuen, 1978.

Innes, Christopher. *Avant Garde Theatre 1892–1992.* London: Routledge, 1993.

Innes. *Modern British Drama 1890–1990.* Cambridge: Cambridge University Press, 1992.

Itzin, Catherine. *Stages in the Revolution: Political Theatre in Britain since 1968.* London: Eyre Methuen, 1980.

Jackson, Anthony, and George Rowell. *The Repertory Movement: A History of Regional Theatre in Britain.* Cambridge: Cambridge University Press, 1984.

Johnston, John. *The Lord Chamberlain's Blue Pencil.* London: Hodder & Stoughton, 1990.

Jones, Dedwydd. *Black Book on the Welsh Theatre.* Lausanne: Iolo, 1980.

Joseph, Stephen. *Theatre in the Round.* London: Barrie & Rockliff, 1967.

Kerensky, Oleg. *The New British Drama: Fourteen Playwrights since Osborne and Pinter.* London: Hamilton, 1977.

Kershaw, Baz. *The Politics of Performance: Radical Theatre as Cultural Intervention.* London: Routledge, 1992.

Keyssar, Helene. *Feminist Theatre: An Introduction to Plays of Contemporary British and American Women.* Basingstoke: Macmillan, 1984.

Kitchin, Laurence. *Mid-Century Drama.* London: Faber & Faber, 1960.

Lacey, Stephen. *British Realist Theatre: The New Wave in Its Context 1956–1965.* London: Routledge, 1995.

Lambert, Jack Walter. *Drama in Britain, 1964–1973.* London: Longman for the British Council, 1974.

Lewis, Justin. *Art, Culture and Enterprise: The Politics of Art and the Cultural Industries.* London: Routledge, 1990.

Lewis, Peter. *The Fifties: Portrait of an Age.* London: Cupid, 1988.

Littlewood, Joan. *Joan's Book: Joan Littlewood's Peculiar History as She Tells It.* London: Methuen, 1994.

Lloyd Evans, Barbara, and Gareth Lloyd Evans, eds. *Plays in Review 1956–1980: British Drama and the Critics.* London: Batsford Academic and Educational, 1985.

Mander, Raymond, and Joe Mitchenson. *The Theatres of London,* revised and enlarged edition. London: New English Library, 1975.

Marowitz, Charles. *Confessions of a Counterfeit Critic: A London Theatre Notebook, 1958–1971.* London: Eyre Methuen, 1973.

Marowitz, Tom Milne, and Owen Hale, eds. *The Encore Reader: A Chronicle of the New Drama.* London: Methuen, 1965.

McFayden, Edward. *The British Theatre, 1956–1977: A Personal View.* London: National Book League, 1977.

McGrath, John. *The Bone Won't Break: On Theatre and Hope in Hard Times.* London: Methuen, 1990.

McGrath. *A Good Night Out: Popular Theatre: Audience, Class and Form.* London: Eyre Methuen, 1981; revised edition, London: Hern, 1996.

McMillan, Joyce. *The Traverse Theatre Story, 1963–1988.* London: Methuen, 1988.

Mikhail, Edward H. *Contemporary British Drama, 1950–1976: An Annotated Critical Bibliography.* London: Macmillan, 1976.

Moore-Gilbert, Bart, and John Seed, eds. *Cultural Revolution?: The Challenge of the Arts in the 1960s.* London & New York: Routledge, 1992.

Murray, Christopher. *Twentieth-Century Irish Drama: Mirror Up to Nation.* Manchester & New York: Manchester University Press, 1997.

Noble, Peter. *British Theatre.* London: British Yearbooks, 1946.

ÓhAodha, Mícheál. *Theatre in Ireland.* Oxford: Blackwell, 1974.

Osborne, John. *A Better Class of Person: An Autobiography 1929–1956.* Harmondsworth: Penguin, 1982.

Peacock, Keith D. *Radical Stages: Alternative History in Modern British Drama.* New York & London: Greenwood Press, 1991.

Pick, John. *The Theatre Industry.* London: Comedia, 1985.

Pick. *The West End: Mismanagement and Snobbery.* Eastbourne: Offord, 1983.

Price, Cecil. *The Professional Theatre in Wales.* Swansea: University College of Swansea, 1984.

Rabey, David Ian. *British and Irish Political Drama in the Twentieth Century: Implicating the Audience.* Basingstoke & London: Macmillan, 1986.

Rebellato, Dan. *1956 and All That: The Making of Modern British Drama.* London: Routledge, 1999.

Richtarik, Marilynn J. *Acting between the Lines: The Field Day Company and Irish Cultural Politics, 1980–1984.* Oxford: Clarendon Press, 1994.

Roberts, Philip. *The Royal Court Theatre 1965–1972.* London: Routledge, 1986.

Roche, Anthony. *Contemporary Irish Drama: From Beckett to McGuiness.* Dublin: Gill & Macmillan, 1994.

Sanderson, Michael. *From Irving to Olivier: A Social History of the Acting Profession in England 1880–1983.* London: Athlone Press, 1984.

Shank, Theodore, ed. *Contemporary British Theatre.* London & Basingstoke: Macmillan, 1994.

Shellard, Dominic. *British Theatre since the War.* New Haven & London: Yale University Press, 1999.

Shellard. *Harold Hobson: Witness and Judge. The Theatre Criticism of Harold Hobson.* Keele: Keele University Press, 1995.

Shellard, ed. *British Theatre in the 1950s.* Sheffield: Sheffield Academic Press, 2000.

Simpson, Alan. *Beckett and Behan and a Theatre in Ireland.* London: Routledge & Kegan Paul, 1962.

Stevenson, Randall, and Gavin Wallace, eds. *Scottish Theatre since the Seventies.* Edinburgh: Edinburgh University Press, 1996.

Taylor, Anna-Marie, ed. *Staging Wales: Welsh Theatre 1979–1997.* Cardiff: University of Wales Press, 1997.

Taylor, John Russell. *Anger and After: A Guide to the New British Drama.* Harmondsworth: Penguin, 1963.

Taylor. *The Rise and Fall of the Well-Made Play.* London: Methuen, 1967.

Taylor. *The Second Wave: British Drama of the Sixties,* revised edition. London: Eyre Methuen, 1978.

Trewin, John Courtenay. *Drama, 1945–1950.* London & New York: Longmans, Green for the British Council, 1951.

Trussler, Simon, ed. *New Theatre Voices of the Seventies: Sixteen Interviews from* Theatre Quarterly, *1970–1980.* London: Eyre Methuen, 1981.

Tushingham, David, ed. *Critical Mass.* London: Methuen, 1996.

Tushingham, ed. *Food for the Soul: A New Generation of British Theatremakers.* London: Methuen, 1994.

Tushingham, ed. *Not What I Am: The Experience of Performing.* London: Methuen, 1995.

Tynan, Kathleen. *The Life of Kenneth Tynan.* London: Methuen, 1988.

Tynan, Kenneth. *Curtains: Selections from the Drama, Criticism and Related Writings.* London: Longmans, 1961.

Tynan. *Tynan Right & Left: Plays, Films, People, Places, and Events.* London: Longmans, 1967.

Tynan. *A View of the English Stage, 1944–1963.* London: Davis-Poynter, 1975.

Wager, Walter, ed. *The Playwrights Speak.* London & Harlow: Longmans, 1969.

Wandor, Michelene. *Carry on, Understudies: Theatre and Sexual Politics,* second edition. London: Routledge & Kegan Paul, 1986.

Wandor. *Drama Today: A Critical Guide to British Drama, 1970–1990.* London: Longman in association with British Council, 1993.

Wandor. *Look Back in Gender: Sexuality and the Family in Post-War British Drama.* London: Methuen, 1987.

White, Michael. *Empty Seats.* London: Hamilton, 1984.

Worth, Katherine J. *Revolutions in Modern English Drama.* London: G. Bell, 1972.

Wu, Duncan. *Six Contemporary Dramatists: Bennett, Potter, Gray, Brenton, Hare, Ayckbourn.* New York: St. Martin's Press / Basingstoke: Macmillan, 1995.

Zeifman, Hersch, and Cynthia Zimmerman, eds. *Contemporary British Drama, 1970–90: Essays from* Modern Drama. Basingstoke: Macmillan, 1993.

Contributors

Elmer Andrews . . . . *University of Ulster*
Pamela Bakker . . . . *British Broadcasting Corporation*
Ute Berns . . . . *Technische Universität Berlin*
Peter Billingham . . . . *Bath Spa University College*
Edward Braun . . . . *University of Bristol*
John Bull . . . . *University of Reading*
Dymphna Callery . . . . *University of Wolverhampton*
Gavin Carver . . . . *University of Kent*
Maria M. Delgado . . . . *Queen Mary, University of London*
Antje Diedrich . . . . *Liverpool John Moores University*
Richard Foulkes . . . . *University of Leicester*
Ben Francombe . . . . *University College Bretton Hall*
Frances Gray . . . . *University of Sheffield*
Trevor R. Griffiths . . . . *University of North London*
Chris Hopkins . . . . *Sheffield Hallam University*
Lucy Kay . . . . *Liverpool Hope University College*
Margaret Llewellyn-Jones . . . . *University of North London*
Michael Mangan . . . . *University of Wales, Aberystwyth*
Ros Merkin . . . . *Liverpool John Moores University*
Steve Nicholson . . . . *University of Huddersfield*
Linden Peach . . . . *Loughborough University*
Jeannie van Rompaey . . . . *University of Leicester*
Sara Soncini . . . . *University of Milan*
Bernadette Sweeney . . . . *University of Dublin*
Anna-Marie Taylor . . . . *University of Wales, Swansea*
Lib Taylor . . . . *University of Reading*
Carole-Anne Upton . . . . *University of Hull*
Mick Wallis . . . . *Loughborough University*
Robert Wilcher . . . . *University of Birmingham*

Cumulative Index

Dictionary of Literary Biography, Volumes 1-245
Dictionary of Literary Biography Yearbook, 1980-2000
Dictionary of Literary Biography Documentary Series, Volumes 1-19
Concise Dictionary of American Literary Biography, Volumes 1-7
Concise Dictionary of British Literary Biography, Volumes 1-8
Concise Dictionary of World Literary Biography, Volumes 1-4

Cumulative Index

DLB before number: *Dictionary of Literary Biography,* Volumes 1-245
Y before number: *Dictionary of Literary Biography Yearbook,* 1980-2000
DS before number: *Dictionary of Literary Biography Documentary Series,* Volumes 1-19
CDALB before number: *Concise Dictionary of American Literary Biography,* Volumes 1-7
CDBLB before number: *Concise Dictionary of British Literary Biography,* Volumes 1-8
CDWLB before number: *Concise Dictionary of World Literary Biography,* Volumes 1-4

A

C

D

E

F

G

H

I

J

K

Cumulative Index

L

M

N

P

Q

R

S

T

Tutuola, Amos 1920-1997 . . DLB-125; CDWLB-3
Twain, Mark (see Clemens, Samuel Langhorne)
Tweedie, Ethel Brilliana circa 1860-1940 . . . . .DLB-174
The 'Twenties and Berlin, by Alex Natan . DLB-66
Two Hundred Years of Rare Books and Literary Collections at the University of South Carolina Y-00
Twombly, Wells 1935-1977 . . . . DLB-241
Twysden, Sir Roger 1597-1672 . . . . DLB-213
Tyler, Anne 1941- DLB-6, 143; Y-82; CDALB-7
Tyler, Mary Palmer 1775-1866 . . . . DLB-200
Tyler, Moses Coit 1835-1900 . . . . .DLB-47, 64
Tyler, Royall 1757-1826 . . . . DLB-37
Tylor, Edward Burnett 1832-1917 . . . . DLB-57
Tynan, Katharine 1861-1931 . . . . . . DLB-153, 240
Tyndale, William circa 1494-1536 . . . . . . DLB-132

U

Uchida, Yoshika 1921-1992 . . . . .CDALB-7
Udall, Nicholas 1504-1556 . . . . DLB-62
Ugrêsić, Dubravka 1949- DLB-181
Uhland, Ludwig 1787-1862 . . . . DLB-90
Uhse, Bodo 1904-1963 . . . . DLB-69
Ujević, Augustin ("Tin") 1891-1955 . . . . . DLB-147
Ulenhart, Niclas flourished circa 1600 . . . DLB-164
Ulibarrí, Sabine R. 1919- DLB-82
Ulica, Jorge 1870-1926 . . . . DLB-82
Ulivi, Ferruccio 1912- DLB-196
Ulizio, B. George 1889-1969 . . . . DLB-140
Ulrich von Liechtenstein circa 1200-circa 1275 . . . . DLB-138
Ulrich von Zatzikhoven before 1194-after 1214 . . . . DLB-138
Ulysses, Reader's Edition Y-97
Unaipon, David 1872-1967 . . . . DLB-230
Unamuno, Miguel de 1864-1936 . . . . DLB-108
Under, Marie 1883-1980 . . . DLB-220; CDWLB-4
Under the Microscope (1872), by A. C. Swinburne DLB-35
Underhill, Evelyn 1875-1941 . . . . DLB-240
Ungaretti, Giuseppe 1888-1970 . . . . DLB-114
Unger, Friederike Helene 1741-1813 . . . . . DLB-94
United States Book Company DLB-49
Universal Publishing and Distributing Corporation DLB-46
The University of Iowa Writers' Workshop Golden Jubilee Y-86
The University of South Carolina Press Y-94
University of Wales Press DLB-112
University Press of Florida Y-00
University Press of Kansas Y-98
University Press of Mississippi Y-99
"The Unknown Public" (1858), by Wilkie Collins [excerpt] DLB-57
Uno, Chiyo 1897-1996 . . . . DLB-180
Unruh, Fritz von 1885-1970 . . . . DLB-56, 118
Unspeakable Practices II: The Festival of Vanguard Narrative at Brown University Y-93
Unsworth, Barry 1930- DLB-194
Unt, Mati 1944- DLB-232
The Unterberg Poetry Center of the 92nd Street Y Y-98
Unwin, T. Fisher [publishing house] DLB-106
Upchurch, Boyd B. (see Boyd, John)
Updike, John 1932- DLB-2, 5, 143, 218, 227; Y-80, Y-82; DS-3; CDALB-6
John Updike on the Internet Y-97
Upīts, Andrejs 1877-1970 . . . . DLB-220
Upton, Bertha 1849-1912 . . . . DLB-141
Upton, Charles 1948- DLB-16
Upton, Florence K. 1873-1922 . . . . DLB-141
Upward, Allen 1863-1926 . . . . DLB-36
Urban, Milo 1904-1982 . . . . DLB-215
Urista, Alberto Baltazar (see Alurista)
Urquhart, Fred 1912- DLB-139
Urrea, Luis Alberto 1955- DLB-209
Urzidil, Johannes 1896-1976 . . . . DLB-85
The Uses of Facsimile Y-90
Usk, Thomas died 1388 . . . . DLB-146
Uslar Pietri, Arturo 1906- DLB-113
Ussher, James 1581-1656 . . . . DLB-213
Ustinov, Peter 1921- DLB-13
Uttley, Alison 1884-1976 . . . . DLB-160
Uz, Johann Peter 1720-1796 . . . . DLB-97

V

Vac, Bertrand 1914- DLB-88
Vācietis, Ojārs 1933-1983 . . . . DLB-232
Vaičiulaitis, Antanas 1906-1992 . . . . DLB-220
Vaculík, Ludvík 1926- DLB-232
Vaičiūnaite, Judita 1937- DLB-232
Vail, Laurence 1891-1968 . . . . DLB-4
Vailland, Roger 1907-1965 . . . . DLB-83
Vaižgantas 1869-1933 . . . . DLB-220
Vajda, Ernest 1887-1954 . . . . DLB-44
Valdés, Gina 1943- DLB-122
Valdez, Luis Miguel 1940- DLB-122
Valduga, Patrizia 1953- DLB-128
Valente, José Angel 1929-2000 . . . . DLB-108
Valenzuela, Luisa 1938- . . .DLB-113; CDWLB-3
Valeri, Diego 1887-1976 . . . . DLB-128
Valerius Flaccus fl. circa A.D. 92 . . . . DLB-211
Valerius Maximus fl. circa A.D. 31 . . . . . DLB-211
Valesio, Paolo 1939- DLB-196
Valgardson, W. D. 1939- DLB-60
Valle, Víctor Manuel 1950- DLB-122
Valle-Inclán, Ramón del 1866-1936 . . . . . DLB-134
Vallejo, Armando 1949- DLB-122
Vallès, Jules 1832-1885 . . . . DLB-123
Vallette, Marguerite Eymery (see Rachilde)
Valverde, José María 1926-1996 . . . . DLB-108
Van Allsburg, Chris 1949- DLB-61
Van Anda, Carr 1864-1945 . . . . DLB-25
van der Post, Laurens 1906-1996 . . . . DLB-204
Van Dine, S. S. (see Wright, Williard Huntington)
Van Doren, Mark 1894-1972 . . . . DLB-45
van Druten, John 1901-1957 . . . . DLB-10
Van Duyn, Mona 1921- DLB-5
Van Dyke, Henry 1852-1933 . . . . . .DLB-71; DS-13
Van Dyke, Henry 1928- DLB-33
Van Dyke, John C. 1856-1932 . . . . DLB-186
van Gulik, Robert Hans 1910-1967 . . . . DS-17
van Itallie, Jean-Claude 1936- DLB-7
Van Loan, Charles E. 1876-1919 . . . . .DLB-171
Van Rensselaer, Mariana Griswold 1851-1934 . . . . DLB-47
Van Rensselaer, Mrs. Schuyler (see Van Rensselaer, Mariana Griswold)
Van Vechten, Carl 1880-1964 . . . . DLB-4, 9
van Vogt, A. E. 1912-2000 . . . . DLB-8
Vanbrugh, Sir John 1664-1726 . . . . DLB-80
Vance, Jack 1916?- DLB-8
Vančura, Vladislav 1891-1942 . . . . .DLB-215; CDWLB-4
Vane, Sutton 1888-1963 . . . . DLB-10
Vanguard Press DLB-46
Vann, Robert L. 1879-1940 . . . . DLB-29
Vargas Llosa, Mario 1936- DLB-145; CDWLB-3
Varley, John 1947- Y-81
Varnhagen von Ense, Karl August 1785-1858 . . . . DLB-90
Varnhagen von Ense, Rahel 1771-1833 . . . . DLB-90
Varro 116 B.C.-27 B.C. DLB-211
Vasiliu, George (see Bacovia, George)
Vásquez, Richard 1928- DLB-209
Vásquez Montalbán, Manuel 1939- . . . DLB-134
Vassa, Gustavus (see Equiano, Olaudah)
Vassalli, Sebastiano 1941- DLB-128, 196
Vaughan, Henry 1621-1695 . . . . DLB-131
Vaughan, Thomas 1621-1666 . . . . DLB-131
Vaughn, Robert 1592?-1667 . . . . DLB-213
Vaux, Thomas, Lord 1509-1556 . . . . DLB-132
Vazov, Ivan 1850-1921 . . . . . .DLB-147; CDWLB-4
Véa Jr., Alfredo 1950- DLB-209
Vega, Janine Pommy 1942- DLB-16
Veiller, Anthony 1903-1965 . . . . DLB-44
Velásquez-Trevino, Gloria 1949- DLB-122
Veley, Margaret 1843-1887 . . . . DLB-199
Velleius Paterculus circa 20 B.C.-circa A.D. 30 . . . . DLB-211
Veloz Maggiolo, Marcio 1936- DLB-145
Vel'tman Aleksandr Fomich 1800-1870 . . . . DLB-198
Venegas, Daniel ?-? DLB-82

W

X

Y

Z